STILL THE RIGHT PLACE:
UTAH'S SECOND HALF-
CENTURY OF STATEHOOD,
1945–1995

Still the Right Place: Utah's Second Half-Century of Statehood, 1945–1995

James B. Allen

Published by
the Charles Redd Center for Western Studies
at Brigham Young University
and the Utah State Historical Society

Redd Center publications are made possible by a grant form Charles Redd. This grant served as the basis for the establishment of the Charles Redd Center for Western Studies at Brigham Young University.

© 2016 Charles Redd Center for Western Studies, Brigham Young University, and the Utah State Historical Society. All rights reserved.

No part of this publication may be reproduced, stored in or introduced into a retrieval system, or transmitted in any form or by any means electronic, mechanical, printing, recording or otherwise—except as permitted under sections 107 or 108 of the United States Copyright Act—without the prior written permission of the author or publisher. To request permission to reproduce selections from this book, email redd_center@byu.edu.

Published by the Charles Redd Center for Western Studies at Brigham Young University and the Utah State Historical Society.

ISBN 978-0-998-69600-3
Retail US $14.99

Edited by Vicky Perry, with contributions from Amy M. Carlin

Cover and interior design by Amy M. Carlin
Cover photograph "Beautiful Sunset Image taken at Arches National Park in Utah" © Josemaria Toscano

The paper used in this publication meets the minimum requirements of the American National Standard for Information Sciences—Permanence of Paper for Printed Library Materials.

CONTENTS

Foreword   1

Introduction
January 1996:
Duhbe, the Crab, and the Beginning of Century Two   6

1. From Swords to Plowshares:
   The Challenge of Converting to Peace, 1945–1948   12

2. "Let 'Em Holler!"
   The Stormy Lee Years, 1949–1956   53

3. Moderate Republicanism:
   The Clyde Years, 1957–1964   107

4. Three-Term Governor:
   The Rampton Administration   159

5. Quest for Balance:
   The Matheson Years, 1977–1984   236

6. Conservatism, But of the Moderate Sort:
   The Bangerter Years, 1985–1992   311

7. Mike Leavitt and the End of Century One, 1993–1995   382

Appendix A
Utah's Ethnic Minorities
and the Quest for a Pluralistic Society   422

Appendix B
Utah and the Arts, 1945–1994   480

Appendix C
Notes on Utah's Religions, 1945–1995   559

Bibliography   620

IMAGES

1.1 Herbert B. Maw
1.2 Reva Beck Bosone
1.3 Geneva Steel
1.4 Gail Halvorsen
2.1 Governor J. Bracken Lee
2.2 Charles Steen
2.3 Senator Arthur V. Watkins
2.4 Ivy Baker Priest
2.5 Ezra Taft Benson
3.1 George Dewey Clyde
3.2 W. Cleaon Skousen with news reporter
3.3 Minuteman missile
3.4 Glen Canyon Dam
3.5 Frank E. Moss
4.1 Calvin L. and Lucybeth Rampton
4.2 Neal A. Maxwell
4.3 Highway I-15 under construction
4.4 Christine Meaders Durham
4.5 Senator Orrin G. Hatch
5.1 Governor Scott M. Matheson
5.2 Governor's Mansion
5.3 Sharlene Wells
5.4 Sagebrush Rebellion
5.5 Thistle covered by water
6.1 Governor Norman Bangerter
6.2 Ski Utah license plate
6.3 Robert F. Bennett
7.1 Governor Michael Leavitt
7.2 Welcome to Utah: Still the Right Place

- A.1 Navajo Family
- A.2 Intermountain Indian School
- A.3 Guadalupe Center
- A.4 NAACP leaders
- B.1 "The Utah Symphony Orchestra performing for a large audience in an amphitheater in Greece"
- B.2 LeConte Stewart
- B.3 Springville Museum of Art
- B.4 Pioneer Memorial Theater
- B.5 Logan Tabernacle
- B.6 Wallace Stegner
- C.1 Salt Lake Temple Square
- C.2 Cathedral of the Madeleine
- C.3 St. Mark's Episcopal Cathedral
- C.4 B'Nai Israel Temple

FOREWORD

The manuscript for this book was originally completed and ready for publication in 1995, the year before Utah celebrated its statehood centennial. The state legislature had funded the publication of several histories, under the auspices of the Utah State Historical Society, to help celebrate the centennial. These included county histories, a one-volume history of the state, and a more detailed four-volume history. Tom Alexander authored the one-volume history, *Utah, the Right Place*, which was published in 1995. I was assigned the final volume in the four-volume series. Unfortunately, this series was never published because not all the volumes were finished and the state wanted to publish them as a set.

My unpublished manuscript sat in my files for years until Brian Cannon, director of the Charles Redd Center for Western Studies, told me that the center would publish it, with support from the Utah State Historical Society. I was delighted, and soon began the time-consuming task of revising and condensing. The result is a much shorter book and, I believe, a much better one.

As a historian I try to free myself from undue bias when making judgements about or interpreting the past. However, writing this book was almost an exercise in autobiography, for I remember so well nearly all the major events discussed. For that reason

I realize that I may not have been completely free of bias in terms of what I chose to include or exclude or in my interpretations. I suspect that most people who will read the book in the next few years have also lived through much, or all, of this era, and may have different impressions than I have. As a result, I know that no matter how carefully I tried to determine what to include or exclude or what conclusions to draw, others will see things differently. To them I can only say that I hope I have interpreted some of the most important aspects of this pivotal era in Utah history in a way that contributes responsibly to understanding it. I have made every effort to recognize my own biases and, to the degree that they may have interfered with responsible analysis, overcome them.

The book is organized according to the administrations of each of Utah's seven governors: one chapter for each. The original (1995) manuscript also had five topical chapters, two of which dealt with economics. As I began the revision, however, I could see, as some reviewers had kindly suggested, that these two chapters were much too detailed and tedious. I therefore condensed the economic material and worked it into the chronological chapters. I also condensed the other three topical chapters and added them as appendices. One deals with the history, problems, and contributions of Utah's ethnic minorities. Because they are so small in number, minorities sometimes receive short shrift in the awareness of others, yet their history is vital to understanding the history of the state as a whole. I have been impressed with how much Utah's involvement in the arts expanded in the fifty years since World War II. Yet I worried that many potential readers were unaware, perhaps even unappreciative, of the rich contributions Utahns have made to the arts and of the remarkable opportunities available in the state for enjoying them. Therefore, I devoted what is now Appendix B to that topic. Similarly, Utah's religious minorities sometimes seem hidden in a state that is still about 70 percent Mormon. Appendix C, therefore, deals with religion. A major portion discusses the Church of Jesus Christ of Latter-day Saints, but more than 80 percent of the space is devoted to the activities of other Utah faiths.

Internally, the major chapters are organized by topics, some of which appear in nearly every chapter. These include education, law and order, Utah's relationship to national problems, economic development, the environment, health and medicine, and politics.

A few general themes pervade the book. One is related to the fact that the history of Utah cannot be studied in a vacuum. After World War II, Utah's political and economic life became more fully integrated than ever before with the rest of the nation and with the world. I have therefore tried to look at the events in each chapter in the context of the larger scene.

Change is another theme running through this book, particularly changes that were inextricably intertwined with the transformations taking place on the larger American stage. For example, as American attitudes toward the role of women changed, so did the attitudes of many Utahns. By the end of the century more than 61 percent of the working-age women made up nearly 44 percent of the total workforce. This was a substantial change over the first half of the century, reflecting a more widespread social acceptance of the idea of working mothers. Even though the Utah legislature rejected the Equal Rights Amendment, and Utahns were actively involved in getting that amendment defeated on other states, the opportunities for women in professions, and the general acceptance of gender equality, was as far along in Utah as in most other places by the end of the century. Likewise, other social attitudes tended to follow broader American patterns.

Utah's changing economy also plays a major role in the book. In the early decades Utah was a "dependent commonwealth," relying on defense-oriented employment, federal government employment, and large firms with headquarters outside the state for much, if not most, of its economic well-being. However, manufacturing became more diverse, tourism became steadily more significant, Utah became home base for a number of major employers, service-oriented industries boomed, and employment patterns changed. Beginning in the 1970s, high-tech manufacturing became a kind of "Cinderella" industry for the state, and some Utah firms became world leaders. At the same time, Utah became increasingly urbanized, as a shift away from agriculture and mining resulted in a move away from rural Utah and into the cities and suburbs, particularly along the Wasatch Front. Utah prospered in the last half of the twentieth century and became an attractive place to establish new businesses.

I have also paid attention to Utah's natural resources, including its land and water, and the environmental concerns associated with their development.

Finally, another theme is politics. In general, Utahns were politically moderate during this era, most often electing governors that were not extreme in their political views, and who were able to work reasonably well with members of the opposite political party. (The exception was Governor J. Bracken Lee.) Although there was extremism in both directions, neither the "far right" nor the "far left" made heavy inroads into the Utah mainstream.

At the end of 1995 Utah completed its first century of statehood. As they celebrated statehood day on January 4, 1996, many Utahns speculated on what Century II would hold for them and for their state. Perhaps the previous fifty years held some of the answers. To the degree that the past portends the future, Utahns could anticipate that many of their problems and challenges would reflect what was going on in the nation at large. They could look forward to political battles over state budgets, education policy, law enforcement, the environment, social welfare, and other ongoing challenges. They could predict that such tragic social problems as drug abuse, juvenile crime, violence, larceny, homelessness, and poverty would not disappear. Nevertheless, most Utahns could look forward to a comfortable, pleasant future in communities noted nationwide for their enviable way of life and high standards. They could anticipate continued economic growth, continuing high achievements in both public and higher education, a steady growth of tourism, and a continuing abundance of artistic talent to enrich the lives of all. In addition, it would not be difficult to predict that the social, economic, and political influence of the LDS Church would remain high, and that discussions over its role in Utah politics would probably never end. At the same time, it was clear that other churches would continue to prosper and provide important religious and social opportunities for a growing number of people. Hopefully, Utahns in another fifty years could echo those in 1995 who beamed: "Utah—Still the right place!"

I wish to give special thanks to a few people who helped me with this revision. I am deeply grateful to Brian Cannon for encouraging me to proceed with the project and for shepherding it along the way to publication. Among other things, he provided two research assistants, Neil Longo and Cameron Nielson, who painstakingly source checked all the endnotes and, thankfully, caused me to correct several of them. I am also grateful for the support of the Utah State Historical Society and to Doug Misner and Greg Walz of the Historical Society for their work in finding photographs for the book. Thomas G. Alexander read the revised manuscript and suggested some valuable corrections. In addition, a good copy editor is probably a writer's best friend. In this case heartfelt thanks goes to Vicki Parry, whose exacting work resulted in a vastly improved text and also in correcting a number of embarrassing errors. She not only knows writing, she knows Utah! I will always be grateful to my daughter, Kristine Allen Card, for putting me in touch with her. I am also grateful to Amy Carlin, office specialist at the Redd Center, who managed the final work of preparing the manuscript for the press. Finally, I thank my wife Renée for her patience with me as I sometimes seemed to ignore what was going on around the house as I worked on this and a few other projects simultaneously, and who read the final manuscript looking for, and finding, those inevitable typos.

James B. Allen
Orem, Utah, September 2016

INTRODUCTION

January 1996:
Duhbe, the Crab, and the Beginning of Century Two

January 4, 1996, was the State of Utah's one hundredth birthday—a century from the day President Grover Cleveland signed the official statehood proclamation. The grand, day-long centennial celebration began at sunrise with a flag-raising ceremony at the state capitol, featuring a forty-five-star American flag (Utah had been the forty-fifth state admitted to the union) and music by the US Army Herald Trumpets. At 9:13 a.m., Max Evans, Director of the Division of State History, ran out of a replica of the 1896 Western Union Telegraph office armed with a double-barreled shotgun. He fired two shots in the air and yelled "Statehood! Statehood at last!" replicating what had happened exactly one hundred years earlier: Marion M. Brown, Western Union manager, had run out of the office announcing his reception of the telegram saying that the official proclamation had been signed. Just as in 1896, the centennial crowd cheered, bells rang, and people danced in the streets. The forty-five-star flag was hoisted over the *Salt Lake Tribune* building, cannons were fired in front of the old *Deseret News* building, and an hour-long parade duplicated, as nearly as possible, the statehood day parade from one hundred years before.

Then came a reenactment of the inaugural ceremony held in the Salt Lake Tabernacle. The Tabernacle was lavishly decorated with red, white, and blue bunting, Utah state flags, and forty-five–

star US flags. Actors portrayed state and church leaders of 1896, but historic speeches were abbreviated because no one wanted to hear anything as long as the entire two-and-a-half-hour speech delivered by Governor Heber M. Wells. The ceremony included musical performances, and speeches by Rev. Robert Sewell of the First United Methodist Church (counterpart of 1896's Thomas Corwin Illiff), Gordon B. Hinckley, President of The Church of Jesus Christ of Latter-day Saints, and Governor Mike Leavitt. In the speech that closed the ceremony, the governor looked to the future:

> Today we celebrate Utah's successes in the last hundred years. But it is also an occasion to examine Utah's role in the next hundred. Utah is not the biggest state in the union nor are we likely to be the most powerful economically or politically. But in a world where many grope for a sustainable core, we can play a vital role.
>
> Utah must be a place of quiet quality, a mentor state, a place where people pass on to future generations the ageless values. Like the youngest brother who preserved the glowing ambers until the flame could be rekindled, Utah can be among the places where the world turns to renew its sense of basic values.
>
> Let it be our role to blow upon the embers when the flame dims. Let this be the place where each person nurtures the flame within themselves and willingly passes a torch to another whose fire has gone out. Let Utah be a "keeper of the flame," not for a century, but forever.[1]

In the evening, a gala celebration at the Delta Center featured the Utah Symphony, the Mormon Tabernacle Choir, the Utah Opera company, the US Army Herald Trumpets, other performing celebrities, a speech by the governor, and fireworks. Other cities throughout the state also held elaborate celebrations. Remembering the past and looking to the future were themes that dominated the beginning of Utah's "Century Two."

Looking at the Stars

Nine days after the centennial celebration, the state legislature opened its annual forty-five–day session with the introduction of 174 bills and resolutions in the House and 82 in the Senate. At least one of these bills led to a bit of fun for Utah's lawmakers: Representative Marda Dillree (R-Farmington) introduced HB140, designating the star Duhbe (rhymes with "tubby") as the Utah state star. Why? Because the light that left Duhbe during the year that Utah became a state arrived in Utah on the state's centennial. There was considerable joking about Dillree's bill, and some legislators chanted the star's name incorrectly—"doobee, doobee, doobee!"—as they approached Dillree. In a mock legal analysis, legislative attorney John Fellows reported that "Denizens of Izar, a planet circling the star Epsilon Bootis, have already claimed the star we know as Dubhe as their own." Further, he warned that naming a dim group of stars in the constellation Cancer "the Beehive Cluster"—another part of Dillree's proposal—could result in interplanetary war. The Klingons, he warned, already claimed those stars, and such action by Utah "might provoke a violent response from the Klingon Empire" and "create an intergalactic incident." Nevertheless, Dillree's bill flew through both the House and Senate to pass unanimously, and Utah gained new astronomical symbols.[2]

There was hardly an urgent need for Utah to have an official star or star cluster; no other state had one.[3] However, because symbols stand as monuments to historical events and significant ideals, they can remind us of our heritage, culture, values, and traditions and portray a state and its wonders to the people of the world.

By 1996, Utah had a variety of official symbols, emblems, and mottos. The state flag and seal are the most obvious, but there are others: the sego lily, designated the state flower in 1911; the blue spruce, named the state tree in 1933; "Utah, We Love Thee," designated the state song in 1937, although it became the state hymn when "Utah, This Is the Place" was adopted as the state song in 1996; the California gull, named the state bird in 1955; the beehive, designated the state emblem in 1959 to emphasize the state motto *industry*; the topaz, named the state gem in 1969; the Rocky

Mountain Elk, designated the state animal in 1971; the honeybee, named the state insect in 1983; Indian ricegrass, designated the state grass in 1990; coal, named the state rock in 1991; and the square dance, designated the official state folk dance in 1994. Shortly after Utah claimed stars as symbols in 1996, the legislature also created an official state tartan. The Utah Centennial Tartan honored the first Scots known to have arrived in Utah, as well as all Utahns of Scottish heritage. In later years, more official symbols were added.[4]

Most Utahns are probably unaware of or care little about most of these symbols. However, each meant something significant to those who promoted it. The stars seemed particularly fitting as Utah remembered its first hundred years and looked forward to its second century of statehood. Stars are among the most widely-used symbols in the world. They stand for many things, including military might, religious ideology, political or philosophical tenets, protection, law and order, and achievement of excellence. Perhaps some Utahns thought of the latter in regard to Utah's new astronomical symbols. A recent publication book from the University of Utah Press, Charles Peterson and Brian Cannon's *The Awkward State of Utah*, reflects on Utah's prosperity and achievements during its first half-century and its signs of continuing those trends. Naming a symbol in the heavens might well reflect Utah's pride in its past and confidence in its future prosperity.

Although the state continued to experience economic fluctuation, political tension, and serious internal controversy, the years 1945 to 1995 were momentous for Utah's economy, educational attainments, and efforts to increase its stature in the world. In a figurative sense, Utah's leaders and citizens had their eyes on the stars as they planned and worked toward making sure that Utah was still "the right place." That phrase, in fact, was officially incorporated into the state slogan adopted by the Statehood Centennial Commission in 1990: "This Is Still the Right Place."

During its second half-century of statehood, Utah's high rates of birth and in-migration caused the state to grow at a remarkable rate. Population jumped from around six hundred thousand in 1945 to more than two million in 1996 and more than 2.2 million by the end of the decade, making Utah the fourth-fastest-growing state in the nation. The economy remained generally robust through the period, although its nature changed somewhat. The state developed an enviable business climate that attracted and helped create new businesses, especially several high-tech companies, and Utah became a leader in technology development. The state also established favorable economic relations with some foreign countries, thanks especially to the efforts of Governor Mike Leavitt, opening foreign markets to Utah's goods. Surveys showed that Utah, despite a low education budget, still had some of the most well-educated children in the nation in the mid-1990s. Fortunately, in 1996 the Utah legislature had the luxury of dealing with a budget surplus of nearly $5.5 million, much of which was applied to education. In 1995 the International Olympics Committee chose Salt Lake City to host the 2001 Winter Olympics. In this and other ways, Utah became an increasingly significant presence on the national stage. Socially, many religious groups, both Christian and non-Christian, contributed to Utah's reputation for a high level of public and private morality. Utah came to be known as one of the best places in the nation to live and do business[5]—a remarkable change from its image a half-century earlier.

When Brigham Young first gazed on the valley of the Great Salt Lake in 1847 he said, "This is the right place!" This book focuses on why, more than 150 years later, Utah's people could say with pride that "This Is Still the Right Place!"

Notes

1. *Deseret News* online document: "Text of Gov. Leavitt's Centennial Speech," January 4, 1996. Accessed online at http://www.deseretnews.com/article/465412/ONLINE-DOCUMENT--TEXT-OF-GOV-LEAVITTS-CENTENNIAL-SPEECH.html?pg=all. Accessed February 2, 2015.
2. Lee Siegel, "Shine On, Shine On, Utah Star, The State Hath Dubbed You, So Thus You Are," *Salt Lake Tribune*, January 22, 1996, A1.
3. In 1999, Delaware became the only other state to name an astronomical symbol. The middle star in the handle of the Big Dipper (Mizar) was designated by Delaware as its state star and officially dubbed the "Delaware Diamond."
4. In 1998, allosaurus, a large carnivore that lived 145 to 150 million years ago, became the state fossil. In 1994 copper was designated the state mineral. The cherry was named the official state fruit in 1997. Also in 1997, Utah designated the Bonneville cutthroat trout (*oncorhynchus clarkii utah*) as the official state fish. In 1998 the historic Ogden Union Station became Utah's official railroad museum. In 2002, Utah

designated the Spanish sweet onion as the official state vegetable and also named the sugar beet as the state historic vegetable. Finally, in 2011, Utah became the first state to have an official state firearm when, against the opposition of the majority of Utah citizens, the M1911 automatic pistol, designed by John M. Browning, was officially designated as such. Most people wondered if this controversial decision would send the wrong message; but Governor Gary Herbert said that he perceived this step as honoring the famous John M. Browning more than honoring the gun.

5. In *Money* magazine's fourth annual "The Best Place to Live" survey, in 1990, the Provo-Orem area placed 11th in the nation. It had placed 65th the year before. Lane Williams & Brooke Adams, "Provo–Orem Area Rated 11th Best Place to Live," *Deseret News*, August 23, 1990, B1. The next year that area was rated number one. Dennis Romboy, "Provo-Orem Tops Survey List of Best Places to Live," *Deseret News*, August 21, 1991, A1. In 1990, the Salt Lake City/Ogden metropolitan area topped *Fortune magazine*'s second annual survey of the "best city for business." Joel Cambell, "Winds of Fortune: S.L. 'in Very Good Company' as Magazine Lauds Its Business Climate and Work Force," *Deseret News*, October 7, 1990, B1. Such rankings continued in later years, and other Utah cities received similar evaluations.

CHAPTER 1

From Swords to Plowshares:
The Challenge of Converting to Peace, 1945–1948

War's End

"Brother, this is it: golf balls, duck-shooting and puh-lenty of gas!" shouted one exhilarated Utahn after he heard the news of Tuesday, August 14, 1945. Japan had surrendered and World War II, the most deadly war in history, was over. The sportsman's lighthearted response was hardly meant to ignore the solemnity of the occasion—it was simply one expression of the euphoria felt by all Americans as the horror of war finally came to a halt. It was time for both celebration and thanksgiving.

The news reached Salt Lake City during its busiest afternoon traffic hour. Almost immediately, the city streets went wild. Horns blared while jubilant, war-weary Utahns danced, shouted, screamed, hugged, and kissed. Downtown thoroughfares were jammed, and tickertape, confetti, and wastebasket paper poured down from office windows almost all night. The revelry seemed even more exciting when it became punctuated by thunder and lightning. The city roped off a section of Main Street to accommodate the merrymaking that was embellished with firecrackers, small cannon blasts and children clanging pots and pans as they marched in little parades. Similar victory celebrations, lasting into the early morning hours, took place almost everywhere in the state.

This jubilation was an outward sign of relief on the part of a people who felt both grateful and prayerful at the end of a nightmare. The next two days, declared national holidays by US President Harry Truman, were devoted to more sober, reflective observances. In the evenings, people gathered around bonfires to sing, and on Thursday, August 16, a band concert was held in Salt Lake City's Liberty Park. Churches held special memorial and thanksgiving services, and the First Presidency of The Church of Jesus Christ of Latter-day Saints[1] advised all bishops and branch presidents to set aside the following Sunday as a day of fasting and prayer.

About 6 p.m. on September 1, Utah time (about 9 a.m. on September 2 in Japan), Japanese officials formally signed surrender documents aboard the battleship Missouri in Tokyo Bay. President Truman designated Sunday, September 2, as "V-J day." Then came the public prayers and sermons. On Tuesday evening, six thousand Utahns met at the Salt Lake Tabernacle, where they heard Governor Herbert B. Maw and the leaders of six major religious denominations utter words of thanksgiving and appeals for permanent peace based on an increase in righteousness, brotherhood, and justice. Prayers were offered by Joseph F. Smith, Patriarch to the LDS Church, and the Reverend W. F. Buckley, Episcopal archdeacon of Utah.[2] In most churches, religious services the following Sunday were devoted to sermons and prayers of thanksgiving and peace.

With World War II behind them, Utahns were anxious to see the nation turn its swords into plowshares and return to peacetime pursuits. However, they knew this would not happen overnight. The state had become dependent upon some of the war machinery itself. In addition, postwar Utah, like the rest of the nation, faced a variety of challenges relating to labor relations, education, and various social issues. The housing shortage was serious, returning veterans would be looking for work as well as places to live, many defense-related jobs would disappear, labor relations were on the verge of exploding, and there was the possibility of a serious postwar economic depression unless the state could maintain something close to the high level of industrial activity generated by the war. Nevertheless, the general mood in Utah was one of optimism. Utahns thought the lifting of wartime restrictions would vitalize business and provide many new jobs. For the most part they were confident of a secure and prosperous future. The years 1945 to 1948 were crucial years of transition.

Impact of World War II[3]

Utah suffered terrible losses in World War II: 71,172 of its citizens (nearly 13 percent of the 1940 population) went to war, 2,501 died, 2,829 were wounded, 36 were reported missing in action, and 511 became prisoners of war.[4] No matter what happened otherwise, nothing could compensate for such human tragedy.

The war changed Utah in many ways. A 1946 study, for example, summarized the economic impact in five categories: (1) a marked increase in production facilities; (2) the discovery of new mineral deposits and the expanded knowledge of others; (3) improved individual and business financial status, including the reduction of mortgages, installment debts, and state and local government bonded indebtedness; (4) an increase in employment and technical training; and (5) the integration of Utah's economy with that of the rest of the West.[5]

Utah's location away from the coast made it an ideal spot for military installations and defense industries. As a result, ten major military bases and an army hospital were established there during the war.[6] In addition, several new firms manufactured munitions, steel, and other military needs, while others provided a variety of defense-related services and commodities.

Perhaps the most important new industry was the giant steel plant in Utah County, built for the government by the United States Steel Company. Operated by the newly-organized Geneva Steel Company, it began producing steel in February 1944, and before the war was over, it had produced 634,000 tons of plate steel, 144,280 tons of structural shapes, and significant amounts of other steel products.[7] At its peak the plant employed approximately ten thousand people.

The war also brought a number of defense-related plants to Salt Lake City, as well as a major expansion of the Utah Oil Refinery. In addition, a refractory was established in Lehi, the Standard

Parachute Company opened in Manti, and the state saw a huge expansion in mining, milling, construction, and agriculture. In all, such wartime operations brought an estimated 49,500 new jobs into the state.[8] It would be disastrous if all these war-related jobs were to disappear.

The war also stimulated Utah's mining industry. There was a huge increase in copper production, the annual output of coal more than doubled, and the production of iron ore increased nearly six times between 1939 and 1944.

In agriculture, the war stimulated price increases and contributed to the creation of 1,104 new farms and ranches and the opening of 1,956,762 new acres of farm land,[9] resulting in a marked increase in other economic indicators and a permanent stimulus to the economy. One prominent economist observed in 1943 that these economic changes were so far-reaching that economists could no longer use past historical trends to forecast Utah's economic future.[10]

The war had significant social consequences, including a permanent change in the role of women in Utah's workforce, and in resulting attitudes toward working women, including working mothers. Previously, about one-sixth of Utah's women were gainfully employed; only one state in the nation ranked lower. However, during the war perhaps as many as thirty-three thousand more women, including married women with children in school, went into the workforce.[11] They found employment in transportation, in wholesale and retail trade, as skilled mechanics, and as unskilled labor. At war's end many remained in the work force, and by 1950, nearly one-fourth of all Utah's women age fourteen and over were employed.[12] Even though Utah was still the ninth lowest state in this regard, an important new pattern had been established.

Anticipating the Postwar Economy

Painfully aware that the economic depression following World War I was more devastating and longer lasting in Utah and the Mountain West than almost anywhere else, Governor Herbert B. Maw and others began early to look at what might happen after World War II. In 1943, two important studies made some valu-

Image 1.1: Herbert B. Maw, governor of Utah, 1941–1949, led out in conversion to a peacetime economy after World War II. Used by permission, Utah State Historical Society, all rights reserved.

able observations and recommendations. One saw Utah as a fertile place for new investment in industry, agriculture, and mining and emphasized the importance of postwar cooperation between government and private enterprise. It also stressed the importance of water development to economic growth.[13]

A second study, made under the direction of J. R. Mahoney of the Bureau of Business and Economic Research, noted that Utah's workforce was better trained than before to engage in industrial pursuits[14] and foresaw that Utah's postwar economy would become more dependent upon industry than before. Mahoney predicted that several manufacturing plants would close but noted also that wartime economic forces had created a number of industries whose products could be used for purposes other than military. The Geneva Steel plant, he said, was the "most significant industrial happening" of the war and would remain open and become part of the United States's growing involvement in international trade.[15] He also predicted that the military storage depots near Ogden and Tooele would remain open and that Hill Field would become a permanent aircraft repair facility.

Mahoney identified steel, mining, and the military as Utah's "basic" postwar industries, but he also foresaw that the state's service industries would grow to support them, helping to ward off any tendency toward economic depression.[16] Equally important was his assurance that the construction industry would boom.[17]

Although Mahoney's economic forecasts were remarkably sound, in at least one projection he did not foresee the war's long-range effect. He observed that many wartime jobs had been filled by women, by young people, and by older people who had not previously been working outside the home. This, he predicted, would alleviate job shortages later as younger people returned to school, older people to retirement, and women to their homes. In the last prediction he was wrong, for women remained in the workforce, as they did in the rest of the nation, and in increasing numbers.

The Signs and Quandaries of Peace

Signs of Utah's conversion to a peacetime atmosphere began to appear in mid-1944 and continued through the year. In July, Utah's prewar speed limit of 60 mph (which had been dropped to 35 mph during the war) was restored. On August 13, the Salt Lake Tabernacle opened for daily noon organ recitals for the first time since the bombing of Pearl Harbor. On August 31, the three-year hiatus in sightseeing ended with the renewal of tours through Salt Lake City and to the famous Bingham copper mine. The first Utah state fair since Pearl Harbor opened on Monday, September 3. By the end of November, the Japanese-American internment camp at Topaz was empty. The people confined there as a result of anti-Japanese wartime hysteria were allowed to return to their homes in other states, although many chose to remain in Utah. On the night of Friday, November 30, Major Harry Ostler, a war veteran, threw an electrical switch in front of the *Tribune*-Telegram building and thousands of Christmas lights suddenly illuminated the streets of Salt Lake City for the first time since America had entered the war. By Christmas, between six and seven thousand Utah servicemen were discharged and returned home.

Among the challenges of reconversion was the question of who would control the process. In July 1945, the annual governors' conference, chaired by Utah's Herbert B. Maw, was held on Mackinac Island, Michigan. In his opening address, Maw declared that the federal government should quickly retreat from its myriad wartime regulations and controls. The states, he said, were fully competent to deal with reconversion, and he decried what he saw as the belief of many federal officials that the government should extend its controls into peacetime. "No system of central control from Washington will replace the simple yet effective democratic processes which have kept men free," he declared.[18] Governor Maw's sentiments reflected the deeply held feelings of most Utahns.

Actually, it did not take long for the federal government to drop its wartime economic controls. Even though Congress extended the authority of the Office of Price Administration to July 1946, popular clamor brought an end to controls on everything but rent, sugar, and rice by the end of 1945. The result was a mixed blessing: business activity stepped up, but prices, particularly food prices, also soared.

Politically, the immediate postwar economy did not bode well for the Democratic party. Shortages, inflation, labor unrest, a rash of strikes, and a witty Republic slogan "Had Enough?" all contributed to the election of a Republican-controlled Congress in 1946—the first in eighteen years. In Utah, voters ousted Democratic senator Abe Murdock in favor of Republican Arthur V. Watkins and replaced Democrat J. Will Robinson with Republican William A. Dawson in the House of Representatives. Walter K. Granger, a Democrat, was returned to the House but only by a slim margin of 104 votes.

America's rapid demobilization after the war had a direct effect on Utahns as thousands of veterans returning to the state were faced with the immediate need for housing, jobs, and schooling.

In addition, a jump in marriage statistics and the beginning of the post-war baby boom added to the large influx of population during the war, all of which resulted in a population increase of 25.2 percent between 1940 and 1950, the ninth highest growth rate in the nation.[19]

By November 1945, with an estimated three thousand veterans expected to make their homes in Salt Lake City, the housing situation seemed critical. City officials called for canvassing all available housing units, a door-to-door campaign to find new units, an advertising campaign, and the possible use of city and county land for temporary shelters. However, some tension arose as local apartment house owners wanted to increase rent. H. Grant Ivins, district director of the federal Office of Price Administration, argued that the owners already had a 44 percent greater net income than before the war, and 8 percent greater than in 1944. Owners called Ivins's statistics "rank propaganda" and argued that their costs were up by 30 percent—triple what Ivins claimed. However, they did not call for immediately abolishing federal controls.[20]

A fortuitous stop-gap measure came in December when the army air base in Salt Lake City was declared surplus and put at the disposal of the city for veterans' housing. The mayor's emergency housing committee soon concluded that even though there were still shortages, the problem was not alarming, no social problems would be created, and housing needs were gradually being met.[21] In the long run, the housing shortage never reached crisis proportions.

Another concern was an unusually high rate of traffic accidents and fatalities. This national problem was especially acute in Utah, where 174 people lost their lives on Utah's highways in 1945—an increase of 45 percent over 1944.[22] This carnage was attributed to old automobiles, bad tires, poor driving, the lifting of wartime gasoline rationing, raising of the speed limit, old roads originally designed for 40 mph traffic, and old bridges unable to handle modern heavy traffic.

In 1946, a hard-working and resourceful judge stepped into the battle. Reva Beck Bosone of Salt Lake City's Police and Traffic Court already had a reputation for being extremely hard on speeders and drunk drivers. Alarmed at the shocking increase in

Image 1.2: Reva Beck Bosone, Salt Lake City Police and Traffic Court judge who did much to reduce slaughter on the highways. Beginning in January 1949, she served two terms in the United States House of Representative, the first Utah woman to be elected to Congress. Used by permission, Utah State Historical Society, all rights reserved.

highway slaughter, she invited city officials from Salt Lake City, Ogden, and Provo to a meeting to plan a crusade against the rising death toll. A Tri-City Traffic Safety Committee was formed, with Bosone as chairperson. The committee agreed that henceforth heavier fines would be imposed for speeding, reckless driving, and hit-and-run convictions, along with fines and jail sentences for drunken driving and driving with licenses revoked. Under Bosone's continual prodding the program worked, but after her election to Congress in 1948, the committee dissolved. In Bosone's mind, however, this was "one of her finest hours on the bench."[23]

Part of the problem was road construction, something that had been long delayed because of the Great Depression and then the war. Early in 1948, the state debated a proposal for an express highway on the west side of Salt Lake City. The state road commission had available $1.2 million in federal road allocations to begin construction, which had to be contracted for by June 1, 1948.[24] However, west side residents were up in arms when they realized that the expressway might be built virtually in their backyards, adding an undesirable environment as well as destroying some homes, schools, and other improvements. Several hundred people attended a protest meeting on January 12, 1948, where someone suggested that a better location for the highway would be farther west, along the salt flats. State engineers replied that they had no intention of bypassing the city and that a highway that far west would only create problems related to the east-west traffic flow in and out of the city.[25] Nothing was done immediately, but in 1949 the state road commission decided to build the expressway just west of downtown (see chapter 2).

Let's Keep 'Em Open: Immediate Postwar Industrial Conversion

J. R. Mahoney's optimistic economic predictions of 1943 were mostly realized. The military supply depots at Ogden and Tooele remained open, as did some other installations, and Hill Field remained a major installation for aircraft service and repair. This meant a continuing reliance upon federal dollars for much of

Image 1.3: Geneva Steel plant, aerial view taken December 19, 1946. The plant was built during World War II and remained an important factor in Utah's economy for many decades after the War. Used by permission, Utah State Historical Society, all rights reserved.

Utah's economic well-being, but it also provided a crucial boost to the existing economy.

Equally significant was what happened in manufacturing. Some plants that produced goods primarily for military use closed, but shortly after V-J Day, Utah's newspapers assured readers that their state would have no problems with postwar reconversion. Already most industries were well into the task. Remodeling and maintenance was enjoying a minor boom, and a considerable new amount of construction was under way. As early as the end of 1945, the *Salt Lake Tribune* reported that the conversion process was nearly complete.[26]

The big question was the fate of Geneva Steel. Politicians, newspaper editors, workers, and other citizens all clamored to find some way to keep this war-born plant open, almost as if it were the lifeblood of the state's future economy. Some said that it was not that essential, but Governor Maw argued in August 1945 that "without steel we are lost," stressing the fact that steel was a basic industry that would attract others to the state. In October, the *Salt Lake Tribune* reported on a nationwide "spot check" on reconversion showing that the future of Geneva was the key to Utah's potential unemployment problem.[27] Many people argued that Geneva was important not only for the economy of Utah but also for a healthy postwar economy in the entire West.

By August 1945, the government was entertaining offers for Geneva. US Steel, Colorado Fuel and Iron, and the Kaiser Company all showed an interest, but on August 9 US Steel withdrew from the bidding. Benjamin Fairless, president of US Steel, said his company withdrew because it understood that the government opposed its involvement on the grounds that it could lead to a monopoly. In response, Stuart Symington, chairman of the Surplus Property Board, wrote to Fairless denying any opposition to US Steel. In less than a month after its withdrawal, US Steel renewed its bid.

State and local leaders were ecstatic,[28] but the process seemed to drag on interminably as it moved through several federal agencies as well as Congress. In September the Reconstruction Finance Corporation (RFC) finally declared Geneva and some other Utah properties to be surplus. However, the law required the Surplus Property Board to present to Congress a report stating its proposed policies for governing disposal of government-owned steel plants. That report was a long time coming, drawing the wrath of the *Tribune*. It had been promised for four months, the editors complained, enough damage had already been done, and the board's continued dallying, plus inevitable "congressional mauling" of the report, left the potential of even more disaster. "Under the circumstances," they chided, "the SPB will run no greater risk of compounding its past errors if it just grabs a report of some kind out of its collection of rejects and sends it along."[29] The report, finally delivered on October 11, outlined what seemed to be responsible policies, including a preference for selling rather than leasing surplus properties.[30]

Seven companies submitted sealed bids for Geneva, and on May 2, 1946, it was announced that US Steel's was the most favorable. It offered $47.5 million for the plant and inventories and agreed to spend at least another $18.6 million for immediate reconversion. The government's acceptance of the offer brought prompt applause from Utahns, some calling it the opening of a golden era for the state.[31]

Geneva Steel may not have been the panacea it was made out to be, but it helped Utah assume a much more prominent role in the economy of the West. Before 1946, Utah and other western manufacturers usually purchased their steel at Chicago prices plus freight, which added one-third to the cost. However, beginning in 1946, Geneva sold to them at competitive prices, capturing a number of western markets and providing a continuing high level of employment in Utah. In addition, Geneva's operations provided employment elsewhere, such as in the iron and coal mines that provided ore and coke for its furnaces as well as in transportation and other businesses necessary to the operation of the giant mill. Within a few years after the war Utah ranked fourth in the nation in production of iron ore and tenth in production of steel.[32] Geneva's impact also extended to mining, manufacturing, and other business activities beyond the boundaries of the state. Geneva, along with the rest of the growing manufacturing industry in Utah, gave a vital boost to housing, construction, and various retail trades. In October, 1948, Benjamin Fairless complimented company officials and civic leaders for the marvelous job Geneva was doing, commending it for "accepting the challenge of those who said steel couldn't be produced on a satisfactory basis in Utah."[33]

More Postwar Economics: Utah's New Look

Demobilization brought numerous economic problems. but there was no postwar depression either in the nation or in Utah. Several economic shock-absorbers helped avert it. One was the rush of Americans to purchase goods they had been denied during the war. Their ability to buy was fortified by federal unemployment compensation and Social Security, reflecting one of the legacies of the New Deal: the permanent commitment to increased responsibility for social welfare on the part of the national government. In addition, the 1944 "GI Bill of Rights" helped millions of former servicemen attend school by paying tuition, books, and a modest living allowance for a period of time based on how long they had served in the military. It also provided medical treatment, unemployment insurance, and low-interest loans for home-building and business. Another shock-absorber appeared when the federal Defense Plant Corporation offered its properties for sale. Many of these properties (such as Geneva Steel) were picked up at bargain prices by private enterprise, which resulted in a round of new investment. At the same time, a continuing high level of government spending after 1945 also helped stave off depression.

World War II stimulated a move toward dependence on heavy manufacturing as Utah's primary industry.[34] But there were hopeful signs in other industries as well. These included, in 1947, a new plant in Nephi for manufacturing brake linings and industrial hose, and an announcement by Standard Oil Company of the forthcoming construction of a $5 million refinery near Salt Lake City. At the end of the year, the secretary of the Utah Manufacturing Association reported that Utah factories employed thirty thousand people, 75 percent more than in the years immediately preceding the war.[35] He also pointed to a healthy diversity of products and of manufacturing locations in the state, including rubber at Nephi, gypsum at Sigurd, cement at Devil's Slide, oil refineries in Salt Lake City, battery plants at Ogden, chemical manufacturing at Garfield, the production of silica at Murray, plaster at Cedar City, fertilizer south of Salt Lake City, and food processing in Salt Lake City and Ogden.

All of these developments helped stimulate Utah's construction industry. By October 1945, about $5 million in new construction, including an estimated three hundred new housing units, was in progress in Salt Lake City.[36] The average monthly employment in construction reached 13,027 by 1951. By 1955 it was up to fourteen thousand—more than four times the average before the war.

Except for a brief decline immediately after the war, mineral production increased, although this did not mean a great jump in employment. Changing technology improved production per man-hour but at the same time decreased the number of men needed in the mines. However, the production of iron ore tripled between 1944 and 1950. Coal production also soared, feeding markets in Utah, other parts of the western United States, and Japan. Utah's production of non-ferrous metals, particularly gold, silver, lead, zinc, and copper, was somewhat erratic, but in 1950 Utah copper, valued at nearly $116 million, accounted for 30.6 percent of the nation's production.[38] Mining declined in terms of the percentage of the population it employed, but it remained a viable and highly important part of Utah's economy and continued to pay the largest average monthly wage of any industry.[39]

Another changing pattern came in agricultural employment as many men left the farm to seek work elsewhere. There was also a significant increase in the number of farmers holding two jobs, one at home and the other at a nearby construction project or industrial plant. The result was more work for wives and children on the farms, as well as more use of migrant labor.[40] Between 1945 and 1950, the total number of farms in Utah declined slightly, down from 26,411 to 24,322, while the total number of acres in farmland remained fairly constant and the average size of farms increased (from 391.7 acres to 449.4).

This pattern continued,[41] suggesting that various factors were making it possible to raise more crops and operate larger farms with fewer people working full-time. One of these factors was mechanization. In the sugar beet industry, for example, mechanical beet harvesters garnered about two-thirds of the Utah-Idaho Sugar Company's crops by 1950. Operators of one sugar factory bragged that its beets were now "untouched by human hands."[42]

This period also saw the beginnings of important changes in livestock industries, particularly Utah's "big four": beef, dairying, poultry, and sheep. In the first five years after the war, there was a general decline in production of most livestock and livestock products. Much of it, with the exception of cattle, milk solids, and chickens, even fell below pre-war levels.[43] At the same time, the processing of poultry became a major segment of Utah's economy. In 1945, for example, Utah was the fourth largest producer of turkey products in the nation, and that year the opening of another major packing plant was announced.[44]

One irony in Utah's rosy economic picture was the fact that even as the state's businessmen and politicians were among those most loudly opposing government spending, emphasizing instead the importance of private enterprise, the changes wrought by World War II made Utah's economy highly dependent upon government (federal, state, and local) employment and federal expenditures in defense-related industries. At the beginning of 1947, for example, nearly 20 percent of Utah's workforce was employed by government. Utah's ratio of 74 government employees per thousand population was second highest in the nation.[45] By 1950, more than 23 percent of Utah's nonagricultural employees were working for government, and 48 percent of these were employed by the federal government.[46] The 1950s saw the beginning of a surge in defense-related industries, eventually making defense spending the major source of income in Utah.[47] The continuing impact of the national government on Utah's economy was considerable. Without it, Utah may well have slipped into the depression so many people had feared. Beating swords into plowshares was a noble ideal, but in practical terms Utah's economy could not have gotten rid of the swords all at once.

The Central Utah Project: More Optimism for Utah's Future

The availability of water was also a major key to Utah's economic development. The Strawberry Valley Project, the first large-scale diversion of water from the Colorado River into the Great Basin, was completed in 1920 and benefitted the Spanish Fork and Payson areas of southern Utah Valley in particular.[48] In 1945, the Bureau of Reclamation investigated possibilities for diverting more water from the Green River into central Utah as an expansion of the Strawberry project, and the name Central Utah Project (CUP) was coined. An interim report called for a 102-mile aqueduct that would carry water along the Uinta Mountains and into Little Brush Creek, from which it would flow into Strawberry Reservoir. The report also proposed a 132-mile aqueduct to Echo Park on the Green River, where the Echo Park Dam would be built, and contemplated eight power plants. The assumption was that water would be available under the terms of the Colorado River

Compact, a 1922 agreement mediated by the federal government between all the states bordering on that river. A project office was located in Spanish Fork in June 1946, and full-scale feasibility studies, which continued for several years, began in August.[49]

Utahns promoted the CUP as eagerly as they had promoted Geneva Steel. An optimistic review of the project, published in September 1948, anticipated that without the CUP Utah could supply the water needs of 850,000 people, but with it there would be enough water for 1.6 million, plus considerably more for farmland, industrial development, and one billion kilowatt hours of low-cost hydroelectric power annually.[50] There was hardly a dissenting voice as the potential of the CUP became one of many factors upon which Utahns based their hopes for a prosperous postwar economy. However, it would be a long time coming.

The Promise of Tourism

Utahns expected tourism to become increasingly important for their state, and it is little wonder that they were outraged when some grossly inaccurate, even unflattering, information went out to the public. In July 1945, the Office of War Information (OWI) published a new edition of *America Illustrated*. The publication, distributed in Russia to help acquaint the people of that nation with the United States, contained greatly misleading information about Utah, as well as several other states. The *Deseret News* angrily editorialized that "So far as we can see, OWI is about as useful to our economy now as a coronet to a cow." Senator Abe Murdock sarcastically told Elmer Davis, head of OWI, that if no one in Davis's organization were capable of describing all parts of the nation accurately, Utah would be glad to send some of its grade school students to Washington to do it. Davis soon publicly admitted that the book contained "some misstatements" that would be corrected in later editions. He also sent letters of apology to each member of Utah's Congressional delegation as well as to the delegations of seven other states who were equally furious.[51]

Meanwhile, in December 1945, Gus P. Backman, executive secretary of Salt Lake City's Chamber of Commerce, reported a tremendous upsurge in the number of tourists—an increase of 100 percent each month since V-J Day and an expected 2,225,000 total for the year. This was more than double the number of visitors in 1940.⁵² Tourism continued to prosper, illustrated in part by the fact that in 1947 over one million people visited Temple Square in Salt Lake City, a jump of 147 percent over the prewar year 1939.⁵³ The major challenge, according to Backman, was not getting people to come to Utah but getting them to extend their stay, and he stressed the importance of promoting the state's superb scenic and recreational attractions. During 1948 an estimated 2,453,000 tourists visited Utah, spending approximately $50 million.⁵⁴

The Pioneer Centennial, 1947

A highlight in this period of transition was Utah's Pioneer Centennial celebration of 1947, a hundred years after the first Mormon pioneers settled the Salt Lake Valley. David O. McKay, second counselor in the First Presidency of the LDS Church, was appointed chair of the State Centennial Commission as early as 1941, but the commission was temporarily disbanded during the war. Gus P. Backman was appointed Centennial Director.

The commission began its most intensive planning early in 1946. Among other things, it sponsored a statewide beautification and cleanup program. In response, many cities and towns promoted their own "cleanup, fixup, and paintup" campaigns.⁵⁵

Public celebration began on January 1, 1947, when Utah entered a float entitled "Pioneer Days" in the annual Tournament of Roses Parade in Pasadena, California. Made up of gold and silver chrysanthemums and blue delphiniums, the float depicted a large beehive and the state flower, the sego lily, and carried Centennial Queen Colleen Robinson. The entry won first prize in its division, class AA for counties and states.

Throughout the year, Utahns involved themselves in numerous and varied festivities: parades; rodeos; festive games and contests reflecting pioneer times; statewide pioneer-style dances; twenty-two concerts by the Utah Symphony Orchestra before a total of ten thousand people in thirteen Utah communities; a tour of the light opera "Blossom Time," which played to a total of twenty thousand people; the production of an original musical, "Promised Valley," commemorating the pioneers, journey to Utah; traveling art exhibits; and a four-month-long exposition at the state fairgrounds featuring Utah industry, manufacturing, agriculture, and natural resources. On July 4 and 5, as part of the national Independence Day observance, a Utah centennial extravaganza was presented at the Brigham Young University stadium in Provo. Depicting the sweep of Utah history, the production included the original Native American inhabitants, Spanish and other explorers, and the coming of the Mormons.[56]

The highlight of the year was the unveiling and dedication on July 24 (Utah's official Pioneer Day) of the majestic "This Is the Place" Monument, at the mouth of Emigration Canyon. Sculpted by Mahonri Young, nationally prominent Utah sculptor and a grandson of Brigham Young, the monument was the apex of his career—the "big job" he had always wanted.

The monument was symbolic of much more than the Mormon entry into the Salt Lake Valley. Rather, it represented all those whose paths met or crossed in the area. One section honored Washakie, the Northern Shoshoni chief who befriended the white men and often roamed into the Utah area. Another section paid tribute to the fur trappers and traders and included such famous men as Peter Skene Ogden, Jedediah Smith, and Joseph Walker. The Spanish explorers, particularly Fathers Domínguez and Escalante, who came through in 1776, were also depicted, as was Father Pierre Jean DeSmet, founder of the Pacific Northwest missions in 1840. There was a statue of Captain Benjamin L. E. Bonneville, a colorful explorer who never actually traveled into Utah but whose exploits in the West were well known. Another celebrated explorer, John C. Fremont, was likewise honored with a statue. Fremont visited the area now known as Utah during three of his expeditions. His report, published in 1845, became one of the Mormons' most valuable sources of information as they considered where to settle in the West. An impressive frieze depicted men and women with their wagons on the Mormon pioneer trail and the ill-fated Donner Party that went through the Salt Lake Valley in 1846. The focal point was the group of three pioneer leaders that crowned the monument: Brigham Young, Heber C. Kimball, and Wilford Woodruff.[57]

Utahns viewed their centennial celebration as a huge success, not only because of the new construction, community cleanups, and myriad celebrations that took place but also because it brought a great deal of welcome, positive publicity to the state.

Social and Cultural Challenges

Utahns faced a number of social and cultural challenges in these transition years, some of them related to the larger national context. Civil rights, for example, received a considerable amount of national attention because of the large numbers of blacks and other minorities who had served in the military or worked in defense plants during the war but who now were experiencing discrimination. In the late 1940s, the federal government and some states made mild, mostly ineffective, efforts to alleviate the problem.

The effort to enhance civil rights in Utah was pitifully unpopular. In 1947 state Senators Sol J. Selvin (D-Tooele) and Lorenzo E. Elgren (D-Salt Lake), members of an interim committee appointed to study racial relations, introduced two bills in the legislature. One would have outlawed racial discrimination in hotels and eating establishments and the other would have kept employers from discriminating on the basis of race, color, or creed. Both failed to pass, receiving only six votes each.[58]

Part of the problem may have been that most of the white majority in Utah had simply never associated with blacks, Native Americans, or other ethnic minorities. In 1950, minorities totaled only 11,953 people or 1.73 percent of the state's population.[59] Of these, 4,201 (0.6 percent) were Native Americans, most whom lived on reservations and were therefore out of the consciousness of most other Utahns. The 2,729 blacks in the state constituted 0.4 percent of the population, while all other groups (mostly Asian and Hispanic) combined made up 0.73 percent. Whatever the reason, the prevailing attitude in Utah toward racial minorities seemed biased.

Another challenging issue was education as Utah's public schools faced serious teacher shortages. In the fall of 1945, nearly 1,500 teachers were employed only on the basis of emergency authorization because they lacked the required state teacher certification. Due to wartime restrictions on renovation and new construction, there was also a shortage of classrooms, with some schools holding classes in churches and other improvised facilities. School administrators were also concerned with other kinds of problems, such as how to provide more adequate vocational education and how to develop more racial tolerance in the schools.[60]

The problem of public school finance was complex. The federal government helped, particularly in areas where military bases made a significant impact on the school population. Utahns were wary of other kinds of federal aid but, at the same time, were reluctant to vote for increased local taxes. Nevertheless, in 1947, the state increased the public education budget to $23 million, a jump of more than $7.4 million from the 1946–47 school year. Under the new budget, each classroom unit in the state would receive a minimum of $3,300 per year, and local districts had the discretion to raise this amount another 30 percent.[61]

Utah's vocational schools, colleges, and universities also experienced postwar challenges. Thousands of returning veterans, taking advantage of the G.I. Bill of Rights, clamored for admittance, resulting in huge strains on school facilities. Some relief came in 1947 when the State Board of Education received funds to expand vocational training in the Salt Lake City area.[62]

Dr. A. Ray Olpin, who became president of the University of Utah on January 1, 1946, hoped to make the school a top research institution that would benefit the entire state. However, the university had a more immediate crisis. With enrollment expanding rapidly, classroom facilities were gone and new student housing was almost nonexistent. One possible solution was to use facilities being vacated at Fort Douglas, but the problem was how to receive permission. On February 18, 1946, Olpin and Salt Lake City Mayor Earl J. Glade met with General Dwight D. Eisenhower, Army Chief of Staff, who was in Salt Lake City. The base was "just through the fence" from the university, Olpin pointed out, and certain buildings would be perfect to alleviate their problems. Eisenhower suggested to Major General William E. Shedd, commander of the Ninth Service Command, that he simply "cut a hole in the fence" and let the university in. Shedd responded that the law forbade such use of military posts, but Eisenhower promised that when he got back to Washington the law would be changed.

Almost immediately the university began to expand its facilities. In March General Shedd turned over an area of Fort Douglas formerly used by the Women's Army Corps. A short time later Olpin and his staff obtained 301 family dwelling units from various places in Utah, Arizona, California, and Oregon and moved them to a location that became known as Stadium Village, where they were available for student housing. Federal laws were changed, making military facilities available for veterans' housing and educational needs. In May, 1946, Olpin descended on Washington with maps of Fort Douglas. Building 105, he told the War Assets Administration, would be especially useful for university classrooms. Other interests, however, also wanted to acquire it, but by the end of the summer the university obtained not only that structure but also others from the fort. Still more buildings were brought in from elsewhere. In addition, working partly through Utah's senators, the university acquired more land as well as a considerable amount of surplus property, laboratory supplies, and furniture. This included 1,800 chairs acquired from Fort Douglas after General Eisenhower cut through the bureaucracy with a simple phone call.[63]

Despite these problems, Utah continued to rank high in educational achievement. In 1945 the average number of school years completed by persons over the age of twenty was 10.8, the highest in the nation. In 1946, the state was second only to Oregon in the percentage of youth finishing eighth grade (97.1 percent), highest in the nation in percent enrolled in high school (91.7 percent), and second only to Washington in percentage graduated from high school (64 percent). At the same time, 24 percent of Utah's college-age youth were enrolled in colleges, second in the nation in this category, and the state led the nation with 12.6 percent of its youth graduated from college. In addition, Utah could boast that its rural population under age forty had more education than the rural population of any other state.[64]

Uncomfortable Interface: Labor, Politics, and Religion

One of the nation's most tense immediate postwar problems was labor unrest. Workers had honored a no-strike pledge all through the war, despite a 30 percent increase in prices. Now, their pent-up uneasiness exploded in a rash of nation–wide strikes, particularly in the automobile, coal, and railroad industries, which in turn affected other industries.

In Utah, major strikes began in Salt Lake City on November 1, 1945, with unions at some grocery store chains seeking wage increases and shorter work weeks. The four-day walkout ended with substantial wage increases but a withdrawal of the demand for a 48-hour week. On January 21, 1946, national strikes broke out in the steel and related industries, taking six thousand Utahns off the job. The steel strike ended in mid-February when the companies agreed to President Truman's proposed 18 ½ cent hourly wage increase, but received in return an inflationary $5-a-ton hike in the price of steel. At the same time, the International Union of Mine, Mill and Smelter Workers continued its strike against Utah Copper Company, American Smelting and Refining Company, and United States Smelting and Refining Company. The strike lasted for 148 days, from July 22 to December 17, becoming the longest strike in the nation during the reconversion period.

Utah's anthracite coal miners went out on strike on April 1, 1946. They returned to work temporarily on May 13, but a week later the federal government seized the mines in order to keep them open. The resulting negotiations with the Secretary of the Interior ended with the union receiving most of its demands with respect to wages, safety regulations, and other technicalities. In November, however, miners were again on strike until, on December 7, they were ordered back to work as the result of a federal court injunction. This was a welcome settlement for most Utahns—it was the beginning of the winter season and many homes and industries were beginning to suffer from lack of coal, the major source of fuel for heating and industrial purposes.

One result of these and other strikes was a generally intensified feeling against the seemingly increasing power of labor and its "bosses."[65] The Wagner Act of 1935, sometimes called the "Magna Carta of labor," had guaranteed the right of collective bargaining and protected unions from employer interference, but many people felt that the pendulum had swung too far. As a result, in 1947 Congress passed, over Truman's veto, the Taft-Hartley Act, which banned the closed shop, where an employer could hire only union members in good standing, but allowed a union shop (where new workers were required to join the union within a specified time), unless prohibited by state law. Members of Utah's Congressional delegation clearly demonstrated their political partisanship in how they stood on this act. Utah's Senator Watkins and Congressman Dawson (Republicans) voted to override Truman's veto, while Congressman Granger (Democrat) voted to sustain it. Democratic senator Elbert D. Thomas supported the veto, but he could not vote because he was in Geneva Switzerland, attending sessions of the international labor conference.

In Utah the Taft-Hartley Act was resented by labor leaders but drew a considerable amount of praise from what seemed to be a majority of the people. The *Deseret News* and the *Salt Lake Tribune*, often at odds editorially, both criticized Truman's veto.

The same year Congress passed the Taft-Hartley Act Utah's legislature also passed a restrictive labor law that, among other things, prohibited secondary boycotts. Governor Maw vehemently opposed the bill and was determined to veto it. However, after labor leaders counted the bill's supporters it was clear that a veto would be overridden.[66] The governor let it become law without his signature.

Unfortunately, the political implications of the labor question took on overtones of church-state relations. While the dominant LDS Church seldom officially embraced a political issue, some of its leaders were often politically outspoken. Elder Joseph F. Merrill of the Council of the Twelve Apostles was such a person.

Next to prohibition, the national issue that drew Elder Merrill's most impassioned political commentary was the growing power of labor unions and particularly the closed shop. As a long-time conservative Democrat he was sympathetic with the need for unions, but he was convinced that they had gone too far. He blamed both business and labor for the growing evils of the day, but he saved his most devastating criticism for the closed shop. One of his early salvos against this policy came in a general conference address on October 5, 1941, in which he declared that liberty was "fast fading away." "When we deny an able-bodied man 'the right to work,'" he said, " we rob him of his independence and destroy his happiness."[67] The next attack came in another general conference just three years later.[68]

During the labor difficulties of 1946, Elder Merrill spoke out again during the October general conference of the church. He decried the strikes, scolding labor for demanding pay increases after having received disproportionate increases in war industry work. Unions were so strong, he complained, that they controlled elections, making politicians subservient to them. The strikes they had called, he argued, had done no one any good. Rather, they had delayed production, brought unrest and civil strife, put millions on public relief rolls, and weakened America abroad. "What difference, in principle, is there between this method of holdup and that of a gun?" he tartly asked. "In both, force is applied. Then are not both methods forms of robbery?"[69]

As might be expected, such strong words brought a storm of criticism. One scorching letter from a non-Mormon in Nevada, who pictured laborers as practically in slavery, vehemently decried what seemed to be the church's general anti-labor stance. Another criticized Merrill for not taking into account the abuses by business associations that conspired to fix prices and thus hurt the consumer.[70] Merrill responded that the writer had been misinformed on his position on labor. He was in sympathy with those who wished to organize unions. His only concern was with the selfishness that, he felt, governed too many of the activities of the unions and led them to strike for unjustly high wages.[71]

Frank H. Jonas, a young assistant professor of political science at Utah State Agricultural College, wrote to Elder Merrill, mentioning, among other things, his understanding that the apostle had been assigned the "problem" of labor by the Quorum of the Twelve. In response, Merrill denied that he had been given any such assignment, saying that any speech he ever gave was totally his own responsibility. He also told Jonas that the church was neither anti-labor nor anti-union, but he affirmed his feeling that most general authorities were opposed to the closed shop.[72]

Elder Merrill's jeremiads reflected, in part, the nationwide reaction to the growing strength of unionism that resulted in the Taft-Hartley Act. It is important to recognize, however, that the public statements of Elder Merrill and other prominent Latter-day Saints helped create an unfortunate assumption in Utah and elsewhere that Mormonism and modern unionism were incompatible. Whether true or not, that assumption had an important impact on Utah politics.

Utahns Look at Other National Issues

The people of Utah also took great interest in other national concerns. One was foreign relations and particularly what was dubbed the "Cold War." Like many other Americans did, they began to see the Soviet Union, a World War II ally but a Communist state, as a threat to world peace. As it expanded its political hegemony over Eastern Europe, by 1949 it had also developed the capability of exploding an atomic bomb. Increasingly fearful of Communism, Americans saw in the actions of the Soviet Union a determination to spread it worldwide.[74]

This was only one indication that America's postwar relationship with the world was taking a 180-degree turn from the isolationism that characterized the nation in the years before World War II. Another manifestation of that change was a new kind of foreign policy, known as "containment," which was aimed directly at stopping Communist expansionism. An early expression of this policy came in March 1947 after Great Britain announced that it no longer had the means to continue supporting the Greek government in its civil war against Communist insurgents. Almost immediately, President Truman asked Congress for money to provide economic aid for Greece as well as Turkey, which was engaged in a similar civil war, and authority to send Americans to train Greek and Turkish soldiers. It must be American policy, Truman declared, to support free people who were resisting attempts at subjugation by armed minorities or outside pressures.

In the end, America's $659 million aid program helped save both countries from Communism.

The Truman Doctrine, as it was called, received mixed reactions from Utahns. Senator Elbert Thomas was concerned about America's intent. He thought the United States might be justified in loaning money to Greece for the purpose of helping that country care for its own people, but he thought it was wrong to do so for the purpose either of stopping Russia or sustaining an "unworthy faction" (i.e., a monarchy) in Greece. The *Salt Lake Tribune*, on the other hand, praised the policy, although it saw a certain irony in the fact that the United States was thus supporting a monarchy.[75]

The Marshall Plan was less controversial. Proposed by Secretary of State George C. Marshall in 1947, this was a program of massive economic aid designed to help Europe recover from the devastation of the war. Between 1948 and 1951, America contributed $13 billion dollars toward European recovery, which not only helped achieve that purpose but in some cases also helped stave off Communism. Utahns were enthusiastic about the program and its purposes. Saving Europe would be a costly and thankless job, said one *Salt Lake Tribune* editorial, but it was necessary for world survival. The writer of the editorial then reminded readers of the new reality that many Utahns may not have grasped, but which would permanently affect the destiny of their state and nation: "Alas, times have changed and the world has shrunk to a fraction of the size it was in the 18th and 19th centuries. No longer is Europe a 'far off country,' but a neighbor. No longer is the Atlantic Ocean a great barrier between the old world and the new one. No longer can Americans or any other people on the globe consider themselves isolated nations."[76]

The most visible political symbol of the deepening East-West tension was Germany, which had been divided at the end of the war into zones of occupation, each controlled by one of the four major powers. However, in 1948, the United States, Britain, and France united their zones and invited the people of western Germany to form a new federal government. The Soviets, who controlled eastern Germany as well as the access route to jointly occupied Berlin, were furious at the plan to unify West Berlin. In retaliation, and in an effort to persuade the western powers either to give up the city

Image 1.4: Gail Halvorsen gained international notoriety because of his dropping candy to children during the Berlin Airlift of 1948–48.

or to back away from unification, the Soviets began in April 1948 to restrict traffic to Berlin. In June they stopped traffic altogether. The Americans, however, immediately organized a massive air lift program that, between June 1948 and mid-May 1949, delivered more than 1.5 million tons of supplies to West Berlin.

Utahns applauded what was happening. They saw the Berlin Airlift as a political necessity. "There can be no US retreat from Berlin without serious loss of prestige," editorialized the *Salt Lake Tribune*. "It would imply that division of Germany is inevitable, and Moscow might reconsider it a green light for its expansion program."[77]

One Utahn, Air Force First Lieutenant Gail Halvorsen, achieved special notoriety as the "candy bomber." One of many pilots flying food and supplies into Berlin, he usually simply landed his plane and then took off as quickly as possible. However, one day during off-duty hours he hitched a ride on another plane and spent four hours touring the city. Among the people he talked with was a group of about thirty children, who impressed him so much that he told them if they were there when he flew over later that day, he would drop them some candy. They could tell which plane he was in because he would wiggle the plane's wings. Before returning, Lieutenant Halvorsen tied chocolate bars to tiny parachutes made of handkerchiefs or pieces of cloth. When he came back, the children were waiting, and he dropped his special cargo through the tube pilots normally used to drop flares. After landing, he taxied to the fence surrounding the airport and could see the children happily waving the white parachutes. He continued his "candy bombing" and his good deed quickly caught on. Thousands of Americans soon began showering him with candy and handkerchiefs, and other pilots also began dropping candy. Near the end of October, the Air Force announced that "Operation Little Vittles" was delivering 1,500 "candy chutes" a day to the sparkly eyed children of Berlin.[78]

A different kind of national issue for the United States, one with deep historical roots, concerned Native Americans. It was a question that other Americans seemed to hope would just go away, but in the fall of 1947 it became a special concern for Utahns.

Many tribes faced serious economic problems, but none were more cruel than those of the sixty-four thousand Navajo living on a reservation that included sections of Arizona, New Mexico, Colorado, and Utah. Their population was 640 percent higher than when their ancestors were placed on the reservation in 1868, yet one of their chief means of livelihood, raising sheep, was becoming increasingly difficult to sustain. As both the human and sheep population increased, the grasslands were nearly destroyed, making it necessary for children to range farther and farther from home to watch and drive the sheep. The problem was exacerbated in 1935 when the federal government, in an effort to halt the devastating erosion, instituted a massive stock reduction program. The result was disastrous for many Navajo. Some families with hundreds of sheep were suddenly forced to survive with only ten per person, and this allotment was reduced by five for each horse or cow the family owned. Then, in 1947, a severe drought threatened not only the Navajo but other western tribes with both freezing and starvation during the coming winter.[79] Something had to be done, and soon, to prevent a total catastrophe.

One of those who took note was Spencer W. Kimball, a member of the LDS Church's Quorum of the Twelve Apostles and a long-time friend of the Native American people. In two angry, two-part articles in both the *Deseret News* (November 28 and 29, 1947) and the church's *Improvement Era* (February and April 1948), he vividly portrayed the shocking conditions of the Navajo. He also excoriated the federal government for violating its treaty commitments to provide Native Americans with a means of livelihood and education in support of their quest to become economically self-sufficient. "America must awaken to its responsibilities!" he declared, giving voice to the pent-up feelings of many that the government had abdicated its duty.

> Shame on any nation which will ignore or repudiate its solemn treaties and promises. When we shall have filled the stomachs and clothed the bodies of the Navajos we shall have only begun to make restitution to them for injury we have imposed upon them. Only a long range program of education can begin to undo the wrong we have inflicted.[80]

The Navajo saw a bitter irony in the lack of attention they were receiving from Washington in the same year that the Truman and Marshall plans were being touted so loudly. One of them asked a very reasonable question: "But, Mr. Kimball, why is it that the government which cannot furnish us schools for our little children talks about hundreds of millions to go to Greece and Turkey with other peoples?"

In the meantime, church, civic, and other groups rallied to help, calling for public donations and organizing efforts to get at least the necessities of life to the stricken people. On November 27, the LDS Church's Welfare Department sent two truckloads of food, clothing, and bedding to the Navajo of southern Utah. The *Deseret News* also organized an Indian Aid Caravan that, by mid-December, had collected in donations for Navajo relief 130 tons of food, clothing, bedding, and Christmas packages.[81]

Such charity was only a stop-gap measure, but the news stories, and particularly the work of one *Deseret News* reporter, helped bring the matter forcefully to the attention of federal officials.[82] On December 2, President Truman announced that he would appeal to Congress for a long-range plan for the improvement of Navajo health and education, and Utah's Congressman William A. Dawson called for quick passage of a proposed $2 million bill. The Secretary of the Interior suggested long-range programs for the development of irrigation, natural resources, and better marketing of Navajo crafts. On December 4, the $2 million Navajo relief bill was approved by Congress, authorizing expenditures for immediate relief, as well as a more extensive, long-range building and employment program.

These hurried measures were hardly enough to turn the situation around immediately, but they were at least a beginning. Such beginnings had been made before, however. The next half-century would see more beginnings, and some hard-won progress, in the march toward self-reliance and economic independence for Native Americans.

Politics: 1948

All of the political, economic, and social cross-currents connected with the transition to peace made 1948 an interesting and pivotal election year. On the national level, Harry S Truman had been trying to carry on the New Deal tradition in the face of opposition from a Republican Congress, but his political fortunes were waning, both in the nation and within his party. They reached a new low when, early in 1948, former Vice-president Henry A. Wallace bolted the party to become a Progressive Party candidate. Democrats, in turn, urged Truman to step aside in favor of the popular General Dwight D. Eisenhower, but when Eisenhower refused offers from both major parties the Democrats reluctantly nominated Truman anyway. Meanwhile, disgruntled southerners also trailed out of the Democratic party, forming a States' Rights Party and nominating Governor Strom Thurmond of South Carolina as their candidate. Republicans scented a political triumph in November and nominated New York governor Thomas E. Dewey. The response in Utah was positive. The *Salt Lake Tribune*, for example, endorsed him, predicting that he would be "a safe, sound, sensible and steadfast leader of the American people in any emergency."

For the most part, political pollsters and commentators around the nation agreed that the Democratic split meant almost certain defeat for Truman. The president himself, however, refused to give up, barnstorming the country and attacking the "do-nothing" Republican

Congress with a vengeance. His "give-'em-hell" tactics appealed to key voters everywhere, including Utah. Dewey, on the other hand, assured of victory, ran a cautious, lackluster campaign. Surprising almost everyone, Truman won by a decisive electoral vote (303 to Dewey's 189 and Thurmond's 39), although his popular majority was thin. He also carried with him enough Democrats to regain control of both houses of Congress.

In 1948 Utah had a Democratic governor, only a one-vote Democratic majority in the state senate and a lopsided Republican House of Representatives. Governor Maw was clearly at odds with the legislature, primarily over the issue of welfare. He accused lawmakers of being more concerned with cutting costs than with human welfare,[83] but many Utah voters also disagreed with his efforts to obtain more social welfare funds. However, believing that welfare needs were acute, in February the governor called a special session of the legislature to meet on March 1 to deal with the problem. This brought the ire of the *Deseret News*, which ridiculed what it called his "tear-jerking radio plea" and cited figures to demonstrate that people on welfare were not in the "perpetual state of insufficient food, inadequate clothing, cold houses and suffering conditions" that Maw had described.[84]

At the special session, Maw declared that the money available simply was not sufficient to care for those needing public welfare. He called for a $3,575,000 appropriation for the remainder of the biennium—an increase of $2,390,000 over the current appropriation. The *Salt Lake Tribune* predicted that the proposal would not pass because there was little public sentiment in favor of it, and the *Deseret News* declared that the state could not afford it and cited figures to show that it was not needed anyway.[85] On March 15, the proposal was killed in the Senate.

Maw's defeat in the special session did nothing for his political career. He was nominated by his party for reelection despite the fact that some anti-administration Democrats opposed him and the fact that he was running for a controversial and unprecedented third term. Few people believed he would win. It seemed almost a foregone conclusion, in fact, that the Republicans would sweep the state.

The Republican gubernatorial nominee was J. Bracken Lee, former mayor of Price and an outspoken advocate of cutting government expenditures. He had previously challenged Maw in 1944. He wanted to return government to the hands of the people, he said, declaring that Utahns were tired of government operated for the benefit of the few at the expense of the majority. His call for cutting both taxes and spending was a welcome sound in the ears of Utah voters.

For seats in the House of Representatives, Republican David J. Wilson challenged the four-term incumbent Walker K. Granger, while Democrat Reva Beck Bosone challenged incumbent William A. Dawson.

A highlight of the campaign was President Truman's whistle-stop tour of Utah. On his way to major appearances in Salt Lake City and Ogden, he also gave speeches in Price, Helper, Springville, Provo, and American Fork. A bit of human interest came in American Fork, the home town of Reva Beck Bosone. She had already introduced the president in Provo, but when people crowding the tracks forced the train to an unscheduled stop in American Fork, the colorful judge saw her chance to win political points by doing it again. This time, however, instead of simply using the traditional and accepted statement, "Ladies and gentlemen, the president of the United States," she surprised everybody by shouting, "President Truman, meet the people of the best home town in the United States—American Fork!" Undaunted, Truman replied good-naturedly, "No, Judge Bosone, you are wrong. The best home town in the United States is Independence, Missouri!"[86]

Such personal warmth may have helped Truman win the hearts of wavering Utahns, but he was also well coached on what issue might be most attractive to the citizens of the state. In both Salt Lake City and Ogden he pledged to put his full effort into water development. He criticized Congress for cutting reclamation appropriations and promised, if he were elected, "the most ambitious irrigation development in all our history." He also stressed hydro-electric resources. In addition, he reminded the people of Ogden that the Ogden River project was the result of the Democratic administration, vowing that "other reclamation projects are in store for you if you return me to office."

Governor Dewey also visited Utah during the campaign. However, the things he talked about were not as immediately vital to Utah voters as Truman's message. Instead of discussing what he would do for Utah, Dewey dwelt on wider issues, particularly foreign affairs and military preparation. He was well received, but in the final analysis the voters were more impressed with Truman.

The gubernatorial campaign became tense—even bitter at times. It included charges and countercharges about corruption, liquor control, taxes, and Mormon influence in politics.[87]

Liquor control was a particularly sensitive issue. Earlier, Lee seemed to favor a liquor by the drink policy, but in 1948 he simply said that the question should be on the ballot for the people to decide. LDS Church leaders clearly opposed liquor by the drink, and the issue was discussed at length in a meeting between Lee and several of the church's General Authorities. There are conflicting accounts of what happened in that meeting, but it seems clear that Joseph F. Merrill was particularly outspoken in his concern for what Lee might do. In the end, church leaders decided not to oppose Lee. This was due, in part, to the influence of J. Reuben Clark, Jr., first counselor in the First Presidency of the church and a friend and supporter of Lee. In effect, Lee had Church support, although not an official endorsement.

The liquor issue provided some of the most heated exchanges of the campaign. Two scandals, one in which the chief enforcement officer of the liquor commission was convicted and jailed for accepting a bribe, had marred the Maw administration. In a radio debate on October 27, Lee accused Maw of consciously ignoring the irregularities in the liquor commission. Maw emphatically denied the charge and then, in response to Lee's claim that local officials could enforce the law better than state officers, said that while Lee was mayor of Price the property of sixteen "dives" had been confiscated by state enforcement officers.

Maw was not averse to using his LDS Church membership to promote his campaign. In an ill-advised "Dear Brother" letter, sent mostly to fellow members, he claimed not to be writing as governor but simply as an "active and devoted member of our Church." It would have taken a great deal of political naïveté not to see through such a ploy. In any case, Maw wrote of his numerous church activities, and then charged that the "underworld" opposed his reelection and was trying to make Utah an "open state." He called on his brothers in the church to oppose the election of "a governor who will eliminate the State Liquor Police Force and close his eyes to law enforcement." Not surprisingly, Maw was widely criticized for such a blatant attempt to get the moral force of the church on his side.

An only slightly more subtle Republican attempt to bring the prestige of the church into the Lee campaign appeared in the *Deseret News* the day before the election and in the *Salt Lake Tribune* the day of the election. It was said that a group calling itself the "Law Observance Committee" of the church had "carefully studied" the positions of both candidates on various moral issues and that "J. Bracken Lee has received the approval of this committee for his stand on these important matters." The Democrats shot back with their own advertisement in the *Tribune*. "Don't be Fooled!" it said, for the church had at no time endorsed Lee. "No one can speak for the church except over the signature of the First Presidency." The Republican statement was actually more misleading than the Democrats said, for the "committee" had never actually endorsed any candidate—it had only listed the position of each candidate on the issues involved.[88] Nevertheless, though there was no open endorsement, Lee apparently had the support of the church's leaders.

Lee also attacked Maw on other issues, and in the end few people were surprised that he overwhelmed the governor at the polls. On the other hand, almost everyone was astounded at the Democratic sweep in the rest of the election. Along with most other states, Utah went for Truman in the presidential election. He won 53.98 percent of the state's popular vote. In this astonishing upset he also carried Utah's Democrat Walter K. Granger back to Congress, along with Reva Beck Bosone, who was elected for the first time. Bosone thus became the first woman to represent Utah in Congress. She also became the first woman to serve on the House Interior Committee. In the Utah legislature, there were no senatorial contests but the Republican majority in the House of Representatives was more than reversed: election result yielded forty-one Democrats to nineteen Republicans.

Thus ended three years of transition, in which both Utah and the nation confronted several important challenges but faced the future with a high degree of optimism. Nationally, the American people seemed to have confidence in Truman's ability to get things done and in his plans for extending some of the trends begun under the New Deal. Utahns seemed to agree. But they elected a colorful, maverick Republican as governor—partly, it appears, because they had lost confidence in the incumbent but also because J. Bracken Lee had the support of leaders of the dominant church and he seemed to speak to the people's innate resistance to rising taxes and expanding bureaucracies. It seems ironic that so many would vote so decisively for a liberal president, Congress, and state legislature and, at the same time, send an ultraconservative to the statehouse. But that's the way it was, and it set the stage for eight years of stormy and exciting politics.

Notes

1. The Church of Jesus Christ of Latter-day Saints has been variously called the Mormon Church, because of its belief in the Book of Mormon, or the LDS Church, as a shortened version of the proper name. In this book we will use both the full name of the church and the shortened version. Members of the church will be referred to either as Latter-day Saints or as Mormons.
2. "V-J Meeting Told to Build Peace," *Salt Lake Tribune*, September 5, 1945, 1, 7.
3. Some of this section is based on John E. Christensen, "The Impact of World War II," in *Utah's History*, ed. Richard D. Poll, Thomas G. Alexander, Eugene E. Campbell, David E. Miller (Logan, UT: Utah State University Press, 1989), 497–514. For a more in-depth discussion, see that chapter and its bibliography.
4. Various estimates were reported in the months after the war, and they increased as more information was tabulated. These figures from the Utah State Historical Society were reported in *Deseret News*, July 14, 1947.
5. J. R. Mahoney, "Economic Changes in Utah During World War II," *Utah Economic and Business Review* 5 (June 1946): 5.
6. These included the Ninth Service Command transferred to Fort Douglas; Kearns Army Base; Wendover Air Force Base; Ogden Arsenal; Utah General Depot, Ogden Air Depot (Hill Field); Clearfield Naval Supply Depot; Tooele Army Depot; Dugway Proving Ground; and Bushnell Military Hospital.

7. Elroy Nelson, *Utah's Economic Patterns* (Salt Lake City: University of Utah Press, 1956), 109.
8. Christensen, "The Impact of World War II," 505.
9. "Jump Shown in Acreage, Number of Farms in Utah," *Deseret News*, November 9, 1945, 14.
10. Rather, in attempting to forecast the nature of the postwar economy, he had to determine what basic industries (many of them new, wartime industries) would survive the war, then forecast employment patterns in those industries, then predict employment in the various service industries, and then let all this help determine the more general economic picture. J. R. Mahoney, "Wartime Economic Changes and Postwar Industrial Readjustment in Utah," *Utah Economic and Business Review* 2 (June 1943): 78.
11. A figure of twenty-four thousand more is given in Maureen Ursenbach Beecher and Kathryn L. McKay, "Women in Twentieth Century Utah," in *Utah's History*, ed. Poll et al., 581. A wartime report from the Utah Bureau of Economic and Business Research, however, indicated that there were approximately thirty-three thousand more women working in 1943 than in 1940. See Mahoney, "Wartime Economic Changes," 83–84. The difference in estimates may be partly explained by whether the comparisons were based on 1940 or 1941 figures.
12. Beecher and McKay, "Women in Twentieth Century Utah," in *Utah's History*, ed. Poll et al., 581–82; *Statistical Abstract of Utah 1993* (Salt Lake City: Bureau of Economic and Business Research, David Eccles School of Business, University of Utah, 1993), 81.
13. Utah State Department of Publicity and Industrial Development, "After Victory: Plans for Utah and the Wasatch Front: Report of the Cooperative Planning Program, Compiled Under the Direction of Ora Bundy" (Salt Lake City: Utah State Department of Publicity and Industrial Development, 1943).
14. Mahoney, "Economic Changes," 7–8.
15. Mahoney, "Economic Changes," 7–8, 94–95. He believed the radio tube plant would also continue, but he wondered whether the Kalunite plant in South Salt Lake could compete with other such plants built elsewhere.
16. Ibid.,79–88.
17. Ibid., 97–98. For a discussion of housing problems during the war, see James B. Allen, "Crisis on the Home Front: The Federal Government and Utah's Defense Housing in World War II," *Pacific Historical Review* 38 (November1969): 407–28.
18. "US Control Must Cease, Maw Avers," *Deseret News*, July 2, 1945, 1, 6.
19. The Utah population jumped from 555,340 in 1940 to 688,862 in 1950. For comparison of the percent of growth with that of other states, see the 1950 tab on the very interesting "Interactive US Census Bureau Chart" at http://www.npg.org/library/population-data.html. Accessed January 19, 2015.
20. "Construction Wage Control Will Remain," *Deseret News*, December 5, 1945, 16; "Apartment Owners Hit Back at OPA," ibid., December 12, 1945, p. 13.
21. "S.L. Speaker Discounts House Crisis," *Salt Lake Tribune*, December 28, 1945, p. 15.
22. "State Reports 45 Percent Increase over 1944 Toll," *Deseret News*, February 5, 1946, 6.
23. Beverly B. Clopton, *Her Honor, the Judge: The Story of Reva Beck Bosone* (Ames, IA: The Iowa State University Press, 1980), 128–30.

24. "State Asks City to Work Out Highway Locale," *Salt Lake Tribune*, January 14, 1948, 15.
25. The argument took on political overtones when Mrs. C. L. Jack, a Democrat from the west side and a member of Utah's House of Representatives, quoted Governor Maw to the effect that he would not sign any paper that would run a highway through the west side. A critic from the rear of the room protested that this was nothing more than "a 1948 campaign speech." "Hundreds Voice Protest to Express Highway," *Salt Lake Tribune*, January 13, 1948, Second Section, 1.
26. O. N. Malmquist, "Utah Industry Well Along in Recovery,"*Salt Lake Tribune*, September 11, 1945, 13, 20; "Most of Utah Industries Reconverted," ibid., December 10, 1945, p. 11-13. For a good general overview of Utah manufacturing through the immediate postwar period, see Nelson, *Utah's Economic Patterns*, chapters 14 and 15.
27. "Geneva Declared Key to Utah Employment," *Salt Lake Tribune*, October 8, 1945, Second Section, 9.
28. As Provo's mayor Maurice Harding said, Geneva was a "vital necessity to the economic well-being of the entire West, Provo City and Utah County." "Geneva News Cheers State, Civic Leaders," *Deseret News*, September 7, 1945, 11.
29. "Reconversion Suffers While Officials Dally," editorial, *Salt Lake Tribune*, October 6, 1945, 8.
30. "Board Sends Congress Geneva File," *Salt Lake Tribune*, October 12, 1945, 4; "Geneva to Continue Partial Operation," ibid., October 13, 1945, 1. The October 12 issue contains the full text of that report.
31. "US Steel Bid Favored for Geneva," *Deseret News*, May 2, 1946, 1,5; "S.L. Leaders Delighted by Geneva Deal," ibid., May 23, 1946, 1.
32. Nelson, *Utah's Economic Patterns*, 100.
33. "Steel Chief Lauds Work on Utah Mills," *Deseret News*, October 13, 1948, A11.
34. In 1939, the food processing industry accounted for 41 percent of the state's employment in manufacturing but by 1955 this had dropped to 25 percent, second to primary metals manufacturing (smelting and/or refining metals), which provided 31 percent of the jobs. Other manufacturing was also making important gains in Utah, dominated by heavy industry. Nelson, *Utah's Economic Patterns*, 204. Nelson provides more interesting figures demonstrating the war's stimulus to manufacturing in general. The most dramatic growth was in metal products, which showed an increase in employees of 470 percent from 1939 to 1955 (438 to 2,500). In other areas, employees in lumber and millwork increased by 352 percent; petroleum processing, 341 percent; manufacturing of machinery and equipment, 261 percent; stone and clay products, 224 percent; furniture and fixtures, 221 percent; primary metals, 190 percent.
35. These figures were given by Ames K. Bagley, secretary of the Utah Manufacturers Association. "An Appropriate Time to Tell About Progress of American West," editorial, *Salt Lake Tribune*, January 18, 1948, A16. More official figures, however, show that in 1947 only 27,050 were employed in manufacturing. *1969 Statistical Abstract of Utah* (Salt Lake City: Bureau of Business and Economic Research, University of Utah, 1969), 69.
36. "S. L. Construction Totals 5 Million," *Salt Lake Tribune*, October 22, 1945, Second Section, 1.
37. Nelson, *Utah's Economic Patterns*, 237-38.

38. The production of iron ore jumped from 1,540,594 long tons, valued at $1,742,876 in 1944 to 3,111,167 long tons, valued at $5,746,808, in 1950. Coal production reached a record 7 million tons in 1944 and 7.4 million in 1948. The total value of non-ferrous metals fell off immediately after the war, jumped to a new peak in 1947, declined again for two years, then began to climb again. *1969 Statistical Abstract of Utah*, 209, 215; Nelson, *Utah's Economic Patterns*, 132.
39. Nelson, *Utah's Economic Patterns*, 19.
40. Mahoney, "Economic Changes, 10. The term "imported labor" used in this report was probably a euphemism for migrant labor. Also, according to this report, some prisoners of war were still being used.
41. *1969 Statistical Abstract of Utah*, 173.
42. Leonard J. Arrington, *Beet Sugar in the West: A History of the Utah-Idaho Sugar Company, 1891–1966* (Seattle: University of Washington Press, 1966): 153.
43. *1969 Statistical Abstract of Utah*, 179–80.
44. "8-Million Pound Turkey Processing Establishment Assured in Salt Lake," *Deseret News*, July 2, 1945, 9.
45. Neighboring Nevada, with 84 per 1,000 population, was first. "Fifth of Utah Workers are on Public Payrolls," *Deseret News* July 1, 1947, 13.
46. *1969 Statistical Abstract of Utah*, 67–68; *Statistical Abstract of Utah 1993*, 226.
47. George Jensen and Leonard J. Arrington, *Impact of Defense Spending on the Economy of Utah* (Logan, UT: Department of Economics, Utah State University 1967), 43–84; Leonard J. Arrington and George Jensen, *The Defense Industry of Utah* (Logan, UT: Department of Economics, Utah State University, 1965), 31.
48. For a thorough survey of the history of the origin and completion of the Strawberry project, see Thomas G. Alexander, "An Investment in Progress: Utah's First Federal Reclamation Project, The Strawberry Valley Project," *Utah Historical Quarterly* 39 (Summer 1971): 286–304.
49. There is a need for a major general history of the CUP. In the meantime, see "CUP History," Central Utah Project, Bureau of Reclamation, 1973 (an eleven-page report) and Craig Fuller, "Central Utah Project," *Utah History Encyclopedia*, ed. Allen Kent Powell (Salt Lake City: University of Utah Press, 1994), 82-85.
50. J. H. Gordon, "Proposed Central Utah Project Envisions Rosy Blossoming of Thousands of Acres," *Deseret News*, September 5, 1948, M2.
51. "Utah Demands OWI Retract False Report on the State," *Deseret News*, July 10, 1945, 1; "Elmer Davis' OWI Offices is Set Right About Utah," ibid., July 11, 1945, 9; "OWI Needs a Lesson in Geography," ibid., July 12, 1945, 4; Katherine Johnson, "OWI Excuses Rejected by Sen. Murdock," ibid., July 13, 1945, 9.
52. "Utah Sees Record Tourist Influx," *Salt Lake Tribune*, December 17, 1945, 11.
53. This and other economic indicators are published in the *Salt Lake Tribune*, January 18, 1948.
54. Nelson, *Utah's Economic Patterns*, 300.
55. In 1946, for example, several towns in Utah Valley encouraged such activities and also planned more development of the mountain areas for hiking and other recreational activities. C. W. McCullough, "Utah Valley Teems with Action," *Utah Magazine* 8 (1946): 43–44.
56. See various newspaper reports during the year, as well as Utah Centennial Commission, "General Report," (Salt Lake City, 1947); Utah Centennial Commission, "Utah Centennial Programs, Magazine Articles, and Newspaper Clippings, 1947"

; David R. Trevithick, "Utah's Centennial Celebration," *Utah Humanities Review* 1 (October 1947): 355-60.

57. For an interesting treatment of the many problems, financial and otherwise, involved in getting the monument approved and completed, see chapter 7, "The Big Job," in Wayne K. Hinton, "A Biographical History of Mahonri M. Young, a Western American Artist" (Ph.D. dissertation, Brigham Young University, 1974). Before his initial model was approved, the sculptor made it clear to the committee that the way the men atop the monument were portrayed was not historically accurate for it did not depict an ill Brigham Young overlooking the valley from Wilford Woodruff's wagon. Rather, the three stood together in powerful perspective, seeming to envision the great future of the people they were leading. His intent was symbolic, Mahonri Young said, so that the figures represented the spirit of the occasion. President Heber J. Grant approved, reminding the other members of the committee that "they weren't erecting a monument to a covered wagon." When the monument was finally unveiled, Young was invited to say a few words. He gave what may have been one of the shortest speeches in the history of such occasions: "Next month, come the ninth of August I will be seventy years old. This is the greatest day of my life."

58. "Senate Killed Racial Bills," *Deseret News*, March 1, 1947, 6.

59. Statistics based on *Statistical Abstract of Utah 1993*, 11.

60. "Utah Senate Faces Crisis in Shortage of Teachers," *Deseret News*, July 26, 1945, 9, 10; E. Allen Bateman, "What Lies Ahead for Education in Utah," *Utah Educational Review* 38 (1945): 261-64; James O. McKinney, "Readin', Ritin', and Remodeling," *Utah Magazine* 8 (1946): 16-17, 38-39.

61. "Education Program Likely to Boost Taxes," *Deseret News*, March 15, 1947, 6.

62. State Superintendent of Public Instruction, *Utah School Report, 1946-47* (Salt Lake City: Utah State Department of Public Instruction, 1948): 1-3.

63. Elinore H. Partridge, "A. Ray Olpin and the Postwar Emergency at the University of Utah," *Utah Historical Quarterly* 48 (Spring 1980): 193-206; Paul W. Hodson, *Crisis on Campus: The Exciting Years of Campus Development at the University of Utah* (Salt Lake City: Keeban Corporation, 1987): 1-8

64. Raymond Hughes and William Lancelot, *Education: America's Magic* (Ames, IA: Iowa State College Press, 1946); John T. Wahlquist, "Education in Utah, 1947," *Utah Educational Review* 40 (September-October 1947): 11-13, 38; John T. Wahlquist, "Utah Schools Rank High," *Utah Educational Review* 41 (December 1947): 20-21, 30; John T. Wahlquist, "Status of Education in Utah," *Proceedings of the Utah Academy of Sciences, Arts, and Letters* 24 (1947): 109-131.

65. See, for example, editorials supporting the Taft-Hartley Act and criticizing Truman's vote, "Veto Message on the Labor Bill," *Deseret News*, June 21, 1947, 4; "Politicians Take Advantage of Voters With Labor Bill," *Salt Lake Tribune*, June 21, 1947, 8. For a scholarly discussion of the prevailing negative attitude toward compulsory unionism, see J. Kenneth Davies, "Mormonism and the Closed Shop," *Labor History* 3 (Spring 1962): 169-87.

66. O. N. Malmquist, "Maw Lashes Welfare, Labor Laws," *Salt Lake Tribune*, August 20, 1947, 1, 7; "AFL Unions Name Latter to Utah Post," *Deseret News*, August 20, 1947, 1, 3.

67. The talk was later circulated in a flyer entitled "The Closed Shop and Personal Liberty," copy in Joseph F. Merrill papers, Brigham Young University. The conference

address contained some introductory remarks that were not reproduced in the flyer. See *Conference Report*, October 3, 4, 5, 1941, pp. 129–35.
68. See *Conference Report*, October 6, 7, 8, 1944, pp. 29–34
69. See *Conference Report*, 4,5,6 October, 1946, pp. 67–71.
70. Carleton S. Jones to "Jos. S. Merrill," November 15, 1946, Merrill papers.
71. Joseph F. Merrill to Carleton Jones, November 19, 1946, Merrill papers. The Merrill papers contain several other such letters, with his replies.
72. Frank H. Jonas to Joseph M. Merrill, October 2, 1946, Merrill papers.
73. Joseph F. Merrill to Frank H. Jonas, October 11, 1946, Merrill papers.
74. By 1948, *Deseret News* editorials were filled with anti-Communist rhetoric. See, for example, "Stalin Gets a Bill of Rights Particulars, *Deseret News*, October 15, 1948, A5; Samuel Pettengill, "The Next Four Years," October 26, 1948, A4; "An Intellectual Iron Curtain," November 4, 1948, A4.
75. "Thomas Scents Peace Threat," *Salt Lake Tribune*, March 12, 1947, 2; "Thermopylae, Marathon Cast Historic Shadows," ibid., editorial, March 13, 1947, 8. Unfortunately, three years later, Senator Thomas's position came back to haunt him, as it became part of the ammunition used in a vicious election campaign to unseat him by charging him, wrongly, with being a Communist sympathizer.
76. "Saving Europe Costly and Thankless Job, But Necessary for World Survival," *Salt Lake Tribune*, editorial, June 30, 1947, 6.
77. "There Can Be No Retreat From Berlin Without Serious Loss of Prestige," *Salt Lake Tribune*, editorial, June 26, 1948, 6.
78. "Operation Little Vittles," *Deseret News*, October 28, 1948, A4; "1500 'Candyshutes' Fall Daily to Hungry Berlin Children," *Salt Lake Tribune*, October 31, 1948, A19; Pat Christian, "Candy man keeps up bombing runs," *Daily Herald* (Provo, UT), March 29, 1994, B1.
79. "Dire Want Grips Navajo Tribe, Chairman Advises Interviewer," *Deseret News*, November 21, 1947, 1; "Utah Indians Found in Dire Hunger, Want," *Deseret News*, November 25, 1947, 1; "Navajos Left in Poverty By Loss of Sheep," ibid., November 27, 1947, 1.
80. "US Breaks Navajo Pact, Church Leader Charges," *Deseret News*, November 28, 1947, 1, 6.
81. "Indian Aid Caravan Totals 130 Tons," *Deseret News*, December 19, 1947, 1, 2.
82. "Indian Donation Made," *Deseret News*, December 2, 1947, 1, 6.
83. "He Doesn't Trust This Legislature, *Deseret News*, editorial February 9, 1948, 4.
84. "Governor Maw and the Special Session," *Deseret News*, editorial, February 20, 1948, 4.
85. "Governor Asks Repeal of Litigation on State Welfare Expenses," *Salt Lake Tribune*, March 10, 1948, 8; "Utah's Welfare Costs," *Deseret News*, March 12, 1948, 4.
86. Clopton, *Her Honor, the Judge*, 133.
87. Unless otherwise noted, the following discussion on the Maw-Lee campaign is based on Dennis L. Lythgoe, *Let 'Em Holler: A Political Biography of J. Bracken Lee* (Salt Lake City: Utah State Historical Society, 1982): 33–39.
88. See "The Battle Corner" Section, *Salt Lake Tribune*, November 2, 1948, 9, for both the Republican statement by Vernon Romney and the Democratic statement by Grant MacFarlane.

CHAPTER 2

"Let 'Em Holler!"
The Stormy Lee Years, 1949–1956

On Monday, January 3, 1949, nearly four thousand people crowded into the rotunda of Utah's state capital building to hear a political maverick, J. Bracken Lee, take the oath of office as Utah's ninth elected governor. Lee soon became the most colorful, controversial, and independent-acting governor in the annals of the state, but he also made more enemies than almost any other politician in Utah's history. Over the next eight years, Lee's fervent economic and political conservatism and his uncompromising tactics were at the heart of numerous controversies, but his administration was also characterized by many important themes.

During Lee's years, Utah's economy remained strong, although the cost-conscious governor frequently fought with the legislature over state budgets. Utah began to improve its highway system, and Utah's schools continued to provide quality education, despite the governor's mistrust of educators and his slashing of education budgets. Utah became more and more influenced by and involved in national and regional concerns, including the Cold War, a Republican political resurgence in 1952, and the Colorado River Storage Project (CRSP). These issues would have made these years a pivotal era no matter who occupied the governor's mansion.[1]

Image 2.1: J. Bracken Lee, perhaps Utah's most controversial governor, held office from 1949–57 and later served three terms as mayor of Salt Lake City (1960–71). Used by permission, Utah State Historical Society, all rights reserved.

The New Governor and His Goals

Lee portrayed himself as an honest, thrifty, and tough-minded populist, once describing his political philosophy this way: "Do it honestly, do the best you know how, and let 'em holler!"[2] He promised his inaugural audience that for the next four years he would dedicate his life "to the service of the people of Utah," also telling them that "although I am your governor, this is your government."

Lee was determined to carry out measures that he believed were essential to the well-being of the state and its people, whether or not he got along with the political establishment. High on his agenda was economic growth, efficiency and economy in government, tax reform, educational reform, and getting government, especially the federal government, out of the lives of the people. He also opposed the income tax, most federal aid, and the United Nations: all issues that had both economic and constitutional implications.

In his inaugural address, Lee asked the people to oppose excessive tax demands and to remember that the government must live within its income. Such sentiment fit perfectly with a report recently published by the Utah Taxpayers Association decrying the fact that the state budget had jumped from $649 million in 1945 to an estimated $783 million in 1948 even though the per capita income had dropped by 16.6 percent. The state, it warned, must avoid the high price tag attached to much of the proposed legislation for 1949. It simply could not stand the $47 million in increases requested by various departments, institutions, and taxing units.[3]

To his credit, Lee practiced in his personal life what he preached in public. In 1953 he accepted a salary increase, from $7,500 to $10,000, only because the legislature refused to raise salaries of state employees without raising the governor's salary at the same time. As his biographer has emphasized, "Lee set the example by trying to economize himself—on his office expenses, his home, his style of living, his salary. The public knew that he was not living in luxury or getting rich off the public trough while he was insisting that they sacrifice."[4]

Lee began his administration with a considerable amount popular support, including editorial support from both the *Salt Lake Tribune* and the *Deseret News*, but he was still, in a sense, a political voice in the wilderness. He was the only Republican among the major elected state officials, and he faced a legislature dominated by Democrats. In addition, he often came in conflict with the other two members of the three-man state board of examiners, which had the constitutional power to examine "all claims against the state." In effect, this undermined the administrative power of the governor because if the other members of the board (the secretary of state and the attorney general) disagreed with him over an expenditure, they could outvote him. This became especially troublesome when the other members were both of the opposite political party.

As Lee's administration proceeded, moreover, it became increasingly clear that he was a maverick within his party, and the Republican establishment became steadily more uncomfortable with him. For example, at a time when most Republicans were happy with the Eisenhower administration, Lee openly criticized the president, convinced that Eisenhower would never reverse the policies and big spending of the New Deal. In February 1955, Lee proposed that conservatives in both parties join together and create a third party. Utah's senator Wallace F. Bennett quickly denounced the governor, saying that this would have immediate repercussions within the party and could hurt the Utah congressional delegation's efforts to get the much-needed Colorado River Storage Project approved. The rest of Utah's solidly Republican delegation agreed, but Lee continued his barrage.[5] He soon became the darling of right-wing conservatives around the country but the object of criticism from Republican governors and other party regulars.

However, Lee did not approve of one highly controversial, ultra-conservative organization that, he believed, went too far in the fight against Communism. In commenting on the John Birch Society, he said: "I do not believe that you can fight a dictatorship—and that's all Communism is—by setting up another dictatorship. Now the whole theory behind the John Birch Society as I understand it is the only way to whip Communism is adopt their tactics."[6]

The Pesky Liquor Issue

The first item on the new governor's agenda was to get rid of the aggravating liquor issue that had plagued him for years and was a central issue in his campaign. Of particular concern were alleged irregularities in the Liquor Control Commission, as well as Lee's belief that local governments could do a better job of enforcing the law than the state could. On his first day in office, Lee asked for, and received, the resignation of the three members of the commission, appointed a new bipartisan commission of two members, and ordered all state liquor stores to close for a three-day period while an audit was conducted. Contrary to Lee's expectation, the audit revealed no major discrepancies.

The new commission quickly abolished the liquor enforcement division and appointed a liaison officer to coordinate commission activities and local police efforts. This erased $108,000 from the state budget. The commission also established policies that were intended to eliminate corruption arising from the fact that some liquor company agents charged the state higher prices than those being charged in other states.

Lee named a twenty-two member committee to study the liquor control problem. Its report included a recommendation, adopted by the administration, that the state refuse to place orders with any liquor firm whose agents worked for commissions rather than salaries. This was intended to eliminated some corruption because the state then bought directly from the companies, whose representatives became liaisons rather than salesmen. However, this did not work as well as anticipated. Representatives were named by the governor, but they were then required to kick back a percentage of their salary to the governor's party. Clearly, this left the door open for possible scandal, but such kickbacks did not end until the Rampton administration.[7]

In 1950 a study by the Utah Foundation revealed that liquor control costs had, indeed, gone down as a result of eliminating the enforcement division, reducing the number of other employees and generally tightening administrative procedures. The study also demonstrated that enforcement of the liquor laws had slightly improved.[8] Over the next two years the number of successful prosecutions increased dramatically. In addition, the annual profits from liquor sales steadily grew, exceeding $4.2 million by the end of Lee's second term.

Lee promised voters that he would never make Utah an "open" state, but the vexatious issue of liquor-by-the-drink continued to spring up. In May 1950, a group of businessmen from Salt Lake City and Ogden began an effort to have a liquor-by-the-drink initiative placed on the November ballot. However, there was virtually no public support for the petition, and it died for lack of signatures.

The liquor issue practically disappeared from public view by the end of Lee's administration. In the long run, however, the matter would not go away. As questions relating to tourism and economic growth set the stage for continuing challenges to the state's liquor laws, the laws remained among the most restrictive in the nation.

Governor Lee and the Economy[9]

Lee's most urgent concern was the state budget, and in his first budget message in January 1949, he called for several reforms. He asked the legislature to cut back or eliminate a number of programs. He challenged the practice of earmarking funds, which, he believed, too often led departments to use money simply because it was there. He noted that some aspects of the welfare program needed correcting, but his main concern was that welfare be divorced from politics. Lee also believed that a good highway program was essential to the state's future, and was willing to spend money for it. However, cost-cutting was necessary somewhere, and with that in mind he took a swipe at education. The state's colleges, he said, were receiving altogether too much money, and the public schools were straying from basic educational principles in their all-too-expensive experiments with new programs. Other agencies also came under his proposed legislative ax. He called for the abolition of the Publicity and Industrial Development Department, a reduction in the number of commissioners in several departments, and a halt to all new state construction, except for a badly needed state prison. He also suggested studying the juvenile court system, which, he believed, was both inefficient and too expensive.

If Lee's budget had been deliberately fashioned to evoke controversy it could not have been more effective. He shaved the requests of nearly every department, but the most massive cuts were reserved for education. Higher education was slashed from $10.58 million to $5.7 million while the Department of Public Instruction's request for $690,800 was cut by more than half. Vocational schools were eliminated entirely from the budget, as were the juvenile courts. Welfare was the only budget request that did not feel the governor's scalpel and this only because it had not asked for an increase from the previous biennium. Many Utahns, especially educators, were stunned at what the governor really meant by economy in government. Not surprisingly, these developments created a rallying point for Lee's political enemies.

Wrestling with what seemed to be impossible recommendations, the legislature passed several bills that Lee promptly vetoed on the basis of cost. One bill would have provided $40,000 for a Utah Symphony deficit. Another would have allowed the expansion of Weber College to a four-year institution, but, Lee argued, this would not be "keeping faith with all sections of the people." Weber president Henry Aldous Dixon's plea that this would be only a limited expansion and would not result in a "full blown" college was to no avail.[10]

The legislature, painfully conscious of the public clamor for economy and urged on by Lee's harangues, trimmed $29 million from various department requests to produce a budget of $53,356,278. But the governor was dissatisfied because it was $9 million higher than what he recommended. Besides, he claimed, it was illegal because it exceeded anticipated revenues. It was time, he decided, to wield the carving knife, but since he was unable, legally, simply to reduce specific appropriations, he proceeded to veto whole items in the general appropriations bill, to the extent of about $3.9 million. Programs sacrificed included the Salt Lake Area Vocational School, the Utah Water and Power Board, a new hospital requested by the Department of Health, an appropriation for a children's crippling disease hospital, $400,000 for airport construction, special education funds, all funds requested by Utah State Agricultural College for soil conservation and certain animal disease controls, and a training school at the University of Utah.

Most people were amazed at Lee's persistence, but laudatory comments in the press were restrained and cautioned against cuts that might have long-range negative consequences. The governor's opponents took some of the issues to court, resulting in the invalidation of some of his vetoes. Finally, in a compromise, the administration and the legislature simply agreed not to spend the disputed amounts.

Lee's astonishing economy measures attracted unusual attention in the national press. In April 1950, *Time* magazine pictured him as leaving a cost-cutting trail "littered with the bones of sacred cows" such as veterans affairs and agriculture. Despite the doubts of politicians, it said, he believed that his "small businessmen's government," could get him reelected in 1952, but "if it does, after he has alienated just about every pressure group in the state, politicians will be flocking to Salt Lake for lessons." In 1951, Raymond Moley, a former New Deal advisor and administrator who, after 1936, became one of Franklin D. Roosevelt's most severe critics, called Lee more than "just another Governor. He embodies principles to which a distracted nation may turn next year."[12] Not all the national publicity was as glowing but, for the most part, it was very positive. Some conservatives even touted Lee for president of the United States. While visiting Salt Lake City in 1951 former US president Herbert Hoover remarked: "If we had governors like yours in every state, they could save this nation."[13]

At the beginning of the 1951 biennium, Lee was again unhappy with the legislature's budget, which amounted to $56.4 million. Again he exercised the veto liberally, disapproving, among other things, the entire recommended appropriation for higher education. This and other vetoes resulted in the need for a special session of the legislature in June (see discussion below).

By 1952, Lee had lowered the state school equalization tax from $6.3 million to nothing. This did not last for long, but, at least for a while, property owners saw some genuine tax relief. Collections of sales taxes increased, but state property taxes were reduced. These reductions, however, often benefitted special business interests.[14]

During the 1953 legislative session, Lee's continuing attack on taxes included a call for the complete elimination of the state property tax. By then, however, there was some public concern that he might go too far. The *Salt Lake Tribune* continued to praise his measures but the *Deseret News*, while pointing to the positive side of governmental economy, predicted that the people of the state would soon complain about the austerity, especially in the field of education. This time the legislature went along with most of Lee's recommendations. Among other things it raised income tax exemptions and approved transfers from the General Fund and the Emergency Relief Fund to the Uniform School Fund. Temporarily, at least, this avoided the need for a state property tax.

By 1955 Utah's financial situation did not seem quite so rosy. Surpluses in both the General Fund and the Emergency Relief Fund were greatly depleted, and there was nothing in the Reserve Building Fund. More money, therefore, had to be found for schools. Because the legislature appropriated $1 million more than the estimated revenue for the biennium, Lee predicted, with some gloom, that the state could incur a $2 million deficit by the end of the period. Actually, however, in the year Lee left office the state still had a working surplus of $8.35 million.

Interpreting J. Bracken Lee's economy and tax-cutting drive is complex. According to his biographer, Dennis Lythgoe, most Utahns would have been content to leave the tax system as it was when Lee came into office, yet their general inclination toward political conservatism, as well as traditional Mormon teachings regarding thrift and the avoidance of debt, tended to make them ready supporters of a governor who seemed to share that ideology. But it was not the small property owners or average citizens who benefitted most. Rather, it was large corporate property owners. Kennecott Copper Corporation, for example, saved at least $1 million by the abolition of the state property tax, while the Denver and Rio Grande Railroad may have saved more than $763,000.[15]

Lee was a man of great personal integrity, sincerely devoted to saving money and making government the tool rather than the master of the people, but his economic program was probably more drastic than the state needed at the time. Utah was in good financial shape when he was elected, and it remained so while he was in office, but in the long run his economizing was costly, divisive, and required expensive catch-up programs during subsequent administrations.

It has been estimated, conservatively, that during Lee's eight years in office the state lost at least $47 million in revenue.[16] In Lee's opinion, this did not mean much. Corporations, he said, passed the expense of higher taxes on to the people, so with lower taxes the people also benefitted from lower prices. But this ignored the fact that these prices benefitted Utahns little because most corporation sales were out-of-state. More significantly, Lee's failure to carry out more state building programs actually cost the state nearly three times as much, because of inflation, when the buildings were actually constructed. "But who's to know that?" retorted Lee when Lythgoe confronted him with the figures later on. "See, I didn't know the government would actually keep cheapening our money until it became valueless."[17]

In 1955, five years into the Lee administration, Utah ranked tenth among the states in the amount of money per capita received from federal grants in aid. In light of the governor's attitude, and that of most conservatives, toward federal aid, this was indeed ironic. In fact, Utah received more money from such grants than Utah tax paid to the federal government.[18]

Despite his strident opposition to massive federal programs, Lee supported the Colorado River Storage Project (CRSP) which he believed was important to the industrial expansion of the entire Mountain West. This was one of the few issues on which he was in at least tacit agreement with Utah's Senator Arthur V. Watkins, who led the fight in Congress.[19] In 1956, the last year of Lee's administration, Congress finally approved the CRSP and appropriated $13 million for it. Construction began the same year. On October 15, President Dwight D. Eisenhower signaled the official beginning by pressing a button that ignited explosions at both the Glen Canyon and Flaming Gorge dam sites. Each of these projects would eventually have a significant economic impact on Utah.

In other aspects of the economy, Utah's labor force continued to grow, from 243,054 workers in 1950 to an estimated 283 thousand in mid-1955, with women making up an increasingly larger portion. Agriculture, mining, and manufacturing remained important sources of wealth, although total farm income dropped as Utah gradually became more urban in nature. Military installations and defense-related industries also remained essential to

Image 2.2: Charles Steen, a geologist who made millions after discovering a rich uranium deposit in Utah in the early 1950s and provoked a "uranium rush" in the region. However, he declared bankruptcy in 1968. Used by permission, Utah State Historical Society, all rights reserved.

the economy. Unemployment rose slightly until 1950 but then dropped significantly during the next few years and maintained a ratio far below the national average. On the negative side, even though the economy was generally healthy, "real" personal income in 1954 was nearly 25 percent below the 1943 wartime high.[20] At the same time (and no doubt much to the governor's delight), in 1952 Utah had the lowest per capita state debt in the nation: twelve cents compared with an average of $33.55.[21] With respect to public welfare, Utah was substantially above the average in the amount it paid to welfare recipients.[22]

An industry that saw a dramatic and well-publicized "boom and bust" during these years was uranium mining. With the huge postwar search for sources of nuclear energy, in the early 1950s prospectors by the hundreds tramped the hills of southern and eastern Utah, where uranium ores had been worked previously in search of radium and vanadium.²³ The first big strike was made by Charles Steen, southeast of Moab, which touched off a veritable stampede. A few fortunes were made, seemingly overnight, as production soared from nothing in the 1940s to 1,239,767 tons of ore containing 8,913,872 pounds of uranium valued at $38.61 million in 1958. The town of Moab, in fact, was dubbed the "Uranium Capital of the World." But the federal government was the only legal purchaser, and in the early 1960s it announced that it had a sufficient stockpile. Production immediately plummeted. A national energy crisis in 1973–74 stimulated new exploration and production, although not with the wild fervor of the 1950s. Uranium was mined on 510 different properties in Utah in 1956, but by 1975 only thirty-three properties remained in production.²⁴

Tax Rebel[25]

Utah's governor attracted national attention through his economy drive and tax cuts, but he was just as much, if not more, a national sensation with his caustic comments on the income tax and, on one occasion, his refusal to pay. Lee complained that the income tax was the worst thing that ever happened to the nation, partly because it allowed the government to use taxpayer money for many things he thought were unnecessary. He also castigated the IRS as a gestapo, often addressing it in correspondence as "Snoopers and Looters." The law that required taxes to be withheld from wages only added insult to injury.²⁶

In his 1954 introduction to a book by Frank Chodrov, *The Income Tax, Root of All Evil*, Lee called for repeal of the 16th Amendment, which he considered unconstitutional. He also tried unsuccessfully to get the rest of the nation's governor's on the bandwagon. Then, in January 1956, he filed his federal tax form but held back the money he owed. It was a test, he said, of the government's right to use taxpayer money for foreign aid.²⁷ He hoped to have his day in court, where the constitutionality of the law could be examined, but he was realistic enough to keep the money in a bank account in case he lost.

Reaction was immediate and mixed. Many conservatives applauded him, but in general the press was critical. The IRS, meanwhile, simply attached his bank account. In 1956 he filed suit in the US Supreme Court, but the court refused to hear the case. Although Lee ultimately paid his taxes, he continued his fight for many years.[28]

Utah's Highways[29]

Highway improvement was one of the most urgent problems of the immediate postwar era. Utah's population was growing, more and faster automobiles were on the roads, highways were in terrible shape, and traffic fatalities were rising at an alarming rate. It was clear that something must be done soon. In the end, despite his scruples against federal spending, Lee was willing to accept federal money to maintain Utah's highways, but only because he saw no alternative.

Lee was fond of saying that Utah's highways were as good as those in most other states,[30] but that did not necessarily mean much. In 1949 the US Bureau of Public Roads reported that only 17 percent of the nation's 37,800 miles of interstate highways met "minimum standards" and that primary and secondary roads were just as bad. Cities and highway users throughout the nation were clamoring for action. That same year, the Utah State Highway Commission estimated that just to bring the state's road system up to "minimum standards" would require a capital outlay of $15.66 million over the next fifteen years.[31]

The hard reality of what was needed, and why, was summarized in a report by the Utah Foundation. Minimum standards, it said, were changing drastically. In 1930, a main-line highway was satisfactory if it had two lanes, was eighteen feet wide, and was designed for a speed of 35 mile per hour. It could also get by with limited sight-distance and unlimited access. By 1949, however, the US Bureau of Public Roads would require a new highway through Parley's Canyon (location of the present Interstate 80) to consist of four twelve-feet wide lanes separated by a four-feet neutral zone and with four-feet wide surfaced shoulders on each side. It must be designed for 55 miles per hour speeds and weight loads of up to 79,900 pounds, have a maximum curvature of seven degrees, and have rigidly controlled access roads. Of Utah's 6,083 miles of state and federal-aid roads and highways, 82 percent did not meet even the approved width requirement.³²

Utah's postwar highway program got its start in 1949, when the state road commission and Salt Lake City officials agreed to build the long-needed expressway west of downtown. Construction began in 1951, and eventually the new highway became part of Interstate 15 that now runs north and south through the state. In November 1951, Congress approved more than $40.7 million in federal funds for Utah in the fiscal year beginning the following July 1. In December the state road commission approved what it said was the greatest road construction program in the state's history, calling for an expenditure of nearly $10.3 million in 1952, in addition to regular maintenance and repair expenses.

In August 1952, Lee reported that highway construction in progress was nearly double that of any previous year in his administration. He also took credit for keeping highway money from being diverted to other uses so that every dollar possible was devoted to new road construction and maintenance.³³ Despite the apparent progress, however, the state road commission estimated in October that the need for $71 million in highway construction was "urgent" and called for a $35 million bond issue for the purpose of catching up.³⁴ Such recommendations were controversial, however, and the matter never made it to the ballot.**

Several long-needed stretches of highway were completed during these years. One was a superhighway in Davis County, eliminating a terrible commuter bottleneck often referred to as the Davis County "death strip." Another, in southern Utah, was an improved connection between US highways 89 and 91. This greatly enhanced the potential of tourism by making it possible to travel safely on a superb scenic loop through Utah's national parks and Cedar Breaks National Monument. Before that time, a very narrow road, largely unpaved, made the trip from Cedar City to Highway 89, via Cedar Breaks, not only uncomfortable for tourists but unsafe for the tour busses that negotiated it daily during tourist season.

Between 1950 and the end of 1954, nearly $48 million was spent on Utah's highways, and $11,166,000 more in federal money was scheduled to be spent for fiscal 1955–56.³⁵ But these outlays still could not fund the anticipated needs. In 1955, as a result of a year-long study, President Eisenhower proposed a vast new expenditure of federal funds in order to complete a huge interstate, limited-access highway system. When Governor Lee heard about it, he had mixed feelings. In principle he opposed the multi-billion dollar federal program as "the wrong thing to do at a time when the federal budget is unbalanced and when we're trying to take care of the rest of the world." Nevertheless, he said, if the bill passed, "self-preservation would force me to accept the funds allocated to Utah. But I would accept them believing still that it was the wrong thing to do."[36] The following year the Federal Aid Highway Act of 1956 authorized the federal government to provide 90 percent of the cost of constructing 42,500 miles of limited-access interstate highways. The states would provide the remaining 10 percent. This new infusion of federal funds, with many later additions, eventually resulted in the completion of a vast interstate highway network. It took nearly four decades to complete Utah's portions of I-15, I-80, I-84 and I-70, along with other projects, such as a major belt route (I-215) around Salt Lake City.

The highway program gradually improved interstate travel, tourism, commuting, and trucking, and did much to enhance the state's economy. But it did not reduce the carnage on the highways resulting from high speeds and other unsafe driving practices. Some argued, in fact, that better highways only enhanced the temptation to travel beyond either the legal limit or reasonably safe speeds.[37] In any case, Utah's traffic toll continued to climb: two hundred fatalities occurred in 1956, 256 (18.4 per 100,000 population) in 1960, and 326 (30.6 per 100,000) in 1970. The problem seemed never-ending.

The Governor Battles the Schools

Between 1940 and 1950, the number of children enrolled in Utah's public schools jumped by 8.8 percent, from 137,434 to 149,553. In addition, E. Allen Bateman, State Superintendent of Public Instruction, estimated that the rising birthrate would bring in an additional fifty thousand students by the 1956–57 school year, creating a vital need for 1,500 more classrooms and that many more teachers.[38] The implication was obvious: Utah was facing a school crisis and the governor's economy drive, interpreted by educators as a war on education, could only make it worse.

Lee believed that Utah's education administrators were spending too much money on unneeded and wasteful programs, and he was determined to see it stopped. His tug-of-war with educators began almost immediately. He vetoed a legislative appropriation for the Extension Division of Utah State Agricultural College and a $20,000 appropriation for the Research Division of the State Department of Education. The Extension Division veto was soon declared unconstitutional because the funds were simply part of a larger budget item. Lee did not appeal that decision, but he somehow persuaded the college to reduce its total budget by the same amount. The state attorney general then issued an opinion to the effect that other vetoes, including that for the Research Division funds, were also unconstitutional, whereupon Superintendent Bateman applied for release of the $20,000. Lee stubbornly refused, and after a markedly angry debate between the two, he told Bateman that he would appoint a special committee to study needed services and that he would authorize the release of no funds until that study was complete. Lee ignored Bateman's suggestion that the committee be impartial and composed of experienced public school teachers. Instead, he appointed Thorpe B. Issacson, whose views on education were similar to his own, Marl Gibson (a political associate from Price), and three other non-educators. The group never submitted a report.[39] In March 1950, the Utah Supreme Court upheld the lower court's ruling, but Lee apparently declined to release the money. He later reported that it was returned to the general fund.[40]

This was only the first skirmish of an acrimonious battle between Lee and educators that raged through the rest of the governor's administration. Much of Lee's criticism was focused directly on Bateman, but he also attacked the "school lobby" frequently and disparagingly.

In 1950, Utah voters approved two constitutional amendments relating to education. One made the state board of education elective and the other made the position of Superintendent of Public Education appointive by the board, thus taking it out of politics. When the new procedures were implemented, the board appointed Bateman and also raised his salary from $6,000 to $10,000 annually. Both moves angered Lee, who tried unsuccessfully to block Bateman's appointment. He also refused to authorize payment of the higher salary but was overridden by the other two members of the state board of examiners, who were both Democrats. But Lee was not finished. The three-man finance commission included two of his own appointees, who blocked the payment again.

After a considerable amount of animosity from both sides, the matter finally went to the state supreme court which, in August 1952, held that Bateman's salary could be determined by the state school board. The following March, the legislature passed a new law affirming the right of the board to appoint the superintendent but claiming for itself the right to determine his salary, which was eventually fixed at $8,000, a figure the governor approved.[41]

The larger question, however, was how the schools would continue to be financed at all. In 1951 the legislature approved Senate Bill 75, modifying the Minimum School Fund Act of 1947. Lawmakers were convinced that the 1947 law did not provide adequate funding at the time and that inflation, along with heavily increased school enrollments, had made matters even worse. They also thought that educators were underpaid. The bill increased the minimum school program from $3,300 per classroom unit to $3,600, increased transportation allotments, made changes in leeway taxation provisions, and allowed local districts to set their own limits on local school taxes. Lee was adamant in his opposition, using the media to attack educators and everything they wanted. He argued, among other things, that Utah ranked second among the states in the percentage of its revenue devoted to schools; that many teachers were, like other public servants, merely mediocre did not merit a raise in salary; and that Utah's average teacher salaries were already above the national average. He also predicted that the new expenditures demanded by "special interests" and "greedy minorities" would lead to socialism.

Lee's most publicly outspoken critics included Bateman, Dr. John T. Bernhard of the political science faculty at Brigham Young University, and Allan M. West, executive secretary of the

Utah Education Association (UEA). The latter two each gave major addresses on public radio harshly discounting most of Lee's assertions. Lee, in turn, attacked both the competency and the motives of educators, accusing them, along with the Parent-Teachers Association, of constituting a disgraceful lobby.[42] This brought an impassioned rejoinder from the *Utah Educational Review*, accusing Lee of exaggeration and near-demagoguery. True to his threats, when Senate Bill 75 made its way to his desk, Lee vetoed it. He also vetoed a subsequent compromise bill.

In addition to striking down Senate Bill 75, Lee eliminated appropriations for two vocational schools, for the teacher retirement fund, and for the school for the blind. He also vetoed the entire budget for higher education. Lee had no intention of destroying Utah's colleges and universities, but eliminating their budgets constituted a challenge to the legislature to produce something more in line with his economic convictions.

The veto made it necessary for a special legislative session to be called in June. As far as Lee's economy drive was concerned, the session was a disaster. The legislature restored all the items he had line-vetoed, along with the full budget for higher education. With reference to Senate Bill 75, it compromised on the increase per classroom unit with a stop-gap measure and plans for a long-range study of certain taxing implications. In the end, the total appropriation for education in the special session amounted to $3.3 million more than that of the regular session. Wisely, Lee contented himself by taking more verbal swipes at the politicians responsible for "excessive appropriations," but he did not veto the new legislation.[43]

The irreconcilability of the conflict between Lee and Utah's educators was perhaps no more evident than in Lee's campaign for reelection in 1952. Lee claimed in a campaign pamphlet that he had actually advanced education in eleven ways, to which the UEA promptly issued a rejoinder. Lee asserted that public school expenditures had increased 42 percent during his first term, but the UEA explained that most of this was in building programs, long delayed by the war, and that actual operating funds had increased only 17 percent, which was more than offset by the increase in the number of students and in the cost of living. Lee took credit for a 40 percent increase in higher education funds, to which the UEA replied that this happened only because the legislature overrode his vetoes and appropriated money that he did not approve. The UEA admitted an increase in average teacher salary, but with the caveat that when Lee took office, it was $277 higher than the national average but four years later was $40 below that average.

One serious problem facing Utah schools was a growing shortage of well-trained teachers. Among the reasons for the shortage was that higher salaries were offered elsewhere, which induced some teachers, especially younger ones, to move out of state.[44] In April 1953, with Lee being pressured to call still another special session of the legislature, thirty-five of Utah's forty school districts withheld teacher contracts on the basis of the possibility that the state could take some action to improve salaries.

After vetoing Senate Bill 75 and its successor, Lee persuaded the legislature to fund a school survey commission, promising to honor its findings and, if necessary, call a special session to implement its recommendations. Chairman of the commission was Adam S. Bennion, a prominent educator and LDS Church leader.[45] The commission made its report in February 1953. Among other things, it recommended raising teacher salaries and studying the establishment of a merit system in order to provide incentive for exceptional work. In all, its recommendations could cost the state $3 million or more.

The legislature had no time to consider the recommendations during its regular session and, contrary to his commitment, Lee stubbornly resisted convening a special session. The resulting summer-long standoff became both bitter and caustic. At one point the UEA advised teachers not to sign contracts for the 1953–54 school year unless Lee called a special session. At the end of August, however, it urged them to go ahead and sign, fearing that failure to do so would simply play into the governor's hands.[46] The teachers signed, but most of them did so with a proviso that they could resign after a ten-day notice. This would protect them if the legislature authorized a raise but the governor refused to approve it.

Finally, after the legislative council worked out a proposal that was somewhat closer to his liking, Lee called the special session, which would convene in December. There the legislature adopted a school finance program that included a $340 greater increase per classroom than Lee recommended. He promptly exercised his veto. A compromise plan finally became law without his signature. In addition, his veto of an improved teacher retirement program was overridden by the legislature. Although education still remained underfinanced, Lee had suffered a major defeat.[47]

One of Lee's most misleading statements was that Utah teachers received salaries higher than the national average and higher than those in adjoining states. In fact, Utah's average teacher salary that year was $3,500, while that of the surrounding states was $3,663. All but two of these states paid higher salaries.[48] The situation continued. The 1953 commission report recommended that Utah teacher salaries be maintained at a level equal to the average of the Rocky Mountain States. Instead, three years later they were significantly lower than those in every Mountain and Pacific Coast state except Idaho.[49]

Lee's reticence to support education is accounted for in part by his general attitude toward the teaching profession itself.[50] He believed Utah's educators were not only overpaid but generally inferior in talent. He also feared they had the potential of becoming much too influential politically. His attempt to get a constitutional amendment barring anyone holding "an office of public profit or trust" from being elected to the legislature was really a not-so-subtle effort to keep teachers from becoming lawmakers. It failed from the start.

School construction was another thorny issue. Lee was adamantly opposed to federal aid for education and, in 1954, refused to send a representative to Washington to participate in hearings on federal aid for public school construction. In addition, he wanted to eliminate state funding of local school construction. Educators, as well as many other people in districts that badly needed new buildings, were irate. In 1955, he vetoed a bill extending the mill levy for such purposes but was overwhelmingly overridden by the legislature (23–0 in the Senate and 51–4 in the House). However, he successfully vetoed a bill that would have permitted

Utah to qualify for federal aid for school construction and maintenance. The Utah Taxpayers Association tended to support him, saying that the state was doing just fine with its school building program and needed no federal help.[51]

Actually, by the 1950s federal aid was becoming increasingly important in Utah public school financing, having grown from half of 1 percent of all school revenue in 1930–31 to 6 percent in 1950–54. Most of these funds went to four school districts heavily affected by federal installations: Davis, Tooele, Weber, and Ogden. In addition, most Utah schools participated in the federal school lunch program, while some also profited from miscellaneous programs such as veterans training. The Davis school district was the largest benefactor from federal money, which accounted for 33.4 percent of its school funds. In nearly half of Utah's 40 districts, however, less than 1 percent of the school revenue came from that source.[52]

How much Lee permanently damaged or set back education in Utah is a matter of conjecture. Lee and his supporters claimed he was a friend of education and that during his administration it fared better than in any comparable period in Utah history. Critics said he harbored ill will toward teachers, that his program hurt both educators and schools, that he undermined both the morale and the public image of teachers, and that any achievements during these years came despite him rather than because of him.[53]

However, a few things are clear. Even though the amount spent per child in public education went up during his administration, there was a definite decline in the relative amount spent when compared with the nation or with nearby states. In 1945–46 the average expenditure per child in Utah was $129.30 compared with $136.41 in the nation, $153.33 in the Mountain States (excluding Utah). Utah ranked 30th among all the states. In 1957–58, it had dropped to 35th place, spending $261.40 per student as compared with $341.14 in the nation, $359.54 in the Mountain States and $369.27 in the western states.[54] To put it another way, before Lee took office Utah's expenditure per child was 94.8 percent of the national average, 84.3 percent of the mountain states average and 81.17 percent of the western states average. When he left office the respective averages were 76.7, 72.7, and 70.8, a decline of more than 10 percent in each instance. It is also clear that critical building needs were not met by the Lee administration. A 1956 report said that Utah needed 3,245 new classrooms but was building only 625 at the time. It also noted that there would be need for an additional 1,072 classrooms in another four years,

On the other hand, Utah had a more severe fund-raising problem than most other states. In 1955 Utah's birthrate was 30 percent higher than the national average, and the state had a significantly higher proportion of its students enrolled in public schools, yet the average income in the state was only 88.4 percent of the national average.[55] At the same time, Utah devoted a larger portion of its individual income, 4 percent, to education than any other state.[56] Also, even though it spent less money per student the Utah spent about the same as the national average per classroom, the result of larger school districts, fewer schools, and larger classroom sizes.

Despite its problems, Utah continued to rank high in educational attainments. It led the nation in the median number of years of schooling its people completed; it was first in the nation in the percentage of population enrolled in colleges and universities; and in 1955, the author of a popular article entitled "How Your State Ranks in Education" placed Utah second in the nation. The Utah Foundation attributed all this to two factors: "organizational efficiency," meaning, in particular, the effective consolidation of school districts; and "superior financial effort," meaning the high percentage of individual income going to education.[57]

Colleges, Universities, and the Governor

As far as Utah's colleges and universities were concerned, the Lee era was a time of notable achievements, including some for which Governor Lee could be credited. For example he encouraged and fully supported an interstate compact for higher education. The compact committed several western states to waive out-of-state tuition for students from other states in the compact that did not have medical, dental, or veterinary schools.

Meanwhile, the four-year medical school at the University of Utah, begun during the war to help alleviate a serious shortage of physicians, attained an enviable reputation and attracted a number of students from outside the state. Dr. A. Cyril Callister, the first dean, conducted an aggressive recruiting campaign in a successful effort to attract people who were fine teachers and also had national reputations for medical research. One such recruit was Maxwell M. Wintrode, world renowned for his research as well as his textbook *Hematology*, who chaired the department of medicine until 1967. He, in turn, brought outstanding people in cardiology, public health, preventive medicine, pathology, radiology, pharmacology, anatomy, biochemistry, and other fields important to a distinguished medical school.[58]

Utah State Agricultural College, at Logan, had a fine reputation in agriculture, forestry, industrial education, and some aspects of engineering, all of which brought in many students from outside the state. It also expanded its curriculum to meet increasingly diverse needs and to support a growing demand for graduate studies. In 1957, more fully representing its new stature, the college's name was changed to Utah State University of Agriculture and Applied Sciences. (Its short name, Utah State University, is now always used, even on official documents.)

Four years earlier, in April 1953, Utah State was the focus of an uncomfortable controversy when the board of trustees, with the approval of the governor, released the school's president, Dr. Louis L. Madsen. The issues were related to differences in administrative philosophy between Madsen and the board, as well as between Madsen and Governor Lee. Madsen's supporters, who included most of the faculty and student body, were outraged. The board made its decision on Saturday, April 25, and the story appeared in the papers on Sunday. On Monday morning, students arriving on campus found their student body president angrily berating the governor and haranguing the students, urging them to take the day off from classes, go to Salt Lake City, and demand Madsen's reinstatement. By mid-morning, seven hundred students were on their way to Salt Lake City in automobiles. Their mile-long caravan was escorted to the capitol building by police, and there, in the rotunda, they noisily shouted their demands. Lee refused to talk to the entire group, but he told their representatives that the matter was out of his hands. The uproar, with photographs, even made the pages of *Life* magazine, but it accomplished little, and Madsen was not retained. With a distinguished national reputation in agricultural sciences, however, he soon accepted a position in the US Department of Agriculture as head of the beef cattle division.

Madsen's successor was Dr. Henry Aldous Dixon, president of Weber College. A distinguished educator and administrator in public schools as well as at the college level, he once served on President Harry Truman's commission for higher education. After Dixon's election to Congress the following year, he was replaced by Dr. Daryl Chase, director of the Branch Agricultural College at Cedar City and former dean of students at Utah State.

The other major institution of higher learning in the state was Brigham Young University, which boasted a full-time student body of more than 7,600 in the 1955–56 school year, and which was the largest church-related college or university in the nation. In 1951 Dr. Ernest L. Wilkinson, a former Utahn and a prominent attorney in the nation's capital, was appointed president. Two years later Wilkinson also became administrator of all LDS Church schools. In this capacity he envisioned a huge network of LDS junior colleges that would serve, in part, as feeders to BYU. Governor Lee's controversial proposal to return three of the state's junior colleges to the church only complemented Wilkinson's goals.

As early as 1951, as part of his economy drive, Governor Lee proposed to the state legislature that it return Weber College (Ogden), Dixie College (St. George) and Snow College (Ephraim) to the LDS Church. All three, originally established and operated by the church, were transferred to the state in 1933 with the stipulation that if the state should ever cease their operation, they would revert to the church. Opposition came from many sources, especially Weber County. In December 1953, Lee made his proposal again, also suggesting the closing of Carbon College in Price. The legislature soon passed a bill, signed by Lee on December 21, returning the three colleges to the church.

However, instead of settling the controversy, this action intensified it. Opponents obtained enough signatures on a referendum petition to place the matter on the ballot in November 1954. Church leaders maintained a position of neutrality, but it was clear that they were willing to take over the schools. Lee told Utahns in a radio broadcast that the state must use its money to support its rapidly growing public schools, but in the end voters soundly rejected the proposal.[59]

Utahns Look at National Politics and Issues

Meanwhile, the United States pursued a futile quest for normality, even though things could never be the same as before the war. More than ever, national politics became an offshoot of international politics as the United States completed its leap away from isolationism and became one of the world's two great superpowers.

Among the most overwhelming political concerns were the heating up of the Cold War and America's involvement in international organizations and undertakings. President Truman's foreign policy emphasized support for the United Nations, the Marshall Plan, NATO, and technical assistance to underdeveloped areas. Utahns supported the last three, but to some, including the governor, the United Nations was little more than a Communist tool for undermining American sovereignty.

In 1949, the Chinese Communists overthrew that country's Nationalist government, leading the United States to end diplomatic relations with China. At the same time, America discovered that the Soviet Union possessed the atom bomb, leading Truman, in January 1950, to order the development of the even more fearful hydrogen bomb. Then, in June 1950, North Korean forces invaded the Republic of South Korea. The United States, acting under the auspices of the United Nations, quickly became involved.

The Korean conflict was different from any Americans had ever known. Never before had the president of the United States committed the country to such extensive military action (it was never officially called a "war" but rather a "police action") under the auspices of an international organization or without the consent of Congress. Nor could they remember a "limited war," in which the objective was not to defeat the enemy but simply to maintain a status quo. Americans, including most Utahns, supported the action in Korea to the extent that they saw it as a means of stopping the spread of Communism, but they were not sure that acting under the umbrella of the U.N. was a good idea. It seemed, somehow, to be a negation of American sovereignty.

General Douglas MacArthur was given overall command of the U.N. (mostly US) forces, with the objective of driving North Korean troops from the area south of the Thirty-eighth Parallel. After China entered the conflict, however, he became irate that he was forbidden from sending troops or bombing missions into China itself in order to cripple or destroy the invaders' support. He began to express his displeasure publicly. President Truman believed that what MacArthur wanted could only lead to full-scale war with China. Besides that, it was contrary to the United Nations mandate. Just as Truman was attempting to negotiate a boundary settlement, MacArthur made it clear that he would attack China if it did not make peace. He also criticized Truman publicly for not realizing that "there is no substitute for victory." Truman, as commander-in-chief, had no choice but to dismiss MacArthur from his command, a decision supported by the Joint Chiefs of Staff. However, Truman's action sent the American people into an uproar. MacArthur was one of their heroes and also, like him, they were suspicious of a political situation that did not allow what they were used to—total "victory," where "good" triumphed over "evil."

The fighting in Korea finally ended with an armistice on July 26, 1953. The political status quo was formalized, but the two sides continued holding truce talks at Panmunjom. Technically, the war was not over, bitter antagonism remained, and the Panmunjom talks continued for decades with no resolution of the major issues.

The Korean war affected Utah in several ways. By February 1952, approximately six thousand Utahns were drafted into the military, while an additional twenty-two thousand joined the armed forces voluntarily.[60] Probably less than half of these actually served in Korea, but at the time the armistice was signed it was reported that 135 Utahns had been killed, nearly three hundred were wounded, and over fifty were prisoners of war or missing in action.[61]

In general, the people of Utah approved America's involvement in Korea, believing it to be a means for stopping the expansion of Communism. They were divided, however, on whether the action should be conducted unilaterally or under the auspices of the United Nations. Some supported the U.N. but others, even though they backed anti-Communist military activity, believed that working through the U.N. in any matter was wrong. Even the *Tribune*, which supported the U.N. as such, quickly became critical of the fact that the United States had tied itself to the U.N. and was not willing to make an independent declaration of war.[62] Most Utahns probably agreed.

Like other Americans, Utahns were outraged when it appeared that political considerations kept the military from defeating the enemy. When MacArthur was fired, Governor Lee became livid, calling the action "but another step of appeasement."[63] Many other Utahns felt the same way, although a *Deseret News* analyst recognized the practical necessity faced by Truman. A military commander, he said, must not "try to coerce his government" by making his views public. The *Salt Lake Tribune* charged that MacArthur had been crippled by the policies of the administration but nevertheless declared that he was "rendering a disservice to our cause and to himself by assuming to make delicate political and diplomatic policy decisions."[64]

Inescapably entangled with the effort to keep Communism in check internationally was the "red scare" at home. In many ways this red scare reached deeper into the American psyche and affected politics more intently than the red scare that followed World War I. Responding to accusations that Communist agents had infiltrated the government, President Truman launched a loyalty review program for federal employees. Most received clean bills of health, but the few revelations of possible Communist influence heightened the hysteria of many to the point that they were willing to believe the irresponsible charges that Senator Joseph R. McCarthy of Wisconsin began to hurl in 1950. Claiming, first, that the State Department was thoroughly infested with Communists (who, by implication, were working for the overthrow of the government), McCarthy claimed to have lists of names. He never produced his list and never uncovered a single agent, but he continued making national headlines with reckless charges of subversion, until after the Korean war. As a result, the reputations of many good and perfectly innocent people were ruined or dam-

Image 2.3: Arthur V. Watkins, Republican Senator from Utah, January 3, 1947–January 3, 1959. In 1954 he chaired the senate committee whose investigation led to the censure of Joseph McCarthy. Used by permission, Utah State Historical Society, all rights reserved.

aged. McCarthy achieved the dubious distinction of having his name turned into a synonym for such tactics.

Unfortunately, Utah was not immune from McCarthyism,[65] illustrated by the senatorial campaign of 1950, perhaps the worst smear campaign in Utah history. One prominent political historian, in fact, said that this campaign "will go down in the history of the state as the most scurrilous since the almost forgotten days of the bitter Mormon and anti-Mormon struggles" of the nineteenth century.[66] (Details are discussed later in this chapter.)

Although Utah's newspapers were critical of McCarthy's smear tactics, Governor Lee supported him. He also joined in the campaign against Senator Elbert D. Thomas by calling him "a stooge who has been too long associated with the Reds, the Pinks, and the Fellow Travelers."[67] Similar tactics were effectively used to help drive other people from office, including Reva Beck Bosone in 1952.[68]

In the midst of this tense political climate, Utah's Senator Watkins received an unwanted and delicate assignment. McCarthy's tactics were increasingly lambasted in the press, and there was a considerable amount of public pressure to do something to check his reckless actions. In response, the Senate appointed a select subcommittee, chaired by Watkins, to consider a censure of McCarthy. Public reactions, including those of Watkins's constituents in Utah, were mixed. While many people were disgusted with McCarthy's actions, they were nevertheless so deeply imbued with anti-Communism that they wondered if the committee would go too far. Others urged Watkins on enthusiastically, while still others were highly critical of him for participating at all. Watkins himself later commented on his thankless assignment: "I should have been most amazed at the time had I realized that in the minds of many Americans it was I who was on trial; not Senator McCarthy."[69] In the end the Watkins committee recommended censuring McCarthy on two specific counts. The Senate approved censure on only one of those counts but also condemned McCarthy for his abusive treatment of the committee.

Another political issue brewing in the nation was civil rights. Segregation in public places was rampant, especially in the South, and racial bias stood in the way of any action concerning it. The problem was particularly tragic in education, where segregation often meant blacks were forced to attend inferior schools. By the 1950s, segregation was being challenged in the courts. In 1954, a pivotal Supreme Court decision, *Brown v. Board of Education*, finally declared unconstitutional the doctrine of "separate but equal" in public education. This had no immediate effect on racism but it established legal parameters and opened the door to years of tense struggles to actually achieve integration.

In Utah, meanwhile, the problems seemed relatively remote because racial minorities there were small in number. Beneath the surface, however, there was a considerable amount of prejudice, including the kind that came simply from lack of association. There were also deep-seated traditional biases and certain religious practices, discussed in the next chapter, that kept ethnic minorities from being fully accepted into Utah society.[70]

A 1950 survey in the public schools revealed that early in their lives Utah children displayed racial attitudes much like those in the nation at large. There was some degree of intolerance toward all minority groups, but more toward Germans, Japanese, African-Americans, and Jews, in that order, than toward Chinese, Italians, Catholics, Filipinos, or Mexicans. The anti-German and anti-Japanese bias was probably a lingering result of the war. Unfortunately, students demonstrated greater intolerance as they became older, continuing through the university level. Illustrating the seriousness of the problematical attitudes was a questionnaire returned by one elementary school teacher. A black line was drawn through the entire questionnaire and the teacher had written at the bottom: "We don't have any racial problems in our town now because we don't have any Negroes here. Studies like this only stir up troubles. Keep Negroes out and avoid prejudice."[71] Clearly, racial prejudice was only perpetuated by teachers with such attitudes.

One illustration of the unfortunate results of Utah's racism occurred in January 1984when Marian Anderson, a world-famous African-American opera star, arrived to perform in Utah. Anderson had experienced segregation and discrimination throughout her life, including a highly publicized denial for her to perform at Constitution Hall in Washington, D.C., in 1939. Outraged at this, Eleanor Roosevelt resigned her membership in the Daughters of the American Revolution, who owned the hall, and arranged for Anderson to perform on the steps of the Lincoln Memorial. When she arrived in Salt Lake City in 1954, she was allowed to stay in the Hotel Utah but not to use the public elevator or dining room. Instead, she was required to use the freight elevator and to take her meals in her room. Later that week, she performed at Utah State Agricultural College in Logan but, unable to find public accommodations, she was invited to stay in the home of music professor Walter Welti. Anderson's experience was only one of many in Utah in which famous entertainers and other prominent blacks, even including Ralph Bunche, American ambassador to the United Nations, received the same treatment.[72]

In other developments, a generally flourishing American economy coming on the heels of wartime limitations on consumer goods led to increased demands for new automobiles, televisions, transistorized radios, and electric household gadgets of all sorts. Utahns were not immune to such wants as their economy, too, remained generally healthy. This increased consumerism led to gradual but significant changes in family life. New shopping malls, a proliferation of credit card use, and other signs of increased consumption characterized both the nation and Utah. Two-car families became more common, making it easier for teenagers to be away from home more often. Another changing social pattern was the fact that the number and ratio of women, including mothers, to men in the workplace continued to grow. In a different kind of development, Utahns benefitted from the new Salk polio vaccine, as children began receiving vaccinations in April 1955. Eventually the disease was practically eradicated in both the nation and the state.

Meanwhile, J. Bracken Lee made such a reputation for himself in his drive for economy, efficiency, and individualism, and in his vociferous denunciation of practically everything the federal government did, that there was speculation about the possibility of his running for national office, perhaps as a candidate for vice-president on a ticket headed either by Robert A. Taft or Dwight D. Eisenhower. Lee professed little interest in such a move, but his particularly indignant address before the national convention of the US Chamber of Commerce in Washington, D.C., on April 28, 1952, endeared him even more to many political right-wingers. It was a long, bitter harangue in which he said that the Constitution was now honored not so much in its application as in its breach. He raged against a "self-seeking, power-hungry few" who had cunningly stolen from and misled the people. "Whose country is this, anyway?" he asked, "Is it the people's or does it belong to the political gangster?" He concluded with a dissertation on what could be done, including political action against the "gangsters" who had taken over the government. He called upon business leaders, "you who may be gifted," to "lead this fight for the return of the government to the state, the county and the city." He also included a blast at the United Nations, which he had detested since its inception.[73] Such rhetoric brought Utah's governor even more to the attention of many conservatives, but he was never seriously considered for national office.

Lee's personal preference for the Republican presidential nomination in 1952 was Senator Robert A. Taft of Ohio. The bid, however, went to the tremendously popular Dwight D. Eisenhower, who in the election overwhelmed his opponent, Adlai Stevenson, with 55 percent of the popular vote and 83 percent of the electoral ballots. Voters in both Utah and the nation were influenced, in part, by Eisenhower's image as a war hero and the hope that he could bring an end to the Korean conflict.

After his election, Eisenhower appointed two Utahns to prominent federal office. One was Ivy Baker Priest, who became Treasurer of the United States.[74] Mrs. Priest had long been an avid Republican party worker, from her early days as a babysitter for Republican women voters in her hometown of Bingham through her enthusiastic work as a member of Utah's Young Republicans. In 1944 she became a member of the national Republican committee, and she was named secretary of the Republican conference of the eleven western states in 1947. Her appointment was certainly, in part, a reward for years of faithful service to the party.

Perhaps Eisenhower's most surprising appointment was that of Ezra Taft Benson, a member of the Quorum of the Twelve Apostles since 1943, to be Secretary of Agriculture. Benson's qualifications seemed excellent. They included a master's degree in agricultural economics from Iowa State College, nine years as head of Idaho's Department of Agricultural Economics and Marketing, and four years (1939–43) as executive secretary of the National Council of Farmer Cooperatives, headquartered in Washington, D.C. He also had strong recommendations from such prominent national figures as Thomas E. Dewey, Senator Robert A. Taft, and Allan Kline, president of the American Farm Bureau Federation.

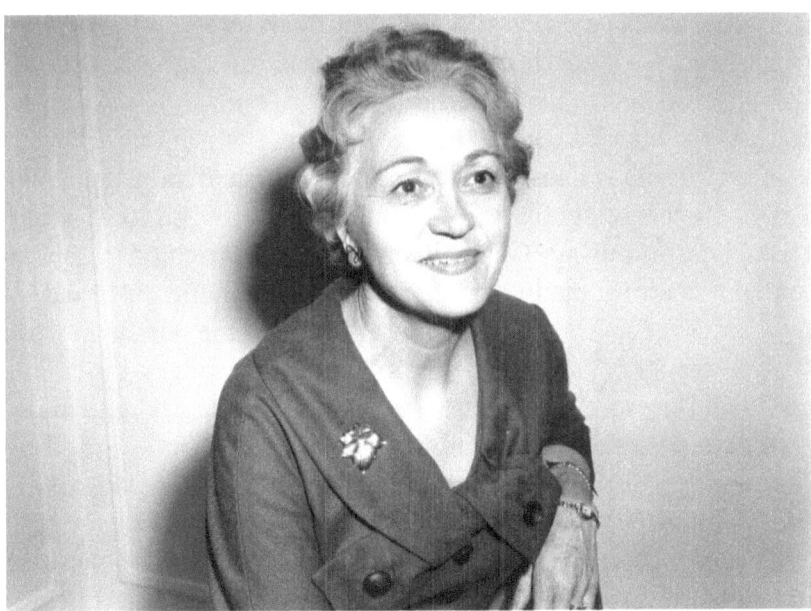

Image 2.4: Ivy Baker Priest, Utah Republican who became the thirtieth United States Secretary of the Treasury, 1953–1961. Used by permission, Utah State Historical Society, all rights reserved.

Image 2.5: Ezra Taft Benson served as Secretary of Agriculture under President Dwight D. Eisenhower. Here he visits Forest Serviced Smokejumpers at the Aerial Fire Depot in Missoula, Montana. Used by permission, Utah State Historical Society, all rights reserved.

The new Secretary of Agriculture had special expertise in marketing. This was an important aspect of his highly conservative political stance that de-emphasized governmental support to farmers in favor of complete free enterprise which, he believed, would promote and reward personal initiative and industry. However, he became controversial immediately after he took office. His uncompromising "General Statement on Agricultural Policy" took direct aim at planned and subsidized economies. Dubbed by political wags as "the epistle from the apostle," the statement worried members of his own department, many farmers, leaders of the Farm Bureau, Republican leaders from the Midwest, and many Democrats. Although Eisenhower and other Republican leaders continued to respect Benson highly and generally agreed with his basic philosophy, which would have eliminated price supports and other subsidies almost at once, the president's farm policy did not reflect everything that Benson wanted. Rather, Eisenhower presented a more moderate, and more politically astute, policy of gradualism and flexibility. Benson agreed with flexibility but continued to push for more quickly lifting all price supports. There were many positive aspects of the Eisenhower-Benson program that greatly helped farmers, but Secretary Benson himself became so controversial that many people began to urge the president to drop him from the Cabinet. Recognizing the political problems he was causing the president, Benson even offered to resign, but Eisenhower remained firm in his support of Benson and in his determination to keep him. Despite the controversy, Benson gained universal respect, both nationally and internationally, for his expertise, hard work, and integrity. In the end, he and Postmaster General Arthur E. Summerfield were the only two Eisenhower Cabinet appointees to remain in office for the president's entire two terms.[75]

The Environment and Related Concerns

It might be said that, in a way, weather and politics complimented each other during the stormy J. Bracken Lee years: the turbulence in both was unusual, devastating to some people, and worth commentary.[76]

It began with the winter of 1948–49, the coldest and most snow-laden winter on record. Ten people lost their lives directly as a result of the weather, and there was a near-ruinous 25 percent loss in livestock. Dairy production fell, fruit trees died, wildlife suffered, and the tourist trade reached an all-time low. The economic loss to stockmen and transportation companies ran into the millions of dollars. Toward the end of January 1949, Governor Lee proclaimed a state of emergency, and plans were made for using bombers to fly feed to many of the state's 1.5 million sheep and an undetermined number of cattle that were both freezing and starving to death. A $50,000 Sheep Emergency Fund was established by President Harry Truman, and military aircraft from Las Vegas as well as other bases operated by the Utah National Guard began the "feedlift" operation.[77] Tragically, a few people died in plane crashes while trying to help, and one Salina sheepherder was killed by a bale of hay dropped from a plane.[78]

Two years later, a series of spring floods ravaged parts of the state. On May 28, 1951, for example, the streams flowing from Little Cottonwood and Big Cottonwood canyons burst their banks in a dozen places. Farms in the Salt Lake Valley were damaged, basements were flooded, and the *Salt Lake Tribune* chided local government for not anticipating these possibilities and not spending more money on conservation and flood control measures.[79] Before the end of the year Salt Lake City began to install better storm drains in at least some areas. Nevertheless, the following year saw even more severe flooding throughout the entire state. The western part of Salt Lake City was flooded, with 13th South becoming a canal. Utah Lake rose two feet above its compromise level, and the junction of two highways at the mouth of Weber Canyon was washed away. In all, the state suffered an estimated $6 million in flood damage that year.

The weather also went to the other extreme as the fall of 1952 brought a drought in the Salt Lake area that equaled the longest on record. The next year saw an average rainfall in the state of only 59 percent of normal. The general dryness was so severe and continued for so long that in 1956 one-third of Utah's counties received federal aid.

Nothing could be done about the weather, but conservationists believed something could, and should, be done about preserving the environmental integrity and scenic beauty of Utah's public lands and national parks. With heavy economic pressure being brought to bear for developing many pristine areas, the controversy over the proposed Echo Park dam in Dinosaur National Monument (located on the border between Colorado and Utah but mostly in Colorado) became one of the most intense debates of the decade. In 1950 the Bureau of Reclamation made the dam part of the CRSP, which was still being argued in Congress. This meant, however, that Echo Park, a beautiful meadow at the confluence of the Green and Yampa rivers, would be inundated.

Ironically, the proposal for the dam was a boon to conservationists in their battle against the threat of economic development in the disappearing wilderness areas, including the national parks. They were also confronted with an early version of the "sagebrush rebellion," an effort to transfer millions of acres of federal land to the states. Echo Park quickly became a rallying point, bringing together diverse conservationists, preservationists, and environmentalists on a clear and immediate issue that they believed the public would understand. To them the proposed dam exemplified the callousness with which economic interests had always treated the delicate environment.

One of the first public blasts against the dam came from the pen of Bernard DeVoto, a Utah expatriate who had achieved national prestige as a novelist, historian, and columnist. Such a dam, he proclaimed in a scathing article in the *Saturday Evening Post*, would not only destroy the beauty of the magnificent canyons in the area but also destroy both Echo Park and Dinosaur National Monument.[80] Following DeVoto's lead, conservationists and preservationists around the country joined in a massive effort to defeat the project. For them it was a major test of their ability to protect all of America's parks and wilderness lands. Dinosaur National Monument had never been as well publicized throughout the nation as it was in the blitz of newspaper and magazine articles drawing attention to what was about to happen.

However, most of the anti-dam publicity came from outside the state because Utahns were not necessarily supportive of the conservationists. To those who promoted the CRSP, and particularly the Central Utah Project, the Echo Park Dam was essential. Senator Arthur V. Watkins of Utah, a member of the Senate subcommittee for irrigation and reclamation, felt just that way.

The debate over Echo Park was inextricably tied up with the proposal for a dam at Glen Canyon in northern Arizona. The Bureau of Reclamation saw these projects as complementing each other. Conservationists did not like either one, but since the Glen Canyon Dam was more likely to pass a congressional test, they decided to concentrate their efforts on Echo Park. In the end, the destiny of both Echo Park and Glen Canyon hinged on a fateful decision by the Council of Conservationists, a temporary lobbying group that served as an umbrella for twenty-eight different organizations. After the Senate voted in 1954 to approve the CRSP, including Echo Park Dam, the Council made it clear that if Echo Park were not removed from the bill all the nation's wilderness groups would oppose the CRSP. If the dam were eliminated, however, they would support the bill. That assurance, which promised to make passage of the still-controversial measure much easier, led lawmakers to take out the Echo Park Dam.

Ironically, by using this tactic the predecessors of today's environmentalists actually joined in the development of the Colorado River and the promotion of Glen Canyon dam. Only later did they recognize the extent of the majestic natural beauty that their creation would destroy, a fact which now sends shivers up the spines of their philosophical descendants. Nevertheless, they helped preserve the integrity of Utah's Dinosaur National Monument and, at least in that way, helped strengthen both the national park system as well as the public awareness of the value and beauty of pristine nature.[81]

The 1950s saw the beginning of still another environmental concern that only grew in intensity over the years. The Korean war raised the specter of a third world war, with the frightful possibility that it could become an atomic war. It was in that context that the United States expanded its nuclear testing program with a major series of open air atomic blasts at a test sight in Nevada, just 120 miles west of St. George, in southern Utah. The nuclear fallout

89

also resulted in medical, social, and political fallouts in Utah that lasted for the rest of the century and beyond.

The first blast was detonated on January 18, 1951. Residents of St. George and other southern Utah towns were awed as they felt the earth rumble and watched the giant mushroom cloud rise ominously in the West. Even though they knew that the clouds soon to drift over their homes were laden with radioactive particles, they had been assured by government agents that any harmful fallout would be minimal. Testing went on for the next seven years. At times people were told to spend part of the day in their homes, and cars traveling through the area were stopped for a few hours. But Utahns still watched, only partially grasping the grim significance of what they were seeing. The Atomic Energy Commission (AEC) held to the deceit that the people had nothing to fear. After one powerful blast in May, 1953, an official was quoted as saying that "a person could have remained outdoors in St. George unclothed for the entire period of the fall-out without receiving a dangerous dose."[82]

By this time, however, some people had serious suspicions that something was wrong, and that either the AEC did not know what it was doing or it was deliberately keeping any knowledge of the real danger from them. In 1953 sheep ranchers and herders began to find sheep giving birth to deformed lambs, losing their wool, breaking out with unusual sores, or dying in unusually high numbers. A few people began to complain of unusual illnesses, rashes, and hair falling out. One blast, dubbed "Dirty Harry," produced a fallout 1,230 times the so-called permissible limit, a fact that was not reported to the public. Instead, the AEC invited Utah's Congressman Douglas Stringfellow to tour the proving grounds and receive an official briefing. Stringfellow then assured the civic and business leaders of St. George that the AEC was telling the truth: there was no danger at all to the health of the people of southern Utah. Incredibly, they believed him.

In Cedar City, meanwhile, many people were convinced that radiation poisoning was killing their sheep, but after what it claimed was one of the most exhaustive investigations in history the AEC declared that there was no evidence to support the accusations. The commission even survived a number of lawsuits for damages caused to livestock, claiming that the sheep died because of malnutrition.

In later years it became clear that, in reality, the deadly radioactive fallout was the cause of much sickness and death, and that the AEC was involved in a sophisticated cover-up and propaganda campaign in order to save the atomic testing program. Some officials may have felt that Communism posed such a serious threat to American security that it was worth both the deception and the risk to develop the nuclear capabilities necessary to ward off that threat. Just how well they did their job was illustrated by two 1955 editorials in the *Salt Lake Tribune*. The editors claimed that most of the propaganda about radiation came from Communists. They agreed that there was some danger to public health but said that this was outweighed by the threat of nuclear destruction at the hands of Communist nations. They criticized the Atomic Energy Commission, nevertheless, for minimizing the radiation dangers. This, they said, "plays directly into the hands of Communists who want to stir up public anxiety sufficiently to stop the atomic tests altogether." They expressed hope that future tests would be conducted elsewhere, but declared that "on the whole, we must agree, the Atomic Energy Commission did an excellent job, particularly in establishing and following rigid safety standards."[83] It would be thirty-five years before the government would finally face up to the actual peril and the damage left in its wake.[84]

State Politics and Resurgent Republicanism

The 1950s saw a Republican resurgence in Utah. By this time, however, mainstream Republicanism was quite different from the old conservatism that characterized the pre-New Deal party. Much to Governor Lee's consternation, the new party, like its leader, Dwight D. Eisenhower, accepted most of the New Deal reforms.

J. Bracken Lee's uncompromising temperament was at the heart of several political feuds. When he took over as governor he attempted to remove from office several appointees from the Maw administration. In at least one case, the effort backfired. Milton B. Taylor, a member of the finance commission, simply refused to resign, whereupon Lee summarily fired him. When Taylor took the matter to court, Lee responded with a list of financial "irregularities" that, he said, were not in the interest of the state. Charges and counter charges flew, but in 1951, the state supreme court upheld an earlier district court order that Taylor should be reinstated.[85]

The Taylor controversy created another political feud. Parnell Black, Taylor's attorney, was responsible for many of the charges hurled against Lee. He was also chair of the state Democratic Party. In 1950 he decided to run for the state senate seat from Salt Lake County, but his main purpose was to undermine Lee. "A vote for me is a vote against the governor," he said.

Lee fought back with a vengeance. He accused Black of such things as overcharging the working man and cheating the state by accepting an unearned retainer from the liquor commission. Black countered by arguing that he was a good lawyer, charged reasonable fees and was second to none in his record of helping the poor. He also argued that Lee's tax program benefitted large corporations but not the ordinary wage earner. Accusations of dishonesty and corruption flew from both sides. Black was defeated, but a by-product of this bitter feud was a strengthening of Lee's long time disdain for lawyers in general.

The most significant event in the political campaigns of 1950 was the defeat of Democratic senator Elbert D. Thomas; perhaps one of the most extreme examples of McCarthyism and "political dynamiting" in the country. Thomas was highly respected both nationally and internationally. His Republican opponent, Wallace F. Bennett, was a successful businessman and former president of the National Association of Manufacturers. The seeming paradox of Thomas's loss amid a generally Democratic victory in the state was accounted for largely by a shameless, McCarthy-like smear campaign as well as strong opposition from Utah's agricultural interests, businessmen, and medical groups. Another factor was what appeared to be the entry of the LDS Church into the political arena.

The Republican campaign began with efforts to brand Thomas as a Communist sympathizer who was active in subversive Communist causes. Both charges were patently false. One particularly shameless piece of literature charged that Thomas had presided at a Communist banquet when, in fact, he had not even accepted the invitation to attend it. Another blow came when, after such softening up, Utahns were suddenly confronted with a one-time publication entitled *United States Senate News*. Prepared by Walter Quigly, a professional "political dynamiter," the publication was nothing more than a vicious attack on Thomas's reputation. It used cartoons, misquotations, unproven accusations, and well-calculated distortions of his voting record to claim that he was an active Communist sympathizer. It is not clear who paid for the mass distribution of these scurrilous publications, but Bennett claimed that he was not responsible for them.

Bennett had no political record to smear but after Senator Arthur V. Watkins joined in the Bennett campaign Democrats tried unsuccessfully to diffuse Watkins's support by tarnishing his reputation. He was called an extreme isolationist who was unwilling to fight the Communists abroad.

The final blow against Thomas came not long before the end of the campaign. A twenty-six member committee calling itself the Salt Lake County LDS Law Observance Committee released a list of candidates it endorsed. Most Democrats, including Thomas, were not on the list. In addition, the committee circulated a letter urging Latter-day Saints to vote on the basis of principle, not party, and to counsel with their bishops if they needed further advice with respect to candidates. The committee did not have official church origins, as its name implied, and church leaders issued a strong denial to the newspapers. Nevertheless, the matter was viewed by political observers as church leaders giving their personal support to Republican candidates.[86] In addition, a whispering campaign, apparently begun by a few local LDS leaders, further tarnished Thomas's reputation by picturing him as an apostate. Nothing could be further from the truth, for Thomas, who once served as president of the church's Japanese mission, was still an active, committed Latter-day Saint.

In the end, Thomas was turned out of office, even though the two Democratic incumbents in the House, Walter K. Granger and Reva Beck Bosone, were returned by comfortable majorities.[87] Bosone was elected for a second term and Granger for a sixth. In addition, Democrats showed significant gains in most local elections. In the legislature, they lost eleven seats in the House of Representatives but gained three in the Senate. The House was thus evenly divided between the two parties (thirty members each), while the Democrats held a 15-8 majority in the Senate.

In 1952 the state moved clearly into the Republican ranks. In the presidential election Utahns gave Eisenhower about 59 percent of their votes. The Republicans, riding happily on Eisenhower's coattails, also sent their two congressional candidates to the House of Representatives. That same year, for the first time in twenty years, Republicans took control of both houses of the Utah legislature.

Perhaps the most interesting races in the state were those for Congress. Both Walter K. Granger and Reva Beck Bosone were challenged on the basis of their presumed leanings toward socialism. Among other things, both were accused of favoring socialized medicine which, it was charged, would automatically lead to socialization of every other profession.[88]

Granger did not even receive the Democratic nomination, which went, instead, to Ernest R. McKay. Key to McKay's ultimate defeat was the dramatic impact on voters of Republican Douglas R. Stringfellow. Having been wounded and paralyzed from the waist down during World War II, he painfully learned to walk again with the use of canes. In 1952 he stumped the First Congressional District with a spell binding tale of leading a secret mission behind German lines in which, among other dangerous exploits, they captured physicist Otto Hahn. According to his story, Stringfellow was wounded by the explosion of a German land mine while on this mission. Only four others, he said, survived the murderous torture inflicted after their capture. The war-hero aura surrounding Stringfellow and his near-theatrical presentations helped defeat his opponent by seventy-seven thousand to fifty thousand votes.

Challenging Reva Beck Bosone was former Congressman William A. Dawson, whom she had defeated in 1948. As Dawson later described the campaign: "It was not the milktoast affair we had in 1948 but a hard hitting campaign based on her record."[89] Since Bosone's was a generally liberal record, he could attack it vigorously in a political climate that was rapidly moving to the right. The inaccurate images painted of her leaning toward socialism were important in the overwhelming 105 thousand to ninety-five thousand vote in favor of Dawson, but Bosone later noted that the heavy pro-Republican political winds would probably have swept him into office anyway.[90]

Governor Lee's opponent in 1952 was the popular Earl J. Glade, mayor of Salt Lake City. During the campaign Lee emphasized his economic program, lower taxes, administrative reform, and the lack of scandal during his first administration. He also claimed that the schools were receiving more money than ever before. Glade attacked Lee's record in education and proposed his own program for restoring confidence in the system. However, Lee still had the general support of LDS Church leaders as well as that of Salt Lake City's two major newspapers. Despite, or perhaps because of, his maverick demeanor and attitudes, Lee was still incredibly popular with the voters and won with a convincing 55.1 percent majority.[91]

On the evening of October 16, 1954, less than three weeks before the next election, Utahns were stunned when they saw Congressman Douglas R. Stringfellow appear on their television sets and admit, with a tear-stained face, that the story of his war exploits was a lie. Almost from the beginning, a few skeptics had detected inconsistencies, but at first there was not enough evidence to arouse serious suspicion in Utah. Later, however, rigorous sleuthing and investigative reporting, including a devastating story in the *Army Times*, demonstrated that his claims were totally fallacious. Apparently the fabrication had simply grown out of control as a result of his constantly being presented as a war hero and then succumbing to the temptation to embellish the image.[92]

The dazed Republican leadership had no choice but to scurry around for another candidate. They persuaded the highly respected H. Aldous Dixon, president of Utah State Agricultural College, to run. Running against Walter K. Granger, he took 54 percent of the vote. In the second Congressional District, Dawson was challenged by Bosone, but he was easily reelected.

In general, even though there was a Democratic trend in the western states during the off-year election of 1954, the Republican party prospered in Utah. This is accounted for partly because of the voters' continuing admiration for Eisenhower as well as the fact that Ezra Taft Benson strongly endorsed Republican candidates.[93]

One of the difficult political issues with both national and local implications was the continuing concern over labor relations and, particularly, compulsory union membership. Following World War II, several states adopted right-to-work laws that made it illegal to require union membership as a condition of employment. Such laws infuriated labor, but the general feeling in Utah was supportive of such laws, and it was apparent that the dominant LDS Church also favored them. The *Deseret News* became a strong advocate of right-to-work legislation and editorialized against any form of compulsory unionism in 1953.[94] Governor Lee, too, strongly supported such legislation, believing it was unconstitutional to require a worker to join and pay dues to any organization as a condition of employment. In 1955 the state legislature passed, and Governor Lee happily signed, a right-to-work law for Utah, which thus became the eighteenth state to have one. Lee believed that his drive for economy and lower taxes showed that he was a friend of the working man, but in this action he lost the support of Utah's labor leaders. Most of them believed that labor-management relations in the state had been good, and that they were being attacked unjustly. But, said the local Utah Federation of Labor president, if big business wants "open warfare" with labor, "I am sure they will find it."[95]

By 1956, Eisenhower's popularity in Utah reached new heights. In that election, running again against Adlai Stevenson, he took 64.6 percent of Utah's votes.[96] In the senatorial campaign, Wallace F. Bennett won easily over Democratic challenger Alonzo F. Hopkins. Utah's two Republican congressmen also won handily. In addition, it was another Republican year state wide, with Republicans dominating both houses of the state legislature.[97]

In the 1956 gubernatorial race, Lee self-confidently decided to run for a third term. In the primary elections, however, he lost his bid for the Republican nomination to political newcomer George D. Clyde. Undaunted, Lee stirred up the political scene in mid-October by announcing that he would run as an independent candidate.

By that time, several factors were working against the governor. As expected, he was the target of stepped-up criticism from educators. He had also lost the support of various other important voting blocs or organizations with political power. Republican leaders generally were antagonized, partly because of Lee's incessant attacks on Eisenhower which, by implication, seemed also to denigrate Secretary of Agriculture Benson. In 1955, dismayed over the fact that Eisenhower had made no attempt to reverse the policies of the hated New Deal, Lee not only charged that in the past two years the president had moved the country farther to the left than in any comparable period in American history, but he also, McCarthy-like, attacked Eisenhower's loyalty.[98] Lee also lost whatever support he previously had from LDS Church leaders. His 1954 veto of a Sunday closing bill did nothing to help his image. While the church did not overtly speak out against Lee, the implication became clear when Albert R. Bowen, son of LDS apostle Albert E. Bowen, pointedly and publicly did so and the church-owned *Deseret News* came out in support of Clyde. At the same time, Lee's signing of the 1955 right-to-work law had drawn the ire of labor.

George D. Clyde was a quiet, calm person who may have appealed to some voters simply because he did not have the bluster of Lee and yet was more articulate. Clyde, age fifty-eight, was an engineer by profession and director of the Utah Water and Power Board. He was also on several commissions concerned with water power and land reclamation. Earlier he had served as chief of engineers in the US Soil Conservation Service. For ten years (1935–45) he was dean of the School of Engineering at Utah State Agricultural College. Vitally interested in water development, Clyde had been active in the successful campaign for passage of the Upper Colorado River bill. Until just a few years before his gubernatorial nomination as a Republican, Clyde actually had been a Democrat.

The Democratic candidate that year was Salt Lake City Commissioner Lorenzo C. Romney, but the most intense battle was between Lee and Clyde. It was a bitter campaign on the part of Lee, who tried to counter charges that he had abandoned the Republican part by asserting that it was the Eisenhower administration, not he, who had done the deserting. He also castigated Clyde as a "new Republican," not a "true Republican." Just a day before the election, much to Lee's surprise, the Clyde forces made public a telegram from President Eisenhower wishing Clyde success. Among other things, it emphasized his support of the Colorado River Project as a demonstration of the fact that he had the interests of the state at heart. In the end, Clyde received 38.2 percent of the vote, as opposed to Romney's 33.4 and Lee's 28.3 percent. For the first time in its history the state of Utah had a governor elected by a minority vote.[99]

Miscellany and Summary

Among the many other events of interest during the Lee years was the unveiling, in June 1950, of a statue of Brigham Young in Statuary Hall in the United States Capitol in Washington, D.C. Each state is authorized two statues in the hall, and this was Utah's first contribution. Appropriately, the statue was sculpted by the famous pioneer leader's grandson, Mahonri M. Young, and unveiled by his only living daughter, Mabel Young Sanborn.

Other bits of miscellany also brought Utah at least fleeting national attention. In 1951 Miss Utah, Coleen Hutchins of Salt Lake City, was named Miss America. Also that year, Brigham Young University achieved national notoriety by winning the basketball championship in the National Invitational Tournament. In 1955, Utah's Mrs. Lavina Christensen Fugal, age seventy-five, was named American mother of the year. That same year the Mormon Tabernacle Choir enhanced Utah's public image when it made a six-week tour of Europe. The choir sang in Great Britain, Belgium, the Netherlands, Germany, and France, receiving enthusiastic notices in every city it visited.

In summary, during the Lee years, Utah continued to be affected by national economic, social, and political trends. It also received national notoriety because of the cost-cutting, tax-slashing policies of the governor as well as his hard-hitting excoriations of every extension of federal power. The state's economy continued to improve, influenced in part by the continuing presence of defense-oriented installations and businesses. Although Utah's highways improved substantially, largely because of the continued infusion of federal funds, there were serious problems ahead because of increasing population pressures and more rapid vehicles. Schools and teachers suffered financially when compared with the rest of the region and the nation, but educational attainments remained remarkably high. Politically, Utah followed the nation into the Republican camp, with most of its successful political leaders showing avid support for Eisenhower and his programs. Some, however, like J. Bracken Lee, never accepted the president as a true conservative, charging him with leading the nation down the road toward socialism. As the period ended, it appeared that Lee was discredited when in 1956 he resoundingly lost his bid for a third term. Two years later he came in third when he ran for the Senate as an independent, but in 1959 he was elected mayor of Salt Lake City. The fortunes of state government, meanwhile, were in the hands of a milder, more middle-of-the-road conservative, George D. Clyde.

Notes

1. For the best general coverage of J. Bracken Lee's political career, see Dennis L. Lythgoe, *Let 'Em Holler: A Political Biography of J. Bracken Lee* (Salt Lake City: Utah State Historical Society, 1982). Much of the material and interpretation in this chapter is based on Lythgoe. See also Dennis L. Lythgoe, "A Special Relationship: J. Bracken Lee and the Mormon Church," *Dialogue: A Journal of Mormon Thought* 11 (Winter 1978): 71–87.
2. Lythgoe, *Let 'Em Holler*, 1.
3. "Utah Tax Unit Hits Costly State Projects," *Salt Lake Tribune*, January 1, 1949, 16.
4. Lythgoe, *Let 'Em Holler*, 79.
5. Ibid., 203–06.
6. As quoted in Lythgoe, *Let 'Em Holler*, 245n.
7. Dr. Rod Julander, professor of political science, Weber State University, telephone interview by James B. Allen, January 25, 1996. Notes in James B. Allen papers, L Tom Perry Special Collections, Harold B. Lee Library, Brigham Young University. Julander has been a long-time political activist in the Democratic party and has personal knowledge of this and other significant political activities.
8. The report indicated that there were 615 arrests reported by the Enforcement Division in fiscal 1948 and 676 reported in fiscal 1949. Utah Foundation, "Utah's Liquor Monopoly," *Research Report* No. 59 (1950).
9. Unless otherwise noted, most of this section is based on Lythgoe, *Let 'Em Holler*, chapters 5 and 6.

10. Richard W. Sadler, ed., *Weber State College: A Centennial History* (Ogden, UT: Weber State College, 1988), 102.
11. "The Man at the Wheel," Time, April 24, 1950, 28.
12. Raymond Moley, "Utah's No-Man," (Portsmouth, Ohio), August 4, 1951, 6. For more details on Lee's national image during his first term, see Lythgoe, *Let 'Em Holler*, 58–64.
13. George B. Russell, *J. Bracken Lee: The Taxpayer's Champion* (New York: Robert Speller & Sons, 1961), viii.
14. Ibid., 71.
15. Floyd Samuel Wilcox, "The Major Financial Policies of Governor J. Bracken Lee of Utah, 1949–1957" (master's thesis, University of Utah, 1967), 93.
16. Ibid.
17. Lythgoe, *Let 'Em Holler*, 77. Lee's economy measures no doubt often went to extremes. He recognized this later, but rationalized it in an interview with his biographer. See ibid., 63.
18. This according to a major study by Dr. Milton R. Merrill, dean of the School of Commerce at Utah State Agricultural College. "Utah Ranks Tenth in Federal Grants in Aid," *Deseret News*, September 3, 1956, B2.
19. There were political accusations that Lee was not supportive of the Colorado River Storage Project, and it is true that at times he seemed to waffle. In general, however, he supported it.
20. Some interesting details on these issues are reported in Utah Foundation, "The Changing Utah Economy," *Research Report* No. 126 (November 1955). See also Elroy Nelson, *Utah's Economic Patterns* (Salt Lake City: University of Utah Press, 1956), 12–20.
21. "Utah Debt Reported Lowest in Nation," *Salt Lake Tribune*, January 13, 1952, B1.
22. "Utah's Welfare Payments Top National Average," *Deseret News*, February 8, 1956, B2.
23. For a comprehensive overview of the prewar activity and how it set the stage for later uranium mining, see Don Sorenson, "Wonder Mineral: Utah's Uranium," *Utah Historical Quarterly* 31 (Summer 1963): 280–90. For brief overviews of Utah's boom, see Raye C. Ringholz, "Uranium Mining in Utah, *Utah History Encyclopedia*, ed. Allen Kent Powell (Salt Lake City: University of Utah Press, 1994), 582–83; Raye C. Ringholz, "Utah's Uranium Boom," *Beehive History* 16 (1990), 25–27. For more detailed accounts, see Amberly Knight, "Hot Rocks Make Big Waves: The Impact of the Uranium Boom on Moab, Utah, 1948-57," *Utah Historical Quarterly* 69 (Winter 2001), 29–45; Raye C. Ringholz, *Uranium Frenzy: Saga of the Nuclear West* (Logan: Utah State University Press, 2002).
24. A detailed year-by-year analysis, with figures reflecting production in various counties, can be seen in the annual issues of *Minerals Yearbook*. For general information and considerable human interest relating to Utah's early uranium industry, see a series of articles in the *Salt Lake Tribune*, May 22–31, 1955.
25. This story is told, in some detail, in Wilcox. "The Major Financial Policies of Governor J. Bracken Lee," 59–65; Lythgoe, *Let 'Em Holler*, 177–90.
26. As Lee complained in his 1952 speech to the US Chamber of Commerce, one of the many strands of wool that had been pulled over the taxpayer's eyes was "the cleverly devised scheme facetiously called the *withholding tax*..... This ill-conceived

hokum merits its rightful name; the tax that snatches your earnings before you see them." Russell, *J. Bracken Lee*, 98.

27. "Lee Files Return–Minus Payment," *Deseret News*, January 13, 1956, B1.
28. Lythgoe notes that, as a result, the IRS audited Lee regularly—a kind of harassment that he probably did not deserve but was the result of his continual attacks on the abuses of a system that he considered little more than "an instrument of police-state mentality." Lythgoe, *Let 'Em Holler*, 187, quoting David Brinkley's characterization of Lee's attitude.
29. For a general survey of highway development into the 1960s, see Ezra Clark Knowlton, *History of Highway Development in Utah* (Salt Lake City: Utah State Department of Highways, 1967).
30. "Lee Promises Road Action," *Salt Lake Tribune*, May 21, 1949, 17; "Lee Describes Utah Roads: 'Not Bad,'" ibid., July 8, 1950, 17.
31. Utah Foundation, "Financing Highways in Utah 1949," *Research Report* No. 60 (1949).
32. Ibid.
33. "Road Condition Best Today, Lee Reports," *Salt Lake Tribune*, August 29, 1952, 42.
34. "$71 Million Road Improvement Project Urged," *Salt Lake Tribune*, October 10, 1952, B1.
35. "Will We Ever Catch Up on Road Building?" *Salt Lake Tribune*, December 18, 1954, 16; "Utah Plans Road Projects to Tune of $11.1 Million," ibid., December 26, 1954, B1.
36. "Eisenhower's Highway Plan Draws Opposition of Lee," *Salt Lake Tribune*, February 24, 1955, 14.
37. For comments on some national statistics suggesting that better highways did not necessarily reduce accidents, see Utah Foundation, "What Price Safety?" in *Research Reports* (December 1954).
38. State Superintendent of Public Instruction, *Utah School Report, 1948–49* (Salt Lake City: Utah State Department of Public Instruction, 1950). Actually, Bateman's dramatic estimates were not far off the mark. In 1956 there were 39,032 more children enrolled in the public schools than in 1950, but this jumped to 45,603 more in 1957 and 53,941 more in 1958. *1969 Statistical Abstract of Utah* (Salt Lake City: Bureau of Business and Economic Research, University of Utah, January 1969), 44.
39. For more complete discussions of this battle see Edwin Lee Reynolds, "J. Bracken Lee and Utah Public Education" (master's thesis, Brigham Young University, 1973), 15–27, with the correspondence between Lee and Bateman reproduced in Appendix A; Lythgoe, *Let 'Em Holler*, 109–15.
40. He said this in a personal interview with Elwin Lee Reynolds, December 5, 1972. Lee also observed that, as a result of this altercation, succeeding legislatures did not itemize various departmental budgets so that the governor could not exercise his item veto. "Thus," commented Reynolds, "for the sum of $20,000 the Governor, in large measure, deprived the taxpayers of the opportunity to scrutinize the budget." Reynolds, "J. Bracken Lee and Utah Public Education," 26–27.
41. Details on Lee's effort to get rid of Bateman and on the salary struggle are contained in Reynolds, "J. Bracken Lee and Utah Public Education," 28–37, and Lythgoe, *Let 'Em Holler*, 112–14. During much of this time Bateman had refused to accept any checks, pending court action, and had been living on borrowed funds since October 1951. He immediately received his back pay.

42. A matter of semantics became part of the discussion when educators claimed that he called them a "vicious lobby," but Lee replied that he had only used the word "disgraceful."
43. For details on the fight over Senate Bill 75, see Reynolds, "J. Bracken Lee and Utah Public Education," 38–64 and Appendix B (which reproduces radio addresses by Lee, Bernhard, and West); Lythgoe, *Let 'Em Holler*, 117–22.
44. The problem is illustrated by the fact that 82 percent of the 773 teachers trained in Utah in 1947–48 remained in the state, but in 1954 only 37 percent of the 802 Utah-trained teachers took jobs in Utah's schools. Lythgoe, *Let 'Em Holler*, 127.
45. Bennion had been a teacher in the public schools, a professor of English at the University of Utah, a professor of education at BYU, superintendent of LDS Church schools, and a member of the board of trustees for BYU. He also held a Ph.D. from the University of Chicago. At the time of his appointment to the commission he was vice president of Utah Power and Light Company in charge of public relations. He was named to the LDS Church's Council of the Twelve Apostles in April 1953, shortly after the commission completed its work.
46. Jack Goodman, "UEA Votes 2 to 1 to Open School," *Salt Lake Tribune*, August 29, 1953, 1–2.
47. He also received bad national press, exemplified by a *Time* magazine article in January, 1954, criticizing him for his "passion for economy" that, it said, had inflicted "definite signs of malnutrition" on Utah's schools. "The Governor and the Schools," Time, January 11, 1954, as quoted in Lythgoe, *Let 'Em Holler*, 135. The governor, furious at this and other charges, fired back.
48. Lythgoe, *Let 'Em Holler*, 136.
49. Utah Foundation, "Service Bulletin," no. 8 (1956), 1. The foundation also found that when Salt Lake City was compared with large cities (over 100,000 population) nationwide, its beginning teacher salaries were $471 below the average, fifth year teachers were $719 below that average, and teachers receiving the maximum salary were $908 below. It took sixteen years for teachers in Salt Lake City to achieve the maximum, but only thirteen years on a national average. Salt Lake City's teacher salaries were similar to those of cities in the southern states.
50. He was convinced, according to his biographer, "that teachers were not in fact professionals but, rather, hired help. He had little respect for the teacher as a necessary, contributing member of society." Lythgoe, *Let 'Em Holler*, 136.
51. "School Building Refutes Aid Bid, Report Declares," *Salt Lake Tribune*, June 19, 1955, B1.
52. Utah Foundation, "Federal Funds for Public Schools in Utah," *Research Briefs* (October 1955).
53. One of Lee's most avid supporters declared that his first-term accomplishments included a 42 percent increase in expenditures for new public school buildings, better school finance and tax equalization laws, greater percentage of individual income devoted to education, a comprehensive study of school programs and problems, and inter-state compacts for higher education. Lee's program, he said, "helped create record surpluses, and without any increases in tax levies. Something like a million and a half dollars had been appropriated for supplemental aid to local school districts. There were two million dollars available for emergency public school building aid; and the greatest four-year building program in history was under way on the college and university level." Russell, *J. Bracken Lee*, 109–10.

For a scholarly study that both reports and accepts the negative evaluations of Lee's impact on education, see Reynolds, "J. Bracken Lee and Utah Public Education." For a more balanced approach that still leans toward criticism, see Lythgoe, *Let 'Em Holler*, 117-46. Both authors show that many of the accomplishments credited to Lee by his supporters were, indeed, achieved during his administration but not with his support. In addition, Reynolds concludes: "His profile was one of constant opposition to any advances in education and not withstanding the advances made in Utah in education during his two terms in office, at the end of that time the state held a position in relation to the other states which was several steps lower than when he took office. The single biggest factor in this slip was the opposition of the Governor to any attempts to maintain excellence in education." Reynolds, "J. Bracken Lee and Public Education," 113-14. Lythgoe says that "Lee's record in education is mixed.... Based on all available evidence, one must conclude that Lee's unfortunate treatment of education and educators was his most serious flaw both as a public servant and as a politician. He made unnecessary enemies who haunted him throughout the remainder of his career, contributing to several subsequent election defeats. Even given his rigid economics, he could have prevented such an albatross through the employment of finesse. His constant battling reduced the quality of education in Utah and did irreparable harm to teacher morale." Lythgoe, *Let 'Em Holler*. 144.

54. Wilcox, "The Major Financial Policies of Governor J. Bracken Lee," 79.
55. Utah Foundation, "Public School Finance in Utah—1955," *Research Report* No. 119 (March 1955).
56. Ibid. See also editorial in *Utah Educational Review* 50 (November 1956): 8-9. The Utah Foundation reported 4 percent in 1955, but other figures for years around this time show even more.
57. Utah Foundation, "Federal Aid and Education," *Research Report* No. 125 (October, 1955).
58. See Henry P. Plenk, "Early History of the Four-Year Medical School of the University of Utah, 1942-1952," in *Medicine in the Beehive State, 1940-1990*, ed. Henry P. Plenk, 3-59 (Salt Lake City: Utah Medical Association, LDS Hospital-Deseret Foundation, University of Utah Health Sciences Center, 1992).
59. Another highly controversial ballot issue that year, also strongly supported by Governor Lee, was legislative reapportionment. It, too, failed. Jedediah Smart Rogers, "'When the People Speak': Mormons and the 1954 Redistricting Campaign in Utah," *Utah Historical Quarterly* 71 (Summer 2003), 233-49.
60. "Four Out of Five Utahns Join Up Voluntarily," *Salt Lake Tribune*, February 15, 1952, 11.
61. O. N. Malmquist, "Korea 'Police Action' Changes Utah," *Salt Lake Tribune*, July 27, 1953, 1.
62. In March1952, it decried the "hypocrisy" evident in the fact that this was a U.N. operation and yet the Soviet Union, a member of the U.N., was supplying China and North Korea. It also decried both the president and Congress for "not labeling a war a war." "The Confusions of Korea," *Salt Lake Tribune*, editorial, 10 March 1952, 10.
63. "Lee Raps US 'Appeasement,'" *Salt Lake Tribune*, April 15, 1951, B1.
64. Vivian Meek, "Interpreting the News," *Deseret News*, April 11, 1951, B3; "Fundamentals of MacArthur Political Row," editorial, *Salt Lake Tribune*, April 11, 1951, 8.

65. For a general overview, see Richard Swanson, "McCarthyism in Utah" (master's thesis, Brigham Young University, 1977). See also F. Ross Peterson, "McCarthyism in the Mountains, 1950-1956" in *Essays in the American West, 1974-75*, ed. Thomas G. Alexander (Provo, UT: BYU Press, 1976), 47-77.
66. Frank H. Jonas, "The 1950 Election in Utah," *Western Historical Quarterly* 4 (March 1951), 90-91.
67. Swanson, "McCarthyism in Utah," 114-15; "Lee Flays Leaders of Democrats," *Deseret News*, September 27, 1950, A10.
68. One unsuccessful campaign, however, was Governor Lee's effort to unseat James M. Wolfe, chief justice of the Utah Supreme Court. A conservative 1953 publication, *Counterattack*, accused Wolfe of having been a Communist front for fifteen years. The evidence was circumstantial, strained, and open to serious question. He was charged, for example, with urging President Eisenhower to commute the death sentence of convicted spies Julius and Ethel Rosenberg. Wolfe had done this, but that certainly did not mean he was a Communist. Lee, however, got hold of Wolfe's file and called for an investigation. The state House of Representatives conducted an investigation that completely cleared Wolfe of any suspicion. Lee, nevertheless, continued to press for his resignation and finally got it, but only after Wolfe became too ill to continue in office. Lythgoe, *Let 'Em Holler*, 171-75.
69. Arthur V. Watkins, *Enough Rope* (Englewood Cliffs, NJ: Prentice-Hall, Inc., 1969), x. This important book is Watkins's own description and assessment of his committee's work.
70. See Richard O. Ulibarri, "Utah's Unassimilated Minorities," in *Utah's History*, ed. Richard D. Poll, Thomas G. Alexander, Eugene E. Campbell, and David E. Miller (Logan, UT: Utah State University Press, 1989), 629-49, and the bibliography attached to that essay.
71. Gilbert Geis, "Do Utah Schools Face the Race Problems?" *Utah Educational Review* 42 (January 1950): 20, 32.
72. For a detailed discussion of discrimination in Utah during this period, see F. Ross Peterson, "'Blindside': Utah on the Eve of *Brown v. Board of Education*," *Utah Historical Quarterly* 73 (Winter 2005), 4-20. Incidentally, I was a student at Utah State when Marion Anderson gave her concert there, and I still remember the outrage I felt when I learned of her treatment in Salt Lake City.
73. The entire speech is recorded in Russell, *J. Bracken Lee*, 93-105. Russell's book is a very one-sided, emotional history of Lee to 1960. It was written partly to promote Lee as a possible presidential candidate. Russell no doubt reflected the feelings of many conservatives in his view that this was one of Lee's most important speeches
74. For an autobiographical, see Ivy Baker Priest, *Green Grows Ivy* (New York: McGraw-Hill Book Company, 1958).
75. For analyses of Ezra Taft Benson's years as Secretary of Agriculture, see Ezra Taft Benson, *Cross Fire: The Eight Years with Eisenhower* (Garden City, NY: Doubleday, 1962); Edward L. Schapsmeier and Frederick H. Schapsmeier, "Eisenhower and Ezra Taft Benson: Farm Policy in the 1950s," *Agricultural History* 44 (October 1970): 369-78; Schapsmeier and Schapsmeier, "Religion and Reform: A Case Study of Henry A. Wallace and Ezra Taft Benson," *Journal of Church and State* 21 (1979): 525-35; Edward L. Schapsmeier and Frederick H. Schapsmeier, *Ezra Taft Benson and the Politics of Agriculture: The Eisenhower Years, 1953-1961* (Danville, IL: Interstate Printers & Publishers, 1975).

76. The following discussion is based, in part, on Mark E. Eubank, *Mark Eubank's Utah Weather* (Bountiful, UT: Horizon Publishers, 1979), 66–70; numerous newspaper accounts during the years mentioned; and annual historical summaries in yearbooks of the *Encyclopedia Americana* and *Encyclopedia Britannica*.
77. Robert C. Blair, "Gov. Lee Decrees 'State of Emergency' As New Storms Menace Livestock," *Salt Lake Tribune*, 23 January 1949, 1, 4; Will Lindley, "'Haylift Fleet' Warms Up To Fly Feed for Sheep," 24 January 1949, 1, 2.
78. "Winter Story Eludes Reporter's Pencil," *Salt Lake Tribune*, editorial, 23 February 1949, 8.
79. "So We Can't Afford It?" *Salt Lake Tribune*, editorial, August 9, 1951, 12.
80. "Shall We Let Them Ruin Our National Parks?" *Saturday Evening Post*, July 22, 1950, 42, as quoted in Mark W. T. Harvey, "Echo Park, Glen Canyon, and the Postwar Wilderness Movement," *Pacific Historical Review* 60 (February 1991), 50.
81. The foregoing discussion is almost wholly based on Mark W. T. Harvey's excellent revisionist article, "Echo Park, Glen Canyon, and the Postwar Wilderness Movement." See also Mark W. T. Harvey, "The Echo Park Controversy and the American Conservation Movement" (Ph.D. dissertation, University of Wyoming, 1986); Mark W. T. Harvey, "Utah, the National Park Service, and Dinosaur National Monument," *Utah Historical Quarterly* 59 (Summer1991): 242–63; Mark W. T. Harvey, *A Symbol of Wilderness: Echo Park and the American Conservation Movement* (Albuquerque: University of New Mexico Press, 1994); Glenn Sandiford, "Bernard DeVoto and His Forgotten Contribution to Echo Park," *Utah Historical Quarterly* 59 (Winter 1991): 72–86; Susan Mae Neel, "Utah and the Echo Park Dam Controversy" (master's Thesis, University of Utah, 1980); Susan Rhodes Neel, "Irreconcilable Differences: Reclamation, Preservation, and the Origins of the Echo Dam Controversy" (Ph.D. dissertation, University of California at Los Angeles, 1989); Jared Farmer, *Glen Canyon Damned: Inventing Lake Powell and the Canyon Country* (Tucson: University of Arizona Press, 1999). For a discussion of what was lost as a result of building the Glen Canyon dam, see P. T. Reilly, "The Lost World of Glen Canyon," *Utah Historical Quarterly* 62 (Spring 1995): 122–34.
82. "St. George Advised to Stay Indoors, Avoid Radiation," *Salt Lake Tribune*, May 20, 1953, 1–2.
83. "Facts and Radiation," *Salt Lake Tribune*, May 16, 1955, 16; "The 'A' Tests End," ibid., May 17, 1955, 10.
84. For discussions of the atomic testing program and its consequences, see A. Costandina Titus, *Bombs in the Backyard: Atomic Testing and American Politics* (Reno and Las Vegas: University of Nevada Press, 1986); John G. Fuller, *The Day We Bombed Utah: America's Most Lethal Secret* (New York: New American Library, 1984); Philip L. Fradkin, *Fallout: An American Nuclear Tragedy* (Tucson: University of Arizona Press, 1989).
85. See Lythgoe, *Let 'Em Holler*, 83–84.
86. See Jonas, "The 1950 Elections in Utah."
87. For a detailed analysis of the tactics that destroyed the reputation of Thomas and several other western political figures, see Frank H. Jonas, ed, *Political Dynamiting* (Salt Lake City: University of Utah Press, 1970). On Thomas, see particularly pp. 47–108. See also Frank H. Jonas, "The Mormon Church and *Political Dynamiting* in the 1950 Election in Utah," *Proceedings of the Utah Academy of Sciences, Arts, and Letters* 40 (1962–63): 94–108; Jonas, "The 1950 Election in Utah"; Swanson, "McCarthyism in Utah," 99–102.

88. See Frank H. Jonas, "The 1952 Elections in Utah," *Proceedings of the Utah Academy of Sciences, Arts, and Letters* 45 (1968): 42-65. Granger was also charged, inaccurately, with using taxpayers' money to improve his ranch.
89. William A. Dawson, "Memoirs of William A. Dawson," typescript, 1972, available L. Tom Perry Special Collections, Harold B. Lee Library, Brigham Young University library, 15.
90. For interesting insight, from Bosone's perspective, on a variety of issues surrounding this political year, see Beverly B. Clopton, *Her Honor, the Judge: The Story of Reva Beck Bosone* (Ames, IA: The Iowa State University Press, 1980), 199-218. To Dawson's credit, after some of his campaign staff presented him with certain "juicy" tidbits that could have been used to embarrass Bosone, he decided not to use them and had all copies of the memorandum destroyed. Bosone's staff, however, had obtained a copy. Believing that Dawson would use the material to make a scurrilous attack on her, Bosone secured television time to make a reply. When the station informed Dawson, he secured the next fifteen minutes. In her presentation, Bosone held the memorandum up to the camera so the voters could see it, and then proceeded to reply to the charges. Dawson, in response, only had to tell the audience that he had destroyed all his copies and that it was Bosone's decision, not his, to bring them up at all. Dawson, "Memoirs," 15-16.
91. For more details, see Lythgoe, *Let 'Em Holler*, 147-58.
92. For numerous discussions of this confession and its political repercussions, see both the *Salt Lake Tribune* and the *Deseret News* for the last part of October and early November 1954. For an exhaustive study of the Stringfellow story and how it was finally discredited, see Frank H. Jonas, *The Story of a Political Hoax* (Salt Lake City: Research Monograph No. 8, Institute of Government, University of Utah, 1966).
93. O. N. Malmquist, "Rally Cheers Benson Appeal to Bolster Ike, Vote GOP," *Salt Lake Tribune*, October 24, 1954, B1. For details on the election, see Frank H. Jonas, "The 1954 Elections in Utah," *Proceedings of the Utah Academy of Sciences, Arts, and Letters* 32 (1955): 155-69. Milton R. Merrill, "The 1954 Elections in the Eleven Western States," *Western Political Quarterly* 7 (December 1954): 588-635, puts the election in a regional context.
94. See J. Kenneth Davies, "Mormonism and the Closed Shop," *Labor History* 3 (Spring 1962): 169-87; J. Kenneth Davies, "The Accommodation of Mormonism and Politico-Economic Reality," *Dialogue: A Journal of Mormon Thought* 3 (Spring 1968): 42-54.
95. Arthur E. Tholey, "Gov. Lee Ratifies 'Right to Work.'" *Salt Lake Tribune*, 25 February 1955, A1-2.
96. In 1896, Utahns gave 85.7 percent of their votes to William Jennings Bryan, the losing candidate. In 1936, they gave Franklin D. Roosevelt, running for his second term, 69.7 percent.
97. For a discussion of the 1956 election, see Frank H. Jonas, "The 1956 Election in Utah," *Western Historical Quarterly* 10 (March 1957): 151-60.
98. Lythgoe, *Let 'Em Holler*, 203.
99. For details on the 1956 gubernatorial campaign, see Lythgoe, *Let 'Em Holler*, 203-220; Jonas, "The 1956 Election in Utah"; Frank H. Jonas, "J. Bracken Lee and the Mormon Church," *Proceedings of the Utah Academy of Sciences, Arts, and Letters* 34 (1957): 109-25; Frank H. Jonas, "The Mormon Church and J. Bracken Lee," *Proceedings of the Utah Academy of Sciences, Arts, and Letters* 36 (1959): 145-69.

CHAPTER 3

Moderate Republicanism:
The Clyde Years, 1957–1964

On the morning of Monday, January 7, 1957, retiring governor J. Bracken Lee celebrated his fifty-eighth birthday by serving cake and coffee to a group of close friends. He may not have shown it at the moment, but Lee was leaving office disgruntled and angry because of his rejection by both the Republican party and the voters. Elsewhere that morning the new governor, politically moderate George D. Clyde, also fifty-eight, served a preinaugural breakfast to the other new state officers. Clyde was exuberant, confident he could maintain the state's economic strength and, at the same time, deal with the nagging problems Lee had left hanging.

Born and raised on a farm, Clyde knew firsthand the importance of irrigation and water management. After serving in the infantry during World War I, he earned a degree in agricultural engineering at Utah State Agricultural College in 1921. Two years later he received a master's degree in civil engineering from the University of California, Berkeley. He then returned to teach at Utah State, where he became dean of the School of Engineering and Technology. He resigned in 1945 to become chief of the division of engineering and water conservation research in the US Department of Agriculture's Soil Conservation Service. In 1953 Governor Lee named him director of the state water and power board and commissioner of interstate streams. An ardent support-

Image 3.1: George D. Clyde, Governor of Utah 1957–1964. Used by permission, Utah State Historical Society, all rights reserved

er of the Colorado River Storage Project (CRSP), by the time he became governor, Clyde had already made significant contributions toward dealing with one of Utah's chief economic concerns. After Congress approved the CRSP, Clyde felt the fight for water development in the West had only begun. "We will not obtain the benefits of the legislation by sitting down," he warned. "We must press the fight for appropriations in every Congress until the project becomes a reality. The opposition will continue until the major dams are built."[1] Clyde's words were prophetic: the battle over

CRSP, and especially the Central Utah Project, raged for another four decades.

The state's economy weighed heavily on the new governor's mind. In his inaugural address, he declared that the development of mining, industrial, and water resources would be among the prime objectives of his administration. He was particularly optimistic about the possibility of economic growth based on new technology and more skilled manpower to exploit Utah's "untold quantities" of mineral resources. Included in his list of resources was fissionable ores—an important reminder of Utah's involvement in the nuclear age.

Clyde suggested no new taxes but instead called for holding spending in check in order to "live within our means." He must have realized, however, that it would not be long before new taxes would be required. The state government he inherited had a surplus, but it was one that would be consumed quickly in catching up on programs his predecessor had slighted.

Education: The Continuing Dilemma

One of those programs was education. At first, Clyde was popular among educators as they saw a considerable amount of improvement in funding, including salary improvements. But good fortune is often fleeting, and before the end of his second term the governor found himself at loggerheads with the Utah Education Association (UEA).

State school support came from the Uniform School Fund, derived from various sources.[2] Any difference between the amount of money in this fund and the state's share of the school program was automatically raised by a state property tax.

When Lee left office, teacher salaries were substantially lower than those of surrounding states, teacher morale was low, classrooms were overcrowded, school supplies were inadequate, and physical facilities were badly deteriorating. The 1957 legislature tackled the problem boldly, making changes that raised both local and state property taxes and increased the basic school finance program from $4,050 per classroom unit to $4,800, plus a transportation supplement. It also raised the maximum local leeway tax. Even with these improvements in funding, however, the estimated costs to the state for the next biennium fell $9,645,000 short of the predicted revenue. This meant an anticipated state property tax averaging 4.0 mills in each of the next two years.[3]

The 1957 legislature also made a major improvement in teacher salaries for the 1957–58 school year that, at least temporarily, raised the average slightly above that of the Mountain States as well as the nation.[4] Lawmakers also financed a badly-needed driver education program, provided funds for educational television, accelerated curriculum revision, and strengthened requirements for teacher certification. In addition, the 1959 legislature provided funds for the state school office to employ a director of special education who would more effectively coordinate the activities of teachers, districts, and other agencies working with children who had disabilities.

Lawmakers also tried to face up to the school building crisis. In 1959 they adopted a continuing program that guaranteed $700 per "building unit" for long-term capital outlay to school districts that levied a tax of at least six mills. The state would make up the difference between the money raised from the mill levy and the $700. Results were disappointing, however, partly because local levies were often spent on current, rather than long-term, capital needs. There remained a critical need to replace obsolete buildings, build additional schools, modernize current facilities, acquire new sites, and provide noninstructional facilities such as lunchrooms, libraries, garages, warehouses, and administrative offices. Despite the fact that between 1945 and 1961 total capital outlay for building construction and improvement amounted to $25 million, analysts estimated that to adequately meet the needs the state must spend an additional $106,357,000 by the end of the 1964–65 school year. In 1961, therefore, the legislature increased local bonding power again and adopted further measures to try to provide additional building construction funds.[5]

Meanwhile, Congress passed the National Defense Education Act of 1958, providing funds for states to enhance their science, math, and modern foreign language curricula. The Utah legislature quickly came up with the required $94,000 in matching funds and the result was a total of $700,000 from the federal government.[6] Federal aid continued to provide an average of 2.8 percent of Utah's overall school funding. The largest amount went to federally impacted districts, in one case amounting to 17 percent of a district's funds.[7]

Unfortunately, all of the new funding seemed only stop-gap. Costs kept spiraling, school-age population soared, and overcrowding continued. In some districts, students went to school only half a day because of the need to double up on classrooms. However, the state's ability to raise more money remained inadequate. Utah still spent a significantly lower amount per student than any other intermountain state except Idaho[8]—even though it continued to devote a higher percentage of its personal income to public schools than any other state in the nation.

It was almost inevitable that teachers should again become disgruntled. Despite improved salaries in 1957, within five years they were once more behind both the nation and the region.[9] This was one reason why Utah was plagued with a high turnover in teachers, with an estimated 12 percent leaving the state's classrooms in 1960. The most common reasons given were better salaries elsewhere, better conditions elsewhere, and Utah's continuing large class size.[10] Further, only about half of the trained teachers graduating from Utah institutions remained in the state to teach. Nearly half the positions available had to be filled with people trained elsewhere or with uncertified teachers who were given emergency authorization. A 1964 report showed that uncertified teachers constituted 5 percent of the teaching force in the state. More than 1,200 educators did not have a college major or minor in the fields they taught.[11]

In the spring and summer of 1963, the continuing frustration over funding finally erupted in an open conflict between the governor and state educators. It began with a UEA-sponsored bill called CAPS (Cooperating Agencies for Public Schools), presented to the 1963 legislature. The irony is that the ensuing struggle was sometimes identified in the public mind as a salary dispute when, in fact, the bill called for increases in everything but salaries. Many Utahns, including the governor, were aghast at the financial implications of the bill, which could have cost taxpayers a minimum of $24.5 million. Clyde declared that raising such an amount was "totally unrealistic" for the tax burden would be too great.[12] The UEA, on the other hand, said that all it wanted was a minimum program at least equal to that of surrounding states.

The bill that finally passed did not provide anything near the amounts CAPS called for. In response, the UEA voted in March to halt all contract negotiations until the impasse was resolved. Even after school boards throughout the state substantially increased salaries the teachers refused to sign, demonstrating their resolve to stay out of the classroom until they were satisfied that minimum standards would be met. The problems they pointed to included outmoded and unsafe buildings, leaky roofs, makeshift cafeterias, small and overcrowded classrooms, inadequate materials, and rocky playgrounds. The teachers demanded that the governor call a special session of the legislature to deal with the issue, but he refused. It was, he said, like "having a pistol to my head." At that point, the issue became, in his mind, not the schools themselves but "whether the state shall remain sovereign or be dictated to by an organized group."[13]

The real question was one of the state's ability to pay. Utah still led the nation in school revenue as a percentage of personal income and was near the top in per-capita expenditures on schools, but it still could not match the amount spent per student or classroom unit in most other states. Utahns wanted good schools,[14] but their comparative ability to finance them seemed strained to the limit. Nevertheless, Governor Clyde agreed to appoint an impartial citizens committee to study school needs and the capacity to finance them. He also promised to "give full attention to" and "be guided by" the findings of the committee, including the calling of a special legislative session if the facts made it appear advisable. The *Salt Lake Tribune* heartily approved, commenting with what must have been the sentiment of most Utahns: "There has been far too much emotion, even vindictiveness, in this school dispute. The time has come to set things straight."[15] The committee was charged with studying the entire problem of education, from elementary schools through college.

In August, teachers voted to sign contracts for the coming school year, pending the committee report and the implementation of the CAPS program. However, when classes opened that fall, the conflict was still simmering. It blew up again after the committee issued an interim report in May, recommending an emergency session of the legislature for the purpose of increasing school finances by $6 million for the 1964–65 school year. However, the governor again refused to call a special session, whereupon the teachers voted for a two-day "recess" on May 18 and 19. According to the UEA, this was the first statewide teacher strike in the history of the nation.[16] Most districts continued classes during the walkout by hiring substitutes, but others simply closed school. In addition, the National Education Association, at the request of the UEA, invoked sanctions against Utah.

The public severely criticized the teachers, but Clyde was the victim of harsh censure from the educational establishment. His wife, Ora, later recalled that people angrily called him at home and he even received threats of violence.[17] Teachers refused to sign contracts until late in the summer, when they decided to take no further action until after the November elections. They then campaigned openly for the election of legislators sympathetic to the state's educational needs. In December, the governor's committee submitted its final report, which called for about $11.5 million additional state school support annually. What to do about it became the challenge of the next governor and the next legislature.

Utah received a different kind of national publicity in 1961 when Sterling M. McMurrin, academic vice-president of the University of Utah, was named US Commissioner of Education by President John F. Kennedy. However, he resigned after a year and returned to the university as a professor of philosophy. An outspoken critic of what he called "declining quality" in American education, McMurrin was "frustrated by the slow motion of the wheels of bureaucracy, the apathy toward bettering public education in Congress and elsewhere and the outright hostility of several powerful lobbies in Washington, some allied with educational groups."[18]

Utah's institutions of higher education also experienced growing pains during the Clyde years. These included the University of Utah, Utah State University (until 1957, known as Utah State Agricultural College), five junior colleges, and two technical colleges, one in Salt Lake City and the other in Provo. The junior colleges included a branch of Utah State in Cedar City, Weber College in Ogden, Dixie College in St. George, Snow College in Ephraim, and Carbon College in Price. Snow College also offered high school classes until 1956, when the local school board voted to transfer all high school work to Manti. The decision was unpopular among some of the citizens of Ephraim, but in the long run it helped Snow strengthen its position as a collegiate institution.[19]

A 1963 report showed that Utah had the highest proportion of its college-age youth attending colleges and universities than any other state. Adding to the challenge was the influx of students from out of state. Four nonresident students attended Utah's public colleges and universities for every resident student that went elsewhere.[20]

For years there was agitation to eliminate duplicate academic services, especially between the two universities, in order to more effectively control costs. Finally, in 1959, the legislature created a Coordinating Council on Higher Education. Its legal power was only advisory in nature, but its major function was to gather all the information necessary to prepare a single budget for all these institutions, rather than have each one present a separate budget request to the legislature. In the process, it would look at what might be a duplication of effort and then recommend that only one institution receive the funds for a particular program, thus eliminating unnecessary overlap.

There was a considerable amount of discussion in the legislature about Utah's junior colleges. In 1959 lawmakers approved bills making Carbon College a branch of the University of Utah and making Weber College (later renamed Weber State University) a four-year institution, offering degrees in arts and sciences, business, education, vocational and technical training, and industrial technology. Weber's first bachelor's degrees were awarded in 1964. The 1959 legislature also considered establishing a junior college in Roosevelt but in 1961 the Coordinating Council of Higher Education advised against it. The 1959 legislature also allocated funds to develop a new site for the Salt Lake Area Vocational School and changed its name to Salt Lake Trade Technical Institute. (In 1967 it was renamed Utah Technical College at Salt Lake and in 1987 it became Salt Lake Community College.)

In 1964, here was a significant change in leadership at the University of Utah when retiring President A. Ray Olpin was replaced by Dr. James C. Fletcher, prominent space scientist, business executive, and educator. Fletcher was deeply involved in numerous committees that directed and evaluated America's space program. Later he became head of the National Aeronautics and Space Administration.

Educational television came to Utah during these years when, in January 1960, station KUED, under the direction of Keith Engar, began to broadcast from the University of Utah. Five years later, in November 1965, KBYU-TV began broadcasting from Brigham Young University. Both stations, as well as the radio stations sponsored by each school, became part of the important National Public Radio network, financed in part by the federal government as well as by donations from numerous private organizations, businesses, and individuals.

Questions of Law and Order

Only a month after Governor Clyde took office, he was confronted with a totally unexpected challenge: the worst riot in the history of Utah State Prison. This was only the first of a series of incidents that raised serious questions relating to law enforcement in the state.

Brooding discontent at the Point of the Mountain prison erupted at 6:30 p.m. on February 6, 1957, when more than five hundred rioting inmates took over most of the main building. During the violence one guard was stabbed, an apparently recalcitrant prisoner was beaten by the rioters, and another inmate attempted suicide because he feared vengeance from the unruly prisoners. Twenty-nine people were taken hostage, including a visiting basketball team from a local LDS ward and a group of student teachers from BYU.

Clyde responded at once. He and members of the State Board of Corrections met with a committee of prisoners, who presented a list of demands. Before agreeing to anything, however, Clyde warned the prisoners to "release the hostages immediately or we'll come in with guns."[21] Six hostages were freed at 11:15 p.m., and the others were released unharmed when the riot ended about 6 a.m. the next day. The prisoners' list of forty-three specific complaints included alleged mishandling of inmate funds by prison personnel, unfair procedures by the board of pardons, poor food, and poor overall working and living conditions. Among their suggestions for improvement were the establishment of a prison newspaper, better inmate organization, including an inmate council, and a prison chapel. Clyde promised to consider their recommendations seriously.

Immediately after the riot, prison warden Marcell Graham initiated changes that helped tighten prison security. The governor, meanwhile, appointed an investigating committee which, by February 20, recommended several improvements. As the investigation continued, experts from California were brought in and Warden Graham was sent to California to study its penal system.

By mid-April a number of changes were instituted, many of them reflecting the specific concerns of the inmates. The State Board of Corrections approved an inmate council, an employee council, and a better system for relaying suggestions. Better recruiting, training, and promotion procedures for guards and other prison staff were also approved.

As reforms continued, ground was broken in August for a new prison chapel built by the inmates themselves and not at state expense. In a show of public spirit, a number of local companies donated building materials as well as architectural and engineering services. In a different kind of reform, a specially trained sixteen-man control unit was formed in December, and a new alert system was installed to help prevent or more effectively control future riots. In the meantime, state officials called for Warden Graham's resignation. He resigned on September 23 and was replaced by his deputy, John W. Turner.

Unfortunately, reform did not keep violence and crime from festering inside the prison. In August the body of a viciously murdered prisoner was found in the maximum security cell block. Officials later discovered that barbiturates were being smuggled into the prison, and in October an investigation revealed that many inmates were involved in an extensive counterfeiting and smuggling ring involving county checks, bogus driver licenses, and duplicate license plates. Inmates were also involved in wholesale narcotics traffic, smuggling phony prescriptions out and smuggling drugs back in. Even a few prison guards were implicated.[22]

The difficulties inside the prison may have been only symptomatic of expanding problems of law and order outside. The incidence of crime was growing around the nation, and Utah was no exception. Between 1960 and 1965, the state's crime rate jumped from 1,118.8 to 1,394.3 per 100,000 population. The greatest increase was in larceny, burglary, and aggravated assault.[23]

On May 13, 1959, a grand jury met in Salt Lake County for the first time since 1948. Among other things, the jury probed alleged irregularities in city offices, eventually returning indictments for misconduct and malfeasance in office against Salt Lake City's finance commissioner, who was ultimately released from office. The grand jury also investigated gambling and illegal liquor sales in Bingham, finally indicting the police chief. In addition, the state prison, the county jail, and other county detention facilities were investigated.

As if crime itself were not enough, in 1960 Utahns were scandalized by the March 21 firing of Salt Lake City's chief of police, Cleon Skousen, over administrative issues.[24] Skousen had spent sixteen years as an FBI agent, devoting much of his time to training police officers. He then taught at Brigham Young University until his appointment as Salt Lake City police chief in 1956. A zealous anti-Communist and an effective public speaker, he was highly popular in Utah, well known around the nation, and well connected with LDS Church officials. He was recommended for the job by FBI director J. Edgar Hoover.

In 1959 former governor J. Bracken Lee was elected mayor of Salt Lake City. Since Lee and Skousen were both avid conservatives and anticommunists, it appeared that they would get along well. However, they soon disagreed on many issues, including their philosophies of what was required to run a police department and effectively enforce the law. The friction erupted into open conflict in connection with Lee's traditional concern for economy. One of Mayor Lee's assignments as a member of the city commission was supervision of the Public Safety Department, which he immediately put under close scrutiny. Skousen responded to the mayor's

Image 3.2: W. Cleon Skousen (left) speaks with Channel 2 newsman Doug Mitchell about his thoughts on law enforcement and on his being fired as Chief of Police by Mayor J. Bracken Lee. Used by permission, Utah State Historical Society, all rights reserved.

concern over costs by recommending modest cuts that he felt would not impair the effectiveness of the department. Lee, however, demanded much larger cuts, leading to strong disagreement between the two over how seriously such reductions would affect law enforcement.

There were other differences between the two officials. Skousen later claimed that the real reason for his dismissal was his refusal to follow Lee's instructions to be soft in his enforcement of laws respecting gambling, liquor by the drink, and other illegal activities in private clubs. Lee, on the other hand, felt that even as Skousen complained that he did not have enough police officers to stop nighttime burglaries and robberies, he placed too much emphasis on cracking down on things that really did little harm, such as raiding private clubs looking for illegal gambling and liquor sales. These and other differences, stemming partly from the different lifestyles of the two men, were irreconcilable. Determined to get rid of Skousen, Lee obtained the support of two other members of the city commission and Skousen was dismissed.

The immediate response was widespread antagonism. The mayor received irate phone calls, angry citizens protested at the City and County Building, and mass meetings were held in an attempt to persuade the city council to reinstate Skousen.[25] On the other hand, the *Salt Lake Tribune* lauded Skousen for his work but did not call for his reinstatement. The *Deseret News*, in a surprisingly mild editorial, noted the strong public reaction but held that since Lee was the public safety commissioner, he was right to release the chief of police when good harmony between them was apparently not possible. However, what the public did not know was that the editors of the *Deseret News* had originally prepared a long, scathing editorial denouncing Lee for his "high-handed autocracy," highly extolling Skousen's accomplishments, and speculating that the firing was connected with Lee's instructions that Skousen "go easy" on illegal activities in private clubs, such as gambling, striptease shows, and dispensing liquor. The editorial urged citizens to protest so strongly that the city commission would feel compelled to reinstate the chief. But that editorial was permanently killed following instructions from LDS Church leaders not to run it. The reason is not clear, but it appears to have been related to their desire to avoid public conflict with certain powerful non-Mormon elements in the community.[26]

Population and Economic Development

One surprise in the years following World War II was what happened with Utah's population. Growing more rapidly than most people anticipated, it passed the one million mark in 1964, about six years earlier than the best estimates had predicted. Moreover, the average annual increase was higher than that of the nation as a whole and also higher than that of the average of the eight Mountain States. One reason for this disparity was Utah's higher than average birthrate and lower death rate. Utah's economic growth was also a factor.

These years were euphoric for many Americans, including the residents of Utah, as the longest period of sustained economic growth in the nation's history continued. The result was the production of more consumer goods and a higher standard of living than ever before.

Much of Utah's economic development in these years was related to national defense. Between 1956 and 1961, eight new plants devoted to developing and manufacturing missile components came to the state. These, along with several smaller plants and four launching and test-firing sites, made Utah a significant contributor to the nation's space-age military activities. Missile technology became a major contributor to Utah's economy. The largest employer in the missile industry was Thiokol Corporation, which built a major plant in Brigham City in 1957 and two years later announced that Utah would become the center of its entire missile program.[27]

It was not long before Utah became essential to the American missile program, especially with regard to the Minuteman intercontinental ballistics missile. Much of the research and development work on the Minuteman, and most of the manufacturing, took place within the state. In 1960 Thiokol received a $45 million contract for producing the first-stage engine, Hercules Powder Company received a $100 million contract to produce the third stage, Hill Air Force Base became the assembly site, and Utah General Depot (Ogden) won the job of providing railroad cars for the trains that would carry the missile. Thiokol's contract allowed for the November groundbreaking of a new $30 million plant. In 1963, Thiokol alone spent $56 million in the state: nearly $49 million on payroll and over $11 million on purchases from Utah suppliers. Utah companies were also involved in producing the Bomarc, the Sergeant, the Polaris, and the Poseidon missiles.

The impact of the missile industry was felt in several ways. At the end of 1960, for example, missile companies employed an estimated thirteen thousand people and paid wages and salaries amounting to $244 million. In addition, the industry had a dramatic effect on the number of people working in related industries, particularly transportation, ordnance manufacturing, and the production of electrical machinery, equipment, and supplies. Between 1956 and 1963, the total number of employees in these industries jumped from 1.6 percent of the total in all manufac-

Image 3.3: An Air Force Minuteman ICBM, newest missile in the nation's arsenal, on its launching pad at Cape Canaveral, Florida, November 15, 1960. The first stage was developed and built by Utah's Thiokol Chemical Corporation. Used by permission, Utah State Historical Society, all rights reserved.

turing to 33.9 percent.[29] At the beginning of 1965, Utah's defense industries provided 10 percent of all employment in the state, and payrolls exceeded $251 million, about one-eighth of the total income of Utah residents.[30] At the time, missile production was the largest manufacturing enterprise in the state.

Beyond missiles, manufacturing in general became the largest single contributor to personal income in the state in these years. Geneva Steel remained a major employer, and a number of new manufacturing plants came into the state. In addition, consistent with Clyde's inaugural hopes, the extractive industries remained strong, even though, in 1957, a drop in copper prices forced Kennecott to reduce the number of its employees. Oil and gas became more economically important as new strikes boosted production and more areas were opened for exploration.

Also contributing to Utah's economic growth was the state's participation in the huge interstate highway program. The Federal-Aid Highway Act of 1956 provided for constructing a forty-one-thousand–mile network of interstate highways across the nation, with the federal government paying 90 percent of the cost. By the end of 1962, 185 miles in Utah were open to traffic. The influx of federal money as well as the improved transportation helped the economy but, unfortunately, it did not stem the tide of traffic fatalities.[31]

George D. Clyde paid close attention to the various reclamation projects finished or begun during his administration, knowing that water resources were essential to a growing economy. The construction of Glen Canyon Dam began the year he became governor and was complete in April 1963. Lake Powell, which formed behind the dam, soon became the second largest man-made lake in the United States, smaller only than Lake Mead, and provided power as well as recreational facilities for residents of Utah and other surrounding states.

Meanwhile, the vital Central Utah Project got under way. Authorized in 1956 as a participating project with the larger Colorado River Storage project, it was eventually expanded to serve the people in a twelve-county area in the central part of the state. The first undertaking, the Steinaker Dam near Vernal, was completed in 1961. At the same time, CUP officials recognized the need to involve representatives of the people in future planning. In 1960, they began to hold meetings throughout the seven counties then directly involved to inform the public of the need. On March 2, 1964, after petitions signed by more than six thousand property

Image 3.4: Glen Canyon Dam in 1966, three years after its completion. Used by permission, Utah State Historical Society, all rights reserved.

owners were filed and approved, the Central Utah Water Conservancy District became a legal agency.

Flaming Gorge Dam, on the Green River near the Utah-Wyoming border, was completed in 1963. On August 17, 1964, Mrs. Lyndon B. Johnson unveiled a plaque at the dam, becoming the first woman in history to dedicate a national reclamation project. This $81 million project provided flood control, hydroelectric power and numerous recreation facilities for both Utah and Wyoming.

However, the various reclamation projects on the Green, Colorado, and other rivers in northern and western Utah did nothing for the southeastern part of the state. Washington and Iron counties, especially, saw tremendous opportunity for growth if they could obtain more water. Developers and other economic interests were delighted, therefore, when Congress authorized the Dixie Reclamation Project in 1964. Designed to regulate the flow of water in the Virgin River and its tributary, the Santa Clara River, it was estimated that the project eventually would provide supplemental water for nearly 9,500 acres already developed and all the water necessary for over 11,600 acres of newly developed land.[32] It was disappointing when the project stalled after it was discovered that bad foundation rock ruled out the best site for a dam on the Virgin River.[33] Only in later years did the residents of southern Utah find other ways to develop water resources.

The Larger Setting: Utahns and the Domestic Scene in America

On the national scene, Dwight D. Eisenhower began his second term as President of the United States the same year Clyde became governor of Utah. Politically, Eisenhower was in a less comfortable position than Clyde; he had a Congress dominated by Democrats, while the Utah legislature was controlled by Republicans. Four years later, in 1960, John F. Kennedy, age forty-three, became the youngest man and the first Roman Catholic to be elected president. Tragically, he was assassinated on November 22, 1963. He was replaced by Lyndon B. Johnson, who then was elected in his own right in 1964.

Although most Utahns had not voted for Kennedy, they were genuinely saddened by his untimely death. He had ingratiated himself with many of them when he visited the state just two months before he died. He gave a major address in the Salt Lake Tabernacle about America's leadership of the free world and, in a special airport ceremony, pressed a button that started a generator at the recently completed Flaming Gorge Dam. At his death, people of all persuasions expressed both shock and remorse. Adults and school children alike were seen crying, religious leaders expressed heartfelt condolences, schools were closed early, and the bells at the Cathedral of the Madeleine tolled for fifteen minutes.

Utahns watched closely the intensifying campaign for civil rights in America. The first civil rights law since Reconstruction was passed in 1957, resulting in more federal protection for blacks in their efforts to register and vote. That same year, the struggle for integration in schools came to a head in Arkansas when Governor Orval Faubus called out the Arkansas National Guard in an effort to keep black students from entering Little Rock High School. After attempting unsuccessfully to negotiate, President Eisenhower sent a thousand federal troops to Little Rock to see that a federal order requiring integration was upheld.

The movement for integration did not stop with schools. Beginning in Greensboro, North Carolina, early in 1960, "sit ins" quickly spread to towns in other southern states. Black protestors, mostly students, sat in prohibited sections of segregated restaurants and other public places. They were usually heckled and often attacked and beaten for their efforts, but they took the punishment without retaliating. In addition, some became "freedom riders" on southern busses. Their leaders, particularly Martin Luther King, Jr., advocated peaceful, nonviolent resistance to segregation laws. Many, including King, were jailed, but their efforts helped dramatize the injustice of segregation and set the stage for passage of the Civil Rights Act of 1964, the most far-reaching civil rights bill in American history.

Utah's reaction to Eisenhower's policy in Little Rock was mixed. Some people cheered but others expressed concern over the implications for states' rights. The *Salt Lake Tribune* characterized events in Little Rock as a national tragedy. "Meanwhile," the paper editorialized, "in the battle for rights, state or racial, education suffers—the children suffer—the nation suffers."[34]

On January 31, 1961, Martin Luther King, Jr., gave a speech before 1,700 people at the University of Utah. "The most important force behind the struggle for first class citizenship for colored citizens is the non-violent resistance movement," he declared. "It's our most potent weapon."[35] The timing of King's visit to Utah was fitting, if not deliberate. It came while the state legislature was in session and a civil rights bill was up for consideration. However, on March 1, the bill failed by one vote to pass the House. An effort to revive it the next day also failed as all the Republicans and ten Democrats voted against it.[36]

Lawmakers' opposition to civil rights legislation no doubt reflected the all-too-prevalent racism of their constituents. Racial minorities were small in Utah, which probably contributed to a lack of association, understanding, and sensitivity on the part of the majority. Blacks constituted only 0.47 percent of the population, and all minorities made up only 1.88 percent. Most Utahns had little sense of the difficulties faced by minorities and may never have examined their own attitudes toward other races. Biases are often hidden, even from those who hold them, yet they surface when challenged by proposals for change, such as the proposed civil rights legislation of 1961. In addition, the LDS Church's policy of denying priesthood to blacks may have contributed to bias on the part of many Utahns. Although church spokesmen officially and repeatedly emphasized their support for equal political and civil rights for all Americans, the mere existence of the priesthood policy could not help but affect the attitudes of many Mormons toward anything that might lead to racial mixing.

Even though Mormon policy did not change until 1978, church leaders considered the possibility of change at least as early as 1963. In June, Hugh B. Brown, a member of the church's First Presidency, told the *New York Times* that they were "in the midst of a survey looking toward the possibility of admitting Negroes" to the priesthood. He cautioned the press that the policy would not change without "divine revelation through the President of the church," but he nevertheless affirmed that the whole issue was being considered "in the light of racial relations everywhere."[37]

In October, President Brown took occasion at the general conference of the church to make a strong, unequivocal statement reaffirming the church's full support of civil rights:

> We would like it to be known that there is in this Church no doctrine, belief, or practice that is intended to deny the enjoyment of full civil rights by any person regardless of race, color, or creed.
>
> We say again, as we have many times before, that we believe that all men are the children of the same God, and that it is a moral evil for any person or group of persons to deny any human being the right to gainful employment, to full educational opportunity, and to every privilege of citizenship, just as it is a moral evil to deny him the right to worship according to the dictates of his own conscience.
>
> We have consistently and persistently upheld the Constitution of the United States, and as far as we are con-

cerned this means upholding the constitutional rights of every citizen of the United States.

We call upon all men, everywhere, both within and outside the Church, to commit themselves to the establishment of full civil equality for all of God's children. Anything less than this defeats our high ideal of the brotherhood of man.[38]

Despite such statements, there was little legislative action on civil rights in Utah, but in 1963 the legislature repealed a statute prohibiting interracial marriages. When Congress passed the national Civil Rights Act of 1964, Utah, Arizona, and Nevada were the only states outside the South that did not have positive civil rights laws prohibiting racial discrimination. In the absence of such state laws, the federal statute allowed the US Department of Justice to step in to fill the void. After the law went into effect, Governor Clyde promised to take steps to provide for its enforcement.[39]

In other domestic affairs, Americans became more acutely aware of the deep, widespread poverty that existed even in the midst of the nation's wealth. Much of the problem lay in the inner cities, where centers of abject poverty bred crime and violence. In 1964 President Johnson called on Americans to join in creating a "Great Society," with the hope of ending both poverty and racial injustice. The Economic Opportunity Act of 1964 was the most far-reaching social welfare program passed in the United States since the New Deal. It included a Job Corps that provided skills training for youth, particularly urban youth, the Head Start program, designed to help disadvantaged preschoolers, a kind of domestic Peace Corps, known as VISTA (Volunteers in Service to America), work-study jobs for college students, and various loans and grants to farmers and rural businesses. Not all of the ideals of these programs were achieved, but some of the programs, particularly Head Start and others affecting education, had a direct and positive impact on Utah.

Utah and National Labor Problems

One national problem that had an immediate effect on Utah was the intense labor unrest that resulted in nationwide steel and copper strikes. In March 1959, some 150 workers left their jobs in iron fabricating plants in Salt Lake City, Provo, and Ogden. The strike lasted for twenty-eight days, ending only after union members accepted a compromise that gave them only half the 10 percent pay raise they demanded and none of the fringe benefits, such as a pension plan.

More serious was the work stoppage that began in July when employees at US Steel's Geneva and Ironton plants joined in a nationwide steel strike and Kennecott Copper employees joined a nationwide copper strike. By October the total number of people out of work directly as a result of the steel strike included 4,600 striking workers at Geneva, 350 at Ironton, 235 strikers at two iron mines near Cedar City, eight hundred coal miners in Carbon County who were laid off because of production cutbacks, fifty men at a quarry near Payson who were let go because their contract was connected with metals, and 250 men at a pipe mill near Geneva. In addition, some seven hundred supervisory personnel were not working, even though they were being paid, and 750 railroad workers were furloughed because of lack of work.[40] In all, some fourteen thousand workers were directly affected. In addition, the spin-off slowdown in related service industries made 1959 one of the most devastating years in Utah's history as far as labor difficulties were concerned.

A Taft-Hartley injunction sent Geneva workers back to work on November 7 for an eighty-day cooling off period, but a new contract was not signed until the first week in January 1960. The copper strike went on, and in January the governor stepped in to try to bring about some reconciliation. The strike ended on January 27.

Another major strike against Kennecott began on July 1, 1964, idling 8,500 workers in three states and lasting eighty days. It ended with slightly improved wages as well as better fringe benefits, which was what the workers said they wanted most. It was estimated that the strike cost them about $1,300 in wages for the time lost, but the *Tribune* complained that it also cost the state millions of dollars in taxes and commercial activity.⁴¹

The Larger Setting: Utahns Observe American Foreign Relations

Utahns were troubled during these years as they observed changes in American foreign relations, worried about the Cold War, and watched the growing power of the Soviet Union. On seemingly alarming portent suddenly appeared on October 4, 1957. Utahns were both awed and stunned that day when they learned that the Soviet Union had put the first man-made satellite, called Sputnik, into orbit around the earth, and when they could actually see the satellite as it passed over them on its rounds. This and a second, much larger, satellite made them fearful that America was not only losing the "space race" but also falling behind the Soviets in the ability to deliver warhead-laden missiles to any part of the world.⁴²

America's missile technology was actually farther ahead than most Americans realized, but the launching of an American satellite the next year did not completely ease their foreboding. However, this event led to a vastly stepped-up program for developing long-range ballistic missiles and helped passage of the National Defense Education Act of 1958.

Early in 1961, the Soviets scooped the United States again by putting the first astronaut into orbit around the earth. A few months later, the United States followed suit, though with a mere fifteen-minute flight in a much less impressive vehicle. Nevertheless, said Governor Clyde with what seemed like a sigh of relief, "it proves that the United States is very much in the space race."⁴³ President Kennedy soon infused new life into the space program by making it a national goal to land a man on the moon, and bring him back alive, before the end of the decade. Congress authorized vast new expenditures, and from then on the American space program enjoyed one triumph after another. The result for Utah, as discussed earlier, was continuing economic prosperity.

In other matters, the United States found itself in diplomatic quandaries over tensions in the Middle East, Soviet repression of Hungarian nationalism, civil war in Lebanon and the threat of Chinese Communist aggression in Asia. In addition, anxiety continued over the problem of access to Berlin, which was tied to American refusal to recognize the legitimacy of the East German government.

In 1961, the impasse in Berlin resulted in a new crisis when the Soviets threw up an ugly, heavily guarded wall between East and West Berlin, intended to prevent East Germans from escaping to the West. The immediate effect on Utah was the activation of nearly a thousand Utah National Guardsmen and two hundred army reservists in anticipation of any increased US involvement in the area.

However, President Kennedy's chief worry was only ninety miles from American shores, in Cuba, where Fidel Castro had established a brutal revolutionary regime supported by the Soviet Union. In October 1962, reconnaissance photos revealed several Soviet missile sites under construction in Cuba. Kennedy quickly "quarantined" Cuba, warning the Soviets that no missile-bearing ships would be allowed to land. After a tense, week-long standoff that brought the two sides to the brink of war, the Soviets finally backed down and removed the missiles.

Utahns watched the Cuban missile crisis with deep apprehension, fearful it would lead to a nuclear holocaust. They fully supported the President, however, agreeing with Governor Clyde that "we cannot stand by and watch the Soviet buildup in Cuba 90 miles from our coast. The time has come when we must fish or cut bait."[44] Hurried, almost panicked, preparations for possible consequences began. Civil defense offices were flooded with inquiries. Buildings licensed as air raid shelters were stocked with food. People rushed to grocery stores, almost denuding the shelves of basic needs. Teachers and PTA groups were given instructions on emergency procedures for schools. All Americans breathed a collective sigh of relief when the short-lived crisis was over. They realized that they had narrowly escaped the tragedy of the Cold War turning hot right at their doorsteps.

The Cold War actually did turn hot in South Vietnam, where America was continually frustrated in its attempt to maintain political stability. There, by late 1963, some sixteen thousand

American military "advisors" were attempting to help the American-supported government in its civil war against the Vietcong (South Vietnamese supporters of North Vietnam communist leader Ho Chi Minh). In the "Golf of Tonkin Resolution," after two American destroyers were attacked, Congress authorized President Johnson to take whatever measures were necessary to repel armed attacks and "prevent future aggression." This "blank check," as critics called it, set the stage for years of failure in Vietnam and mounting anti-government protests at home. For the time being, however, it appeared that most Utahns supported what they interpreted as a show of strength and unity between the President and Congress in the war against "creeping communism."

The Environment: Natural and Man-made Problems

The weather and the environment were matters of unusual concern during these years, heightened by another severe drought in 1961. In May, Utah was declared a drought disaster area, and federal grants and low-cost loans were made available to farmers to get them through the year. The drought became so severe that Utah's crop production dropped 8 percent below the ten-year average and 10 percent below the 1960 figures. Especially hard hit was sugar beet production, which was down 40 percent from the previous year.[45]

The year of drought was followed by a wet winter and extreme flooding conditions. In 1962 flood damages of more than $20 million were reported in Utah and surrounding Intermountain states. Hard-hit areas in Utah included Goshen, where an irrigation dam gave way, Ogden, Gunnison, Nephi, Scipio, Mona, and parts of Box Elder County. In September five hikers were killed as the result of a flash flood in the Narrows of Zion's National Park.

As if floods were not enough, two unusually strong earthquakes hit Utah in August and September 1962. The epicenter of the first was in Cache Valley, and the second was in the Salt Lake Valley. There were no fatalities, but the Cache Valley quake was among the most severe in the state's recorded history and caused extensive property damage.

Still another concern was the persistent problem of mine fatalities. On August 27, 1963, a huge explosion occurred 2,712 feet underground in a Texas Gulf Sulphur Company mine near Moab. Eighteen men were killed. The company soon improved the ventilation system in order to prevent such accidents in the future, but many people thought it lamentable that it took such tragedies to force companies to adopt more adequate safety standards. Just four months later, on December 16, nine men were killed in an underground explosion at a Carbon Fuel Company mine near Helper. That company, too, soon installed better ventilation equipment and established better safety procedures.

In a different kind of environmental concern, the problem of radioactive fallout reared its troublesome head again in 1962. The Atomic Energy Commission had replaced the open air blasts of the 1950s with underground nuclear testing, but the explosions still created radioactive clouds that carried enough fallout to cause anxiety in Utah, especially over the effect it would have on milk. Monitoring by US public health officials revealed that after a blast on July 6 the levels of radioactive iodine in milk increased significantly, and after a July 12 explosion the levels literally soared.

Apparently not aware of the earlier cover up by the AEC, or not convinced of the problem's seriousness, Senator Wallace F. Bennett tried to reassure the people of Utah that there was no danger.[46] Nevertheless, the state director of public health, Dr. Carlyle Thomas, secured the cooperation of several major milk producers on measures intended to reduce possible hazards. These included placing cows on uncontaminated dry feed or sending milk only from cows on fresh feed to processors. By August 3, the radioactive levels were receding, but the state health department, the US Public Health Service, and the Department of Radiation Protection at the University of Utah continued to cooperate in promoting protective measures. The latter began conducting monthly spot checks of sixty-two milk producing stations around the state.[47]

At Dugway Proving Grounds, meanwhile, potentially dangerous releases of radiation in the late 1950s resulted in more government cover-ups. In an effort to design and build a nuclear-powered aircraft—which had already been rejected by the Air Force—Dugway officials conducted tests designed to simulate the meltdown of a small nuclear reactor. In the process, about 215.57 curies of radiation escaped, but military officials did not disclose that information. It became public knowledge only after a newsman's investigation in 1994. By then, no one knew whether the radiation actually caused any damage, but there was great concern over the growing list of secret tests conducted in the 1950s related to chemical and biological warfare as well as radiation.[48]

The Canyonlands Controversy[49]

The most politically heated environmental debate of the 1960s concerned the creation of Canyonlands National Park near the confluence of the Green and Colorado rivers. The sheer grandeur of this area's diverse and spectacular mountains, canyons, and panoramas made it a national treasure.

Efforts to preserve this incredibly breathtaking region from despoilment were intensified in the 1950s after the superintendent of Arches National Monument and the chair of the National Parks Advisory Board urged the National Park Service (NPS) to recommend the area for national park status. This would preclude any economic development or usage, including grazing, hunting, and mining. The NPS conducted field investigations in 1959 and 1960.

Meanwhile, Utah's State Parks and Recreation Commission conducted its own studies and, in 1959, recommended that the state acquire certain federal lands in the area and create a state park that would allow multiple use. The question of a single-use national park versus a multiple-use area soon became as politically divisive as any other issue in recent state history.

In 1961, Stewart L. Udall of Arizona, a leading environmentalist, became United States Secretary of the Interior. In February, less than two months after taking office, Udall suggested that this "still untouched" region be made a park. "There is nothing like it anywhere else," he said after flying over the area in May and then visiting it for five days in July. "It has extraordinary beauty. It would be one of the few parks (in the United States) that will remain relatively remote."⁵⁰ His announcement of his intent to establish a park in the area received mixed reaction in Utah, the governor and various commercial interests objected to a single-use park and environmentalists demanded it.

Udall's deep emotional and philosophical attachment to the land was captured in his important book, *The Quiet Crisis*, published in 1963. There he briefly reviewed the history of man's relationship to the land in America, calmly pleading for renewed dedication to keep it from being further despoiled. "In this increasingly commercial civilization," he wrote, "there must be natural sanctuaries where commercialism is barred, where factories, subdivisions, billboards, power plants, dams and all forms of economic use are completely and permanently prohibited, where every man may enjoy the spiritual exhilaration of the wilderness."[51] The opposite sentiment was typified by Senator Bennett. Commercial use would be banned forever, Bennet argued, and "nearly all of Southern Utah's growth would be forever stunted" by Udall's "grandiose pie-in-the-sky scheme."[52]

Senator Frank Moss, sometimes called the "father of Canyonlands," joined with Udall in promoting the park. However, they realized that they would not get a park at all unless they were willing to make at least some compromises. Moss prepared the appropriate legislation, introducing it in the Senate in August 1961, and worked tirelessly for the next three years to guide it through Congress. His bill envisioned a three hundred thousand–acre park where grazing would be allowed as well as mining, but only on claims held at the time the law was enacted. Bennett introduced alternate legislation calling for three small parks and leaving room outside their borders for commercial activity. Neither plan was considered that year.

As the debate went on, Udall and Moss felt attacked from all sides despite their proposed compromise. Bennett and powerful business interests complained at the idea of restricting commercial activity in any way, while the mere fact that Udall and Moss compromised at all raised the ire of die-hard environmentalists. It came as welcome news. therefore, when David Brower, execu-

Image 3.5: Three-term US Senator Frank E. Moss (1959–1977), sometimes called the "father of Canyonlands." Used by permission, Utah State Historical Society, all rights reserved.

tive director of the Sierra Club, made known his support of their middle-of-the-road position. A realist, Brower said it made him "boiling mad" when purists insisted upon "100% standards or forget about new parks."[53]

In February 1962, Moss introduced a bill that compromised even more but it only resulted in more scathing denunciations from Bennett and a letter-writing campaign by Moss against the positions taken by Bennett and Governor Clyde. Meanwhile,

Utah's State Fish and Game Department as well as the State Land Board came out publicly against a large park that did not allow for multiple use.[54] Udall, in turn, released a report prepared by the University of Utah's Bureau of Economic and Business Research that predicted that in the first twenty-five years of the park's operation, tourism and Interior Department expenditures would bring $220 million into the state. The report also emphasized the permanence of the towurist trade as opposed to the inevitable exhaustion of mineral deposits. However, the year ended with no action on the bill on the floor of either the Senate or the House.

Moss amended his plan again before reintroducing it in January 1963. Later in the year he and the Utah Republicans, including the governor, reached an accommodation in which Moss agreed, among other things, to fight any effort in Congress to create a park without multiple use. The compromise backfired, however, when Bennett withdrew his support. Nevertheless, after more hearings, on August 7 the Senate approved Moss's bill. In the House, a bill calling for a large, single-purpose park ran into difficulty, but it was finally approved on April 19, 1964.

Ironically, Moss had what he originally wanted, but he was not happy about it because it undermined his genuine effort at political compromise. True to his bargain, in the conference committee he fought for multiple usage, but even Utah's Congressman Laurence Burton stood firmly with the other conferees against it. The final bill was passed on September 3, 1964, and was signed by President Lyndon B. Johnson two weeks later.

In the end, Canyonlands National Park was not tainted with the multiple-use provisions that park enthusiasts and environmentalists so abhorred. The "crown jewel of the sandstone kingdom," as one writer called it,[55] was the outcome of a long and often caustic battle. Today, however, it is one of Utah's premier tourist attractions.

Health and Medicine

Several issues affecting the health and well-being of Utahns came to a head during the Clyde years. One was the continuing campaign against polio. In 1955, after two years of field testing, the announcement was made to the world that the Salk vaccine was safe and successful in battling this terribly crippling disease. After Utah physicians began administering the vaccine that year, results were dramatic. While 280 new cases had been reported in 1954, only seventy-five appeared in 1955. In an all-out drive in 1956, doctors, civic organizations, schools, and industry around the state cooperated in giving low-cost shots. The number of new cases in 1958 was down to twelve. In 1963 another major campaign was mounted, in which vaccine-coated sugar cubes were administered to people in 160 clinics throughout the state. By the end of May it was estimated that more than 80 percent of the total population had received the vaccinations. In 1965 and 1966 no new cases of polio were reported.[56]

A more controversial nationwide issue was fluoridation of community drinking water as a protection against tooth decay. Dentists argued that the process was perfectly safe and would bring about dramatic improvements in dental health. Opponents argued that putting the chemical in public drinking water was dangerous, too costly, an infringement of personal rights, and another step toward socialism. In 1961 the issue went to voters in four Utah communities: Salt Lake City, Sunset, American Fork, and Springville. In Salt Lake City, the board of health pointed out that many American cities already fluoridated their waters and that doing so had reduced tooth decay by about 50 percent. Others, however, used all the standard arguments against it, and a prominent Utah physician, Dr. Nephi Kezerian, argued vehemently that having a government agency dispense medication in that way really amounted to socialized medicine and would hasten the coming of a welfare state.[57] In November the proposal was soundly defeated in all four cities.

Statistically, in 1961 Utah showed many positive signs of improving health, partly because of stepped-up vaccination programs in schools and clinics as well as increased parental awareness. Dramatically declining numbers included diseases such as diphtheria, scarlet fever, and whooping cough. Infant mortality rates were well below the national average. However, with respect to available health care, Utah had the lowest number of hospital beds per 100,000 population than any western state and only slightly more than half the national average. At the same time, it ranked third in the Mountain States in terms of number of physicians per 100,000 population and highest in the number of dentists.[58]

The medical school at the University of Utah continued to achieve national recognition. The achievements of Dr. Hans H. Hecht in cardiology, for example, received national attention and support that resulted in the establishment at the university of the first modern cardiac catheterization laboratory in the western United States and the first cardiac microelectrode laboratory in the world. In addition to its various studies, the lab conducted cardiology training at both the undergraduate and graduate levels. From these beginnings, catheterization labs were eventually established at other major hospitals in the state. In addition, President Lyndon B. Johnson's "Great Society" programs brought into the state funds that were aimed at conquering cancer, heart disease, and stroke. Under the auspices of what was formally called the Regional Medical Program (RPM), these funds were used to help physicians, nurses, and paramedics in state-of-the-art diagnosis and management of heart attack. RPM also helped establish acute coronary care units in several Utah hospitals.[59]

State Politics During the Clyde Years

The political fortunes of Utah's Democratic and Republican parties tended to follow national patterns during the Clyde years. At the same time, the potential influence of the LDS Church on Utah politics became especially apparent. Although officially the church did not try to influence particular elections, the fact that some people still persisted in the belief that Mormonism and Republicanism were politically synonymous contributed to some interesting political dialogue.

The Republican resurgence in Congress of 1952 declined over the next six years as farmers and laborers became increasingly dissatisfied with Republican programs. In addition, an economic recession in 1957 and 1958 added to Republican woes. These and other issues gave Democrats a nearly two-to-one majority in each house of Congress after the election of 1958.

The Democratic surge was reflected in Utah's 1958 Congressional elections. Even though popular Republican Henry Aldous Dixon retained his seat in the House, William A. Dawson lost to Democratic newcomer David S. King and the venerable Senator Arthur V. Watkins was replaced by the Democratic candidate, Salt Lake County Attorney Frank E. Moss. Democrats also gained control of both houses of the state legislature, for the first time in ten years.

The 1958 senatorial campaign was unique, with three seemingly viable candidates on the final ballot.[60] Senator Watkins had little doubt that he would be reelected. He had served Utah well, he believed his constituents liked him, and he had the public support of President Eisenhower and Secretary of Agriculture Ezra Taft Benson. But farm, labor, and other interests in Utah were not as persuaded by Eisenhower and Benson as they once had been, and the vigorous campaign of Frank E. Moss surprised everyone. In addition, J. Bracken Lee complicated the race by running as an independent, splitting the Republican vote and helping to throw the election to Moss.

Lee's campaign reflected, in part, his bitter, ongoing feud with Arthur Watkins. He was furious with Watkins for several reasons, including the senator's role in the McCarthy hearings and the help he gave to Clyde in obtaining the 1956 gubernatorial nomination. At first he thought of opposing Watkins for the Republican nomination. However, he soon realized that he probably could not win the nomination anyway, and he believed that his popularity among independent voters would give him strength enough to win the election when others would split their votes between Watkins and the Democratic candidate.

Frank Moss, meanwhile, began his drive for the Democratic nomination in 1957 by vigorously stumping all parts of the state, making himself known while Lee was barnstorming the nation in behalf of "For America" (a right-wing group whose objectives included the elimination of the income tax) and Watkins was taking care of his senatorial duties in Washington. In March 1958, Moss formally announced his candidacy. It was clear to voters that he was articulate, well-informed, and would be a formidable campaigner. In the September primaries he handily won his party's nomination.

In the final campaign Moss attacked both Watkins and Lee as well as the Republican administration in Washington. He also argued that he could be more effective in the Senate than either Watkins or Lee because it was practically a foregone conclusion that there would be a Democratic Congress, making a Democratic senator more influential than a Republican.

Watkins ran on his record, his experience, and the fact that he had some seniority in the Senate. He also received the public support of Secretary Benson and a few other Republican luminaries who visited Utah and spoke in his behalf. In addition, he published a letter from President Eisenhower praising his work in Congress. Lee, in turn, inveighed against both Watkins and Moss, although his most vehement denunciations targeted Watkins and the way the nation was going in general. Toward the end of the campaign, Lee lost his composure during a three-way debate at the University of Utah, which may have contributed to his subsequent steady decline in the polls. In the final tally, Moss received 113,000 votes, Watkins 101,000, and Lee seventy-seven thousand. Moss remained in the Senate for eighteen years.

One of the factors contributing to Moss's victory was the labor vote, which until then had not been a major factor in Utah elections. However, this time labor was rallied effectively by Esther Peterson (the first woman lobbyist for the AFL-CIO) and other labor leaders who, among other things, were dismayed by the recession as well as by Utah's right-to-work law. Moss's election also may have been helped when an LDS apostle, Elder Hugh B. Brown, openly campaigned for the Democrats.

In the Second Congressional District, David King upset William A. Dawson, partly because Dawson lost the confidence of a number of businessmen when he voted against a natural gas bill that would have removed federal price controls. Dawson's vote was not a willing one, but he was placed on the horns of a dilemma when Speaker of the House Sam Rayburn threatened to withdraw support for the Colorado River Project unless Dawson supported him on the gas bill. Unfortunately for Dawson, such pragmatic trade-offs are seldom understood by voters.[61] One of the most significant keys to King's success, however, was the endorsement of Elder Hugh B. Brown. After Ezra Taft Benson stumped the country delivering 123 speeches for Republican candidates, the Democratic state chairman, accompanied by King and other party members, visited President David O. McKay. They asked him to permit Elder Brown to become a public part of the Democratic campaign, offsetting Benson's efforts in behalf of Republicans. The church president agreed, and Brown gave the keynote address at the Democratic state convention. Later, he appeared in public several times. personally endorsing all Democratic candidates. On three occasions, he specifically endorsed King on television. This clearly helped clinch the election for King, who won by a narrow margin of ninety-one thousand to eighty-seven thousand, or 51 percent of the vote.

In 1959, J. Bracken Lee decided to run for mayor of Salt Lake City. Still independent, feisty, and economy minded, he ran on the promise of economic frugality and no new taxes. Opposed by Bruce Jenkins, who was endorsed by prominent Republicans and Democrats alike, Lee won with 54 percent of the popular vote.

In the 1960 gubernatorial race, Governor Clyde was challenged by William Barlocker, popular mayor of St. George. Clyde was behind in early public opinion polls, but Barlocker's popularity dropped partly because of his ineffectiveness in televised debate and partly because of rumors of moral misconduct. In the words of one historian, Clyde was promoted by his supporters as an "experienced, responsible, trusted, and efficient, if sometimes dull, public servant."[62] He won with 52.6 percent of the vote.

In that year's Congressional elections David M. King was returned to the House and Democrat N. Blaine Peterson was elected to the House, both by very narrow majorities. In addition, the Democrats retained control of both houses of the state legislature.

The 1960 presidential campaign in Utah was spiced by the appearance in the state of the two presidential candidates and the implications of their visits for Mormon voters. John F. Kennedy, speaking in the Salt Lake Tabernacle, made a brilliant appeal to the Mormon populace by praising many of their leaders and showing familiarity with tenets of their religion. Before the speech, President David O. McKay promised him the church's support if he were elected. Vice president Richard M. Nixon, on the other hand, fell far short of Kennedy's eloquence, but when he met with President McKay, the church leader told him that he hoped he would be elected. Inevitably, that remark hit the news media, making press far outside Utah, with many people assuming that the "Mormon vote" was in Nixon's pocket. The *Washington Star* made a particularly interesting comment: "In a year when 'religion in politics' has been a burning issue, the first candidate to receive the formal endorsement of the head of a major church is not Senator Kennedy, the Catholic, but Mr. Nixon, the Quaker, who yesterday won the endorsement of the No. 1 Mormon in the land. [President McKay's] action was seen as having significance even beyond the borders of Utah."[63] President McKay was chagrined and immediately made it clear that, as a Republican, he supported Nixon but that his statement should no way be interpreted as church endorsement. Sometime later, a careful political analysis showed that "President McKay's statement had little effect on Mormon voting behavior."[64] In any case, 54.8 percent of Utah's voters cast their ballots for Nixon, an impressive majority but not overwhelming if the "Mormon vote" were as solid as some commentators presumed it to be.

The election of 1962 brought another Republican resurgence as Utahns returned Wallace F. Bennett to the Senate, elected two Republicans, Laurence J. Burton and Sherman P. Lloyd, to the House of Representatives, and gave the Republicans slim majorities in both houses of the state legislature. This outcome followed a more modest national trend in which the Republicans made a few gains in the House of Representatives.[65]

The most interesting races in 1962 were those in the Republican primaries. J. Bracken Lee, in his second year as mayor of Salt Lake City, considered running for the Senate as an independent, but he finally challenged Senator Bennett for the Republican nomination. Lee conducted a relatively mild campaign, not attacking Bennett in his usually ruthless style. This and the fact that he publicly endorsed Bennett after the primaries led some observers to conclude that Lee was making a "good will" move, hoping to obtain Republican endorsement in some future campaign. In the end, Bennett received 52.3 percent of the popular vote, defeating David S. King, who had given up his seat in the House for the Democratic nomination.

The other interesting primary was in the Second Congressional District, where state senator Sherman P. Lloyd vied with Reed Benson for the nomination. Benson, an ultraconservative, had been secretary of the right-wing All-America Society and was the son of Ezra Taft Benson. This family connection gave his campaign unusual prominence, but Republican voters demonstrated their moderation by nominating Lloyd by a resounding majority of 60.4 percent. Benson later became Utah Coordinator of the John Birch Society, but his brand of political extremism never attracted the Utah mainstream.

The 1962 Republican resurgence was short-lived, both in the nation and the state. In national elections two years later, President Lyndon B. Johnson overwhelmed Republican challenger Barry Goldwater, a conservative senator from Arizona, by carrying every state except Arizona and garnering 61 percent of the popular vote. Goldwater argued for elimination of such things as welfare payments, farm subsidies, the progressive income tax, aid to education, and compulsory Social Security. He also wanted to give military commanders more latitude to launch tactical nuclear weapons without waiting for presidential approval. Johnson's resounding victory was probably as much a repudiation of Goldwater's apparent extremism as it was support for Johnson himself. Nevertheless, the Democratic landslide also produced two-to-one majorities in both houses of Congress.

Following this trend, Utahns gave Johnson 54.6 percent of their votes, demonstrating again their tendency to shy away from political extremism on either end of the spectrum. Utah voters also elected a Democratic governor, returned Frank Moss to the Senate, and gave David S. King another term in the House of Representatives. In addition, the Democrats regained control of both houses of the legislature and filled all five elective state offices. The major exception in this Democratic landslide was Republican Congressman Laurence J. Burton, who easily retained his seat with 58 percent of the votes in his district.[66]

The role of the LDS Church was more vague in this election than in some previous ones. In the background was a warm friendship between US President Lyndon B. Johnson and church President David O. McKay. Cynics suggested that Johnson cultivated the friendship primarily to gain the Utah vote. He may have used it pragmatically for that purpose, but most analysts believe it was genuine on the part of both men. Whatever the case, it appears that Utahns built up an affection for Johnson partly because of the attention he showed to the church and its leader. In January 1964 he invited President and Mrs. McKay to the White House for a well-publicized visit. During the summer he invited the Tabernacle Choir to sing at the White House. In August Mrs. Johnson dedicated the Flaming Gorge Dam, spoke at the University of Utah's commencement exercises, and paid a high-profile visit to the McKays bearing greetings and gifts from her husband. In September Johnson himself made a surprise visit to Salt Lake City, for the sole purpose of meeting with President McKay. In October he visited the state again as part of his campaign. With that kind of warmth exuded toward Utah, a warmth that seemed to be reciprocated by many Utahns, the Democratic candidates naturally scrambled to have their names and pictures identified with Johnson. Johnson's friendship with President McKay and the church were clearly sincere, but it also worked as good political strategy for himself as well as Utah's Democrats.[67] After his reelection, Johnson invited the Tabernacle Choir to sing at his inauguration. This was "the greatest honor that has ever come to the choir," said President McKay in his response to the invitation.[68]

Tensions over education played a significant role in the 1964 gubernatorial race. Early in the year, a carefully selected political action committee met at the invitation of the Board of Trustees of the Utah Education Association and formed the Utah Council for the Improvement of Education (UCIE). This group persuaded about one-third of Utah's teachers to join and pay dues, giving it an operating fund of $35,000. Teachers were then urged to attend political party mass meetings and use all the influence they could to elect delegates to the party conventions. George D. Clyde, meanwhile, chose not to seek a third term, but Salt Lake City Mayor J. Bracken Lee filed his candidacy on the Republican ticket. This was enough to bring out many teachers who had never before attended mass meetings but were fearful of Lee. Possibly because of their influence, Lee came in third in the convention balloting.[69] The Republican nominee was Mitchell Melich, a businessman from Moab. The Democrats nominated Calvin L. Rampton, a Salt Lake City attorney, who soon received the support of the educators. Rampton had been unsuccessful in previous political ventures,[70] but this time he won easily, with 57 percent of the vote.

In Utah's senatorial race, the Republican primaries were particularly close. Congressman Sherman P. Lloyd put in his bid for the nomination, but he was opposed by the much more conservative Ernest L. Wilkinson, who had resigned his position as president of Brigham Young University in order to run. An interesting sidelight to the highly intense campaign came when, in response to hints by the Lloyd forces that he was too old to take on the task of being a United States senator, the sixty-five-year-old Wilkinson took off his coat during half-time at a BYU basketball game and did forty-seven pushups. He won the nomination by a slim margin.

Wilkinson campaigned against federal programs of all sorts, including federal aid to education. His chief target was the national debt, which he believed must be drastically cut back by reducing federal expenditures. He also tried unsuccessfully to portray Moss as an extreme liberal who would take the country down the road to ruin. In the end, partly because of the Johnson landslide but also because of Moss's record in behalf of Utah, Moss won with 57 percent of the vote.[71] Wilkinson then returned to BYU as its president.

Religion and Partisan Politics: Some Observations

The sensitive question of the LDS Church's involvement in partisan politics seemed to gain renewed intensity in the 1950s and 1960s. Church leaders tried to keep the church itself aloof from partisanship, but the general impression that they favored the Republican party continued. Nevertheless, even though most of those elected in Utah over the years were Mormons, they represented both parties. As seen in the discussion above, in most election years the fortunes of the Democratic and Republican parties in Utah tended to reflect national patterns rather than to favor either party consistently.

No survey at the time reflected Mormon versus non-Mormon voting patterns, but it seems likely that the demographic makeup, employment patterns, social attitudes, and economic status of both groups were similar, except for the ethnic minorities that made up less than 2 percent of the population. The presence of the church, which usually fostered moderation, may have encouraged viable candidates from both parties to take moderate stances on many controversial issues, but this appealed to Mormons and non-Mormons alike. Non-Mormons, like Lee, generally made political friends as well as political enemies among the Mormons. For the most part, if candidates appealed to the Mormons it was not because they supported some supposed LDS Church line. Rather, they were simply effective politicians who were persuasive in their campaigning, appeared to be men and women of integrity, and did not usually espouse politically extreme positions. Lee was an exception, but Clyde, an active Mormon, was a good example of moderate, middle-of-the road Republicanism, while his successor, an inactive Mormon, was much the same kind of Democrat.

Hugh B. Brown's involvement in the 1958 election made it clear to those who still may have been in doubt that Mormons should feel no animosity toward those who chose to become members of the Democratic party. In an atmosphere where too many people assumed that the Mormon leadership was almost *ipso facto* Republican, this was indeed refreshing. After that, however, church leaders increasingly shied away from endorsing political candidates. The church's continuing official stance, emphasized in some manner before every election, was that it took no position on political issues or candidates, unless there were clear moral implications. Instead, the church simply advised its members to study the issues and vote for honest, upright candidates of either party who would support the principles they (the voters) believed in.

Nonetheless, Mormon leaders continued to make their positions clear on those they considered to be moral issues. One was legalized gambling, which appeared on the ballot in 1958 in the form of an initiative to legalize pari-mutuel betting on horse races legal. The church did not campaign against the proposition, but it did not have to. Its position was well known. Other religious leaders also opposed the move and made efforts to have it taken off the ballot. Utah voters turned it down by an eight to five margin.

Although the *Salt Lake Tribune* and the *Deseret News* agreed on the gambling issue, their sometimes differing political perspectives were indicative of the fact that the *News* was owned and controlled by the LDS Church and the *Tribune* was independent. The *Tribune* was often thought of as representing a non-Mormon view. In some instances, however, active and politically prominent Mormons also disagreed with what seemed to be the church position, as expressed by the *News*, and they acted accordingly. The Sunday closing bill, passed by the legislature in 1959, was a case in point. LDS Church leaders clearly favored the bill, though they did not openly campaign for it. Other people, including many Mormons, felt it was unfair to minorities, especially those whose day of worship fell on a day other than Sunday. After the bill passed, Governor Clyde courageously vetoed it, largely for that reason. The *Salt Lake Tribune* praised the veto, arguing that "to trample upon these rights is to violate a basic principle of American free, democratic society." The *Deseret News*, on the other hand roundly criticized the veto, gloomily predicting that the "clear and immediate" effect would be to accelerate the "alarming trend toward opening all sorts of business on the Sabbath. Within five years, if nothing is done, the retail business that takes a rest on the Sabbath will be the exception."[72] For the time being, however, the *News* was wrong. In most Utah communities, retail businesses that were not already opening on Sunday showed little sign of doing so. Nevertheless, by the end of the century the pattern was changing.

Another political issue that, in the minds of some Utahns, had religious overtones was Utah's right-to-work-law. In 1959, an effort by labor groups to get the law repealed failed when it was killed by a substantial majority in the Utah House of Representatives. Mormon leaders did not take a public position, as some had done in the 1940s, but there was a general understanding that they strongly supported it.

An interesting survey taken in the 1960s revealed that, in general, Utah Mormons believed that church leaders should not give advice on specific political issues, including labor-management relations, taxation, foreign aid, compulsory health insurance, and agricultural surpluses. On the other hand, Mormon voters felt good about receiving political advice on issues that had clear moral or religious overtones, such as juvenile delinquency, gambling, government corruption, and liquor control. Communism and fascism were also on the list,[73] but this did not imply what form anticommunism or antifascism should take.

Perhaps the most important statement, at least for Mormons, to come from this era was the official position of the church on politics issued on August 22, 1962:

> The General Authorities of the Church as such do not favor one political party over another; the Church has no candidates or candidate for political office; we do not undertake to tell people how to vote. We do, however, most earnestly urge every citizen of our beloved country to take advantage of the privilege and opportunity to participate in the local primaries where representatives of both political parties will be selected and that they exercise their God-given franchise to make their wishes known at the election polls.[74]

The statement reflected a sentiment that had been expressed many times before and would continue to be echoed in years to come.

Representative Government: The Question of Reapportionment

In the early 1960s, one of the most active US supreme courts in history, headed by Chief Justice Earl Warren, handed down a series of controversial, far-reaching decisions that had a direct effect on Utah. Many Utahns were especially incensed over *Engle v. Vitale* (1962), which outlawed prayer in public schools, calling it a violation of the principle of separation of church and state. In *Abington v. Schempp* (1963), the court banned even the reading of the Bible and the Lord's Prayer in schools. The decisions with perhaps the most far-reaching political consequences, however, were *Baker v. Carr* (1962) and a few subsequent rulings that required Utah, along with most other states, to revamp its legislative apportionment to conform with the "one-man-one-vote" principle.

Legislative reapportionment was a long-standing, slippery issue in Utah.[75] The state constitution called for reapportioning the legislature after every federal census, but during the first fifty years of statehood (1896–1946) there seemed to be little concern for doing so. In 1951, however, Governor Lee reminded the legislature of the constitutional requirement, which touched off the introduction of a series of bills over the next four years. In particular, residents of Utah's rural counties were concerned over the possibility that the three most populous counties of the state (Salt Lake, Weber, and Utah) might control both houses of the legislature.

The 1951 legislature failed to pass any of the reapportionment bills that were introduced, but by 1953, the issue was so hot that it could no longer be put off. After lawmakers again failed to agree they finally passed a joint resolution that would go before the voters in November as a referendum. It would have established what some people called the "little federal" principle. Just as states were represented equally in the United States Senate, so counties would be represented equally in the Utah senate, with one senator from each. What this meant, in practical terms, was that rural areas with less than 27 percent of Utah's population would have held 83.1 percent of the seats in the Senate. A proportionate representation in the House of Representatives, not determined by county boundaries, would favor the more populous areas.

The public debate was heated, especially after it became clear that some LDS Church leaders privately supported the proposal and some local leaders even used church meetings to promote it. However, opponents included an impressive cross-section of other prominent Mormons as well as prominent people from other faiths, Chamber of Commerce personnel, teachers, labor leaders, and business interests. Significantly, the referendum was overwhelmingly defeated in 1954.

In 1955, the legislature finally passed a reapportionment bill, thus completing the first successful reapportionment attempt since 1931. The plan represented somewhat of a compromise between "little federalism" and the "one-man-one-vote" principle. Representation in the Senate, which consisted of twenty-five members, was allocated strictly according to population. In the House, however, even though the sixty-four seats were apportioned by population, each of the twenty-nine counties was guaranteed at least one representative.

This plan lasted for the next decade, during which time the Utah supreme court upheld its constitutionality. After the 1960 census, the 1961 legislature passed another reapportionment bill that kept representation the same in the House but increased Senate membership to twenty-six. It also took representation away from some areas that were losing population. Governor Clyde, doubting its constitutionality, vetoed the bill.

At that point, a series of historic decisions by the US Supreme Court triggered new consternation over reapportionment. In 1962, in *Baker v. Carr*,[76] the court ruled that the federal judiciary had the constitutional right to review apportionment of state legislatures to determine whether they provided a "republican" form of government as guaranteed by the Constitution. The implication for implementing a "one-man-one-vote" rule was clear. Then, in June, 1964, came *Reynolds v. Sims*, wherein the court ruled that both houses of a bicameral state legislature must be "based substantially on population," although the states were given a little leeway with the recognition that it might not be possible to meet the requirement with "mathematical exactness or precision." In justifying the decision, Chief Justice Earl Warren wrote: "Legislators represent people, not trees or acres. To the extent that a citizen's right to vote is debased, he is that much less a citizen. Simply stated, an individual's right to vote for state legislators is unconstitutionally impaired when its weight is in a substantial fashion diluted when compared with votes of citizens living in other parts of the State."[77] This meant "one-man-one-vote," and it had serious implications for Utah's legislative districting.

The uproar from states–rights advocates around the country was almost deafening. Observers noted that *Baker v. Carr* was a victory for urban dwellers in every state. Several lawmakers, including Utah legislators, angrily scored the decision as unreasonable interference by the federal government in the rights of the states.[78] After the *Reynolds* decision the *Salt Lake Tribune* observed, probably with some exaggeration, that not since the school segregation cases of 1954 had the court interpreted the Constitution in a way that would require such a fundamental change in the country's institutions. "This decision is wrong and not good for the states," declared state Senate president Reed Bullen, while state senator Orval Hafen reflected the feeling of many lawmakers and citizens, especially those from less populous areas, in his comment that "there is no point in having two houses unless there is a difference in apportionment. Nearly every state has felt it can use a different method and make one house a check and balance for the other."[79]

At issue was the question of whether the states had the right to make up their legislatures according to the pattern for Congress established by the Constitution, with counties being considered analogous to states. What many critics did not seem to recognize was that, unlike states, counties had never been sovereign. They were, in fact, creatures of the state that could be created or discontinued by the state and whose boundaries could be changed.[80] A "republican" form of government meant, unequivocally, that all citizens within a sovereign state must be represented equally. Both houses of a legislature, therefore, must be apportioned according to population.

There was little Utah could do but reapportion its legislature according to the new federal guidelines. In 1965, therefore, a reapportionment bill cut back sharply on representation from rural areas in both the Senate and the House. In order to meet the Supreme Court's requirements, lawmakers disregarded the state constitutional provision that allocated each county at least one representative. Counties too small to justify a full member were grouped with others to make the combined population enough to warrant one seat. The House retained sixty-nine members, but the Senate gained one extra seat, bringing its membership to twenty-eight. The numbers changed slightly in subsequent years. Representation was still not mathematically equal, but was well within what federal courts allowed. Other reapportionments took place later, but the 1965 bill remained as the permanent general pattern.

The US Supreme Court also looked at congressional representation, handing down guidelines in *Wesberry v. Sanders*, in February 1964, that also required "one-man-one-vote" for members of the House of Representatives. Utah was one of thirty-seven states whose districts were in need of realignment. Utah had not been redistricted since 1913, yet, according to the 1960 census, the First Congressional District contained less than 36 percent of the state's population while the Second District contained more than 64 percent. In 1965, these districts were restructured so that the most populous county, Salt Lake, was split from the next most populous counties: Utah, Davis and Weber. The population split was as near a 1:1 ratio as could be achieved at the time. However, in order to accomplish this Salt Lake County had to be aligned with Iron and Washington counties. Congressional districts were not realigned again until after the 1980 census, when Utah had achieved enough population growth to merit three members in the House of Representatives. (A fourth district was added after the 2010 census.)

Clyde Looks Back

At the end of 1964, as George D. Clyde prepared to leave the governor's mansion, he looked back with mixed emotions. He was still in the good graces of his party and of the people of Utah in general. As a moderate Republican, he had made every effort to run the state with efficiency and economy but also to fill in some of the gaps left by Lee. Ironically, he thought of education as both his most important accomplishment and the most serious problem left hanging. The major goal of his administration, he reflected, was to do more for education at all levels, including school operation and maintenance as well as construction of new facilities. He recognized that the National Education Association and others still felt he was niggardly in his spending on education, but he had spent more than his predecessor, and someone still had to "put the brakes on." NEA sanctions aside, he pointed to progress in equalizing educational opportunities, nearly doubling teacher salaries, and nearly doubling the state's overall financial support for public education. He also emphasized that there was a state building program in place (something Lee had not dealt with) that showed promise of solving the problem of physical facilities within the next six years. In addition, state administrative offices had been reorganized and a reorganization of the road department had resulted in what Clyde called the best road-building record in the nation. Finally, he looked with justifiable pride at the progress in water development, with federal reclamation projects proceeding on schedule and a State Water and Power Board in place. This board, he said, was "the best investment the state has ever made," evidently because it had developed a comprehensive state water plan and was keeping it current. He anticipated, however, that the national water program (which had direct implications for the state water plan) would need constant attention for the next fifty years.[81]

The Clyde administration thus began and ended with commentary on two of Utah's most important ongoing problems, education and water. Clyde took satisfaction in what had been achieved in both areas during his eight years, but he also saw that the problems were far from solved. Both issues, but especially education, would plague each succeeding administration for the rest of the century.

Notes

1. "River Efforts to Continue, Meet Decides," *Salt Lake Tribune*, April 11, 1956, 19.
2. The Uniform School Fund came from various sources. As explained by the Utah Foundation, "This Fund consists of the new revenues from the individual income tax, the income-based portion of the corporation franchise tax, one half the state cigarette tax, Federal mineral royalties, receipts from rentals and proceeds from school lands, contributions of excess property tax collections by certain local school districts (namely: Jordan and Iron), other miscellaneous sources, and legislative appropriations." Utah Foundation, "1957 Revisions in Utah's Public School Finance Laws," Report No. 139 (April, 1957).
3. Ibid.
4. Utah Foundation, *Research Briefs*, No. 58–1 (January, 1958).
5. Utah Foundation, "Utah's Public School Building Program–1961," *Research Report* No. 188 (September 1961). This was the estimate of the Utah State School Office. The Utah Legislative Council estimated emergency public school building needs at only $66.35 million. The School Office estimate included all the items mentioned

above, while the Legislative Council included only the money needed to provide necessary classrooms because of overcrowding and enrollment growth.

6. State Superintendent of Public Instruction, *Utah School Report, 1958-1960* (Salt Lake City: Utah State Department of Public Instruction, 1960).

7. Utah Foundation, "The Role of the Federal Government in the Public Schools," *Research Report* No. 192 (February, 1962). For the viewpoint of one of the most outspoken opponents to federal aid, see Ernest L. Wilkinson, "Fallacies of Federal Aid to Education," address before the Salt Lake City Kiwanis Club, January 26, 1961, available in L Tom Perry Special Collections, Harold B. Lee Library, Brigham Young University. Wilkinson argued that federal aid was simply not needed and would lead toward socialism and an increase federal taxes.

8. The figures, in order, were as follows: Wyoming, $512.92; Arizona, $473.09; Nevada, $438,33; Colorado, $434.76; New Mexico, $414.38; Montana, $410.04; Utah $354.56; Idaho, $323.00. Spencer Wyatt, "Comparative Study of the 1962–1963 School District Expenditures for Eight Rocky Mountain States" (Salt Lake City: Utah State Department of Public Instruction, 1964).

9. By 1962, the average beginning salary was $4,100, approximately $293 below the Mountain States average. The longer people remained in teaching, moreover, the further behind they got, so that after nine years they were $390 below the Mountain States average. It also took Utah teachers longer to reach the maximum. Utah Foundation, "1962–63 Teacher Salary Survey."

10. Jefferson N. Eastmond, "Why Teachers Leave Utah Classes," *Utah Educational Review* 54 (January 1961): 22–23.

11. State Superintendent of Public Instruction, *Utah School Report, 1962-64* (Salt Lake City: Utah State Department of Public Instruction, 1964).

12. As quoted in "Showdown in Utah," *Time* 81 (May 24, 1963): 62–63.

13. William F. Smiley, "'Schools to Open This Fall,' Clyde Insists to NEA Panel," *Salt Lake Tribune*, June 6, 1963, B1.

14. A detailed analysis of this issue as it stood in 1961–62 is found in Utah Foundation, Service Bulletin, No. 32 (May 1963).

15. "Clyde's Plan: Logical School Solution," *Salt Lake Tribune*, editorial, May 28, 1963, A14.

16. Michael T. McCoy and James B. Eldredge, "The Evolution of the Utah Education Association into Collective Bargaining In Utah" (December 4, 2003), 4. Online at http://myuea.org/Uploads/files/Resources/Research/HistOfCollectBargInUtah.pdf. Accessed February 9, 2015

17. Ora P. Clyde, oral history interview by Keith Melville, November 23, 1979, p. 9. Brigham Young University Archives. Mrs. Clyde also noted that their youngest daughter was a first-year teacher. Security forces at the capitol building thought she should have some protection when she left, so when she drove her car to school (apparently after the walkout ended) a patrolman followed. Some teachers told her, "we think your father is right but we daresn't say so. We're afraid we'll be let go out of school."

18. "U. Job Calls McMurrin from East," *Salt Lake Tribune*, July 28, 1962, 1; "Back to the Classroom," ibid., editorial, July 29, 1962, A14.

19. Edward L. Christensen, *Snow College Historical Highlights: The First 100 Years* (Provo, UT: Community Press, 1988): 81–92

20. Utah Coordinating Council of Higher Education, "Coordination of Utah Higher Education" (Salt Lake City: n.p., 1963).
21. Jim Baldwin, et al., "Rampaging Convicts Seize Utah Prison, Lock Up Hostages in Defiance of Guns," *Salt Lake Tribune*, February 7, 1957, 1.
22. Stan Bowman, "Board Moves to Rectify Prison Setup," *Salt Lake Tribune*, October 24, 1958, B1-2. In addition, the public was shocked at the revelation of homosexual activities in the prison. A member of the board of corrections quickly pointed out, however, that only a small percentage of the prisoners were involved. Prisoners were angry, he said, at the implication that the practice was widespread, because this made their rehabilitation after release more difficult.
23. Figures relating may be found in the Federal Bureau of Investigation's *Uniform Crime Reports*, which appear annually.
24. The following account is based on Dennis Lythgoe, "Political Feud in Salt Lake City: J. Bracken Lee and the Firing of W. Cleon Skousen," *Utah Historical Quarterly* 42 (Fall 1974): 316-43, and Dennis Lythgoe, *Let 'Em Holler: A Political Biography of J. Bracken Lee* (Salt Lake City: Utah State Historical Society, 1982), 265-94. That same year, the Ogden police chief, Golden Jensen, was also fired.
25. Will, Fehr, "Utah's Top 10 News Stories Run Gamut from Skousen Firing to 1960 Census," *Deseret News*, December 31, 1960, B1, in discussion of the year's "top ten" news stories.
26. For the controversial story of this incident, see Lythgoe, "Political Feud in Salt Lake City," 327-32; Lythgoe, *Let 'Em Holler*, 175-79.
27. For details on the development of the missile industry in Utah, see Leonard J. Arrington and Jon G. Perry, "Utah's Spectacular Missiles Industry: Its History and Impact," *Utah Historical Quarterly* 30 (Winter 1962): 3-39. See also "Missiles Industry Carries Utah to a New Peak of Prosperity," *Business Week* (February 27, 1960), 146-48, 150. For the history of Thiokol, see Eric G. Swedin, "Thiokol in Utah," *Utah Historical Quarterly* 75 (Winter 2007): 63-77.
28. "Thiokol Dollars Add to Utah's Stability," *Deseret News*, October 29, 1963, M8.
29. George Jensen and Leonard J. Arrington, *Impact of Defense Spending on the Economy of Utah* (Logan, UT: Department of Economics, Utah State University 1967), 54-55, 61.
30. Leonard J. Arrington and George Jensen, *The Defense Industry of Utah* (Logan, UT: Department of Economics, Utah State University, 1965), 31.
31. Traffic fatalities rose steadily from 237 in 1961 to 351 in 1966, or an increase of 48.1 percent. Phillip R. Kunz and Merlin B. Brinkerhoff, *Utah in Numbers: Comparisons, Trends, and Descriptions* (Provo, UT: Brigham Young University Press, 1969), 173. There seemed to be little law enforcement officers could do to persuade people to help stop the carnage by slowing down and by not mixing drinking with driving.
32. "LBJ Signature Authorizes Dixie's Irrigation Project," *Salt Lake Tribune*, September 3, 1964, A6.
33. "Dixie Project Impasse," *Deseret News*, March 4, 1966, B18.
34. "Ominous Deadlock," *Salt Lake Tribune*, editorial, October 5, 1957, 14.
35. "Speaker Sees Battle for Integration," *Salt Lake Tribune*, February 1, 1961, 13.
36. Jerome K. Full, "'Rights' Dies in Vote by Utah House," *Salt Lake Tribune*, March 3, 1961, 1.
37. Wallace Turner, "Mormons Consider Ending Bar on Full Membership for Negro," *New York Times*, Eastern edition, June 7, 1963, 17.

38. *The Improvement Era* 66 (December 1963): 1058. For a brief discussion of President Brown's effort to have the priesthood policy changed, see Edwin Brown Firmage, "Hugh B. Brown in His Final Years: The Joys and Trials of an Aging Apostle," *Sunstone* 11 (November 1987): 7–11.
39. "Clyde Plans Utah Agency To Enforce Rights Law," *Salt Lake Tribune*, July 13, 1964, 19.
40. Jerry Voros, "Strikes Pile Up Mountainous Losses in Payrolls, Taxes," *Salt Lake Tribune*, October 4, 1959, C4.
41. "Utah Welcomes End of Copper Strike," *Salt Lake Tribune*, editorial, September 20, 1964, A14.
42. See, for example, an editorial comment in the *Salt Lake Tribune*: "Soviet 'Moon' and American Dream World," October 6, 1957, 12A.
43. "Utahn's Hail Astronaut Space Trip," *Salt Lake Tribune*, May 6, 1961, 4.
44. "Utah Leaders Strongly Back JFK," *Salt Lake Tribune*, October 23, 1962, 4.
45. "Utah Crop Tonnage Dips 10 Per Cent under 1961," *Salt Lake Tribune*, December 25, 1961, B12.
46. As quoted in William C. Patrick, "Fallout in Utah Milk Spurs State Action," *Salt Lake Tribune*, August 1, 1962, 17. On July 6, the day before the first blast, the level of I-131 in milk was "not detectable," but on July 20 it was 1,660 micro-micro-curies. Then, after dropping to 450, it rose on July 28 to 2,050 mmcs.
47. William C. Patrick, "A-Expert Hits Delay by Health Chief," *Salt Lake Tribune*, August 2, 1962, B1; William C. Patrick, "Milk Radioactivity Continues to Drop," ibid., August 3, 1962, B1.
48. See editorial, "Report of Radiation Tests Shows Need for Openness," *Deseret News*, October 12, 1994, A8.
49. The following account is based largely on Thomas G. Smith, "The Canyonlands National Park Controversy, 1961–64," *Utah Historical Quarterly* 59 (Summer 1991): 216–42.
50. "Udall on Utah," *Salt Lake Tribune*, July 2, 1961, A10.
51. Stewart L. Udall, *The Quiet Crisis* (New York: Avon Books, 1963), 137.
52. As quoted in Smith, "Canyonlands National Park Controversy," 221.
53. David Brower to Udall, December 8, 1961, as cited in Smith, "Canyonlands National Park Controversy," 226.
54. "2 Utah Departments Oppose Large Park," *Salt Lake Tribune*, February 10, 1962, 19.
55. Smith, "Canyonlands National Park Controversy," 242.
56. Statistics are from Kunz and Brinkerhoff, *Utah in Numbers*, 146. See also *Deseret News*, March 26, 1958; *Salt Lake Tribune* May 21, 1963. Figures vary slightly in different reports.
57. "Fluoridation Gets Rap by Doctor," *Salt Lake Tribune*, November 2, 1961, 14.
58. Kunz and Brinkerhoff, *Utah in Numbers*, 143–57.
59. Hirosho Kuida, "Cardiology," in *Medicine in the Beehive State, 1940–1990*, ed. Henry P. Plenk (Salt Lake City: Utah Medical Association, LDS Hospital–Deseret Foundation, University of Utah Health Sciences Center, 1992), 107, 101–111.
60. For discussions of this unusual election, see Frank H. Jonas, "The 1958 Election in Utah," *Western Political Quarterly* 12 (March 1959): 345–54; Frank H. Jonas, "The Third Man in Utah Politics," Proceedings of the Utah Academy of Sciences, Arts

and Letters 37 (1960): 103–25; Roger Bryan Madsen, "Analysis of the 1958 Senatorial Campaign in Utah" (Master's thesis, Brigham Young University, 1973). There have been other elections where more than two candidates have been on the ballot, but up to that time there was virtually no expectation that anyone other than the two major party candidates had a chance.

61. Jonas, "The Third Man in Utah Politics," 110.
62. Allan Kent Powell, "Elections in the State of Utah," in *Utah History Encyclopedia*, ed. Allan Kent Powell (Salt Lake City: University of Utah Press, 1994), 164.
63. David S. Broder, "Mormon Church Leader Strongly Backs Nixon," *Washington Star*, October 11, 1960, as quoted in Gregory A. Prince and Wm. Robert Wright, *David O. McKay and the Rise of Modern Mormonism* (Salt Lake City: University of Utah Press, 2005), 337.
64. A detailed, in-depth analysis of the impact of this statement is made in Dean E. Mann, "Mormon Attitudes toward the Political Roles of Church Leaders," *Dialogue: A Journal of Mormon Thought* 2 (Summer 1967):32–48. See p. 47 for the statement quoted above. The article also gives considerable insight into the general question of the political role and impact of the Mormon church.
65. For the story of this election, see Stewart L. Grow, "The 1962 Election in Utah," *Western Political Quarterly* 16 (June 1963): 460–66.
66. For the story of this election, see Frank H. Jonas, "The 1964 Election in Utah," *Western Political Quarterly* 18 (June 1965): 509–13. In reporting this and other elections, the figures and percentages given above are slightly at variance with those given in the appendix of Poll, et al, *Utah's History*. I have tended to follow the latter, though often the figures there are rounded off.
67. See Frank H. Jonas, "President Lyndon Johnson, the Mormon Church and the 1964 Political Campaign," Proceedings of the Utah Academy of Sciences, Arts and Letters 44 (1967): 67–90; Frank H. Jonas, "Utah," in Jonas, ed. *Politics in the American West* (Salt Lake City: University of Utah Press, 1969): 336–7.
68. Harold Lundstrom, "Greatest Honor for the Choir," *Deseret News*, January 4, 1965, 1.
69. Jonas, "Utah," 348–49.
70. Several years earlier Rampton ran for the position of state chairman of the Democratic party but lost. In 1952 he was defeated in his bid for the position of national chairman. In 1962 he lost to David S. King in his effort to obtain the Democratic nomination for the US Senate.
71. For a detailed, behind-the-scenes account of the Wilkinson campaign, see Gary James Bergera, "'A Sad and Expensive Experience': Ernest L. Wilkinson's 1964 Bid for the US Senate," *Utah Historical Quarterly* 61 (Fall 1993): 304–24.
72. "Governor Clyde's Forthright Veto," *Salt Lake Tribune*, editorial, February 20, 1959, A18; "A Disappointing Veto," *Deseret News*, editorial, February 20, 1959, A16.
73. Mann, "Mormon Attitudes toward the Political Roles of Church Leaders," 44.
74. "Statement of the First Presidency," *Deseret News*, August 23, 1962, A1.
75. For full discussions of these issues see Brad Hainsworth, "Reapportionment in Utah, 1954–1965" (master's thesis, University of Utah, 1966); Frank H. Jonas, "Reapportionment in Utah and the Mormon Church," Proceedings of the Utah Academy of Sciences, Arts and Letters 46 (1969): 11–26; Eleanor Bushnell, ed., *Impact of Reapportionment on the Thirteen Western States* (Salt Lake City: University of Utah Press, 1970); League of Women Voters in Utah, *Reapportionment in Utah:*

Political Game or Fair Representation? (Salt Lake City: League of Women Voters of Utah, 1980).

76. See *Baker v. Carr*, 369 US 186. For an overview of the broad issues, see Gene Graham, *One Man, One Vote* (Boston: Little, Brown and Company, 1972).
77. See *Reynolds v. Sims*, 377 US 533.
78. Two Supreme Court justices dissented. Senator Herman E. Talmage (D-Georgia), called the decision unconstitutional and said that "it is beyond the comprehension of anyone who ever has been exposed to a law book, how a court at any level could compel a state legislature to take or not take action on any question." Utah's lawmakers had varied opinions, mostly negative, although they generally expressed resignation to the reality that something must be done to bring the state into line with the court. *Salt Lake Tribune*, March 27, 1962.
79. Anthony Lewis, "Historic Ruling Orders States to Reapportion," *Salt Lake Tribune*, June 16, 1964, 1.
80. For a discussion of when and how Utah's counties were created and various boundary changes, see James B. Allen, "The Evolution of County Boundaries in Utah," *Utah Historical Quarterly* 23 (July 1955): 261–78.
81. O. N. Malmquist, "Clyde's Glad—and Sad—to Go," *Salt Lake Tribune*, December 30, 1964, 15.

CHAPTER 4

Three-Term Governor:
The Rampton Administration

Fifty-one-year-old Calvin L. Rampton, inaugurated on January 4, 1965, was the first Democrat in sixteen years to occupy Utah's statehouse. Born and raised in Bountiful, Rampton graduated from the University of Utah in 1936 and from the University Law School in 1940. He attended George Washington University law school from 1936 to 1938 and worked as an administrative assistant for Utah Congressman J. Will Robinson. From 1941 to 1942 he was Assistant Attorney General for Utah. He served in the army during World War II, at the end of which he was Chief of the US Army Claims Commission in Paris. He then practiced law in Salt Lake City until he was elected governor. A man of rare political balance, he became the only Utah governor to serve for three terms.

The Rampton era was a fascinating period of accomplishment, conflict, and change. During his twelve years in office, the state saw several new programs for stimulating economic growth, important refinements in state government, a host of difficult issues in education, advances in health care, and such perpetual controversies as Sunday closing, right-to-work, and liquor-by-the-drink policies. The state was also caught up in the economic and political cross-currents affecting the nation as a whole, including a stream of social welfare legislation emanating from

Image 4.1: Calvin L. Rampton, Utah's only three-term to governor, and his wife Lucybeth. Used by permission, Utah State Historical Society, all rights reserved.

President Lyndon B. Johnson's "Great Society," urban renewal, land use planning, the civil rights movement, and feminism. In addition, Utah had more than its share of crime problems, and its continuing environmental challenges included several man-made disasters as well as the rejection of a major industry because of environmental concerns. The people of Utah also shared with other Americans the tragedy and disillusionment of the Vietnam War and the embarrassment of Watergate.

Democrats in Power: Agenda and Administrative Decisions

As Rampton looked forward to his first term in office, he reflected on problems remaining from the Clyde administration, including serious difficulties in the public schools and a critical need for more buildings at state colleges and universities. He worried over Utah's unemployment rate, which had risen above the national average, and the fact that Utah workers received lower wages than the national average. He was also concerned that there was no industrial promotion department in state government, and that promotion of tourism was inadequately funded.[1] Because of its dependence for employment upon the federal government and upon large corporations from outside the state, Utah has been aptly described as a "dependent commonwealth" during that era.[2] Calvin Rampton was determined to change that dependency as rapidly as possible. "We must dare to move forward," he said in his inaugural address. "We will risk error and will no doubt make errors. We must produce the courage and the vision to adopt new remedies for new problems. in quest of this goal, I solicit your support—and your prayers."[3]

Rampton's "state of the state" address, delivered on January 12, was perhaps the longest such speech in state history.[4] He spoke for two hours, with a short recess, devoting most of the time to economics and anticipating the most vigorous program of industrial development in state history. He called for the creation of an industrial promotion commission, urged the legislature to pass a "proper and effective" freeport law, and called for a $1 million annual appropriation to stimulate tourism. "If this figure looms large," he said, "let me remind you that this appropriation will repay itself many times over in direct tax income to the state." He also called for state legislative and congressional reapportionment, legislation that would permit the establishment of metropolitan governments, the creation of a committee on the reorganization of state government, a more effective merit system for state employees, strengthening state civil rights laws, a revamping of the juvenile court system, and a $67 million bonding program, $65 million of which would be used for state building needs and $2 million for state parks. He also promised to convene a special session of the legislature in 1966 to review progress and make adjustments. In addition, he asked for repeal of Utah's right-to-work law. This, he recalled later, "was a futile gesture but I felt that I should do it anyhow."[5]

At the end of his lengthy speech, Rampton engaged in a bit of humorous, local-color banter with state senator Reed Bullen. As the governor stepped down from the rostrum, Bullen remarked: "I think, governor, that's the longest speech I ever listened to." Rampton replied: "I'll have to watch that, Reed, because when a Mormon stake president complains about the length of a speech, there's certainly room for concern."[6]

Rampton asked Clyde's department heads to remain until he had time to choose new ones, and most of them did. However, one of his first administrative orders, issued on the afternoon of the inaugural, surprised them. He directed that there would be no more lobbying of state legislators by heads of departments. They could testify before legislative committees and give full and frank opinions, but they were not to make initial contacts. This was something new for this group of administrators, and they took it in somewhat sullen silence.[7]

The 1965 legislature was quick to act on most of the governor's proposals. It passed the bonding bill, approved a $14.9 million increase in state expenditures for public schools, established the State Industrial Promotion commission, passed a freeport law, and acted favorably on the governor's proposal for a merit system for state employees. At the same time, Rampton and the legislature turned down a Republican proposal for merit pay for teachers. Rampton wanted to use whatever money was available to give all Utah teachers a living wage. The legislature also established a committee on the reorganization of state government, known popularly as the Little Hoover Commission.[8] In addition, it responded to the new reapportionment requirement and to the need to redistrict the legislature and passed Utah's first civil rights legislation.

Rampton was particularly delighted that his budget passed, almost without change, even though it called for an increase in the state sales tax as well as an increase in both corporate and personal income taxes. The tax proposals tended to alienate some Democrats and Republicans alike, but his pledge to lower the state property tax when he took office won over enough Republicans to ensure passage of the budget. The next year the property tax was down by 1.1 mills, and before the end of Rampton's second term it was eliminated.[9]

But not everything was sweetness and light within the Democratic party. Rampton made political appointments carefully, but in a few cases appointed or opposed certain people against the wishes of his own party. Some party members even tried to have him censured for this.[10] But such independence was one of Rampton's traits that helped him get elected twice more.

Among the things that appealed to the public were the visits made by Rampton and his wife, Lucybeth, to each county in the state during his first year in office. At each visit Rampton typically met with county commissioners in the morning, left time for other county and city officials to visit and express their concerns, and then met with school officials. In the afternoon he talked with whoever cared to come in. Lucybeth, meanwhile, met with some of the women of the county. The good resulting from such visits was demonstrated on the first one, to Duchesne County. There the women made clear to Lucybeth that the state had failed in its responsibility for maintaining the state highway between Hanna and Tabiona. Upon investigation, Rampton found that the highway department had, indeed, ignored this road. He immediately instructed the head of the department to rearrange his budget so that the road could be repaired, which was done before fall.[11] Another reason for the dramatic success of these visits was that the

Ramptons ate and slept in the homes of the people of the communities. For years afterward Democrats in rural areas continued to brag that the governor and his wife had stayed with them.[12] Rampton continued his county visits throughout his administration.

A Hard Look at State Government: The Dilemma of Constitutional Change

One of the most politically difficult challenges that came to a head during the Rampton years was that of governmental and constitutional reform. The seventy-two-year-old state constitution was badly in need of revision. As the *Salt Lake Tribune* noted in 1972, the original 1896 constitution "contained every desperate compromise demanded by a hostile congress as the price of statehood."[13] Even though it had been altered fifty times since statehood, much of the constitution was still out of date. In addition, the government itself was greatly in need of administrative reorganization.

Actually, this was part of a national dilemma; many other states were also wrestling with outdated constitutions. Montana adopted a new one in 1972, but voters in other states rejected such a move as too radical and instead made piecemeal changes.

Rampton began to tackle the problem when he called a special session of the legislature in January 1966. There lawmakers passed twenty-two bills and also ratified the proposed amendment to the US Constitution on presidential succession (the Twenty-Fifth Amendment, which went into effect the following year). In Rampton's mind, however, the most important reason for the session was to deal with the report of the bipartisan Little Hoover Commission. Calling for a thorough overhaul of the executive branch of the government, the commission recommended combining its 157 different state agencies into eleven, which could be done without constitutional amendment. Unfortunately for the governor, the report raised so much controversy that the legislature took no action.

Rampton called a second special session for May and, realizing that he may not have enough support in the next legislature to get the recommendations of the commission through, he again put the report on the agenda.[14] Lawmakers also considered recommendations for legislative reform made by a special task force headed by Neal A. Maxwell of the University of Utah. After two weeks of deliberation they showed little enthusiasm for the Little Hoover Commission's recommendations, although one of them, a proposal to abolish the state board of examiners, was placed on the November ballot. The ballot also carried four proposals of the special task force, designed to strengthen the role of the legislature. All of these proposals, as well as a proposition calling for a state constitutional convention, were defeated in November.

Nevertheless, some important administrative reforms proceeded. During the May special session lawmakers authorized the governor to make changes in the groupings of state agencies, as the Little Hoover Commission had suggested. Rampton consolidated those agencies under six general groupings: health and welfare, budget services and general services, natural resources, recreation, public safety, and revenue services.[15] In 1970, as the result of a 1968 constitutional amendment, the state legislature held its first budget session. Previously the legislature met every other year but under the new requirements it met in regular session for sixty days on odd-numbered years and in a budget session for twenty days on even-numbered years. In 1984, the constitution was changed again, requiring a regular forty-five-day session each year.

However, none of these actions got to the real heart of the problem, for the Constitution still needed fundamental revision. There were only two ways to accomplish this. One was to call a constitutional convention, but that idea had already been rejected by Utah voters. The other procedure was the amendment process, but this was complicated by the fact that Utah law did not allow an entire article to be changed at once. Only sections within an article could be modified. The result was that the ballot was frequently loaded with several constitutional propositions, which tended to confuse voters. What was needed was a way of amending an entire article, thereby simplifying the ballot and allowing a full overhaul of particular branches or functions of government at the same time.

Image 4.2: Neal A. Maxwell, chair of Utah's newly-formed Constitutional Revision Commission, 1969. Later he became an LDS apostle and a member of the Church's Special Affairs Committee. © By Intellectual Reserve, Inc.

In 1969, the legislature established a temporary Constitutional Revision Commission, with Neal A. Maxwell as chairman. The following year that commission prepared an amendment, identified popularly as the Gateway Amendment, authorizing the legislature to propose changes to an entire article as a single ballot proposition rather than making piecemeal corrections. Maxwell emphasized that this was not so much a revision as a tool for revision later on. Opponents argued that it was much too broad.[16] In November voters approved Gateway, finally opening the way for smoother, more effective, Constitutional reform.

The Constitutional Revision Commission immediately began work on a series of fundamental, long-needed changes. However, the idea of overhauling the constitution still did not sit well with some people, which may have been what led to a strong statement of support by N. Eldon Tanner, second counselor in the First Presidency of the LDS Church, on May 11, 1972. The occasion was a banquet sponsored by Brigham Young University's Institute of Public Management and honoring Governor Rampton, who received the "Outstanding Executive of the Year" award. As principal speaker, Tanner took the occasion to make it clear to Utahns that church leaders had no objection to constitutional revision. "The Constitution of Utah was not sanctioned by the Lord in the same manner as the Federal Constitution, and is therefore not a sacred document," he said. He also noted that a "special committee of knowledgeable men" was studying it in order to suggest amendments that would meet changing conditions and be in the best interest of the citizens of the state.[17]

The first full article of the constitution to be amended was the legislative article. Approved in 1972, the amended article made a variety of housekeeping changes that helped modernize the legislative process and also incorporated some fundamental additions. One addition, for example, gave the legislature the authority to hire its own legal counsel and its own auditor. Up to that point, lawmakers received their legal advice from the office of the state attorney general. Providing the legislature with its own legal counsel not only enhanced the legislative process but also strengthened the principle of separation of powers.[18] The amendment appeared on the ballot as Proposition 1.

Three other constitutional amendments went before the voters that year, but only Proposition 1 was prepared by the commission. In his support of the legislative amendment and of Proposition 4, which authorized counties to establish alternate forms of government, Maxwell made an important comment about the broader significance of constitutional reform around the nation. America, he said, was being given an opportunity to "re-federalize our republic by improving local and state government. More than accusatory rhetoric about the federal government is required. What is needed to offset ponderous federal government is not more power but more representative government within the limited, and properly so, power already delegated by the people to state and local governments." These amendments were a step in that direction.[19] All four propositions were approved by the voters in November.[20]

By the end of 1972, then, the first hurdles in the process of constitutional revision had been crossed—the passage of the Gateway Amendment and the revision of an entire article as authorized by that amendment. The Constitutional Revision Commission then turned its attention to a more complicated and politically inflammatory issue, the revision of the executive article. However, it would be several years before this and three other articles were changed (see Chapter 5). Meanwhile, the authorized life of this commission expired in 1975, but at that point the legislature created a permanent Constitutional Revision Commission. State senator Karl N. Snow, author of the bill creating the new commission, served as chair for the next twelve years.[21]

Quest for Industrial Development

Nothing enthused Calvin Rampton more than promoting Utah's industrial development. The 1965 legislature handed him two laws that were key to this goal. One established the State Industrial Promotion Commission, and the other was a freeport bill that exempted goods from Utah taxation if they were stored in the state only for transshipment elsewhere. Rampton named Milton Weilenman to head the Industrial Promotion Commission.[22] Meanwhile, a group known as Pro-Utah was formed by Gus Backman, former executive secretary of the Salt Lake Chamber of Commerce. Representing private business interests, Pro-Utah worked closely with Rampton and with Weilenman's department in their efforts to attract new business to the state.

The immediate results of the freeport bill seemed to bear out all of Rampton's hopes. At a Business Preview Conference in January 1966, it was reported that as a result of firms taking advantage of this legislation, Utah had an increase of 1,280 new jobs. Twenty-two companies had established themselves in the state during the year, citing the freeport bill as their major consideration in choosing Utah.[23]

Rampton, along with various state officials and business leaders, lost no time in spreading the gospel of Utah. Stumping the country and meeting with key industrial and financial leaders in a number of major cities, they explained how Utah's tax structure, social climate, and schools made it an ideal place for business investment. In February, 1968, for example, "Rampton's Raiders," as they were dubbed,[24] visited some of the most concentrated industrial sites in the nation. In what the local newspaper called an "industry raiding expedition" they stopped first in Columbus, Ohio. This characterization was a bit of good-natured play on the fact that Ohio's governor, James Rhodes, was known for his own expeditions outside the state in search of new industries, leading a group nicknamed "Rhodes' Raiders." Rampton addressed the state Senate on the evening of Monday, February 12. "We are not attempting to take any business from Ohio to Utah," he said, probably with a smile. "But we had heard out there that your industrial development program was so successful that you have more than you can handle and we are just here to accommodate that overflow."[25]

Rampton and his group were in Cleveland the next day, where Rampton went into great detail as he told a large group of industrial and business leaders that Utah had five qualities they would want in seeking new locations: a stable, highly productive workforce; new markets or better access to old ones; research ability; abundant natural resources; and ample energy. But above all, he said, Utah had an adequate supply of trained, highly educated people.[26]

"Rampton's Raiders" made close to a hundred trips, often paying several visits to key places such as New York, Los Angeles, San Francisco, and Chicago. Results were not immediate, but by the early 1970s, at least partly because of these business promotion tours, Utah's unemployment rate was in decline.[27]

One interesting aspect of economic development grew out of a disagreement with the federal government over the reliction lands around the Great Salt Lake (lands from which the lake had receded since statehood). The question was whether the right to lease them to industry belonged to the state or to the federal government, and whether either could grant title. Senator Frank Moss pushed a bill through Congress that allowed the state to lease the lands, put the money in escrow, and then let the courts decide who owned them. This meant that Utah could develop the economic potential of the reliction lands immediately. Department of Interior officials urged President Lyndon B. Johnson to veto the bill because, they said, it undermined their authority. However, Rampton made an emergency call to the president, who was flying from Washington to Texas, urging him to sign the bill. Johnson ultimately did so.[28]

Economic Resurgence

With these and other developments the early years of the Rampton administration saw a clear resurgence of Utah's economy. Mining was stimulated by an increased demand for copper, silver, lead, zinc, phosphate rock, and potassium salts, which resulted in mineral production reaching a record value. New facilities for manufacturing truck trailers, kitchen equipment, and filters were completed north of Salt Lake City, and several small clothing factories began production in various Utah communities. Federal aerospace and missile contracts were increased, and Hill Air Force Base was enlarged in order to support the Air Force in Vietnam and to absorb the functions of other bases that were being closed. The Rampton administration also continued to work with bankers and utility and transportation executives in an effort to attract more business by lowering freight rates and property taxes and developing more industrial parks. The first industrial park had opened in 1955 and by 1976 there were forty-four in the state.[29]

Another sign of the vitality of Utah's economy was the growth of the banking industry, one aspect of which was the expansion of branch banking. In 1966, there were fifty-five banks in Utah and 109 branches. By 1978, there were twelve additional banks and 142 additional branches.[30]

The growth of wholesale and retail trade was still another indication of Utah's economic strength. There was a trend toward larger retail shopping centers, and huge sums were spent on location development, parking, beautification of stores, merchandising techniques, and so forth. In 1965, wholesale firms alone employed 18,100 people, an increase of 5.23 percent over the previous year. One factor was the freeport law, which strengthened Utah's role as a distribution center. Wholesale and retail trade together provided more than 22 percent of all nonagricultural employment in Utah.[31]

Another bright spot was the electronics industry where between 1960 and 1970 the number of manufacturing plants jumped from five to twenty-two, most of them shipping goods out of the state.[32] Utah's major utilities also reflected the state's economic health. Production of electrical power grew from 3.5 million kilowatt hours in 1955 to 7.4 million in 1975. Also, as natural gas gradually replaced coal as the heating fuel of choice, Utah's natural gas industry increased its customers from 76,300 in 1950 to 275,000 in 1975.[33]

Utah relied heavily on the transportation industry for its economic well-being and its strategic location provided some advantages. As the geographic center of the eleven western states, Utah became a distribution point for products from its own factories as well as those of other states. As a result, by the mid-1970s, Utah had developed a strong network of transportation services, including railroads, trucklines, airlines, and pipelines.

Traffic in and out of the Salt Lake City International Airport reflected Utah's increasing regional and national significance. Between 1950 and 1975 the number of aircraft movements more than tripled, from about 19,400 to over 61,600, the number of passengers arriving annually jumped from 82,800 to just over 1.4 million, and the number of outgoing passengers rose from just over eighty-eight thousand to over 1.43 million.[34] Airport facilities were strained to the limit but in December 1970 Salt Lake City voters approved a $25 million bond to renovate and expand it.

This era marked a turning point in Utah's dependence upon the federal government for employment. In 1955, the federal government employed 12.1 percent of all Utah's nonagricultural workers. By 1975 the figure was only 8.4 percent. The loss of federal jobs was more than offset by the increase in state and local government employment, including in education.

The general economy improved so much during Rampton's first administration that at the beginning of his second term, in 1969, he felt comfortable proposing a tax increase. His purpose was to consolidate the gains already made in financing various state programs, including education, and to make sure there would be enough money in state coffers to continue them. Accordingly, the Republican legislature went along with his proposed increase in the sales tax as well as increases in several license and franchise taxes. These taxes, along with a previous income tax hike, gave the state a comfortable surplus by the time Rampton faced the budget session in 1970.[35]

On a regional note, some significant changes came to Washington County, and particularly St. George, during these years. In 1970, the population of St. George was double that of 1940, setting the stage for a literal population explosion over the next two decades. In 1968, Terracor, a land development company, founded a new community, Bloomington, adjacent to St. George. Several other new housing subdivisions also helped draw more people to the area, including a significantly larger proportion of residents over age sixty than most Utah communities. Retirees poured in because of the warm climate, strategic location, recreational potential, and, for Latter-day Saints, the Mormon temple.

All of this growth brought new businesses, particularly those related to trade and services. Between 1940 and 1970 St. George changed from a community in which the percentage of its people employed in agriculture dropped from 40 to 10 percent. Equally important, St. George was no longer as economically tied to Salt Lake City as it once was. Instead, it developed greater economic ties to Las Vegas and Los Angeles. Whatever agricultural exports it still had, one of which was milk, went largely to Las Vegas, California, and Colorado. Well over half the water from Washington County's Virgin River went into the Colorado River system and helped feed the municipal and industrial needs of southern California (although no profit came to Washington County as a result). Half the visitors to Zion National Park came from Califor-

Image 4.3: Interstate 15 under construction, interchange at 2400 South and 2nd West, Salt Lake City, March 30, 1963. Used by permission, Utah State Historical Society, all rights reserved.

nia. Moreover, most of the nonresidents who owned property in the county were from California or Nevada.[36]

A Demographic Sidelight: Urbanization and Suburbanization

The 1970 census demonstrated that Utah, like other parts of the nation, was becoming more urban.[37] In the decade between 1960 and 1970, counties with the smallest population—all of them rural—declined even more while those with large urban centers, and their adjacent counties, gained in population. The portion of Utahns who lived in urban areas jumped from 65.3 percent in 1950 to 80.4 percent in 1970.

At the same time, the state was also becoming more suburban. The population of both Salt Lake City and Ogden dropped, while that of adjacent communities increased substantially. For example, one of Ogden's suburbs, North Ogden, grew by 2,636 people, or an amazing 100.6 percent. Significant gains also came in communities surrounding Salt Lake City: Murray grew by 4,400 or 26.2 percent, Sandy grew by 3,116 or 93.8 percent, and South Jordan by1,588 or 117.3 percent.

One effect of suburbanization was the disappearance of orchards in southern Davis Count and the blossoming of suburban bedroom communities for people working in Salt Lake. Another was a strong shift in business patterns within Salt Lake County, as firms moved away from central business districts and into suburban shopping locations. Between 1960 and 1970, business volume in Salt Lake City rose 36 percent, while the volume in the unincorporated areas of Salt Lake County rose 158 percent. In Murray, one of the fastest growing suburbs in the state, sales increased 190 percent.[38]

Highways and the Economy

Essential to the state's economy was its highway program. Federal grants, matched by state funds, went toward both rural and urban highways, but the state's most urgent need was the Interstate highway system. One reason was that further economic development depended, in part, on better highway access to the state.

The Clyde administration wisely spent federal highway money on completing the more difficult and costly urban sections first because building in such areas would become more expensive later on.

When the federal interstate program began in the 1950s, the target date for completion was 1972. Unfortunately, this date was continually set back and in the process Utah fell substantially behind the nation. The year 1965 saw the opening of a portion of both I-15 and I-80, but by mid-1973 only 60 percent of Utah's projected 939 miles was finished. According to even the most optimistic projections the completion date was still more than a decade away. The Federal Highway Act of 1973 only complicated matters, shifting the emphasis from urban to rural highway construction and to non-interstate roads. The result was a substantial reduction of federal money available for interstate construction in the state.[39]

Utah's highway program was also affected by other national problems and policies. In an effort to control inflation, both the Johnson and Nixon administrations impounded federal highway funds. In addition, after the 1973 decision of the Organization of Petroleum Exporting Countries (OPEC) to withhold oil shipments from any country supporting Israel, and raising its prices by 400 percent, a major petroleum crisis hit the United States. The result was a significant drop in highway travel, with an accompanying reduction in the principal source of state highway funds, the motor fuel tax. To help alleviate this problem as well as a generally sagging national economy, early in 1975 President Gerald Ford released to the states $2 billion of impounded federal funds. This created a problem in some states that had already committed their available highway funds for the year and therefore lacked the money needed to match the federal grants. In Utah, however, the legislature appropriated enough traditionally non-highway funds to meet most of the federal matching requirements. Slightly more than 74 percent of Utah's Interstate was complete by April 1976.[40]

Tourism and the Public Image

One of Utah's most promising economic potentials lay in promoting tourism, and Governor Rampton pushed it hard. In April 1965, he appointed Manny Floor, a Salt Lake City advertising executive, as director of the Tourist and Publicity Council. With a greatly enhanced budget, Floor's effective efforts eventually attracted many new visitors and brought important new revenue to the state.

In his 1966 address to the Business Preview Conference, Rampton noted that tourism had already achieved gains beyond their expectations. Preliminary figures indicated that in the last six months of 1965 the number of visitors to the state increased by perhaps as much as 20 percent, compared with a national average of 8 percent for the year. The Tourist and Publicity Council estimated that Utah's tourist industry grossed over $150 million in 1965 and expected to see a $1 billion industry within ten years. Tourism was big business, Rampton emphasized, noting that in the last six months of 1965 the increase in gasoline taxes alone brought about by sales to travelers repaid the state for the entire six-month program. Beyond that, he pointed out, "The gain in sales tax revenue and increased business revenue can be classified as 'profit' on our investment."[41] Actually, the economic impact of tourism was even greater than Rampton thought. During 1965 visitors (mostly tourists, but also some who came for business purposes only) actually spent $183 million in Utah—$33 million more than the gross reported by the Tourist and Publicity Council.[42]

One effort to attract visitors to Utah was the construction of the Salt Palace in Salt Lake City, conceived as a combination civic auditorium, convention center, sports arena, and arts center. An effort by Salt Lake City's economy-minded mayor J. Bracken Lee to stop the project, even after voters approved a bond issue, failed, and the Salt Palace was dedicated in July 1969. The new complex proved to be a turning point in the history of Salt Lake City, attracting conventions and meetings of various groups. It also led to the rehabilitation of much of the surrounding area with new restaurants, a major new shopping center, and attractive new hotel facilities. A proposed concert hall was eliminated from the original Salt Palace because the cost would have exceeded the bond limit. Before the end of Rampton's administration, however, another bond was issued. With this money, as well as the generous support of Obert C. Tanner and other private donors, the elegant $10 million concert hall adjacent to the Salt Palace was completed in 1979. Its magnificent acoustics rivaled those of any auditorium in the world, and it became the home of the world-famous Utah Symphony.

Utah's stepped-up efforts to attract tourists also included promoting various sports activities, particularly the fantastic skiing available in the Wasatch Mountains. In 1966 and again in 1973, Utah was the American entry in bidding for the Winter Olympics but lost both times. The 1966 effort brought Utah's great skiing potential into sharp focus but also raised the question as to why this industry was not more well developed and why nearby states drew more ski enthusiasts. A study revealed two major drawbacks: inadequate facilities, which would require much heavier investment by the resorts as well as some new resorts, and poor access by air. What Utah needed most in order to develop skiing as a tourist attraction was better airline service.[43] In the 1970s, this problem was at least partially remedied with the expansion of the airport at Salt Lake City.

Utahns also used the state's unique history to attract national attention. A special occasion for doing this was the centennial anniversary of the completion of the first transcontinental railroad and the driving of the famous golden spike near Promontory Point in 1869. In 1965, Congress created the Golden Spike National Historic Site at Promontory. A visitors' center was constructed, tracks were laid, and full-scale replicas were built of the two locomotives present when the spike was driven. On May 10, 1969, some twelve thousand people were on the spot to witness a well-publicized re-enactment of that famous ceremony.[44]

By 1970, efforts to promote Utah tourism achieved some welcome results. In 1969 a record 3.5 million people visited Utah's national parks, monuments, and historic sites. Another 725,000 went to Flaming Gorge.[45] In the twelve months ending in May 1970, some seven million non-resident, private vehicles, carrying a total of nearly 21 million people, passed through the state.[46] This did not include one million people who came into the Salt Lake City International Airport, many of whom did more than simply pass through the terminal on their way to somewhere else. Salt Lake City, primarily Temple Square, was still the most popular attraction, followed by Zion National Park and Bryce Canyon.

Public Education, The Perennial Crisis

Like his predecessor, Governor Rampton began his administration with a crisis in public education. NEA sanctions against Utah were still in place, and educators were still disgruntled over low salaries and inadequate funding for classroom needs. When Rampton went before the legislature in January 1965, he called for huge increases in educational spending. On March 9 he signed an education finance bill that provided $24.6 million in additional state and local funds. Six days later the NEA sanctions were lifted.[47]

However, that did not end the problem in Box Elder County, where teachers and the school board remained at an impasse. Rampton intervened, calling Terrel H. Bell, state superintendent of public instruction, Darrold Long, executive secretary of the Utah School Board, and John Evans, executive secretary of UEA, into his office. He told them bluntly that he wanted the pressure from both sides to stop and asked Superintendent Bell to go to Box Elder County and negotiate. As the time drew near for school to open, Rampton himself made a few trips to the county. After the problem was resolved, Bell quipped to Rampton that "you've discovered one of the secrets of mediation. You get each side so angry at the mediator that they cease to be angry with each other and settle."[48]

But Utah was not out of the woods in its ability to support education. By almost every standard of comparison, Utah's ability to pay remained low, reflected, in part, in teacher salaries, which dropped from 25th in the nation in 1965–66 to 31st in 1969–70. This was despite the fact that Utah's effort was still well above average, with nearly 50 percent of all state and local expenditures going for education in 1966, as compared with 38 percent for the nation. Utah ranked first in the nation in this category and second in the percentage of personal income going for state and local school taxes.

Nevertheless, the quality of education remained relatively high in some fields of study. In examinations administered by the American College Testing Program (ACT) between 1968 and 1974, Utah's students scored above the national average in English and the Natural Sciences and also scored high in mathematics.[49]

At the same time, Utah's school system was frequently criticized for failing to provide the kind of vocational and technical training needed in a society that was rapidly become more dependent upon technology. In 1970, more than 93 percent of the dollars spent for post-high school education went toward academic degrees but less than 15 percent of the jobs in Utah required such training. Forty-five percent of those entering the ninth grade had no education beyond high school, emphasizing the need for better vocational and technical training in order to help them secure adequate employment.[50]

On the other hand, these years saw substantial improvement in some aspects of public education. An infusion of federal funds during the 1964–66 biennium, as part of the national war on poverty, provided badly needed equipment, instructional material, and minor remodeling. The 1967 legislature passed a mandatory driver education law and driving ranges and driving simulation equipment were soon added to many school programs. During the same year federal funds allowed the development of several bilingual programs to meet the special needs of children who had limited English-speaking ability.[51] Utah also expanded its emphasis on special education, although some students remained unserved, or served inappropriately, while some districts apparently received a disproportionate amount of the funds available.[52]

In addition, Utah schools increased their efforts to deal with drug abuse, which, in the late 1960s, exploded among adolescents and young adults throughout the nation as well as in Utah. In 1968, an alarming 50 percent of Utah's teenagers knew students who had used narcotics and 26 percent knew where to obtain them.[53]

In the fall of 1969, school districts were given new curriculum guidelines for teaching the effects of drug abuse. As curriculum materials were distributed, State Board of Education health specialist Robert L. Leake noted that a decade earlier there was little reference to drugs in the schools, partly because police officers had asked educators to "tread lightly" on the issue. "This has all changed in the last three to four years," he said. "As drug abuse has spread from college campuses to high schools, junior high schools and even to some elementary students, drug education has become a necessity."[54] In the summer of 1970, a one-week "live-in" drug abuse prevention program was held for over 180 educators, students, parents, and community leaders. This was followed by twenty-one regional workshops throughout the state. From 1972 through 1975, supported by federal funding, Utah's drug abuse team promoted other special projects, including teacher in-service training on drug abuse prevention, programs for parent-student-teacher involvement and interaction, developing interpersonal relationship skills, and values education.[55] The immediate results were difficult to ascertain, but Utah educators were trying to respond as aggressively as possible to this national social disaster.

Higher Education

Meanwhile, higher education in America continued to face serious challenges with a rapidly increasing college-age population. This was especially serious in light of the crucial need for the younger generation to be more well educated and more well trained than their parents had been. Overcrowded schools could deprive them of the opportunity.

These concerns led to the development of a new kind of educational institution, the comprehensive community college. This was seen as "an institution which is neither an upward extension of the high school nor a downward retraction of the University."[56] It provided a wider range of courses for a wider range of purposes than traditional colleges. These included terminal technical training; training for vocations or trades; general education programs designed to train students in citizenship responsibility; daytime and evening classes designed to meet a variety of academic, technical, vocational, and avocational interests of adults in the community; remedial programs for "late bloomers" and others with poor academic records; special community services; and strong guidance and counseling programs.

In 1965, the Utah legislature made Cedar City's branch of Utah State University into a four-year college. Four years later, the school's name was changed to the College of Southern Utah. This left only three junior colleges in the state (Snow, Dixie, and College of Eastern Utah), none of which met the criteria of a comprehensive community college. At the same time, the state continued to operate two small technical and vocational schools, the Utah Trade Technical Institute in Provo and the Salt Lake Trade Technical Institute. These institutes performed some of the functions of the comprehensive junior college. Primarily vocational in nature, however, they did not offer all the courses necessary for those wanting to complete their first two years of a senior college degree.

The changing educational challenges of this decade became part of an intense public debate over what the state should do about the fact that all its colleges and technical institutes were literally bursting at the seams. Both the state school board and the Utah Coordinating Council of Higher Education recommended establishing a junior college in Salt Lake City, but the Coordinating Council recommended that, for cost-saving purposes, it be combined with the Salt Lake Trade Technical Institute. This would have resulted in the creation of a model comprehensive junior college. However, the state school board resisted that idea, arguing that combining the two would result in a de-emphasis, if not the elimination, of industrial and technical training. Others complained that the combination would degrade the academic aspects of the program. The argument went on without an immediate solution.

In 1967, the name of the Salt Lake Trade Technical Institute was changed to Utah Technical College. However, debate raged over whether the school should remain as it was or become a comprehensive community college with both vocational and general education components. The community college concept eventually prevailed, and in 1987 the name was changed to Salt Lake Community College.[57]

The Utah Technical Institute in Provo went through a similar transition. In 1967, its name was changed to Utah Technical College at Provo. It grew rapidly, a new site was located in south-west Orem, and a new campus was dedicated in 1977. In July 1982, the Board of Regents officially designated the school as a comprehensive community college, charging it with retaining a vocational/technical emphasis. In 1987, the legislature approved changing the name to Utah Valley Community College. The emphasis remained on vocational education, but a strong general education curriculum, which had been developing over many years, remained.[58] In 1993, it became Utah Valley State College, and became Utah Valley University in 2008.[59]

The College of Eastern Utah (CEU), too, eventually became a comprehensive community college. In that spirit, the Board of Regents also established the CEU San Juan Center at Blanding. By the 1990s, this center served about 350 students each quarter. CEU also enhanced its vocational-technical programs. Among its specialized programs was mine safety training, for which the school received an exclusive state assignment. It also established a nursing program, in cooperation with Weber State College, in 1970.[60]

The stepped-up pace of college and university enrollment caused educators and legislators to take a hard look at the future. A report produced by the Coordinating Council of Higher Education in 1967 revealed some astonishing projections for the next decade, including a 50 percent jump in enrollment in Utah's public and private universities and colleges. As in the case of public schools, however, Utah's ability to pay for higher education was already severely strained.

In a pathbreaking effort to plan responsibly for the future, Governor Rampton assigned the Coordinating Council the task of producing a "Master Plan for Higher Education in Utah" and the 1967 legislature authorized a budget for the project. The Coordinating Council began by organizing two dozen committees, including a citizen's advisory committee.[61] In 1968, Governor Rampton and the Coordinating Council sponsored Utah's first Governor's Conference on Higher Education. Its major theme was master planning. "Education is much too vital to our future for us to continue without carefully laid plans which will point the way toward quality, economy and efficiency in our education programs," the governor declared.[62] That year the committee's effort resulted in a working document titled *Utah's Master Plan for Higher Education*.

Concerns for the future sparked a lively debate over how to govern higher education. With costs skyrocketing, and with the recognition that there was considerable duplication of effort among the various schools, two major proposals surfaced. One called for strengthening the authority of the Coordinating Council, while the other called for the creation of a single board to govern all the institutions of higher learning. The 1968 master plan recommended a single board that would represent all schools equally, rather than a continuation of the six boards that for decades had engaged in a biennial battle before the legislature for funds. Funds would be spent more efficiently, advocates maintained, and duplication of programs could more easily be eliminated.[63]

The issue reached the legislature in January 1969. There was no unanimity but those arguing for a single board prevailed. The Higher Education Act of 1969 created a fifteen-member State Board of Higher Education, five members appointed by the governor, five by the state Senate, and five by the state House of Representatives.[64] The president of each of the state's institutions of higher learning reported directly to the board. G. Homer Durham, former vice-president of the University of Utah and president of Arizona State University, became the first Commissioner of Higher Education. He was succeeded in 1976 by Terrel H. Bell, former State Superintendent of Public Instruction and also former United States Commissioner of Education. In 1974, the legislature changed the name of the board to the State Board of Regents.

Utahns and the Nation: The "Great Society"

Utahns seemed to have a kind of love-hate relationship with Lyndon B. Johnson, who began his second term as President of the United States by inviting the Mormon Tabernacle Choir to sing at his inauguration ceremony on January 20, 1965. Among the three numbers performed by the choir was the stirring "Battle Hymn of the Republic." "I've never seen them sing more beautifully," Governor Rampton said later. "Anyone from Utah who was there that day, whether Mormon or not, could not have helped being very proud of that group which performed so well."[65] Despite Johnson's friendship with the people of Utah, however, and despite the fact that Utahns gave him their electoral votes in 1964, many of his programs were not overwhelmingly popular in the state.

Several pieces of federal legislation during these years had long-range consequences for every state. A series of controversial laws in the mid-1960s was designed to implement Lyndon Johnson's "Great Society." In 1970 Congress gave eighteen-year-olds the right to vote in national elections. This was followed by the Twenty-Sixth Amendment to the Constitution, passed by Congress in March 1971 and ratified by the states before the end of June, extending to eighteen-year-olds the right to vote in all elections. Social Security benefits were continually increased. The Occupational Safety and Health Act of 1970 established a federal agency to oversee state and local efforts to control pollution, and several acts in 1970 and 1972 established new standards for water pollution. These and many other laws were designed to improve the quality of life in America but, to the dislike of many Utahns, also contributed to the ever-growing involvement of the federal government in the affairs of the states, businesses, and individuals.

Johnson's "Great Society" was a case in point. Many voters were uncomfortable with the burgeoning federal bureaucracy and the expanding number of federal programs, which probably helped account for Utah's dramatic return to the Republican fold in 1966. But under Johnson's prodding, the Eighty-ninth Congress (1965-1966) rolled out a stream of social legislation unequaled since the New Deal of the 1930s. Long-standing concerns over health insurance for those over the age of sixty-five came to fruition in the Medicare (health insurance for those over age 65) and Medicaid (grants to the states to provide medical care for the indigent) programs. "Great Society" legislation also included federal aid to elementary and secondary education; the Appalachian Regional Development Act of 1966; the Housing and Urban Development Act of 1965 that provided massive funds for housing as well as for urban renewal (a program that had been going on for years but was drastically underfunded); rent supplements for low-income families; and a new, Cabinet-level Department of Housing and Urban Development. Each of these programs would have a direct effect on many Utahns and would also affect the way some Utahns voted.

With national concerns mounting over the deterioration of America's "inner cities," funds for urban renewal were welcomed by many cities as a means of revitalizing and beautifying the community and helping to control vice and crime. However, in September 1965, the people of Salt Lake City decisively rejected these funds. Both Salt Lake City newspapers supported the idea of funds for urban renewal, as did Governor Rampton and the League of Women Voters. Congressman David S. King assured the people that "after 15 years' experience, we can say with some confidence that urban renewal works."[66] Nevertheless, spurred on by ultraconservative Mayor J. Bracken Lee, opponents denounced the plan on the grounds that it would expand bureaucracy, increase taxes, wrongly take property from unwilling owners at a fraction of its value, and that it was socialistic. Wary voters turned it down by a six-to-one margin.

A similar debate took place in Provo, where urban renewal was also defeated. Unfortunately for Provo's immediate economic future, its rejection of urban renewal funds helped developers decide to build a huge new shopping mall in nearby Orem rather than in Provo.

But Salt Lake City did not neglect urban renewal for long. A 1972 report to newly elected Mayor E. J. (Jake) Garn said that the city had become a metropolis characterized by blighted neighborhoods. Garn and the city council quickly launched a community improvement program, establishing a Salt Lake Redevelopment Agency in January 1973. With Lee gone from the mayor's office, the city also accepted federal funds to help finance the agency's projects. The long-range plan was to eventually tear down houses that could not be rehabilitated and to use better zoning laws to promote more balanced growth. In 1974, in preparation for the 1976 bicentennial of the American Revolution, the city established a beautification committee. Its major project that year was the Main Street Beautification Project, designed to change the appearance of downtown Salt Lake City. In a close vote, property owners along the affected part of the street agreed to finance the face-lift. By the end of the year the first phase was under way.

Utahns and the Nation: Civil Rights

The national civil rights movement continued during these years, with both positive and negative consequences. On the positive side was the Voting Rights Act of 1965, which prohibited states from imposing any qualification or prerequisite to voting that would deny or abridge the right of any citizen to vote on account of race or color. The intent was to outlaw the practice of some southern states of requiring voters who were otherwise qualified to pass literacy tests. This was a way of preventing African-Americans from exercising their franchise.

On the negative side was continuing racial tension. That same year, beginning with devastating riots in the Watts area of

Los Angeles, racial strife throughout the country resulted in millions of dollars worth of damage in many urban areas. Concurrently, a new "black power" movement, representing the frustration of blacks who could no longer accept Martin Luther King's philosophy of nonviolent integration, promoted black separatism.

Meanwhile, school integration continued even as the Nixon administration attempted to slow it down by calling for a more gradual middle road between instant integration and permanent segregation. African Americans and other civil rights advocates saw this only as further evidence of prejudice, and the Supreme Court ordered integration to proceed. Schools continued to be desegregated at a steady pace through policies that included bussing students from one school district to another in order to achieve a balance. However, both Congress and the courts eventually accepted more moderate approaches.

The 1965 legislature passed Utah's first civil rights legislation, a public accommodations law, signed by Governor Rampton on February 18. Like its federal counterpart, the new law prohibited racial discrimination in restaurants, theaters, motels, and other public places, and it went beyond the federal law by including taverns, bars, and service establishments such as doctor's offices and beauty salons. The legislature also finally passed a fair employment law, although it excluded from the provisions of the law those firms hiring fewer than twenty-five people as well as businesses owned by religious organizations. There were questions in the minds of some people as to whether the new legislation was finally a courageous recognition by the legislature of its responsibilities in civil rights or simply a minimal response intended to preclude federal intervention.[67]

Still complicating the picture in Utah was the LDS policy that did not allow blacks to hold the priesthood, although many Mormon leaders continued to express strong support for civil rights legislation. They also explained that they did not know why the priesthood was denied but that they were powerless to make a change unless directed by divine revelation. Nevertheless, public pressure mounted. In July, 1965, acting on a proposal offered by its Salt Lake City and Ogden branches, the NAACP passed a resolution criticizing the church's "discrimination practices." It also urged embassies in South America, Asia, and Africa to "refuse to grant visas to missionaries and representatives of The Church of Jesus Christ of Latter-day Saints until such time as the doctrine of non-White inferiority is changed and rescinded by the church and a positive policy of support for civil rights, is taken by the same."[68]

Protests spread to some universities. In October 1969, about 250 Arizona State University students, mostly black, urged a boycott of the ASU-BYU football game. In other instances, students wore black arm bands in protest when BYU came to play. In November 1969, Stanford University took the most drastic action when it officially announced that it would schedule no more athletic contests with BYU. After receiving a letter from BYU showing that it was in complete compliance with the Civil Rights Act, with no discrimination on campus, Stanford officials rescinded their decision. But such incidents illustrated the continuing tenseness that the policy engendered both in and out of the state.

Utah and the Nation: The Status of Women

In 1966, feminist author Betty Friedan organized the National Organization for Women (NOW), which became a strong political force in agitating for such things as child-care centers for working women, lawsuits against sexual discrimination in the workplace, and legalized abortion. The intensity of the movement subsided somewhat by the end of the 1970s, but it was a catalyst for numerous changes in the role of, and attitudes toward, women in America. The following discussion deals with some of those changes in the period covered by this and the next two chapters.

In Utah, the changing role of women was illustrated in part by the growing proportion of women in the workforce. In 1980, 52.4 percent of eligible women worked outside the home, compared with 51.6 percent in the nation. Women accounted for 40.7 percent of the labor force, compared with a national figure of 41.9 percent.[69] A study in the mid-1970s showed that Utah women actually entered the job market at a more rapid rate than women nationally, and married women and mothers were working at increasingly higher rates. Women also enjoyed an increasing share of the available jobs. They were especially prominent in Utah's public school classrooms.[70]

By 1987, women made up 44 percent of Utah's labor force. In addition, 60 percent of all Utah women age sixteen and over were in the workforce, higher than the national average. Among married women, 58 percent were working, and 71 percent of those in the typical childbearing years (ages 20–35) were employed. Nevertheless, surveys demonstrated that women made up the largest share of "discouraged workers" in Utah—those who gave up looking for work because of real or perceived barriers to finding it.[71]

Women moved slowly into professions traditionally dominated by men. Between 1950 and 1980, in the "white collar" occupations—professional, managerial, sales, and clerical—women increased their share of the jobs from 38 percent to 50.4 percent. They also improved their share of the blue collar jobs, from 7.4 percent to 16.8 percent.[72] In some areas, however, women still lagged behind the nation. In the medical profession, for example, slightly more than 13 percent of the American MDs in 1984 were women, compared with only 6 percent in Utah.[73]

Women concerned about continuing discrimination in the marketplace found support in the Utah Anti-Discrimination Act of 1965 that prohibited discrimination in employment based on race, color, national origin, sex, religion, or age. They were also encouraged by the fact that major employers paid increasing attention to providing adequate time off for employees who had babies. An important symbol of the changing attitude toward mothers in the workplace was seen in the mid-1970s, when the LDS Church dropped its policy of not allowing women who had babies or young children to work for the church.

But Utah women continued to lag behind men, as well as behind the national average for women, in terms of income. Numerous explanations were offered for this earning gap, but research completed under the auspices of the Department of Employment Security indicated that most of them were valid only in a minority of the cases. The more important fact seemed to be that women often received less pay simply *because* they were women. However, the figures were skewed by the fact that many young, uneducated women were "marrying too young, becoming pregnant too soon,

Image 4.4: Christine Meaders Durham. In 1982 she became the first woman to be appointed to the Utah Supreme Court. She served as Chief Justice 2002–2012. Used by permission, Utah State Historical Society, all rights reserved.

and divorcing at young ages," ending up in the most low-paying jobs and dragging down the average.[74]

However, by the mid-1980s real progress was being made toward more equal pay, more equal job distribution between men and women, and more equal treatment before the law. In addition, more women found places in traditionally male-dominated professions such as business, law, medicine, and higher education. More were also elected and appointed to public office, serving as mayors, legislators, heads of government departments, and other traditionally male positions. One noteworthy appointment was that of Christine Meaders Durham who, in 1982, became the first female justice on the Utah Supreme Court. A mother of four, she and her husband, George Durham, a Salt Lake City pediatrician, seemed to represent an ideal balance as they each pursued significant careers and, at the same time, shared household and family responsibilities.

When asked why they worked, Utah's women gave several reasons. Because technology had made many traditional household tasks obsolete, some no longer felt as tied to the home. Equally important, they became increasingly aware of and interested in career opportunities. A growing portion of those seeking work were divorced with families. For other women, caught in the trap of spiraling inflation, the possibility of a two-paycheck household became increasingly attractive. Other reasons given included personal satisfaction, the need to "make ends meet," the desire to improve living standards, the need for a family "nest egg" in case of emergency, and the need to provide for the education of a spouse or children. These reasons were all consistent with national patterns, but in Mormon-dominated Utah many women worked for the additional reason of providing funds to send a son or a daughter on a mission.[75]

Women were becoming more well-educated in the last part of the twentieth century, but by the mid-1970s only half as many women as men received bachelors degrees and about a third as many earned graduate degrees.[76] This became gradually more equal: in 1988, 47.3 percent of Utah's college students were women, up from 43 percent in 1983. This was not enough, however, to raise Utah from its position as number fifty in the nation. The fact that Utah women married at an average age of twenty-one, three years younger than the national norm, may have been a contributing reason.[77]

Utah college women tended to major in the traditionally female-dominated fields of humanities, education, homemaking, liberal arts, and nursing, but by the 1980s there was a noticeable increase in the number studying business, law, and medicine.[78]

About 1982 the Young Women's Christian Association of Salt Lake City published an interesting and highly useful booklet entitled *Women's Guide to Salt Lake City*. Designed to help women newly arrived in Utah, it noted that some had heard they might feel uncomfortable or out of place in the state. It set about to change that image by listing numerous agencies, services, and resources that could be of specific help to women. In many ways, the kinds of services listed, the groups providing those services, and the concerns they represented suggested that in this as well as other matters of interest Utah was rapidly becoming much more like the nation as a whole.[79]

Utah's women were highly active in social work. Various women's clubs and church groups provided substantial volunteer service for a variety of social welfare groups. In addition, the LDS Relief Society was an important licensed social work agency.

Utah women also belonged to numerous professional organizations, many of which worked together through the Utah Federation of Business and Professional Women's Clubs. The resurgence of the women's movement in the 1960s and 1970s spurred the founding of even more women's organizations in Utah, exceeding 160 in number by 1978.[80] In addition, the LDS Relief Society enjoyed membership in many national women's organizations. President Belle Smith Spafford was president of the National Council of Women from 1968 to 1970.

Women gradually became more visible in Utah politics. Several Utah communities, including Alpine, Orem, Spanish Fork, Springville, and, in 1991, Salt Lake City, elected women as mayors. Women were also elected to the state legislature, although Utah ranked among the lowest states in the nation in terms of the percentage of women in the makeup of the legislature.[81]

State government demonstrated a growing interest in the status, conditions, and opportunities for women, including the kinds of legal problems they faced. In 1986, the Utah Judicial Council established the Utah Task Force on Gender and Justice. The idea came to Chief Justice Gordon R. Hall of the Utah Supreme Court while attending a session dealing with gender bias at the annual Conference of Chief Justices. After approval from the Utah Judicial Council, he asked Aileen H. Clyde, who had served for years as a volunteer with the Utah judiciary and was highly respected for her work, to chair the task force. Members included judges, lawyers, court personnel, and community leaders. The purpose of the task force was to "inquire into the nature, extent, and consequences of gender bias as it might exist within the Utah court system."[82]

The highly detailed report, published in 1990, revealed that women simply did not have equal access to Utah's courts, partly for financial reasons but also because of other factors such as role stereotypes or religious norms and attitudes.[83] These same factors discriminated against them in most kinds of court settlements. In the distribution of alimony and property in divorce cases, for example, the task force found that Utah judges seemed to underestimate difficulties faced by women when they went back into the workforce after long absences, and they did not respond "adequately" to well-documented differences in earning abilities between men and women.[84] Even though improvements were being made in the court system, by 1990 there was still a long way to go before complete gender equity was achieved. In many instances the fact that women had to appear before male judges who were also male ecclesiastical leaders tended to intimidate them. The report carried specific recommendations for judges and court administrators, the bar, law schools, the legislature, and religious leaders.

Unlike many governmental reports, this one did not languish on the shelves gathering dust. It was taken seriously by lawyers, judges, and the legislature. It seemed, in fact, to take on a life of its own, becoming a kind of measuring stick for progress or lack of progress. A year after it was published, reports indicated that progress had been slow on some recommendations but surprisingly rapid on others. The report noted that women were disgracefully underrepresented on the bench, and that Governor Norman Bangerter had named only three women judges out of seventeen judicial appointments. During the following year, three out of four appointments went to qualified women. The legislature, too, responded to some of the concerns expressed in the report. A 1991 law, for example, removed spousal exception for rape, one of the main issues in the concern over domestic violence. During the year members of the task force also met with religious leaders and police officers in an effort to ensure that the first person a woman talked to when she became a victim of domestic violence would take her complaint seriously.[85]

In 1987. the Utah Governor's Commission for Women and Families published the first edition of *Utah Women and the Law: A Resource Handbook*. Revised editions appeared later. This helpful publication provided an overview of laws that dealt with the most common problems faced by women, suggesting agencies to contact and questions to ask. Intended as a practical guide on basic legal matters, though not a substitute for competent legal counsel, the book consisted of sixteen chapters in which legal issues were spelled out clearly and, on some kinds of cases, advice was given on specific courses of action.[86]

The National Organization for Women's Legal Defense and Education Fund published a book in 1987 that rated each state in terms of how its laws treated women. It also ranked the states, based on information concerning laws related to marriage, divorce, child support, education, employment, and whether there was an equal rights clause in the constitution. Utah ranked 29th among the fifty states, though the publication pointed out that the lot of women had improved greatly in Utah during the previous ten years.[87]

Utah and the Nation: The Equal Rights Amendment

Perhaps the most intense political debate in Utah during the Rampton era concerned the Equal Rights Amendment (ERA).[88]

In the late nineteenth and early twentieth centuries, women's organizations pushed for legislation that would specifically protect working women through minimum wages, maximum hours, and regulated working conditions. Shortly after World War I, however, the emphasis shifted. Rather than gender-based laws that specifically protected women, they wanted general equal rights laws, or, better still, a Constitutional amendment that would make it illegal to discriminate in any way on the basis of sex. Beginning in 1923, an equal rights measure was proposed in every session of Congress. In 1972, Congress finally approved an Equal Rights Amendment and sent it to the states for ratification. It stated, simply, that "Equality of rights under the law shall not be denied or abridged by the United States or any state on account of sex." In the US Senate, Utah's Wallace F. Bennett voted against it, while Frank E. Moss supported it. In the House, Republican Sherman P. Lloyd abstained, while Democrat Gunn McKay voted against it.

The new amendment would become part of the Constitution when approved by thirty-eight states. Within a year, it was ratified by twenty-two states, but at that point the campaign bogged down as the amendment met increasingly fierce resistance in several states. Opponents argued that, taken to its possible extremes, it could undermine traditional family values and, through radical interpretation, it could become untenable and lead to endless lawsuits. They also argued that there was no real need for the amendment because women already had equal protection under the laws. Proponents argued that the amendment would put an end once and for all to any possible discrimination against women in employment, political activity, and social life. In Utah, there seemed to be widespread support for the amendment. A *Deseret News* poll in November 1974 demonstrated that well over 60 percent of Utah's population supported it.[89]

In 1973, Representative Rita Urie, supported by the Governor's Commission on the Status of Women, presented the Equal Rights Amendment to the state legislature for ratification. However, a sudden showing of strong conservative opposition helped defeat it. Shocked at the setback, promoters soon formed an organization known as the Equal Rights Coalition that led out in intensive and well organized campaigns, both in 1975 and 1977, to get the amendment through the legislature. Each time, however, it went down in defeat.

Among the opponents of the ERA were several religious groups, including Catholics, Protestants, Mormons, and Jews. In Utah, the role of the LDS Church was pivotal. Church leaders considered it a moral issue because, they concluded, it had the potential of striking a blow at the family. At first they did not make public statements, presumably because the issue was so volatile, but by the end of 1974 they decided to make their opposition more open. On December 13, Barbara B. Smith, general president of the LDS Relief Society, took a strong public stand against the amendment in an address at the Institute of Religion adjacent to the University of Utah. Although she was not speaking officially for the church, Smith did not make her statement until she had been given the go-ahead by two members of the Quorum of the Twelve Apostles.[90]

According to Smith, the amendment was imperfect, dangerous, and "a confused step backward in time." It would create "endless litigation," she said, leading to decisions that might be detrimental to the family and to the "optimum protection of children." Further, it would nullify laws providing favorable treatment for women in cases dealing with the custody of children and lead to several other undesirable consequences for women, including a denial of the right of privacy. The amendment, she said, "is so broad that it is inadequate, inflexible and vague—so all-encompassing that it is nondefinitive." Instead of such a "blanket approach," redress for injustices and unfair practices should be sought in the courts, through presidential decrees, and in group action.

Kathy Collard, a Salt Lake City attorney and spokesperson for the Equal Rights Coalition, responded to Smith's address by saying that the broadness of the amendment was not a fault but, rather, one of its virtues. A piecemeal approach to getting rid of sexist legislation, she said, would take the next twenty-five years because biases were so pervasive in American society. Denying each of Smith's major assertions against the ERA, she argued that care for children involved in custody battles would be improved because instead of basing custody on traditional sexual bias favoring women, it would be based on "objective factors—the fitness of each parent, concern, interest and ability to care for the child."[91] The differences between Smith and Collard on these and other issues related to the amendment constituted a classic microcosm of the continuing debate around the nation.

Barbara Smith's address was followed in less than a month, on January 11, 1975, by an anti-ERA editorial in the *Church News* section of the *Deseret News*. The editorial quoted Smith extensively, affirmed the progress already made in America toward equality of opportunity in political, civil, and economic activities, and cited the lead story in the January 1975 issue of *Nation's Business* to the effect that the amendment was unnecessary, uncertain, and undesirable.[92] While this was not a First Presidency statement, such an editorial could not have been written without the approval of church leaders. It was widely assumed that it was written by Mark E. Petersen, a member of the Council of the Twelve who often wrote *Church News* editorials.

Finally, in October 1976, the First Presidency issued an official statement. It recognized the injustices done to women in the past, as well as the fact that women were entitled to additional rights, but declared that "we firmly believe that the Equal Rights Amendment is not the answer." It could, indeed, bring women "far more restraints and repressions. We fear it will even stifle many God-given feminine instincts." The statement repeated other standard arguments against the amendment, concluding with the observation that men and women were equal before the Lord but were different biologically, emotionally, and in other ways. "ERA, we believe, does not recognize these differences. There are better means for giving women, and men, the rights they deserve."[93]

The LDS Church apparently played a crucial role in the ultimate defeat of the amendment. By the fall of 1976 thirty-four states had ratified it, leaving only four more needed to meet the Constitutional requirement. As a result of open opposition from church leaders, some Mormon legislators who had previously supported ratification switched sides, thus helping to defeat ratification in Utah. Mormon opposition in Idaho in 1977 led the voters of that state to rescind the legislature's previous ratification. Local church leaders in a number of other states, including Virginia and Nevada, also joined in sponsoring well-organized and successful anti-ERA campaigns. However, even though church leaders were kept apprised of what was happening in other states, no church funds were distributed to the various political action groups formed by local LDS church members.[94] Proponents succeeded in getting Congress to extend the 1979 deadline for ratification to 1982, but no additional states took action.

Utah's original constitution included a statement that was much like the ERA: "Both male and female citizens of the State shall enjoy equally all civil, political, and religious rights and privileges." However, state court rulings over the years weakened the implications of this provision by emphasizing biological gender differences and traditional husband-wife relationships. Nevertheless, the defeat of the ERA did not prevent the Utah legislature from taking action to correct some Utah statutes in order to bring them into conformity with the state constitution and equalize the status of men and women before the law. But the truth was that Utah had not been guilty of as much repressive legislation as some other states, and Utah women enjoyed a comparatively enviable legal status.[95]

Utah and the Nation: Other Domestic Issues

Economically, most of this period was characterized by rapid inflation, which rose from 3 percent in 1967 to 9 percent in 1973. But unemployment also rose, leading political wits to coin the term "stagflation" to describe the confusing economic malaise. On top of that, OPEC's 1973 embargo on oil shipments caused gasoline prices to skyrocket, fueling even more severe inflation. When the Federal Reserve Board finally raised interest rates (a standard way of fighting inflation), the stock market collapsed, and the "Nixon recession" set in.

The gasoline shortage had many implications for Utah, even putting some independent service stations out of business. Utahns found themselves standing in long lines waiting their turns at the gasoline pumps and fearing the possibility of rationing. The shortage eased off after a few years, but prices never returned to where they were in 1972.

The worst political scandal of the era was the Watergate affair, which revealed how far Richard Nixon would go to cover up political mistakes and to discredit opponents. At least as early as 1970, the White House began using illegal tactics, such as unauthorized wiretaps on telephones, to spy on political enemies. By 1972, the Committee to Re-elect the President, appropriately abbreviated CREEP, was conducting various acts of political sabotage. These included breaking into the headquarters of the Democratic party in Washington's Watergate Hotel. The public had received only hints of such activity by the time of the 1972 election, but early in 1973 the whole story began to unravel in the press. In the ensuing investigation, a number of Nixon aides were convicted and sent to prison, and in 1974 the president himself was publicly humiliated when the Supreme Court ordered him to release tapes of White House conversations that clearly implicated him in the cover-up of these illegal activities. An outraged nation turned against him, the House Judiciary Committee voted to impeach him, and on August 9, 1974, Nixon became the only American president ever to resign from office. He was succeeded by Vice-President Gerald Ford. In the aftermath, the aura once surrounding the office of president seemed gone. Nevertheless, the remarkable resiliency of the American constitutional system was demonstrated once again with the peaceful and orderly transition of government in the face of a national crisis.

Reaction in Utah to the Watergate scandal was one of shock, anger, and disappointment in the president most voters had supported so avidly. Utahns were also dismayed when President Ford officially pardoned Nixon.

At least two Utahns were involved in different aspects of the Watergate affair. Thomas J. Gregory, a BYU student enrolled in the university's Washington Seminar, was apparently hired by one of Nixon's operatives to spy on certain Democrats. When found out, Gregory was dismissed from BYU for at least two semesters.[96] After the White House tapes were released, it was discovered that 18½ minutes of one of the tapes was blank. Dr. Thomas G. Stockham, professor of computer science at the University of Utah, was part of a six-member team put together to examine the tape. With its highly sophisticated electronic gear, the team concluded that the segment in question had been intentionally erased.[97]

Utah and the Nation: The Costly, Useless War

In foreign affairs, the Vietnam war dragged on but Americans were becoming weary of the conflict and open protests became frequent nationwide. In 1968, violating a holiday truce, the North Vietnamese and the Vietcong (South Vietnamese who opposed the US-supported government) launched heavy new attacks on US military bases as well as many cities and towns in South Vietnam. This intensified the political war in America, and more impassioned anti-war protests and violence broke out all over the country. In 1969, President Nixon began a phased withdrawal of American troops, but the process was too slow for many Americans, who mounted increasingly vehement protests. The next year, reports of a massacre by American troops at the village of My Lai touched off even more fierce protest, which only expanded when Nixon ordered troops into Cambodia (a staging area for the Vietcong). The most devastating protest took place at Kent State University, where the Reserve Officers Training Corps building was burned and the Ohio National Guard was called out to quell the riot. It was seen as a national tragedy when guardsmen opened fire on the demonstrators, killing four of their fellow Americans.

Utah's reaction to the Vietnam war was, at first, generally supportive; Utahns saw the conflict as a fight against Communist expansion. In 1965, Hack Miller, a popular sports writer for the *Deseret News* and a colonel in the Utah National Guard, went to Vietnam. In a series of articles published in 1965 and 1966, Miller described the country and gave glowing reports of the war and the activities of some Utahns.

No Utah National Guard unit saw action in Vietnam, but the Utah Air National Guard, operating out of Hill Field, flew ninety-six missions between 1966 and 1971, carrying 1,340 tons of cargo in direct support of the war. Indirectly, it also supported the war with 110 cargo-carrying missions to Southeast Asia, Korea, Europe, and Central and South America. Some members of the Utah National Guard volunteered directly for active duty. With these and other volunteers and draftees, Utah sent a larger percentage of its young men to Vietnam than most other states. The 1970 census showed that 27,910 served in the war, or 8.6 percent of the men ages sixteen and over. This figure, compared with a national average of 6.9 percent, placed Utah fifth in the nation. Some of these soldiers, as might be expected, were decorated with hero's laurels.[98]

At home, many Utahns participated in a variety of supportive activities. Some took part in projects such as "Operation Friendship," organized to collect food, clothing, and medicine for the victimized peasants in South Vietnam, and "Operation Schoolhouse," which raised funds for the construction of schoolhouses there.

Nevertheless, opposition to the war gradually mounted in Utah. Prominent Utah banker Marriner Eccles was one of the first to speak out, declaring in 1966 that the United States was in Vietnam as an aggressor. University of Utah history professor James L. Clayton received national publicity when he pointed to the excessive costs, both in terms of current expenditures and future obligations, incurred by the war. On October 15, 1969, more than four thousand demonstrators took part in a full-day "moratorium." It began with speeches on the campus of the University of Utah and concluded with a march downtown and the reading, by the Reverend G. Edward Howlett of St. Mark's Episcopal Cathedral, of the names of Utahns killed in the war. Protests and antiwar speeches also took place on other Utah campuses that day, all part of what the *Salt Lake Tribune* called the largest peace demonstration in Utah history. But that was not the only protest in town—on that same day more than two hundred counterdemonstrators held a pro-war rally at the City and County Building. Other antiwar protests followed, although none were on the scale of the October 15 moratorium.[99] As far as public opinion was concerned, most Utahns expressed disapproval of such protests.[100]

Meanwhile, President Nixon continued troop withdrawals but intensified the air war. By October 1972, he had succeeded in negotiating a cease-fire, the return of American prisoners of war, and the withdrawal of all American military forces. In December, however, he resumed bombing North Vietnam, charging that country with not bargaining in good faith. In January North Vietnam agreed to release the prisoners within sixty days, whereupon the bombing ceased. On January 27, 1973, the United States signed an agreement that was supposed to end the war and restore peace in Vietnam. By the end of March, all American troops were gone.

Utahns, like the rest of the nation, were exuberant, except for the discomforting feeling that America had won nothing. The fact that the fighting was over, however, was enough to celebrate. At 5 p.m. on January 27, at the governor's request, people around the state joined the rest of the nation in honking horns, ringing bells, and cheering. Then they bowed their heads or went to church, responding to the governor's proclamation designating this as a "day of prayer for a lasting world peace."[101]

In the end, the United States really had accomplished nothing in Vietnam except for postponing the inevitable takeover by the Communists. None of the announced American aims were achieved. The fighting continued after the Americans were gone, and in 1975 Saigon fell to the North Vietnamese. It was a sad day for all Americans. Even though they were glad the slaughter was finally over, they had a profound sense of disillusionment at the apparent uselessness of it all.

The disaster to America lay not only in its loss of prestige abroad, bitter political divisiveness at home, and a cost of some $200 billion, but, more tragically, in its human casualties: more than forty-seven thousand Americans were killed and more than three-hundred thousand were wounded. Today, an impressive memorial stands in Washington D.C., honoring those who served in the Vietnam War. The names of the dead are forever enshrined on an elegant wall of polished granite that faces a powerful sculpture of four fighting men. In Utah, the Utah Vietnam Veterans Memorial, dedicated in 1989, stands on the grounds of the state capitol. In a theme similar to the national memorial, it includes a larger-than-life-size statue of a soldier returning from battle, carrying a comrade's rifle. The statue is flanked by a gray granite wall with black granite panels inscribed with the names of those Utahns, 388 men and one woman, listed as killed or missing in action.

Part of the tragedy was felt with the return of Utahns who had been prisoners of war. It was a powerful emotional experience to see and read of men coming home to families they had not seen for six or seven years. Some told tales of mistreatment and torture at the hands of their captors that would remain as constant reminders of the hellishness of war. Others said little or nothing as they tried to put the past behind them and pick up the threads of their lives.

The Environment

In the 1960s and 1970s, Utah's environmental concerns seemed to multiply more rapidly than ever before. Some, such as numerous natural disasters, demonstrated the dangers of wind, rain, and the sun. Others, such as testing of nerve gas and transporting hazardous waste across the state, reflected a variety of national problems and issues.

The potential fury of Mother Nature was displayed in 1965, when Salt Lake County sustained $1 million in damages due to flooding. In the aftermath, planners came up with a $10 million long-range master flood control plan. Its implementation began in 1966 when the county let contracts that would pay for enlarging storm drains and making other improvements in Salt Lake City. Elsewhere in the state, June floods killed seven people. Also in 1966, for the second year in a row, much of Utah's multimillion dollar fruit crop was decimated by frost. The following year, one of the most savage winter snowstorms in the history of southeastern Utah left the town of Monticello marooned for several days. It also stranded thousands of miners, Native Americans, and livestock so that the state had to mount special rescue operations. Massive rainstorms in September 1970 triggered more destructive floods in Utah. In 1972, icy temperatures in March, April, and the first few days of May caused more than $10 million in damages to Utah fruit crops and delayed the growing period for many other crops.

Following this catastrophe, in the mid-1970s Utah experienced the most severe drought in the state's history. The drought was statewide, resulting in water rationing as well as emergency transportation of water in many communities. Alfalfa fields in parts of the state were destroyed because they had no snow cover to protect them from freezing. The lack of enough feed and the high cost of that which was available forced many ranchers out of business, while ski resorts and other businesses depending on snow were financially decimated. The drought did not end until generous amounts of rain began to fall in January 1978.[102] Such natural disasters were not uncommon in Utah, but their frequent recurrences provided regular and uncomfortable reminders of how helpless man really is in the face of nature's fierceness.

It was man-made environmental disasters, however, that concerned Utahns the most, especially since they came on the heels of the suspected atomic fallout problems of the 1950s. Between March 14 and 19, 1968, more than six thousand sheep were found dead in Skull Valley, a remote desert range in Tooele County. An extensive investigation revealed that on March 14, the spray tanks of an F-4C Phantom jet fighter malfunctioned and deadly nerve gas was accidentally released outside the boundaries of Dugway Proving Ground. No human life was lost, but the cost to sheep owners was devastating and the fear of the potential impact of future accidents raised serious questions about the safety of any operations like those at Dugway. Military officials gave the people of the state every assurance that in the future greater precautions would be taken not to endanger either humans or sheep. Meanwhile, the Army paid the sheep owners $376,000 in damages.[103] Finally, in December 1969, the Army suspended all further open-air tests of lethal chemicals, including nerve gas, at Dugway.[104]

Beyond the hazards of military chemical testing, America's efforts to find solutions to some of the most pressing environmental questions required cooperation at state, regional, national, and international levels. It also required federal legislation because both the causes and effects of many environmental problems transcended state boundaries. Some such legislation came but not without complaint from many Americans, including Utahns.

In 1969, Congress passed the National Environmental Policy Act, which required federal agencies to prepare environmental impact statements for any project conducted by them, including private projects that were in part financed by the federal government. This, of course, impacted private individuals or companies that wanted to develop federal land or asked for federal funding. Businesses, as well as state and local governments, were thus required to recognize the possible harmful effects of major development activities, such as building new factories and power plants, erecting dams, and developing new mines or oil wells. They were also required to examine alternatives.

Protecting the environment included preserving wildlife, whose habitat was increasingly threatened with destruction. The Endangered Species Preservation Act of 1966 was only one of many pieces of legislation in the 1960s and 1970s that established programs to help save wildlife from extinction.

In the 1970s, the Utah State Department of Natural Resources, Division of Wildlife, undertook a major reevaluation of its program of fish and game management and established a number of new goals and objectives. The loss of habitat, said a report published in 1975, was the major reason why some species of wildlife were classified as "endangered."[105] The revised goals called for the protection of all species from waste, exploitation, deterioration, or extinction. They also reflected the concerns of sportsmen and others interested in wildlife by calling for maintaining numbers of game animals sufficient to perpetuate hunting, fishing, and trapping while, at the same time, "providing for other—recreational, educational, scientific, aesthetic, therapeutic, and economic— uses of all wildlife."[106]

One major accomplishment of the Nixon administration that would directly affect Utah as well as every other state was the establishment of the Environmental Protection Agency (EPA). Public concern over the impact of human activity on the environment had been building for years and a number of clean air acts had been passed. As part of Nixon's broader governmental reorganization plan, the EPA was officially established on December 2, 1970, in order to consolidate all federal environmental research, monitoring and enforcement activities in a single agency. As the EPA's current website states, its mission "is to protect human health and the environment."[107] The Clean Air Act of 1970, signed by the President on December 31, authorized the EPA to set national air quality, auto emission, and antipollution standards.

The EPA was not universally welcomed or loved. Governor Rampton had concerns about the federal government entering that field; he saw a built-in potential for conflict between the EPA and state governments. However, he recognized the need for some kind of environmental regulation, and he had difficulty persuading the state legislature to pass what he considered reasonable antipollution laws. Lawmakers no doubt reflected various interests in the state who were opposed to stronger regulations. Industrialists in urban areas saw them as too expensive and therefore potentially detrimental to their businesses and to the economy of the state. Farmers saw possible limitations on agricultural burning, and ranchers feared restrictions based on the assumption that animals were a major source of water pollution. To the degree that he was unable to overcome such objections to state regulation, Rampton welcomed the EPA. What made him uncomfortable with it was the fact that many of Utah's problems were different in nature from those of other states, and it did not seem to him that the EPA, at first, recognized those differences.[108]

One of the industrial concerns most highly criticized by environmentalists was Geneva Steel in Orem. Utah coal, used by Geneva, contained a much higher content of fluorides than coal from other sources, and fluoride emissions into the atmosphere from Geneva fell on the feed and grass eaten by livestock. As a result, as early as the 1950s Geneva settled claims from farmers in the area that eventually amounted to nearly $450 million. Company officials expressed some concerns over who had brought the lawsuits, claiming that most of them were actually nonresidents of Utah County, "outside agitators," who really wanted Geneva closed.[109]

Charges against Geneva mounted in the 1960s, becoming highly controversial and causing considerable amount of local agitation. Actor Robert Redford, who resided in the Sundance area of Provo Canyon, was one of the most prominent critics.

Geneva responded to the agitation of the 1960s and the establishment of the EPA with major efforts to clean up its manufacturing process. It improved existing equipment, refined many operations, and mounted a campaign to make employees conscious of the nature of the problem and how they could help solve it. By the end of 1970, the company claimed to have improved its air pollution control system by 70 to 80 percent. Furthermore, company officials said, its water pollution problems appeared to be solved for cages of fish at mill outlets showed no contamination effects. The validity of these claims remained to be proved, and Geneva received continuing pressure from the EPA and negative publicity from environmentalists.

Utahns had other running battles with the EPA. In 1974, for example, the federal agency proposed plans for controlling automobile traffic in Salt Lake City as part of its anti-pollution effort. City officials were outraged, claiming that the EPA was interfering in areas that rightly belonged to state and local government. The EPA also attempted to set emission standards for the Kennecott smelter at Magna. Kennecott complained at the severity of the standards and state agencies criticized the EPA for rushing in too fast while the state itself was still establishing its own standards. In 1976, the state legislature passed the Utah Air Conservation Act that set up a committee with legal responsibility to monitor and control air pollution in the state. Although jurisdictional questions were never completely solved, in later years federal, state, and local agencies attempted to work cooperatively to deal with this highly complex problem.

Perhaps the most heated environmental argument of the decade centered around plans for building a power plant, fueled by coal, near the Kaiparowits Plateau in Kane County. Utahns first heard of the proposal in the fall of 1965. Designed to develop Utah coal supplies to provide power for southern California, it would, if successful, integrate Utah even more fully with the regional economy.

Many Utahns, especially in southern Utah, were ecstatic about the idea. The project would clearly become a major boon to a region that was both economically isolated and economically depressed. Utility companies argued that the project would create more than six thousand new jobs and provide many other economic benefits. But environmentalist groups were convinced that the enormous amount of coal dust and smoke produced by the plant would destroy the delicate ecology at Kaiparowits, pollute air in the entire region, and damage some of Utah's most spectacular natural wonders. The proposed site, after all, was only one hundred miles from Bryce Canyon, Grand Canyon, and Capitol Reef National Parks. There were many other objections and the battle raged for ten years. Finally, in 1975, after federal hearings sparked some especially bitter controversy, the project was abandoned.[110]

Health Care and Public Policy

A number of changes affected the delivery of health care in Utah during the 1960s and 1970s. Among them was the introduction of Medicare in 1965. Many doctors and conservative politicians vigorously opposed Medicare on the grounds that it would impose too many regulations, require too much paperwork, invite abuse, and actually diminish the quality of health care. As predicted, paper work increased and there were some abuses, but after a year of operation, with more than sixty thousand senior citizens enrolled, the Utah Medical Association, the Utah Hospital Association, the State Welfare Department, and the Blue Cross–Blue Shield insurance agency (which handled Medicare claims) all agreed that Medicare was working smoothly.[111]

A serious health care dilemma grew as more specialization began to eat away at the number of general practitioners available in small rural communities. Some help came in 1970, when Rocky Mountain Helicopters began to provide emergency service to rural areas. In 1972, LDS Health Services Corporation inaugurated the LDS Rural Health Project in an effort to extend the resources of Provo's Utah Valley Hospital to rural areas. In addition, the increased use of physician's assistants was spurred in 1970 when the medical school at the University of Utah began a program for training them. Graduates from the program eventually found their way not just into rural areas but into various other positions, including Health Maintenance Organizations (HMOs).[112] Also in 1970, the medical school created a Department of Family and Preventive Medicine, which stressed broad training in general medicine, pediatrics, obstetrics, surgery, and psychiatry tailored somewhat toward the needs of more isolated rural communities.

Meanwhile, in the 1970s, the mushrooming cost of both medical care and medical insurance helped stimulate some important trends in the process of delivering medical care. One was an increase in the number of HMOs around the country. Utah's first HMO, Family Health Plan (FHP), was established in 1976. Another significant development was the rise of corporate hospital chains, both for-profit and nonprofit in nature. In Utah, the nonprofit Intermountain Health Care, Inc. (IHC), was formed as a result of a 1974 decision by the LDS Church to divest itself of all fifteen of its hospitals in Utah, Idaho, Arizona, and Wyoming. IHC began to function as an autonomous corporation in 1975 and became the major health care organization in the state.[113]

The most controversial public health issue in this era concerned the fluoridation of community drinking water, which had been turned down by four Utah cities in 1961. The next major battle was fought in Brigham City, where the city council approved adding sodium fluoride to the water supply in 1965. Angry opponents soon obtained enough signatures to have the matter referred to the public in the November elections. At the ballot box, 53 percent of the voters supported the city council.[114]

But fluoridation did not fare well in other areas. In 1972, it was on the ballot in Salt Lake County and was soundly defeated,[115] despite the fact that dentists and physicians argued that it was perhaps the most effective tool available against tooth decay.

Fluoridation became a statewide political issue in 1976, when anti-fluoridationists obtained enough signatures on an initiative petition to put it on the November ballot. Titled the "Freedom from Compulsory Fluoridation and Medication Act," the proposed law would prohibit the state Board of Health from adding fluorides or any other medications to public water supplies. It would also prohibit the addition of these chemicals to a public water supply in any area except when authorized by an initiative petition approved by a majority of the voters of that area.

Opponents of the initiative, including the *Salt Lake Tribune*, argued that, somehow, it would give the state power to dictate how and when local governments could treat their water supplies. The *Tribune* called it "a malignant extension of state power, a precedent-setting intrusion into whatever independence Utah city, town and county governments have left." The *Deseret News*, while taking no position on the controversy, pointed out that the chief defect in the proposal was that the legal language was so restrictive that it could rule out not only fluoridation but also chlorination, which had been used for years to purify the water supply. The *News* also conducted a poll in September 1976 which showed that 42.1 percent of those polled favored the proposal, 50.5 percent opposed it, and 7.4 percent were undecided. However, many voters found the initiative confusing; if they favored fluoridation they were urged to vote against it and if they were opposed to fluoridation they were urged to vote for it. As election day approached, Salt Lake's city-county health department was swamped with calls asking for an explanation of what the proposal said. In the end, voters approved the initiative by a narrow 52 to 48 percent margin.[116]

Fluoridation was adopted in most other states by 1985. That year Utah, with only 2 percent of its people drinking fluoridated water, ranked next to the lowest in the nation.[117]

Continuing Concerns with Law and Order

This was an era of rising crime rates, including violent crimes, brutally symbolized on the national scene by three political assassinations. One of the "black power" movement's most articulate spokesmen, Malcolm X, was shot by unknown killers in 1965. Martin Luther King, Jr., was gunned down by a white assassin in April 1968. Two months later, Robert F. Kennedy, brother of assassinated President John F. Kennedy, was shot to death by a Palestinian who resented his support of Israel.

In Utah, crime rose at an alarming rate, faster than that of the nation as a whole. Between 1960 and 1975, the national crime rate increased by 179.9 percent, while Utah's rose by a disheartening 357 percent.[118] Violent crime jumped by 214.5 percent, while crime against property, including "white collar crimes," rose by 367 percent. At the end of the 1970s, Utahns still seemed to be more safe from violence than residents of most other states. It ranked 37th in the nation in terms of all violent crimes, but, as the authors of an article on the crime rate in 1979 concluded, "Utah may be a safe place to live in terms of one's chances of avoiding homicide, robbery, or assault, but the state has a lower-than-average quality of life in terms of protection of personal property."[119]

Larceny and theft sent Utah's crime rate higher than national and regional averages.[120] Some analysts suggested that part of the explanation might lie in Utah's religious nature, which made its citizens more susceptible to scams because they were more trusting, especially if scam artists claimed membership in or held local leadership positions in the LDS Church.

Not included in the FBI's crime reports was vice and prostitution, yet these, too, were growing problems in Utah's metropolitan centers. In 1967, one national health group portrayed Salt Lake City as "soft" on vice, but throughout this period a number of political squabbles involving Mayor Lee, as well as a few court rulings, kept the city from strengthening its laws against prostitution.[121] Also not included in the reports were child abuse and child neglect, both of which had long-range physical, emotional, and social consequences for victims and perpetrators alike. In 1976, a "valid report" (i.e., a report found to be true) of child abuse or child neglect was received by the Utah Division of Family Services on the average of every two hours and thirty-seven minutes. One in ten cases were abuse (including sexual abuse, mental abuse, and physical injury), while the others were neglect. Moreover, abuse or neglect was the cause of one or two deaths each month. Evidence suggested that there were also numerous unreported cases.

Concerns over law enforcement were exacerbated in 1968 with the mass escape of nine men, including two convicted multiple murderers, from the state penitentiary. All were eventually recaptured.

By 1970 state officials were deeply worried about overcrowding at the prison. In August Governor Rampton decided that it was time to try out a program of halfway houses for prisoners about to be released. He approached legislative leaders as well as the press in an effort to gain support for the idea. "Everyone was enthusiastic," he recalled later, "until it came to the matter of selecting where the halfway house would be located."[122] Over the next few years, a number of halfway houses were set up, but even though the people of the state recognized the need for such facilities, they just were not comfortable with having them in their own backyards.

In 1969, widespread concerns over crime as well as the problems of school dropouts and juvenile delinquency led to the creation of "Women Alert" in the Salt Lake area. This action program was designed to help in law enforcement by watching the courts, promoting better law enforcement legislation, fighting drug abuse, helping the youth in various ways, improving street lighting, and assisting in other such positive activities. Initially more than ten thousand women in Salt Lake City united themselves in the cause. They provided welcome support to the "Crime Alert" program, inaugurated by the Salt Lake City police and the *Deseret News*, that got citizens involved in law enforcement.[123]

A few of Utah's crime sprees made national headlines. One was the daring escapade of Richard Floyd McCoy, a student at Brigham Young University. In 1972, McCoy hijacked an airliner after it had taken off from Los Angeles, forced the pilot to land in San Francisco, collected a $500,000 ransom while the plane was on the ground, and then, while flying over Provo, parachuted out with the money After a massive manhunt in Utah's mountains, McCoy was captured and eventually sentenced to forty-five years in prison. Two years later, he escaped from a maximum-security federal prison and was killed in Virginia during the ensuing manhunt.[124]

The nation also followed the horrific story of Theodore Bundy, the most notorious killer to operate in Utah during this era. In 1974, he murdered several attractive young women in the Seattle area. That fall, he enrolled in law school at the University of Utah. Before the year was over he attempted to abduct another young woman and succeeded in abducting and killing at least three others. He was arrested in August 1975. There was not enough evidence to prove the murders but he was found guilty of aggravated kidnapping and sentenced to confinement in the Utah State Prison. Meanwhile, evidence began to mount that he was also involved in several Colorado murders that had taken place while he lived in Utah. Extradited to Colorado, he escaped from custody there, was recaptured, but then escaped again at the end of December, 1977. He went to Chicago, Atlanta, and then Tallahassee, Florida, changed his name, and went on another binge of violence and murder. Convicted of two Florida murders and one Utah murder, he was finally executed in a Florida electric chair in 1989. Shortly before his execution he confessed to more murders, at least eight, and possibly eleven of which took place in Utah.[125]

Continuing Impact of the LDS Church

The Church of Jesus Christ of Latter-day Saints continued to take an interest in the economic and political affairs of the state and to play a significant role in its economy. Deseret Management Corporation, founded in 1968, became a holding company for church-owned businesses. Investments, such as real estate holdings and the church's stock portfolio, were brought together under Zion's Securities Corporation. About the same time the church also created Bonneville International Corporation, which took over existing church-owned broadcasting facilities and also purchased companies in key cities around the nation. Eventually Bonneville began producing films as well as television and audio productions and stood at the center of the church's worldwide media and broadcasting activities.

Politically, the turmoil over civil rights and Vietnam stimulated the creation of a new church Special Affairs Committee in 1974. It consisted, at first, of apostles Gordon B. Hinckley, James E. Faust, David B. Haight, and Neal A. Maxwell, all of whom were highly skilled and knowledgeable in dealing with public issues. The committee examined such issues as the MX missile, the effect of land policy on the church, the Central Utah Project, and the Indian Child Welfare Act of 1976, all of which had possible consequences for church policy and programs. While this committee was by no means overt in using church influence on the issues, it kept its leaders informed on their possible consequences for the church.

Other Political Issues, 1965–76

Calvin Rampton was a remarkably astute and well-balanced political leader. He warmed up to the populace easily, and made friends among people of both parties. Nevertheless, he disliked what he considered extremes in the Republican party, and sometimes found himself seriously at odds with certain Republican leaders. One was Cache County's Franklin Gunnell, who, much to Rampton's dismay, became speaker of Utah's House of Representatives in 1967. The two disliked each other with a passion. However, Rampton wisely modified his budget message to the legislature that year, trimming much of what he really wanted. For the most part, lawmakers went along with his proposals. Not even the Gunnell faction found much to complain about.[126]

Despite his quarrels with Gunnell, Rampton genuinely respected and got along well with many other Republicans, which helped account for his continued success even though Republicans controlled the legislature throughout most of his administration. He expressed particular admiration for Wallace Gardner, state senator from Utah County and chairman of the Joint Appropriations Committee. The two worked well together. He also appreciated, and felt dependent upon, other Republican senators, including Warren Pugh, Hughes Brockbank, and Karl N. Snow, for their lack of unbending partisanship.[127]

Among the seemingly perennial political issues in Utah was Sunday closing of business. Governor Clyde had vetoed a Sunday closing law in 1959, but in 1967 another one appeared in the legislature. Strongly supported by the LDS Church, it was the most controversial bill of the session. As expected, the two major newspapers were on opposite sides of the fence, and the debate in the legislature was intense. The bill passed, and Rampton was faced with a bitter dilemma over whether to sign or veto it. Personally, he liked the idea of stores closing on Sunday, and it was clear that most Utahns favored the law. He also received several personal calls from Mormon leaders, including general authorities, urging him to sign it, even though they did not specifically use religious teachings in their reasoning. Nevertheless, Rampton did not believe it proper for the state to intervene in such matters and he had strong constitutional reservations about the bill. After listening to all sides, he finally decided, as his Republican predecessor had, to veto it. Among his objections were its inequities. Under the bill, he observed in his lengthy veto message, magazine stores could stay open, but bookstores could not; shops associated with recreational promotion, such as pro-shops, could stay open, but sporting-goods stores could not; service stations could stay open and hire mechanics to perform auto repairs, but auto repair shops must close. He also believed the bill to be unconstitutional. But despite his reasoning, Rampton was the object of bitter criticism by many people, including the editors of the *Deseret News*, for his veto.[128]

The Sunday closing forces tried again, this time during the 1970 budget session of the legislature. As one of the few non-budget items on the calendar, lawmakers passed a "Common Day of Rest Act" that, in effect, required most Utah businesses to close either on Sunday or Saturday. According to Rampton, the new law met all the objections he raised against the 1967 bill, but still he did not like it. Caught in the trap of not having any constitutional objections and yet not wanting to sign the law, he let it become law without his signature.[129] However, the bill was soon tested in the courts, and in April 1971, a unanimous Utah Supreme Court held it to be unconstitutional. The measure, said the court, constituted "one of those areas where the state seeks to regulate private conduct" and was "so vague a person of ordinary intelligence could only guess at its meaning."[130] That decision put the issue permanently to rest.

Another seemingly perennial issue was liquor-by-the-drink. It came up again in 1968 after proponents obtained nearly seventy thousand signatures in order to have it placed on the November ballot as an initiative. The proposed law was a local-option measure that would permit state-controlled sale of alcoholic beverages as individual drinks in licensed hotels, resorts, nonprofit private clubs, and certain restaurant facilities. Proponents argued that the law would attract business and conventions as well as provide incentives to those who wanted to promote tourism.[131] Opponents argued that passing the initiative would contribute to greater crime and drunkenness in the state and to a deterioration in the quality of life. The controversy was extremely heated, with the *Deseret News* and the *Salt Lake Tribune* opposing each other more vehemently than they had on any issue since statehood.[132] Governor Rampton did not take sides, claiming to be personally indifferent. At the polls, the initiative was defeated by almost a two-to-one margin.

But the liquor issue would not die. Continuing agitation over the enforceability of the existing liquor statute led the legislature, in 1969, to pass two controversial measures designed to tighten enforcement as well as loosen a few restrictions. The new legislation permitted the sale of liquor in state stores located in specially licensed restaurants and private clubs, though it placed severe restrictions on the location of such clubs. It also provided stronger means and more funding for the "prevention, detection or control" of liquor law violators. Governor Rampton signed the new legislation on March 10.[133]

Another extremely volatile issue was land use planning. Communities nationwide faced increasingly serious problems related to growing population densities, pollution, deterioration of neighborhoods, and the possible disappearance, or diminution, of parks and recreational facilities. State legislatures and city and county governments around the nation took great pains to reevaluate zoning regulations in order to more effectively regulate the use of the remaining lands and control the unplanned, often environmentally detrimental, development of housing and business complexes.

In that spirit, Governor Rampton was anxious to strengthen Utah's laws in order to require cities to review community development more carefully. The Utah Land Use Act of 1974 did just that. The law authorized a Land Use Commission to establish guidelines and to review local plans. It required cities and counties to begin their own planning, but it also allowed them wide latitude in formulating their plans. It was a compromise between the wishes of ardent land use planners on the one hand and, on the other, those of many real estate developers who wanted no restrictions at all. As a *Salt Lake Tribune* editorial observed, it was designed to make certain that Utah's land was used wisely, that airports were not built in the wrong places, that housing was not constructed on locations better suited for industry, and that cities could continue to provide good, clean drinking water.[134] The new commission was primarily an educational body, with the responsibility of making recommendations to the state legislature and to local governments but with no enforcement authority.

Despite the mildness of the new law, and despite the fact that Utah had a strong historical tradition of land use planning dating back to Brigham Young and the pioneers, angry special interests succeeded in getting the law placed on the November ballot as a referendum. The debate was intense. Those supporting the law tried to make it clear that land use planning was essential but that the new law allowed it to take place at the "lowest possible level of government." Supporters included Congressman Gunn McKay, Salt Lake City Mayor Jake Garn, and Governor Rampton, who, along with other political leaders were particularly concerned that rejecting the new legislation could only open the door to more federal intervention with its attendant bureaucracy and even stronger regulation. Opponents included the John Birch Society and other politically conservative groups. In addition, the real estate industry, which originally supported the compromise measures that finally were enacted, made a last-minute switch to the opposition. These groups argued that land use planning was an unconstitutional invasion of the rights of property owners. This was just not true, Rampton fired back, for "the right to zone is as old as the country itself. as fundamental as the Bill of Rights," and the act in no way infringed on local planning and zoning authority.[135] Nevertheless, the referendum was roundly defeated, thus nullifying the bill. This defeat, said Rampton, "was the biggest disappointment that I had in my twelve years as governor."[136] As one political historian has observed, "those two great urban and rural planners—Joseph Smith and Brigham Young—would have been dismayed to see Utah's people trade quality for quantity."[137]

Politics and Elections, 1966–76

Election patterns during the Rampton years showed that Utahns retained their generally conservative political orientation. In 1966, Republicans won a stunning victory at the polls, giving them an overwhelming majority in the state legislature and in most county governments. They also returned Republican incumbent Laurence J. Burton to the US House of Representatives and, in the Second Congressional District, replaced David S. King with former Republican Congressman Sherman P. Lloyd.[138] The Republican party also gained in the national elections that year, winning new seats in both houses of Congress but not enough to gain control.

Governor Rampton was reelected in both 1968 and 1972. In 1968, he received 68.7 percent of the vote, as compared with Republican contender Carl W. Buehner's 31.3 percent. This was clear evidence that even Utah's conservative voters did not see Rampton as a rigid partisan. They saw him as a man of political balance and astuteness, and they voted for the man rather than the party.

This did not mean that the campaign was mild or that Rampton took the voters for granted. Rampton feared that Buehner would make a particularly good showing because of his status as a former member of the LDS Church's Presiding Bishopric. But he also believed that he could overcome Buehner's advantage in their public debates. In their first direct confrontation, Rampton reminded Buehner of his promise during the primaries that he would reduce state expenditures by 30 percent and then asked what he would cut. Buehner responded that he had made no such promise, whereupon Rampton produced a tape recording of the speech. This clearly embarrassed Buehner and, in effect, brought an end to the debates. Buehner's campaign committee canceled the rest.

The remainder of the campaign was heated and sometimes vicious, even though it was through no direct fault of Buehner's. Never before nor since, Rampton recalled later, was he subjected to such malicious underground rumors. Die-hard anti-Rampton forces, not controlled by Buehner, spread totally false gossip, including claims that Rampton and Lucybeth were alcoholics, that Rampton was once divorced, and that the two were having domestic problems. Thoroughly disgusted, Rampton finally wrote to N. Eldon Tanner of the LDS First Presidency, suggesting that Buehner's former ecclesiastical position seemed to give credence to these tactics. Tanner responded that he and other general authorities were disturbed at the tone of the campaign and would do what they could to improve it. The situation did improve, but what probably hurt Buehner most was his refusal to meet Rampton in any more debates. As Rampton later noted, "We made all we could of this, and stated what was already beginning to appear to people—that Buehner had no concept of what state government was about or what the issues were in the campaign."[139]

Rampton seemed almost the lone Democrat in a sea of Republicans, but voters also reelected Democrat Clyde Miller as secretary of state. This was tremendously important to Rampton, for Miller was also one of his staunch supporters on the three-man state board of examiners. Ironically, Democratic attorney general Phil Hansen, also a member of the board, had opposed nearly everything the governor wanted to do. Hansen was replaced in 1968 by Republican Vernon Romney, who, for the next eight years, was an even greater thorn in the governor's side.[140]

In Utah's 1968 Congressional races, Wallace F. Bennett won his fourth, and final, term in the US Senate, defeating Rampton's close friend Milton L. Weilenman. Utah's two Republicans in the House of Representatives, Burton and Lloyd, also retained their seats.

As the 1968 presidential campaign approached, the Democratic party was badly divided over President Johnson's conduct of the Vietnam War. Senator Eugene McCarthy and Robert F. Kennedy, both outspoken opponents of the war, each announced that they would challenge the president for the nomination. But, at the end of March, Johnson outlined plans for ending the war and announced that he would neither seek nor accept the nomination for another term. This was the only way he could remove himself from the politics of the war in his effort to find a solution. This opened the way for Vice President Hubert Humphrey, who quickly threw his own hat into the ring. The three-way contest was cut short in June when Kennedy was shot and killed just after a dramatic victory in the California presidential primary. At the Democratic convention in Chicago, Humphrey won the nomination easily, but the occasion was marred by violence outside the convention hall. Thousands of radical anti-war protestors had descended on the city, hoping to goad the police into a violent response and gain national publicity. They did just that, and the nationally televised images of Chicago police clubbing protestors and bystanders alike, in an effort to maintain law and order, did little to promote the image of the Democratic party as the party of peace and order.

Republicans nominated Richard M. Nixon, who made the most of the Democratic dilemma by promising to make America free from domestic violence and also by attacking the "Great Society." Nixon appealed to many conservatives and white southerners when he asserted that the public schools were for education, not integration. The American Independent Party, meanwhile, nominated George C. Wallace, former segregationist governor of Alabama, whose fiery rhetoric against integrationists, radicals and liberals of all sorts, and even welfare mothers, appealed to many working-class men and women.

Early in the year, the Wallace candidacy took on a special interest for Utahns, who heard rumors that LDS apostle Ezra Taft Benson, former secretary of agriculture and an outspoken critic of communism and radical liberalism, might become Wallace's running mate. The rumor has some basis in fact. As early as February, Wallace had contacted President David O. McKay, asking him to give Benson permission to become a vice-presidential candidate. Elder Benson seriously considered the possibility of running, but he would not do so with President McKay's approval. Apparently feeling that it was more important for Benson to continue in his ecclesiastical role, and not wanting any implied church endorsement of partisan political activity, President McKay advised against the move and Elder Benson declined the invitation.

All three candidates appeared in Utah during the campaign and spoke in the Salt Lake Tabernacle. Many national issues weighed heavily on the minds of the voters, but the deteriorating and increasingly unpopular war in Vietnam seemed uppermost. Nixon promised, if elected, to bring the war to an honorable end. Hubert Humphrey appeared too closely tied to the Johnson administration, which was blamed for escalating the war, but his visit to Utah was a kind of turning point in his public image. When he appeared in the Tabernacle he finally told a nationwide audience that he favored a halt to the bombing of North Vietnam. His fortunes began to improve at that point, but it was too little too late. Nixon won the election with a remarkably narrow popular majority, 43 percent of the vote compared to Humphrey's 42.7 percent and Wallace's 13.5 percent. Nixon, however, received a decisive 301 electoral votes to Humphrey's 191 and Wallace's 46.

Utahns, more conservative than the nation, gave Nixon their electoral votes by a 54.6 percent margin: Humphrey received 39 percent and Wallace 6.4 percent.

In Utah's 1970 Congressional campaign, Congressman Laurence J. Burton tried to unseat Senator Frank Moss, who was running for a third term. The election had national significance, for during the campaign President Nixon devoted most of his personal efforts toward winning control of the Senate. On July 24, Pioneer Day, Nixon was in Utah on what was billed as a non-political visit, but after starting out as a non-partisan address his speech in the Tabernacle became an obvious anti-Moss and pro-Burton campaign speech. Governor Rampton was particularly upset by Nixon's appearance in the Tabernacle, because the church's general authorities were seated on the stand and the Tabernacle Choir provided the music, all of which seemed to lend church support to the political intent of the speech. However, Rampton thought it was rather humorous that as soon as Nixon shifted to the political harangue, the presidential seal hanging on the podium fell to the floor.[141]

On the Saturday evening before the election, Nixon was back in town, attacking Moss and other Democrats and telling voters that he needed Burton in Congress.[142] Moss, nevertheless, won with a 57 percent majority. Voters still had confidence that he was working in Utah's best interest. In the same election, Democrat Gunn McKay defeated Richard Richards, who was trying to take Burton's First District seat in the House of Representatives, and the Second District returned Lloyd.[143]

Nationally, despite Nixon's all-out efforts to win control of the Senate, the Democrats retained control of Congress.In Utah, much to Rampton's delight, the Democrats regained control of the House of Representatives, by a substantial margin, and increased their strength in the Senate.

In 1971, an important local election brought E. J. (Jake) Garn into the mayor's seat in Salt Lake City. Handpicked to run by his predecessor, J. Bracken Lee, Garn thus began an illustrious political career. He was a popular and effective mayor, much more open to innovation than Lee. He brought Salt Lake City into the National League of Cities, through which many major cities pooled their

Image 4.5: US Senator Orrin G. Hatch. In 1976 he defeated three-term incumbent Frank E. Moss. A moderate conservative Republican, he was subsequently re-elected six times and became the longest-serving Senator in Utah history. Used by permission, Utah State Historical Society, all rights reserved.

resources and talents to find solutions to common problems, and he successfully promoted efforts to modernize city government. After serving as mayor for less than three years, he resigned to run for the US Senate.

Early in 1972, Governor Rampton announced his intention to run for an unprecedented third term. He was nominated without opposition by his party, but about two weeks after the convention he publicly announced that there were seven planks in the Democratic platform that he did not support. This brought a considerable amount of carping from the liberal wing of the party, but it demonstrated once again his political independence and balance. Utah voters liked that. Republicans, meanwhile, nominated Salt Lake businessman Nicholas L. Strike.

As in the previous gubernatorial campaign, a series of debates were scheduled. At one point Rampton depicted his opponent as not properly briefed and totally unprepared. Strike made a political blunder, for example, when he criticized Rampton for completing a stretch of highway I-70 in southern Utah before I-80 was finished. There was nobody in southern Utah but jackrabbits, Strike blurted, which immediately alienated one of the strongest Republican sections of the state.[144] In the end it was an easy victory for Rampton—69.7 percent to 30.3 percent.

Utah's Democratic candidates for Congress also did well in 1972. Gunn McKay retained his seat, while Wayne Owens upset Republican Sherman P. Lloyd. Owens, a relative newcomer to Utah politics, was the western states coordinator for Robert F. Kennedy's presidential campaign in 1968 and administrative assistant to Senator Edward Kennedy from 1969 to 1971. For the next year he served as administrative assistant to Senator Frank E. Moss. To overcome his lack of personal identity with Utah voters, Owens conducted a unique campaign by walking through every county of the state, logging over 1,200 miles. He stunned the Republicans by attracting 54.4 percent of the vote in the Second Congressional District. In other Utah elections, however, the Republicans retained their hold on the state Senate and regained control of the House.

In the 1972 presidential campaign, the American people gave Nixon 60.7 percent of the popular vote and 520 electoral votes. Democratic challenger George S. McGovern simply had no chance against Nixon's foreign policy record, which included an amazing breakthrough in relations with China, "détente" with the Soviet Union, and the fact that there seemed to be progress toward disengaging in Vietnam. Utahns gave Nixon 67.6 percent of their votes. He was riding high, but within a year, as a result of the Watergate scandal, his ratings in both Utah and the nation plummeted.

One citizen of Utah, Jean Westwood, became particularly prominent during the campaign. An active Democrat since the 1950s, in 1972 she became vice-chair of the national McGovern-for-President Committee, and when he received the nomination he named her as chair of the Democratic National Committee. She resigned under pressure at the end of the year, but remained highly visible in Democratic politics.

In 1974, encouraged by his upset victory over Lloyd two years earlier, Wayne Owens announced his bid for the United States Senate and won the Democratic nomination. With the venerable Wallace F. Bennett retiring after twenty-four years, Democrats saw this as their best chance in decades to have two members of their party in the Senate. But they did not reckon with Salt Lake City's Mayor Jake Garn, who obtained the Republican nomination and ultimately won the election. Garn's campaign was given an important boost with the visit to Utah of President Gerald Ford just three days before the election. Garn captured 53.2 percent of the votes, compared with Owens's 46.8. At age forty-two, Garn was the youngest senator yet to be elected from Utah.

In the races for the House of Representatives, Gunn McKay retained his seat with 63 percent of the First Congressional District vote, while Democrat Allen T. Howe, a Salt Lake City attorney and former administrative assistant to Rampton, upset Salt Lake City Commissioner Stephen Harmsen by a narrow margin of 51 percent. It was a good election year for the Democrats, who also gained control of both houses of the Utah legislature for the first time since Rampton's election ten years earlier.

The 1976 election was marred by the embarrassment that came to the Democratic party when Congressman Howe was arrested in June and convicted in July on a charge of soliciting sex from a Salt Lake City prostitute. Throughout the period of the trial, there was a heated debate over whether Howe should withdraw as the party candidate. The party withdrew its official support, but Howe decided to stay in the race anyway. The result was a victory for Republican newcomer Dan Marriott, who took 53.5 percent of the votes compared to 38.8 percent for Howe. In the First Congressional District, Gunn McKay won an impressive 58.1 percent victory over Republican ultraconservative Joe Ferguson.

In the presidential campaign, the aftermath of the Watergate scandal and Gerald Ford's inability to deal effectively with national economic and energy problems made it seem as if almost any Democratic opponent was a near shoein. It was not quite that easy, however. Jimmy Carter garnered only 50.1 percent of the popular vote, even though he won 489 of the electoral votes compared with Ford's 240. Utahns thought better of Ford, giving him their electoral votes by a majority of 62.3 percent.

In the race for the Senate, it appeared that Frank Moss had been living on borrowed time. Elected three times, sometimes helped by splits in the Republican party, Moss was unable to capitalize on his seniority, which, he argued, gave Utah an investment in keeping him in Washington. Young (age forty-two), highly conservative Orrin Hatch, who had only recently moved from Pennsylvania to Utah, mounted an effective challenge, convincing 54.5 percent of the voters that he could better represent them.

The brightest spot for the Democrats that year was the race for governor. After Rampton announced that he would not seek a fourth term, the party nominated Scott M. Matheson, an attorney for the Union Pacific Railroad. His opponent was Attorney General Vernon B. Romney. Rampton, of course, was active in the campaign, praising Matheson as having both greater ability and greater intellectual capacity than his opponent. Matheson won with 53.1 percent of the votes.

Much like Rampton, Matheson cultivated an image of political balance and lack of party fanaticism. Unlike his predecessor, he entered the state house with a divided legislature. In the election, Democrats retained control of the Senate but lost to the Republicans in the House of Representative. To be effective as governor,

Matheson would need to maintain a delicate political balance and good relations with leaders of both parties.

The 1976 election was noteworthy for at least one more significant reason. That year a black minister from Ogden, Reverend Robert Harris, and a Hispanic, John Ulibarri, became the first of their races to be elected to the state legislature.

Reflections

Almost any period in history may be characterized as a time of change, but the period of the Rampton administration was a time of particularly fundamental and far-reaching change for Utah. Administratively, the executive branch of government was simplified. Constitutionally, the Gateway Amendment paved the way for a complete restructuring, a few years later, of several key articles in the state constitution and, eventually, some fundamental changes in the very nature of state government. Changes in philosophy and administration led to significant developments in higher education, particularly the emergence of the comprehensive community college. The "Great Society" brought new, and often unwelcome, federal incursions in the affairs of the state, but it also brought some worthwhile programs that helped increase the well-being of Utah's underprivileged. During this period, Utah experienced an economic resurgence sparked by new business, industrial parks, and an increase in tourism. Some parts of the state also began an ongoing process of urban renewal. Utah joined the rest of the nation in finally approving far-reaching civil rights legislation and in passing laws to improve the legal status of women, even though, in refusing to ratify the ERA, it helped keep that controversial amendment from becoming part of the US Constitution. There were numerous political controversies, some of them bitter, many problems still hung over the state, and frustrating new challenges were emerging. But on the whole, these were twelve years of positive change that justified the optimism with which Rampton assumed office in 1965.

On another note, the interparty strife, the bitterness that sometimes broke out between members of different parties, the friction generated by the ERA, the sometimes extreme rhetoric poured out in the battle over issues such as Sunday closing or liquor-by-the-drink, and the fervent disagreement over numerous other national and local issues—all these issues caused Utahns extreme discomfort. But these things were no more nor less than what was natural in the kind of democratic society that Utahns deeply cherished. In looking back over his own political wars, Rampton made a telling comment that once again illustrated his political astuteness and at the same time reflected his continuing faith in the democratic form of government, as imperfect as it is:

> I learned as a political figure what I already knew as a trial lawyer—you should not underestimate the average juror or the average voter. If you have a good cause and present it fairly, you would be listened to and will receive a fair verdict. However, if you attempt to deceive jurors or citizens or patronize them, your cause is certain to be lost.
>
> I believe that government is generally somewhat less efficient than business and industry. This is because democracy is inherently less efficient. The division of powers concept found in government, which is necessary for the preservation of our freedoms, often makes government cumbersome—but it also tends to guard against abuses. I believe that next to the ministry, government service, and particularly service in elective offices, offers the greatest opportunity for public service available to our people. I tell my children and my grandchildren that they owe it to themselves and to their neighbors to be involved in public affairs. Those who disdain such involvement are doing a disservice to our society.[145]

Notes

1. Calvin L. Rampton, *As I Recall*, ed. Floyd A. O'Neil and Gregory C. Thompson (Salt Lake City: University of Utah Press, 1989), 119–20.
2. See PeterWiley and Robert Gottlieb, *Empires in the Sun: The Rise of the New American West* (New York: G. P. Putnam's Sons, 1982), section entitled "The Dependent Commonwealth," 141–50. Economic historian James L. Clayton concluded in 1978: "If one word had to be chosen to summarize the economic history of Utah for the past thirty years, a good choice would be *dependency*," although he also noted some

trends away from dependency. James L. Clayton, "Contemporary Economic Developments," in *Utah's History*, ed. Richard D. Poll, Thomas G. Alexander, Eugene E. Campbell, David E. Miller (Logan, UT: Utah State University Press, 1989), 542.

3. M. DeMar Teuscher, "Rampton Takes Oath—Utah's 11th Governor," *Deseret News*, January 4, 1965, A6.
4. For a review of the address, see M. DeMar Teuscher, "Rampton Maps Goals for Utah Legislature," *Deseret News*, January 12, 1965, A1.
5. Rampton, *As I Recall*, 135.
6. Ibid., 134. The governor's address was generally well received. The *Salt Lake Tribune* and *Deseret News* were both highly supportive. The only major criticism came from the *News*, which was concerned with his failure to recommend teacher incentives and an extended school year, and his proposal for repeal of the right-to-work law. "Big Blueprint for Utah," *Deseret News*, January 13, 1965, A22.
7. Rampton, *As I Recall*, 130–31. Some administrators apparently continued to lobby anyway, though much more subtly. As one of them later quipped to Rod Julander, "He can't deny me the constitutional right to talk to my legislator." Rod Julander, telephone interview by James B. Allen, January 25, 1996, notes in James B. Allen papers, L. Tom Perry Special Collections, Harold B. Lee Library, Brigham Young University. Mr. Julander is professor of political science at Weber State University.
8. It was so named after the commission headed by Herbert Hoover, under the Truman administration, that recommended changes in the federal bureaucracy.
9. Rampton, *As I Recall*, 147.
10. Ibid., 151–52.
11. Ibid. 253–54.
12. Julander interview.
13. "Evolving Constitutions," *Salt Lake Tribune*, editorial, June 11, 1972, A22.
14. Rampton, *As I Recall*, 168.
15. Ibid., 170–71.
16. "Confrontation: 'Gateway,' Pro, Con," *Salt Lake Tribune*, September 27, 1970, B1.
17. "Utah Constitution 'Not Sacred,'" *Deseret News*, May 12, 1972, B1; "BYU Hails Governor as Administrator of Year," *Salt Lake Tribune*, May 12, 1972, B1; text of N. Eldon's Tanner's statement regarding the constitution, in James B. Allen papers, L. Tom Perry Special Collections, Harold B. Lee Library, Brigham Young University.
18. Maxwell noted that thirty-one states already had legislative auditors and thirty-seven had legislative legal counsels. Neal A. Maxwell in "Common Carrier," in *Salt Lake Tribune*, November 5, 1972.
19. Ibid.
20. Proposition 2 allowed the courts to deny bail to suspects already at liberty on bail in connection with previous criminal charges. Proposition 3 did away with the requirement that first- and second-class cities constitute a single school district.
21. There is no available history of Utah's state government, yet such a history is badly needed. As indicated here and in chapter 5, the Constitutional Revision Commission was instrumental in bringing about many highly important changes. Some of the information presented here and in chapter 5 was obtained from Karl N. Snow, interview by James B. Allen, February 5, 1996, notes in James B. Allen papers, L. Tom Perry Special Collections, Harold B. Lee Library, Brigham Young University. For a thorough look at the Constitution itself as it stood in 1998, including

discussions of the various amendments, see Jean Bickmore White, *The Utah State Constitution: A Reference Guide* (Greenwood Press: Westport, Connecticut, 1998).

22. Weilenman remained in that position beyond the Rampton years. When his and other agencies, including the Tourist and Publicity Council, were combined under the Department of Developmental Services, Weilenman became head of the new agency.
23. "Utah's Economy: A Further Outlook," *Salt Lake Tribune*, January 9, 1966, C1, 3.
24. Actually, the term "Rampton's Raiders" was originally coined by his wife, Lucybeth, to describe those who helped in his campaign for the Democratic nomination in the 1962 US Senate race. Julander interview.
25. "Utah Governor Turns Tables in Industry Speech," *The Daily Times* (New Philadelphia, Ohio), February 13, 1968, 3.
26. "Tour Nears to Lure New Firms," *Salt Lake Tribune*, February 8, 1968, D6; "Utahns Urged To Prospect For Industry," ibid., February 14, B1; "'Raiders' Lay Groundwork for New Industry," ibid., February 16, 1968, A14. "Ohio Leaders Get 'Hard Sell' From Rampton," *Daily Herald* (Provo, UT), February 14, 1968, 5.
27. Rampton, *As I Recall*, 156.
28. Ibid., 170.
29. See "Industrial Parks" in Deon C. Greer, et al., *Atlas of Utah* (Ogden, UT, and Provo, UT: Weber State College and BYU Press, 1981) 236–37; Mark E. Linford, "Industrial Park Growth in Utah," *Utah Economic and Business Review* 37 (February 1977):1-5.
30. "Banks and Savings and Loan Associations" in Greer, et al., *Atlas of Utah*, 227.
31. Retail trade employed by far the largest number. See Howard W. Price, "Retailing and Wholesaling in Utah, *Utah Economic and Business Review* 26 (January 1966): 9–13, 16; (Salt Lake City: Bureau of Economic and Business Research, David Eccles School of Business, University of Utah, 1993), 393.
32. See Bruce A. Kirchhoff, "The Electronics Industry in Utah," *Utah Economic and Business Review* 30 (September–October 1970): n.p.
33. *Statistical Abstract of Utah 1993*, 386–88, 302.
34. Ibid., 379.
35. Rampton, *As I Recall*, 197, 214.
36. For an analysis by two prominent geographers of developments in Washington County in this era, see Lowell C. Bennion and Merrill K. Ridd, "Utah's Dynamic Dixie: Satellite of Salt Lake, Las Vegas, or Los Angeles?" *Utah Historical Quarterly* 47 (Summer 1979): 311–27.
37. See Iver E. Bradley, "Census of Population, 1970," *Utah Economic and Business Review* 31 (January 1971): 1-13; Elroy Nelson and Osmond S. Harline, *Utah's Changing Economic Patterns 1964* (Salt Lake City: University of Utah Press, 1964), passim; *1969 Statistical Abstract of Utah*, passim; *Statistical Abstract of Utah 1993*, passim.
38. Glen M. Leonard, *A History of Davis County* (Salt Lake City: Utah State Historical Society, 1999), 360; Utah Foundation, "*Research Briefs*," June 17, 1970.
39. See a full discussion of the Federal Highway Act of 1973 and its consequences for Utah in "Utah and the Federal Highway Act of 1973," Utah Foundation, *Research Report* (October 1973), 163–66.
40. For full discussions of these and related developments, see "1975 Highway Problems–Utah and the Nation," Utah Foundation, *Research Report* (May 1975), 239–

42; "Problems Confronting Utah's Highway Program," Utah Foundation, *Research Report* (July 1976), 25–28.

41. Governor Calvin L. Rampton, address to the Business Preview Conference, January 3, 1966, *Utah Economic and Business Review* 26 (January 1966), 3.
42. David Wetzel, "Utah's Visitors 1965," *Utah Economic and Business Review* 26 (September 1966): 1, 4–7.
43. John M. Bagley, "Utah Ski Industry Needs Air Carrier Support," *Utah Economic and Business Review* 26 (June 1966): 1–5.
44. "Utah's Date with History—1969," pamphlet printed by the Golden Spike Centennial Commission, n.p.
45. "Travel Tops Record in Utah Parks," *Salt Lake Tribune*, January 28, 1970, 20.
46. "7 Million Tour Utah in Year, Council Notes," *Salt Lake Tribune*, September 5, 1970, 17.
47. While there was disagreement over the effectiveness of the sanctions themselves, school administrators tended to believe that they had helped. Howard J. Carroll, "Sanctions Work in Utah," *Michigan Educational Journal* (May 1965): 8–9, 74.
48. Rampton, *As I Recall*, 157–58.
49. David E. Nelson, *Utah Educational Quality Indicators*, No. 3 in *How Good are Utah Public Schools?* series (Salt Lake City: Utah State Board of Education, 1974), 93–95, 100–101.
50. "But What about Utah's Vital 80%?" *1970 Annual Report, Utah State Advisory Council for Vocational and Technical Education* (Salt Lake City: January 1971).
51. State Superintendent of Public Instruction, *Utah School Report, 1969–70* (Salt Lake City: Utah State Department of Public Instruction, 1970).
52. By 1977, the amount of money available for the handicapped from federal, state, and local funds was more than 10 percent more per student than that available for regular students. Utah Legislature, Handicapped Children's Research Team, "Utah Schools Special Education Study: A Report to the Education Study Committee of the Utah State Legislature" (Salt Lake City, 1977?), 1–2, 27.
53. "Survey of Attitudes of Teenagers Regarding Drugs," *Utah Educational Review* 62 (March–April 1969), 21.
54. "Aids, Guidelines to Boost Drug Abuse Education," *Salt Lake Tribune*, February 5, 1970, B8.
55. For a full discussion, see *A Review of the Federal and State Funded Utah Drug Abuse Education Project, 1970–1976* (Salt Lake City: State Board of Education, 1976).
56. "Utah's Junior College Program," Utah Foundation, *Research Report* (October 1965), 268.
57. See Jay L. Nelson, *The First Thirty Years: A History of Utah Technical College* (Salt Lake City: Utah Technical College at Salt Lake, 1982); John S. McCormick, "Salt Lake Community College," in *Utah History Encyclopedia*, ed. Allen Kent Powell (Salt Lake City: University of Utah Press, 1994), 482–83.
58. See Wilson W. Sorenson, *A Miracle in Utah Valley: The Story of Utah Technical College 1941–1982* (Provo: Utah Technical College at Provo, 1985); Dennis Farnsworth, "Utah Valley Community College," in *Utah History Encyclopedia*, ed. Powell, 606–7.
59. This change in status was authorized by the legislature in February 2007.

60. Michael Petersen, "The College of Eastern Utah," in *Utah History Encyclopedia*, ed. Powell, 105
61. See *Higher Education in Utah: Facts for Master Planning for the Decade Ahead* (Salt Lake City: Utah Coordinating Council of Higher Education, 1967).
62. Utah Coordinating Council of Higher Education, *News of Higher Education* 1 (June 1968).
63. Edward L. Christensen, *Snow College Historical Highlights: The First 100 Years* (Ephraim, UT: Snow College, 1988), 112–113.
64. This arrangement was challenged by Rampton, who argued that it was unconstitutional to allow the legislature to make appointments because the Utah Constitution gave the governor such appointive responsibility. In April the Utah State Supreme Court refused to accept jurisdiction in the case, which sent it to the Third District Court. On June 20, 1969, the federal court ruled against the governor. "Rampton's School Suit Moves to Lower Court," *Salt Lake Tribune*, April 29,1969, 26; "Rampton Loses Higher Board Makeup Action," ibid., June 21, 1969, 21. For an overview of efforts to create a single governing board, see Mary Jane Stewart Hair, "History of the Efforts to Coordinate Higher Education in Utah" (Ph.D. dissertation, University of Utah, 1974).
65. Rampton, *As I Recall*, 140.
66. "Urban Renewal Needed, Civic Leaders Declare," *Salt Lake Tribune*, August 16, 1965, 19.
67. "Utah Initiates First Civil Rights Law," *Salt Lake Tribune*, February 19, A3; "Utah's Civil Rights Laws–Courageous or Minimal?"ibid., March 13, 1965, 5.
68. "NAACP Claims LDS Bias," *Salt Lake Tribune*, July 2, 1965, 4B; "Negro Rally Acts to Censor LDS Policies," ibid., July 4, 1965, A3.
69. The figure jumped to 54.4 percent by 1984. *Women in Utah's Labor Force 1950–1980* (Salt Lake City: Utah Department of Employment Security, Labor Market Information Services Section, 1981), 13–15; Lecia Parks, *Hard at Work: Women in the Utah Labor Force* (Salt Lake City: Labor Market Information Services, Utah Department of Employment Security, 1985), 4. See also Howard M. Bahr, "The Declining Distinctiveness of Utah's Working Women," *BYU Studies* 10 (Summer 1979): 525–43.
70. Donald L. Hughes, "Aspirations and Goals of 1976 Utah Women Educators for Public School Administration" (Ed.D. dissertation, Brigham Young University, 1976), 126–28.
71. See Lecia Parks Langston, *Hard at Work: Women in the Utah Labor Force* (Salt Lake City: Labor Market Information Services, Utah Department of Employment Security, 1989), for a detailed analysis of all the available data. This summary is based on that source..
72. *Women in Utah's Labor Force*, 1950–1980, 29–31.
73. David Walden,"Utah's Health Care Revolution: Pluralism and Professionalization Since World War II" (master's thesis, Brigham Young University, 1989), 20–21.
74. Ibid., 7.
75. Utah Department of Employment Security, *Women in the Labor Force, 1950–1980* (Salt Lake City: Utah Department of Employment Security, 1981), 1. See also Langston, *Hard at Work* (1989), passim.
76. Maureen Ursenbach Beecher and Kathryn L. MacKay, "Women in Twentieth Century Utah," in *Utah's History*, ed. Poll, et al., 569.
77. Elaine Jarvik, "Last on the List," *Deseret News*, December 28, 1990, C1.

78. Langston, *Hard at Work* (1989), 3.
79. This booklet is available in libraries. The exact publication date is not clear.
80. Beecher and McKay, "Women in Twentieth Century Utah," 566–67. Among the more prominent in the 1960s were the Women's Democratic Club, the Republican Women's Club, the Utah Federation of Women's Clubs (which included five thousand members in 150 clubs around the state), Utah Federation of Business and Professional Women's Clubs, the American Association of University Women, and the League of Women Voters. *Women in Utah [1966]*, (Report of the Governor's Committee on the Status of Women in Utah, June 15, 1966), 34–38.
81. As late as 2014, Utah was still only 45th in the nation in terms of the percentage of women in the legislature. Center for American Women in Politics, Rutgers University, Fact Sheet, "Women in State Legislatures 2014," http://www.cawp.rutgers.edu/fast_facts/levels_of_office/documents/stleg.pdf. Accessed November 17, 2014.
82. *Utah Task Force on Gender and Justice: Report to the Judicial Council* (March 1990), S1.
83. Ibid., S4, 11–19.
84. Ibid., S5, 30–32.
85. Susan Lyman-Whitney, "Did Gender Report Change Utah Justice?" *Deseret News*, March 21, 1991, C1.
86. Governor's Commission for Women and the Family, *Utah Women and the Law: A Resource Handbook* (2d ed., rev., Salt Lake City: University of Utah Press, 1991), xii.
87. "Utah Ranks 29th in Women's Rights Laws," *Salt Lake Tribune*, February 3, 1987, A10.
88. For one of the most effective publications arguing against the ERA, see Rex E. Lee, *A Lawyer Looks at the Equal Rights Amendment* (Provo, UT: Brigham Young University Press, 1980). For discussions of the ERA struggle in Utah as well as Mormon influence on the anti-ERA campaign elsewhere, see Beverly Campbell, "A Conversation with Beverly Campbell," *Dialogue: A Journal of Mormon Thought* 14 (Spring 1981): 45–57; Linda Sillitoe, "The New Mormon Activists: Fighting the ERA in Virginia," *Utah Holiday* 8 (March 1979): 12, 14; Linda Sillitoe, "Fear and Anger in Virginia: The New Mormon Activists (Part II)," *Utah Holiday* 8 (April 1979): 9–10, 12; O. Kendall White, Jr., "Overt and Covert Politics: The Mormon Church's Anti-ERA Campaign in Virginia," *Virginia Social Science Journal* 19 (Winter 1984): 11–16; O. Kendall White, Jr., "A Feminist Challenge: 'Mormons for ERA' as an Internal Social Movement," *Journal of Ethnic Studies* 13 (Spring 1985): 29–50; O. Kendall White, Jr., "Mormonism and the Equal Rights Amendment," *Journal of Church and State* 31 (Spring 1989): 249–67; Lorie Winder, "LDS Position on the ERA: An Historical View," *Exponent II* 6 (Winter 1980): 6–7; D. Michael Quinn, "The LDS Church's Campaign Against the Equal Rights Amendment," *Journal of Mormon History* 20 (Fall 1994): 85–155; section on "The Church and the Era" in Martha Sonntag Bradley, "The Mormon Relief Society and the International Women's Year," *Journal of Mormon History* 21 (Spring 1995): 115–18. For a national perspective on the failure of the ERA, see Mary Francis Berry *Why ERA Failed: Politics, Women's Rights, and the Amending Process of the Constitution* (Bloomington: Indiana University Press, 1986).
89. Hal Knight and Dan Jones, "Most Favor Full Rights for Women," *Deseret News*, November 15, 1974, A1.
90. Smith said in 1977 that before giving the talk at the Institute of Religion she had met with Elders Gordon B. Hinckley and James E. Faust, telling them that "I had

given it careful consideration and I would like to make that kind of statement if it would be in keeping with the policy of the Church. They said they thought it would be very appropriate and that they would arrange for an audience for me to speak to." Barbara Bradshaw Smith, Oral History, interviewed by Jessie L. Embry, June-July 1977, 3. James H. Moyle Oral History Collection, LDS Church Archives, as cited in Bradley, "The Mormon Relief Society and the International Women's Year," 116-17.

91. Jane Cartwright, "Relief Society President Assails ERA," *Salt Lake Tribune*, December 14, 1974, B1. See also Gerry Avant, "Equal Right Amendment Is Opposed by R.S. President," *Church News* section of *Deseret News*, December 21, 1974, 7.

92. "Equal Rights Amendment,"*Church News* section of *Deseret News*, editorial, January 11, 1975, 16.

93. "LDS Leaders Oppose ERA," *Deseret News*, October 22, 1976, B1.

94. Quinn, "The LDS Church's Campaign against the Equal Rights Amendment," 148-49.

95. Beecher and MacKay, "Women in Twentieth Century Utah," 575.

96. Bob Woodward and Carl Bernstein, "Y. Student Plays Bugging Role," *Salt Lake Tribune*, January 11, 1973, A14; "Y. Student Fails Course after Watergate Spying," ibid., February 7, 1973, 34.

97. Harry F. Rosenthal, "Tape Experts Cite Erasures," *Salt Lake Tribune*, January 27, 1974, 1.

98. In 1966, for example, Major Bernard Fisher, a native Utahn living in Idaho, received nationwide acclaim for his daring rescue of a fellow pilot from a besieged airstrip in Vietnam. As described in the *Salt Lake Tribune*, Fisher "plopped" his battered, propeller-driven AIE Skyraider to the ground in a near-stall and, "in the middle of a savage crossfire" plucked his downed wingman to safety." Two other pilots zoomed in to protect him with strafing, and, while Viet Cong "watched pop-eyed," the downed pilot sprinted to the open cockpit of Fisher's plane and dived in. Slamming on the throttle, Fisher "roared head on at a machine gun post and took off." "It was the bravest thing I've ever seen a pilot do," remarked a fellow pilot later. "Ex-Utahn Snatches Pilot From Cong," *Salt Lake Tribune*, March 11, 1966, B1.

99. Allan Kent Powell, "The Vietnam Conflict in Utah," in *Utah History Encyclopedia*, ed. Powell, 612-14; Linda Sillitoe, "War and Protest," *Utah History to Go* website, http://historytogo.utah.gov/utah_chapters/utah_today/warandprotest.html. See also Denny Roy, Grant Paul Skabelund, and Ray C Hillam, *A Time To Kill: Reflections on War* (Salt Lake City: Signature Books, 1992).

100. A survey conducted in Salt Lake City in July1970, revealed that 73 percent of the respondents disapproved, 7 percent said it depended on whether the protests were violent or not, 18 percent approved, and 2 percent were undecided. J. Roy Bardsley, "Public Records Opposition to Student Unrest," *Salt Lake Tribune*, July 12, 1970, A1.

101. "Utahns Hail Peace In Sound of Joy," *Salt Lake Tribune*, January 28, 1973, 10A.

102. See Trevor C. Hughes, *Utah's 1977 Drought* (Logan, UT: Water Research Laboratory, College of Engineering, Utah State University, 1978). For a general overview of Utah's weather patterns, see Mark Eubank, *Mark Eubank's Utah Weather* (Bountiful, UT: Horizon Publishers, 1979).

103. This story is summarized in Paul Swenson, "Sheep Deaths Top Local News," *Deseret News*, December 31, 1968, B1.

104. Frank Hewlett, "Army Halts Dugway Open Tests," *Salt Lake Tribune*, December 16, 1969, 17.
105. Edwin U. Rawley, *A Decade in Review and a Look Ahead* (Salt Lake City: Utah State Department of Natural Resources, Division of Wildlife Resources, 1975), 173.
106. Ibid., 4–5.
107. United States Environmental Protection Agency, "Our Mission and What We Do," http://www2.epa.gov/aboutepa/our-mission-and-what-we-do. Accessed November 11, 2104.
108. Rampton, *As I Recall*, 239.
109. This complaint against "outside agitators" who had no real understanding of the economic consequences of closing down the plant foreshadowed arguments used by the company through the rest of the century. This and some other information on Geneva was obtained from an unpublished working paper, "Geneva and the Environment," prepared for Garth L. Mangum by Scott McNab. Copy in James B. Allen papers, L. Tom Perry Special Collections, Harold B. Lee Library, Brigham Young University. Used by permission.
110. For further comment on Kaiparowits, see Ronald Jepperson, *The Kaiparowits Coal Project and the Environment: A Case Study* (Ann Arbor: Ann Arbor Science Publishers, 1981); David Kent Sproul, "Environmentalism and th Kaiparowits Power Project," *Utah Historical Quarterly* 70 (Fall 2002), 356–71; Peter Wiley and Robert Gottlieb, *Empires in the Sun: The Rise of the New American West* (New York: G. T. Putnam's Sons, 1982), 150–51; Rampton, *As I Recall*, 171.
111. Clark Lobb, "Medicare's Not So Bad--So Far," *Salt Lake Tribune*, July 9, 1967, B1.
112. Walden, "Utah's Health Care Revolution," 14–19.
113. For an overview of the activities of IHC, see Walden, "Utah's Health Care Revolution," 47–70.
114. Barbara Springer, "A Report on Fluoridation: A Red-Hot Controversy Returns for Vote in S.L.," *Salt Lake Tribune*, October 23, 1972, B1.
115. "Concern, Experience, Wisdom Favor Vote for Fluoridation," *Salt Lake Tribune*, November 4, 1972, 24; "County Voters Nix Fluoridation by Wide Margin," ibid., November 8, 1972, E7.
116. "Dangerous Health Trade-Off," *Salt Lake Tribune*, September 27, 1976, A14; "Fluoridation Ballot Proposition Downgrades Local Government," October 7, 1976, A20. "All 3 Vote Proposals Contain Significant Defects," *Deseret News*, September 29, 1976, A5. "Confusing 'Anti-Fluoride' Proposal Passes," *Salt Lake Tribune*, November 4, 1976, B4. For an interesting discussion of the nature of the debate in Utah, see Richard B. Dwore, "A Case Study of the 1976 Referendum in Utah on Fluoridation," *Public Health Reports* 93 (January–February 1978), 73–78.
117. Walden, "Utah's Health Care Revolution," 33, citing US Department of Health and Human Services, Centers for Disease Control, *Fluoridation Census 1985* (Atlanta: 1988), v, xi.
118. Statistical data compiled from *Uniform Crime Reports of the United States*, printed annually by the Federal Bureau of Investigation, US Department of Justice, Washington, D.C.
119. Spencer J. Condie and Thomas K. Martin, "Crime," chapter III in *Utah in Demographic Perspective: Regional and National Contrasts*, ed. Howard M. Bahr (Provo, UT: Family and Demographic Research Institute, Brigham Young University, 1981), 29.

120. In 1975, Utah was still significantly below the national average in all other categories except burglary. In larceny/theft, however, Utah's rate was 3,372.6 per hundred thousand population, 20 percent above that of the nation as a whole.
121. Various articles on this may be found in the newspapers for 1967, and the *Deseret News* rated it one of the "top ten" stories for 1967. See "Utah Copper Strike Rated Top '67 Story," *Deseret News*, January 1, 1968, B1.
122. Rampton, *As I Recall*, 223–24.
123. See various news stories throughout 1969 and summary in Paul Swenson, "'Buck' Jones–Top Story," *Deseret News*, December 31, 1969, B1.
124. See Bernie Rhodes, *D.B. Cooper: The Real McCoy* (Salt Lake City: University of Utah Press, 1991). Rhodes, a federal parole officer and investigator on the McCoy case, became convinced that McCoy was also the mysterious D.B. Cooper, who had hijacked a plane flying between Portland and Seattle in 1971 and parachuted out with $200,000 of airline money. His book tells the story of McCoy and presents convincing evidence of the Cooper connection.
125. There are numerous books and articles on Bundy and his exploits. Among them are Steven Winn and David Merrill, *Ted Bundy: The Killer Next Door* (New York: Bantam Books, 1979); Richard W. Larson, *Bundy: The Deliberate Stranger* (Englewood Cliffs, NJ: Prentice-Hall, 1980); Stephen G. Michaud, *The Only Living Witness* (New York: Linden Press; Simon and Schuster, 1983); Stephen G. Michaud, *Ted Bundy: Conversations With a Killer* (New York: New American Library, 1989).
126. Rampton, *As I Recall*, 174–75.
127. Ibid., 213.
128. For discussion of this veto, see Rampton, *As I Recall*, 175–76; Robert W. Nixon, "Anti-Sunday-Law Strategy Forecast in Utah Governor's Veto," *Liberty* 63 (January-February 1968), 20–22; *Deseret News* and *Salt Lake Tribune*, various issues, January–March, 1967.
129. Rampton, *As I Recall*, 215–16.
130. As reported in Dave Jonsson, "Top Utah Court Nullifies Sunday Closing Act," *Salt Lake Tribune*, April 17, 1971, 23.
131. "Sign the Petition with Full Confidence," *Salt Lake Tribune*, editorial, June 2, 1968, A14.
132. Raymond E. Beckham, "The Utah Newspaper War of 1968: Liquor-by-the-Drink" (master's thesis, Brigham Young University, 1969), 116–18.
133. Dave Jonsson, "Gov. Rampton Signs Bills on Liquor, Poses Queries," *Salt Lake Tribune*, March 11, A1; Robert S. Halliday, "Liquor Act to Allow Mini-Bottle Outlets," ibid., March 16, 1969, A19.
134. "Senate Bill 23 an Able Deterrent to Future Land Use Mistakes," *Salt Lake Tribune*, January 27, 1974, A16.
135. Robert S. Halliday," Rampton Appeal Urges Okay of Land Use Act," *Salt Lake Tribune*, November 1, 1974, B1.
136. Rampton, *As I Recall*, 255.
137. F. Ross Peterson, "Utah Politics Since 1945," in *Utah's History*, ed. Poll, et al., 528.
138. For a full discussion of this campaign, see Frank H. Jonas, "The 1966 Election in Utah," *Utah Historical Quarterly* 20 (June 1967): 602–6.
139. For Rampton's account of this campaign, see Rampton, *As I Recall*, 190–94.
140. Ibid., 196.

141. Douglas L. Parker and Clark Lobb, "S.L. Hails Nixon on Days of '47 Visit; Pioneer Parade Delights Thousands," *Salt Lake Tribune*, July 25, 1970, A1; Rampton, *As I Recall*, 221–22.
142. Douglas L. Parker, "Nixon Solicits Support to Meet 'Great Issues,'" *Salt Lake Tribune*, November 1, 1970, A1.
143. For a discussion of this election, see Frank H. Jonas and Dan E. Jones, "The 1970 Election in Utah," *Western Political Quarterly* 24 (June 1971): 339–49.
144. Rampton, *As I Recall*, 235.
145. Ibid., 281–82.

CHAPTER 5

Quest for Balance:
The Matheson Years, 1977–1984

Forty-eight-year-old Scott M. Matheson became the state of Utah's twelfth governor on January 3, 1977. He was a man with extensive legal and business-related background. After receiving his law degree from Stanford University in 1952, he practiced in Cedar City, and then became Deputy Salt Lake County Attorney. He joined the legal department of the Union Pacific Railroad Company in 1958, accepted a position as assistant general counsel for the Anaconda Copper Company in 1969, and then returned to Union Pacific two years later. He remained there until he was elected governor.

Matheson got off to a good start: nineteen of the twenty policy proposals he made to the legislature on January 10 were passed in some form. These included funding an Executive Reorganization Committee, establishing a State Energy and Conservation Council, creating a Community Impact Board, and establishing a "circuit breaker" program that allowed modest home property tax relief to senior citizens.[1]

Three interrelated issues were of special urgency to the new governor: energy resource development, the environment, and the relationship between the state and federal governments. Each of these problems was critically important to both the nation and the state, but the fact that they were so inextricably intertwined pro-

Image 5.1: Governor Scott M. Matheson, governor of Utah 1977–1984. He spent much this time attempting to reverse the flight of power from the states to the federal government. Used by permission, Utah State Historical Society, all rights reserved.

duced increasingly complex political controversy. At its heart was the fact that many people, including Matheson, were convinced that the American federal system was out of balance. As conceived by the Founders, federalism meant a division of responsibilities between the national government and the states, but in the twentieth century, and especially since the Great Depression of the 1930s, many traditional areas of state responsibility had been taken over by Washington. Matheson believed that the states had simply abrogated their responsibilities, leaving a void that was all too easy for the national government to fill.

During his eight years in office, Matheson spent much of his time trying to reverse this trend. He was only partially successful, but he later published a book, *Out of Balance*, that provides a remarkable overview of his efforts. Much of this chapter is drawn from that work.[2]

The Governor's Mansion

In 1901 Thomas Kearns, a public-spirited millionaire, mining magnate, and US Senator from Utah, completed one of the state's most elegant mansions. This magnificent building (located at 603 East South Temple in Salt Lake City) served as a Kearns family residence until 1937, when Jennie Kearns, Thomas's widow, moved out and donated it to the state to be used as an official governor's residence.

Beginning in 1938, the mansion was the residence of three governors (Blood, Maw, and Lee), but during the Lee administration it was found unsuitable to be used as a home. Adequate renovation would be highly expensive, but it was too valuable as a historic landmark simply to let it go. The legislature, therefore, turned it over to the Utah State Historical Society, which happily occupied it from 1957 to 1977, the year Governor Matheson was inaugurated. The governors, meanwhile, occupied an official residence built by the state on Fairfax Road.

But the Fairfax residence lacked the charm, historical significance, and gracious decor of the stately Kearns Mansion. Besides, thought the governor's wife, Norma Matheson, it was inadequate to take care of her family's needs as well as official functions. The governor, legislators, and much of the public, too, wanted the mansion restored to its original grandeur. So, in 1977 the legislature passed the following resolution: "The legislature finds and declares that the State property known as the Kearns Mansion is an irreplaceable historic landmark possessing special and unique architectural qualities which should be preserved and the deterioration which has taken place will continue unless remedial measures are taken." The mansion was reestablished as the official residence, and the state Historical Society was appropriately relocated in the historic Denver and Rio Grande Railroad Depot. Restoration of the mansion began in March 1978.

The restoration project was a model of community cooperation, lovingly nurtured by many people, including Norma Matheson. Restoration of the various rooms was designed by ten members of the Utah chapter of the American Society of Interior Designers, who donated their time. Except for kitchen equipment and some carpeting, no state money was spent on interior furnishings. These were purchased with funds donated by corporations or private citizens. Many beautiful needlepoint pieces, including seats and cushions, a piano bench cover, and numerous couch pillows, were stitched by members of the Salt Lake Needlepoint Guild. In addition, a talented prison inmate volunteered to restore the white-oak cabinets in the pantry.

In January 1980, the Mathesons moved into the restored Governor's Mansion. At the public opening, March 7–11, thousands of citizens stood in line, sometimes for as long as two hours, to view the elegant residence with its exquisite woodwork, magnificent furnishings, and fine sculpting and paintings. Terry Rampton, daughter-in-law of the former governor, summed up its significance well when she said that the mansion "gains its greatest strength from the pride of each of us in our state's past. By returning this mansion to its owner's original intent, a governor's residence, we are not making it a museum but a symbol of a gracious life style."[3]

The National Setting, 1977–84

On the national scene, Georgia's Jimmy Carter was inaugurated as president of the United States the same month that Matheson became governor of Utah. During his single term in office, Carter led out in the reorganization of federal agencies and departments, similar to what both Rampton and Matheson tried to accomplish in Utah government. Carter was also deeply concerned over energy policy, and the Department of Energy was created during the first year of his administration. In foreign affairs, Carter successfully mediated negotiations between Egypt and Israel, leading to a remarkable peace treaty in 1978. He also signed a treaty turning the Panama Canal over to the Panamanians by the year 2000 and entered into full diplomatic relations with China in 1979.

Image 5.2: Utah Governor's Mansion, 1967. Originally the home of millionaire Thomas Kearns, it became the Governor's Mansion n 1938, then the home of the Utah Historical Society from 1957–1977, then restored during the Matheson administration as the Governor's Mansion. Used by permission, Utah State Historical Society, all rights reserved.

However, it was Ronald Reagan's administration, beginning in 1981, that seemed to create a domestic atmosphere more conducive to dealing with Matheson's concern over the imbalance in federal-state relationships. Reagan's call for a "new federalism" was an effort to curb the size of the federal behemoth by getting it out of some programs, retrenching others, providing block grants to states to help them take over some programs from Washington, eliminating federally imposed mandates, and attempting to substitute state governments for the federal government in dealing with cities and counties.

As a start, federal taxes were cut in 1981, but Reagan soon found himself in trouble because the federal deficit kept burgeoning. Although he tried to scale down, his refusal either to cut defense spending (which amounted to about 70 percent of the federal budget) or to raise taxes in order to finance more block grants to states, as well as the refusal of many Congressmen to let go of federal power, doomed his efforts. Reagan was also hurt by a severe economic recession in 1982–83, which diminished government revenues even more and, ironically, forced him to obtain Democratic support in order to push through a $98-billion tax increase. However, a strong recovery in 1984 helped assure his reelection that year.

Meanwhile, the United States was passing through an era of continuing social change. Among other things, Americans were living longer and they were becoming more well educated. Both of these factors were related to a remarkable population growth in the West and the South, even as population remained stagnant or declined in the Northeast and Midwest. With many major corporations moving their offices and plants to the Sunbelt and other western states, including Utah, college-educated professionals as well as blue-collar workers followed them. The West also grew as a retirement haven.

Another important social transition was the growing significance of women in the work force, not only in various skilled jobs but also in the professions. The Reagan administration helped set the tone when the president appointed Sandra Day O'Connor, the first woman justice to sit on the Supreme Court of the United States. In 1983 he also named two women to Cabinet positions: Elizabeth Dole as Secretary of Transportation and Margaret Heckler as Secretary of Health and Human Services.

Meanwhile, the concerns of Utah and the nation became increasingly interrelated. The MX missile debate, pollution, water, energy, and the Sagebrush Rebellion were all two-way issues: federal policy directly affected Utah, and Utah had an influence on federal policy. In addition, Utah continued to attract national publicity for a variety of other reasons. These included the LDS announcement in 1978 of the extension of the priesthood to males of all races; the continuing activities of the Utah Symphony and the Mormon Tabernacle choir; the 1977 arrival of the Utah Jazz, formerly the New Orleans Jazz, and the team's first-ever entry into the NBA playoffs in 1984; Brigham Young University's football team being named number one in the nation in 1984; Utah's

Image 5.3: Utah's Sharlene Wells, named Miss America in 1984. Courtesy of the Miss America Organization.

Sharlene Wells being named Miss America in 1984. On the other hand, Utah received a bit of unwelcome national attention because of a few ruthless crimes and some unusual problems in law enforcement.

Crime and Punishment: Frustration at Many Levels

Matheson had hardly taken office before he got a sobering lesson on what it meant to be governor. Almost immediately he and the state of Utah were thrust into the national and international limelight over an event that, he said, "was one of the most traumatically emotional experiences I've ever had. The pressure that grew out of that internationally was just incredible."[4]

The controversy surrounded the execution of Gary Gilmore, a habitual criminal who had cold-bloodedly murdered two people in July, 1976. Found guilty, he was sentenced to death and refused to appeal the sentence. The execution was originally set for November 15, but after several delays stemming from appeals by attorneys and anti-death penalty groups, Governor Rampton granted a stay until the January meeting of the Board of Pardons. As a result, any further gubernatorial action fell to Matheson.

The issue could not have come at a more untimely moment for Utah. There had not been an execution in the United States since 1967, but in 1976 the US Supreme Court ruled that the death penalty for murder was not necessarily cruel and unusual punishment. By default, Utah was the state where the traumatic confrontation over the resumption of executions took place.

The Gilmore case soon became a cause célèbre. Anti-death penalty groups grabbed media attention when they descended upon the state in force, making Gilmore himself a focus of both national and international attention. Complicating the matter was the fact that Utah's death penalty statute, revised in 1973, had yet to be tested in the state Supreme Court. Opponents of capital punishment were fearful that Gilmore's execution would diminish the chances of such a test.

The drama took on elements of the macabre. While those who fed the media sometimes seemed to revel in glorifying the murderer, the state prison received telephone calls from dozens of men offering to join the volunteer firing squad. Gilmore, who had no desire to continue living, antagonized those attempting to save him by making a written public appeal to be allowed to die, claiming that it was cruel and unusual punishment to prolong the inevitable. He even made two attempts at suicide. At the same time, he sold book and movie rights and had the money distributed to his family, the families of his victims, and his girl friend. He sent out invitations to his execution to his girlfriend, an uncle, two attorneys, and a Hollywood promoter. He also planned his own funeral and made arrangements to donate his organs and eyes to the University of Utah Medical Center. His last words, after being strapped in a chair and blindfolded before the firing squad, were a thankful "Let's do it."

Governor Matheson was caught in a trap of public misunderstanding and deep personal emotion. Contrary to a popular perception, Utah law did not permit the governor to stay an execution permanently. He could issue a stay only until the next regularly scheduled session of the Board of Pardons. Rampton had already done that, and after the board met in January and refused to back down, Matheson felt there would be no point in prolonging the matter again. But hundreds of telegrams and letters arrived daily, and a number of anti-capital punishment groups, including religious leaders, flew to Salt Lake City from all over the world to meet with him in his home all pressuring him to postpone the execution, which was rescheduled for January 17. It was an emotional time for everyone, but especially for the new governor, who knew he would receive the brunt of the publicity, both positive and negative, after the sentence was carried out.

Then came a bizarre ending to the story. Almost at the last minute, Chief Judge Willis W. Ritter of the US District Court for Utah responded to a class action suit by the American Civil Liberties Union and issued a temporary restraining order. Immediately, however, Utah Attorney General Robert B. Hansen flew to Denver with an appeal to the Tenth Circuit Court of Appeals. Ritter was overruled, the decision was delivered to the Utah State Prison at

7:42 a.m., and the firing squad did its work almost immediately. Gilmore thus become the first person to be executed in the United States in ten years and the first in Utah in nearly seventeen years.

After the execution, Matheson felt numb, but he had to face a press conference. When that ordeal was over, he went for a long walk with his chief executive assistant. It was there, he later wrote, that "I first began to feel the total responsibilities of my role as governor. Even though I could not personally affect the outcome, for the first time, I clearly understood that I *was* governor."[5]

In the Gilmore case, the brutality of the crime seemed almost to be lost in the national outcry against capital punishment, making the state itself appear harsh and inhumane. Unfortunately, there were other crimes in Utah that also brought unwelcome national attention, but for different reasons.

One incident began in May 1977, when Dr. Rulon Allred, leader of a large Utah polygamist group, was shot to death. After a multistate manhunt, police arrested five members of a small rival polygamist faction led by Ervil LeBaron, who apparently had ordered Allred's killing on the grounds that dissenters must be exterminated. LeBaron himself was arrested in 1979, convicted in 1980, and eventually died in prison.[6]

Another incident also involved polygamy and, in addition, the issue of private rights versus public rights. The question was whether individuals have the legal or constitutional right to teach their children at home instead of sending them to public schools if the quality of their home education does not meet state-imposed standards. As Matheson recalled later, this was one of the most complex individual rights issues he had to face as governor.[7]

It began in 1973, when John and Vickie Singer, who lived on a farm in Summit County, took their children out of public schools. Singer was an ex-Mormon who held several heretical beliefs, including a belief in polygamy. Among the things he objected to in the public schools were sex education, the teaching of evolution, failure to teach religion, and a textbook that praised Martin Luther King, Jr. School officials tried to work with the family, explaining that home schools must be monitored, but the Singers rejected all their overtures. They allowed their children to be tested twice, but in the spring of 1976 declined even that. In 1977 and 1978 they also spurned the state's offer of a private tutor. Finally, in March 1978, after five years of virtual stalemate, a juvenile court ordered Singer's arrest. Gun in hand, Singer refused to submit, and the sheriff backed off.

Later that year, Singer took a second wife, Shirley Black, who moved into the Singer compound with her children. But Black was not divorced from her first husband, who immediately petitioned the court to award him custody of their children. The Third District Court ordered the children removed from the Singer home.

In October, with two court orders in force, County Sheriff Ron Robinson asked for state help in arresting Singer. This forced Matheson to make another soul-searching decision. Singer was doing no harm to the public, even though his children were receiving an inferior education. But Matheson believed that the law requiring a minimum school standard must be upheld, and that the Black children must be returned to their rightful father. He approved state assistance but then, without his knowledge, officers made a tactical error. Not wanting to show force, three of them went to the Singer farm posing as reporters and photographers. After being let into the house, they identified themselves, whereupon a free-for-all broke out. Vickie Singer, the children, and a friend of the family all jumped the officers, Singer broke loose and pulled a gun, and the police soon left. The affair made headlines, with some of the media castigating the police for approaching under false pretenses.

Matheson quickly instructed the public safety department to make no further plans without consulting him, but he still believed that Singer must be held accountable to the law. Among the various proposals presented to him were the use of SWAT teams to raid the Singer compound and the utilization of an armored weapons carrier to crash through the compound gate and teargas the home. Both were rejected because of the likelihood of causing injury or accidental deaths. However, it all came to an end for Singer on January 18, 1979, when five uniformed and armed sheriff's deputies on snowmobiles bore down on him while he was outside, on his way to the mailbox. They hoped to isolate him and, by sheer show of force, persuade him to surrender. But Singer pulled a pistol from his belt and aimed at one of the officers, whereupon the officer shot and killed him.

Emotions ran high that day. Most Utahns supported the effort to arrest Singer but, like Matheson, were dismayed at his killing. Others sympathized with Singer so much that they made threatening calls to the governor's office. Concerned state officers took the Singer children into seclusion for a day as a safety precaution. In the aftermath, Vickie Singer was given custody of her own children and taught them in an approved home school. Meanwhile, her lawyer filed a $110 million suit, arguing that Singer was wrongfully slain. In a decision that was upheld by the Tenth Circuit Court of Appeals, the judge ruled that the police were acting responsibly and that the First Amendment did not give parents the broad right to educate their children according to their private religious beliefs without some reasonable governmental oversight.

There could be no better example of the dilemma over personal rights versus public responsibility, and the extent to which the state may go to uphold the latter, than the Singer case. The debate over these issues will probably never end in America, whose people place heavy emphasis on important principles that sometimes come into ironic conflict with each other: personal freedom, the value system of a society, and the rule of law. Matheson summed up his feelings as follows:

> People have suggested that the issues involved were not worth Singer's death. But what kind of precedent would we have set by turning our backs on the situation? That clearly would not be in the public interest. We live under a system of laws. If such a system espouses values, those values must be protected. I firmly believe we were protecting society's values.[8]

Tragically, even beyond the Gilmore and Singer cases there were enough bizarre or atrocious incidents to keep crime in Utah the focus of national attention for several years. An unusual rash of child kidnappings was among them. In 1982, three-year-old Rachael Runyon of Sunset was kidnapped and murdered, her body found in a remote part of Morgan County. Her killer was not found, but the case had a nationwide impact when she became a national symbol of the problem of missing children. As a result of the publicity, over thirty thousand children in Utah were fingerprinted that year, their blood types were put on file, and their parents received identification packets. In addition, a 1982 federal law gave parents of missing children access to a national clearinghouse, administered by the FBI, containing information sent in from around the nation.[9] The case also led to the development of Utah's Amber Alert system, which was originally called Rachael Alert. In 1983, as a direct result of several kidnappings, the Utah state legislature unanimously approved the toughest child kidnapping and molestation law in the United States. It established minimum five-years-to-life sentences for first-time offenders for kidnapping or sexual abuse of children under fourteen and fifteen years-to-life sentences for those who were convicted three times.

That same year, a particularly nefarious kidnapping spree came to an end when Arthur Gary Bishop was arrested on eleven felony counts, including capital homicide and aggravated kidnapping, in connection with the murder of five boys, ages six to thirteen, who had disappeared between 1979 and 1982. Bishop was convicted in 1984 on five counts of first-degree murder, five of aggravated kidnapping, and one count of sexual abuse of a minor. He was executed four years later.

In still another grotesque case, in 1983 a New York socialite, Frances Schreuder, was convicted of first-degree murder in connection with the 1977 death of her wealthy father in Salt Lake City. Her teenage son, Marc, who had earlier been convicted of the crime, testified in court that his mother had ordered him to kill her father because the father was taking steps to keep her from inheriting part of his fortune. Frances was sentenced to life in prison. The case received national news coverage and led to two books, two television miniseries, and eventually to a documentary on Court TV.[10]

The following year, another Utah polygamy group appeared in national headlines. The brothers Ron and Dan Lafferty were arrested for killing their sister-in-law, Brenda Wright Lafferty, and her infant daughter in American Fork and for conspiring to kill two local LDS leaders. The Laffertys claimed that God had commanded them to do this. Dan was sentenced to two life terms. His brother was sentenced to death but later appealed on the grounds of incompetency to stand trial. The case was still pending after eleven years as defense attorneys questioned the validity of Utah's insanity defense law, which held that a person could not use this defense if he knew he was killing someone. In April 1995, however, the Utah Supreme Court upheld the law.[11] In March 1996, a judge found Lafferty competent to stand trial. In April he was convicted of two counts of murder and sentenced to death. However, ongoing appeals claiming mental incompetence kept him alive at least until the time this book was finished. The Lafferty story eventually led to the publication in 2003 of a highly controversial book, *Under the Banner of Heaven: A Story of Violent Faith*.

The national publicity given to these particularly devilish crimes tended to hide a more positive picture in Utah. According to the FBI's *Uniform Crime Report*, Utah's total crime rate actually fell by 6.8 percent between 1975 and 1984, a record considerably better than the national average. Unfortunately, the decline was not reflected in figures for the violent crimes of murder, manslaughter, and aggravated assault. The major decline was in burglary and motor vehicle theft.[12] In addition, some crimes, including child abuse and neglect, were not even included in the *Uniform Crime Report*. Both of these rates continued to climb.[13]

There was also a national increase in "white-collar" crime, particularly larceny and theft, and Utah was sometimes stigmatized as the "stock-fraud capital of the nation." One example was a corporation known as AFCO, which bilked some 750 investors out of $25 million through offering returns as high as 30 percent on securities that, in fact, had no assets behind them. AFCO folded in 1982, and its founder, C. Grant Affleck, was sent to prison. In February 1984, Matheson formed the Governor's Securities Fraud Task Force for the purpose of analyzing the problem and making specific recommendations to the legislature. That year the task force identified ten frauds that had involved over nine thousand Utahns at a loss of about $200 million and the next year a national magazine reported that perhaps twelve thousand citizens had been bilked out of $215 million. Victims included many LDS Church members who had placed their money in fraudulent trust funds, believing they were building up money to send their children on church missions. Also included were many senior citizens, who were particularly vulnerable to investment scams. At the recommendation of the task force, Matheson beefed up the Utah Securities Division and asked the legislature to outlaw or bridle blind trusts, where people put up money without knowing where it would be invested. Such pools were legal in several states, but Utah was at the top of the list in terms of the number registered: 211 in 1984 as opposed to only seventeen in Colorado, the next-highest state. Nevertheless, the task force concluded, most of Utah's citizens were blissfully ignorant of fraud, and their trusting nature made them ready targets for the continuing wiles of con artists.[14]

Constitutional Revision: The Process Continues

Meanwhile, the vital process of bringing Utah's constitution up to date continued, as the Constitutional Revision Commission carried on its difficult and often thankless task. Between 1979 and 1986, voters approved the overhaul of four pivotal articles.[15]

Getting constitutional amendments approved, first by the legislature and then selling them to the public, was no easy task. The commission could not rely on detailed voter education because many issues were so complex that the details resulted in more confusion. Instead, the commission relied heavily on obtaining the endorsement of prominent, respected groups and citizens whom the public recognized as knowledgeable on the subject. The League of Women Voters, for example, studied the commission's proposals carefully and usually supported them. The support of former governors helped promote the amended executive article. On the judicial article, the commission obtained the endorsement of Gordon R. Hall, chief justice of the Utah Supreme Court, as well as Associate Justice Dallin H. Oaks, both of whom appeared before the legislature in March, 1984.[16] Less than two weeks before that appearance Oaks had become a member of the LDS Church's Quorum of Twelve Apostles. James E. Faust, also a member of the Quorum of Twelve Apostles and a highly respected Salt Lake

City attorney, also supported the measure, as did by then former governor Scott M. Matheson. Such endorsements went a long way toward convincing the public that the amendments were sound.

The executive article was the first to be changed. The board of examiners consisted of the governor, the secretary of state, and the attorney general. The executive article gave the board authority to examine "all claims against the state," but since all three members were elected officials, it often happened that two were of a different party than the governor and disagreed with him over expenditures that he considered vital. This was hardly the way to allow the chief executive to do the job he was elected to do. In addition, the secretary of state became acting governor whenever the governor was out of the state, which left some chief executives in the awkward position of not wanting to leave the state for fear the secretary of state would take action they disapproved of.

The temporary Constitutional Revision Commission turned its attention to the executive article as early as 1971, but the revised article, drafted by the permanent commission, did not go before the legislature until 1979. It went on the ballot in 1980 and took effect in 1981.

The revised article stated unequivocally that the "executive power of the State shall be vested in the Governor," something that was not clearly spelled out in the original Constitution. It also changed the authority of the board of examiners. Instead of examining "all claims against the state" the board could examine only "all unliquidated claims against the state," which meant only claims not covered by appropriations, such as accidents for which the state might be liable. In practical political terms, the board was stripped of any administrative power over finance, freeing the governor from the threat of veto by the board in his effort to spend funds appropriated by the legislature. The revised article also abolished the office of secretary of state, created the office of lieutenant governor, and provided that candidates for governor and lieutenant governor must run in tandem. This assured that, if elected, they would be of the same party. It also included unambiguous provisions for gubernatorial succession.

The revenue and taxation article caused the most vehement opposition to change.[17] It dealt mainly with the administration and limitation of property tax, which was the main source of revenue for state and local governments at the time the state constitution was written. Since the rules were inflexible, they could not be adapted to changing realities. For example. under the old system all property owned by local government, no matter where that property was located, was exempt from taxation. The Constitutional Revision Commission wanted to meet the needs of a rapidly changing economy by giving the legislature the power to determine the conditions of tax exemption. Under the new article the state could tax those properties if they lay outside the geographic boundaries of the local units. The legislature, then, had the flexibility to determine what property of local government should be exempt from or subject to taxation. The example used by the commission was the Intermountain Power Project, which was owned jointly by several cities and rural cooperatives but was exempt from taxation. The legislature needed flexibility, said the commission, in order to respond to the impact of such facilities without relying on other tax programs. The new article also changed the confusing property tax exemptions for religious and charitable purposes. It provided that all property, not just lots with buildings on them, used for "religious, charitable, hospital, educational, employee representation, or welfare purposes" were exempt. The amendment also removed the limitation on what the state could contribute to the minimum school program, which allowed more reductions in local property tax. The important principle was legislative flexibility in the face of changing needs.

The most significant, and most controversial, change was a provision that allowed the legislature to exempt primary residences and tangible personal property from taxation. If local governments were hurt by such exceptions, the legislature could provide for reimbursement from general state funds. This was a direct response to the unpopularity of the property tax. The new article did not require anything, but it gave the legislature flexibility, and this, argued the commission, was one of its strengths. Opponents argued that the amendment would undermine local authority and ability to deal with local problems, would further shift the tax burden to business and industry, would have inconsistent effects around the state, and would have numerous other dire consequences. But the Utah Foundation was correct when it observed that even if the amendment passed, it was unlikely that much property tax relief would be given in the foreseeable future. Approximately 59 percent of the property tax in the state was used for school purposes, and with enrollments rising it was unlikely that the state could come up with enough money to replace what would be lost through exemptions.[18] The new article was approved by the legislature in 1980, went on the ballot that fall and, along with the executive article, went into effect in January 1981.

The third article to be changed was the judicial article. The amendment was presented to the voters in 1984 and became effective July 1, 1985. The proposed changes were politically volatile, however, because they went to the heart of judicial discipline, dealt with questions that had been raised about improprieties relating to admission to the bar, changed the system for selecting judges, and had the effect of cutting down on the number of appeals a convicted felon could initiate.

For the first time in Utah history, the amended article created an integrated judicial system, with the Supreme Court clearly at the head, a trial court known as the district court, and such other intermediate courts as the legislature might establish. It also gave the legislature wide latitude to determine the number of district and other court judges, but the state Supreme Court was given the exclusive right to "govern the practice of law" in the state, "including admission to practice law and the conduct and discipline of persons admitted to the practice of law." This brought the bar more fully under the Supreme Court's jurisdiction than ever before. In addition, the method of selecting judges was changed. Previously, judges were elected in the same way as other public officials were, but this tended to politicize the judiciary and undermine the independence necessary for fair and impartial judgments. Under the new system, a new judge in a court of record (that is, a court in which a full record, which becomes the basis of an appeal, is kept) was appointed by the governor from a list of three nominees named by a judicial nominating commission. At the expiration of his or her term, the judge then stood, unopposed, for retention by a "yes" or "no" vote.

The Constitutional Revision Commission also proposed a revision of the education article, which was approved by voters in 1986. The State Board of Education claimed that the Board of Regents was unconstitutional because the original Constitution gave the state board full power over education in the state. It appeared that technically, because the framers of the original Constitution simply did not foresee the development of an elaborate system of higher education, the state board's claim had some basis. Practically, however, the commission saw that this could lead to numerous complications. The proposed revision simply brought the constitution up to date by clearly designating two educational systems and defining their jurisdiction. There were also other changes, including a provision that all public elementary and secondary schools, instead of just grades 1–8, should be free.

The revision of these major articles were not the only accomplishments of the Constitutional Revision Commission. Its long-range importance lay in the fact that, as a result of its work, the manner of conducting government was changed in many ways, numerous outdated or unworkable provisions were taken out of the constitution, and the constitution was brought up to date in order to conform to some practices already instituted but not clearly authorized. The governance of higher education was one example, as was a 1980 amendment that authorized convicts to be released for contract work on a voluntary basis. The movement for constitutional reform that began with the Little Hoover Commission still goes on, although less dramatically, as the permanent Constitutional Revision Commission continues to study the constitution in the light of changing needs.

Quest for Balance: Defense, Environment, and the Federal Leviathan

As noted earlier, one of Governor Matheson's overriding concerns was the need to restore a proper balance between the actions of state and federal governments. But the issues were complex and involved many programs with myriad long-range consequences. The environment, atomic testing, national defense, control of public lands, and numerous other problems were all interrelated in a perplexing pattern that complicated inter-governmental relations.

One persistent dilemma was the continuing revelation of damage done by the fallout from atomic testing in Nevada in the 1950s. In the late 1970s, higher-than-normal rates of leukemia and other forms of cancer were reported in southern Utah. Lawsuits mounted into the hundreds, and more extensive studies than ever before were carried out on the population that had been exposed.

Governor Matheson was highly concerned, especially because several members of his own family from southern Utah had died of cancer. His dismay heightened when an investigation revealed that in the 1960s the Division of Public Health received numerous important reports but simply filed them away with no comment and no action. Matheson ordered further study and, in November 1978, he went to Washington seeking help in getting federal files open for inspection. At first meetings with federal officials seemed fruitless. President Carter's assistant for intergovernmental affairs, Jack Watson, had not even read the briefing materials Matheson sent ahead, and he offered no assistance. His lack of concern for Utah was a perfect example of the breakdown in intergovernmental relations that troubled many state governors.

Matheson was angry and disheartened, but when he met with Joseph Califano, Secretary of Health, Education, and Welfare, things suddenly changed. Califano had been thoroughly briefed on the subject, understood the issues, and was anxious to help. He also promised to work with President Carter on the matter. This was an especially opportune time because Carter was scheduled to speak in the Tabernacle in Salt Lake City at the National Conference on Families on November 27. During his address, Carter announced his intent to have Califano reevaluate earlier studies on the rate of leukemia in southern Utah, reopen a study on thyroid disease conducted in the 1960s, and consult with Utah officials on the possibility of a new and more complete investigation. As a result, Califano established a joint Federal-State Radiation Effects Management Committee to supervise the reevaluation and to implement new studies. This was, indeed, a major breakthrough.

A series of investigations ensued, and at an April 1979 congressional hearing Matheson reported some of the findings. With reference to the 1953–57 investigation of sheep deaths, Matheson told the lawmakers that the documents "read like a case study in government misfeasance and callous disregard for health and property."[19] He also lambasted the Atomic Energy Commission for its lack of willingness even to consider the possibility that atomic fallout was the cause of the sheep deaths. More importantly, there was no evidence of any concern for the implications the deaths might have had for the safety of humans living downwind from the atomic test site. What were the health risks, Matheson wanted to know, and what could be done about them in the future? He was also concerned about assessing the responsibility of those who did not take proper precautions and who were involved in the subsequent cover-up.

Essential to a thorough study was a large federal grant expected by the University of Utah. In May1979, representatives of the National Institute of Health assured university officials that their proposal would likely be funded. The next three years, however, were a bureaucratic nightmare as the proposal bounced from one agency to another, got involved with questions over competitive bidding, was sidetracked by changing rules, and came close to being rejected altogether. Frequently Matheson was promised that the funds were forthcoming, sometimes within two weeks, but each time the date went by with no action. The contract finally came in May 1982, but, said Matheson later, the evidence of "bureaucratic foot-dragging, if not actual sabotage of the grant proposal," was substantial. In the labyrinth of the federal bureaucracy, even though top policy makers were fully behind the study, middle management had sidetracked it. Still angry after he left office, Matheson pointed again to his concern over policymaking in general and the necessity for local watchfulness. There was a continuing need, he stressed, "for governors to be vigilant concerning both short-term and long-term impacts of federal decisions on their residents. If the citizens of a state are to be sacrificed for the 'national interest,' then, at the very least, those citizens need to be fully informed and protected as much as possible."[20]

Before Matheson left office, there were at least some positive results from the many efforts to place responsibility for the fallout deaths where it should have been placed. Late in 1982 the federal government was dragged into the US District Court in Salt Lake City. The trial lasted ten weeks, and the judge's verdict was not given for another seventeen months. Finally, in May 1984, Judge Bruce S. Jenkins ruled that the federal government failed to warn residents living downwind from the Nevada Test Site of the dangers from fallout and that exposure to radiation from open-air blasts caused cancer among some of them. The government had failed to carry out its legal responsibilities, he said, and he ordered compensation to be paid in ten specific cases. This was a small beginning because it covered only a handful of victims and included only three types of cancer. But it was a landmark case and it became the catalyst for many more suits and for the introduction of bills in Congress to compensate all fallout victims. The fight over those bills would go on for years.

The most time-consuming and divisive issue involving federal-state relations during Matheson's eight years as governor concerned a weapon system known as MX (an acronym for Missile Experimental) and its proposed basing in Utah. In the end, "with a significant nudge from the Mormon Church," the state won its campaign against it.[21]

Matheson received his first detailed briefing on MX in March 1979. America's missile defense system was getting old and increasingly vulnerable, he was told. The Air Force's answer was a huge, ten-warhead missile that was mobile, making it a less vulnerable target. The vast desert in western Utah and eastern Nevada was among the proposed locations.

Matheson initially supported the project, but as he learned more about it he became less enthusiastic. The plan was to build twenty-three shelters for each individual missile, spacing the shelters seven thousand feet apart. A missile would be deployed on launchers that could be moved quickly from one shelter to another. The SALT II treaty with the Soviet Union (which was never ratified but nevertheless had to be considered) required that the shelters be open to satellite "inspection" to ensure that each of them housed only one missile. But a missile could be moved, on its launcher, to another shelter long before a Soviet missile could be fired and reach the initial location. The Department of Defense planned to begin with two hundred missiles and 4,600 shelters, and then expand to a possible ten thousand shelters by 1989. This understanding took on ominous dimensions, leading Matheson to conclude that the people of Utah needed to know more about it and to participate more fully in the debate. Congressman Gunn McKay responded by scheduling public hearings in Cedar City on November 5. Matheson, meanwhile, organized an MX Task Force, encouraged the formation of a Four County MX Policy Board, which worked closely with the task force, and obtained the cooperation of the state of Nevada.

Matheson still supported the MX concept, but at the November 5 hearings he shocked Congressman McKay and the Air Force by expressing serious reservations about its impact on the quality of life in Utah. The massive construction project could overwhelm all other projects in Utah combined, possibly creating a labor crisis in the state. The populations of Juab, Millard, Beaver, and Iron counties would double in six years, creating a variety of social problems and straining public service and educational facilities beyond their limits. Other potential problems included the possible impact on public lands, security measures required for the huge network of roads suddenly created in large parts of the state, the availability of water, and a variety of environmental concerns.

Later in the month, Matheson learned that the Air Force was planning an end run around his efforts at caution. Its proposed "fast track" legislation would allow it to withdraw seven thousand square miles of land in Utah and Nevada from the public domain, then return the unused portion when it wanted to. In addition, the MX would be exempt from the environmental impact statement required by law. Matheson was irate, and the Air Force eventually backed off. But from that point on Matheson saw the Air Force as the enemy. Everything the Air Force did, especially with regard to environmental issues that might affect the selection of a site for a project, was carefully monitored, and a complete record was kept in case the state ever had to go to court.

At Matheson's urging, the public soon became more involved in the debate. Beginning in February 1980, a series of town meetings were held in key locations throughout the state. Interest and emotions ran high, every point of view was aired, and the press coverage was extraordinary. For two years in a row the MX controversy was number one in the *Deseret News*'s year-end list of "top ten" stories. Among the most vocal opponents were the people of Delta, who were closest to the proposed basing site. Both Matheson and Governor Robert List of Nevada testified before Congressional committees early in 1980, expressing their concerns over the possible socioeconomic impact of MX. Both still generally supported the idea but urged breaking up the deployment into smaller units in a larger number of states.

In a private "spirited conversation" with Congressman Joseph Addabbo (Dem., NewYork) during these hearings, the issue of states rights versus national interest came into sharp focus. Matheson and List insisted that they were just as much concerned over national security as anyone, but they also believed that they, as representatives of the citizens of the states involved, had a right to be part of the resolution of the issue. Addabbo responded by giving them a "tongue lashing," implying that they were somehow unpatriotic. "This has got to go somewhere in the United States, Governor Matheson!" he said. Matheson did not have time to give him a full reply, which he later regretted, but, he wrote in his book,

> I should have explained to him that the people in Utah are fully cognizant of their responsibilities to national causes; that we are fully supportive of national defense and want to be helpful in solving problems. But that I also had the responsibility of maintaining the integrity of Utah's ability to survive as a viable, economic, political and social entity. National security involves economic success as well, and to destroy the ability of a state to maintain its economic integrity in the name of national security absolutely defeats the principle.[22]

The issue became even more focused for Matheson when a $1 million grant was obtained by Congressman McKay for the purpose of funding studies associated with the MX basing proposal. The Air Force wanted to handle the grant in a way that, it seemed to Matheson, imposed restrictions that violated the intent of Congress. He was particularly upset with the attitude of Undersecretary of the Air Force Antonia Handler Chays, who refused to cooperate with him and Governor List on any of the controversial issues. Convinced that it was time to draw the line, the two governors went directly to President Carter. As a result of that meeting, Carter assigned people to work with them who seemed more compatible than the current bureaucrats. He also agreed to review the question of alternative deployment sites and basing strategy. In principle, however, the president was still committed to the "racetrack" system which the governor was convinced by this time was completely wrong for Utah.

The ongoing controversy included a ninety-minute, nationally televised debate originating at Symphony Hall in Salt Lake City on April 24, 1980. Particularly strident in her presentation was Undersecretary Chays, who continued to advocate the racetrack basing mode. On June 16 the governor issued an official public statement strongly opposing the racetrack system, convinced that such a "shell game" would only proliferate the nuclear arms race. In December 1980, the Air Force issued its Draft Environmental Impact Statement, but Matheson followed with a detailed statement in opposition. Meanwhile, Ronald Reagan was elected President of the United States. Matheson was encouraged because it appeared that both Reagan and Secretary of Defense Casper Weinberger were willing to reconsider everything. In March the president appointed a committee to conduct a review.

At that point the LDS Church became involved, throwing what was probably the knockout punch in the long and complicated contest. After careful study and extensive discussion, church leaders concluded that the matter was a moral issue. They decided to take a public position not only against the Utah basing plan but also against the MX itself.

The "First Presidency Statement on Basing of the MX Missile" was issued on May 5, 1981. It evoked widespread attention and was the target of both criticism and praise. It repeated, first, a long-standing general warning against the arms race. "We deplore in particular," the statement read, "the building of vast arsenals of nuclear weaponry." Then, with specific reference to the fact that so many missiles could be concentrated in one place, it recognized the possibility that such a concentration might invite a first-strike attack by an aggressor, bringing deadly fallout to much of the nation. After reviewing several other objections, the First Presidency then pointed to the great irony of what was happening on the doorstep of a people whose whole religious tradition was devoted to peace:

> Our fathers came to this western area to establish a base from which to carry the gospel of peace to the peoples of the earth. It is ironic, and a denial of the very essence of that gospel, that in this same general area there should be constructed a mammoth weapons system potentially capable of destroying much of civilization.
>
> With the most serious concern over the pressing moral question of possible nuclear conflict, we plead with our national leaders to marshal the genius of the nation to find viable alternatives which will secure at an earlier date and with fewer hazards the protection from possible enemy aggression, which is our common concern.[23]

In Matheson's mind, anything he and his staff had done previously "paled by comparison to the position of the church."[24] Not only did it help solidify public opinion in Utah, but it brought Utah's Congressional delegation on board. Senator Jake Garn, for example, although still an advocate of MX, began to work on alternative basing schemes. Whether President Reagan was directly influenced by the LDS stance is unclear, but in October 1981, he came out in opposition to racetrack basing in Utah and Nevada. As far as Matheson was concerned, the battle was won. Years later, even though a site in Texas was agreed upon and millions of dollars were spent in initial preparation for it, the MX system was abandoned.

Matheson had more battles to fight with the federal leviathan. One concerned the transfer of nearly nine hundred Weteye bombs, filled with deadly nerve gas, from the Rocky Mountain Arsenal in Denver to the Tooele (Utah)Army Depot. In 1939, Matheson learned that the Department of Defense had decided to make the transfer, and he was angered by the fact that no one had notified him. It was another example of a "failure of the federal-state partnership and illustrated the callous disregard federal agencies have for the states, particularly those involved in national security matters."[25]

Concerned with the implications for health and safety because of possible leakage from the bombs, Matheson filed suit in federal court. When it became apparent that the matter could be settled out of court, the suit was withdrawn. On February 26, 1980, the Carter administration announced its decision to back off the transfer. But the victory was short-lived. Later in the year Colorado's Senator Gary Hart got an amendment on a bill going through Congress that, ultimately, required the move. Utah's only advantage was that Governor Matheson's efforts resulted in the Army imposing much more stringent safety requirements during the move. The Weteyes arrived in Utah in August 1981. Twenty years later, they were destroyed.[26]

Beginning in 1982, Matheson became involved in a battle to prevent the federal government from locating a nuclear waste dump at Gibson Dome, close to Canyonlands National Park. By that time Utah's governor considered himself a "scarred veteran of intergovernmental relations,"[27] and he mounted an effective campaign against the dump being placed in Utah. The debate went on for more than two years, but finally, at the end of 1984, the Department of Energy removed Gibson Dome from its list of possible locations.

Each of these issues involved the relationship between the states and the federal government. Matheson believed that the federal bureaucracy had grown so huge and powerful that it too easily overrode the legitimate interests and prerogatives of the state. The history of Utah, he reflected, had been a "perfect example" of acceptance and compliance with federal demands. This, he believed, must change, and it was up to the governors to lead out in working for change. "While we are citizens of the federal system and have a solemn obligation to help solve national security problems, we must also speak for the people of the states. Our duty is not only to accommodate federal interests but to protect state interests as well."[28]

Sagebrush, Land, and Water: National, State, and Private Interests

As if atomic testing, MX, nerve gas, and nuclear waste were not enough to worry about, Utah also found itself in the thick of a different kind of debate over federal-state relations. The Sagebrush Rebellion was a controversial effort to persuade the federal government to transfer its public lands to the states in which they were located.

One thing that distinguished most western states from others was the fact that much of their land area was not settled in the nineteenth century and therefore remained under the ownership and management of the federal government. In the twentieth century, under the prodding of various groups concerned with conservation and with the environment, federal land policy gradually shifted from disposal to retention and regulation for public purposes and in the national interest. In 1946 the Bureau of Land Management (BLM) was created, and a 1964 law provided for multiple-use management. Five years later the National Environmental Policy Act required the filing of an Environmental Impact Statement when any major actions affecting the environment were contemplated on federal lands. This was followed, over the next several years, by other laws designed to protect endangered species and to deal with a host of additional environmental concerns. The Federal Land Policy and Management Act (FLPMA) of 1976 proclaimed that it was the policy of the United States government to retain public lands, and it mandated multiple-use management under the BLM.[29] At the end of the 1980s, about 67 percent of Utah's land area belonged to the federal government. The BLM managed 22 million acres, or about 42 percent, while the rest of the federal domain consisted of national forest land, wildlife reserves, and land under the administration of the Department of Defense, the Bureau of Reclamation, or the Park Service.

In the years following World War II, Utah was involved in several disputes over the use of federal lands.[30] After Matheson become governor, he made an extensive reexamination of federal land policy and concluded that there was a clear need for a more effective partnership between the state and the federal government. One of his concerns was the fact that much state-owned land consisted of isolated sections completely surrounded by federal lands, thus limiting both access and the possibility of economic development.

Meanwhile, many private citizens and special interests in the West grew weary of the proliferation of federal environmental legislation. They saw the public lands as an economic resource that the government was over-regulating, making it almost impossible for growth and development to take place. Such concerns gave birth to the Sagebrush Rebellion."[31]

In 1979, the state of Nevada fired one of the early salvos when its legislature claimed title to all BLM lands within the state's boundaries.[32] The federal government owned and managed 85 percent of all of the land in Nevada, and the BLM managed 80 percent of that.[33] The federal government paid little attention to Nevada's attack, but the idea spread and Utah's Senator Orrin Hatch embraced it with enthusiasm. He even obtained several influential cosponsors for his proposed Western Lands Distribution and Regional Equalization Bill, which would have provided a mechanism for transferring federal lands to the states. But the bill died in committee.

By the fall of 1979, the Sagebrush Rebellion was in full bloom, but so was a counterattack from environmentalists and other opponents who saw it as an effort to ultimately turn the public lands over to private ownership. But even if the states retained ownership, opponents had no confidence that the states could manage the public lands any more effectively than the federal government. In fact, they feared that state legislatures and bureaucrats might be more amenable to the demands of ranchers, mining companies, developers, and other special interests, thus effectively undermining environmental, conservation, and multiple-use efforts.

An incident of civil disobedience outside Moab, county seat for Grand County, represented in microcosm what the Sagebrush Rebellion was all about.[34] Most of Grand County was on federal land, and about 33 percent of its labor force was employed in agriculture and mining, both of which were heavily affected by federal land policy. On July 4, 1980, about three hundred people gathered outside Moab, many wearing insignias reading "I am a Sage-

Image 5.4: Sagebrush Rebellion. The gathering of over three hundred people outside Moab on July 4, 1980, was an apt microcosm of this widespread protest against federal land policies. Photo courtesy of https://commons.wikimedia.org/wiki/File:Sagebrush_Rebellion_July_4th,_1980_Grand_County_Utah.JPG

brush Rebel." The colors were presented, the national anthem was sung, and political speeches were given from the back of a Caterpillar bulldozer decorated with a "SAGEBRUSH REBEL" sticker. County commissioners angrily berated the federal bureaucracy, particularly the BLM, declaring that the people of the area were going to take over their own destiny *and* preserve the freedoms guaranteed them by the US Constitution. Then, at the end of the speech-making, a bulldozer began to illegally scrape a road across a BLM wilderness study area that blocked access to a parcel of state-owned land that had potential for mineral development. The BLM responded by informing the Grand County Commission that within ten days the area must be restored to its original condition or the BLM would do it and the cost would be deducted from whatever federal grants were coming to the area. Ultimately the commissioners agreed to pay for the restoration.

No one believed that the county commissioners could actually get away with violating the law. Rather, they were making what Matheson called "a symbolic protest against what they felt was an attempt by the federal government to deprive them of their right to use the land and to earn a living."[35] Their action was no different in principle from a long American tradition of deliberate but peaceful violation of laws the people considered unjust. The idea was to bring such laws dramatically to the awareness of the public. Such action was almost a tradition in Utah a century earlier,[36] and was exemplified in twentieth century America by "sit-ins" in behalf of civil rights. The Grand County protest encouraged angry, sometimes extreme, harangues against the government from other sagebrush rebels. John L. Harmer, a leader of the rebellion in Utah, grumbled in print that the confrontation at Moab demonstrated "the federal government's contempt for local authority and interests and their determination to eliminate any vestige of local control over the public domain."[37] Harmer perhaps overstated the case, but his comment tellingly captured the outrage and frustration of a growing number of citizens and special interests in Utah and the West.

Governor Matheson did not support the Sagebrush Rebellion, but he was as upset as anyone with what he characterized as "inflexibility and insularity on the part of federal land managers." He wanted to find an alternative that would give the states a greater voice in managing federal lands, and he hoped to take advantage of the rebellion in his effort to get the West "back in the driver's seat."[38]

When the 1980 legislature began debate on a bill similar to that of Nevada's, claiming title to BLM lands within its borders, it seemed apparent that public opinion in Utah supported it. Matheson, skeptical of this solution, promised to sign the bill only if it contained a provision that it would not go into effect until Nevada's law had been sustained in the United States Supreme Court. The proviso was included, Matheson signed the bill, but Nevada chose not to enter into litigation. Utah's law, therefore, never went into effect. Arizona, New Mexico, and Wyoming also passed legislation patterned after that of Nevada, but they all raised serious constitutional questions, and none were ever set in motion.[39]

In 1980 it appeared that, if elected president of the United States, Ronald Reagan would add the prestige of the White House to the rebellion. In August, in a campaign speech in Salt Lake City, he made his position known by declaring, "I am a sagebrush rebel." After his election he sent a telegram to the "Sagebrush Convention" convening in Salt Lake City. "Best wishes to all my fellow Sagebrush Rebels," he said, and he promised to work toward a "sagebrush solution."[40] In 1981 he named James Watt, another sagebrush rebel, as Secretary of the Interior. But as the two came face-to-face with all the movement's intricate political ramifications, and saw the original support for the rebellion dwindling, they gradually shifted strategy. Watt, in fact, said that he thought conveying the land to the states was wasteful. The real problem, he said, was that the Department of the Interior had "become almost hostile to many interests in the West." He promised that the new administration would manage the public lands as a "good neighbor. and let the 'Sagebrush Rebellion' die because of friendly relations."[41]

This was exactly the attitude Matheson appreciated because it was designed to diffuse the rebellion and, at the same time, obtain more state and local input into the way the public lands were administered. Encouraged, the Matheson administration developed a plan, called Project BOLD, which was designed to trade isolated sections of state land for federal land in order to create larger state blocks that would be more practical to oversee and develop. To his great disappointment, Matheson was unable to get the federal government to accept the plan.[42]

In the end, the Sagebrush Rebellion did not fail completely. As the author of an important, detailed analysis of its history observed, the rebellion "left an identifiable mark on the policy landscape." Its initial impetus was the plethora of environmental regulations, but during the Reagan administration there was a "policy tilt" that paid serious attention to the demands of the sagebrush rebels and slowed down the environmental movement.[43] From Matheson's perspective, the Sagebrush Rebellion did some good in terms of his overriding concern for improved federal-state relations. It increased public involvement in planning and improved relationships between the state and federal land managers, who, Matheson observed, became "sensitive to state interests" and were more willing to cooperate with state officials.[44]

Even more contentious than the Sagebrush Rebellion was the wilderness issue. The 1964 National Wilderness Preservation System Act defined wilderness as "an area where the earth and its community of life are untrammeled by man, where man himself is a visitor who does not remain." Under the Act, the National Forest Service, the Bureau of Land Management, and the National Park Service were required to make recommendations as to what areas should be set aside as wilderness. At the beginning of the Matheson administration, Utah was the only state in the nation with no specified wilderness areas, but the governor soon received a letter from the Forest Service telling him that it planned to so designate certain areas as part of its Roadless Area Review and Evaluation process. The first location to be set aside as wilderness was the Lone Peak area in the mountains east of Salt Lake City.

This was the beginning of open controversy. Wilderness enthusiasts felt encouraged to push for more, while some opponents nursed an exaggerated fear that if the process continued most of the state could be designated as wilderness. Many county officials and businessmen quickly jumped on the anti-wilderness bandwagon while Matheson tried to plot a middle curse that would take into account private interests, state concerns, and the perspectives of federal land managers.

But at that point, wilderness planning seemed completely uncoordinated, leading Matheson to approve the formation of a State Wilderness Committee. Early in 1978 the state also adopted a wilderness policy that defined wilderness in much the same way as the federal Wilderness Act but with the proviso that the need to protect wilderness resources must be balanced with the need for future resource development. It also said that the state and affected local governments must participate in plans for managing designated wilderness areas.

The first State Wilderness Committee consisted of representatives from relevant state offices, representatives from five counties, and a staff representative from each of Utah's congressional delegates. Unfortunately, the structure of the committee itself represented a potential for conflict. In the fall of 1978 the committee recommended that 684,000 acres be designated as wilderness and that further study be conducted on another 123,400 acres. This was far less area than avid conservationist and wilderness groups wanted but much more than the five county officials on the committee thought proper. The county officials were livid and complained to the governor that they were outnumbered by state officials and therefore had no effective voice.

State and federal studies continued, with livestock and other agricultural interests letting it be known that they were opposed to any wilderness designation at all. Matheson, meanwhile, reconstituted the Wilderness Committee so that it consisted of five state department heads and five local representatives. Matheson also coordinated state efforts with Senator Jake Garn, who worked to keep Utah's Congressional delegation together in seeking the right kind of national legislation.

In March 1979, Matheson endorsed the State Wilderness Committee's final recommendation that 408,000 acres be designated as wilderness. The proposal, though smaller than the Forest Service recommendation, had the advantage of not interfering with the completion of the Central Utah Project, not conflicting significantly with grazing, and affecting timber interests only marginally. But as he worked toward getting legislation through Congress, Matheson had to walk a tightrope between various outspoken interest groups. In order to present a united front he had to convince county commissioners that most of their concerns were taken care of. On the other hand, he had to persuade members of the Utah Wilderness Association, who were pressing for considerably more acreage, that without their cooperation Congress would probably pass no wilderness bill at all. Until Utahns seemed united, their Congressional delegation could hardly be expected to push for the bill Matheson thought would be in the state's best interest. But suddenly the Reagan administration announced its intent to conduct a new roadless area review and evaluation. This was more than anyone in Utah could stomach and led to a refreshing meeting of the minds, or at least a willingness to compromise, between various Utah groups.

When legislation was introduced in Congress in November 1983, Utah environmentalists gave it restrained but favorable support, as did various elected officials throughout the state. The proposed bill called for more than 706,000 acres of wilderness—more than most county officials wanted and less than environmentalists were really happy with, but it was a reasonable compromise.[46] Finally, with the support of Utah's Congressional delegation, the Utah Wilderness Act was passed and signed by President Reagan in 1984. That, along with the thirty thousand–acre Lone Peak area and a 22,500-acre BLM wilderness on the border of Arizona, gave Utah close to 760,000 acres of wilderness at the end of Matheson's administration.

Although it was a compromise, Matheson considered the Wilderness Act "a unique intergovernmental success, involving federal, state and local deliberation and needing substantial input from affected citizens and interest groups."[47]

Another matter of vital concern to the Matheson administration was water, and especially the continuing battle over the Bureau of Reclamation's Central Utah Project. Authorized in 1956, the project was only one-third complete and at least twenty years behind schedule. There were still objections to the CUP, even from some Utahns, but more critical were federal budget considerations. President Jimmy Carter threatened the project's very existence when in February 1977 he placed the Bonneville unit of the CUP on a list of nineteen federal projects for which funding would be eliminated.

Matheson learned of Carter's announcement only when he landed at the Denver airport en route to a meeting with other western governors and Secretary of the Interior Cecil Andrus concerning a devastating drought. The other governors were also caught off guard, and the meeting turned into an angry questioning of Andrus about what they felt were poorly informed decisions made with neither the knowledge nor the participation of the states. But Andrus, too, was surprised—the president had not consulted with him on the final decision—and he promised to conduct public hearings on the threatened projects. Carter's announcement and the furious response of the governors opened another long debate over federal water policy.

Matheson and his staff immediately began to gather information to present at an open hearing in Salt Lake City on March 23 and before a Congressional committee on March 25. In both places they reiterated the benefits of the project and carefully pointed out that all the relevant issues had been addressed fully in the original environmental impact statement. There would be some environmental damage but the plans provided funds for the best mitigation possible.[48] Matheson later observed that, in the long run, Carter actually did Utah a favor: by forcing a new public debate he allowed Matheson's administration to educate a whole new generation of Utahns on the importance of water policy.

Members of Utah's Congressional delegation, meanwhile, used all their influence to keep the budget intact. They inundated the president with information, to the extent that by mid-September he changed his mind. When Congressmen Gunn McKay and Dan Marriott emerged from a meeting with Carter, McKay observed that, after learning more, Carter had actually "singled out" the CUP as a reclamation project he was willing to support. As a result, nearly $33 million dollars were appropriated to the CUP for the following fiscal year.[49]

The Carter administration also instituted a national water study, in an effort to develop a comprehensive, unified development program. At the same time, in November 1977, the Western Governors' Conference organized the Western Governors' Policy Office (WESTPO). The national administration and the governors had to work together on water policy, they said, and Secretary Andrus agreed. A comprehensive national policy was never agreed upon, but when President Carter issued his national water policy message in June 1978, better federal-state cooperation in water resource planning was among its major objectives.

Matheson was also concerned with developing a state water policy, which meant sharing the costs of large irrigation and power projects that were not part of the CUP. During his administration he was able to persuade the legislature to appropriate $70 million in general obligation bonds for such purposes. By 1985 the Board of Water Resources administered more than $125 million in revolving cash and repayable loans.[50]

Other Resource Development and Environmental Problems

Land management, water, and the environment were all parts of a large, complicated, and interrelated economic and social system. Another part, fraught with equal potential for conflict, was energy resource development, which was inseparably intertwined with environmental issues.

The Intermountain Power Project (IPP) was initiated in the 1970s by the Intermountain Consumer Power Association (ICPA), composed of twenty-three Utah cities that had developed their own public power program. After extensive resource and environmental studies, it was determined that a new plant would be located at Salt Wash, a site eight miles east of the northern end of Capitol Reef National Monument. However, after more studies at the federal level, Secretary of the Interior Andrus was convinced that the proposed plant presented a great potential danger to the monument, and he urged Governor Matheson to come up with an alternative site.

The issue could have been explosive. Several people urged the governor not to give in to Washington but, if necessary, to go to court over the matter. But Matheson was convinced that litigation would be both costly and useless, so he instructed the Energy Conservation Development Council to look for alternatives that would meet federal air quality requirements. In addition, Secretary Andrus agreed to have federal officials participate in the search for other sites. This was an ideal situation for federal-state cooperation as diverse elements from the federal government, the state government, environmental groups, and private agencies all became involved. In the end, the IPP agreed to a site near Lynndyl, in Millard County.

But the project raised other environmental concerns, including adverse effects on Carbon and Emery counties, where coal for the huge power plant would be mined. The federal government agreed to provide funds to help mitigate the effect in those two counties as well as in Millard County. IPP itself also provided funds to assist the affected communities. At the same time, IPP was given tax-exempt status because a significant portion of its power was going to public power entities.⁵¹ Groundbreaking for the $9 billion, three thousand megawatt project took place in October 1981.

The IPP could have gone the way of the Kaiparowits project (see chapter 4), ending not only in failure but also in distrust and recrimination. Instead, it ended up in a reasonable compromise. Few people were completely happy, yet most were convinced that this solution did the best job of balancing all interests. It worked because responsible people at both the federal and state levels were willing to use the National Environmental Policy Act (NEPA) of 1969 and the Environmental Impact Statement (EIS) as means to responsible ends, not as ends themselves. In the case of MX and the Weteye, the state used the EIS to help bar an unwanted action. In other cases, such as IPP, wilderness, various water projects, mining, and road building, the EIS was used to improve decision making. As Matheson observed, neither the NEPA nor the EIS was perfect, but they provided a way to achieve a balance in decision making as well as between the often conflicting aims of development and environmental protection. His plea for continuing in the tradition of reasonable compromise was impassioned but sensible:

> We can develop our natural resources and preserve the environment if we are willing to follow the spirit of NEPA, utilize the EIS or a similar process in making decisions; in so doing we can find the right balance in our decision making. Success or failure will affect both present and future generations in a dramatic way. The extra paperwork and time is a small price if we can make better decisions as a result.⁵²

There were other difficult environmental issues, each laden with heavy economic consequences. One was the continuing story of US Steel's Geneva plant, in Utah County, and its efforts to bring its air and water pollution in line with federal standards. The Clean Air Act of 1977 required more heavy investment than ever before in order to meet new emission standards. As a result, there were increasingly frequent hints that Geneva might be forced to close. But the company was already in the process of installing

Image 5.5: The town of Thistle after the disastrous landslide and flood of 1983 covered it with water. Used by permission, Utah State Historical Society, all rights reserved.

a considerable amount of new equipment and company officials were livid at a report of a nonprofit New York ecological group claiming that Geneva showed the worst record of deterioration in pollution abatement of all the forty-seven plants studied. "These charges are totally unfounded!" replied Henry Huish, plant general superintendent. "How could any responsible, investigative group not know about Geneva's $9 million baghouse collector being constructed at the power house?"[53]

Meanwhile, the EPA established 1982 as a deadline for meeting minimum standards, and Geneva agreed to spend $50 million on improvements over three years. But the EPA rejected Geneva's plan in favor of an alternate plan that could have cost an additional $128 million. This prompted a group of Utah County residents called the Citizens Coalition to Save Geneva to put heavy pressure on Utah's Congressional delegation and urge mass letter writing to the EPA in an effort to get it to accept the more economical plan. Newspaper editorials and letters to the editor were overwhelmingly critical of what they pictured as an unbending federal bureaucracy that was insensitive to local needs and wishes. Governor Matheson promised that the state would go to court, if necessary, to defend Geneva against the EPA, and Congressman Gunn McKay worked tirelessly to keep negotiators talking to each other. Finally, in October 1980, Geneva agreed to up its expenditures on new pollution controls to $94.5 million. The compromise was accepted.[54]

As usual, only some of the environmental problems of these years were man-made, and those caused by nature had devastating consequences. With the 1982–83 snowpack ranging from 150 to 400 percent above normal, the year 1983 was especially brutal. On April 14 over four million yards of mud slid down a mountain in Spanish Fork Canyon. The slide blocked the Spanish Fork River, created a mile-long artificial lake, destroyed over a mile of highway and railroad track, and caused the town of Thistle to be almost completely submerged. The lake was drained in October, but the state had to build in the area a completely new highway that was higher and hopefully drier. Later, a massive slide east of Gunnison dammed up Twelve Mile River, but the dam broke on May 25 sending a thirty-foot wall of water down the canyon.

On May 30, an area three blocks square in Farmington was inundated by water and mud from Rudd Creek. The following night, an even worse disaster hit the east side of Bountiful. Residents knew of the potential danger because of the spring warming in the water-logged hills. They had worked for days building dikes and dredging creeks, but most of the barriers simply crumbled under the force of mud and water that rushed into the area about 11:30 p.m. Also late in May, flooding in Salt Lake City became so severe that waters were diverted down two major streets, 1200 South and State Street. For two weeks, twenty-five to thirty thousand volunteers placed sandbags in order to prevent worse damage. *Newsweek* reported that a fourteen-mile river ran through Salt Lake City, with rumored good fishing near the Federal Building.[55] Near Delta, the spillway of the DMAD dam developed problems because of high runoff. On June 16, crews began working to shore up the dam, but a week later it broke, dumping ten billion gallons of water into the Sevier River, swamping the desert farming communities of Deseret and Oasis and causing millions of dollars' worth of damage to farms and homes. The floods and landslides of May and June alone wreaked at least $250 million worth of damages in Utah and caused twenty-two of the state's twenty-nine counties to be declared federal disaster areas. As if this were not enough, an unusually hot July brought fires that destroyed hundreds of thousands of acres of brushlands, and then the storms of August brought more flooding to the state.

Nature continued its tirade in 1984. Heavy snows threatened the food supply for the wildlife, driving starving deer into the foothills and leading to an all-out effort to provide food for them. The plight of Utah's deer, in fact, received nationwide publicity, including television coverage, and attracted contributions from all over the country. Flooding recurred in the spring, with more damaging mudslides, especially in the Salt Lake Valley.

Much of the 1983-84 flood damage took place around the Great Salt Lake, which in 1984 reached a peak of 4,209.25 feet, the highest level in 106 years. In order to lower the water level in the south end of the lake, the Southern Pacific causeway was breached. The possibility that the water would not subside for many years presented serious problems for the commercial development of the lakeshore area and gave rise to talk of various other remedies, including building dams along the Bear River to halt the flow of water into the lake. Another proposal, which presented the next governor with one of his most difficult and controversial decisions, was to pump water from the lake into the west desert.

On December 19, 1984, still another kind of disaster grabbed national headlines. The most deadly coal mine fire in the history of Utah killed eighteen miners and nine company officials at the Wilberg mine in Emery County. Burning out of control, the fire quelled every attempt even to recover the bodies, which was not accomplished until a year later. After a lengthy investigation. the Mine Safety and Health Administration (MSHA) finally concluded that the fire was touched off by a faulty air compressor running unattended in a non-fireproofed area. Thirty-four citations, including nine that related directly to the fire, were issued against

Utah Power and Light, owner of the mine, and Emery Mining Company, the mine operator. However, the United Mine Workers of America (UMWA) criticized MSHA for focusing just on the cause of the fire and not on the cause of the deaths as well. The union asserted that casualties could have been prevented if there had been an escape route. After a Senate hearing on the disaster, Utah's Senator Orrin G. Hatch asked the General Accounting Office (GAO) to investigate MSHA. In November 1987, GAO cited MSHA on several serious counts, including allowing the Wilberg Mine to operate under outdated plans for firefighting and evacuation.[56]

Matheson and the West: The Quest for Regional Cooperation

No one ever doubted that Utah's economic destiny was unalterably tied to the larger scene, but during Matheson's administration the implications of this reality became more clear than ever before. Matheson became more involved in regional and national organizations—and in making substantive changes in some of them—than any previous governor, although much of what he did was built on a foundation laid by Governor Rampton.

One problem was overlapping jurisdictions. The Economic Development Act of 1965 encouraged states to work together in regional organizations in order to deal with regional economic problems. Ten years later, regional commissions, such as the Four Corners Regional Commission to which Utah belonged, had sprung up all over the nation. However, during the Nixon administration ten federal regions were created, which did not correspond geographically with the regional commissions previously developed by the states. In this illogical arrangement Utah, Colorado, New Mexico, Arizona, and Nevada all belonged to the Four Corners Regional Commission, but Utah and Colorado were also part of a federal region headquartered in Denver, New Mexico was in a region headquartered in Dallas, and Nevada and Arizona were part of a region with headquarters in San Francisco. In addition, a number of other interstate organizations were formed to deal with special issues, such as energy.

Just sorting out the maze of administrative arrangements was complex in itself, but by the time Matheson came on the scene, governors everywhere wondered whether any of these regional organizations provided effective assistance to state and local governments. At its 1977 meeting the Western Governors' Conference (WGC) eliminated two regional organizations and created the Western Governors' Policy Office (WESTPO), which served as a regional forum where governors could deal with national, regional, interstate, and federal-state issues.

Thirteen western states eventually became part of the new organization. It worked well in dealing with some questions, but its activities still overlapped with those of WGC. Moreover, a newly elected governor was not automatically a member of either organization. Matheson argued that, as a distinctive region with distinctive problems, the western states needed an organization in which all new governors became members automatically. His proposal was adopted at the 1984 midwinter meeting of the National Governors Association (NGA). A new entity, the Western Governors' Association (WGA) was formed, replacing both WESTPO and WGC and including eighteen states and the Pacific territories.[57] Matheson also had an effect on the NGA. Becoming its president in 1982, he implemented a series of important reforms.[58]

Utah and the Nation: Selected Economic Issues

Although these administrative issues had important economic implications for Utah, the ramifications were not immediately apparent to the public. More evident was the ever-growing need to improve Utah's highway system, and the apparently sluggish progress on Utah's share of the interstate highway program. The legislature raised the fuel tax by two cents per gallon in both 1978 and 1982, but these increases barely kept up with inflation. In mid-1982, with 15.3 percent of the 938 miles of projected interstate not yet complete, Utah was still the second highest among the states in the number of miles not yet open. However, the estimated cost of completing even that much was $600 million. By some estimates, unless both the federal and state fuel taxes were increased substantially the system would never be complete. Alternatives included reducing or eliminating federal aid to highway programs that seemed to be of predominantly local interest.[59] Understandably, neither alternative was very popular.

What was popular in Utah was the idea of tax relief, especially in light of rapidly spiraling inflation. In 1978, amid a widely publicized "taxpayer revolt," California captured national attention with its voter-initiated Proposition 13 that placed heavy restrictions on property taxes. Seven other states followed suit that year by limiting property taxes or government spending. In October 1978, Governor Matheson's Tax Revision Study Committee recommended a five-year program of gradual tax relief, focusing primarily on property and income taxes.[60] In 1979 the legislature passed some $74.5 million in tax relief. It included property tax rebates for homeowners and renters, "circuit breaker" relief for senior citizens and widows and widowers, a four-mill reduction in local property tax levies for schools, and other taxing restrictions. A problem with these reductions and limitations, however, was that they carried potentially serious consequences for funding public schools.[61]

Utah also experienced a number of labor problems during these years. In 1980, a strike at Kennecott Copper was part of a nationwide copper strike that idled about thirty-six thousand workers. It ended on September 10, after union members voted to accept a contract that would raise their hourly wage from $10.23 to $14.20 over a three-year period. Observers estimated, however, that the seventy-one day strike cost the Utah economy nearly $100 million, including $25 million in lost wages and more than $70 million in purchases of goods and services.[62]

At the same time, reflecting a deepening national depression, Utah's unemployment rate reached 9 percent in 1982, as compared with only 5.8 percent the previous year. There were layoffs in mining, manufacturing, and construction. In an effort to cope with the recession, the governor ordered a 2 percent cut in state spending and called a special session of the legislature to consider a major bonding program for water projects, highways, and state building construction. When the legislature met on December 15

279

and 16 it approved $40 million in federal grant anticipation notes for accelerating interstate highway construction and a $25 million general obligation bond that would assure payment on the notes until the state received federal reimbursement.[63]

The recession became more severe in 1984 with layoffs at Kennecott Copper and Geneva. Kennecott's July layoff of a thousand workers, blamed on foreign competition and sagging demand, was the largest one-time layoff in Utah history. Early the next year the company announced the layoff of another 2,200 workers over the next six months,[64] resulting in a cessation of mining operations at Bingham Canyon. However, after modernization efforts, the mine reopened two years later. At Geneva Steel, the number of employees dwindled from five thousand in 1981 to 2,500 in 1984, primarily because of the company's inability to remain fully competitive in the international market.[65]

Utah and the Nation: Women's Issues

Of all the public activities in Utah during these years, perhaps none evoked more widespread interest and diversity of opinion than the International Women's Year (IWY) Conference in Salt Lake City in 1977. Coming in the wake of Utah's rejection of the Equal Rights Amendment (see chapter 4), the conference had an equally polarizing effect. However, it also made many Utahns more aware of the multifaceted nature of the issues facing women throughout the world. Feminism was not a monolithic force dedicated to a single political agenda but, rather, a movement that incorporated a variety of perspectives in its quest for equal rights and opportunities for women.[66]

Prior to 1977, in an effort to promote worldwide discussion of the status of women, the United Nations had designated the year 1975 as "International Women's Year." From June 19 to July 2 of that year, the U.N.'s International Women's Year Conference met in Mexico City. Among the 8,300 people attending this unprecedented meeting were forty-one women from Utah, there as unofficial delegates. The conference produced a declaration that set the tone for many conferences to follow. It also had a profoundly moving effect on all the women there by showing them the international nature of their concerns and inspiring them with increasing commitment to working for a better world.

Meanwhile, commensurate with President Gerald Ford's 1975 executive order creating a National Commission for the Observance of IWY, preparations were made for a series of state IWY conferences that culminated in a national conference in Houston, Texas, in November 1977. National legislation provided funding as well as broad, well-balanced guidelines for the conferences.[67] Of major importance was the fact that they were not to be gatherings of the intellectual, social, or political elite among women. Rather, they were intended to include women from every walk of life and to represent the diversity of women's interests and concerns. The hope was that the conferences would provide forums for open discussion of differing views in an atmosphere of mutual respect and tolerance.

Most of the state conferences were held between January and July 1977, drawing more than 150,000 women. In some states there was open conflict between the forces of change and the supporters of the status quo, particularly in those states, like Utah, that had not ratified the ERA.

The Utah IWY conference drew the largest attendance of any in the nation and gave conservative forces their most resounding victory. More than fourteen thousand women jammed the Salt Palace in Salt Lake City on June 24 and 25. Most were Mormon women ready to vote against every recommendation of the national committee in their belief that by doing so they would be defending correct principles. In some ways the conference was one of the most significant social-political episodes in this era of Utah history because it poignantly reflected deep-seated and sometimes conflicting aspects of Utah culture: the continuing quest for equality and for greater understanding of the proper roles of women in society; support of many Utah women for much of the national feminist agenda; conservative political forces who were opposed to that agenda and that knew how to take advantage of Utah's unique religious makeup; policies of the LDS Church; and, mixed with but not necessarily limited to the conservative agenda, fear of the growing influence of the federal government. It was partly for the latter reason that many women were persuaded to vote against anything the national committee wanted, for that committee seemed to rely on new national legislation.

Chair of Utah's state coordinating committee was Jan L. Tyler, a professor of education at Brigham Young University, who had been appointed by Governor Rampton in 1976. Although it was attacked by critics as being liberal and pro-ERA, the state committee actually represented a wide diversity of voices. The thirty-two members of the committee represented various ecclesiastical organizations, ethnic groups, and political interests and included such well-known women as Norma Matheson, a long-time participant in community activities, and Belle S. Spafford, former general president of the LDS Women's Relief Society. After six months of work, the resolutions subcommittee formulated with a set of resolutions that its members felt represented a consensus of women's interests. They did not, however, represent a complete consensus of the members of the coordinating committee, and some ran counter to the resolutions of the national committee.[68]

In April 1977, twenty-two task forces began working on plans for the conference workshops. They trained coordinators to hold mass meetings throughout the state. Jan Tyler and her committee wanted to disseminate the kind of information that would lead to responsible, informed, and amiable discussion of issues that might be highly controversial.

Tyler asked Barbara Smith, general president of the LDS Women's Relief Society, to invite Mormon women to attend the mass meetings and to prepare a fact sheet on the national recommendations so that the women would arrive at the meetings well acquainted with the issues. Smith, in turn, assigned Relief Society board members to study the resolutions and to present their findings to the board. Board members also conducted surveys in order to ascertain what Mormon women around the state felt were the most important issues. On some issues, such as the ERA, abortion, and homosexuality, the Relief Society leaders felt compelled to take a stand when the national recommendations violated their religious beliefs. Nevertheless, contrary to the misinformation some Mormon women received through other sources, there was no attempt on the part of the Relief Society to get the women to automatically vote "no" on every national recommendation.[69]

The Relief Society, not wanting to hold its own seminars for fear of being accused of indoctrinating people, proposed asking the *Deseret News* to publish a series of articles on the issues and sending a letter to the wards urging women's participation in the conference and suggesting that they read the articles in the newspaper. church leaders liked the idea but instead of having the Relief Society initiate the recommendation they telephoned regional representatives, asking them to inform the wards of the conference and suggest that each ward assign ten women to attend. A follow-up letter then went out from the office of Ezra Taft Benson, president of the Quorum of the Twelve, though on Relief Society letterhead. Addressed to regional representatives, with enough copies attached for all wards and stakes, the letter urged the reading of the *Deseret News* articles and participation in the conference. The Relief Society then sent another followup letter to stake Relief Society presidents. The request was quickly translated into action in LDS wards around the state as Relief Society presidents and ward bishops selected women who would be asked to attend the conference.

Unfortunately, the involvement of the church opened the door for some unauthorized maneuvering by others. In May, mass meetings were held throughout the state, most of them conducted with little rancor. But the lines of information became confused, leaving many women with the impression that certain information was coming from the church when in fact it was not. An organization called Let's Govern Ourselves (LGO), led by Georgia B. Peterson, a Republican state legislator, sponsored its own meetings in an attempt to get a list of chosen candidates named as official delegates to the conference. Because of Peterson's close association with the Relief Society and LDS general authorities, there was a widely-held assumption that LGO represented a church view. In addition, certain conservative groups asked Barbara Smith for permission to hold instructional meetings, but Smith consistently refused to officially involve the Relief Society in such activities. Nevertheless, some of these non-Church, right-wing groups, such as the Eagle Forum and the Conservative Caucus, proceeded on their own to organize and instruct Mormon women about participation in the conference.

It was during these meetings that women received instructions to vote "no" on every national recommendation and to vote for a certain set of delegates. This action reflected a wrongly held assumption that the state IWYs were little more than parts of a national agenda designed to pass the ERA and pro-abortion laws. The literature circulated by these groups sounded so much like Relief Society literature that many women did not know the difference. Both before and during the conference, therefore, "feminists were pitted against homemakers who were portrayed as guardians of the home and family values, an unfortunate and inaccurate dichotomy that tainted debate on virtually every issue."[70] When Barbara Smith realized what was happening, she notified Dennis Ker, head of the Conservative Caucus, that using her name and the name of the church was entirely inappropriate, but by that time the damage was done.

The women who attended the conference came for a variety of reasons—some for information, some with a desire to debate the issues openly, some with a hope of getting most of the feminist agenda adopted, some with a determination to save their religious traditions from what they perceived to be the threat of feminism, and others simply because they were assigned. Many of the latter had never attended preliminary meetings and knew little or nothing about the issues. They attended plenary sessions, workshops, lectures, discussion groups, and movies. Some workshops went well, but in others bitterness and rancor broke out to the point of causing near disruption. In the final voting, the delegates defeated by an overwhelming majority every national resolution. In most cases the vote was nearly one thousand in favor, approximately eight thousand opposed, and two hundred or fewer "don't know." Conservative forces could have asked for no greater victory. Ironically, several of the state recommendations were approved, and some of these represented exactly the same position as some of the national recommendations that were so soundly defeated.

The conference also elected the fourteen anti-ERA candidates who appeared on the LGO list as delegates to the national convention. Whether they would have been elected anyway is conjectural, but the fact is that, as a group, they and their five alternates were highly capable, intelligent representatives of what was still a mainstream Utah perspective. In addition, as one writer characterized them, they were "united by a strong commitment to traditional religion as the source of their political beliefs."[71] Chair of the delegation was Georgia Peterson.

Although not an elected delegate to the Houston meeting, Jan Tyler attended as an invited guest and at her own expense. She was delighted to find an atmosphere of warmth and friendliness, in which she could converse freely with women from around the country with whom she shared many concerns. She was especially thrilled with the opening ceremony, when a torch was carried into the convention, representative of the one carried to the first women's rights conference in Seneca Fall, New York, in 1848. "The past telescoped in and the link was made with the present," she said. "I felt a real closeness with our foremothers. It was thrilling." Tyler was concerned for the members of the Utah delegation because they seemed unable to have the impact she felt they could have had. This was partly because they remained somewhat aloof but also, according to Tyler, because they had not grasped parliamentary procedure well enough to work effectively.[72] At the same time, some members of the delegation felt they were not treated with the same respect as other delegates. At times they were shouted down when they tried to express an opinion, chided in the press, and openly criticized in plenary sessions. This did nothing to allay their fears that the IWY was little more than a pressure group with a pre-determined agenda that did not allow for free discussion.[73] Nevertheless, the IWY was concerned with numerous issues of special interest to all women, although some of the resolutions that passed, such as those dealing with abortion and sexual preference, clearly were not to the liking of the Utah delegation.

The IWY came at a time when Americans were becoming more aware than ever before of issues involving women and when remarkable progress was being made toward more equal treatment in the workplace and under the law. Utah was no exception.

Education: Continuing Challenges and Achievements

The presence of the LDS Church affected not only women's issues in Utah but other social issues as well, including education. In 1978, the Logan school district became involved in a lawsuit related to the policy of granting a limited amount of high school credit for Bible classes taught in the LDS seminary program. Since early in the century, the state had allowed local school districts to grant released time for students to take religion classes at LDS seminaries or in programs offered by other churches. Courses limited to the Bible were granted high school credit on the theory that they were nondenominational and therefore not an unconstitutional mixing of church and state. That assumption, as well as the entire released-time program, was challenged by the American Civil Liberties Union. After a lengthy trial, a federal judge ruled that granting credit was unconstitutional but upheld the released-time practice.

The question of credit for Bible classes seemed to make little difference either to seminaries or to the schools. But the released-time program itself was another issue, and many school administrators were relieved that it remained intact. The reason was purely pragmatic: released time classes made a significant contribution toward alleviating the problem of overcrowding in the schools.

Mushrooming enrollment and school finance continued to plague school administrators during these years. There were at least three important reasons for the exploding enrollment: Utah's birthrate continued to climb, there was continuing in-migration of population, and there was a decline in the number of students attending private schools.[74] In 1982, the number of school-age children as a percentage of total population was the highest in the nation. All this resulted in an unfortunate paradox: although Utah collected and spent more per capita for public schools, and continued to lead the nation in the percentage of all state and local government expenditures for education.[75] The amount spent per student was smaller than any state except Alabama.[76]

General academic achievement remained high, but there were signs that Utah was not doing as well as it had in earlier years. Between 1972 and 1982 the performance of Utah students slipped from 14th to 17th place among the twenty-eight states administering the American College Test (ACT). Utah remained slightly above average in English, social science, and natural science, but fell below in mathematics. The implications of this caused school administrators to worry about students who were preparing for college.[77]

In some instances, Utah's educators did an especially remarkable job. In 1983, for example, six Utah schools were commended by President Ronald Reagan as being among the 144 most effective high schools in the country.[78] Utah schools also made noteworthy accomplishments in various kinds of specialized education. In 1983, approximately 3,200 out of nearly twenty thousand graduating seniors had taken advanced placement classes—a higher proportion than in any other state.[79] The state also began to place emphasis on a Limited English Proficiency (LEP) Program. The problems faced by non-English speaking students became especially apparent in 1975, when the first group of refugees from Southeast Asia arrived in the state. In 1977, recognizing that Utah was not doing enough to help these students, the legislature authorized an initial $317,100 for a bilingual program in school districts serving students with bilingual needs. But this was only a beginning. In the early 1980s the State Office of Education pointed out that considerable more help was needed for LEP students.[80]

The state also paid attention to migrant children, whose parents came to selected areas to work as farm laborers. Initially established in 1968, the migrant education program was an attempt to provide well-rounded academic work as well as recreational, vocational, and cultural activities. The children involved in the program were mostly Hispanic, but there were also Asian, Native American, and some Anglo students. Most were in the age range from kindergarten to sixth grade. There were some problems with the program, such as the need for better trained teachers, but by the 1980s the state was making a commendable effort to meet the needs of this important distinctive group. In 1985, Jerry Ortega, Director of Migrant Education, reported that many migrant students went on to high school, with ninety enrolled in grades 9 through 12 that year. Some had been recognized as runners-up for Utah's prestigious Sterling Scholarships. Migrant students were respected in their communities, said Ortega, and some had been involved in helping fellow migrants and in promoting pride in their ethnic heritage.[81]

The perennial problem of teacher salaries continued to nag at school boards and the legislature. In the 1978–79 school year, with an average public school salary of $13,910, Utah was 28th in the nation. In the previous ten years, the gap between Utah salaries and the average of the other surrounding had narrowed significantly,[82] but State Superintendent of Public Instruction Walter Talbot warned that unless something more was done about salaries the state would be unable to attract and keep high quality teachers.[83] The following year a 7.1 percent average boost made Utah salaries roughly equivalent to the average of the surrounding States.[84]

That increase was good news, as was a 1983 study that revealed that teacher turnover rate in Utah was the lowest in the nation. The Utah Foundation attributed this to the fact that salaries were becoming better while the general economy was doing poorly, prompting people to stay in education. The report also noted that most teaching positions were filled by certified teachers (a marked improvement over previous decades), although mathematics and sciences (the areas where Utah students were falling behind on ACT tests) still suffered from teachers with inadequate training.[85]

That same year, Americans everywhere were stirred by a National Commission on Excellence in Education report entitled *A Nation at Risk: The Imperative for Educational Reform*. Warning of a "rising tide of mediocrity" in the schools that threatened the well-being of the nation at large, the report was a scathing indictment of the whole public school system. The result was an intense national and local campaign to reform education systems throughout the country. Utah educators and concerned political leaders took the report seriously. Governor Matheson was clearly alarmed, and he declared that Utah must act immediately, while the subject was in the national limelight, and make sweeping reforms.[86]

In the summer of 1983, responding to *A Nation at Risk* and other reports on the declining quality of American education, Utah's State Board of Education appointed a 21-member Commission on Education Excellence. That fall the board began to implement the commission's recommendations for reform by establishing five goals: "(1) curriculum reform; (2) enhancing teaching as a profession; (3) improved planning for vocational-technical education; (4) utilization of physical resources; and (5) public and parental involvement in decision-making."[87] Governor Matheson, meanwhile, formed an eleven-member Utah Education Reform Steering Committee. In November that committee published *Education in Utah: A Call to Action*, which called upon the people of Utah to support efforts to raise more funds to enhance the quality of both public and higher education.

In January 1984 a number of educational support groups, such as the Utah School Boards Association and the Utah State Congress of Parents and Teachers, launched an intensive campaign aimed at generating legislative support for the needed reforms. The legislature considered a package calling for a $109 million increase in appropriations for the public schools but eventually approved only $69.4 million. This represented a 10.4 percent increase over the previous spending level and was considered by most educators to be an important step toward meeting the state's critical needs.[88] But, as Matheson's administration came to a close, it also put severe pressure on the incoming Republican administration and Republican legislature to make education a top priority.[89]

In an effort to make teaching more attractive as a lifetime profession, in 1984 the legislature also appropriated $15.2 million for inaugurating a career ladder program For the first time, teachers would be given clear financial incentives to improve their effectiveness, which would be determined by student performance and other criteria spelled out by the legislature. According to one study, as much as $1,000 per year might be added to the average salary.[90] Some teachers scoffed at the idea, calling for across-the-board increases in salary before such merit increases were implemented. In the face of their embarrassingly low salaries, they said, a career ladder only added insult to injury. Governor Matheson disagreed, and at the opening session of the Utah Education Association's annual convention in October 1984 he scolded these teachers for their lack of foresight. In the long run, he believed, the career ladder would make teaching a more attractive and rewarding profession, particularly if teachers themselves helped design it.[91] Significantly, a UEA survey demonstrated that approximately 65 percent of teachers throughout the state wanted the association to work with the legislature in refining and improving career ladder guidelines. Unfortunately, by the end of the year only one school district, the Provo School District, had raised enough money to provide the matching funds required by state legislation to fully fund the career ladder program.[92]

Funding from the legislature also allowed the State School Board to press for curriculum reform and strengthen graduation requirements. The legislature also increased its funding of scholarships to outstanding high school graduates and some students who were already in college in order to recruit them into teaching careers. Increased support in 1984 provided for 365 such scholarships.

The legislature also raised the amount available for productivity incentives from $300,000 to $1 million. School districts were encouraged to propose ways to increase efficiency and productivity. These proposals included year-round school, which provided more efficient use of both human and physical resources and extra pay for teachers. The first year-round program in the state began in the fall of 1984 at Westridge Elementary School in Provo. In 1985 schools in Washington, Jordan, and other districts were preparing to follow suit.

In another effort at effective reform, the legislature more than tripled the budget for vocational training, from $300,000 to $1 million. This came in response to a long-standing concern on the part of government, business leaders, and educators that the rapid growth of business and industry was increasing the need for workers with many different vocational skills. In 1980 a blue-ribbon commission appointed by Governor Matheson made a number of recommendations for improvement, but it was estimated that their full implementation would require $16 million over the next five years.[93] The financial boost in 1984 was only a fraction of what most people agreed was needed.

Another of the many efforts to improve school administration was the Principals Academy, endorsed by the Utah State Board of Education in 1984. Because half of the state's school principals would be retiring within a decade, some three hundred new, well-trained principals would be needed by 1994. At the academy, new and practicing principals would be able to sharpen their skills in curriculum, community outreach, teacher evaluation, and many other areas of importance.[94]

Utah continued to face serious problems in financing higher education as well. The escalating student population at the state's colleges and universities reached sixty thousand in 1981,[95] but the national recession, a resistance to raising taxes, and the federal government's policy of shifting more funding responsibility to state and local agencies only magnified the financial woes of the higher education system. Since part of the answer lay in receiving huge private donations, college presidents and governing boards around the country found themselves increasingly preoccupied with fund raising.[96]

Utah's dilemma was emphasized during the 1978–79 academic year: the nine state operated institutions of higher learning were required to make a 4 percent budget cut even though they experienced an unexpected 4 percent increase in enrollment, and, at the same time, the board was being bombarded with requests for strengthening academic programs.[97] Budget cuts had a disastrous effect. The Board of Regents reported in 1983 that over the previous four years nearly ten thousand additional students had been admitted with no equivalent increase in state funding, but that year, 3,500 qualified students were turned away simply because there were not enough funds to admit them. The regents also imposed a salary freeze on faculty members, leading some teachers to leave the profession for higher-paying jobs in private industry.[98] Teachers were finally given substantial raises in 1984, ranging from 9.2 percent at the University of Utah to 14.1 percent at Southern Utah State College.[99]

During these years, many Utah educators received national recognition for their research contributions or administrative skills. Terrel H. Bell, state Commissioner of Higher Education and a professor of education at the University of Utah, was named United States Secretary of Education by President Ronald Reagan. He served from 1981 to 1985. In 1983 University of Utah President David P. Gardner was named president of the highly prestigious University of California nine-campus system. During Gardner's ten years in Utah the university had risen from 35th to 25th in national rankings of major universities. Among its highest rated programs, each of which had enviable national ratings, were engineering and mines, mathematics, computer science, biology, and chemistry.[100] Gardner, who headed the presidential commission that produced *A Nation at Risk*, was replaced by Dr. Chase N. Peterson, who had served as vice-president of health sciences since 1978. Peterson was a graduate of the Harvard Medical School and before arriving at the University of Utah he had been in the administration at Harvard University.[101]

Other Social Issues

Among the persistent social issues affecting Utah, and particularly its public image, was the continuing LDS Church policy of denying the priesthood to blacks, which meant that they could neither serve in the most significant leadership positions nor participate in the church's sacred temple ordinances. During a time when the United States was making great strides in civil rights and equal racial opportunity, the Mormon practice seemed incongruous to many people. However, on June 8, 1978, the church's First Presidency announced that President Spencer W. Kimball had received a divine revelation that "all worthy male members of the church may be ordained to the priesthood without regard for race or color," thus opening the priesthood to blacks and ending any trace of official discrimination. This announcement, the most far-reaching to come from the church in the twentieth century, immediately made national and international headlines, enhancing not only the positive image of Mormonism but also that of the state.

A different kind of social issue was the soaring cost of medical care. A 1981 report showed that in the previous five years Medicaid hospital charges had more than doubled, from $11.7 million to $24.5 million annually. Utah traditionally had lower medical costs than the national average, but the rate of increase in that period exceeded the average. As a result, the Utah Department of Health was forced to make changes in Utah's Medicaid program, including reducing the limit on in-patient hospital care to twenty-eight days.[102] Because of these rising costs health insurance costs also soared. By the 1990s it was estimated that about 35 percent of Utah's population lacked this vital coverage.[103]

Utah received national attention for some noteworthy medical accomplishments during this period. In 1979, for example, Lisa and Elisa Hansen, 20-month-old Siamese twins whose heads were joined at birth, were separated in a Salt Lake City hospital. Another was Utah's leadership in the development of artificial organs, such as the heart, ear, arm, and kidney. As a result of the involvement of the University of Utah and several Utah biomedical firms, Salt Lake City was once nicknamed "Bionic Valley."[104]

The most widely covered medical event in Utah was the first-ever artificial heart implant, a project doctors at the University of Utah had been working on for years. In 1981, the US Food and Drug Administration gave its approval for an artificial heart to be transplanted when an appropriate patient was found. That patient was Dr. Barney Clark, a Seattle dentist with congestive heart failure. On the morning of December 2, 1982, with Clark's thoroughly informed consent, and at a point when it seemed clear that he probably would not survive his condition, a team under the direction of Dr. William DeVries performed the surgery. After receiving his Jarvik-7 artificial heart, Dr. Clark made a remarkable temporary recovery and lived for another 112 days. The operation raised a variety of legal, ethical, and scientific questions, but it also provided a vast amount of knowledge and experience to assist in the continuing exploration of ways and means to better understand and care for the human body. Clark himself said, "All in all, it's been a pleasure to be able to help people."[105]

Utah wrestled with many other social problems that were growing in intensity throughout the nation. One, that caused increasing dismay in parents, educators, and many public servants, was the alarming rise of sex, violence, and profanity in movies and on television. The rise of cable television only enhanced the dilemma.

In the 1950s and 1960s, cable television was limited largely to rural areas, as a way to bring programs to homes and communities that regular television transmission could not reach. However, as satellite transmission became more feasible in the 1970s and various legal barriers were swept away, the availability of cable television mushroomed. By 1975, here were 3,506 cable systems serving nearly 10 million subscribers, but by 1985 this had jumped to 6,600 systems serving nearly 40 million subscribers. Cable television, and the rise of huge cable networks, thus dramatically expanded the amount of context that could come into the home—in addition to what was traditionally available through national networks and local broadcasts.[106]

In the early 1980s, there were efforts at both the state and local levels to regulate cable companies by banning "indecent" material, These efforts, however, ran into legal and constitutional difficulties in defining "indecent" as well as First Amendment protection of free speech. In 1983, for example, Utah's legislature passed the Cable Television Programming Decency Act, which banned sexually explicit programs. However, Governor Matheson received national attention when he vetoed the act, along with another regulatory bill, saying they would have a "chilling effect'" on freedom of choice. "Individuals in a free society must honor different tastes and opinions," he said. "I oppose as much as anyone the intrusion of unwanted material into my home, but individuals must assume the responsibility to decide for themselves whether to subscribe."[107] The legislature promptly overrode the veto, but a federal court reversed that action and in 1987 the US Supreme Court upheld the lower court's ruling.[108] Meanwhile, in 1984, Utah voters defeated an initiative that would have placed restrictions on broadcasting sexually explicit material, but arguments and legal action over the issue continued. That same year Congress passed the Cable Community Policy Act of 1984, which said that regulating content was the responsibility of the Federal Communications Commission, not the states.

Cable television was only one facet of Utah's concern for family values. The state continued to enjoy a well-deserved public image of stable families with high moral and ethical values, but there were some discouraging trends. A 1982 report indicated that Utah's divorce rate, which had been the same as the national average in 1981, had now climbed to 5.4 per 1,000 population, slightly higher than the national average. On the plus side, however, was the fact that Utah's abortion rate was dropping, with a total of 3,600 that year, 162 percent lower than the rest of the country.[109] Contributing factors may have been Utah's law restricting Medicaid abortion funding in cases where the mother's life was threatened and another law that required physicians to give notice to parents of minors before performing abortions. Both laws were upheld by the United States Supreme Court in 1981.[110]

Those concerned with family values were dismayed also at the rate of teenage pregnancy and teenage abortion in Utah (although, because many of the pregnant teens were married teenage pregnancy alone did not necessarily reflect negative family values). A 1983 report by the Utah Department of Health revealed that between 1975 and 1981 the pregnancy rate for white females ages 15 to17 increased from 36.6 per 1,000 population to 42.5, while the national average jumped from 46.1 to 50.0, a 9 percent increase. Among young women ages 18 to19, the pregnancy rate went from 104.2 in 1975 to 125.3 in 1981, an increase of 20 percent. National figures for 1981 were not available, but the rate in 1980 was 232.6, approximately double Utah's rate. With respect to induced abortions, among white females ages 15 to19, Utah's rate was 12.8 per 1,000 population in 1980, or 29th among the thirty states reporting. The department also gathered a few statistics for the non-white population but cautioned that the sample was so small that it was unreliable. The reported rates were higher than those for whites but still significantly below the national average.[111]

These figures suggest that even though many people were rightly alarmed over the increasing rates of teenage pregnancies, particularly out-of-wedlock pregnancies, and abortions, the problems were of significantly less magnitude in Utah than in most of the rest of the nation. Even though Utah's rate was climbing slightly faster than the rest of the nation, it was still well below the average. At the same time, a number of local projects were under way to combat teenage pregnancy by counseling with youth and helping them make informed decisions about sexual activity. These included the Youth Caring and Sharing program in Weber County and a similar program in Utah County.[112]

Another national problem affecting many Utahns, especially teenagers, was a startling increase in the use of illegal drugs, particularly in urban areas. Although much of the public seemed unaware of it, by the 1980s the sale of drugs was taking place almost openly in high school parking lots, in parks near schools, and outside fast-food restaurants close to schools. While marijuana, much of it grown in the state, was the most common drug, teenagers were also using cocaine, amphetamines, and barbiturates. It was reported in 1983 that drug trafficking was the most serious crime problem in the state.[113] School officials and law enforcement agencies were desperately working on better ways to apprehend dealers and educate the youth on the evils of drugs, but funds for enforcing anti-drug activities were severely limited.

Still another social issue that grew in intensity in the 1980s was the problem of poverty and homelessness. As a result of the national recession, many people who had lost jobs elsewhere came to Utah seeking work in the energy-related industries that were appearing in the state and helping to keep its economy more stable. There were fewer jobs than job-seekers, however, which forced many unemployed men and women, some married and with children, to rely on emergency food and shelter programs. Many Utahns suddenly received a new perspective on poverty and homelessness. While traditionally thought of as nonindustrious beggars, many of the homeless were now the "new poor" who had come from good middle class employment and were both industrious and eager to find work. Others were mentally ill and were unable to hold jobs but were left on the streets by cutbacks in the budgets of facilities designed to help them.

Utahns along the Wasatch Front often responded with kindness. Both government and private funds helped open new shelters, with separate facilities for women and children. Among the private donors was the George S. Eccles Foundation, which contributed $18,000 toward an emergency shelter in 1982 and another $20,000 in 1984.[114] State and local employment agencies also increased their efforts in counseling and job placement. Ted Wilson, Salt Lake City's mayor later commented, "While some Rocky Mountain communities were escorting the homeless out of town, the Wasatch Front responded with concern and aid."[115] Utah, nevertheless, like the nation as a whole, still had far to go in dealing with the fundamental causes of homelessness and poverty. Because of the recession, fewer federal resources were available, yet in 1983 it was estimated that 13.2 percent of all Utahns lived at or below the poverty level. Utah was slightly below the national average, but the gap was narrowing.[116]

The homeless problem, as well as the accompanying problems of health care for the poor, were exacerbated in the mid-1980s when downtown Salt Lake City was revitalized and, in the process, eight hundred low-income housing units were demolished and about a thousand poor residents were displaced. The problem was not just housing but also health. As a result, a few non-profit groups began to help. One, for example, was the Fourth Street Clinic, founded in 1988. It began as a small triage clinic but by 2013 it had a staff of fifty as well as a network of over 150 volunteers.[117]

Utah also dealt kindly with a host of refugees from Southeast Asia who began flowing to the state in 1975 after the Vietnam ceasefire. During the next fifteen years, about twelve thousand of these refugees settled in Utah, although by 1990 more than half of them had decided to go elsewhere. Most were initially located in the Salt Lake Valley, but many also went to other urban areas such as Logan, Ogden, and Provo. They were helped in the process of resettlement by a variety of public and private, nonprofit agencies. In 1983 Salt Lake County received a $326,000 federal grant to assist Asian refugees, one of twenty-six metropolitan areas in the United States to obtain such an award. The county commissioners awarded $87,200 to the Asian Association of Utah because of its good track record in finding jobs for refugees, $55,315 to the Career Guidance Center for guaranteeing forty jobs, $27,000 to Granite Community Education for providing technical assistance and skills training, $62,000 to the Utah Indochinese Mutual Assistance Agency, and $34,601 to the state job service.[118] (See chapter 7 for more details on Asian refugees.)

State and Local Politics[119]

Politically, Utah voters moved strongly into the Republican camp during the Matheson years. In 1978 the Republican party took control of both houses of the state legislature, remaining in control throughout the next two decades. While some observers attribute this development mostly to the conservative influence of the Mormon Church,[120] others see it as the result of a set of much more complex economic and political changes. Thomas G. Alexander, for example, has shown that the emergence of a Republican majority was closely associated with Utah's shift from an economy dominated by the federal government and eastern capital to one in which a substantial percentage of the business enterprise was controlled by local people.[121] The natural political and social conservatism related to business enterprise only complemented that of the LDS Church. In addition, Democrats often seemed stigmatized by what was perceived as too-radical liberalism. In actuality, Utah Democrats were usually more conservative than their national counterparts, but in the latter part of the century not many of them more than overcame the image of their party.

In 1978, Democrats were stunned as Republicans won their most sweeping victory in over a decade. Democrat Gunn McKay narrowly retained his seat in the First Congressional District, but Republican Dan Marriott was reelected in the Second District with more than 62 percent of the vote. In the Utah Senate, Democrats lost seven seats, turning control over to the GOP by a margin of nineteen to ten. This number was one short of the two-thirds majority needed to override vetoes, clearly presenting a challenge to the governor. In the House of Representatives, Republicans gained ten new seats, widening their margin to fifty to twenty-five. Many long-time office holders from traditionally Democratic strongholds lost their seats as voters sent a clear anti-tax, anti-regulation message to elected officials.

That same year, citizens of Utah's largest metropolitan area wrestled with the problem of whether to combine Salt Lake City and Salt Lake County governments. A proposition on the November ballot provided for a single government for the city and the unincorporated areas of the county, creating an incorporated entity of approximately 450,000 people. Arguing that this move would increase efficiency, reduce costs, and have the effect of a tax cut, proponents represented an impressive bipartisan coalition. They were led by former governors Calvin Rampton and J. Bracken Lee and included Salt Lake City's mayor Ted Wilson, and Senator Jake Garn. The proposal was hotly contested, however, by a coalition of politicians, businessmen, and city and county commissioners calling themselves "We the People." They included Senator Orrin Hatch, ten of the eleven mayors in the county, and the administrators of several special taxing districts. Calling the "tax cut" assertion a lie, opponents of unification trotted out police and fire department studies that demonstrated it would take $30 million to equalize these services under a unified government. Proponents countered with charges of "scare tactics." Unification forces spent $80,000 on the campaign, while "We the People" spent $40,000. The proposition was soundly defeated by a vote of 60,709 in favor to 91,781 in opposition. Later, however, city and county commissioners voted to negotiate for "functional consolidation" in various departments, such as personnel, parks, and some law enforcement activities. The following year, Salt Lake City's commission form of government was replaced by a council-mayor form.

On February 26, 1980, a new city was formed in the Salt Lake Valley when residents of the Granger, Hunter, and Redwood areas incorporated themselves as West Valley City. Some people fought the idea, even forcing a July 9 vote on disincorporating the new entity. They lost, however, and, with a population of approximately seventy thousand people, the new community became Utah's third largest city.

The continuing growth of political conservatism in Utah was demonstrated in 1980 when Republican presidential challenger Ronald Reagan captured 73 percent of the popular vote, compared with only 51 percent in the nation at large. Jake Garn retained his seat in the Senate by defeating Democratic challenger Dan Berman by 74 to 26 percent, the highest portion of the popular vote yet won by a Utah senatorial candidate. At the same time, in the

Second Congressional district incumbent Dan Marriott won a decisive victory over Democratic challenger Arthur Monson, and in the First District Republican James V. Hansen narrowly defeated five-term Congressman Gunn McKay 52 to 48 percent. McKay's defeat surprised some people because of his solidly conservative record as chair of an important appropriations subcommittee. However, his opponent's campaigners smeared him as a liberal Democrat who was soft on moral issues. The major exception to Utah's convincing Republican trend was the reelection of Governor Matheson, who defeated former Republican state chairman Robert Wright by a margin of 55 to 45 percent. All other major state and county offices also went to Republicans.

The amazing growth of Republican strength in Utah brought state party leaders to the attention of national leaders. Ogden native Richard Richards, for example, had been an avid party member from his youth, chairman of Utah Young Republicans, chairman of the state Republican Party for three terms, western states coordinator for Richard Nixon in 1972 and Ronald Reagan in 1980, and a congressional candidate in 1980.[122] In 1981, he was appointed chairman of the Republican National Committee, although he remained in that post only until January 1983.

In 1980 Utahns voted on two politically heated tax initiatives. One would have removed the sales tax from food, while the other was a limitation on property tax. Both initiatives were defeated. Also on the ballot were two important constitutional amendments, both of which easily passed. One, discussed earlier in this chapter, provided that the governor and the lieutenant governor must belong to the same party. The other struck down any constitutional restrictions on work-release programs for prisoners as well as the employment of women in mines.

In 1981, as a result of population increases revealed in the 1980 census, reapportionment again became a bitter political issue. Beginning with the next election, the number of Utah congressmen in the United States House of Representatives would be increased from two to three. Changes would also be made in state legislative districts. In what seemed to be a tug-of-war between the governor and the Republican-controlled legislature, the report of the Utah Advisory Commission on Reapportionment, appointed by Governor Matheson to study the alternatives, was challenged by the State Legislative Reapportionment Committee. In October, with accusations flying from both sides that the redistricting process was being manipulated for partisan benefit, the governor called the legislature into special session to act on the issue. Lawmakers favored the Republicans as they realigned Congressional as well as state legislative districts. Complaining that the bill reapportioning the state House of Representatives created a three hundred–mile long district, Matheson vetoed it. However, after forcing the legislature back into session twice, the governor finally allowed a compromise measure to become law without his signature.

In the 1982 Congressional elections, Democrats predictably failed to break the Republican hold on Utah. Senator Hatch and Congressmen Marriott and Hansen were all reelected, and Republican Howard Nielson, a former professor of economics at Brigham Young University, easily won election in the new third Congressional district.

Although he was still generally popular among the electorate, Matheson decided not to run for a third term in 1984. Democrats nominated former Congressman Wayne Owens who, after losing his bid for the Senate in 1974, had served as an LDS mission president from 1975 to 1978, practiced law in Salt Lake City, and was western states coordinator in 1980 for Edward M. Kennedy's bid for the Democratic presidential nomination. Owens was unable to garner enough strength, however, even with Matheson's support, to stave off the strongest Republican assault on the governorship in many years. He was defeated by Norman H. Bangerter, who garnered 56 percent of the popular vote and became the first Republican governor in twenty years. Bangerter, a home builder and real estate developer, had served for two terms as speaker of the Utah House of Representatives. His business background and his moderately conservative political image appealed to the ever-more-conservative voters in Utah, some of whom castigated Owens as a Kennedy-type liberal whose ideology would only contribute to the growth of federal programs and power.

Republicans made practically a clean sweep in both state and federal offices that year. Two incumbents, Hansen and Nielson, regained their Congressional seats, each with more than 71 percent of the vote. Marriott did not run, which paved the way for some extra excitement in the First Congressional District. Republicans nominated Lieutenant Governor David S. Monson, who faced the vigorous challenge of Frances Farley, former state senator from Salt Lake City. Farley hoped to appeal to voters by campaigning against the MX missile deployment as well as for repeal of the state sales tax on food, while Monson emphasized his well-known fiscal conservatism and criticized Farley for her vote in the legislature on abortion. Monson also expected to run on the coattails of President Ronald Reagan who, as expected, took 75 percent of Utah's popular vote. Monson's prospects may have been hurt, however, when he was named as a defendant in a federal lawsuit and charged with violating securities and banking laws as a director of Diversified Energy Corporation. He was found innocent, but the publicity did nothing to help his campaign. Farley fought with tremendous energy, hoping to be the first Utah woman to be sent to Congress since Reva Beck Bosone. She came close, but in the end Monson narrowly edged her out by a margin of 49.4 percent to 49.1 percent. Interestingly enough, Farley, a sixty-one-year-old grandmother, won 53 percent of the women's vote that year, while Monson took 69 percent of the Mormon vote. As one historian quipped, "For Monson, President Ronald Reagan's coattails extended to the loose threads of his suit coat."[123]

Scott Matheson was disappointed with the fact that the Republican tide swept so strongly through Utah. Nevertheless, he was not a liberal ideologue, and his legacy fit well with the state's traditionally moderate political climate. He left office convinced that during his tenure most states, including Utah, had made enough changes in the nature of their governments to put themselves in a better position to take over many federal programs. He also believed that the Balanced Budget and Emergency Deficit Control Act of 1985 (the Gramm-Rudman bill) would, within a few years, force the federal government out of many areas that the states could take over—but that never happened. Nevertheless, a major goal of Matheson's administration was to see that Utah began to more fully meet its own responsibilities in areas such as education and social welfare, instead of continuing to draw so heavily upon Washington. His successors shared that ideal.

Notes

1. Scott M. Matheson, with James Edwin Kee, *Out of Balance* (Salt Lake City: Gibbs M. Smith, Inc., Peregrine Smith Books, 1986), 192.
2. An overview of Matheson's perspectives on the imbalance between federal and state governments, the possible effects of the Gramm-Rudman bill, and the restructuring of federal-state relations he thought would, or should, take place is found in *Out of Balance*, chapters 1–5.
3. The story of the Kearns Mansion is beautifully told in Leonard J. Arrington, *In the Utah Tradition: A History of the Governors' Mansion* (Salt Lake City: Governor's Mansion Foundation, 1987). The Rampton quotation is found on p. 118.
4. Scott Matheson, "Scott Matheson: Oral History Interview," by J. Keith Melville, November 21, 1979, L Tom Perry Special Collections, Harold B. Lee Library, Brigham Young University.
5. Matheson, *Out of Balance*, 195. For further commentary on this national cause célèbre, see Norman Mailer, "Crime and Punishment: Gary Gilmore," in J. Michael Lennon, ed., *Conversations with Norman Mailer* (Jackson, Miss.: University Press of Mississippi, 1988), 228–51; Earl F. Dorius, "Personal Recollections of My Involvement and the Involvement of the Attorney General's Staff with the Gary Gilmore Case, between November 1, 1976 and January 17, 1977," unpublished manuscript, Howard W. Hunter Law Library, Brigham Young University; Mikal Gilmore, "A Death in the Family," *Rolling Stone* (June 11, 1992): 111–12; Mikal Gilmore, *Shot in the Heart* (New York: Doubleday, 1994); Norman Mailer, *The Executioner's Song* (Boston: Little, Brown, 1979), a fictionalized account; "Gary Gilmore Promoter Called a Good Hustler," *The Ledger* [Lakeland, Florida], January 23, 1977, A8.
6. See Scott Anderson, *The 4 O'Clock Murders: A True Story of a Mormon Family's Vengeance* (New York: Doubleday, 1993); Rena Chynoweth, *The Blood Covenant* (Austin, TX: Diamond Books, 1990); Bella Stumbo, "No Tidy Stereotype: Polygamists: Tale of Two Families," *Los Angeles Times*, May 3, 1988; Pamela Abramson, "A Hand from the Grave: The Polygamy Murders," *Newsweek*, December 21, 1987; Verlan M. LeBaron, *The LeBaron Story* (Lubbock, TX: Verlan M. LeBaron, Keels & Co, 1981); Ben Bradlee, Jr., and Dale Van Atta, *Prophet of Blood: The Untold Story of Ervil LeBaron and the Lambs of God* (New York, G. P. Putnam's Sons, 1981).
7. Matheson, *Out of Balance*, 256.
8. Ibid., 260. For further discussion of these issues, see ibid., 256–60; David Fleisher, *Death of An American: The Killing of John Singer* (New York: Continuum, 1983); Raye G. Ringholz, "Armageddon at Marion, Utah," Parts I and II, *Utah Holiday* (January 1979): 39–48 and (February 1979): 36–41.
9. Paul Rolly, "Rachel Becomes a National Symbol," *Salt Lake Tribune*, October 24, 1982, S3.
10. Immediately after Schreuder died, the story was reviewed briefly in Douglas Martin, "Frances Schreuder, 65, Manhattan Socialite Who Was Convicted in Murder Case, Is Dead," *New York Times*, April 1, 2004, A21.

11. Marianne Frank, "3-2 Ruling Upholds Insanity Defense Law," *Deseret News*, April 22, 1995, B1.
12. Generalizations based on data reported in *Uniform Crime Reports of the United States*, printed annually by the Federal Bureau of Investigation, US Department of Justice, Washington, D.C.
13. See Utah Department of Human Services, Division of Family Services, *Report on Child Abuse and Neglect* (Salt Lake City: The Division, 1984), charts 1, 3, 4.
14. See Governor's Securities Fraud Task Force, *Report* (Salt Lake City: The Task Force, 1984) as well as the many national articles on Utah scams during this period. They include: "The 'Stock-Fraud Capital' Tries to Clean up its Act," *Business Week* (February 6, 1984), 76; "Bilking Utah's Faithful," *Newsweek* (December 24, 1984), 31; "Purity in Utah," *Forbes* (March 11, 1985), 12; "The Wild West Days May be Back for Utah Brokers," *Business Week* (July 1, 1985), 69-70.
15. The following discussion is based largely on Karl N. Snow, interview by James B. Allen, February 5, 1996, notes in James B. Allen papers, L Tom Perry Special Collections, Harold B. Lee Library, Brigham Young University.
16. Dan Bates, "Constitution Revise Looks Long Way Off," *Salt Lake Tribune*, March 27, 1984, 6A.
17. See discussion in "Revision of the Constitutional Tax Article," Utah Foundation, *Research Report* No. 405 (July 1980).
18. Utah Foundation, *Research Report* No. 405 (July 1980): 231-32.
19. Matheson, *Out of Balance*, 97.
20. For Matheson's extensive discussion of this issue, see Matheson, *Out of Balance*, 87-103.
21. This debate, and Matheson's role in it, is covered extensively in ibid., 55-86.
22. Ibid., 67.
23. For full text, see "First Presidency Statement on Basing of the MX Missile," The Church of Jesus Christ of Latter-day Saints, Salt Lake City, May 5, 1981, reprinted in *Ensign* 11 (June 1981): 76. For discussion, see Steven A. Hildreth, "The First Presidency Statement on MX in Perspective," *BYU Studies* 22 (Spring 1982): 215-25; Steven A. Hildreth, "Mormon Concerns over MX: Parochialism or Enduring Mormon Theology," *Journal of Church and State* 26 (1984): 227-55; Joan Elbert, "Mormons and the MX Missile," *Christian Century* 98 (July 15-22, 1981): 725-26; Matthew Glass, *Citizens Against the MX: Public Languages in the Nuclear Age* (Urbana: University of Illinois Press, 1993), which contains various references to the LDS Church, in the context of a broader discussion.
24. Matheson, *Out of Balance*, 83.
25. Ibid., 104. For Matheson's full discussion of this issue, see pp. 104-113.
26. For a brief discussion, see Joe Bauman, "Final Goodbye for the 'Weteye,'" *Deseret News*, December 26, 2001, B1.
27. Matheson, *Out of Balance*, 112.
28. Ibid., 112-113.
29. For brief reviews of this legislation, see Terry Graham, "The Bureau of Land Management in Utah," in *Utah History Encyclopedia*, ed. Allen Kent Powell (Salt Lake City: University of Utah Press, 1994), 118- 20.
30. See brief review of some of these in Matheson, *Out of Balance*, 121-23.

31. For a scholarly, well-documented analysis of the Sagebrush Rebellion, see R. Mc-Greggor Cawley, *Federal Land, Western Anger: The Sagebrush Rebellion and Environmental Politics* (Lawrence: University Press of Kansas, 1993). For Matheson's perspective, see Matheson, *Out of Balance*, 117–34
32. For a brief discussion of this as well as a recent call for Nevada's federal lands to be turned over to the state, see Geoffrey Lawrence, "It's Time to Free the West: Federal Lands Belong under State Control," in the online publication of the National Policy Research Institute, January 23, 2012, http://www.npri.org/publications/its-time-to-free-the-west, Accessed November 15, 2014.
33. See table in "Nevada Summary Policy Plan for Public Lands," Chapter 1 in *Nevada Statewide Policy Plan for Public Lands* (Nevada Division of State Lands and Nevada's Cities and Counties), 1985. Available online at http://lands.nv.gov/forms/chapter1.pdf.
34. See Cawley, *Federal Land*, 5–9; Matheson, *Out of Balance*, 117.
35. Matheson, *Out of Balance*, 117.
36. See, for example, James B. Allen, "'Good Guys' vs. 'Good Guys': Rudger Clawson, John Sharp, and Civil Disobedience in Nineteenth-Century Utah," *Utah Historical Quarterly* 48 (Spring, 1980): 148–74.
37. John L. Harmer, "A LASER Foundation Editorial," *LASER Beam* (August 1980): 3, as cited in Cawley, *Federal Land*, 7.
38. Matheson, *Out of Balance*, 124, 126.
39. Arizona's Governor Bruce Babbit vetoed his state's law, but he was overridden by the legislature. Wyoming went beyond the other states by including US Forest Service lands in its legislation. In other western states, California, Colorado, Idaho, Montana, Oregon, Washington, and South Dakota, Sagebrush Rebellion legislation was defeated in the legislature, or by executive veto. In the case of Washington, the bill passed but with a stipulation that it would not go into effect without a state constitutional amendment. The amendment was defeated. Cawley, *Federal Land*, 2. For a discussion of some of the Constitutional issues involved and Nevada's decision not to enter into litigation with the federal government, see ibid., 97–101.
40. From a brief entry, "1980 Sagebrush Rebellion," in the Forest History Society's "US Forest Service History," http://www.foresthistory.org/ASPNET/Policy/States_Rights/1980_Sagebrush.aspx, November 15, 2014. Accessed November 15, 2014.
41. As quoted in Cawley, *Federal Land*, 114.
42. For details, see Matheson, *Out of Balance*, 129–34.
43. These and other observations on the contribution of the Sagebrush Rebellion are discussed at length in Cawley, *Federal Land*, 143–68.
44. Matheson, *Out of Balance*, 128.
45. For Matheson's perspective and a fine overview of what happened on this issue during his administration, see Matheson, *Out of Balance*, 135–45. The following discussion is based primarily on that source.
46. Gordon Eliot White, "706, 736 Acres in Revised Wilds Bill," *Deseret News*, November 19, 1983, B1; Jim Woolf and Tom Gorey, "All Agree Utah Wilderness Bill Is a Masterpiece of Compromise," *Salt Lake Tribune*, November 19, 1983, C8.
47. Matheson, *Out of Balance*, 145.
48. For a discussion of these meetings, see Robert S. Halliday, "Battle Rages on Central Utah Project," *Salt Lake Tribune*, March 24 1977, B1, B6; Frank Hewlett, "CUP Plans Defended," ibid., April 5, 1977, 17, 19.

49. Frank Hewlett, "Carter Withdraws Opposition to Bonneville Unit," ibid., September 16, 1977, B1; Frank Hewlett, "Early Completion Eyed for CUP," ibid., October 15, 1977, B1; ibid., "In 'Hot Water' at Times," October 16, 1977, F2.
50. Matheson, *Out of Balance*, 160.
51. Ibid., 179. For a general discussion of the overall impact of the Intermountain Power Project and a proposed expansion, see Jan Crispin-Little, "The Economic and Fiscal Impacts of Expanding the Intermountain Power Project," *Utah Economic and Business Review* 63 (September/October 2003): 1-7.
52. Matheson, *Out of Balance*, 182. See pp. 165-82 for Matheson's full discussion of the IPP and other energy and environmental issues.
53. "Geneva and the Environment," *research report* prepared for Garth L. Mangum by Scott McNab, 17-18. Copy in James B. Allen papers, L Tom Perry Special Collections, Harold B. Lee Library, Brigham Young University, used by permission.
54. Ibid., 17-23; Robert S. Halliday, "Officials Laud Pact On Geneva Curbs," *Salt Lake Tribune*, October 17, 1980, B1; Robert S. Halliday, "McKay Lauded for Efforts In Geneva–EPA Accord," ibid., October 24, 1980, B1.
55. George Raine, "Utah Helping Thy Neighbor," *Newsweek* (June 20, 1983): 27. See also Loren R. Anderson, *The Utah Landslides, Debris Flows, and Floods of May and June 1983* (Springfield, VA: National Technical Information Service, 1984); Diane Dickman, "Riding Out a Deseret Tide," *This People* 6 (September 1983): 27-29, 49, 51.
56. See Elizabeth Cocke, "The Wilberg Mine Fire," in *Utah History Encyclopedia*, ed. Powell, 636-37; Barry R. Norton, "Wilberg Coal Mine Fire and Recovery" (master's thesis, Brigham Young University, 1991).
57. Matheson, *Out of Balance*, 230-36.
58. See Matheson's discussion in ibid., 236-41. For further discussion of Matheson and economic regionalism, see Peter Wiley and Robert Gottlieb, *Empires in the Sun: The Rise of the New American West* (New York: G. P. Putnam's Sons, 1982), 152-55.
59. "Completion of Utah's Interstate Highway System," Utah Foundation *Research Report* No. 432, October, 1982.
60. For full discussion, see "Tax Relief and the 1979 Utah Legislature," Utah Foundation *Research Report* No. 387, January, 1979.
61. See discussion in "Tax and Spending Limitations in Utah," Utah Foundation *Research Report* No. 393, July 1979.
62. "Kennecott Package Wins OK by Union," *Salt Lake Tribune*, August 30, 1980, B1; Robert H. Woody, "No Pleasure in Copper Strike," ibid., September 20, 1980, B7.
63. Douglas L. Parker and Dave Jonsson, "Lawmakers Pass Highway Issue," *Salt Lake Tribune*, December 17, 1982, A1.
64. Robert H. Woody, "Kennecott Lays Off 2,200, Shuts Down Utah Division," *Salt Lake Tribune*., March 26, 1985, A1.
65. "More US Steel Layoffs Likely," *Salt Lake Tribune*, August 4, 1984, B11.
66. The leading scholarly article on the IWY in Utah is Martha Sonntag Bradley, "The Mormon Relief Society and the International Women's Year," *Journal of Mormon History* 21 (Spring 1995): 105-67. See also Linda Sillitoe, "Inside Utah's IWY Conference: Women Scorned," *Utah Holiday* 6 (August 1977): 26; Dixie Snow Huefner, "Church and Politics at the Utah IWY Conference," *Dialogue: A Journal of Mormon Thought* 11 (Spring 1978): 58-75; Linda Sillitoe, "A Foot in Both Camps, an Interview with Jan Tyler," *Sunstone* 3 (January/February 1979): 11-14.

67. The conferences were required to "recognize the contributions of women in the development of our country; assess the role of women in economic, social, cultural and political development; assess the progress that has been made toward insuring equality for all women; identify the barriers that prevent women from participating fully in all aspects of our national life; set goals and a timetable for the elimination of all barriers to the full and equal participation of women in all aspects of American life; and recognize the importance of the contribution of women to the development of friendly relations and cooperation among nations and to the strengthening of world peace." National Commission, "Manual," 7, as quoted in Bradley, "The Mormon Relief Society and the International Women's Year," 113.
68. For a listing of those that contradicted the national committee resolutions, see Bradley, "The Mormon Relief Society and the International Women's Year," 121–22. For a summary of all the recommendations of the various state task forces, as well as a listing of the national recommendations, see pp. 156–67.
69. Bradley, "The Mormon Relief Society and the International Women's Year," 125, 135.
70. Ibid., 135.
71. Ibid., 148.
72. Sillitoe, "A Foot in Both Camps," 13–14
73. See excerpt from a letter to the IWY Commission, by Ruth Funk, in Bradley, "The Mormon Relief Society and the International Women's Year," 149.
74. "Utah School Enrollment Projections Through 1988–89," Utah Foundation *Research Briefs*, No. 78-18, December 11, 1978. The number of students enrolled in private schools in the fall of 1978 totaled 4,111, compared with 5,388 a decade earlier. See also "Rising School Enrollment in Utah," Utah Foundation *Research Briefs*, No. 79-13, December 3, 1979.
75. Lavor K. Chaffin, "Utah Education Statistics Paradoxical," *Deseret News*, July 6, 1979, B3.
76. "39% of Utah Teachers Are Male; Ratio Has Dropped Since 1964," *Deseret News*, September 1, 1983, B4.
77. "Teacher Productivity Rates High, UEA Says," *Deseret News*, June 10, 1981, E7; Vicki Varela, "Education Review Cites Utah Shortages," ibid., May 30, 1983, B2; Vicki Varela, "Utah's Education Issue," ibid., January 22, 1984, A13.
78. Vicki Varela, "6 Schools in Utah Called Exemplary," *Deseret News*, July 1, 1983, B1. The schools so honored were Brigham High School, Butler Middle School, and Highland High School in Salt Lake City; Wasatch Middle School in Heber City; Logan High School in Logan; and Bountiful High School in Bountiful.
79. Students participated at the highest rate in English and history and at the lowest rate in biology and chemistry. "Utah Gets an A-Plus in Motivating the Gifted," *Deseret News*, May 22, 1983, A1.
80. *Survival Communication Instruction for Classroom Teachers of Students with Limited English Proficiency (LEP)* (Salt Lake City: Utah State Office of Education, Division of Program Administration, 1981), iv.
81. See annual reports (variously titled) of the migrant education program, published by the Utah State Office of Education; *Migrant Education in Utah: Portraits of Success* (Salt Lake City: Migrant Education Section, Curriculum and Instruction, Utah State Office of Education, 1985), 3. The latter publication is devoted mostly to por-

traits and personal sketches of migrant students who have graduated from high school in recent years.

82. Lavor K. Chaffin, "Utah Education Statistics Paradoxical," *Deseret News*, July 6, 1979, B3; "Analysis of 1978-79 Teacher Salaries," Utah Foundation *Research Briefs*, No. 78-15, October 16, 1978. The Utah Foundation did not list the average of all salaries, but its report showed that the average minimum salary among the various districts was $9,768 and average maximum was $14,911. It also pointed out that Utah paid 5 percent of the employee's share of the required contribution to a retirement fund. Since this benefit was not generally available in surrounding states, the Foundation said, Utah teachers actually received 1.8 percent more than the average of the Mountain States.

83. State Superintendent of Public Instruction, *School Report, 1978-79* (Salt Lake City: Utah State Department of Public Instruction, 1979), 9.

84. "Analysis of 1979-89 Teachers' Salaries," Utah Foundation Research Briefs, Number 79-12, October 8, 1979.

85. "Fewer Utah Teachers Leaving Their Jobs," *Deseret News*, October 17, 1983, B1.

86. He outlined six key areas the state must work on: revising sources of funding for education; guaranteeing a strong basic education program in every school; making the teaching profession more attractive financially, including some kind of merit pay; making equity adjustments in higher education; advanced use of technology in the classroom; and improving vocational-educational programs. David Heylen, "Matheson: Help Schools Now," *Deseret News*, July 1, 1983, B1.

87. *Twelfth Annual Report of the Superintendent of Public Instruction of the State of Utah, for the Period Ending June 30, 1984*, 4.

88. Ibid., 4.

89. Everyone agreed that this was necessary, and the UEA had drawn up a list of ambitious objectives for the next five years. They included full funding, within three years, of a career ladder program for teachers. Jennifer Brandion, "Pressure for Better Schools Is on Republican Legislators," *Deseret News*, November 29, 1984, B13.

90. Vicki Varela, "Teacher Pay Reforms under Scrutiny," *Deseret News*, May 20, 1984, B2; "Teacher Paychecks 9% Fatter," ibid., December 3, 1984, B1.

91. Vicki Varela, "Matheson Scolds Teachers at Parley," *Deseret News*, October 11, 1984, B1.

92. Vicki Varela, "Career Ladders Get an 'A' in Giving Teachers Extra Days," *Deseret News*, November 4, 1984, B4.

93. "Vocational Education in Utah," Utah Foundation *Research Report* No. 400, February 1980.

94. "State Endorses an Academy to Train Principals," *Deseret News*, July 24, 1984, B2; *Twelfth Annual Report of the Superintendent of Public Instruction*, 41.

95. Lavor K. Chaffin, "Colleges Busier Than Ever," *Deseret News*, November 3, 1981, B1.

96. Jackson Newell and Takeyuki Ueyama, "Higher Education in Utah," in *Utah History Encyclopedia*, ed. Powell, 155-57.

97. The most pressing problem, board members felt, was the serious nursing shortage in Utah, which prompted them to seek a $1 million appropriation to expand nursing training programs. Utah State Board of Regents, *Annual Report to the Governor and the Legislature, 1978-79*.

98. Utah State Board of Regents, Annual Report to the Governor, 1982-83.

99. "SUSC Faculty Will Get 14.1% Salary Boosts," *Deseret News*, June 21, 1984, B8.
100. Diane Cole, "Gardner Accepts Berkeley's Offer," *Salt Lake Tribune*, March 3, 1983, B1; Derin Lea Head, "At the Helm of an (Academic) Empire," *This People* (February 1984): 40–41.
101. "Congratulations to U. Of U. on New President Choice," *Salt Lake Tribune*, June 15, 1983, A18.
102. "Health Care at Crossroad," *Deseret News*, December 9, 1981, B4.
103. See Henry K. Plenk, "Medicine in Utah," in *Utah History Encyclopedia*, ed. Powell,, 353–59. Plenk, a medical historian and prominent Utah radiologist, discusses here several factors that, he believed, contributed to the rising costs.
104. David Walden, "Utah's Health Care Revolution: Pluralism and Professionalization Since World War II" (master's thesis, Brigham Young University, 1989), 26. See also Gode Davis, "Biomedical Breakthroughs: Utah's Bionic Valley Needs A Venture-Capital Boost," *Utah Holiday* (January 1988): 30–37; Constance C. Steffen, "Development Potential: Medical Supply and Biomedical Research Industries in Utah," *Utah Economic and Business Review* (November 1983): 1–9, 12.
105. For a thorough discussion of the complex implications of the Barney Clark operation, see Margery W. Shaw, ed., *After Barney Clark: Reflections on the Utah Artificial Heart Program* (Austin: University of Texas Press, 1984). See also Renée C. Fox, *Spare Parts: Organ Replacement in American Society* (New York: Oxford University Press, 1992), chapter 7. On pp. 162–69 is an interesting discussion on "The Role of Mormonism" in the heart transplant program. After Clark's death, controversy arose over proposed new guidelines for the next artificial heart patient. Some members of the university's Institutional Review Board felt that the case showed that the artificial heart was not ready for human tests. In 1984 DeVries left Utah and joined the staff of Humana's Audubon Hospital in Louisville, Kentucky.
106. Sharon Strove, "Cable Television: United States," in *Encyclopedia of Television*, 2d ed., Vol. 1, ed. Horace Newcomb (New York: Fitzroy Dearborn and the Museum of Broadcast Communications, 2004), 393.
107. "Utah Governor Vetoes Bills to Regulate Sex on Cable TV," *New York Times*, April 2, 1983, 37.
108. Stuart Taylor Jr., "Justices Strike Down Curbs on 'Indecent' Cable TV Programs," *New York Times*, March 24, 1987, A22.
109. "Utah Marriage, Abortion Rates Down, Divorces Up," *Deseret News*, March 6, 1983, B14.
110. "Utahn Pushes State Powers," *Deseret News*, June 12, 1981, B1.
111. See *Teenage Pregnancy in Utah 1975–1981* (Salt Lake City: Utah Department of Health, Office of Management Planning and Division of Family Health Services, 1983). Figures given here are found on charts throughout this booklet.
112. "Statistics Do About-Face: Utah Low in Teen Pregnancies," *Deseret News*, April 29, 1981, A21.
113. See Janice Perry, "School Drug Pushers Deal Openly," *Deseret News*, October 19, 1979, B1; "Utah Waging War against Drug Trade," ibid., January 19, 1983, B1.
114. Brian Wilkinson, "Eccles Foundation Gives $20,000 for Transients,"*Salt Lake Tribune*, November 21, 1984, B1.
115. Ted Wilson, *Utah's Wasatch Front* (Salt Lake City, Utah: Utah Geographic Series, Inc., 1987), 110.

116. "Report to the Governor: *Poverty in Utah*," (Salt Lake City: Utah State Community Service Office, 1983), 95.
117. According to its website, today the Fourth Street Clinic is a comprehensive health care home that serves 3,783 homeless men, women and children with 22,300 primary care, behavioral health and specialty care visits. Its pharmacy dispenses 44,600 medications annually. "By increasing homeless Utahns' access to primary care, Fourth Street Clinic is a major partner in ending homelessness, promoting community health, and achieving across-the-board health care savings." See the clinic's website, http://www.fourthstreetclinic.org/get-educated/health-homelessness. Accessed November 15, 2014.
118. "Funds Granted for Jobs for Refugees," *Salt Lake Tribune*, August 11, 1983, B4.
119. For a short overview of the elections of 1980 and 1984, see Alan Kent Powell, "Elections in the State of Utah," in *Utah History Encyclopedia*, ed. Powell, 157–67.
120. See John Heinerman and Anson Shupe, *The Mormon Corporate Empire* (Boston: Beacon Press, 1985); "Utah: Inner Sanctum of the Right," *The Economist* (May 6, 1978): 48, 51.
121. Thomas G. Alexander, "The Emergence of a Republican Majority in Utah, 1970–1992," in *Politics in the Postwar American West*, ed. Richard Lowitt (Norman: University of Oklahoma Press, 1995), 260–76.
122. For an interesting, though somewhat biased, analysis of the Republican rise to power and the 1980 election in Utah, see Ronald J. Hrebenar, "Utah: The Most Republican State in the Union," *The Social Science Journal* 18 (October 1981): 103–14.
123. Craig Fuller, "David Smith Monson," in *Utah History Encyclopedia*, ed. Powell, 372.

CHAPTER 6

Conservatism, But of the Moderate Sort:
The Bangerter Years, 1985–1992

With the inauguration of Norman H. Bangerter on January 7, 1985, the Republican-dominated state of Utah had a Republican governor for the first time in twenty years. In terms of goals, however, not much would change. Many of Bangerter's economic objectives and moderate political views were similar to those of his predecessor. In his inaugural address he praised Scott Matheson and called for some of the same objectives the former governor had tried to achieve. In particular, he stressed three things: high quality education, economic expansion, and efficiency and responsiveness in state government. He was especially concerned that government not lose sight of its proper—and limited—role. "Government must allow individuals to be modern pioneers of private enterprise," he said. "It must not limit the vision or opportunity of business innovators."[1]

In his first address to the legislature, Bangerter expounded on the forthcoming challenges.[2] The school-age population, he observed, would grow by ten to twelve thousand every year. Changes in the workforce, particularly an increase in the number of working mothers, would require more child care and support services. Structural changes in the economy would displace some of the workforce, creating a need for more job training to support new industries. Bangerter promised to review carefully before carrying out new policies, but some people felt that many challenges must be dealt with immediately and with a heavy hand. A cartoon appearing on the front page of the *Deseret News* on the day of his inaugural depicted the new governor in golf clothes, facing a giant golf ball covered with words such as "taxes," "education," "economy," and "flooding" (referring to problems occurring on the shores of the Great Salt Lake). The governor seemed a bit diminutive, with an even more diminutive club in hand, as his caddie said to him: "May I suggest the sledge-hammer, Governor Bangerter." Over the next eight years the governor may have used the "sledge hammer" occasionally, but in most cases he took a moderate, but effective, approach. His administration, in fact, was a model of moderate conservatism.

Utah and the Nation: General Observations, 1985–1992

Two Republican presidents led the nation during Norman Bangerter's stint as governor: Ronald Reagan (1981–89) and George H. W. Bush (1989–93). Among the accomplishments of the Regan administration was the Tax Reform Act of 1986, the most extensive revision in the United States tax code since World War II. The act simplified the code, decreased individual tax rates, broadened the tax base, and eliminated a number of tax shelters and loopholes. However, it was revenue-neutral and did not greatly help most taxpayers. That same year Congress also rewrote America's immigration laws and passed several environmental bills.

Among the major pieces of domestic legislation passed by Congress during the Bush administration were the Clean Air Act of 1990 (which called for greater reduction in some of the most dangerous emissions and increased EPA monitoring of the number of chemicals from seven to about 250), the Americans with Disabilities Act of 1990, and the Civil Rights Bill of 1991. However, Bush failed to keep his campaign promise that he would not raise taxes. Faced with a mounting federal deficit, he finally asked for and Congress approved a tax increase. This brought him more criticism than praise, and the deficit continued to grow anyway

Conservatism, But of the Moderate Sort: The Bangerter Years, 1985-1992

Image 6.1: Norman H. Bangerter, Governor of Utah 1985-1992. Used by permission, Utah State Historical Society, all rights reserved.

because Congress refused to make the spending cuts necessary to confine it. In 1990 the country slipped into another recession.

Meanwhile, in connection with America's adventures in space, Utahns continued to make a name for themselves and the state. In April 1985, Senator Jake Garn, chair of the Senate subcommittee that oversaw the space program, went along on the space shuttle *Discovery's* five-day mission, becoming the first person who was not an astronaut or a technician to orbit the earth. That same year, Utah astronaut Don Lind flew a mission in *Discovery's* sister shuttle, *Challenger*. However, in January 1986 a tragedy turned national eyes on the Thiokol plant in Box Elder County when *Challenger* exploded on takeoff, killing all five astronauts aboard. The accident was blamed on failure of an O-ring, a seal in a solid rocket booster manufactured by Thiokol. The space shuttle program was grounded for more than two-and-a-half years while Thiokol engineers, led by one of their number who had tried unsuccessfully to stop the launch in the first place, redesigned the faulty part. Finally, in September 1988, *Discovery* was launched on a highly successful mission that went without incident.

In another matter of national concern, pressure intensified on the federal government to face its responsibility to victims of fallout from atomic testing in the 1950s and from other nuclear projects. In 1987, the Tenth Circuit Court of Appeals reversed Judge Bruce Jenkins's 1984 decision compensating ten Utah victims. However, Jenkins's decision became an important guide for others as the fight continued. Before the end of the decade, the Department of Energy awarded residents of Ferdinand, Ohio, $78 million for harm caused by a uranium processing plant. In addition, the Department of Veterans Affairs was ordered to pay disability benefits to veterans who had participated in the Nevada testing and later contracted any of thirteen different kinds of cancer. Meanwhile, Utah's Congressman Wayne Owens and Senator Orrin Hatch lobbied for years for a Congressional compensation bill. Finally, on October 15, 1990, President Bush signed the Radiation Exposure Compensation Act, in which the government apologized for its behavior and established a trust fund that would provide $50,000 each for those contracting cancer from the Nevada tests and $100,000 each for uranium miners whom the government failed to warn of potential risks in the mines.[3]

It was a bittersweet victory, however, for even though financial compensation eventually came to many victims, some had feelings like those expressed by a resident of Enterprise, Utah: "I feel like we were really used, and I'll never trust our government again."[4] In addition, those who deserved compensation often found it extremely difficult to prove. The law was too narrowly drafted and too narrowly interpreted, complained Elizabeth Wright, a Utah resident and vice president of the Association of Radiation Survivors. It covered only certain kinds of cancer, applied only to people living in certain counties, and did not cover birth defects and other problems that were probably caused by fallout but were not classified as cancer. By January 1994, the government had rejected 44 percent of all claims by "downwinders," 45 percent of the claims presented by miners, and 80 percent of the claims from workers at test sites.[5]

Among the international crises of this era was the rise in terrorism, aimed largely at Israel but also at western Europe and the United States because of their support of Israel. There was also considerable amount of anti-American activity in certain South American countries, some of which had a direct effect on Utah families. Some terrorists, for example, interpreted the presence of the LDS Church as another aspect of an unwanted American influence, and they sometimes attacked not only LDS buildings but also missionaries. In May 1989 two Utah missionaries serving in Bolivia were murdered in one such incident.[6]

One of the most momentous international events since World War II was the end of the Cold War. Utahns were as anxious as anyone to see the wearisome struggle come to a close, and many participated directly in efforts to bring about more good will with Communist nations and to stop the proliferation of nuclear arms. Some Utah citizens belonged to small private groups that maintained contact with similar Soviet organizations attempting to promote disarmament and peace. In June 1987, thirteen Utahns participated in a joint Soviet-American "march for peace" between Leningrad and Moscow. Among them was William Logan Hebner and his future wife Angie, who met each other on that walk. Later the two of them founded International Legislative Exchange, which worked with new parliaments emerging from ex-Soviet republics.[7] After the march Soviet Premier Mikhail Gorbachev sent personal congratulations to the Utah marchers for their efforts.[8]

That same year the Utah branch of International Physicians for the Prevention of Nuclear War hosted four Soviet physicians as they visited the University of Utah medical facilities for four days.[9] In July 1988 Utahns welcomed twenty-three Soviet technicians and linguists who were part of a team permanently located in the state. They were monitoring Hercules Corporation and other missile manufacturers to be certain that the United States conformed to a disarmament treaty that prohibited building more Pershing II and other missiles. A similar team of Americans were monitoring sites in the USSR. A report in the Soviet newspaper, *Pravda*, said that of all the areas the Soviet inspectors visited, Utah was the most receptive and welcoming.[10]

In 1989, several Communist regimes in Eastern Europe began to crumble. That same year the infamous Berlin Wall came down, leading to the reunification of Germany in 1990. The following year the Soviet Union fell apart, resulting in the creation of several independent states, the largest and most dominant of which was Russia. The Cold War was over and, for all practical purposes, Marxian socialist governments were dead almost everywhere but China, Cuba, and North Korea. Utahns, along with America and the rest of the western world, breathed a long-anticipated sigh of deep relief. Among other things, the new political realities led to increased travel and cultural exchange. In June 1991, the Mormon Tabernacle Choir conducted a twenty-one-day tour in eight European countries, including its first-ever tour to Eastern Europe and Russia.

The winding down of the Cold War did not usher in an era of world peace or American popularity, however, and President Bush found himself sending American troops to three different parts of the world. In 1989 troops entered Panama to depose that country's dictator, General Manuel Noriega, who directed a huge drug trafficking empire and snubbed American efforts to stop it. In August 1990 Iraq's dictator, Saddam Hussein, used military force to annex the small but oil-rich country of Kuwait, on the

Persian Gulf. Bush immediately obtained United Nations support for sending a military expedition to expel the invaders. In December and January, through a massive five-week effort known as Operation Desert Storm, U.N. forces (mostly American) drove out the Iraqis and restored the Kuwaiti government.

Utahns felt deeply and personally involved in the Persian Gulf operation. More than a thousand Utah reservists were called to active duty. In addition, nearly a quarter of Utah's National Guard was mobilized and more than three hundred members of the Utah Air National Guard volunteered for active service. The mobilization was unique because, for the first time, many women were called into active duty. Husbands and wives were sometimes activated together, although in some cases a wife was called up while her husband remained at home to care for the children.[11]

An estimated four thousand Utahns, including reservists, Guard units, and regular military personnel, participated in the Gulf War. Two men, both from Bountiful, were killed: Marine Lance Corporal Dion J. Stephenson and Army Sergeant Jeffrey A. Rollins. Two National Guard units received citations for their accomplishments. Deactivated between March and June 1991, Utah Guardsmen received heroes' welcomes in homecoming celebrations and patriotic parades throughout the state.

The Gulf War was popular in both Utah and the nation, but there were significant pockets of antiwar sentiment. Bush claimed that it was a humanitarian war, intended simply to restore the legitimate government of Kuwait. Others charged that it was purely economic in nature, designed to retain access to Kuwait's oil. On January 19, 1991, in a peaceful antiwar rally sponsored by a group known as the Utah Coalition against US War in the Middle East, some 1,500 banner-carrying protesters demonstrated in the streets of Salt Lake City.

In late 1992, President Bush sent thirty thousand American marines to famine-plagued Somalia to ensure the proper delivery and distribution of food supplies. The troops faced violent opposition from dissident elements in Somalia itself, and in 1993 they were withdrawn. During the crisis, volunteers from the Utah Air National Guard were activated to support American efforts

Utah and the Nation: Economic Issues

One of Bangerter's chief concerns was economic development, and toward the end of his first year in office the Utah Department of Community and Economic Development published a detailed plan for the future. Already, the publication noted, the administration had taken several steps toward redirecting and more sharply focusing the department's activities.[13] One development was the establishment of the Utah Centers of Excellence Program, a partnership between the state and Utah's universities designed to help market products resulting from university research. By 1986, thirteen Centers of Excellence were located on the campus of the University of Utah, eight at Brigham Young University, seven at Utah State University, and one on the campus of Weber State College. The result, by 1992, was fifty new companies that provided more than two thousand high tech jobs. Another initiative, the Utah Procurement Outreach program, helped small businesses obtain contracts to supply goods and services to the federal government and large companies. In addition, the Utah Business Expansion and Retention Office and the Rural Development Office were created to help Utah business, and Small Business Development Centers were set up throughout the state. These and other programs helped insure the success of many business enterprises, including "high tech" (high technology) firms. The administration also expanded the state's efforts to promote exports, paying increased attention to foreign investors, and helping to convince several international firms to establish operations in Utah.[14]

The economy continued to be sluggish, however, and a prolonged strike at Kennecott Copper and the eventual closure of Geneva Steel (see below) did not help. The 1986 legislature passed a $2.7 billion state budget, but Bangerter was forced to reduce spending by $48 million as deficits began to surface. At a special session in November, anticipating a $95.5 million shortfall, legislators not only accepted the governor's cuts but slashed $11 million more.

The state, nevertheless, could not ignore ballooning school enrollments and the ever-expanding need for human services. Having little choice but to take drastic, though unpopular, action, in 1987 Bangerter proposed a $207 million tax increase. The legislature responded with a smaller figure, but it was still the largest one-time tax increase thus far in the history of the state: more than $150 million in new sales, income, motor fuels, and cigarette taxes. The state also closed several branch offices, consolidated some positions and divisions, turned a few programs over to private enterprise, and centralized others. Not surprisingly, the tax increase brought on a statewide tax protest movement (see below). In 1988, three tax-related initiatives were put on the ballot. One was intended to place limits on state taxes and spending, another would have reduced taxes, and a third would have given income tax credit for private education. These measures failed, but the fact that they were on the ballot in the first place sent an important message to the legislature. At a special session late in the year, lawmakers voted a one-time tax rebate totaling $77 million and provided a few cuts in the state income tax. The next year they enacted a major income tax reduction, but to protect the state the legislature also established a "rainy day fund" intended as a shield against future financial crises.

Despite these necessary measures, Utah was still the pride of economic conservatives, as the state continued to boast consistent budget surpluses. It was one of the few states, in fact, to show a surplus during each of the eight years of the Bangerter administration.[15] *Financial World* magazine called Governor Bangerter one of the most tough-minded state money managers in the country.[16]

Unfortunately, however, Utah did not escape the crisis in the savings and loan industry (S&Ls) that startled the nation in the mid-1980s. After Congress voted in 1982 to allow S&Ls to invest in more risky real estate projects, many over-invested, prices plunged, and billions of dollars were lost. Also contributing to the crisis were a sharp rise in operating costs, unusually high interest rates paid to depositors to entice them to keep their money in savings, speculation in junk bonds and other risky enterprises, and various mistakes by government regulators.[17] In 1986 Utah assumed control of five failing S&Ls with more than $100 million in deposits belonging to about fifteen thousand depositors. It then suspended deposit activity and liquidated those that could not qualify for federal deposit insurance. The silver lining was that in the final distribution Utah depositors, unlike those in some other states, received about 95 percent of their account balances.[18]

A larger potential problem arose when the Credit Union Insurance Corporation failed in 1987. Nearly one-third of the households in Utah were represented in more than 130 credit unions. However, the National Credit Union Administration soon extended federal deposit insurance coverage to all privately insured credit unions.[19]

By the end of the 1970s, One of the most intriguing economic stories of this era was the continuing saga of Geneva Steel.[20] United States Steel, seriously hurt by foreign competition, had closed sixteen of its facilities in the United States. In the early 1980s, USX (the acronym for the newly diversified United States Steel Corporation) promised to modernize Geneva in order to keep it open, but it never happened. Instead, in 1985 USX completed a contract allowing a Korean steel manufacturer to supply the company's plant in Pittsburgh, California, beginning in 1989. Utahns were irate, feeling they had been betrayed.[21] The announcement made it clear that Geneva's life would end in 1989, if not sooner. One angry union member reflected the feeling of many others when he called it a "stab in the back."[22] The plant closed in mid-1986 and more than two thousand people were suddenly out of work.

At that point, Joseph A. Cannon stepped into the picture. A Utah native, Cannon had been an assistant EPA administrator, and in 1986 he was a partner in a Washington, D.C. law firm. When he heard of the problems at Geneva Steel he immediately tried to persuade various Utah business leaders to purchase the plant. Concerned about the impact of the closure on the economy of his home state, Cannon was convinced that, if properly managed, Geneva could make a profit. His efforts with business leaders failed, but he then decided to assemble his own team and try to buy the plant himself. The new company, Basic Manufacturing and Technologies of Utah (BMT), was organized early in 1987.

In a series of events that almost took on the aura of a suspense story, Cannon worked tirelessly to find financiers to lend BMT the $58 million needed to buy the plant. A deadline, originally set by USX as July 1, 1987, was moved to July 31. After one financial deal disintegrated, Senator Orin Hatch intervened and set up a meeting with USX at which the price, surprisingly, was cut to $40 million and the deadline extended to August 31. More complications followed, but on the day of the deadline the deal was closed. Geneva Steel, with Joseph A. Cannon as president, would soon reopen.

Meanwhile, other negotiations were necessary if the plant were to operate at a profit. Local members of the Steelworkers Union agreed to accept a cut of about 30 percent in their total wage and benefits package, the state legislature helped with a sales tax reduction, and potential suppliers offered price concessions.

Geneva again became a major factor in the economic life of Utah County. Beginning with fewer than a thousand workers, the plant employed more than 1,500 by the end of November 1987. With the installation of modern equipment, effective management, and the cooperation of a model labor force, Geneva competed successfully in several markets both at home and abroad. In 1989 it was listed by *Fortune* magazine as one of the top fifty exporters in the United States. The November 20, 1991, issue of the *Wall Street Journal* featured Geneva in a front-page story, calling it a "miracle mill" that rose phoenix-like from the ashes of USX. Its stock had risen from $10 a share in March 1990 to between $18 and $19 a share. In 1992, with imported steel flooding the American market, Geneva led the nation in low-cost domestic production.[23]

It was not easy sailing for Geneva though, as, among other things, the plant inevitably became involved in the political-economic problem of air pollution. In Utah County, pollution came from many sources, but Geneva Steel received the brunt of the criticism as the chief source of PM10 (airborne particulates that measured ten microns or less in diameter and were a major cause of respiratory problems). It was ironic that, four decades earlier, Geneva had been heralded as the economic savior of the county, yet by the 1990s many residents were saying just the opposite. The economy had changed, they argued, the county no longer needed the plant, and if the cost of drastically reducing harmful emissions was too great, then it would not hurt for Geneva to close. Company officials constantly pointed out that they were in compliance with current regulations and were making every reasonable effort, and spending millions of dollars, to improve.

The battle was partly one of conflicting statistics and interpretations. In June 1989, John A. Cooper, an air quality expert hired by Geneva Steel, reported that the plant was responsible for about 44 percent of the airborne particulates over Lindon and North Provo. Road dust, wood smoke, and automobile exhaust contributed most of the rest. But a citizens group questioned Cooper's estimate, arguing that Geneva contributed about 60 percent of the PM10 in the county.[24] Some critics heralded the findings of C. Arden Pope, associate professor of economics at Brigham Young University. In 1988 and again in 1991, he produced papers claiming that the Geneva plant was the direct cause of respiratory problems in the area, particularly in children. He reported in 1991 that hospital admissions of preschool children with bronchitis or asthma were twice as high when the mill was operating than when it was closed. Geneva officials replied that Pope's data was flawed because he was unable to explain why hospital admissions were actually lower in 1988–89 when PM10 levels were high. They also criticized him for not looking at monthly and annual variations. One Geneva researcher suggested that the rise in hospital admissions was due to a "respiratory syncytial virus," to which Pope responded that if that were the cause, similar increases would be seen in neighboring communities, but they were not.[25]

In 1991 a state implementation plan called for a 43 percent reduction of PM10 in Utah County by the end of 1993. Geneva claimed that it was already in compliance with current air quality regulations and was in the process of implementing an $84 million modernization plan intended to conform with future regulations.[26] Many critics were still not satisfied, but they were treated to a stinging editorial rebuff by *Daily Herald* columnist Ed Haroldsen. "What more would critics have Geneva do?" he asked. "So far, says Cannon, no one has ever said anything except things like close the plant down. But that makes little sense considering that the efficient Geneva plant provides jobs for 2,800, produces 1.4 million tons of steel a year and adds $300 million to our economy. Geneva is making a super effort to be as environmentally clean as humanly possible, as soon as possible. . . . Let's give Geneva a fair shake."[27]

In the fall of 1991 Geneva installed its first Q-BOP, an enclosed steelmaking system that captured emissions inside itself and emitted, instead of white-orange plumes, a long, much cleaner, blue flame. Q-BOPs also produced steel faster and more economically, and ultimately the Q-BOP process replaced all of the old open-hearth furnaces. In addition, Geneva planned a system for using coal rather than coke in the steelmaking process, which would reduce sulfur emissions by 95 percent. Eventually, the company estimated, its total modernization program would eliminate 90 percent of all the emissions that had resulted from the open hearth process.[28]

With rapidly changing economic realities, however, Geneva could not last much longer. Throughout the 1990s the plant was plagued increasingly by cheap foreign steel and it began to show substantial financial losses. Geneva Steel closed for good in 2001.

On another front, Utah continued to carefully watch the progress of the Central Utah Project and to promote other water development plans. But finding suitable sites for dams and reservoirs became increasingly difficult, and in 1986 the Utah Foundation warned that it was time to reexamine basic state water policy. The projects handled by the state's Division of Water Resources were small compared to those handled by the Federal Bureau of Reclamation, but the foundation urged the state to consider employing an independent review panel to check on engineering plans for new projects. Already there were problems with the year-old Quail Creek Dam, yet it was the most costly program to be undertaken by the division.[29] The dam burst three years later, In 1990 the state completed a comprehensive state water plan designed to coordinate water-related activities of local, state, and federal agencies.[30]

Meanwhile, the Central Utah Project gradually neared completion. Its most controversial segment, the Jordanelle Dam near Park City, continually ran into difficulty in Congress, with allegations that the proposed site was unsafe and that the engineering was faulty. The funds were eventually allocated, and the dam was finished in 1993.

Utah's Congressional delegation, spearheaded by Senator Jake Garn, urgently pressed for funding to complete the entire CUP. Finally, on October 30, 1992, after three years of wrangling, Congress passed the Central Utah Project Completion Act and President Bush signed it into law. This was a red-letter day for all Utah water users and recreational enthusiasts. The bill authorized $922 million for completing the project and the state of Utah had to raise only $179 million in matching funds. The bill included many projects designed to stabilize mountain lakes, improve irrigation and drainage systems, improve and develop more fish hatcheries, rehabilitate various fish habitats, enhance water-related recreational activities, and conduct special studies relating to water management and conservation.

Travel, Tourism, Sports, and Recreation

The travel and tourist industry was one of Utah's major economic boons in this era. Visitors to the state's national parks, monuments, recreation areas, and historic sites numbered 7.6 million in 1985 and 10.4 million in 1991. In addition, visitors to Utah's state parks, monuments, and recreation areas jumped from 4.8 million in 1985 to 5.4 million in 1991. Out-of-state visitors purchased nearly 30 percent of all the hunting and fishing licenses sold in 1989, bringing into state coffers some $4.4 million in revenue. Moreover, travel, tourism, and recreation accounted for 8.1 percent of all nonagricultural employment in the state in 1991. The direct dollar impact is suggested by the fact that total taxable room rents collected from travelers grew from $113.3 million in 1982 to $295.5 million in 1990, while state and local tax revenues grew from $65.2 million to $171.4 million. Significantly, the increasingly active Utah Travel Council saw its budget for promoting tourism raised from nearly $2 million in 1982–83 to $4.2 million in 1990–91.[31]

By the 1980s, however, it was clear that sports, particularly skiing, could garner an increasingly major share of traveler dollars. A Sports Development Office, created by the Bangerter administration in 1986 but soon turned over to private enterprise, booked many amateur sporting events in the state and played an

Image 6.2: New license plate issued in 1985 boasting "Ski Utah—The Greatest Snow on Earth." In 1986 the new tag was given the "Best Plate of the Year" award by the Automobile License Plate Collectors Association. Photo courtesy of Special Collections, J. Willard Marriott Library, University of Utah. Used with permission.

important role in Utah's efforts to bring the Winter Olympics to Salt Lake City.

More than anything else, the Utah Travel Council promoted Utah's skiing, with its magnificent powder snow, attractive resorts, and dozens of lifts. New license plates depicted a skier and trumpeted the slogan "Ski Utah!" while brochures and travel folders distributed worldwide boasted that Utah had the "greatest snow on earth." In 1989 the administration worked with Nippon Airways in launching a program that soon brought thousands of Japanese skiers to Utah slopes each year. From 1990 to 1991 the number of skiers visiting Utah's resorts reached 2.75 million and 60 percent of these were from out-of-state. They remained in Utah an average of five nights, often visiting Temple Square or attending professional basketball games, a symphony, a ballet, or an opera. The bottom line was that out-of-state skiers spent an estimated $308 million while in Utah, generating an estimated 12,300 jobs, providing $180 million in direct income to wage earners, and adding more than $23 million to state and local tax coffers.[32]

In 1966 Utah lost its bid to host 1972 Winter Olympics and the question of whether the state should try again met with mixed responses. The Bangerter administration and many private interests were enthusiastic about the idea, but their efforts proved frustrating. In May 1985 Salt Lake City was pursuing a belated bid for the 1992 games, but the United States Olympic Committee chose Anchorage, Alaska, as the American entry in the international competition.[33] The administration immediately created the Governor's Task Force on Amateur Athletics, which soon developed a blueprint for a winter sports training area in Utah. This would become the basis for future Olympic bids.

In 1989 Salt Lake City was the US Olympic Committee's choice to bid for the 1998 winter games, and in November voters approved plans to use public money for certain up-front construction costs, including a speed-skating oval, a bobsled and luge run, ski jumps, and other facilities. Opponents continued the fight anyway, claiming that promoters vastly overstated anticipated revenues and that there was no way to guarantee that the fragile environment of the Wasatch Front would not be permanently damaged. The hopes of Olympics boosters dimmed when Atlanta, Georgia, was chosen for the 1996 Summer Olympics, for it did not seem likely that a US city would be selected for two Olympic events in a row. Nevertheless, the following year Utah made a strong bid to host the 1998 games. This time the international committee chose Nagano, Japan. Utahns then began laying plans for a final attempt—a bid for the 2002 Winter Olympics—which, to the joy of many, was ultimately successful.

In January 1985, Brigham Young University's football team, after being undefeated in its 1984 season and beating Michigan in the Holiday Bowl, was rated number one in the nation. Also in 1985, the University of Utah women's gymnasts won their fifth straight NCAA championship. In 1990, for the first time in history, the Heisman Trophy, college football's most coveted award, went to a Utah player. BYU's Ty Detmer had set an NCAA record with 4,188 yards passing, held forty-two NCAA records, and tied five more.

In professional sports, in 1985 auto dealer Larry H. Miller invested $8 million in the Jazz basketball team, buying half of it from Sam Battistone, in order to keep the team in Utah. The following year he purchased the other half after it appeared that the team might otherwise move to Minnesota. In 1989 Jazz fans were exuberant when Miller announced plans to build a larger arena for the team in downtown Salt Lake City in place of the old, inadequate Salt Palace. The $93 million arena, named the Delta Center because of Delta Airline's sponsorship, was completed in October 1991. It seated 20,400 people—the third largest sports area in the nation for National Basketball Association teams.

Other Aspects of the Economy

A variety of significant changes were taking place In other aspects of the economy. For one thing, the move from a goods-producing to a service-producing economy seemed almost complete. This transition was part of an important national trend, where the service-producing sector of the economy increased its share of total nonfarm employment from 41 percent in 1950 to 75 percent in 1985. Utah was ahead of the nation, jumping from 71.3 percent in 1950 to 77.7 percent in 1985 and 80 percent in 1993. In the 1980s, the service industry alone created eighty thousand new jobs, some 97 percent of all new jobs in the state.[34]

Other segments of the economy were also in transition. One was the defense industry, where continuing cutbacks in spending had a significant impact. Between 1952 and 1989 direct defense employment dropped from 13.1 percent of Utah's nonagricultural workforce to 3.2 percent.[35] This affected not only direct defense-related jobs but also many non-defense jobs that were dependent upon defense employment. Some saw this as a serious problem and wondered how the state could deal with it, but over the long run the vitality of the market system was the ultimate solution.[36]

Agriculture too, saw a slight decline but it remained especially important to the well-being of several rural counties, whose economies would be seriously crippled without it. Most of Utah's farm production was in field and seed crops, with hay (largely alfalfa) leading the way in total value, but production of most such crops except corn and potatoes went down.[37] At the same time, the fruit industry expanded as ranchers began to develop less expensive land away from urban areas.[38] In the livestock industry, the production of cattle remained generally stable but sheep growers were hurt by a rapidly diminishing market. The most impressive gain was in the turkey business, which expanded faster than any other part of the livestock industry. Between 1980 and 1991 the number of turkeys sold jumped by 68 percent, from 2.4 million to 4.1 million.[39]

Employment in manufacturing had dropped slightly by 1991, but it still made up 14.1 percent of the work force.[40]

Even though mining employed only a small fraction of the workforce, the industry continued to play a vital role in the state's economy. Employment continued to decline, down to 1 percent of the nonagricultural workforce by 1993. Between 1977 and 1990 the number of metal mining companies fell from 157 to sixty-eight.[41] However, improved technology kept production growing. The coal industry saw a dramatic increase in production when an oil embargo in the 1970s led energy companies that used coal to generate electricity to acquire several coal mines. Production reached an all-time high of 27 million tons in 1996.[42]

Kennecott Corporation remained one of the state's largest employers and it continued to have a major impact on the economy. Beginning in the second quarter of 1986 and extending through the first quarter of 1992, Kennecott invested an estimated $630 million in modernization and expansion. Most of that amount went for labor, equipment, and materials contracted for to Utah construction firms. Approximately six hundred different companies were involved, leading to non-payroll purchases of $173 million. Beyond that, Utah construction workers received $145 million in wages and benefits, and $32 million went to state and local governments for payroll, sales, and property taxes. In 1990 Kennecott purchased $217 million worth of goods and services from more than 2,500 Utah companies, and it was estimated that the direct and indirect impact of these purchases generated another $238 million in household earnings. Kennecott's average employment during the year was 2,725, but the direct, indirect, and induced effects of the company's operations resulted in the creation of approximately 8,800 jobs in the state. When all of this growth was taken into account, it was estimated that in 1990 Kennecott benefitted state and local governments by generating a total of $52 million in taxes.[43]

Utah did not ignore foreign markets as viable contributors to its economy. In 1983 the state established an International Trade

Office that by 1990 was spending $1 million annually to promote exports and also to attract foreign investment.[44] Bangerter's administration opened offices in Japan, Korea, Taiwan, Belgium, and Mexico City to promote the sale of Utah products and to encourage foreign tourists to visit the state.[45] Utah was not as dependent upon foreign trade as most other states, but beginning in the late 1980s its exports increased more rapidly than those of any other part of the nation. By 1992, they were at a total value of $2.9 billion. That did not include the export of information technology from Utah firms which, it was estimated, amounted to an additional $500 million.

At the top of the list of Utah exports were primary metal products, followed by electrical and electronic machinery, equipment, and supplies; metallic ores and concentrates; transportation equipment; and industrial machinery. The most rapidly growing exports included lumber and wood products, furniture and fixtures, chemicals and allied products, nonmetallic minerals (except fuels), and miscellaneous manufactured products.

In 1992, Utah entered the market in thirteen new countries, bringing its total world market to 130 nations. Five countries consumed 70 percent of the total exports: The United Kingdom, Taiwan, Hong Kong, Canada, and Japan. Other important countries included the Republic of Korea, Thailand, Germany, the Netherlands, and Singapore. Mainland China took 1.7 percent of the total exports.

There were, of course, potential weak spots in Utah's effort to improve its position in world trade. One was the fact that two of its top exports, primary metal products and metallic ores and concentrates, were highly vulnerable to fluctuations in the international market. Another was the state's disadvantage with respect to trade corridors. Mexico was the United States' third best trading partner in 1992, but most Mexican trade went through Texas, and Utah did not have adequate transportation routes to that state. In general, however, Utah's involvement in the global economy was another in aligning the state with national trends. Whether Utahns favored protectionism or free trade, the fact was that Utah was part of a world that was becoming increasingly interdependent, and Utah's political and economic leaders made every effort to turn that reality to the state's economic advantage.

High Tech

If Utah had an economic "Cinderella story" in the 1980s, it was the story of its emerging high tech industry. By the end of 1992, at least 464 high tech companies made their homes in the state, employing more than 42,300 people, spending $588 million annually in research and development, and taking in revenues of nearly $7.5 billion.[46] By 1992 high tech represented approximately 30 percent of Utah's manufacturing base, including almost half of the durable goods manufacturing. In addition, the industry paid relatively high wages, and the businesses involved demonstrated great resilience.[47]

High tech manufacturing got its start in Utah during World War II and continued during the following two decades with the expansion of America's defense and aerospace industry. Later, as these industries declined, there was a veritable explosion in the founding and expansion of computer and software companies, both in Utah and elsewhere in the nation. In the years between 1980 and 1990, Utah was home to the birth of 184 new software companies. The boom was fueled by a rising demand for information processing in almost every business and profession, a recognition of the potential of high tech in biological and medical research and development, the demand for high tech developments in every kind of research and business activity, the advent of the personal computer, and the fact that start-up costs associated with software companies were only a fraction of those entailed in forming other kinds of manufacturing firms. By 1992 Utah's high tech firms employed approximately fifty thousand people. Some observers quipped that the state was becoming the next "Silicon Valley," and the one hundred–mile stretch from Provo to Logan was sometimes called the "info-tech corridor."[48]

Several factors contributed to the remarkable flowering of Utah's high tech industry. One was simply the fact that the founders of many companies lived in Utah, liked it, and therefore established their companies in the state. The existence of three research universities (the University of Utah, Utah State University, and Brigham Young University) provided excellent high tech training and willing interaction with developing firms. At least half the founders of Utah high tech firms in the 1980s came from university environments, and some of them maintained university faculty positions. The University of Utah Research Park, for example, was highly successful in promoting technological research and development, and in getting the faculty involved in entrepreneurial enterprises.[49] Utah's skilled and dedicated labor force was another factor contributing to the state's success, particularly in attracting outside companies to settle in Utah locations.

Many of the early high tech companies in Utah were electronics manufacturers, founded by Utah citizens who kept their headquarters as well as their major operations within the state. Thirty-eight such companies were founded in Utah before 1970, but the 1970s saw 101 new companies formed and the 1980s saw 273.[50] An example was Evans and Sutherland, a highly successful developer of computer graphics technology. Founded in 1968 by David Evans and Ivan Sutherland, by 1989 this company employed about 1,200 people and reported annual sales of $136 million.

Employment related to computers became especially important to the economy of Utah County, which in the early 1990s was home to more than 33 percent of all software companies doing business in Utah. Especially significant was the success of two key companies, WordPerfect Corporation and Novell, Inc. "Without the presence of these veritable giants of the software industry," one economist reported in 1992, "it is doubtful that the agglomeration of software companies in the Provo/Orem Area would have occurred."[51]

WordPerfect Corporation, originally named Satellite Software International, was created in 1979 by Alan Ashton, a professor of computer science at BYU, and Bruce Bastian, a graduate student who worked closely with Ashton. Their novel word processing software was developed and improved just in time to take advantage of the computer explosion after IBM introduced its personal computer in 1981. By 1988 WordPerfect had captured more than 20 percent of the entire word processing market and employed 1,100 people. The company also sold six additional products for office automation, and boasted sales of more than $102 million.[52] By the end of 1992 WordPerfect employed 4,500 people. But word processing and office automation was highly competitive, which made streamlining and cost reduction essential in order to stay in business. Beginning in 1993, therefore, the company was forced to reduce employment, even though it maintained its high sales profile. In 1994, WordPerfect was acquired by Novell, Inc., who said it needed WordPerfect's business applications to supplement and support its highly popular networking software. But the acquisition did not work to Novell's advantage, and early in 1996 WordPerfect was purchased by Corel Corporation, an Ottawa, Ontario, firm that was a proven leader in advertising and selling software.

Novell, Inc., was formed in 1983, built on the remnants of the failed Novell Data Systems, Inc. The previous company had developed a series of products that, working together, formed a LAN (local access network) that allowed several computers to share resources. But the company was plagued with management and other problems, and its major investor, Safeguard Scientifics, Inc., of Pennsylvania, finally insisted that it clean house. It persuaded David Noorda, a native Utahn working in California who had a reputation for turning around failing businesses, to return to Utah and take over the new entity. Noorda quickly boosted employee morale, reorganized development, and began marketing a product that soon became the leader in the networking market. By 1989 the company employed 1,600 people and enjoyed annual sales of $400 million.[53] In 1992 it generated $933 million in revenue and controlled about 70 percent of all the networking software business.[54] But by the end of the century intense competition had cut into Novell's dominant market position.

There were hundreds of other high tech companies, producing many diverse products.[55] Utah's high tech industry was here to stay, although its growth would slow as competition, especially in software and computer equipment, became more fierce.

The high tech industry, along with tourism, the continuing impact of mining and manufacturing, the growth of service industries, as well as other factors all combined to give Utah an enviable economic outlook at the end of the Bangerter administration. In

1992 the authors of an article in *Forbes* magazine observed that the economy of the Mountain States (Colorado, Idaho, Montana, Nevada, Utah, and Wyoming) was doing better than the US economy in general. Salt Lake City's central location, the authors stressed, made it a natural traffic hub for shipments to the West Coast, and a steel-furniture manufacturer with operations in Tennessee and Texas, for example, had chosen to expand his activities along I-15 in southern Utah because of low shipping costs. In addition, the authors underscored the same attractive factors that were voiced almost endlessly by the new wave of Utah boosters: the state was known for its young, well-educated, family-values working force. Indeed, as the title of the article said, Utah was "A Helluva Place to Have a Business."[56]

Utah and the Nation: The Environmental Challenge

The frustrations of modern life, with its economic challenges and technological wonders, were well illustrated in the challenge of caring for the environment. Mining often left unsightly, and sometimes dangerous, waste. Large construction projects, including highways, subdivisions, and new industrial plants, not only diminished air quality but often caused irreparable damage to watersheds and wildlife habitats. Manufacturing had the same side effects. In addition, vehicular traffic spewed deadly particulates and other hazards into the air, yet it appeared that little could be done to halt the burgeoning traffic growth. The only solution Utah voters seemed to want was more and bigger roads and highways to accommodate the ever-increasing, pollutant-emitting traffic.

Dealing with environmental problems was both costly and perplexing. If control devices became too expensive, they could lead to closure of plants, but if they were not installed they could adversely affect community health. Governmental regulation affected profits, interfered with free enterprise, and often only added to the continuing dissatisfaction with more and bigger government. On the other hand, few people trusted big business to regulate itself and to voluntarily do all that could be done to invest in cleaning up the air and water. The economic, public health, and other social issues involved all became emotionally charged, sometimes leading to extremism as angry or disenchanted citizens on both sides saw their respective "rights" being undermined or trammeled. Politicians, in turn, found themselves walking a tightrope as they attempted to find realistic solutions that would satisfy voters and still deal effectively with the problem.

In 1991, reflecting heightened concern for the environment, and at Bangerter's urging, the legislature created a new executive department, the Department of Environmental Quality. The department moved quickly to develop a pollution prevention program that encouraged industry-community cooperation in reducing contamination at reasonable cost. In April 1992 the administration also instituted the "Utah's Environment Next Century" project. Its aim was to involve the public, along with scientific investigation, in looking at the environment and using "comparative risk" analysis to determine the dangers posed to health, ecology, and quality of life.[57]

The legislature also passed several laws specifically designed to deal with air pollution. Prior to 1991, each of the Wasatch Front counties (where the most extensive pollution from vehicle emissions occurred) had its own vehicle emissions inspection program. That year, however, the legislature instituted a standard inspection program for the entire Wasatch Front. In addition, under pressure from the EPA, the 1992 legislature tightened vehicle emission requirements, encouraged use of cleaner fuels, and provided tax incentives for clean vehicle fuels, low-emission fireplaces, and wood-burning stoves.

With respect to water quality, between 1985 and 1992 the state's Drinking Water Board arranged for nearly $29 million in loans to communities for the purpose of upgrading water treatment and delivery systems. The state also provided more than $134 million in loans and grants for Utah communities to construct better wastewater facilities. It also developed a revolving fund to better utilize federal monies available for that same purpose.

In the 1980s, Utahns also became more aware of the dangers lurking in uranium tailings and in radon (a radioactive gaseous element produced by disintegrating radium) coming from the ground under buildings. In the Vitro Project, the state finally removed 4.2 million tons of tailings from an old uranium mill in Salt Lake City. It also removed and capped 1.2 million tons of tailings from Green River. In addition, a year-long radon study, completed in 1991, provided data by which concentrations of radon in public schools could be effectively evaluated. The state also received grants from the US Environmental Protection Agency to test for radon in homes.

Utah's most visible, and perhaps most health-hazardous, problem was air pollution, which became progressively worse in the 1980s and continued to violate federal clean air standards. In 1989, the Magnesium Corporation of America's plant at Tooele was judged by the national Environmental Protection Agency to be the largest toxic air polluter in the nation, spewing fifty-one thousand tons of chlorine into the atmosphere in 1988.[58] So serious were the state's environmental hazards in 1991 that a national insurance firm, which otherwise would have rated Utah as having the third most healthy population in the nation, rated it as twenty-sixth.[59]

Most people seemed to recognize that the most practical approach to the pollution problem would be a cease-fire between environmentalists and business interests, as well as more cooperation in finding solutions. This was the theme at a clean air symposium held at Utah Valley Community College in March 1991 and attended by several environmental and industrial leaders.[60] By that time cooperative efforts were taking place between the Utah Bureau of Air Quality, the Utah County Clean Air Coalition, the Utah County Clean Air Commission, and Geneva Steel Corporation. So effective was this cooperation that in April 1991 the EPA officially honored the four groups for their work in developing the first major PM10 control plan in the nation.[61]

Utah also continued to fight the battle of hazardous waste resulting from various manufacturing processes. Formerly much of the work was buried, but this practice became unsatisfactory because containers often leaked and materials could leach into subterranean water supplies. Incineration was a better solution. In 1991 Utah obtained its first hazardous waste incinerator, located in Tooele County, which had created a 135-square-mile "hazardous industries zone."[62] Several hazardous waste sites, approved by the state, were located in Utah by 1991, most of them in Tooele County.[63]

Disposing of hazardous waste created by Utah manufacturing was one thing, but accepting waste from other states was, to most Utahns, quite another. Several states did not have their own disposal sites, while manufacturers in others, such as California, found it less expensive to send their waste to Utah. Utahns, especially environmentalists, were deeply upset at the possibility that their state could become a hazardous waste dump for the nation, but federal law prohibited the state from restricting such movement as long as the material was disposed of according to federal regulations.[64] High drama surrounded the issues when soil was contaminated by acrylic acid from a spill during a 1989 Michigan train accident. Even though the soil removed from the crash site was of such low toxicity that it fell below both Utah and federal limits, environmentalists raised an alarm when two thousand tons of it was put on another train and hauled toward dump sites elsewhere. One man chained himself to the train twice in an effort to keep it from moving until the soil was put through an expensive treatment. Over the next two years, the thirty-two-car "cancer cannonball," as it was dubbed by critics, wended its way through several states, where privately-owned disposal sites refused to accept its controversial cargo. It arrived in Utah in April 1991, where it was permitted to dump the load.[65] This comic-opera story only emphasized how politically-laden the dumping controversy was.

Many environmental problems were created not by humans, but by nature. The Great Salt Lake presented one such quandary. With an average precipitation of 259 percent of normal from 1983–1986, the lake rose so high that it caused more than $240 million in damages to Interstate 80, railroads, several minerals industries, sewage treatment plants, parks, wildlife habitats, and considerable amount of private property. Intensive study of how to deal with the problem began during the Matheson administration, but no decision was made. Bangerter studied the issue for months, but he faced a crisis that seemed to call for immediate action. Concluding that the most cost-effective way to prevent more damage was to lower the lake level by pumping surplus water to the West Desert, he made one of the most controversial decisions of his gubernatorial career and recommended to the legislature a massive pumping project. The $70 million project, approved in May 1986, took eleven months to complete. It included thirty-two miles of dikes, a pumping station, a ten-mile access road, three huge pumps, and a thirty-seven-mile long natural gas pipeline needed to fire their engines. During the first year in operation, the pumps moved nearly 1.55 million acre-feet of water to an evaporation pond in the West Desert, lowering the lake by thirteen inches. After another year, the pumps were shut down because they were no longer necessary. They remained on location, however, carefully maintained, in case of future need. As an engineering accomplishment, the West Desert Project received the prestigious Award of Merit from the American Society of Civil Engineers.[66]

Utah and the Nation: Politics of Abortion

Of all the national issues affecting Utah, none was more politically or emotionally charged than that of abortion. The dominant attitude in Utah, consistent with that of the LDS Church, was against abortion except in cases where the life of the mother was threatened, the fetus was clearly deformed, or the pregnancy was the result of rape or incest. However, any proposed law based on this position flew in the face of the perspectives of so-called pro-choice groups. Supported by the American Civil Liberties Union, these people were not necessarily pro-abortion. Rather, they simply felt that the decision must be left entirely to the woman, who should have control of her own body and her own destiny. Physicians, they also believed, should have the right to perform abortions without fear of criminal prosecution. Their position was supported by the controversial 1973 US Supreme Court decision, *Roe v. Wade*, which affirmed the legality of abortion.

After *Roe v. Wade*, right-to-life groups mounted well-financed political campaigns and took to the streets in public demonstrations. A few even turned to violence, including bombing abortion clinics. In several states, anti-abortionists succeeded in getting tough laws through the legislatures that, they hoped, would pass the scrutiny of the Supreme Court and modify, if not completely overturn, the 1973 decision. They almost succeeded when, in both *Webster v. Reproductive Health Services* (1989) and *Planned Parenthood v. Casey* (1992), the court stopped short, by a vote of 5 to 4, of overturning *Roe*. But it upheld the power of the states to impose restrictions on abortion. The *Webster* decision was vague enough that it implicitly invited states to pass such restrictions and then present them to the court for scrutiny.

In Utah, the controversy took on both religious and political overtones. Some pro-life groups did everything they could to obtain legislation that was even more restrictive than the LDS Church's stand. Other antiabortionists, including Governor Bangerter, were realistically concerned with the probability that such a law would never pass judicial scrutiny and would therefore be merely an empty gesture. The issue came to a head after the *Webster* decision, when some people claimed that a Missouri law upheld by the court was very similar to Utah law, thus negating the need for any further legislation in Utah. Others, however, quickly pointed to several provisions in the Missouri law that were absent in Utah's code. In addition, because of Utah's predominantly Mormon population, national right-to-lifers targeted the state as the ideal place to promote a law that could be used as a test case for finally overturning *Roe*. The 1990 legislature considered a highly restrictive law but soon abandoned it. Most considered it foolish to pass a law that could cost up to $1 million to defend in court and was doomed to failure anyway. Pro-choice groups were delighted with the decision, while pro-life forces were bitterly disappointed.

The next year was a different story. The 1990 legislature appointed a committee to study the issue and propose new legislation for 1991. But the committee was dominated by conservative pro-lifers who voted 11 to 3 to propose a bill much like the one that had failed. Bangerter felt that such a law was only tilting at windmills, because it could not stand up in court. On January 14, in his State of the State address, he made it clear that he would veto the proposed bill if passed, although he would support a revised bill. In a flurry of activity over the next few days, legislative leaders and representatives from the governor's office devised an innovative compromise: a two-tiered bill. The first tier contained all the restrictive language of the original bill, but the second tier contained more permissive provisions that would go into effect if the first tier were struck down. The bill sailed through the Senate by a vote of 23 to 4 but ran into problems in the House where, in the end, the restrictive first tier was eliminated. On January 25, the Senate agreed and the governor signed the bill into law three hours later.[67] The next day 2,500 people jammed the state capitol building in protest and then proceeded to the Governor's Mansion.

The new law banned all abortions except in the cases of rape, incest, and the endangerment of the life and health of the mother and baby. It was the toughest abortion law in the country and brought immediate nationwide attention. Utah's chapter of the National Organization for Women (NOW) angrily charged that Utah had "declared war on women," and called for a worldwide boycott of the state by vacationers, conventioneers, and Olympic athletes. The national organization soon agreed. The Utah Association of Women countered by saying that, despite NOW's charges, the law represented the women of Utah. It also published a four-page travel guide for pro-life supporters that highlighted "Ten Spectacular Utah Vacations." The American Civil Liberties Union took out a full-page ad in the asking for money to support its fight against the bill. In a highly distorted comment on the law's intent, the ACLU stated that since an illegal abortion was considered murder according to a 1983 law, Utah women guilty of abortion could even be executed. "In Utah, they know how to punish a woman who has an abortion," the headline read. "Shoot her." The governor's office called the statement ridiculous but said that if a loophole existed it would be plugged in the upcoming special session of the legislature. Utah's attorney general, Paul Van Dam, called the ad "one of the ultimate cheap shots I've ever seen."[68]

Van Dam agreed that the state would not enforce the new law until it was tested in the courts. With the support of the ACLU, suit was brought against the state by several women and a women's clinic. The state hired the law firm of Jones, Waldo, Holbrook, & McDonough to handle the case. That firm was later replaced, because of a conflict of interest, by Brigham Young University law professor Mary Ann Wood. By late August 1991, the state had spent more than $126,000 for legal services and, with costs mounting, the Utah Association of Women sent out letters soliciting contributions. The state also sought a stay in the lawsuit, pending the outcome of a Supreme Court test of an even tougher law adopted during the summer by the state of Louisiana. Utah would "piggyback" on this case, filing an "amicus curiae" brief with the court. However, on August 30 a federal appeals court refused to put the Louisiana case on a fast track, thus derailing hopes for a quick decision. The ACLU successfully fought the stay in the Utah suit, and in November, US District Judge Thomas L. Greene set the trial to begin in April 1992.

As Utah prepared to go to court, many people entered the public fray. An announcement early in April that the Rocky Mountain Conference of the United Methodist Church was filing a friend-of-the-court brief in support of the ACLU's challenge tended to emphasize the charge that the law was little more than an effort to codify LDS beliefs. That charge was defused when seventy-seven representatives from Protestant and Catholic churches around the state signed a letter in support of the law. Debbie Ashman, executive director of the Salt Lake Christian Association Action Council, declared that the law "is not a Mormon law but reflects the teaching of the Biblical scriptures for all who take God at his word."[69]

In June 1992, the US Supreme Court further eroded *Roe v. Wade* by upholding most of Pennsylvania's sweeping law, including the provision that women must wait twenty-four hours after asking a doctor for an abortion. But it struck down a provision similar to one in the Utah law that required women to notify their husbands of their plans. Then, in December, Judge Greene struck down the heart of Pennsylvania's law, the prohibition against elective abortions, as unconstitutional. By that time the fight had cost the state approximately $750,000.

Law and Order

In general, Utah's crime rate remained close to or above the national average during these years, although homicide was well below the average.[70] But the state was still embarrassed by its public image as a stock-fraud capital. The Bangerter administration made every effort to stamp out that image by implementing the recommendations included in the Governor's Securities Fraud Task Force Report that had been prepared at the end of the Matheson administration. One move was a ruling by the Department of Commerce that restricted, and practically eliminated, blind pool securities offerings, which had been one of the most prevalent tools for fraud.

However, other problems of law enforcement were mounting. One was the rising number of juvenile gangs, which, nationwide, often resulted not only in street warfare against each other but also indiscriminate violence against the public. Gangs were not as prevalent in Utah as elsewhere, and at first some people even questioned whether a problem existed at all. However, by 1990 it was clear that Utah was no gang-free haven. As of June, Salt Lake City's gang unit had identified approximately 137 gangs and 717 individuals who were members of gangs.[71] In 1991 police chiefs in the Salt Lake area reported that the number of identified gangs had increased by five times in three years and the number of gang members had more than doubled. Gang activities covered a broad range, including homicide, drive-by shootings, drug distribution, and extortion. Gang members even extorted lunch money from third-grade school children.

In January 1991, partly in response to public clamor for a "blue ribbon" task force, the state formed a Gang Project Advisory Board. Its members included representatives from the clergy, minority groups, juvenile courts, the legislature, prosecutors, educators and others. Its purpose was to develop a master plan and make recommendations about gang-related issues along the Wasatch Front.[72] In Salt Lake City, Mayor Deedee Corradini announced in March 1992 the formation of a midnight basketball league, which was intended to attract young people who might otherwise become involved in gangs. The program was modeled after similar programs that had been successful in other major cities. It incorporated not only basketball but also role-modeling, substance-abuse counseling, and programs for help in employment and behavior modification and it was endorsed by such public sports figures as basketball coach Rick Majerus of the University of Utah and Utah Jazz president Frank Layden.[73] Law enforcement officials, meanwhile, attempted to persuade the public that police could not deal with the gang problem effectively without help from citizens. They urged everyone to become acquainted with the kind of attire gang members wore and to learn how to recognize and interpret gang graffiti on neighborhood walls.[74]

Officials were also concerned with victims of gang violence, and Utah's first "victim's bill of rights" became effective on January 1, 1987. In addition, a "victim's coordinator" was added to the staff of the Office of Crime and Victims Reparations, whose job it was to administer funds coming to the state as a result of the federal Victim of Crime Act. This office also had the task of seeing that those who perpetrated crime reimbursed their victims for out-of-pocket losses. By the end of 1992 the office had distributed approximately $3 million annually, all collected from offenders.[75]

Perhaps the most calculating criminal in Utah history was Mark Hofmann, whose long-term white-collar crime spree ended in a tragic double murder in 1985. After years of scheming, Hofmann became a master forger and, on the basis of his forgeries, gained a national reputation as a dealer in historical documents and artifacts. He sold perhaps hundreds of forged documents to libraries and collectors around the nation. Some were purportedly in the handwriting of such luminaries as Betsy Ross, Daniel Boone, Mark Twain, Jack London, Charles Dickens, and others. It was estimated that total sales of his forgeries amounted to more than $3 million.

In Utah, Hofmann claimed to have discovered several rare manuscripts, some in the handwriting of Joseph Smith, Brigham Young, and other historically prominent Mormons. Some of these decisions could have modified LDS Church history in highly controversial ways. They were so sophisticated and fit so well in their presumed historical context that they fooled handwriting experts and historians alike. Hofmann collected a small fortune by selling them to the church and to private collectors. But on October 15, 1985, thinking that his Mormon forgeries were about to be revealed by victims who had begun to suspect him, Hofmann killed two people. One was Salt Lake City businessman Steven C. Christensen, who picked up a package containing a bomb outside his office. The other was Kathleen W. Sheets, wife of Christensen's former business associate. She picked up a bomb-laden package left at their home and intended for her husband. The next day Hofmann himself was seriously injured when another bomb went off in his car. Hofmann soon became a suspect in the two deaths.

The investigation was long and complex because it involved obtaining evidence that Hofmann was indeed a forger. Finally, on February 4, 1986, he was charged with two counts of murder, several counts of theft by deception, and a number of other criminal activities. In January 1987, after a plea bargain agreement, Hofmann pleaded guilty to two counts of second-degree murder and two counts of theft by deception. He was sentenced to life in prison. A year later he appeared before the Board of Pardons, where he coolly described his cold-hearted motives for murder. The board could have granted him a parole after seven years. Instead, it decided that he should serve the rest of his life behind bars.[76]

In January 1988, after a Mormon meetinghouse in Summit County was bombed, John Singer's family again made national headlines (see chapter 5 for earlier confrontations and the death of Singer). One of the bombers, Addam Swapp, had married two of John and Vickie Singer's daughters. He and the rest of the Singer clan were still protesting what they called the murder of Singer nine years earlier. Following the bombing, Vickie, Swapp, and twelve other people armed themselves and holed up in the Singer farmhouse, which was then surrounded by 150 police officers.

Utahns agonized daily as polygamy, religious fundamentalism, the bombing, and the bizarre events of the thirteen-day siege of the Singer compound made national and international headlines. The Singer family apparently believed they must confront the law in order for predictions that John Singer would soon be resurrected to come true. Law enforcement officers used sirens, floodlights, and buzzing aircraft to try to wear down the tiny cult but to no avail. Ogden Kraut, prominent Utah polygamist and a friend of the Singer family, was allowed to take food to the children, but Swapp denied a request, sent through Kraut, that he plug in the telephone and speak to negotiators. On a second visit, Kraut delivered a letter from Governor Bangerter, asking the family to surrender peacefully, but the plea was refused. The bombing of the chapel, Vickie responded in a letter to the governor, was "God making bare his arm through His servant Addam Swapp."[77] Lieutenant Fred House, part of a trained team sent in with dogs to infiltrate the compound, was killed by a shot from the farmhouse as he urged the dogs forward.

The siege ended with the arrest of four people. In a federal court trial, Addam Swapp, his brother Jonathan, and John Timothy Singer were found guilty of attempted murder of federal officers. Addam Swapp was sentenced to fifteen years in prison, the other two were given ten years, and Vickie Singer, found guilty of resisting arrest, was sentenced to five years. In December, a Utah state court sentenced Addam Swapp and John Timothy Singer to one to fifteen years in the state prison (to be served concurrently with their federal sentences) for negligent homicide, in connection with the death of Fred House. Jonathan Swapp was given twelve months.

The Continuing Problem of Child Abuse

An especially tragic continuing problem was child abuse and neglect, which was on the rise in both Utah and the nation. It was difficult to obtain accurate figures on how extensive the increase really was, but the best data available indicated that between 1983 and 1991 the number of child abuse and neglect victims in the state jumped from 4,794 to 10,179. The number of child sexual abuse victims rose from 611 to 2,316. During that same period, the number of reported (not necessarily actual) cases of all kinds of abuse and neglect rose from 5.3 per 1,000 population to 8.2.[78]

The legal difficulties of dealing with abusers were illustrated in 1988 when a man convicted of seven counts of child sex abuse and sodomy involving his son and daughter, both under age thirteen, was given only six months in jail and a ten-year probation. Utah law mandated a ten-year-to-life sentence, but it contained an "incest exception" and the judge ruled that the criteria necessary for probation under that exception had been met. The man was required to undergo psychiatric counseling, however, as a condition of his probation.

The extent of the problem was dramatically portrayed in a 1989 report by the State Task Force on Child Sexual Abuse. It found 1,316 substantiated cases of child sexual abuse in the state during the fiscal year 1988–89 but, it said, only 6 percent of all actual cases were reported. The implication that there could be as many as twenty thousand cases was horrendous. The task force recommended, among other things, providing mandatory psychological counseling for both the victim and the abuser at the expense of the abuser. Meanwhile, the problem continued to mount. Incidence of child sexual abuse in Utah climbed by 24 percent in 1991 (a total of 2,316 cases) and all child abuse rose by 19 percent.[80]

Dealing with child abuse was not just a matter of how to help the abused and punish the abuser but also of seeing that innocent people were not accused of being abusers. In addition, there were differing philosophies on how best to deal with victims, as well as a confusing lack of coordination between various state and private agencies. As a result of the task force's recommendations, three centers were established where all the agencies worked together. In addition, the attorney general's office set up a special child abuse unit to train police and prosecutors in how to deal with the more difficult problems.[81]

Meanwhile, the Division of Family Services of the state's Department of Human Services put in place several programs that, in one way or another, took care of victims of child abuse. One was home-based protective services counseling, which in 1990 helped 1,693 families who had volunteered for the services. It also provided 1,409 families with protective service supervision ordered by the court for families where abuse and neglect had previously occurred. In addition, 3,470 women and children received 21,822 days of protection in domestic violence shelters; however, this number included only 12 percent of the actual victims of violence. Other services were also available, as well as a child abuse prevention program. In 1990, under the auspices of a Children's Trust Account, fifty prevention programs were in existence throughout the state. In addition, eight Family Support Centers provided respite care and training in parental skills.[82] Such efforts were commendable, and much good was done, but they reached only a fraction of those who needed them. Meanwhile, the debate over how best to deal with offenders, as well as what more should be done for victims, continued.

Health and Welfare

By most measurements, Utahns were in relatively good health during the waning years of the twentieth century. The infant death rate declined steadily, standing at 6.2 per one thousand live births in 1992, compared with a national rate of 8.9. The incidence of Acquired Immunodeficiency Syndrome (AIDS), on the other hand, rose in both Utah and the nation, although Utah's rate remained about a third that of the national average.[83] Utah's lung cancer rate was about half that of the nation. But in other maladies Utah was much closer to national norms.

Hanging like a cloud over Utah's health picture was a problem that plagued all of America: the rapid, disproportionate rise in the cost of health care. In the 1980s the medical component of the national Consumer Price Index rose at almost twice the rate of all other items combined. One factor was rising hospital costs, but another, according to a 1990 study by the Utah Foundation, was that a major portion of charges billed to patients were uncollectible. Many Medicare and Medicaid patients could not pay their share of the costs. In addition, mandated charity care only added to the rising "uncollectible" category. As a result, hospitals passed on the cost to paying patients. Everyone thought this, unfair, yet no one knew how to solve the dilemma.

In 1987 the governor appointed a task force to examine health care costs and to study the effects of a market-oriented solution. Reporting a year later, the task force could only suggest that neither a strictly hands-off policy nor a completely regulatory policy was satisfactory; it recommended working toward facilitating market mechanisms. The report noted several positive efforts to contain costs, but the problem remained serious, and the stage was set for some major state and national confrontations over the issue in the next few years.[84] A silver lining to this cloudy issue was the fact that in 1991 Utah ranked 44th among the fifty states in the average level of hospital costs. Compared to the rest of the nation, Utah's health care was still a bargain.[85]

Another Utah problem that followed a national trend was the growing number of hungry children, due mainly to increasing poverty in the state. A 1991 study conducted by the Food Research and Action Center of Washington, D.C., found that an astonishing 51,700 Utah children under age twelve, 11.3 percent, went hungry each day, compared with a national average of 12.8 percent. With more than two hundred thousand Utahns living below the federal poverty level, many more children were also "at risk" of going hungry.[86]

Following still another disturbing national trend, during the 1980s Utah saw a rise in the number of homeless people. Between 1986 and 1992, the number of persons in Utah's homeless shelters rose from 355 to 1,330, an increase of 275 percent. Contrary to popular belief, the typical homeless person was neither mentally ill nor an alcoholic male. Rather, in 1992 families with children, often headed by women, were the fastest growing segment of the homeless population. Most of Utah's homeless were located along the Wasatch Front.[87]

Two state funds, the Homeless Trust Fund and the Housing Trust Fund, were established during the Bangerter administration, and the state also agreed to accept responsibility for four federal programs. By 1992 the state's Housing Trust Fund had grown to $2.4 million. The state also operated the Critical Needs Housing Program, funded by the state, and the federally-funded Rental Rehabilitation Program. From a national perspective, Utah performed well in these programs, and frequently won bonuses of more than 34 percent above the federal government's base allocations.[88]

In 1987 the legislature raised the tax on cigarettes from twelve cents to twenty-four cents per pack. The increase was partly the result of lobbying for a five-year Department of Health program known as "Baby Your Baby," which was intended to reduce infant mortality. The new program, which actually received only part of the money, included state-supported prenatal services as well as a huge public information campaign. One result was a savings to the state of nearly $14 million as the rate of normal births to low income mothers on Medicaid jumped from 55 percent to 66 percent. After four years, Utah's infant death rate dropped from 8.8 to 6.1 per thousand live births.[89]

The Department of Health was also concerned the state's immunization program, especially after a survey of two-year-olds conducted in 1991 revealed that more than half the children were not adequately immunized. Measles and whooping cough, especially, were on the rise, and even a major public awareness program initiated by the department did not seem to help. As a result of the survey, the department supported the national "Every Child by Two" campaign, hoping to increase measles immunization in two-year-olds from 41.3 percent to 50 percent by the end of 1995.[90]

Utahns became increasingly aware of the national AIDS crisis in the 1980s, and the Department of Health initiated an AIDS Control Program to try to reduce the spread of the dreaded HIV virus. The program included screening, counseling, and increased public information. Legislation was drafted to help protect both patients and health-care workers. In addition, in 1987 Utah's Medicaid program became one of the first in the nation to pay for providing AIDS patients with the drug AZT.[91]

The Bangerter administration also showed continuing concern for improving health care in Utah's rural areas. The Department of Health, working with community groups and health centers, obtained federal funding for three community health clinics in rural areas. It also obtained funds for training some two hundred home health aides for rural areas. In 1990 the legislature provided funds for loan repayment and scholarships to physicians who would agree to practice in rural areas, and a similar bill in 1992 provided funds for nurses.[92]

In 1990, the legislature approved the creation of the Utah Comprehensive Health Insurance Pool to help with the medical expenses of the needy who were uninsured. The governor approved an initial $3-million, one-time fund to begin the program, after which the legislature appropriated $2 million in both the 1992 and 1993 fiscal years. By the end of 1992, the program had assisted more than 350 uninsured Utahns.[93]

State funding for Medicaid doubled between 1985 and 1992. One reason for this was simply that more people every year were faced with the inability to purchase health insurance, either through lack of employment or the prohibitive cost of premiums. The biggest factor in the increase, however, was the rise in federal mandates, with more than fifty new ones imposed by Congress in eight years. These developments came at an especially inopportune time as revenue was falling and angry citizens were attempting to roll back taxes. In response, the Department of Health initiated programs intended to extend the use of available Medicaid dollars. Through Home and Community Service Waivers, Medicaid recipients could receive services in their own homes rather than in institutions, often saving tens of thousands of dollars per person.[94]

On the average, Utah did remarkably well on the *Public Health Report Card* issued by the American Public Health Association in 1992. The report was organized into five categories. On "Healthy Behavior," Utah ranked in the first quartile (the top 25 percent). Utah was also in the first quartile in a second category, "Healthy Neighborhoods." In two other major categories, "Medical Care Costs" and "Community Health Service," Utah was in the second quartile—still above national norms in most subcategories.[95]

Utah's good showing in these four categories was all the more remarkable in light of its poor showing in the remaining category, "Healthy Environment," where it placed in the fourth quartile. The state was 44th in the nation on pollution, 49th on unsafe drinking water, and 50th on fluoridated water. On work-related injuries it ranked higher, placing 26th. The Utah Department of Environmental Quality responded to the report card by arguing that the "unsafe drinking water" data was distorted.[96]

As far as delivery of health care was concerned, Utah had fewer physicians per 100,000 population than the national average. Citizens of the state also spent less per capita on health care than the national average, spent fewer days in the hospital per illness, and had a lower hospital occupancy rate than most of the nation.[97]

Alcohol and Drugs

The problem of illicit drug distribution became increasingly acute during these years. In 1986 alone the state's Bureau of Narcotics and Drug Enforcement seized more than $7 million worth of controlled substances.[98] There were major cocaine seizures on highways in central Utah, crackdowns at Hill Air Force Base and the Utah State Penitentiary, and drug arrest sweeps in Utah and Salt Lake counties. Most of the contraband was on its way through Utah, headed for other states, but much of it was also intended for drug users in the state. Drug enforcement officers also found marijuana growing in the state and, in 1985, discovered a multi-million dollar methamphetamine laboratory in Summit County.[99] In 1989 the Substance Abuse Division estimated that 155,000 Utah workers suffered from "severe or extreme" substance abuse.[100]

The legislature passed several laws designed to reduce both alcohol and drug abuse in the state. The so-called "Not a Drop Bill" imposed sanctions on underage drivers who tested positive in alcohol tests. Another law established drug-free zones around schools by increasing the penalties for those who sold drugs near schools or other places where children were gathered. The 1987 Utah Alcohol and Drug Testing Act authorized employers to set up programs for testing both employees and management. Several major employers quickly did so. Thiokol Corporation, for example, Utah's largest employer, required a pre-employment test, a mandatory test for anyone involved in an accident, and random testing for employees involved in safety-sensitive positions. Anyone failing a test twice was automatically suspended, although they were usually offered treatment. Finally, in 1988 the legislature established a Drug Diversion Program designed to short-circuit and eliminate diversion of legal drugs for illegal purposes. Within a year, according to official reports, drug use was down by as much as 44 percent in about half of the groups being tracked.[101]

The state was not left to its own resources in the war on drugs. The United States Department of Justice administered funds authorized by Congress to help the states. In 1991 Utah was awarded more than $3.53 million.

Public Education: Efforts to Minimize the Risk

The story of public education during the Bangerter years contained all of the familiar elements: rising enrollment, crowded classrooms, one of the lowest per-capita student budgets in the nation—despite one of the highest percentage of state income going to education, intensive efforts by the governor and lawmakers to increase both commitment to and quality of education; and continuing teacher dissatisfaction—but remarkable student achievement.[102]

As *A Nation at Risk* (see chapter 5) and other reports heightened concern over the quality of public education in America, Utah's government and school officials tried various means of minimizing the risk by improving education and raising teacher morale.[103] The 1985 legislature provided for permanent funding of the teacher career ladder program begun in 1984. Lawmakers also continued to appropriate more money for the purpose of reducing class size, but rising enrollment made this objective difficult to achieve. In addition, the governor successfully urged the inauguration of a program called the Governor's Schools of Excellence, in which twenty schools each year were selected for special gubernatorial recognition and a cash award of $10,000.

The state also expanded year-round education, in an effort to save money through more efficient buildings and classrooms. During the 1990–91 school year, sixty-five Utah schools, with 12.4 percent of the total enrollment, were involved in year-round scheduling. An evaluation conducted late in 1989 by the State Board of Education demonstrated that 83 percent of the parents with children involved in year-round schools were happy with the program and that 84 percent of the teachers preferred it.[104]

In 1988, the State Office of Education implemented a significant change in its basic approach to public education. Known as "A Shift in Focus," the new program was the result of a year-long study by the Strategic Planning Commission, a group of more than thirty community, legislative, and education leaders. It was based on a new state core curriculum that was adopted in 1984, but it also emphasized individual student education plans (SEPs) and innovative teaching methods.[105] Efforts to achieve the goals of "A Shift in Focus" did not necessarily involve inaugurating new programs but, for the most part, enhancing and improving those already in place. The volunteer program was a case in point. Volunteers provided one-on-one help to individual students who needed tutoring or academic enrichment. During the 1988–89 school year the state volunteer specialist held one-day training sessions in Ogden, Jordan, Kane, Iron, and Murray districts. Through these sessions, approximately 1,200 teachers and parents were trained in setting up local volunteer programs. As the effort grew throughout the state, volunteers came from increasingly diverse segments of the community, including senior citizens, businesses, and service organizations.[106] The results were often outstanding.

In connection with the effort to provide a more positive learning climate as part of the shift in focus, a reform known as Outcome-Based Education (OBE) was gradually instituted in Utah schools. Somewhat controversial in nature because many parents saw it as a loosening rather than a tightening of educational standards, OBE was designed to help all students achieve higher levels of learning by focusing more on individuals and their personal abilities. By the 1987–88 school year, all forty school districts had adopted OBE "to some degree," and a statewide survey credited the program with "sparking curriculum modifications in subject areas ranging from world geography and ancient world studies in Alpine District to science courses in Grand District" and giving educators "a deeper conviction that all students are capable of achieving high level learning."[107] By 1991 the program had spread to more schools within each district and continued, said the State Superintendent of Public Instruction, to exert "a positive impact on student learning, teacher satisfaction, and the support of administrators, board members, and parents to a varying extent in all Utah School districts."[108]

The Bangerter administration also began an important initiative in education technology. In 1990 the state allocated an initial $15 million, to be matched by contributions from local districts and the private sector, to help schools purchase computers for classroom instruction and to train faculty and staff in the use of computers. As the program grew the state also completed a statewide telecommunication network (EDNET) that gave students access to many instructional programs not otherwise available to them. This was especially helpful in remote and rural areas. By 1992 some $40 million had been allocated to this program.[109]

The story of education was not without its usual controversies. A particularly bitter battle was fought after the Salt Lake City school board announced in February 1987 that it intended to close South High School that June. One reason was a bill being considered in the legislature that would penalize school districts financially for underutilizing available space. Enrollment at South High was the lowest of the city's four high schools and continued to drop. The board planned to create three high school districts with approximately equal enrollment. Angry parents, however, charging that the decision had been made without their input, besieged the board with criticism. The board delayed the closing for a year and appointed a community committee to investigate the matter further. In June the committee voted unanimously to close the school, and the board officially voted to do so at the end of the 1988–89 school year. Three years later the renovated building became the home of expanded facilities for Salt Lake Community College, known as South City Campus.

One educational phenomenon spreading across the nation in the 1980s was home schooling. As more parents became dissatisfied with public education and demanded the right to teach their children at home, many state legislatures passed laws allowing them to do so. In most cases school districts were given the responsibility of regulating the home schools to see that they maintained minimum educational standards. The state of Utah had allowed home education since 1953, but in 1986, responding to vagueness in the law and problems with interpretation, the attorney general issued a formal opinion that clarified school district responsibilities and home education requirements. Parents were required to demonstrate that their programs were equivalent with public education, and to reapply annually for exceptions to the compulsory public school statutes. School superintendents could administer standardized tests but could not require such things as the submission of daily teaching plans. In 1992 approximately 3,500 Utah students were involved in home schooling.[110]

In September 1989, President George W. Bush and the nation's governors met in a remarkable educational summit, where they agreed to establish a set of national education goals and to monitor progress toward achieving them. Six comprehensive goals were adopted the following year. In 1992 the governor's office and the State Office of Education prepared a thirty-four-page report entitled *A Utah Perspective on the National Education Goals 1992*. Intended to inform citizens of Utah's progress toward those goals, the report showed both strengths and weaknesses of the state's programs.

With respect to Goal 1, "All children in America will start school ready to learn," the state was concerned that 30 percent of Utah's children between one and two years of age were not adequately immunized. It was also concerned about nutrition, pointing out that the increasing number of parents employed outside the home placed heavy responsibility on day-care centers for adequate nutrition of children. There were, however, several state-sponsored activities that helped prepare children for school. These included "Baby your Baby"; programs to enhance awareness of nutritional needs; PTA initiatives that, among other things, supported preschools, intervened for at-risk students, funded care of disabled preschool children, helped train parents, and conducted preventative programs regarding child abuse; migrant education programs; special education programs serving more than 3,500 disabled children statewide; and the highly successful, federally funded Headstart Program.

Utah had an exceptional record on Goal 2, which called for increasing the high school graduation rate to at least 90 percent. It also sponsored a number of programs to help educate high school dropouts and to prevent dropouts. Goal 3 called for vastly improved student achievement and citizenship. Among the several programs designed to improve Utah's record was Outcome-Based Education, the Educational Technology Initiative authorized by the legislature in 1990, the Advanced Placement Program, and the Utah Character Education Consortium (a multi-district group that focused on citizenship and community service as positive elements in the curriculum). Goal 4 ambitiously called for the United States to become first in the world in science and mathematics. The report pointed out that one reason for Utah's below average performance in mathematics was that only 32 percent of the teachers whose primary assignment was mathematics had a college major in the field, compared to 47 percent in the nation. Utah's effort to change this situation included a stronger requirement of subject-specific endorsement.

Utah also did well on Goal 5, which emphasized adult literacy and lifelong learning. On Goal 6, making American schools free of drugs and violence, Utah's record seemed to be only slightly better than that of the nation and the figures presented cause for concern.[111] Utah, however, was pursuing a vigorous program aimed at drug and violence prevention in the schools.

Higher Education

Higher education, too, faced familiar problems in these years. Enrollment continued to mount, jumping from 70,215 students in Utah's nine public colleges and universities in the fall of 1984 to 99,168 in 1992—an increase of 41 percent in eight years. Part of the challenge was to manage the growth in such a way that it would be spread more evenly among the various institutions. With this in mind, the governor strongly supported the idea of turning Utah's two technical colleges into comprehensive community colleges, increasing the likelihood of students attending community colleges for their first two years. The college's names were changed accordingly in 1987. This was one element of the master plan for higher education adopted by the Board of Regents in 1986. Like earlier plans, this one also encouraged greater diversity and less duplication of programs among Utah's institutions of higher learning.[112]

An important educational innovation during these years was the creation of the Utah Partnership for Educational and Economic Development. Made up of representatives from higher education, public education, business, industry, and government, the partnership appraised the contribution to state economic development being made by both public and higher education, identified areas for improvement, and recommended new programs. The partnership, unique in the nation, received plaudits from many states that were attempting to initiate similar programs.[113]

Private and federal funding continued to be important sources of support for Utah's colleges and universities,[114] but funding sometimes led to controversy. In 1989, the University of Utah agreed to name the University Medical Center and School of Medicine after philanthropist James L. Sorenson in exchange for a gift of $15 million in stock. Immediately an angry outcry went up from faculty, students, legislators, and much of the public, who did not want the name changed, whereupon Sorenson took back the stock. The medical school retained its former name and the embarrassing incident did not stop other donations from coming in. In 1991, for example, President Chase N. Peterson announced that the late Emma Eccles Jones had left an endowment of $15 million to the university, with the stipulation that the graduate school of business bear the name of her father, David Eccles.

In 1985, the Board of Regents appointed a new Commissioner of Higher Education, William Rolfe Kerr. In 1990 Southern Utah State College and Weber State College were both designated as universities. Their names were changed accordingly, to become effective January 1, 1991. The Board of Regents stipulated, however, that both should continue to focus on their roles as teaching institutions, with only limited graduate programs and no substantial research responsibilities for teachers.

A major financial challenge to Utah's institutions of higher learning was the fact that along with increasing enrollment came shrinking per-student revenues. While most other states raised tuition and fees to offset rising costs, the average raise in Utah grew only from $903 per semester in 1978 to $1,021 in 1990. As a result, Utah's real per student revenues dropped from a high of $4,685 in 1985 to $4,005 in 1990. The colleges and universities responded with several adjustments, some of which did not make good educational sense but nevertheless seemed necessary to meet the economic crunch. Among these adjustments was a reduction in the number and regularity of classes, leading to larger classes and frustration on the part of students who could not get the classes they needed and sometimes had to delay graduation. Another problem was comparatively low faculty salaries, which resulted in higher faculty turnover and the loss of some outstanding professors who took jobs at other universities. In addition, library facilities suffered. Because of these issues, the independent Utah Foundation declared in 1992 that the state must look seriously at increased funding, limiting enrollments, and cost-cutting reforms.[115]

State and Local Politics

Utah politics during the Bangerter years was dominated by Republicans, who, like Bangerter, were generally moderately conservative. But elected Democrats were hardly left-wing liberals. Rather, their political stances put them closer to center, emphasizing again that, in general, Utahns accepted the politics of moderation. At the same time, ultraconservatism gained some strength, but not enough to win any elections.

There were a few exceptions to the domination by the Republican party. In 1985, after serving ten years as mayor of Salt Lake City, the popular Democrat Ted Wilson resigned, to become director of the Hinckley Institute of Politics at the University of Utah. Palmer DePaulis, the city's public works director and, like Wilson, a Democrat, was named interim mayor. In November, DePaulis was elected to a two-year term, defeating Merrill Cook. In 1986, moreover, Democrats made a notable comeback from their political rout two years earlier. In local elections, Dave Watson broke the Republican hold on the Salt Lake County Commission by winning over Merrill Cook. In addition, former Congressman Wayne Owens regained his seat in the US House of Representatives, defeating Republican Tom Shimizu in the Second Congressional district. Republicans James Hansen and Howard Nielson retained their seats, however, and Jake Garn was elected to his third term in the United States Senate. Garn was extremely popular, but a great many people were especially sympathetic with him when he donated a kidney to his daughter earlier in the year.

In 1987, it surprised no one when the national Democratic party announced that one of the people it would target for defeat in 1988 was Governor Norman H. Bangerter.[116] It was a good year for such a move because Bangerter had just proposed the largest one-time tax increase in the history of the state. This not only sent his popularity plummeting in the polls but also marked the beginning of an angry tax protest movement (see below). Bangerter decided to seek a second term, however, even after Jon Huntsman, Utah's most well-known industrialist, announced in mid-March 1988 that he would seek the GOP nomination. A month later Huntsman dropped out, but, in the meantime, perennial candidate Merrill Cook cast his lot in the race as an independent. While Cook had practically no chance of winning, his populist appeal had the potential of drawing votes from Bangerter, thus threatening to give a plurality to a popular Democratic challenger. There is some evidence, too, that Bangerter had trouble with his own party, partly because of his moderate position on education and some other issues and partly because he did not throw out some Democratic officials and fill their positions with Republicans.[117]

As their gubernatorial candidate, Utah Democrats chose Ted Wilson, who, according to some public opinion polls, was favored to win. But Bangerter waged a powerful campaign, winning a narrow victory with 40.1 percent of the vote. Wilson's aggressive campaign garnered 38.3 percent, while Cook collected 21.1 percent. Even though it was not enough to unseat Bangerter, the Democrats were making new inroads into Utah politics and they did win one state office. Democrat Paul Van Dam, former Salt Lake County Attorney, defeated incumbent David L. Wilkinson in the race for attorney general. There was virtually no change in the Republican-dominated legislature, with a net Democratic gain of one seat in the House and a loss of one seat in the Senate.

In Congressional elections, Orrin Hatch won his third term in the United States Senate, and all three incumbents were returned to the House of Representatives. Republicans also retained control of both houses of the Utah legislature. In the presidential election, Utahns gave 65.9 percent of their vote to George H. W. Bush, as opposed to 32.4 percent to Michael Dukakis. This was a considerably wider margin than the national average of 53.9 percent to 46.1.

Next to the gubernatorial race, the most fervently fought battle in 1988 was over taxes. Angered at the 1987 tax increase, Merrill Cook and the Tax Limitation Coalition obtained enough signatures to put three tax limitation initiatives on the ballot. The initiative would have reduced residential property taxes and income, gasoline, sales, and cigarette taxes and provided tuition tax credits for students in private and home schools. The cuts would amount to an estimated $330 million, or 15.7 percent of the total general tax revenue of the state.

Claiming that "prosperity follows tax cuts," the coalition argued that tax reduction would bring about economic growth by increasing consumer spending, bringing more companies into the state, and adding more jobs. They also claimed that the loss in revenue to state and local government and to education could be absorbed without undue difficulty. Opponents, who included Republicans and Democrats, business people and labor leaders, parents and teachers, argued that the losses would result in heavy curtailment of vital governmental services and would have a disastrous effect on education. In addition, the Bureau of Economic and Business Research at the University of Utah published a detailed analysis of the potential impact of the reduction, showing that it would, in fact, hurt the economy, that there was no evidence that tax cuts alone would attract more business, and that Utah's situation was much different from that of other states cited by proponents. In addition, the report asked the logical question, "If one argues that prosperity follows tax cuts, how do we explain the significant economic growth in Utah since the tax increase of 1987?"[118] In the end, voters soundly rejected all three proposals.

In the elections of 1990, Democrats staged another slight comeback, ousting two Republican commissioners in Salt Lake County and replacing them with Bart Barker and Randy Horiuchi. They also easily returned Wayne Owens to Congress. In addition, they made small inroads into the Republican majority in both houses of the legislature, although the balance was still nineteen Republicans to ten Democrats in the Senate and forty-four Republicans to thirty-one Democrats in the House.

The most surprising race, however, came in the Third Congressional District, which was dominated by Utah County and usually considered to be one of the safest districts for republicans in the nation. Newcomer William Orton, a conservative Democrat, defeated veteran Republican Karl Snow by an impressive majority of 58 to 37 percent of the vote. Snow had served with distinction in several important state positions, including state

Legislative Analyst, several terms as a state senator, and chair of the state constitutional revision committee. His favor in the public mind was hurt by an unfortunate mud-slinging campaign for the Republican nomination between himself and John Harmer. After his victory over Harmer, though, most observers believed he would win in November. But he was hurt again by an ad placed in the newspapers by some of his campaigners, without his permission, that implied criticism of Orton's unmarried status. At the same time, Orton was able to convince voters that he was, indeed, a conservative, even though he carried the Democratic label, and that he would serve the district well.

Orton's resounding victory astounded pollsters and analysts alike and sent shudders through Republican ranks. This, along with a respectable Democratic showing elsewhere, raised serious questions about how long Utah would remain a firm Republican stronghold. As the *Deseret News* political editor looked at everything that had happened, he asked, "How did Republican Karl Snow lose the 3rd District? How did Democrat Kenley Brunsdale get so close to Jim Hansen in the 1st District? Where were the Republicans who were supposed to vote for Genevieve Atwood and unseat Democrat Wayne Owens in the 2nd District? What happened? A whole lot of Republicans voted for a Democrat, that's what." He then cited pollster Dan Jones, who said that the election was the "most bizarre I've seen in 20 years. I've never seen so many Republicans voting for Democrats, especially in the 3rd District."[119]

If anything, the 1988 election demonstrated once again that Utahns were not impressed only by party labels. Rather, they were conservative in their political orientation but not so dogmatic or extreme that they would not consider voting for anyone, regardless of label, who seemed to match their stance.

The moderation of Utah voters was also demonstrated in 1990 by what occurred with another controversial tax initiative spearheaded by Merrill Cook. This one would have eliminated the sales tax on food, with supporters claiming that Utah's budget surplus could easily absorb the loss. With the powerful opposition of Bangerter, most of the Republican leadership, the State Board of Regents, the business community, and local government, the initiative was easily defeated.

In 1991 Salt Lake City elected its first woman mayor, Democratic businesswoman Deedee Corradini. Aggressive in her economic and administrative views, she became embroiled in several controversies during her first year in office. One if these concerned a proposal to eliminate the rank of police sergeant, while another concerned the raising of greens fees at city golf courses. Unfortunately, Corradini's image was marred in 1992 when the Bonneville Pacific Corporation filed for bankruptcy and it was discovered that some officers, including Corradini, may have profited at the expense of shareholders. The allegations became public and an investigation ensued. Corradini denied any wrongdoing, and voters retained enough confidence in her to ensure her reelection in 1995.

Between 1983 and 1990, Merrill Cook either ran for public office or led a citizen's political movement every year but 1987.[120] Despite the fact that he was defeated every time, Cook simply would not give up. A wealthy businessman, he was dedicated to free enterprise, limited government, tax limitation, and effective judicial and educational institutions. His populist appeal may have gained him supporters in both Republican and Democratic ranks. He believed he was becoming more well known in Utah and that eventually the citizens would pay more attention to what he stood for. In 1989, therefore, he became the leader of an official third party, the newly registered Independent Party of Utah. When questioned about the improbability of a third-party political breakthrough, based on historical precedent, he replied that it was not impossible because it had happened in other states. In Utah, he complained, no one was focusing on "Utah's poor wages, industrial growth or key tax issues. The pocketbook, bread-and-butter issues are being ignored."[121] These steps were, no doubt, in preparation for another bid for the governorship in 1992.

The 1992 election seemed especially crucial for Utah Democrats. Some people wondered whether Bill Orton's victory in 1990 was just a fluke, or whether he could hold on to his seat in a district that was still considered a Republican stronghold. The Democrats now had a chance at the governorship, since Bangerter

Image 6.3: Robert F. Bennett. Elected to the United States Senate in 1992, he served three terms. Used by permission, Utah State Historical Society, all rights reserved.

had announced as early as 1990 that he would not seek a third term. In addition, Democrats hoped to replace Senator Jake Garn, who had declined to seek a fourth term, with four-term Congressman Wayne Owens. Finally, with Owens leaving the House of Representatives, it was essential that they replace him with another Democrat. In the end, however, the state maintained what amounted to political status quo.

Nationally, the 1992 presidential campaign saw President George H. W. Bush challenged by Democrat Bill Clinton, governor of Arkansas, and a third-party candidate, millionaire Ross Perot of Texas. Clinton won the election, but in Utah only 25 percent of the voters gave him their support. Bush received 42 percent of the votes, while Perot garnered 27 percent. Utah was the only state in the nation where Perot took second place and Clinton came in third.

In Utah's Congressional contests, by 1992 Bill Orton was known as one of the most conservative Democrats in the House of Representatives—conservative enough that Utah County voters from either party could support him. During the campaign some observers even wondered if he and his Republican opponent, Richard Harrington, were not reading from the same script. Both wanted to reduce government bureaucracy and spending, for example, although Harrington appeared to propose more drastic measures.[122] Orton easily won the election.

In the Second Congressional District, Karen Shepherd was nominated by the Democrats to fill the place of Wayne Owens. Shepherd, a prominent businesswoman, became Director of Development and Community Relations at the University of Utah in 1988 and was elected to the state Senate in 1990. Republicans nominated Enid Greene, an experienced trial attorney and, since 1990, Governor Bangerter's deputy chief of staff. Although she was not a Mormon, Shepherd appealed to the values of the Mormon community by stressing child-oriented issues. She promoted a ten-point plan that included cracking down on parents who did not pay child support and fully funding the Head Start program for disadvantaged preschool children. Shepherd won by a comparatively narrow 51 percent to Greene's 47 percent. Representative James V. Hansen, meanwhile, was secure in the Third Congressional District, easily defeating challenger Ron Holt.

To fill Jake Garn's seat in the US Senate, Utah saw a hard-fought though clean and respectful battle for the Republican nomination between two well-known millionaires: Joseph A. Cannon, head of Geneva Steel, and Robert F. Bennett, son of former Senator Wallace F. Bennett, an official with the US Department of Transportation during the Nixon administration and a successful businessman who made his fortune with Franklin Quest. Bennett won the nomination in the primary elections by a very narrow margin.[123]

The final senatorial campaign was tinged with innuendoes about Bennett's alleged connection with the 1972 Watergate break-in. Voters were reminded that, at one point, Bennett was accused of being the mysterious "Deep Throat," who fed information to reporters investigating the scandal. Bennett as well as the reporters denied that there was any truth to the allegation. Owens, on the other hand, was embarrassed by a scandal in the House of Representatives when it was revealed that many Congressmen regularly drew overdrafts on their checking accounts, without penalty, in a bank operated especially for them. Owens demonstrated that he was not among the blatant offenders, but the affair tarnished his image nevertheless. Bennett defeated Owens by a margin of 55 percent to 40 percent. Pollster Dan Jones observed later that the bank scandal in the House of Representatives, Owens's stand on environmental issues, and the fact that he was "tagged as a liberal" hurt him at the polls.[124] It also appeared as if Owens's negative campaign against Bennett hurt him more than it hurt Bennett, because Owens had begun gaining in the polls until he stepped up his attack with the Watergate issue.[125]

The 1992 gubernatorial race was a hard-fought three-way contest. Republicans nominated Michael O. Leavitt, chief executive officer of the Leavitt Group, a major insurance firm in Utah and the West. The Democratic nominee was Stewart Hansen, an attorney and a former judge. In addition, Merrill Cook was on the ballot as the nominee of the Independent Party of Utah.

On several occasions, the candidates met in three-way debates, some of which were televised throughout the state. One of the leading issues was health care. Cook proposed a mandatory health insurance plan, which Leavitt strenuously opposed. Hansen suggested waiting until after the election and then getting all parties together to devise a solution to the problem. On abortion, Leavitt supported Utah's strong antiabortion statute (not yet declared unconstitutional), and promised to defend it vigorously in the courts. Cook took a similar position, while Hansen, although personally opposed to abortion on religious and moral grounds, was pro-choice. Leavitt and Cook promised not to raise taxes, while Hansen said such a promise was unrealistic and that he might consider a tax raise for the benefit of education. Leavitt called for major improvements in education, while Cook and Hansen said Leavitt would be unable to achieve that goal without raising taxes. Leavitt and Cook favored the death penalty, while Hansen opposed it but said he would obey the law of the land. Leavitt, confident of victory and well ahead in the polls in mid-October, was emphatic about what he intended to do in his first one hundred days in office. His most pressing objective was a radical reform in education, including a proposed pilot program for giving schools a much greater degree of self-governance. In addition, he was concerned with finding ways to deal with problems created by a six-year drought and how to deal more effectively with the growing problem of gangs.[126]

Leavitt won with a plurality of 42 percent of the votes. Merrill Cook came in second with 34 percent, the first time in state history that a third-party candidate had done so well. Hansen received a disappointing 23 percent. Even though he lost again, Cook was neither dejected nor discouraged. One of his next objectives was to lead out in getting a term limitation initiative, for both state and federal officeholders, on the 1994 ballot.

The race for attorney general was extremely close, with Democrat Jan Graham eking out a narrow victory over Iron County Attorney Scott Burns. Graham stressed her proven record of good management skills as well as her concern for women's and children's issues.

Women were more prominent as candidates in this election year than ever before. Karen Shepherd was the first Utah woman to be elected to the House of Representatives in forty years. Jan

Graham was the first woman ever to be elected attorney general. In the race for lieutenant governor, all three contenders were women: Olene Walker (Republican), Frances Hatch Merrill (Independent), and Paula Julander (Democrat). Walker, the winner, became the first woman ever to hold that office.

Although the election of 1992 was potentially one of the most pivotal in decades, Utah ended up, politically, much the same as it was before. It had a Republican governor, a Republican US Senator, and a state legislature with both houses controlled by Republicans. Even though two of its three US Congressmen were Democrats, as was its attorney general, Utah was still one of the most Republican states in the nation.

On other issues, in 1992 Utah voters turned down a highly controversial light-rail mass transit proposal. A *Deseret News* editorial decried this action, arguing that what they had really opted for was "future gridlock on the main highways."[127] Voters also rejected an initiative that would have allowed pari-mutuel betting on horse races in the state.

Religion and the State: A Delicate Relationship

There could hardly be more emotionally charged political issues than those involving religion. The question of school prayer became this kind of issue throughout the United States. Opponents argued that allowing prayers in school was an unconstitutional imposition of religion on school children by the state, while proponents argued that prohibiting prayer was an unconstitutional violation of freedom of speech. The issue was especially delicate in Utah, where it came under particularly harsh scrutiny by critics who felt that school prayers represented not only religion in general but the LDS religion in particular.

In a 1962 case the US Supreme Court held that causing a prayer, approved by a New York School Board, to be read aloud at the beginning of each school day violated the First Amendment to the Constitution. It was, said the court, "part of a governmental program to further religious beliefs" that "breach[ed] the constitutional wall of separation between church and state."[128] Protests went up from all over the country, and a variety of issues were raised. Could the schools provide a moment of silence for private devotion? Was voluntary prayer on school property, acceptable? What about prayers at graduation ceremonies, especially if they were planned by students and not by the administration? What about prayers in other public places, such as city council meetings? The ACLU supported many lawsuits that were designed to eliminate all such practices.

The debate came to a head in Utah in 1988 when two students at Brighton High School filed a lawsuit against officials of the Jordan School District. They also sent a letter to the district, through their ACLU attorney, demanding either that prayer at graduation be "non-denominational" or that there be none at all. They charged that recent graduation prayers reflected the practices and perspectives of the LDS Church. Rather than face extensive litigation costs, the district agreed to discontinue prayers at all commencements. But not all Utahns were so acquiescent. Many were furious, fearing that this was only the opening wedge in a campaign to remove all reference to religion, even teaching about it in a historical or social context, from the public schools. Some school boards followed Jordan's lead, but others resisted and continued to hold prayers.

The public debate became larger than simply the issue of graduation prayers, extending again to whether schools should allow prayer at any time for any reason. Proponents of school prayer argued that, as long as representatives of all denominations, including non-Christians, were called on, there was no conflict with the First Amendment. They also felt that prayer helped boost the moral and ethical perspectives of students. Some felt comfortable with the 1962 decision outlawing prayers *prescribed* or written by the state but felt uncomfortable with the idea that a state could *proscribe* words, or censor what was said.[129] Opponents argued that school-sanctioned prayer, whether silent, voluntary, or ordered by teachers, interfered with students' rights to worship freely because it tended to set apart those with unpopular beliefs and undermine their own religious self-worth. Religious values, they said, were rooted in the home, not in the schools.[130]

In 1990 the ACLU filed suit against the Alpine and Granite school districts, as representative targets, in order to stop future graduation prayers. Polls showed that about 70 percent of Utahns favored school prayer in general and that more than 70 percent favored having prayer at graduation exercises. Most Mormons supported school prayer, and in July the Catholic Diocese of Salt Lake City released a statement saying that it supported prayer at public school functions if representatives of all religious denominations were called upon. A conservative group known as Families Alert, countering the ACLU action, threatened to sue any school district that did not allow prayer. Governor Bangerter considered asking the state legislature for a one-time special appropriation to help the two districts fight the suit in court, noting that numerous private individuals had also offered money to help out and that several attorneys had offered free legal services.[131] Both the Granite and Alpine districts, supported by the governor and the State Board of Education, decided to fight the suit, even though it would be expensive and there were only limited funds available. To some degree, the fight became a national *cause célèbre* as newspapers around the country picked up the story.

Complications arose when a US Circuit Court of Appeals ruled, in a case involving a school in Providence, Rhode Island, that prayers acknowledging God in graduation ceremonies were illegal. After Rhode Island appealed to the Supreme Court, Utah's attorney general filed a friend-of-the-court brief supporting the appeal, and the State School Board set aside $10,000 from its discretionary fund to assist with Rhode Island's expenses. The Utah chapter of the Society of Separationists immediately hired an attorney to bring suit against the school board for using public funds to promote school prayer.

Meanwhile, as the 1991 graduation season approached, students in other districts made it clear that they wanted graduation prayers, leading to a threat from the ACLU to add the Weber and Davis school districts to its lawsuit. At the end of March, however, US District Judge Thomas Greene put the suit on hold, pending the outcome of Rhode Island's appeal. He also refused to issue an injunction against prayers at upcoming graduations. Granite School District then allowed its student body to vote and, on the basis of that vote, ruled against prayer in that year's graduation. In the Alpine district, Orem High School proceeded with prayer on the basis of a similar student poll. The Alpine district also filed its own brief in support of Rhode Island with the Supreme Court, whereupon the Society of Separationists brought suit against Alpine.

The Supreme Court did not rule on the matter for another year, but finally, on June 24, 1992, in a 5 to 4 decision, it upheld the ban on prayers at graduation. "The government involvement with religious activity in this case is pervasive, to the point of creating a state-sponsored and state-directed religious exercise in a public school," wrote Justice Anthony M. Kennedy for the court.[132] Although they were shocked, Utahns submitted gracefully and moved on to other matters.

The issue of prayer expanded beyond the schools and into other public meetings. City councils, for example, came under scrutiny, and in March 1992 a judge ruled that prayers in the Salt Lake City Council meeting were unconstitutional. Other cities also dropped prayer while still others refused to bow to a letter from the ACLU urging them to stop.[133] Some cities had never held prayer. The court decision was appealed and in 1993 the Utah Supreme Court ruled that prayer, along with the Pledge of Allegiance, as part of an opening ceremony of a city council meeting was constitutional.[134]

Other political issues also had religious overtones, although in other states they may not have been so readily interpreted as church-state issues. One topic was gambling. In 1992, a proposal for legalizing pari-mutuel betting on horse racing in Utah came before the legislature. It was easily defeated, but during the process LDS Church leaders issued a public statement reiterating the church's opposition to gambling. They encouraged regional representatives to urge members to write to their lawmakers and newspapers, but to do it as citizens and not as church members. They also encouraged talks on the issue in church meetings. Some people were angered at what they interpreted as religious influence in the legislative process, but church leaders justified taking a political stance because the issue involved was a moral one.

But the matter did not end there. A group calling itself "Put Utah First" obtained enough petitions to put pari-mutual betting on the November ballot. This led to the organization of another group, the bi-partisan, non-denominational Utah Citizens against Pari-Mutuel Gambling, which included people from civic and religious groups in the state. Public debate raged in the newspapers, on radio and television, and in speeches before civic and religious groups. Proponents of legalized betting argued that the state, and particularly the Education Fund, would benefit financially and that if the initiative were not approved, Utahns would simply take their money to surrounding states and wager anyway. Opponents argued that the economic benefits to education would be minimal, with the majority of the profits going to winners of bets, owners of horses, and owners of racetracks (usually the counties),[135] and that Utahns simply did not want gambling, with all its negative ethical implications, in their state. Surprisingly, early polls showed a slim plurality favoring the initiative, although as election time grew closer, the opposition pulled comfortably ahead. In the final balloting, voters turned thumbs down on the initiative.

Concluding Notes

The Bangerter years saw many other events of note in Utah. Among them was deep concern over plans by the federal government, as a cost-saving move, to close several military installations around the nation. Utah's Tooele Army Depot was on the list, but in 1991 the government decided not to close it. At the same time a heavy reduction in the workforce at Hill Air Force Base took place, although that facility itself was not seriously threatened. That same year Utah's oldest military installation, the historic Camp Douglas east of Salt Lake City, was permanently closed.

On a different note, many Utahns felt a deep sense of loss at the closing, on August 31, 1987, of the Hotel Utah, an elegant Salt Lake City landmark owned by the LDS Church.[136] The hotel had been a favorite meeting place and center of community pride for more than seventy-five years. Nevertheless, said church officials, in recent years the hotel had lost millions of dollars and they simply did not feel it appropriate to use church funds to continue its operation. The announcement sparked citizens' campaigns to prevent its closure but to no avail. Renovations began immediately to turn the hotel into a church office building and place of worship, and, in 1993 it reopened as the Joseph Smith Memorial Building. Its elegant lobby was intact, and the building included offices, worship facilities, a theater, two restaurants, and a modern computer research facility for people interested in family history.

In 1988, Governor Bangerter announced the creation of the Utah Statehood Centennial Commission. This commission would lead out in planning events and activities to recognize and celebrate the one hundred-year anniversary of Utah's statehood, which was achieved on January 4, 1896. As the state looked forward to this important anniversary, committees were formed in every county and a number of interesting projects were instituted to promote the "Spirit of Utah." The state also introduced attractive new Centennial license plates which Utahns could purchase for a special fee that would go toward funding Centennial activities. In addition, the state funded the writing of several new volumes of state history.[137]

As Bangerter's administration came to a close, Utah still faced numerous important challenges. The pollution problem was far from solved, as Utah, and particularly Utah County, still recorded some of the poorest air quality in the nation. Contributing to the problem was the rapidly growing number of vehicles on the road which, in turn, contributed to more traffic congestion and even more air pollution. With little support for alternate transportation, such as light-rail, Utah seemed doomed to a continuing, costly program of highway expansion and even more problems from vehicle emissions. The troublesome abortion issue would not go away, and the question of whether to continue costly litigation regarding abortion laws was very much up in the air. Women were still underpaid and mostly under-represented in the professions. There was still a considerable way to go to achieve complete gender equity in the courts. Gangs and violence among the youth continued to increase, and drug abuse was still a worrisome problem. Utahns, like other Americans, were caught in the midst of ever-spiraling health care costs, but there seemed little that they could do about them. Public schools were still overcrowded and underfunded, as were the state's colleges and universities. All of these challenges and more would provide plenty for the next administration to worry about.

Nevertheless, the Bangerter administration ended with an enviable record. In his final State of the State address, on January 13, 1992, Bangerter noted that since he took office public education had received an increasing share of the total state budget annually, personal income had increased by 58 percent, 167,400 new jobs had been created, sales and personal income taxes had dropped slightly, and the state budget had been cut by 1.4 percent when adjusted for population growth and inflation.[138] In general, the state's economy was extremely healthy, and so were its people.

Particularly satisfying to Utahns was the fact that in the previous few years their state had been recognized nationally, and positively, in ways that seemed unprecedented. While the strength of the state's economy was one of the magnets that drew people's attention, Utah was recognized for a wide variety of other characteristics. The workforce was well known for its high quality, quantity, and productivity. Words such as "best-educated," "well-trained," "bi-lingual," "young," "loyal," and "hardworking" were used regularly to describe Utah workers, who were also lauded as low users of alcohol and drugs. The state was praised as having an attractive business climate, with a good infrastructure, good public services, sound fiscal management, and low overall business costs (including low wages). In addition, Utah's quality of life was widely praised, along with its wide diversity of sports and recreational facilities.[139]

In 1991 *Money* magazine listed the Provo-Orem area at the top of its list of "best places to live" in the United States. In addition, at the US Conference of Mayors that year, Provo received the annual City Liveability Award as the best place to live among cities under 100,000 population. In another study that year, conducted by a national real estate firm, Salt Lake City was named as the city with the nation's most affordable housing. Also in 1991, Norman H. Bangerter received high compliments nationally when he was rated by his peers as among the ten best governors in the United States.[140] That same year, *Financial World* magazine ranked Utah as the best financially managed state in the nation. The state received second place in the same category in 1990 and 1992. It also received national recognition on Wall Street for its responsible, professional bonding and debt management.[141] For Bangerter, this meant that Utah was becoming well known as a state with a strong economy, responsible economic management, and a good place to do business.[142]

Notes

1. LaVarr Webb, "Bangerter worn in as 13th Governor," *Deseret News*, January 7, 1985, A1. For a detailed, though highly sympathetic and laudatory, overview of the accomplishments of the Bangerter administration, see *Building a Better Utah: The Bangerter Administration 1985-1992* (Salt Lake City: Office of the Governor?, 1992?).
2. LaVarr Webb, "Bangerter Stresses Excellence, Efficiency," *Deseret News*, January 14, 1985, A1.
3. Carole Gallagher, American Ground Zero: The Secret Nuclear War (Cambridge, MA: MIT Press, 1993), xviii–xix.
4. Ibid., 137.
5. Lee Davidson, "Downwinders Suffer 49% Rejection Rate," January 23, 1994, A1.
6. For details and commentary, see David Knowlton, "Missionaries and Terror: The Assassination of Two Elders in Bolivia," *Sunstone* 13 (August 1989): 10–15.
7. See http://www.utahhumanities.org/BookFestival/2010/BookFestivalSaltLakeCityAuthors.htm. Accessed November 18, 2014.
8. "Step toward Peace? Utahns Return from Russian Walk," *Salt Lake Tribune*, July 12, 1987, B1; "Gorbachev Congratulates Utah Peace Marchers," ibid., September 25, 1987, B5.
9. "4 Soviet Doctors Coming to S.L. on Peace Visit," ibid., October 1, 1987, C3.
10. Dawn House, "Soviet Paper Reports Utah Isn't Top Secret Anymore," ibid., January 16, 1989, B1.
11. Richard C. Roberts, "The Utah National Guard and Territorial Militias," in *Utah History Encyclopedia*, ed. Allen Kent Powell (Salt Lake City: University of Utah Press, 1994), 596–98. Utah Guardsmen participated in such diverse logistical support activities as water purification, military intelligence, military police, engineers, medical, air refueling, tactical control, and airborne intelligence.
12. "Bangerter Calls for Salute of Utahns in Desert Storm," *Salt Lake Tribune*, March 13, 1991, B3.
13. Developing Utah's Economy: Guidelines, Policies and Plans, Executive Summary (Salt Lake City: Department of Community and Economic Development, November 26, 1985), 4.
14. See *Building a Better Utah*, 8–10.
15. Ibid., 36–37.
16. Ken Shelton, "First in Finance," *Utah Business* 6 (August 1991): 32–36.
17. Gary Hector, "S&Ls: Where Did All Those Billions Go?" *Fortune* (September 10, 1990), 82–88; Mortimer B. Zuckerman, "The Bad Guys of the S&L Fiasco," US News & World Report (June 18, 1990), 92.
18. *Building a Better Utah*, 15. In the process, there was a considerable controversy in the state, including the resignation of Elaine Wells, commissioner of the Utah De-

partment of Financial Institutions, in a controversy over her handling of efforts to liquidate the failed institutions. See various newspaper reports from 1986 to1988.

19. *Building a Better Utah*, 15.
20. The following information is based largely on material gathered by Rick Fish, who, in 1994 and 1995, was involved in writing a history of Geneva Steel. The author is indebted to Mr. Fish for allowing me to see an early draft of some of his work, and for sharing various articles with him. Much of the story may be traced through the pages of American Metal Market, during the years 1986 to1987, copies of which were provided to the author by Mr. Fish. See also Susan Adams, "Rescue Mission," The American Lawyer (December 1987): 83–86; "Geneva Resurrection," Intermountain Contractor 39 (September 5, 1988): 8-10.
21. In May 1985 the company chairman had said that "We have no intention of leaving" and the senior vice-president declared in June that "We will not abandon Geneva for greener pastures." "US Steel Abandons Utah," *The Progressive* (May 1986), 19.
22. Michael Morris, "Orem Union Leaders Begin Fighting "Stab in Back' by U. S. Steel," *Deseret News*, December 17, 1985. A2.
23. Robb Hicken, "Geneva Leads Nation in Low-Cost Production," *Daily Herald* (Provo, UT), May 19, 1992, A1.
24. The state's Bureau of Air Quality said that the figure was more like 56 percent. Jim Woolf, "Scope of Geneva Pollution Remains a Cloudy Issue," *Salt Lake Tribune*, June 10, 1989, B1; Sharon Morrey, "New Numbers Say Geneva Pollution Less Than Before," *Daily Herald*, June 22, 1989, A1.
25. Brooke Adams, "2nd Study Links Geneva to Troubles with Respiration," *Deseret News*, March 29, 1991, B6.
26. Robb Hicken, "Regional EPA Oks Utah County Air Cleanup Plan," *Daily Herald*, February 26, 1991, A1. The modernization, said Cannon, would cut all remaining emissions by 57 percent and remove 95 percent of the particulates.
27. Ed Haroldsen, "Let's Give Geneva Steel a Fair Shake," ibid., March 27, 1991, B6.
28. Dennis May, "Q-BOP Steel Will Flow Soon," *Utah County Journal*, September 17, 1991, A1.
29. "Water in Utah: Too Much or Too Little," Utah Foundation *Research Report* No. 480 (October 1986).
30. *Building a Better Utah*, 45.
31. *Statistical Abstract of Utah 1993*, 451–65.
32. See Boyd L. Fjeldsted and Frank C. Hachman, "Results of the 1990–91 Utah Skier Survey," *Utah Economic and Business Review* 51 (August/September 1991), 7-8.
33. However, the international committee chose Albertville, France.
34. For discussions of the service industry see Lecia Parks, At Your Service: A Look at Utah's Service Economy (Salt Lake City: Utah Department of Employment Security, January 1987); B. Jade Crittenden and Austin Sargent, "Utah's Service Industry Continues to Grow," *Utah Economic and Business Review* 52 (February 1992): 1-9; Michael E. Christensen, "Service-Producing Industries in Utah," in *Utah History Encyclopedia*, ed. Powell, 491–93. The service industry encompasses a myriad of business activities, including agricultural services; hotels, and other lodging places; personal, business amusement and recreation, medical and health, legal, educational, NS repair services; and many others.
35. Economic Diversification: Utah's Adjustment to Declining Defense Spending, prepared for the Department of Community and Economic Development (Salt Lake

City: Bureau of Economic and Business Research, University of Utah, December 1990), 26.

36. As predicted by Jan Crispin-Little and James A. Wood, "Utah's Adjustment to Declining Defense Budgets," *Utah Economic and Business Review* 50 (November–December 1990): 11

37. For various statistics of farm production, see *Statistical Abstract of Utah 1993*.

38. Stephen R. Wood, "Fruit Industry in Utah," in *Utah History Encyclopedia*, ed. Powell, 207–08; *Statistical Abstract of Utah 1993*, 270–71.

39. *Statistical Abstract of Utah 1993*, 272–73.

40. Ibid., 86.

41. Ibid., 295–98.

42. Ibid., 296–98; Nancy J. Taniguchi, "Coal Mining in Utah," in *Utah History Encyclopedia*, ed. Powell, 101–02; Utah Geologic Survey, "Utah's Fossil Fuels," updated October 14, 2014, at http://www.geology.utah.gov/utahgeo/energy/fossil_fuels.htm. Accessed January 19, 2015. See also Garth Mangum and MacLeans Geo-Jaja, "The Prospects for Utah Coal," *Utah Economic and Business Review* 48 (July-August 1986): 1-15.

43. R. Thayne Robson and Boyd Fjeldsted, "Kennecott Corporation and the Utah Economy," paper prepared under the auspices of the Bureau of Economic and Business Research, University of Utah, December 1991, copy in James B. Allen papers, L. Tom Perry Special Collections, Harold B. Lee Library, Brigham Young University

44. Economic Report to the Governor 1990, 18.

45. *Building a Better Utah*, 10.

46. Jan Elise Crispin, "Growth in Software Continues to Fuel Utah's High Tech Sector," *Utah Economic and Business Review* 53 (May/June 1993): 1–7. See also Jan Elise Crispin, "Software Companies Lead Growth in Utah's High Technology Industry," *Utah Economic and Business Review* 52 (March 1992): 1–9; Jan E. Crispin-Little, "Utah's High Technology Industry 1986-1995," *Utah Economic and Business Review* 56 (July/August 1996): 1–9.

47. Crispin, "Software Companies Lead Growth," 9.

48. Pat Birkedahl, "Utah as the Next Silicon Valley: Rhetoric or Reality?" Utah Business 6 (June 1992): 14–17; Jim Impoco, "How Utah Created a Mountain of Jobs: A Pro-Business Climate Lures High-Tech Industry," US News and World Report (February 22, 1993): 43–44; Crispin, "Growth in Software," 5. Birkedahl indicated that there were fifty-five thousand people employed, but this may be exaggerated. The *Utah Economic and Business Review* reported a total employment in high technology in 1992 of 42,340.

49. Michael I. Luger and Harvey A. Goldstein, Technology in the Garden: Research Parks and Regional Economic Development (Chapel Hill: University of North Carolina Press, 1991), chapter 6, "The University of Utah Research Park."

50. The diversity included companies involved in aerospace components, analytical/measuring devices, biomedical and medical products, chemicals, communication equipment, composite materials, electronic components, lasers and +optics, pharmaceutical, plant genetics, robotics, software nd software systems, and a few others. See Table 4 in Jan Crispin-Little, "Is the Bloom Off Utah's High Tech Rose," *Utah Economic and Business Review* 50 (August 1990): 8.

51. Crispin, "Software Companies Lead Growth," 6. For studies on the high tech potential in Utah County, see William R. Michael, "High Technology Industries in

Utah Valley: A Survey and Needs Analysis for Growth and Development" (master's thesis, Brigham Young University, 1986); Darral G. Clarke, Gene W. Dalton, W. Gibb Dyer, and Alan L. Wilkins, "High Tech Business in Utah Valley: A Multidisciplinary Study for the Utah Technology Finance Corporation," (Provo, UT: J. Willard and Alice S. Marriott School of Management, Brigham Young University, 1989. Manuscript available Harold B. Lee Library, Brigham Young University.)

52. For a detailed history of WordPerfect to 1988, see Jan Elise Crispin-Little, "WordPerfect Corporation," *Utah Economic and Business Review* 48 (October 1988): 1-13.

53. For a detailed overview of Novell, Inc.'s history, see Jan Elise Crispin-Little, "Novell, Inc.," *Utah Economic and Business Review* 49 (February 1989):1-13.

54. Impoco, "How Utah Created a Mountain of Jobs," 43–44.

55. See Crispin, "Growth in Software," 5.

56. Richard L. Stern and Toddi Gutner, "A Helluva Place to Have a Business," *Forbes* 15 (December 21, 1992): 114–36.

57. *Building a Better Utah*, 41.

58. Jim Woolf, "Air Emissions Up 50% at Tooele Plant," *Salt Lake Tribune*, February 17, 1990, B1. The company, however, was in the process of completing a chlorine burner that, when installed, would reduce the emissions by 40 percent. Whether this was enough to meet EPA standards, however, was not certain.

59. Joe Costanzo, "Utah's Environment Taints Health Ranking," *Deseret News*, September 19, 1991, B1.

60. "The issue of jobs versus the environment is wrong," said Jon Lear of the Sundance Institute for Resource Management. "They are not mutual contradictions. We must have ultimately both." Joseph Cannon commented on the complexities of modern society that precluded any simple answers to such problems. There was no "time, room [or] energy for polarization in our society," he said. "To the extent we are diverting energy, we are diverting attention, and we are not drawing on the resources of everybody in our community to solve problems." Brooke Adams, "Symposium Panelists Call for a Cease-Fire in Clean-Air Tug of War," *Deseret News*, March 25, 1991, B3.

61. Brooke Adams, "EPA Honors 4 Utah Groups for Clean-Air Work," *Deseret News*, April 23, 1991, B3.

62. "Utah Closing Industrial Circle, Permitting Waste Incineration," *Salt Lake Tribune*, April 1, 1990, A16; Jim Woolf, "Out-of-State Waste in Utah Raises Ire of State Senator," ibid., May 2, 1991, B1.

63. For a partial list, see "Hazardous Waste Facilities Becoming Popular in Utah," ibid., May 2, 1991, B1. One such plant was located in Iron County.

64. In 1992, lawmakers attempted to ameliorate the problem by increasing fees for out-of-state waste by 75 percent. That same year, however, the US Supreme Court nullified a similar Alabama law, saying that the state could not charge higher fees for disposing of out-of-state waste than for disposing of waste produced within the state. How this would affect Utah was not clear.

65. "Contaminated Soil Bound for Utah," *Deseret News*, April 29, 1991, B3; Jim Woolf, "'Cancer Cannonball' Finds Home for Toxic Soil: Utah," *Salt Lake Tribune*, April 30, 1991, A1; Bill Dermody, "Utah Has No Say in Waste," Daily Universe (Brigham Young University), May 7, 1991, 1.

66. *Building a Better Utah*, 44. See also Gode Davis, "Lake Pumper," *Popular Science* 231 (September 1987): 68–71.

67. For a thorough discussion of how this bill came into being and made its way through the legislature, see Richard Sherlock, "Supreme Court Challenge: Inside the Making of the Utah Abortion Law," Policy Review 56 (Spring 1991): 85–87.
68. Cherrill Crosby and Dawn House, "Attorney General Calls Ad on Abortion Law 'Ultimate Cheap Shot,'" *Salt Lake Tribune*, March 28, 1991, B1.
69. "Clerics Back Abortion Law," ibid., April 4, 1992, B1.
70. In 1990, for example, Utah's homicide rate was 3.1 per 100,000 population while the national rate was 10.2. See the chart on homicide, *Utah's Health: An Annual Review 1* (June 1993): 32; Lee Davidson and Brian T. West, "S.L. Crime Rate Outruns US Average," *Deseret News*, October 28, 1991, A1.
71. Brooke Adams, "Locals Part of Utah Gang Problem, Police Say," *Deseret News*, August 5, 1990; available online at http://www.deseretnews.com/article/115930/LOCALS-PART-OF-UTAH-GANG-PROBLEM-POLICE-SAY.html. Accessed, November 18, 2013.
72. "Police Chiefs: Gangs Growing," *Daily Herald*, March 26, 1991, B3.
73. Daniel Piedra, "An Analysis of Downtown Revitalization in Salt Lake City" (master's thesis, Brigham Young University, 1992), 28–29.
74. Dagi P. Binggell, "Learn the Language of S.L.-Area Gangs," *Deseret News*, August 23, 1991, A1.
75. *Building a Better Utah*, 56. See also *Deseret News*, January 28, 1994, B1, for an article dealing with the positive effects of the state fund for crime victims.
76. Numerous books and articles have been published about the Hofmann affair. The two best studies are Linda Sillitoe and Allen Roberts, *Salamander: The Story of the Mormon Forger Murders* (Salt Lake City: Signature Books, 1988) and Richard E. Turley, Jr., *Victims: The LDS Church and the Mark Hofmann Case* (Urbana: University of Illinois Press, 1992). Appended to the Sillitoe and Roberts book is "A Forensic Analysis of Twenty-One Hofmann Documents," by George J. Throckmorton, who played the key role in proving the documents to be forgeries. Appended to the Turley book is a fascinating list of 445 "Suspect Items Acquired by the LDS Church." These included not only documents but also coins and tokens. Some were complete forgeries, others were partial forgeries, and still others are open to question. The list, however, as Turley explains, "though the most extensive ever published, represents only a fraction of the documents that passed through Hofmann's hands. It is hoped that in the future other institutions and individuals will publish similar lists of their Hofmann-related holdings. Some collectors, of course, may be unaware that their documents come from Hofmann; others may be unwilling to admit it. For these reasons, it is unlikely that a complete list of Hofmann documents will ever be compiled." Turley, Victims, 348.
77. As reported in "Here's What Vickie Told the Governor," *Salt Lake Tribune*, January 29, 1988, A4. For an interesting perspective on the Singers, written by a friend, see Ogden Kraut, "The Singer/Swapp Siege: Revelation or Retaliation?" 12 (November 1988): 10–17.
78. "Child Physical and Sexual Abuse," Utah's Health: An Annual Review 1 (June 1993): 51–52. National data was available only through 1987, but it appears that Utah was ahead of the national average until 1985, then fell below it.
79. Paul Rolly, "Scourge of Child Sexual Abuse Growing," *Salt Lake Tribune*, September 14, 1989, B1.
80. Lois M. Collins, "Utah Documents a 19% Increase in Child Abuse," *Deseret News*, January 29, 1992, B1.

81. *Building a Better Utah*, 56.
82. Division of Family Services, State of Utah Department of Human Services, *Report on Child Abuse and Neglect* (1990).
83. In 1990, Utah's AIDS morbidity ratewas 5.7 per 100,000 population, compared with 16.7 nationally, while the death rate was 3.4 compared with 9.6. See "Acquired Immunodeficiency Syndrome (AIDS)," Utah's Health: An Annual Review 1 (June 1993): 17.
84. See "Problems of Rising Health Care Costs," Utah Foundation *Research Report* No. 522 (April 1990). See also Governor's Task Force on Health Care Costs. "Report of the Governor's Task Force on Health Care Costs: Executive Summary." (Salt Lake City: Governor's Task Force on Health Care Costs and Utah Department of Health, Bureau of Health Planning and Policy Analysis, 1988.)
85. See Frank C. Hachman and Boyd L. Fjeldsted, "Utah Hospital Charges Compared to Other States," *Utah Economic and Business Review* 51 (November 1991): 1-5.
86. Lee Davidson and Lois M. Collins, "Hunger Stalks 1 in 4 Utah Children," *Deseret News*, March 27, 1991, A1.
87. "Utah's Homeless," Utah's Health: An Annual Review 1 (June 1993): 9. See also Lois M. Collins, "Portrait of Utah's Homeless is Changing, *Deseret News*, January 29, 1993, B1. Many of Salt Lake City's homeless seemed to be jobless transients who were simply wandering from state to state, and rumor abounded that they were being "dumped" onto Utah by other cities that provided them with one-way bus tickets to the state. See Piedra, "An Analysis of Downtown Revitalization," 26-28.
88. *Building a Better Utah*, 20.
89. Ibid., 46. For a detailed analysis of the beginnings of the Baby Your Baby program, see John C. Nelson, "A Real Solution to a Real Problem: Baby Your Baby," *Utah's Health: An Annual Review 1* (June 1993): 117-23.
90. *Building a Better Utah*, 47.
91. Ibid., 47.
92. Ibid., 47.
93. Ibid., 48.
94. Ibid., 49-50.
95. "*Public Health Report Card*," Utah's Health: An Annual Review 1 (June 1993): 60-63.
96. First, the department said, violations were due largely to failure to monitor rather than to actual poor water quality. The department also claimed that the reliability of the bacterial tests used by the Environmental Protection Agency was questionable, and that the many systems in violation of federal law were used by only a small number of people. Most Utahns, the department concluded, still drank from safe water supplies. Ibid., 60.
97. "Health Care," *Utah's Health: An Annual Review 1* (June 1993): 64-72.
98. *Building a Better Utah*, 54.
99. Jerry Spangler, "Number of Busts is Impressive, but Drug War Hasn't Been Won," *Deseret News*, August 5, 1985, B1.
100. Suzanne Dean, "Utah Fights the Drugs War: Testing in the Workplace," *Utah Holiday* 19 (October 1989): 11.
101. Dean, "Utah Fights the Drug War," 10-11; *Building a Better Utah*, 57.
102. In 1988, Utah ranked first in the nation in literacy rate. With a dropout rate much lower than the national average, in 1992 the state was second in percentage of its

adult population holding high school diplomas and first in the median years of education. Utah also exceeded the national average in most subjects on the Standard Achievement Test (SAT), the American College Test (ACT), and the Advanced Placement examinations. In addition, the state ranked first in the nation in the percentage of its adult population that had completed between one and three years of college. *Building a Better Utah*, 25. For various reports on Utah's comparative statues, see "The School Finance Problem in Utah-1985," Utah Foundation *Research Report* No. 468 (October 1985); "Educational Expenditures in Utah-1986," Utah Foundation *Research Report* No. 485 (March 1987); "Educational Expenditures in Utah-1987," Utah Foundation *Research Report* No. 498 (April 1988); "Public Education Trends and Comparisons 1987," Utah Foundation *Research Report* No. 492 (October 1987); James R. Moss, "Utah: A Case Study," Kappan (September 1988): 25–26; "How Valid Are School Test Scores?" Utah Foundation *Research Briefs* No. 88-18 (November 2, 1988); "Utah School Trends and Comparisons," Utah Foundation *Research Briefs* No. 90-17 (October 8, 1990); "Class Size in Utah Schools," Utah Foundation *Research Report* No. 532 (February 1991); "Public School Issues in Utah," Utah Foundation *Research Briefs* No. 91-13 (September 16, 1991). See also the *Annual Report of the State Superintendent of Public Instruction*.

103. For a highly detailed, incisive study of the interrelationship between the different groups involved and the dilemmas encountered in making educational policy in Utah, see Douglas M. Abrams, *Conflict, Competition, or Cooperation? Dilemmas of State Education Policymaking* (New York: State University of New York Press, 1993).

104. For a summary of the arguments for and against year-round schools, as well as the survey, see "Evaluation of Year-Round Schools in Utah," Utah Foundation *Research Report* No. 530 (December 1990).

105. For discussion of the origins of "A Shift in Focus," see Utah State Office of Education, *Annual Report of the State Superintendent of Public Instruction* 1988–89, 1–4. For pros and cons of the new program, see "A New Focus for Utah Public Schools?," Utah Foundation *Research Report* No. 527 (September 1990). The program had six major goals: (1) "Involve students as full partners in their pursuit of learning, accountable for their actions"; (2) "Enlarge parental and community involvement to enhance student success"; (3) "Establish a curriculum and instruction delivery system that has measurable outcomes"; (4) "Ensure that every school is an effective learning center with a positive learning climate"; (5) "Increase the sensitivity, effectiveness, efficiency, and satisfactions of teachers, administrators, and other educational professionals"; (6) "Increase learning and productivity through technology." Utah State Office of Education, *Annual Report of the State Superintendent of Public Instruction* 1989–90, 9–29.

106. Utah State Office of Education, *Annual Report of the State Superintendent of Public Instruction* 1988–89, 13–14.

107. Utah State Office of Education, *Annual Report of the State Superintendent of Public Instruction* 1989–90, 22.

108. Utah State Office of Education, *Annual Report of the State Superintendent of Public Instruction* 1990–1991, 7.

109. *Building a Better Utah*, 27–28, 31.

110. Stacey Elizabeth Marlow, "Home Schools, Public Schools, Policies, and Practice: Superintendents Implementing Home Education Policy in Four Western States" (Ed.D. thesis, University of Michigan, 1992), passim, 121–130.

111. Office of the Governor, *A Utah Perspective on the National Education Goals* (Salt Lake City, Utah Office of the Governor and Utah State Office of Education,1992):, 27.
112. For a summary of development of master planning in the state, see Utah State Board of Regents, *Utah Higher Education Master Plan* (Salt Lake City: The Board, 1987).
113. The Educational Technology Initiative was one of this program's successful contributions. *Building a Better Utah*, 30–31.
114. Among the particularly noteworthy results of such funding were the Eccles Institute of Human Genetics Building at the University of Utah, completed at a cost of $28 million; a $5.5 million Eccles Broadcast Center at the University of Utah; the Space Engineering Building at Utah State University, the result of $10 million in federal funding; a $5 million grant from Union Pacific to complete the Science and Industry Building at Salt Lake Community College; and the Udvar-Hazy Business Building at Dixie College, the result of a $3 million donation. *Building a Better Utah*, 32.
115. "Utah Higher Education: Challenges of Growth," Utah Foundation *Research Report* No. 548 (June 1992). Among the reforms suggested were eliminating entire academic disciplines, administrative consolidation of some schools, and changing from a four-quarter to a three-semester system like that conducted at Brigham Young University.
116. Douglas L. Parker, "National Democrats Target Bangerter for Defeat," *Salt Lake Tribune*, March 20, 1987, B1.
117. Dr. Rod Julander, professor of political Science, Weber State University, telephone interview by James B. Allen, January 25, 1996. Notes in James B. Allen papers, L. Tom Perry Special Collections, Harold B. Lee Library, Brigham Young University.
118. Brad T. Barber, Michael E. Christensen, Gary C. Cornia, "The Impact of Tax Limitation on the Utah Economy," *Utah Economic and Business Review* 48, No. 9 (September 1988): 7.
119. Bob Bernick, Jr., "Utah Loses its Long-Held Claim to Title of Most Republican State," *Deseret News*, November 7, 1990, A1.
120. Bob Bernick, Jr., "Win or Lose, Cook Vows to be Back in '94," ibid., October 8, 1992, B1.
121. Douglas L. Parker, "Cook Becomes Proud Father of Newborn Political Party," *Salt Lake Tribune*, June 10, 1989, B1.
122. Kelly Burch, "Desperate Attacks," *Salt Lake Tribune.*, letter to the editor, October 22, 1992, A31.
123. Cannon spent more than $4 million of his own money in seeking the nomination, while Bennett spent more than $1.4 million.
124. Douglas Palmer, "Many Things Hurt Owens' Senate Bid, Pollster Says," *Deseret News*, November 5, 1992, E1.
125. Bob Bernick, Jr., "Utahns Buck National Trend, Keep Change to a Minimum," ibid., November 4, 1992, A1.
126. Bob Bernick, Jr., "Leavitt Sets Agenda for His 'First 100 Days,'" ibid., October 23, 1992, B1.
127. "What Lessons in Utah Vote?" ibid., November 4, 1992, A18.
128. *Engle v. Vitale*, 370 US 421 (1962). For a brief but general survey of some other relevant court decisions, placed in historical context, see Richard G. Wilkins, "One

Moment Please: Private Devotion in the Public Schools," *The BYU Journal of Public Law 2* (1988): 1-13.

129. A strong statement of this perspective came from LDS apostle Dallin H. Oaks. See "On the Issue of Public Prayer," *Wall Street Journal*, May 23, 1990, reprinted in BYU Today (July 1990): 2-3.

130. See "School Prayer-Bad Penny," editorial, *Salt Lake Tribune*, June 18, 1989, A12.

131. Twila Van Leer, "Give Schools a Prayer in Fighting Lawsuits?" *Deseret News*, July 27, 1990, A1; Bob Bernick, Jr., "69% of Utahns Favor School Prayer," ibid., July 28, 1990, A1; Bob Bernick Jr., "The Best of All Worlds for Bangerter," ibid., August 10, 1990, A6.

132. Lee v. Weisman, 505 US 577 (1992); available online at various places, including http://www.law.cornell.edu/supct/html/90-1014.ZS.html. Accessed November 18, 2014

133. Joe Costanzo, "S.L. Council Will Fight Prayer Ban," *Deseret News*, March 18, 1992, B1; Dan Rosebrock, "Court ruling on S.L. Prayers Rankles Davis Officials," ibid., March 22, 1992, B3; "Orem Council Decides to Keep Prayers," ibid., March 25, 1992, B2.

134. Society of Separationists v. Whitehead, 870 P.2d 916 (1993); available online at http://www.leagle.com/xmlResult.aspx?xmldoc=19931786870P2d916_11775.xml&docbase=CSLWAR2-1986-2006. Accessed November 18, 2014. This, along with another case, upheld the constitutionality of prayer as long as it was neutral in every way, not favoring particular religions (or even religion in general) and as long as anyone, including nonreligious groups, be given equal representation.

135. For an independent evaluation of the possible economic impact of the proposition, see "Pari-Mutuel Wagering Initiative in Utah," Utah Foundation *Research Report* No. 550 (August 1992).

136. For a history of the Hotel Utah, see Leonard J. Arrington, *The Hotel: Salt Lake's Classy Lady, the Hotel Utah, 1911-1986* (Salt Lake City: Westin Hotel Utah, 1986).

137. These included a detailed, four-volume history of the state; a one-volume "popular" history of the state; and histories of each of the state's twenty-nine counties. Unfortunately the four-volume history was never published, for only one of the volumes was completed on time and the state did not want to publish it separately. That volume, revised, is now this book. Another, authored by Charles Peterson and Brian Cannon, was recently published by the University of Utah Press. The one-volume history is Thomas G. Alexander, Utah The Right Place: The Official Centennial History (Salt Lake City: Gibbs Smith Publisher, 1995).

138. These were the accomplishments listed by Bangerter in his final State of the State address, January 13, 1992. Bob Bernick, Jr., "Bangerter Talks of Past and Future," *Deseret News*, January 14, 1992, A1.

139. For details, see "Utah's National Recognition," Utah Foundation *Research Report* No. 549 (July 1992).

140. In this Gallup poll, published in the July 1, 1991 issue of *Newsweek*, governors were not allowed to vote for themselves. "Ranking the Governors," p. 27.

141. *Building a Better Utah*, 37.

142. Ibid., 34.

CHAPTER 7

Mike Leavitt and the End of Century One, 1993–1995

On January 4, 1996, Utah celebrated its hundredth anniversary of statehood. This historic milestone did not seem far away just three years earlier, when forty-two-year old Michael O. Leavitt, the second youngest chief executive in state history, took up residence in the Governor's Mansion. In a way, Leavitt's relative youth, and the fact that the press usually referred to him by the youthful-sounding nickname Mike, symbolized the new age in which Utah and the nation lived. Leavitt was Utah's first chief executive to have been born after World War II and the first to live *only* in the time covered by this book. A popular and somewhat liberal-minded Republican, Leavitt would become the second Utah governor to serve three terms.[1]

Leavitt, who grew up in Cedar City, had a great deal of business and political experience before he became Utah's chief executive. His positions included success as CEO of the Leavitt Group; a member of the board of directors of Utah Power and Light, as well as various other local and regional companies; a member of the Utah State Board of Regents; and a political campaigner for Senators Jake Garn and Orrin Hatch.

Image 7.1: Michael Leavitt, Utah's fourteenth governor, was inaugurated January 4, 1993. Re-elected twice, he resigned in 2003 to become Administrator of the Environmental Protection Agency. In January 2005 he became Secretary of Health and Human Services. Photo courtesy Leavitt Partners, used by permission.

Looking Toward Century II

The world at the end of Utah's Century I was a much different place than the one Mike Leavitt entered in 1951. Although serious international tensions still existed, the Cold War (which was in one of its "hot" spells when Leavitt was born) was a thing of the past. The amazing revolution in transportation and communication —the result of jet airline travel, space satellites, television, and computers—made it possible to be almost anywhere on the earth within a day, and to communicate with anyone almost instantaneously. But what made modern life even more revolutionary was the fact that the many marvels of the technological revolution were not only available, but they were *essential* to the economy and physical well-being of both the nation and the state. Trade, economic management, public health, traffic management, crime detection and law enforcement, public and private record keeping, publishing and other forms of communication, engineering, medical research—all of these things and more were totally dependent upon technologies that, for the most part, were only dreams in 1951 and had not even been thought of when Utah's Century I began.

Nearly all of the state's newest manufacturing establishments were high-tech firms and older mining and manufacturing companies, such as Kennecott and Geneva Steel, depended on new technology for their profits and to keep pollution within state and federal limits. Farmers, ranchers, and dairymen, too, relied upon technologies hardly known when Leavitt was born, as did every food processing plant in the state. Computer know-how, something Mike Leavitt was anxious to expand as rapidly as possible, was becoming a "must" in public schools, and it was almost impossible for anyone to get through college without knowing at least enough about computers to write a paper and to look up a reference in the computerized library catalog. The old card catalog was rapidly becoming a thing of the past.

No one knew what new wonders Mike Leavitt's grandchildren would become dependent upon in Century II, but everyone knew that their lives would be much different. Forecasters might have seen the immediate future not just in the technology of the age but also in the strengths and weakness that characterized the state in 1994. If the trends of 1993 and 1994 continued, the economy would keep budget-makers in a state of near-euphoria because Utah would be one of the few states in the union to end every fiscal year with a healthy surplus. Utah would be one of the most healthy states in the nation, its people would live longer, and its population would grow faster.[2] Utah would spend a larger portion of its income on public education than most other states, and its children would be more well-educated than those in most of the nation, even though the total amount of money spent per child would still be less than the average. Women would play an increasingly prominent role in Utah's political and economic life.

Religious values, as expressed by many religious groups, both Christian and non-Christian, would constitute the underlying basis for both public and private morality in the state. And Utah's image as a great place to visit, to live, and to do business would be among the best in the nation: a vast change from the negative images that bombarded the American public at the beginning of Century I.

On the other hand, those who observed the trends of 1993 and 1994 detected serious problems. The cost of health care, particularly for the elderly, was mushrooming. There were problems such as gang violence, alcohol and drug abuse, child abuse, and the deterioration of the family. The overall crime rate was slowing down, but the incidence of murder, robbery, auto theft, and aggravated assault was going up. Divorce, teen age pregnancy, and other social ills were continuing their slow rise, while poverty and homelessness remained as blights on an otherwise healthy economy. Most of these problems remained extremely serious, but fortunately the upward trend did not continue. Violent crime, divorce, teen pregnancy and other social problems declined slightly in the first few years of Century II.

As they observed their changing society, most Utahns were concerned with maintaining the social values that seemed threatened by so much of what was happening in the world around them. Family values, in particular, seemed to be eroding in the nation at large, and the people of Utah, a strong family-oriented state, worried about how best to live in the real world and still teach their children traditional ethical and moral standards. Most seemed to believe, as did their new governor, that the ultimate solution to most social ills lay not with government but with families. They also clung to moderately conservative political values, because they interpreted conservatism, in part, as promoting traditional values of self-reliance, thrift, and industry. This did not mean that they wanted to eliminate welfare aid or had disdain for the needy, but they continued to mistrust solutions promoted by big government, even though they also continued to willingly support welfare programs with their taxes. They also believed in limited government and as much local control as possible and tended to interpret the United States Constitution in ways that protected states' rights. As the Leavitt administration prepared for Utah's Century II, one of its most complex challenges was how to balance all of these concerns with the pressing and legitimate need for government action in many areas.

Although Governor Leavitt did not stress it in his inaugural address, much of what he did in his first two years in office had the objective of beginning Century II with the state in the best possible position, financially, educationally, legally, socially, and otherwise. The final three-year count-down to the centennial began with a feeling of optimism about Utah's ability to handle its most pressing problems. In his January 4, 1993, inaugural address, Leavitt's promises included focusing on education, improving the economy with higher paying jobs, promoting responsible health care and welfare reform, maintaining Utah's quality of life, and making state government more efficient and effective. He also promised that state government would grow no faster than the private sector. In commenting on education, which was clearly his first priority, Leavitt recognized how rapidly and surely the fast-paced, technologically oriented modern world would continue to impact everything that happened in Utah, including education. He said that he realized that some teachers, administrators, parents, and even students were worried about the changes he would demand, yearning, perhaps, for a return to "normal." But, he emphasized,

> Normal as it existed in the past will not return. The momentum of change and technological growth is too rapid. ... Now is the time to take the quantum leap forward. We will be focused like a laser in seeing that it is successful. I will not back down. We prepare the work force of the future, and they are our children.[3]

Fire in the Mansion

Governor Leavitt's first year in office ended well, except for a terribly unfortunate fire in the stately Governor's Mansion one night in December. Faulty electrical wiring in a Christmas tree ignited the fire, which spread through the mansion so quickly that the governor's family and resident staff barely had time to escape. (The governor was not home at the time.) The mansion was ruined, with nearly every room damaged by fire or smoke and most of the elegant woodwork and artifacts destroyed.

Fortunately, the quick action of Salt Lake City's firefighters and disaster cleanup workers kept the destruction from becoming worse. When various state agencies studied the situation, they decided that enough of the original materials remained to justify a complete restoration. The painstaking work included replicating the grand French oak staircase as well as all the other elegant woodwork in the mansion. The restoration took much longer than expected but it was finished in 1996–a fitting conclusion to Utah's first century of statehood.[4] At that point Governor Leavitt decided not to move his family back into the mansion, but every succeeding governor has lived there.

A Population Note

In 1994, Utah's population grew by an estimated fifty thousand people, an annual growth rate of 2.7 percent and the highest in twelve years. Approximately 46 percent of that growth was the result of in-migration due in part to a remarkable growth in employment of 6.4 percent. More than half the new residents settled outside the Wasatch Front, and more than four thousand of those took up residence in Washington County, a haven for retirees.[5] At the same time, the thirty-year trend of population movement out of Salt Lake City seemed to have reversed itself. The city added 5,900 people between 1990 and 1992.[6]

Utah's anticipated population growth presented some serious challenges for those who would lead the state into Century II. In 1994 the governor's Office of Planning and Budget estimated that the population would jump from the current 1.9 million to about 3.1 million by the year 2020—just a quarter of a century away.[7] The number of school-age children would jump from 493,000 to an anticipated seven hundred thousand in that same period of time, which meant an average of 7,600 new students per year.

The potential strain on the state's educational resources, already among the lowest per capita in the nation, was staggering.[8]

Riding High, but with Glitches: Utah's Economy at the End of Century I

At that point, however, Utah's economy was riding high. It was so heady, in fact, that at the end of 1993 one national banking leader called it the "single strongest economy in the nation by a wide margin."[9] In 1993 Utah led the nation in job-growth rate as well as in the growth of services and products and showed a 16 percent decline in bankruptcies. Gross taxable sales were the highest in nine years. Construction employment soared as new businesses moved into various communities, and both residential and non-residential construction boomed. In 1994 five Utah companies were on *Inc.* magazine's list of the five hundred fastest-growing companies in America.[10]

This enviable business climate continued to attract new businesses to the state, resulting in thousands of new jobs, but not all of these companies' high expectations were met. In 1994, for example, Packard Bell, the nation's fourth largest manufacturer of computers, announced that it would move one of its divisions to Arbor Park, near Magna. This created six hundred new jobs in Utah immediately, and had the potential of generating up to 1,500 more. However, this optimistic estimate was not realized. By 1999 Packard Bell had nine hundred employees at Magna but then laid off two hundred of them. Also in 1994, Fingerhut Companies, Inc., a national distributing firm, announced plans to build a huge distribution center near Spanish Fork. It promised to provide 527 permanent jobs when the century was completed in 1996. But even though Fingerhut built a huge plant—the size of twenty-four football fields—it never opened.[11]

What seemed like the most exciting new business story was the decision of Micron Technology Inc., early in 1995, to build a $1.3 million semiconductor plant at Lehi. Micron chose Lehi over other sites in the United States because of the high-quality engineering programs at nearby University of Utah and Brigham

Young University, the highly educated labor pool it could draw on, the area's pro-business environment, easy accessibility, and various tax and other economic incentives offered by the state of Utah and Utah County. The boon to Utah, and particularly Utah County, was an estimated 3,500 new jobs, plus a multiplier effect that would stimulate economic activity in construction, housing, retail trade, and all the other areas affected by economic growth. Everyone was excited, even though it would mean some up-front costs for Lehi and surrounding communities: more roads and businesses as well as a sudden need to expand school facilities. Construction on the plant began almost immediately, the state included anticipated tax revenues from Micron in its 1996 budget, and Utah County communities made budget and construction plans accordingly.

Unfortunately, the excitement came to a sudden halt in February 1996 when Micron announced that, because of financial troubles, it was cutting back on some operations and temporarily shutting down construction in Lehi. One result for the state was a scurry during the closing days of the 1996 legislature to cut $20 million from the estimated $100 tax reduction planned for the coming fiscal year. By the end of the twentieth century, Micron was operating a chip testing facility at its still-unfinished plant, employing only about five hundred people—but how long it would be before full operations would commence was anybody's guess.

International trade continued to grow in importance for Utah, and Governor Leavitt paid special attention to cultivating foreign markets. He avidly supported the controversial North American Free Trade Agreement (NAFTA), which passed Congress in November 1993 and paved the way for letting down trade barriers throughout the continent. Within a month Leavitt was on his way to Mexico on a trade mission. In May 1994, he went on a similar mission to South Korea and Japan. The state must think more globally, he reminded Utahns on his return, and must also learn how to better treat foreign guests when they came to the state. He planned several more overseas trips in the interest of trade, especially after he crossed paths with the governors of Montana and Maine on his Asian trip.[12]

In 1994, Salt Lake City's International Airport received a $12 million check from the US Department of Transportation to aid in the building of a new runway, which had already been underway for two years. When completed, the new runway would dramatically increase the airport's capacity.

Travel, tourism, and recreation continued to make up one of the largest segments of Utah's economy. In 1994 alone it accounted for some sixty-nine thousand jobs and $3.5 billion in spending, which generated approximately $247 million in tax revenue for state and local governments. The impact on some areas was particularly important; the industry provided more than 40 percent of the jobs in Garfield, Summit, Grand, and Kane Counties. Over 15 million out-of-state visitors arrived in Utah during the year, and practically every tourist destination showed the highest level of visitation in its history. As usual, the attraction receiving the most visitors (from both in and out of the state) was LDS Temple Square (5 million), followed, in order, by Glen Canyon National Recreation Area (3.6 million), Zion National Park (2.4 million), Flaming Gorge National Recreation Area (2 million), Wasatch Mountain State Park (1.2 million), Bryce Canyon National Park (1.1 million), Park City (1.1 million), Lagoon Amusement Park (1 million); Utah Jazz Basketball (eight hundred thousand), and Hogle Zoo (788,600).[13] Utah skiing received a boost in 1994 when *Snow Country* magazine listed Park City as the fifth top ski area in the nation. In addition, *Life* magazine chose to feature Salt Lake City as one of five great vacation spots for 1995.

Tourism's economic impact on the state was welcome, but in some cases mere numbers created serious problems. In Zion National Park, for example, the increasingly heavy traffic not only brought more people than concessionaires could easily handle, but it also put terrible strains on the roads and had the potential of causing serious environmental damage. One proposed solution included operating a mandatory shuttle system into the park from Springdale and closing all camping areas within park boundaries. The shuttle system was finally adopted, beginning in May 2000, and operating between late March and the end of October each year.

Tourism also threatened valuable historical and prehistorical sites. Archeological sites were sometimes severely damaged, unintentionally, by tourists, but vandals and selfish looters often created even more harm. The Cedar Mesa in southeastern Utah, for example, was a popular backpacking area, but it also contained extensive ruins from the Anasazi and Basketmaker Indians. Its concentration of archeological remains was one of the highest in the world and of inestimable importance to southwestern prehistory. Plagued by a long history of looting, the area was inundated by tourists in the 1990s but only one archaeologist was assigned to its two million acres and nothing effective was being done to protect it.[14]

Despite such problems, state officials were still enthused about the possibility that tourism would continue to boom. An expected increase in foreign travelers, improved national economic conditions, the growth of the LDS Church, the popularity of national parks and historic and prehistoric sites in the American Southwest, and many other factors all seemed to foreshadow continued growth.[15]

For many Utahns, though, the most exciting hope for raising the state's image as a tourist attraction was Salt Lake City's successful bid to host the 2002 Winter Olympics. The quest was long and hard, and support from within Utah waxed hot and cool over the years. Opponents were concerned over possible damage to the environment from more than two hundred thousand people converging on the state all at once. They predicted that the state would lose money and wondered how much of the bill for attracting the bid and building the needed venues would be passed on to taxpayers. Proponents argued that if the Olympics came, employment would increase by almost twenty thousand people, state and local governments would see $108 million in increased revenues, and Utahns would see a total economic boost of $1.7 billion. Even though tax money would be used to help bring the Olympics to Utah, they promised it would all be paid back.[16] By the time the International Olympic Committee met in Budapest, Hungary, in June 1995, Salt Lake City was the front-runner and nearly 70 percent of Utahns polled said they favored holding the Olympics in the state. Their hopes were realized when finally, after decades of effort,[17] Salt Lake City was chosen for the 2002 Winter Games. Governor Leavitt and several other dignitaries were on hand in Budapest for the announcement, and as it was broadcast over international television the people of Salt Lake City demonstrated and danced in the streets.

Utah's economic strength in the 1990s was consistent with a general economic upturn in the entire Mountain West. But there were downsides that should have tempered the euphoria somewhat. Acting together, economic growth and population growth spawned more crowded freeways, more pollution, and higher home building costs. In September 1994, Utah's inflation rate, at 1.7 percent, was nearly six times the national average. More serious, scholars working on a book on Utah demographics pointed out that Utah was susceptible to the same national economic trends that tended to make the poor poorer and to economically pinch middle-income families. The percentage of Utahns in poverty was still below the national average, but their numbers had increased since 1980 at nearly double the average. Moreover, the fact that Utah's middle-income families had more children than the average household caused them to struggle harder to make ends meet than people elsewhere with smaller households. The additional fact that Utah's tax rate was sixteenth highest in the nation did not help. The researchers also noted that 56 percent of the state's mothers with children under age five and 78 percent of those with children between the ages of six and seventeen were working, compared with national figures of 54 and 76 percent, respectively. A large portion of these mothers worked out of necessity rather than by choice.[18]

Fiscal Euphoria

Utah's economic health, nevertheless, gave the new governor and the legislature a case of fiscal euphoria. Still wanting to do more for education, transportation, and Utah's correction programs, Mike Leavitt at first opposed any immediate tax cuts. In 1994, however, legislators estimated that the state would have between $200 and $300 million in extra revenue the following year. Many felt it was time for a tax cut, although voters were divided on the issue.

A poll in February showed that 42 percent of voters felt the surplus should go toward a permanent tax cut or toward rebates, but another 42 percent felt that it should be spent on state programs that needed it the most.[19] The result was a legislative compromise. Lawmakers cut about $32 million in sales and property taxes but at the same time increased the budget of most state agencies and provided money for major reforms in health care and child welfare. "To do all that was done and still cut taxes speaks to the fiscal discipline of the state," said Leavitt.[20]

By the end of 1994, the state was in such good financial health that the governor recommended to the 1995 legislature a $30 million income tax cut along with a record $4.9 billion state spending package. The major increases were in education, transportation, and the justice system.[21] However, indicative of the relative economic comfort of Utah voters was the fact that now 61 percent of them felt that there should be no tax cut at all but rather that the state should spend the extra money on needed programs.[22] Lawmakers passed a record budget but fought with the governor over the tax cut, finally passing an even larger one than he recommended. In 1995, moreover, the state ended the fiscal year with another surplus of over $100 million.

Of Poverty and Wealth

The personal income of Utah's citizens continued to climb slowly. In 1993 total personal income grew by 7.3 percent, compared with an estimated national growth of 4.6 percent. That same year the per capita personal income (i.e., total personal income divided by total population) was $16,300, or 78.4 percent of the national average. But that ratio was not as good as that of the 1970s, when per capita income was more than 81 percent every year.[23] In general, however, the average middle-class family in Utah seemed to be doing well.

There were still troublesome inequities, however. Utah had some of the most serious pockets of poverty in the nation. San Juan County, where part of the Navajo reservation was located, ranked tenth lowest in the United States in terms of overcrowded housing and fourteenth lowest in per-capita personal income.[24]

In other parts of the state, homelessness and hunger continued to rise, even among the working poor. A national report issued in December, 1993, showed that 40 percent of those seeking food and shelter in Salt Lake City had jobs but simply did not earn enough money to pay for both rent and food. This was the second highest such percentage among the twenty-six cities surveyed.[25] This situation, along with even more serious hard-core poverty, kept homeless shelters full and soup kitchens busy. The Community Development Division of the Department of Community and Economic Development estimated that on any given night in 1993 there were as many as 2,425 homeless people on the streets.[26]

Utah continued to carry thousands of people on its welfare rolls, the overwhelming majority of whom were single mothers who were anxious to get off welfare and into paying jobs. Many simply had inadequate skills, partially because only half of them had high school diplomas.[27] In January 1993, Utah began a pilot program, the Single Parent Employment Demonstration (SPED), that was designed to encourage and help people to obtain permanent employment and become self-sufficient. However, the bureaucratic difficulties facing any reform effort were demonstrated when, in order to begin the experiment, Utah had to obtain waivers of forty-six federal regulations in connection with the Aid to Families with Dependent Children (AFDC), food stamp, Medicaid, and various child-care programs. Nevertheless, four pilot centers were established around the state. Families enrolled in the program were allowed to keep substantial portions of any earned income without fear of having their AFDC grants cut. Instead of penalizing people for working, the program encouraged it and helped build family income. Transitional medical and child-care coverage were also continued for substantial periods of time after the head of household found full-time work. The program also assisted with training and education in order to help heads of households acquire necessary skills.

After two years of operation, SPED appeared to be working. The Kearns site, for example, showed a savings of more than $81,000 in AFDC payments and child care expenses as people moved into the workforce. Statewide, 27 percent of those who went on the SPED program in January 1993 were no longer receiving public assistance a year later, and 35 percent had left the welfare system within eighteen months. While these rates may still seem low, they were better than the control group designated for the study.[28] In addition, the federal Job Training Partnership Act (JTPA) helped low-income, older, and displaced workers find on-the-job training with cooperating companies. Between 1992 and 1994, JTPA helped nearly seven thousand Utahns find jobs. This, in turn, saved the state some $10 million in welfare grants and gained $4 million in taxes.[29] Despite these and other programs, however, the poverty problem did not improve. One of Utah's great needs as it moved toward Century II was serious and far-reaching welfare reform. SPED, said Governor Leavitt, could provide a good model.

At the other end of the economic scale was a handful of the very rich. There were many of them, and seven of Utah's most wealthy men made *Forbes* magazine's 1994 annual list of the 400 richest Americans. Their individual net worth ranged from $440 million to $1 billion.[30] But many of Utah's super-rich, at least according to one report, eschewed the most flashy and flamboyant trappings of wealth, preferring a relatively frugal life style and contributing heavily to philanthropic projects.[31]

However, it was not the super-rich who gave Utah its well-deserved reputation for charity. Many Utahns were quick to volunteer for work in all kinds of charitable programs. Volunteers staffed homeless shelters and soup kitchens and found many other opportunities for community service. Numerous unheralded citizens spent many hours collecting clothing, money, and provisions for the needy and working with the needy in a variety of self-help programs. Physicians, dentists, attorneys, and other professional people often donated numerous hours to assist those who could not otherwise afford their services. Volunteers staffed programs designed to help senior citizens, underprivileged youth, and shut-ins, and they continued to enrich the public schools with their assistance to classroom teachers. In some areas, church groups worked side-by-side with other church and civic organizations in providing a variety of community services, including canning food for the needy.[32] Charity of the best quality was found at every level of Utah society.

Miscellanous National Issues: Social and Political

Meanwhile, all the national controversies that had been going on for years also continued to plague the state of Utah. One of the most emotionally-charged was the question of legalized abortion. Many Utahns were unhappy with the fact that the state's prohibition against elective abortions had been struck down, but in January 1993 Governor Leavitt and Attorney General Jan Graham announced a joint decision to abandon the state's appeal, which had already cost taxpayers $750,000. The state continued some aspects of the appeal, however, particularly those relating to fetal experimentation and attorney's fees. Leavitt tried to drop the entire appeal quietly in September 1994, after the cost to the state had skyrocketed to nearly $1 million. It seemed foolish to continue a suit that the state had no chance to win.[33] That did not help his popularity among anti-abortion groups, and the state still persisted in pursuing some questions. The matter was finally resolved in December 1995 when the Tenth Circuit Court of Appeals ruled against the state on all issues.

Leavitt, nevertheless, reaffirmed his commitment to restricting abortions as much as possible, and promised to support new anti-abortion legislation modeled after a Pennsylvania law that had been upheld by the Supreme Court. That law required women to receive counseling about the nature of abortions and about alternatives, and then to wait for twenty-four hours before undergoing the procedure. Utah passed a near-identical law in 1993, and it was upheld a year later by a federal district court.

Meanwhile, a ruling by the Clinton administration in December 1993 required states to use Medicaid money to pay for abortions for poor women who were pregnant from rape or incest. How much this action would cost the state was unclear, but one objection to the rule was simply that it was another unfunded federal mandate. Beyond that, said the director of Utah's Health Department, it flew in the face of Utah law, which prohibited the use of Medicaid funds (provided jointly by the federal and state governments) unless the mother's life were in danger. Utah, like Colorado and other states with similar laws, was in no hurry to implement the new rule. In May 1994 Colorado's law was declared invalid in a Colorado court on the presumption that federal law took precedence over state law. But Utah did not feel bound by that decision unless it was upheld by a federal district court. At the end of 1994 at least one pro-choice group was threatening still another lawsuit against the state unless it began to use Medicaid funds to pay for the abortions in question. To Leavitt, this was only one more reason to fight the continuing incursions by the federal bureaucracy. "Something is seriously wrong," he complained, "when the ruling of an appointed bureaucrat takes precedence over state constitutions."[34]

Another troublesome issue facing most states was the debate over legal recognition of same-sex marriages. Utah law already banned them, but the 1995 legislature strengthened that ban with another law prohibiting recognition by the state of same-sex marriages performed elsewhere. Utah thus became the first state to pass such a law. Opponents prepared immediately to challenge the law in court, but the challenge would not take place until a court decision in Hawaii outlawing that state's ban on same-sex marriages was tested in the US Supreme Court.[35]

Other social concerns in Utah included the divorce rate, which remained constant at about 5.2 divorces for every 1,000 people in the state but above the national average of 4.8. Research demonstrated that even though divorce was becoming more accepted in society, its effect on children was still as tragic as ever.[36] One bright spot was Utah's Provo-Orem area, which remained at the top of the national rankings of children living in married households and at the bottom of the rankings of single-parent families.[37]

Tragically, Utah also ranked high in suicide rates. At 14.1 suicides per 100,000 population, it was in the nation and 18 percent above the national average.[38]

The rapidly rising cost of health care was the catalyst for one of the most intensive national debates of the era. President Clinton's controversial effort at national health care reform died in Congress, but various states, including Utah, worked on their own plans to make health care more affordable for everyone and more available to the poor. In 1994 the legislature passed two bills that began to phase in some reforms and constituted what Governor Leavitt called the "Utah Healthprint." One law established a thirteen-member Health Policy Commission to advise the legislature as it continued its reform efforts in future years. The other expanded Medicaid coverage by including all children up to the federal poverty guideline and, when phased in over the next two years, would include all adults below the poverty level. It also provided the beginning of health insurance reform by improving renewability, setting some price boundaries, and providing for improved portability.

Another national debate arose over the growing evidence that smoking tobacco was injurious not only to the health of the smoker but also to nonsmokers who breathed in second hand smoke. After January 1, 1961, federal law had required health warnings on all cigarette packages, and ten years later cigarette advertising on television was banned. In 1985 the American Medical Association called for an end to all cigarette advertising. In Utah, the 1994 legislature passed a landmark ban on smoking in public places, including restaurants, lobbies, waiting rooms, bowling alleys, truck stops, sports arenas, stores, malls, and many more such locations.[39]

Concerned with the rise of violent crime, in February 1994 Congress, over the loud objections of the National Rifle Association and many conservative politicians, passed a mild form of gun-control legislation known as the Brady Bill. Intended simply to make it more difficult for criminals to purchase handguns, the bill required a five-day waiting period and a background check before a person could legally purchase a handgun.

Utahns had mixed reactions to the Brady Bill, but before it went into effect gun sales around the state skyrocketed. Meanwhile, after a teenager was wounded at the Utah State Fair in a gang-related shooting, Salt Lake City passed its own bill in October 1993. The new law required a waiting period for the purchase of handguns by anyone under age 25, and, to the dismay of many gun owners, several other cities followed suit. But in 1994 a bill was introduced in the state legislature that would have overturned such local ordinances and prohibited any city from enacting gun-control laws that were tougher than those of the state. Salt

Lake City's mayor, Deedee Corradini, led a powerful, relentless campaign to kill the bill. After a bitter fight in the legislature, in which a conference committee was unable to wipe out differences between the House and Senate bills, sponsors had to settle for compromise legislation that did not overturn existing local laws but placed a one-year moratorium on any new gun laws by local governments. It also called for the establishment of a gun-control task force to study the issue and make recommendations to the 1995 legislature. In addition, lawmakers came up with $4 million in various bills to help fight gangs. This included $1.7 million to set up a work camp for the most troublesome gang members. At the governor's prodding, the legislature also made it illegal for anyone under age eighteen to possess a handgun or for anyone under age fourteen to carry any firearm unless accompanied by an adult.

The gun-control task force worked through the end of the year to prepare recommendations for the legislature. One of its first decisions, which was severely criticized by representatives of community governments and by antiviolence groups, was that gun regulations should be set by the state and not by cities or counties. This, said supporters, was necessary to make the laws less confusing statewide and thus protect citizens from breaking laws unwittingly.[40] At the same time, the task force recommended legislation that would make it more difficult to obtain permits to carry concealed weapons.[41] But, with that exception, it did not recommend tougher state laws. By the time the legislature met in January 1995, feelings were intense throughout the state. Gun control had been the most frequent topic of letters to the editors of Utah's newspapers in 1994, with 161 letters opposing it and only fifty-three favoring it.[42] Attorney General Jan Graham, an advocate of gun-control, proposed legislation that would prohibit anyone who was the subject of a domestic violence court order from purchasing firearms. She admitted, however, that, given the makeup of the legislature, this would be a bad year for gun control.[43] The *Deseret News*, which often reflected and perhaps influenced general public opinion, seemed to be running against the tide when it came out editorially in favor of tougher gun laws.[44]

Jan Graham was right. The 1995 legislature was unsympathetic with almost any kind of gun-control legislation, even laws that some conservatives thought would result in responsible gun control. The Senate, for example, refused even to debate a bill that would have banned the purchase of handguns by people whom domestic violence protective orders had deemed to be violent. On the other hand, the legislature overturned city and county laws that were more restrictive than state laws and also passed a law making it less difficult to obtain permits to carry concealed weapons.[45] The latter followed a national trend in which twenty states already had liberalized concealed-weapons laws by granting permits to practically any adult without a criminal record or a history of mental illness. At least thirteen other states were considering similarly easing restrictions. About twenty states, on the other hand, still required people to demonstrate need before they could carry a handgun.[46] But by the end of the year the *Deseret News* was still not convinced that Utah's law was a good one. Although the law was too new to draw any conclusions, the editors observed, the experience with such laws in other states was not convincing. "Relaxed permit standards remain a bad idea—one that the Legislature should rethink."[47]

Another national issue that remained a stumbling block for Utah was public land policy. It was not just a matter of federal-state relationships but also one of differing perspectives between environmentalists and government bureaucrats. One hopeful step came early in 1994 when federal, state, and local agencies, along with business interests and other private groups and citizens in southern Utah, decided they should work together. forming the "Canyon Country Partnership." They chose a "facilitator" to coordinate activities, whose salary would be paid for by Project 2000, a private, nonprofit group dedicated to improving Utah's future.[48] To the degree that such efforts at cooperation worked, Utah would be well served in Century II, but the work proceeded slowly. Lack of sufficient funding along with skepticism by local officials about the role of the federal government in the partnership, led to its becoming more of a discussion group than an action group.[49]

There seemed to be little room for compromise between the strongly held opinions of some groups when it came to Utah's proposed wilderness lands. In 1995, the heavily environmentalist Utah Wilderness Coalition, supported by more than a third of Utah residents, called for 5.7 million acres to be set aside as wilderness. Such a bill was introduced in Congress early that year. However, the House Committee on Public Lands was headed by Utah Congressman James Hansen, who preferred a less ambitious bill calling for setting aside only 1.8 million acres, even though only about a fourth of Utah residents supported that idea.[50] Governor Leavitt also supported setting aside 1.8 million acres, which angered county commissioners who wanted only 1 million acres set aside. Utah Congressman Bill Orton, on the other hand, wanted slightly less land put into wilderness and more put under a special resource management program. But Congress refused to act because Utah wilderness issues became embroiled in other political debates.

Term limitation was the focus of another heated national political debate. In 1994 the Utah legislature agreed to a twelve-year limitation on the terms of governors and state legislators, beginning in the year 2006. It also adopted a similar limitation on members of Congress, but this would not apply unless twenty-four other states adopted federal term limits. One reason for this action was to stop Merrill Cook's attempt to put his own term-limitation initiative on the November 1994 ballot. Not satisfied, Cook obtained enough signatures to put his initiative on the ballot anyway. His proposed law would have unilaterally limited the terms of Utah Senators and Congressmen, something that most Utah voters felt was unwise, because without similar limitations on members of Congress from other states, Utah could be put at a great disadvantage in Congress. The law would also have provided run-off elections in the state in case a candidate did not receive a clear majority of votes. Opponents saw this as providing too much opportunity for political intrigue by minority organizations attempting to use the run-off to gain control of a public office. They also thought it was unfair to voters to include both term limitations and run-off elections in the same initiative, because these were completely different issues and should be voted on separately. Voters overwhelmingly turned down the maverick proposal by a 65 to 35 percent margin. In addition, the earlier term limitation law never went into effect because it was repealed in 2003.

401

More Continuing Issues and Challenges

The state faced many other challenges as it approached Century II. Highways were crowded, finding enough clean water for the growing population was an ever-present problem, and open spaces were being eaten up by business development and residential subdivisions. It was unrealistic to try to stop either population or economic growth. The problem was simply how to maintain and improve the quality of life while growth went on.

Air pollution remained one of Utah's most visible health problems, and projections indicated that PM10 and other dangerous pollutants would only increase as the population mushroomed along the Wasatch Front and as auto traffic grew proportionately. Industry continued to account for 54 percent of PM10 particulates in the air, compared with a vehicular rate of 28 percent, but autos, trucks, and other vehicles poured 79 percent of the odorless, colorless, and highly toxic carbon monoxide into the atmosphere. There was intense disagreement over how serious the carbon monoxide threat really was, especially in Utah County where all forms of air pollution were higher than anywhere else in the state, but the EPA was unyielding in demands for better control. One partial solution was the use of oxygenated gasoline, which was more expensive but which was required in Utah County during the winter. But county officials argued that while such fuels cut down on carbon monoxide, they actually increased the PM10 problem.[51] And so the fight went on.

Trying to determine how to meet the transportation challenge of Century II was mind-boggling. It involved not only heavy expense but also wide differences of opinion on what ought to be done. Even though the US interstate highway program was complete, in 1993 Utah still had $2.3 billion in unfunded highway needs. Revenue resources were declining, not only because of dwindling federal aid but also because increased automobile efficiency was cutting into gasoline sales and therefore gasoline tax revenue. Already Utah collected nineteen cents per gallon in taxes, but highway officials estimated that to finance the unfunded needs over a twenty-year period would require a fifteen cents per gallon increase unless other revenues could be found. Such an increase was probably politically impossible. The first major project officials wanted to fund was improvement of the I-15 corridor from Bountiful to Sandy but they pointed out that even after this was accomplished, that stretch of freeway would be just as crowded by the year 2020 as it was in 1993.

This dilemma caused the question of some form of light-rail transportation system to be raised again. For years, highway engineers and planners nationwide had stressed the impossibility of keeping up with demands simply by building and expanding more highways. The Utah Department of Transportation continually urged approval of a light-rail system similar to that adopted by many other major cities in America, but the idea was simply not politically popular. In November, 1992, for example, Salt Lake County voters rejected a proposed quarter-cent sales tax increase for an expanded transportation system that would include a light-rail connection between downtown Salt Lake City and the shopping mall in Sandy.[52] The following year the Salt Lake County Commission voted two to one against including light-rail in a long-range transportation plan for the Wasatch Front, even though the Wasatch Front Regional Council voted to keep such an option in its master plan. The *Deseret News* called the County Commission's view shortsighted, pointing out that most experts believed it was just a matter of time before oil shortages would send gasoline prices skyrocketing, the growing population produced more traffic gridlock, rising pollution levels resulting from traffic caused the federal government to sharply restrict the use of cars in Salt Lake Valley, and increasingly high taxes made mass transit more attractive. By that time, however, it would not be easy to revive light-rail. "Utahns must not get so caught up in the present that they forget to plan for the future," the editor opined.[53]

In 1993, Congress refused to spend $12 million originally earmarked for improvement of I-15, making it questionable how far Utah could go in widening the highway. The next year a House subcommittee approved an appropriation of $6 million for I-15 and another $13 million for a few other projects in Utah. But this was a far cry from the $253 million that had been requested to shore up deteriorating highways throughout the state. The fact that Salt Lake City was vying to host the 2002 Winter Olympics, which would result in extra heavy traffic, made the issue more crucial. But even the lesser amount was cut back because the state did not conform to federal guidelines on tough seatbelt laws and on requiring motorcyclists to wear helmets.[54]

In 1995, Utah Transit Authority (UTA) announced plans to build a fifteen-mile commuter train line between Sandy and downtown Salt Lake City, relying on the promise of the Clinton administration to provide federal funding for most of the $330 million it would cost. Governor Leavitt supported the plan, but it took on severe political overtones when, early in 1996, his own party's central committee voted two to one for calling a halt to the idea. This followed a demand by Republican Congressman James Hansen that federal transportation dollars be spent, instead, on highways. But UTA believed that light-rail was inevitable and had actually begun initial planning in the 1980s. In 1987 Congress appropriated $3.8 million for preliminary engineering studies and in 1988 it approved $5 million to purchase a right of way from Union Pacific along the proposed corridor paralleling I-15.[55] Then, after Utah's bid for the 2002 Winter Olympics was successful, UTA was able to obtain initial funding through the Federal Transportation Administration. Construction began in 1997, and in December 1999 Utah's light-rail system, TRAX, opened a 17.3-mile line between downtown Salt Lake City and Sandy.

On another controversial issue, it appeared that, despite the defeat of the 1992 referendum on pari-mutuel betting, Utahns would be faced with continuing pressure to legalize at least some form of gambling in the state, but voters would also continue to reject it. Nevertheless, gambling was growing on Utah's borders, and Utahns increasingly crossed state lines to participate. In Wyoming, an estimated 90 to 95 percent of those making wagers at the Wyoming Downs Race Track in Evanston were from Utah. After Idaho instituted a state lottery in 1994, a large portion of the tickets sold were purchased by Utahns. Unfortunately, gambling was a popular pastime for many Utah college students, who regularly spent weekends at various Nevada gambling spots. Utahns in general, however, including their legislators and Governor Leavitt, remained adamantly opposed to gambling of any kind despite the economic temptation. Utah and Hawaii remained the only states in the union that did not allow gambling of some sort. Governor

Leavitt appeared twice on national news shows defending Utah's antigambling status. The state simply was not willing to put up with the social ills that accompanied it, he said.[56]

Religion and the State

Prayer in public functions, religion in the schools, and other issues affecting the relationship between church and state remained sensitive. In December 1993, the matter of prayer in city councils was finally settled when the Utah Supreme Court overturned a 1992 lower court ruling against prayer in the Salt Lake City Council. Ironically, while some city councils continued the practice, in 1994 the Salt Lake City Council voted not to resume having prayer.

In the ongoing debate over prayer in the public schools, in 1993 the Utah Supreme Court upheld Utah's 1992 contribution of $10,000 toward Rhode Island's unsuccessful effort to defend graduation prayers. The suit brought against the state by the Society of Separationists had no logic, the court said, because litigation itself was not a religious exercise. However, the question still remained as to whether a majority of students themselves, not acting under the direction of school administrators, could opt for graduation prayers. In June 1993, the US Supreme Court refused to review a lower court ruling in favor of three states where such action was allowed. At some Utah high schools, meanwhile, despite the state court ban, some students spontaneously uttered prayers during their particular parts on the graduation program. The whole issue of school prayer seemed headed for another round of debate.

By the 1990s, the question of religion in public schools became so delicate that all over the nation teachers feared even mentioning religion in the classroom, let alone allowing prayer. Numerous questions arose, including the tax-exempt status of churches and religious organizations, the legality of a person who was declaring bankruptcy to first donate money to a church, whether or not religion could be discussed in the workplace, and whether or not church-owned schools or institutions could be required by federal law to adopt gay-rights provisions. In addition, the atmosphere became particularly tense in Utah when it appeared that teachers might be disciplined just for teaching *about* religion, even in a cultural or historical context. In some parts of the nation, critics charged, the teaching of history had become so sanitized that the role of religion was entirely absent from the textbooks as well as the classroom. To the degree that such charges were true, this distortion of historical truth was tragic. Some Utah parents complained, whether correctly or incorrectly, that teachers in Utah schools were prohibited even from mentioning why the Mormons settled in the Great Basin.

While Utah law did not actually forbid broad coverage of religion, the matter became so sensitive that some teachers may have avoided mentioning it simply to avoid any pressure on themselves.[57] In November, 1994, in an attempt to lay the matter finally to rest, the legislature placed a proposed constitutional amendment on the ballot. The amendment simply provided that the study of religion in schools did not constitute a "sectarian practice." But the arguments for and against the measure apparently seemed confusing to most voters. Feeling cautious, they defeated the amendment by a 54 percent majority.

The next contest was over choral singing at graduation exercise. Prior to graduation exercises at West High School in June 1995, a student brought suit against the school in order to restrain a chorus from singing two songs that were "devotional" in nature, containing references to God. A federal judge banned the songs. As a result, the chorus did not sing them officially, but after it sang its approved numbers a student "spontaneously" went to the microphone and asked everyone to sing one of the banned songs. Nearly everyone joined in, and efforts to halt the singing were to no avail. In a poll taken later, 72 percent of the Utahns questioned said they approved this defiance of the court order. The issue of what did nor did not constitute state support of religion in the public schools remained a heated open question.

Education: Another Never-Ending Story

In part, the story of public education in Utah maintained a familiar ring: remarkably high achievement in the face of underfunding. Utah students continued to attain scores well above average on most national tests, and the number of high school students taking and passing college-level advanced placement courses remained high. In addition, two Utah schools, Cyprus High School in Magna and Municipal Elementary School in Roy, were among seventy-nine schools nationwide cited by the US Department of Education in 1994 as schools to copy for their discipline and drug-free programs.[58]

But, of course, not everything was perfect, and at the end of 1993 Governor Leavitt and others complained that Utah's Strategic Plan for Education, adopted in 1991, was off track. The extremely high goals, such as having 100 percent of all Utah students achieve the goals of individual education plans, were not being met at the hoped-for rate. One unfortunate reason for this was that while most of Utah's forty district superintendents were aware of the plan, more than a third of them had never seen it.[59]

School finance continued to present problems, but by 1994 a new complication was painfully apparent: the widening gap between the richest and poorest districts in the state. Previously, Utah had been viewed as a model of equity, but with per-student spending ranging from $1,500 annually in Sanpete, Tintic, and Piute districts to more than $3,000 in Millard and Park City districts, this image had changed. The reason for the discrepancy was the that, beyond the equal amount received per child from the state's Uniform School Fund, each district could levy a local property tax for school purposes. Some districts with large numbers of students, low property evaluation, and much-higher-than-average property taxes still could not spend as much money per student as other districts with fewer students, high property value, and low taxes. By the end of 1994, even though a number of proposals had been presented, an equitable formula had not been found. These proposals included raising state support for poorer districts, equalizing all property tax revenues in the state, and withdrawing property tax exceptions from certain businesses in order to raise the tax base in their districts.

Utahns were hoping that the federal government would act to provide up to a 7 percent increase in federal school funds. They also felt reasonably sure they would receive as much as $640,000 from the federally funded Goal 2000 project. The year 1994 was actually considered a good one for people in public education because of the state's enviable financial status. That year the legislature voted a 4.5 percent increase in the minimum school program which, among other things, gave teachers more than a cost-of-living increase. On the negative side, however, was the fact that legislators were intent on giving a tax cut and did not provide enough money to reduce class sizes or to enhance technology in the schools as much as many educators thought necessary.

Among Leavitt's goals for public education was a restructuring process that would decentralize administration and involve parents, teachers, and school principals in more effective planning and administration of local schools. The hoped-for results would be greater flexibility and better and more innovative educational experiences. In 1993 the legislature appropriated $2.6 million to inaugurate the governor's Centennial School program, whereby schools could apply for money to institute special programs, including self-governing ones. Schools designated as Centennial Schools could reapply and receive financing, in diminishing amounts, for up to three years, after which they were expected to continue their programs from regular budgets. During the first year of operation, ninety-seven schools were designated as Centennial Schools. After two years there were nearly two hundred Centennial Schools in the state. The schools, however, received mixed reviews. In some cases school district offices were not enthusiastic about giving up some aspects of curriculum control, especially because they were ultimately held responsible for the quality of education in their districts. Some principles, too, were reluctant to share authority. In addition, except for the areas where the Centennial Schools were located, they were not well known to a majority of citizens in the state.

It was too early to tell whether the governor's goal of several hundred Centennial Schools would lead to a new century of educational excellence, but in at least a few cases there seemed to be some warmly satisfying results. North Sevier High School, for example, negotiated with the district school office to reorganize its budget, raise teacher salaries by 50 percent and extend their contracts to a full year. The result was a truly full-time teaching staff that spent its summers working hard on curriculum and advising students. At the Bryant Intermediate School in Salt Lake City, an interesting business-school partnership provided tutors for students needing help.[60]

Among the many private institutions to show an interest in supporting public education were the *Deseret News* and KSL Television. In 1962 they had initiated the Sterling Scholar program, which recognized outstanding academic performance in Utah's high schools. At first the program gave only recognition, but over the years cash prizes were added in order to help the recipients attend colleges of their choice. In 1994 the program awarded $19,500 in cash to thirteen Sterling Scholars and two runners-up in each of thirteen categories, and $70,000 in scholarships were offered by various colleges, universities, and technical institutions.[61]

In higher education, on July 1, 1993, Cecilia H. Foxley became the first woman to hold the office of State Commissioner of Higher Education. Foxley had previously served as deputy commissioner and associate commissioner for academic affairs. Having been a teacher and administrator at universities in Iowa and Minnesota, as well as at Utah State University, she was eminently well prepared for her new challenge to lead Utah's nine student-jammed public colleges and universities. Among her aims was the continued clarification and refining of institutional roles, including eliminating unnecessary duplications of services. She also hoped to create more links between higher education and private industry, to expand the use of technology, and to work more closely with public education in preparing students for college work.

Federal Versus State Authority: The Continuing Quest for Balance

In 1994, Mike Leavitt was elected chair of the Western Governors' Association as well as chairman of the Republican Governors Association. This immediately thrust Utah's energetic, youthful governor into the national limelight, especially because of an idea that he began to float in May at a two-day conference of state legislators in Phoenix, Arizona. Like both Matheson and Bangerter before him, Leavitt believed the scales of power had tipped far too much in the direction of the federal government, and certainly much further than the framers of the Constitution had ever intended (see, especially, Chapter 5 for a discussion of Matheson's efforts to restore federal-state balance). He spent his 1993 Thanksgiving weekend studying the ideas of the framers and reviewing what had been said about restoring the balance (including Matheson's book).

Leavitt was concerned with several problems, not the least of which was the fact that over the previous half-century federal mandates had infringed on every aspect of state responsibility, including education, and a large portion of those mandates were unfunded. Moreover, he complained during his June 14 acceptance speech to the Western Governors' Association, in the past sixty years the federal government's share of total local, state, and federal taxation had doubled—from 31 percent to 62 percent. "Today the federal government has become too powerful, too prescriptive and too pervasive," he said.[62]

The complications of the question of federal versus state authority were well illustrated in continuing discussions over issues such as the environment and public land. Leavitt's natural predisposition was to favor as much state control as possible, but after attending the two-day conference of state legislators in Phoenix in May 1994, his views were modified. "I have migrated ideologically from a point where I thought states ought to have the predominant role of government to one where I more fully appreciate the need for a federal government role," he said. "The environment is a prime example. Air pollution can drift from one state to another. There are other multistate concerns, like rivers. You've got to have a federal government that can deal with those cross-boundary issues." His option was for the federal government to set broad mandates but to leave it to local governments to determine how to meet them. He continued to resent "one-size-fits-all" federal regulations. He also recognized that the federal government's ownership of public lands was legitimate and necessary, but he called for boards composed of local ranchers and environmentalists to work together on how to manage those lands. Broad, specific federal regulations simply did not take local differences well enough into account.[63]

But Leavitt did not back away from his major concern of restoring states' rights. His approach was three-fold. He called upon the states to focus jointly on several specific legal principles that could be pursued in the courts; he called for a legislative strategy that would eliminate unfunded federal mandates; and he called for a constitutional amendment that would restore the balance of power.[64] The idea of an amendment was hardly new, but Leavitt's way of trying to achieve it was innovative. He called for a "conference of the states," in which every state would be represented equally and where the issue of federal-state relations could be discussed openly and amicably. The conference would convene only after three-fourths of the state legislatures passed resolutions calling for it, thereby giving its deliberations and recommendations a kind of unity that would send a powerful message to Congress. He hoped the conference would be nonpartisan in nature and that it would end with a proposal for a constitutional amendment requiring the federal government to respect the proper role of the states.

The governor avidly pursued his agenda, and he received wide national, bipartisan support. This zeal came at a time when national legislative leaders, in a Congress controlled by Republicans, were promising constitutional as well as legislative approaches to restoring the federal-state balance and also requiring a balanced federal budget. With respect to the balanced budget, however, Leavitt and other governors were concerned that such an amendment might lead to balancing the federal budget simply by shifting responsibilities to the states and, again, providing no funding. They heard promises that Congress would pass a law preventing that, but whether such promises—or even the promise of a balanced budget—would be kept remained questionable. Nevertheless, the climate was right for something like Leavitt was proposing, and by the end of 1994 people around the country were taking him and his proposal seriously.

Leavitt had hopes that the conference of the states would be held in Philadelphia in the fall of 1995, but early that year it became derailed. Although the conference had bipartisan support, some liberals, and particularly labor leaders and leaders of the National Education Association, feared that the conference could lead to the destruction of certain federal programs that helped them. More serious, and surprising, however, was the opposition from the right-wing fringe, including the John Birch Society, the Eagle Forum, radical militia militants, and certain radio talk-show hosts. As one national columnist put it, "their faxes poured into state legislatures considering whether to support the conference, and local politicians did what they usually do. They ran for the hills."[65]

Some saw the proposed conference as nothing more than a clandestine effort to convene a constitutional convention that would replace the US Constitution with something that would destroy basic American rights and perhaps even lead to a world government. Leavitt and his supporters adamantly denied that the conference could, in any way, be construed as a constitutional convention. It would have no authority to pass a resolution that, because of the representation at the conference, would have to be taken seriously by Congress. The Utah legislature approved it with little question, as did those of at least fourteen other states. But the conference died aborning as the political clamor led some state legislatures to refuse to pass the resolutions necessary for its convening, and others to refuse even to debate it.

Politics 1994

The 1994 election emphasized again the moderately conservative nature of the Utah electorate. Republicans swept the state, with the notable exception of the Third Congressional District where conservative Democrat Bill Orton won a third term. In the First District, James Hansen overwhelmed Democratic challenger Bobbie Coray, while in the Second District Enid Greene Waldholz pushed Karen Shepherd out of office with 45.8 percent of the vote to Shepherd's 35.8 percent. Independent Party candidate Merrill Cook ran a poor third with 18.3 percent. In the senatorial race, Orrin Hatch easily won a fourth term.

Nationally, the 1994 race was a disaster for the Democratic party, as voters sent a powerful message to President Clinton by giving control of both houses of Congress to the Republican Party. Utah and the nation then waited to see what would happen to the much-touted "Contract with America," which had been signed during the campaign by many Republican Congressional candidates, including James Hansen and Enid Greene Waldholz. Calling for term limitations, a balanced budget, the death penalty and other tough anti-crime measures, welfare reform, strengthening the family, tax cuts, strengthening American defense, reforms in Social Security that would increase the earnings threshold and repeal the Social Security benefits tax, and various economic and legal reforms, the "Contract" promised to provide plenty of controversy in the upcoming Congress. In the long run, some parts of the "Contract" were enacted, some were never acted on, and some of the enacted parts were vetoed or modified by negotiation with President Clinton. Its major effect was its appeal to voters: many analysts believed that it put the Republicans in the driver's seat for the 104th Congress.

Comemmoration

As Century II approached, Utahns prepared to celebrate. Centennial license plates appeared on vehicles. In 1995, Thomas G. Alexander's *Utah, The Right Place*, the new, one-volume centennial history commissioned by the state, was complete and ready for the bookstores. The authors of the county histories were nearing completion of their works, most of which were published over the next few years. To report on other activities, the Utah Statehood Centennial Commission, chaired by Stephen Studdert, published, beginning in 1994, a periodical report entitled *Utah Centennial Spirit*. To support the Centennial, many Utah businesses licensed their products to carry the official Centennial logo—a representation of Delicate Arch in Arches National Park.

Counties planned their own celebrations, and some sent out invitations as early as 1994. Millard County, for example, planned an Inaugural Ball on the eve of Statehood Day in Fillmore, the first capital of the Territory of Utah. In Emery County, officials made plans to preserve Native American culture. Among other things, they instituted a project for cleaning Native American rock art, and they began a program of education in fourth-grade classes to teach children the harmful effects of vandalism. The Kane

County Travel Council planned a visitor center and museum, and the County Centennial Committee made plans to develop historic trails. In addition, the Utah Centennial Commission provided numerous financial grants to communities and organizations that were bringing to life important historical landmarks, people, community traditions, and legends. One such grant went to the Utah Science Center, whose project called "Leonardo on Wheels" would take science and art throughout the state. Washington County received a grant for renovating the historic opera house in St. George. Brent Palmer and the Daughters of Utah Pioneers were awarded a grant for restoring a 1902 steam fire engine and conducting fire musters around the state. A Centennial Season of the Arts, a Centennial Season of Sports, and a Centennial Winter Games were all in the offing.

These and scores of other publishing, art, restoration, performance, production, and other imaginative projects were all planned as part of the effort to conduct one of the most impressive and important centennial celebrations in America.

The Mountain West Center at Utah State University and the Utah Humanities Council cosponsored a project in which they asked Utahns of all ages to write short essays on "What Living in Utah Means to Me," to be collected for a Centennial social history. At Orem High School, two English teachers took the project so seriously that they expanded on it, assigning their junior and senior students to interview their parents and grandparents. The resulted were printed in a book the students called "Faces of Utah."[66] Hundreds of Utahns, from children to adults, contributed personal essays of varying lengths that would provide future historians some interesting and valuable insights into life in Utah in Century I.

Meanwhile, Utah's major cities prepared for Century II with a number of revitalization projects. By 1994, Salt Lake City's Salt Palace, completed in 1968, had outlived its usefulness. A larger facility was needed to attract conventions and other activities to downtown Salt Lake City. That year the old central arena was destroyed and a major $70.6 million renovation project was begun. Completion was planned for January 1996 in order to accommodate a four-month-long convention of the American Bowling Congress that would begin in February. In Ogden, city fathers

Image 7.3: From 1992 to 1999, this sign welcomed visitors to Utah. Photo copyright Americanspirit/Dreamstime.com.

promoted a major transformation of the city's central district. Beginning in January 1995, a long-planned $60 million construction program got under way when ground was broken for a $36.3 million downtown conference center. Future projects included a county office complex, a baseball stadium, a state courts building, and expansion of the Union Station Railroad Museum.

Looking Ahead

With all of Utah's progress and problems, the key to the future was effective planning. Late in 1993 Governor Mike Leavitt appointed a thirteen-member Strategic Planning Committee, consisting of representatives from the legislature, the judiciary, executive departments, local governments, and the public at large. Its purpose was to define goals for Utah's future as well as the means for achieving and measuring those goals. In July 1994, Leavitt gave what he called a midyear State of the State address in Logan. There he called upon Utahns to help the state meet six challenges: (1) "Use technology, not brick and mortar, to solve Utah's growing school population problems"; (2) "Conserve, both water and highways. Utahns must get out of the family car and into mass transit, carpooling or working out of one's home. Conserve water, or residents will drown in repaying expensive water projects"; (3) "Work together for the 'economic resettlement' of rural Utah, using a statewide electronic highway to allow students and workers to connect to urban centers"; (4) "Become a generation of planners, not regulators"; (5) "Work toward improving the quality of life, not the quantity"; (6) "Rekindle a feeling of individual responsibility and community values, for they will carry the state forward."

These were Utah's goals for Century II, and unless Utahns rose to the occasion, the governor reminded them, the state would become like other states—crowded, inefficient, crime-ridden. Then, commenting on the population growth that clearly would continue, he said,

> The Wasatch Front could become a mega-metropolitan area of 2.5 million. When my four-year-old son Weston is fifty, it could reach four or five million. When we celebrate the bicentennial of Utah, it could be seven or eight million. That day will come. What will our children and grandchildren think of us then? Have we sown the seeds of their solutions?

These were good questions for the people of Utah.
Governor Leavitt's contribution to the Centennial series of personal essays was published in the *Deseret News* on January 5, 1995. There, he not only reminisced on the past but looked to the future. "Future generations depend upon the clarity of our view and the courage of our action," he said.

> As we plan for the years ahead, it will be a time to reflect upon the values that make living in Utah desirable. It will not be a time to strive for the biggest, fastest or loudest. It will be a time to cultivate a sense of quiet, competent quality. Our aim must be to make life in Utah steady, safe and secure.

> Perhaps the greatest challenge will be to rekindle the sense of personal community feeling that made possible the legacy of strength the settlers left for us.
>
> As we move progressively forward, we must also look thoughtfully back, to find, in the lessons of yesterday, values with which to steady our course. As pioneer men and women hoisted onto their shoulders the children of those who faltered on the trek, our success in keeping this place nourishing and safe will depend greatly upon the measure of personal strength every Utahn is willing to lend.[68]

Meanwhile, as Utahns looked toward the future they could feel with pride the meaning of the words on the new centennial highway signs that had welcomed people to the state since 1992: "Utah, Still the Right Place."

Notes

1. Leavitt did not complete his third term, which began in 2001. In 2003, during the George W. Bush administration, he was appointed administrator of the Environmental Protection Agency. Then, in 2005, he was appointed Secretary of Health and Human Services.
2. In 1993, a survey released by the Northwest National Health Insurance Company ranked Utah as the fifth-healthiest state in the nation. Joseph Bauman, "Utah Ranks No. 5 in Healthiness among States," *Deseret News*, September 21, 1993, B2.
3. Bob Bernick, Jr., "Leavitt Vows to Set New Standards for Utah Government," *Deseret News*, January 4, 1993, A1–A2.
4. For information on the Governor's Mansion, including tours, go online to http://www.utah.gov/governor/mansion/index.html. Accessed November 25, 2014. See also Jerry Spangler, "Good as Old: Leavitt Hails Restoration as Governor's Mansion Gets Ready for Public View," *Deseret News*, July 26, 1996, B1.
5. Matthew Brown, "Growth Rate Is Fastest in Twelve Years," *Deseret News*, April 12 1995, A11.
6. Joel Campbell, "S.L. Adds 5,900 Residents in 2 Years," *Deseret News*, February 8, 1994, A1.
7. A later estimate indicated even higher growth—3.5 million by 2020. "The Impacts of Utah's Population Growth," Utah Foundation *Research Briefs*, October 9, 2008.
8. Karl Cates, "It's Coming: Agency Urges Utah to Brace for 'the Third Wave,'" *Deseret News*, October 10, 1994. A1–A2.
9. So said Jeff Thredgold, senior vice president and chief economist for Key Corp. Marianne Funk, "Utah Leads Nation in Fiscal Health," *Deseret News*, January 8, 1994, A1.

10. These were Advantage Computing (Number 63), a Salt Lake City firm; Enrich International (Number 93), an Orem distributor of herbal products; Teltrust (Number 157), a company in Salt Lake City that provided operator services for public pay telephones; System Connection (Number 379), a Provo company that manufactured computer cable and accessories; Covey Leadership Center (Number 404), a Provo company that provided leadership and development training nationwide. Max Knudson, "Utah on the Go with 5 Firms on Inc. Magazine 500 List," *Deseret News*, October 15, 1994, B1.
11. See "Gigantic Spanish Fork Center Taking Big Steps," *Deseret News*, October 20, 2003, B1.
12. Lisa Riley Roche, "Leavitt Energized by Trade Mission," *Deseret News*, May 29, 1994, B1.
13. For details, see *1994 Economic Report to the Governor* (Salt Lake City: Office of the Govenor,1995), 179–86; "1994 Economic and Travel Industry Profiles for Utah Counties," a report prepared by the Division of Travel Development, Utah Department of Community and Economic Development (July 1995).
14. Jerry Spangler, "Tourism Called Top Threat to Ancient Indian Ruins," *Deseret News*, October 10, 1994, B1.
15. *1995 Economic Report to the Governor* (Salt Lake City: Office of the Governor, 1995), 181.
16. Later reports about the total economic impact of the Olympics were mixed. A 2006 report by the University of Utah's Center for Public Policy and Administration stated that the Olympics provided a significant stimulus to the economy. That stimulus was transitory, though, because most of the economic activity, such as building highways and venues or providing media and security services, concluded after the games were over. See "Economic Impact of the 2002 Olympic Winter Games," Policy Brief: 07-25-2006, available online at http://cppa.utah.edu/_documents/publications/econ-dev/olympics-econ-impact.pdf Accessed November 25, 2014. More optimistically, a decade after the 2000 Olympics Salt Lake City's Chamber of Commerce reported some of the same figures as the 2002 report: an estimated $4.8 billion in sales, thirty-five thousand "job years" of employment, and $1.5 billion in earnings for Utahns in 2002. It also pointed out a yeild of $100 million in community profits, including a $72 million endowment to maintain facilities, $10.2 million for Olympic Legacy Plazas and $11.5 million in charitable donations. Further, said the report, there was a 42 percent increase in skier visits to Utah in the ten years after 2002 and the ski and hotel lodging industries enjoyed record-setting profits. At the same time, he president and chief executive officer of the Salt Lake Organizing Committee pointed out that since the Olympic games several globally recognized winter sports companies had moved their American headquarters to Utah. In addition, the Olympics were at least partly responsible for several area venues that were still in use and were significant sources of revenue for their respective communities. It was also observed that the Olympics helped attract other major sports events to Utah. "Utah Economy Still Benefits from 2002 Winter Olympic Games," Salt Lake City Chamber of Commerce blog, posted February 6, 2012, at http://slchamber.com/blog/utah-economy-still-benefits-from-2002-winter-olympic-games-10002750.htm; Jason Lee,"Economic Impact of 2002 Olympics Still Felt," a 2012 KSL report, available online at http://www.ksl.com/?nid=960&sid=19155597. Both items accessed November 25, 2014.
17. As discussed in chapters 4 and 6, in 1963 Salt Lake City was the United States' candidate for the 1972 Games, but the International Olympic Committee chose Sap-

poro, Japan. Salt Lake City tried again in 1967, for the 1976 games, but the United States chose to nominate Denver. Later, however, Denver dropped out and the US Olympic Committee fell back to Salt Lake City. The IOC choice, however, was Innsbruck, Austria. Salt Lake City again sought the bid in 1985, for the 1992 games, but the USOC first nominated Anchorage Alaska. In 1989 the choice was changed to Salt Lake City, but this time it was beaten out in the final decision by Nagano, Japan.

18. Peg McEntee, "Professors Look at Dark Side of Utah's Economic Boom," *Daily Herald* (Provo, UT), July 10, 1994, A1. The scholars were business professor Alan Hamlin and sociologist Richard H. Ropers from Southern Utah University.
19. Bob Bernick, Jr., "Utahns Split on What to Do with Surplus," *Deseret News*, February 16, 1994, A1.
20. Jerry Spangler, "Tax Cut, Other Laws Signed by Leavitt," *Deseret News*, March 23, 1994, p. B1–B2.
21. Mike Carter, "Leavitt Proposes Budget for 1995," *Daily Herald*, December 20, 1994, A1.
22. Bob Bernick, Jr., "Surprise! Utahns Not Clamoring for Leavitt's $30 Million Tax cut,"*Deseret News*, January 8, 1995, A1.
23. *1994 Economic Report to the Governor* (Salt Lake City: Office of the Governor, 1994), 7, 57–59.
24. Joel Campbell, "Census Study Shows Extremes in Utah Counties," *Deseret News*, September 4, 1994, B1.
25. "Homelessness and Hunger on the Rise in Salt Lake City," *Daily Herald*, December 22, 1993, B3.
26. Lois M. Collins, "Homeless Kids Have Doubled Ranks Since '90," *Deseret News*, February 15, 1994, B1.
27. Peg McEntee, "Survey: Most on Welfare are Single Mothers," *Daily Herald*, December 29, 1993, D3.
28. "Governor Says Utah's SPED Could Be Model," *Daily Herald*, January 30 1995, C3.
29. Lois M. Collins, "Program Helps Participants Find Niche in the Work Force," *Deseret News*, August 25, 1994, A1, A4.
30. "7 Utahns Make *Forbes*' Annual List," *Deseret News*, October 3, 1994, B5.The seven were Jon M. Huntsman, worth $1 billion; James LeVoy Sorenson, $885 million; Leonard Samuel Skaggs, Jr., $630 million; Robert Earl Holding, $600 million; Raymond J. Noorda, $500 million; Alan G. Ashton, $440 million; Bruce W. Bastian, $440 million.
31. Joel Campbell, "Money Men," *Deseret News*, September 4, 1994, B1. One of numerous examples was a $10 million gift from the Jon Huntsman family, in 1993, to help the University of Utah develop a world-class cancer center. The anticipation was that this would act as seed money that would eventually attract up to $100 million in resources for this vital project. One of the most innovative projects was announced early in 1995 by Alan Ashton and his wife, Karen. They planned to develop a 400-acre tree and flower garden and animal park to be named Thanksgiving Point, in Lehi, just off Interstate 15. Although not a public charity or welfare project, the park would be open to the public and provide both educational and aesthetic experiences for Utah schoolchildren as well as adult visitors, and provide a welcome vista for those driving by. In addition, there would be an eighteen-hole golf course also open to the public. The plan was especially significant for many Utah Valley residents who were concerned that the continuing inundation of busi-

ness parks and industrial facilities would erode the landscape. Thanksgiving Point preserved a welcome green space. These families and other affluent Utahns made numerous other kinds of donations to universities, hospitals, the arts, other charitable institutions, and the public welfare. Many, if not most, of these donations were private and unheralded.

32. An interesting summary of several examples of cooperation between Mormons and non-Mormons in providing food and services is found in Matthew S. Brown, "LDS, Non-LDS Linking Arms in Service," *Deseret News*, December 26, 1993, A1.
33. Marianne Funk, "Pro-Lifers Angry over Withdrawal of State's Appeal," *Deseret News*, October 9, 1994, B1.
34. Jerry Spangler and Bob Bernick, Jr., "Leavitt Takes on the Feds," *Deseret News*, May 19, 1994, A1, A3.
35. Same-sex marriage became legal in Hawaii in 2013 and by the end of 2014 it was also legal in Utah.
36. Joel Campbell, "Utah Divorce Rate Staying Constant after Its Big Surge," *Deseret News*, May 23, 1994, A1.
37. Jim Rayburn, "Rate of 2-Parent Families Singles Out Utah County," *Deseret News*, January 10, 1995, A1.
38. Dion M. Harris, "Utah Suicide Rate Nearly 18% Higher Than US Average," *Deseret News*, April 23, 1995, B3.
39. The bill was introduced in the House of Representatives by Jordan Tanner. For his story on the background of the bill and how it was passed, see Jordan Tanner, "Smoking and Health: Showdown on Utah's Capitol Hill," *The Religious Educator* 9:3 (2008), 85–90.
40. Paul Parkinson, "State Control of Gun Laws Urged," *Deseret News*, October 25, 1994, D12.
41. Paul Parkinson, "Panel Frowns on Local Regulation of Arms," *Deseret News*, November 18, 1994, B6.
42. Bob Kuesterman, "Utah Letters," *Deseret News*, January 8, 1995, V1.
43. Jerry Spangler, "Graham Doesn't Want Guns in Abusive Hands," *Deseret News*, December 29, 1994, B5.
44. "Utah Should Not Retreat on Tough Local Gun Laws," *Deseret News*, February 2, 1995, A26.
45. Jerry Spangler, "Lack of New Gun Curbs Makes Many Conservatives Blush," *Deseret News*, March 2, 1995, A20.
46. "States Trying to Ease Rules on Weapons," *Deseret News*, March 11, 1995, A8.
47. "More Evidence That Utah Passed a Bad Weapons Law," *Deseret News*, November 11, 1995, A10.
48. Brent Israelsen, "Bureaucrats, Others Will Try Cooperation," *Deseret News*, January 22, 1994, B1–B2; "New Group Wants to Save Canyons," *Salt Lake Tribune*, January 25, 1994, B8.
49. See "Canyon Country Partnership," online at http://www.snre.umich.edu/ecomgt/cases/pubs/em_96/Canyon%20Country%20Partnership%20%28EM%2096%29.pdf. Accessed November 25, 2014.
50. Brent Israelsen, "Utahns Give Little Support to Wilds Bill," *Deseret News*, June 10, 1995, B1.

51. Brent Israelsen and Brooke Adams, "Toxic Haze,"*Deseret News*, "Extra" on pollution, January 27, 1994, A17.
52. For a detailed analysis of Utah's transportation needs in 1993, see "Highway Spending Needs in Utah," Utah Foundation *Research Report* Number 560 (June 1993).
53. "Keep the Light-Rail Option Open on Wasatch Front," *Deseret News*, September 24, 1993, A10.
54. Joel Campbell, "Lack of Laws Puts Brakes on Federal Highway Funds," *Deseret News*, May 4, 1994, A1.
55. "$5 Million OK'd for Light Rail," *Deseret News*, October 10, 1988, B1.
56. "Leavitt Defends Utah's Gambling Stance," *Daily Herald*, April 12, 1994, B3.
57. See Carrie Moore, "Religious Freedoms Facing Challenge From Bureaucracy," *Deseret News*, October 29, 1994, B1.
58. Lee Davidson, "US Schools Are Urged to Copy Utah Projects," *Deseret News*, April 24, 1995, B3, citing a US Department of Education publication, *Success Stories '94: A Guide to Safe, Disciplined and Drug-Free Schools*.
59. "Report: Education Strategic Plan in Trouble," *Daily Herald*, December 15, 1993, B3.
60. Twila Van Leer, "Climbing Together," *Deseret News*, January 30, 1994, B1.
61. "Sterling Scholar Awards," *Deseret News*, special section, March 22, 1994, S1–S8.
62. Doug Willis, "West's Turf War: Leavitt Sounds Battle Cry, Urges 'United' States to Take on Tyrants in D.C.," *Salt Lake Tribune*, June 15, 1994, A1.
63. "Leavitt Softens Land Stance," *Daily Herald*, May 22, 1994, A6.
64. Jerry Spangler, "Will Special Interests Debase Leavitt's States' Rights Debate?" *Deseret News*, June 12, 1994, A1.
65. Marianne Means, "Setback for Conference Shows Wild-Eyed Zealots Have Clout," *Deseret News*, May 24, 1995, A12. See also Dirk Johnson (*New York Times* News Service), "States of Paranoia," *Deseret News*, May 16, 1995, V1. Other reports on the proposed conference of the states appear regularly in the *Deseret News* and *Salt Lake Tribune* in 1994 and 1995.
66. Jeff Vice, "Pages and Pages of 'Faces of Utah,'"*Deseret News*, May 30, 1995, B1.
67. Bob Bernick Jr., "Leavitt Urges Utahns to Meet 6 Challenges," *Deseret News*, July 22, 1994, B1.
68. Michael O. Leavitt, "Living in Utah Builds Sweet Memories," *Deseret News*, January 5, 1995, A25.

Appendix A

Utah's Ethnic Minorities and the Quest for a Pluralistic Society

Early twentieth century Americans, especially Anglo-Americans, often referred to their nation as a great "melting pot," evoking images of many races and ethnic groups becoming assimilated into a unified, almost indistinct mélange. Actually, this never happened, and some Americans wanted to make sure it didn't. Any suggestion of racial assimilation was anathema to many so-called WASPS (White-Anglo-Saxon-Protestants), whose racial biases, often couched in flag-waving rationalization, led to calls for heavy restrictions on immigration and discriminatory laws against African Americans, Native Americans, Asians, and Jews.

Such racist attitudes had mellowed dramatically by the late twentieth century. The nation had outlawed discrimination in the marketplace, in schools, in housing, and in public accommodations in general. What's more, most Americans had put behind them the outmoded "melting pot" idea, replacing it with what might be called the "salad bowl" metaphor. This suggested a genuine unity that came from citizenship, pride in the nation, and devotion to such "American" ideals as personal freedom, equality before the law, and other Constitutional principles, but it also suggested appreciation for the wide cultural diversity that made up the national population, with no need to erase differences. This ideal was not universally shared, and problems related to racial bias and inequality were not completely solved, but Utah and the nation were much closer to becoming a genuinely pluralistic society.

Defining the ideal, let alone achieving it, however, was complex. Each ethnic group developed its own organization for the purpose of preserving its culture, helping its people achieve, and obtaining better access to government services. These diverse groups also worked together on state and local government councils concerned with all minorities. But some people, including members of minority groups, warned that such efforts had the potential of going too far, so that, instead of unifying minorities and the larger society, they could lead to even greater fragmentation.[1]

In 1990, Utah's ethnic minorities made up 8.8 percent of the total state population. By far the largest portion, 56 percent, were Hispanic, followed by Asians or Pacific Islanders (21 percent), Native Americans, including Eskimo and Aleut (15 percent), African Americans (7 percent), and those classified as "others" (1 percent). Except for Native Americans, most of these minorities lived in Salt Lake, Utah, Davis, Weber, or Cache counties. Many Native Americans resided along the Wasatch Front, but approximately 65 percent were located in either San Juan, Uintah, or Wasatch counties.[2]

Although small in numbers, minorities played a vital role in Utah's life and culture. They were important parts of the workforce at every level; their folk culture, as represented in the arts and in various ethnic and multi-cultural festivals, richly enhanced the cultural awareness of other citizens; and their presence sometimes challenged the racial biases of the majority, resulting in a healthy undermining of prejudice. But the fact that they were spread so thinly through the population contributed to a lack of familiarity that tended to slow down the process of acceptance.

Equality of Opportunity: The Continuing Quest

In the nation at large important steps were taken in the latter part of the twentieth century toward the goals of racial equality before the law and a society without prejudice. The activities of various civil rights groups, for example, contributed to a growing public awareness of the evils of discrimination. In 1954 an activist Supreme Court outlawed segregation in the public schools (*Brown v. Board of Education*). Three years later Congress enacted the first civil rights law since Reconstruction, resulting in better federal protection for African Americans in their efforts to vote. Ten years later, partly as an outgrowth of "sit ins," bus boycotts, and other peaceful protests against segregation (often resulting in violence), Congress passed the Civil Rights Act of 1964, the most far-reaching civil rights bill in American history. None of these actions solved all the problems, but they at least helped move the United states toward a more positive tone in race relations.

In Utah, efforts to achieve greater equality before the law were renewed shortly after World War II but these efforts were, at first, largely unsuccessful. African Americans, especially, were the objects of open discrimination, often required to sit in theater balconies, unable to register in many hotels, and segregated in restaurants. Some observers believed that The Church of Jesus Christ of Latter-day Saints' policy of denying the priesthood to blacks exacerbated the situation.[3]

One indication of the biases extant in Utah was seen in the underwhelming response to a 1945 questionnaire sent by a legislative committee to a thousand hotels, restaurants, theaters, dance halls, swimming pools, and other facilities. Only 150 replies were returned, suggesting a lack of interest in the problem, but of these, twenty-seven out of one hundred reported that they did not serve blacks, twelve did not serve Native Americans, and some refused service to Asians, Filipinos, and Hispanics.[4] Two years later, the state senate killed two bills that would have ended racial discrimination in public places.

By the 1950s, public swimming pools and clubs were legally open to all minorities, but discrimination persisted in some private clubs and organizations.[5] A 1953 state law prohibited segregation in restaurants, but some establishments were slow to implement the requirement. In 1956, a surprising 47.6 percent of Utah restaurants responding to a *Host Magazine* survey reported that they would not serve blacks, while only 19.6 percent indicated that they served all races. However, 80.4 percent said they would serve all racial groups if such a policy were the practice of the community, suggesting the potential impact of public pressure. There were similar discriminatory practices in employment and housing.[6]

A pioneer in ending discrimination in places open to the public was the Lagoon amusement park. In the late 1940s the park was taken over by Robert E. Freed and Ranch Kimball, who opened it to black patrons. Later the two businessmen did the same thing at Rainbow Rendezvous, a popular dance hall in Salt Lake City. In 1975 the National Association for the Advancement of Colored People (NAACP) posthumously honored Freed for his contribution to advancing civil rights in the state.[7]

Several attempts in the 1960s to enact more stringent civil rights legislation met with little success. But beginning in 1965, after passage of the federal Civil Rights Act of 1964, the Rampton administration pursued the matter more vigorously. Others in Utah caught the spirit, and by the late 1960s it was no longer common for African Americans to be excluded from hotels and other public accommodations. An exception was housing. A 1968 study revealed that delaying tactics, selective showing of real estate, and other questionable practices effectively prevented blacks in Salt Lake City from moving into traditionally white neighborhoods. The real estate industry, the study concluded, simply did not police itself well enough.[8]

Some Utahns were particularly demeaned when, as partners in mixed-racial marriages, they found themselves in violation of Utah's anti-miscegenation law. This outmoded statute was finally repealed in 1963, and two years later another bill automatically validated all previously performed marriages. This not only helped alleviate the stigma sometimes attached to interracial marriages, but it also had a special meaning for hundreds of Japanese "war brides" who had immigrated to Utah to live with their husbands.[9]

In 1972, concerned over lack of minority representation at the state level in efforts to improve conditions for all ethnic groups, Governor Calvin L. Rampton began to hire ombudsmen from among the minorities.[10] By the mid-1980s a number of state offices existed specifically to work with minority groups in obtaining community and social services. These included the Division of Indian Affairs, the Office of Asian Affairs, the Office of Black Affairs, and the Office of Hispanic Affairs. The Office of Community Services also supported minorities, as did private, community, and educational organizations.

Unfortunately, pockets of overt racism still remained in Utah. In the 1970s, for example, the Ku Klux Klan stepped up its activities, exemplified by a cross-burning and a series of mock hangings staged in the Riverton area in 1979. The Klan's membership was only slightly more than one hundred people but evidence suggests that its mere presence encouraged other kinds of racial intimidation.[11] As late as the 1990s, racist, white separatist flyers were distributed by extremists in some parts of the state.[12]

Meanwhile, leaders of the LDS Church spoke out strongly against racial prejudice and discrimination, making it clear that the policy regarding priesthood should not be interpreted in any way to justify opposition to anti-discrimination laws.[13] As far as the Mormons were concerned, the 1978 announcement that President Spencer W. Kimball had received a revelation granting the priesthood to males of all races finally removed any hint of theological opposition to integration.

In the mid-1970s the public schools increased efforts to encourage teachers' sensitivity to the cultures of ethnic minorities, to provide multicultural materials for classrooms, and to recruit educators from among the minorities.[14] Nevertheless, by 1993 the school dropout rate among minorities was still higher than for other students, and their general educational attainment remained lower. Reasons for these statistics included the persistence of teaching styles geared to the white majority, the fact that some minority families (i.e., migrant workers) moved frequently, and the fact that low-income parents with less education usually spent less time than their middle-class counterparts talking to their children about their school work.[15] By the 1990s, however, the lot of most minorities had improved substantially, and the worst evidences of racism were receding.[16]

Utah's minorities were as different from each other as they were from the Anglo majority. Each had unique characteristics and traditions. The following is a discussion of each major ethnic group, intended to reveal its unique problems and challenges, as well as its distinctive contributions to the cultural tapestry of the state.

Native Americans[17]

The relationship of Native American tribes to the state was much different from that of other minorities. They were still recognized under federal law as sovereign entities, their reservations were outside the jurisdiction of the state, and their treaty rights were still valid. The Native American population in Utah jumped from about 4,200 in 1950 to nearly 24,300 people in 1990. Perhaps half of them lived off reservations, mostly in urban areas along the Wasatch Front.

Utah's Native Americans were directly affected by changing federal policies.[18] The Dawes Act of 1887 attempted to end the reservation system by breaking up the reservations into individual farms—making farmers of the Indians and thereby "assimilating" them into white society—and then selling off the remaining land. The policy was a failure, but by 1930 the Indians had lost more than 80 percent of their land. The Indian Reorganization Act of 1934 ended this misguided effort at assimilation. Instead, this new act was an attempt to promote self-determination by encouraging the tribes to elect tribal governments and to begin their own economic planning. Most Utah tribes did so, but they had difficulty working with private and government agencies that promoted economic mechanisms they were not used to. In 1948 the Bureau of Indian Affairs (BIA) began to offer job placement services that would allow Indians to move their families off reservations. Many Utah Navajos, especially, accepted the opportunity, but many of these found themselves culturally alienated and some finally returned to the reservations.

For many Native Americans, the most damaging step backward since the Dawes Act came with the "termination" policy, begun in the 1940s. The policy was more fully implemented in 1953 when Utah's Senator Arthur V. Watkins, chairman of the Senate Indian Affairs Subcommittee, successfully urged passage of a resolution that called for "terminating" all federal responsibility toward Indians.[19] In effect, this and the implementation of later legislation was a renewal of the failed assimilation policy and was promulgated in the belief that Indians would be better off if they were fully integrated into the larger society. The policy was a disaster and, after several tribes lost their land and status, it was gradually abandoned and officially repudiated by President Richard Nixon in 1969.

Implementation of the termination policy in Utah began with several small tribes. Most lost control of nearly all of their land, although some of it was regained after the policy was abandoned. After that, the government moved back toward a more acceptable policy of self-determination. It also began to provide assistance through agencies such as the Public Health Service and the Office of Economic Employment. In addition, Utah created an advisory body known as the State Board of Indian Affairs as well as a Division of Indian Affairs within the Department of Social Services.

One of the positive factors in promoting self-determination was the federal policy of awarding compensation to Native American tribes for losses sustained through violations of nineteenth-century treaty agreements. Some tribes were represented by the Washington law firm of Wilkinson, Cragun, and Barker, headed by BYU president Ernest L. Wilkinson. In 1962 the comprehensive claims of the Utes resulted in a $47.7 million settlement, $30.5 million of which went to Utah's Northern Ute tribe. In the 1970s, the Southern Paiutes and the Goshutes were each awarded more than seven million dollars.

Under the self-determination policy, many tribes were successful in developing mineral and water resources on reservation lands as well as promoting tourism, recreation, and industry, all of which provided employment opportunities. In addition, Indians living off the reservations were allowed to become active members of tribal councils.

As history professor Richard Ulibarri noted in 1978, Utah's Indians were "caught between cultures."[20] It was impossible to maintain all the old ways, but they tried valiantly to preserve some of them even as they tried to accommodate to the predominant society. On the Navajo reservation, for example, one could observe both Native American dress and white fashions. Nava-

Image A.1: Navajo family on the reservation in Monument Valley, 1960's. Used by permission, Utah State Historical Society, all rights reserved.

jos maintained ancient tribal religious practices while belonging to various Christian denominations, and while medicine men were consulted when they were ill the Navajos also went to nearby American medical facilities. In public schools Indian children were sometimes shortchanged when little attention was paid to cultural differences, but by the 1990s this situation had changed substantially.

One example of the knotty problems involved in dealing with cultural differences concerned the use of peyote, a powerful hallucinogenic drug, by members of the Native American Church as a sacrament in their most sacred ceremonies. Many states outlawed the use of peyote, and in 1990 the US Supreme Court upheld Oregon's ban. Nevertheless, federal regulation had actually protected the ceremonial use of peyote since 1965, and twenty-eight states had passed laws similar to or in conformance with that regulation. There was still lack of uniformity, however. In 1994, therefore, Congress stepped in with Public Law 103–344, which provided that the use of peyote in connection with the practice of a traditional Indian religion could not be prohibited by the United States or by any state. The federal government could adopt reasonable regulations relating to the harvesting and distribution of the drug, however, and states could enforce reasonable traffic safety regulations (i.e., prohibiting anyone under the influence of peyote to drive).[21] This sensible solution fully protected Indian religious freedom but also protected the larger society's right to prohibit the use of peyote in other circumstances.

Among the numerous efforts of whites to educate Native Americans were programs that took children from their natural homes and placing them in boarding schools, foster homes, or adoptive homes. Motives were mixed: some people wanted merely to help Indian children gain enough education to do what was best for themselves. Others wanted to "Americanize" them, even hoping to erase their cultural heritage. After BIA boarding schools were begun in the nineteenth century, some Indian agents even removed children forcibly from their homes. Moreover, treatment received at the schools was often unusually harsh.[22] Boarding schools improved in the twentieth century and some, such as the Intermountain Indian School in Brigham City, became model educational facilities. In 1979 approximately forty-four thousand students were enrolled in BIA boarding, day, and dormitory schools around the country.

The Intermountain Indian School (later identified simply as the Intermountain School) was founded in 1949 when, at the urging of Senator Arthur V. Watkins, the US Army gave the abandoned facilities of Bushnell General Hospital in Brigham City to the Bureau of Indian Affairs. Its purpose was to help the eighteen thousand Navajo children who were not in school. The first group of 542 students arrived in January 1950. Enrollment grew to 2,150 students annually, including many from Utah. Eventually it became an intertribal school for high school students, offering a wide variety of academic and vocational programs and providing students an opportunity to participate in such activities as student government, publications, and athletics. Its placement office helped those who wanted work to obtain weekend jobs in and around Brigham City. The school closed in 1984.

BIA boarding schools were often criticized for not paying enough attention to building appreciation in children for their native heritage. The same criticism was levied, even more strongly, at the foster home and adoption program. As late as 1974 an estimated 25–35 percent of all Indian children were in foster homes or other institutions, most of which had the reputation of doing little or nothing to preserve Native American pride or culture.[23] Although many foster parents conscientiously tried to help students appreciate their Indian heritage, cultural abuse was widespread enough to justify serious concerns on the part of Indian families.[24]

Criticism of these programs finally gave rise to the Indian Child Welfare Act of 1978. That year one hundred thousand children in various placement programs were living in homes other than their own.[25] The new law gave the tribes, rather than the federal government or the states, complete jurisdiction in child custody cases. It also required that children be placed in foster homes only with the consent of their parents.[26]

The most prominent placement program in Utah was the LDS Indian Student Placement Program.[27] It began with a young Navajo, Helen John. In 1948, Helen and her family, along with other members of the tribe, were hiring out to sugar beet farmers near Richfield. Helen wanted to remain in Richfield and go to school, but there seemed to be no way for this to happen. Then Golden Buchanan, who had been appointed by local LDS Church leaders to work with the Indian people, heard about Helen's desire and felt compelled to do something about it. There must be a way, he thought, to get a family to take her in so she could go to school. He wrote to Spencer W. Kimball, a member of the LDS Quorum of the Twelve Apostles and chairman of the church's Committee on Indian Relationships. Sensing the possibilities, Kimball made a special trip to Richfield, called on the Buchanans, and asked them to take Helen into their home, not as a guest but as if she were a member of the family, and give her an opportunity to attend high school. The Buchanans agreed and also arranged for a few other children to be taken into other homes.

By the 1953–54 school year there were sixty-eight students involved in the still-experimental program. The results were rewarding enough that in July 1954 it became an official church

Image A.2: Students at Intermountain Indian School, Brigham City. Used by permission, Utah State Historical Society, all rights reserved.

program but with some firm guidelines. Mormon families were not to be pressured into taking Indian children. They were also to understand that no child was to be considered "a mere guest," nor a servant, but "he or she would be expected to assume such responsibilities of service as all children ought to have and share." The host families must be willing to assume all financial responsibilities because most Indian families had no means to provide what was needed.[28] Also, participating students must be members of the LDS Church. At first the program was directed by the Social Service Department of the church's Relief Society, a licensed agency for placing children, but after 1969 it came under the umbrella of LDS Social Services.

As the program expanded, children in all grades were admitted. The majority were Navajo, but by the end of the 1960s children from at least sixty-three tribes in the United States and Canada had participated.[29] The program also expanded into other states and at its peak in 1970 and 1971 it served approximately five thousand students. After that the numbers declined, and, by the early 1990s, the program served only about 350 to four hundred students, most of them outside Utah.

Contributing to the decline was the greater accessibility of educational opportunities for younger children on reservations or near their homes. Also, in 1992, the state of Utah began to enforce its rule requiring out-of-state students to pay out-of-state tuition, amounting to about $2,500, depending upon which school district was involved.[30] This made it prohibitive for students from reservations outside the state to come to Utah.

Indian Placement inevitably faced a number of problems. Native American families were torn by mixed emotions as their children left home and as it seemed that some of them might forget their tribal traditions. The intercultural social challenges were overwhelming for some students and foster families alike, and some were unable to adapt. A few foster families gave up in just a few months, others after the first year. Nevertheless, the program achieved many of its educational goals and did much to help break down racial prejudice. By 1967, more than half the graduates of the program had received post-high-school training. Many foster families enjoyed the experience, had a positive impact on their foster children, and were pleased to take more. They also learned much about cultural differences and became more tolerant.

Numerous systematic evaluations of the placement program were conducted.[31] In one thorough survey, a team of BYU sociologists found that 34 percent of participating students remained in the program until they graduated from high school.[32] They also concluded that the program had reasonable success in encouraging post-high school training. Among former participants who were age twenty-five or older, 52 percent had obtained at least one year of college, as opposed to 21 percent of the control group. On the question of ethnic identity, the investigators found that participants were more likely than others to consider themselves "partly white," while nonparticipants were more than twice as likely to consider themselves "totally" Indian. Some participants felt that they were "reasonably competent" in both worlds, but that they belonged fully to neither. Nevertheless, two-thirds believed that their experience actually made them feel closer to their Indian heritage than they would have been without it.

Despite tribal economic activities, improved educational attainments, and all the efforts of the BIA, at the end of the 1980s poverty remained a fact of life for most Native Americans living on reservations, including those in Utah, and they remained the poorest of any US minority group. But tribal leaders were optimistic that further natural resource development, various other business ventures, and tourism on and around reservations would speed up economic improvement.[33]

For those Indians who sought post-high-school training, Utah's colleges and universities offered an impressive array of special programs and assistance. These included scholarships and grants as well as courses geared especially to the needs and special interests of Native Americans. Some schools also offered a variety of off-campus programs to help with economic and social development.[34]

As elsewhere, however, Native Americans on Utah's reservations still lived under an often confusing and conflicting web of federal and state regulations. At issue was the question of tribal sovereignty, which became more pressing after the Indian Civil Rights Act of 1968 shifted government policy from one of federal domination to the principle of Indian self-determination. It was not always clear just who had legal jurisdiction. In some states, such as Idaho, Native American tribes had little trouble instituting gambling on reservations as a means of fund-raising. In Utah, the Skull Valley Goshutes considered doing the same thing, even though gambling was against state law. The question was whether Indian sovereignty was complete enough on the reservations that tribal governments could institute practices not condoned by the people of the state or allowable under state law. For the foreseeable future Utah law prevailed.

There was also the confusing question of what activities on tribal lands were subject to both federal and tribal law, and where the dividing line lay. Whether someone who committed a crime on the reservation should be prosecuted in a federal or a tribal court depended on the severity of the felony. There was also confusion about whether tribal law or federal law took precedence when it came to environmental issues on tribal lands. But what seemed to be the most bureaucratically confusing relationship between the tribes and federal and state governments were the rules relating to oil and gas development on tribal lands. The BIA worked with the tribe in selling leases to developers; the tribe issued permits for drilling, but only after the BLM reviewed all applications and authorized the permit; royalties were collected by the Mineral Management Service (an agency within the Department of the Interior), which funneled the funds to the tribe via the BIA; and, finally, severance taxes were paid by the drilling companies to both the tribe and the state of Utah.[35]

Another question was how much land the tribes were entitled to control. In 1986 the tenth circuit court stunned the white citizens of Duchesne and Uintah Counties by ruling that executive orders issued in 1861 and 1862 had created permanent reservation boundaries, within which the Utes could exercise jurisdiction. If this ruling held, much of the property owned and controlled by whites would come under the jurisdiction of the tribes. However, in 1987 the ruling was tested after Ute tribal member Robert Hagen was arrested in Myton for illegally selling marijuana. Hagen argued in state court that the state had no jurisdiction in this because Myton was within the historic boundaries of the reservation. In 1992 the Utah Supreme Court ruled against Hagen, saying that the state had jurisdiction because in 1902 and 1905 Congress had reduced the size of the original reservation, and the town of Myton was no longer under tribal jurisdiction. The matter came before the US Supreme Court and its decision, on February 23, 1994, upheld the state ruling.[36]

Another sticky legal question concerned voting rights. Until 1940 Utah law prohibited Indians living on reservations from voting. An opinion issued by the state attorney general that year changed the policy, but it was reversed again in 1956 by another attorney general opinion, which held that Indians must reside off the reservations in order to establish eligibility for voting. This policy was upheld by the Utah Supreme Court after a resident of the Uintah-Ouray reservation was stopped from voting in the 1956 election in Duchesne County. But the following year Utah repealed the original law so that reservation Indians could vote in both state and federal elections.[37]

In addition to becoming heavily involved in business ventures, Native Americans also became more deeply involved in political affairs. While it was unheard of before World War II for Indians to serve on school boards, county commissions, or in the state legislature, fifty years after the war it was not uncommon. In addition, instead of working strictly through the Bureau of Indian Affairs, tribal councils worked directly with national and local governments. "All in all," wrote Clyde J. Benally, a Navajo educator and historian, in 1976, "the Navajo, a great learner, has mastered the white man's politics."[38] Although Utah Navajos profited from the work of the tribal council, they also, at times, felt overlooked and out of touch because they were so far away from the seat of tribal government in Window Rock, Arizona. State and county governments also seemed out of reach, but an upsurge of political activism, including massive voter registration on the reservation, changed that situation. By the 1990s the Navajos, who constituted about half of San Juan County's population, played a significant role in county politics, mainly through the Democratic party.

But mastering the white man's politics and adopting the white man's economic measures did not mean that most Native Americans were disposed to adopt his culture. Those who remained on the reservations, especially, tried steadfastly to preserve their historic religions and tribal customs. The Navajo reservation, for example, was dotted with traditional hogans, built according to religious dictates.[39] Chants and complex rituals, based on a rich tradition of history, myth, and folk tale, all related to the Navajo ideal "to live in sacred harmony, in beauty, and in blessedness."[40] Tribal medicine men spent years as apprentices under older medicine men, memorizing ceremonies and finally being ceremonially ordained for each one they could perform. In addition to the words and actions of the ceremonies themselves, medicine men were also required to identify all the herbs and plants needed for particular rituals. So strong were traditional ways of life, in fact, that two sociologists who had studied the Navajo Mountain community (on the Utah-Arizona border) wrote in 1970 that "persistence in Navajo Mountain is perhaps even more striking than change when we consider that this small traditional community is surrounded by the most highly industrialized country in the world."[41]

Navajos constituted the largest Native American tribe in Utah and made up approximately 45 percent of the state's total Indian population.[42] Many lived in the cities, particularly in Salt Lake City, but most lived on the reservation in San Juan County. Urban dwellers were generally not as well off as their Caucasian counterparts, but, when compared with the middle class American standard of living, the Navajos in San Juan County were especially deprived. In 1970, some 80 percent lived at or below the federally-defined poverty level, compared with 40 percent for all Utah Indians; the incidence of tuberculosis was fifty times the state average; death rates from pneumonia were four times higher than the state; and there were distressingly low rates of education and employment.[43]

The next two decades showed considerable improvement as more young people went to school and the continued development of oil and mineral resources improved the tribe's economic well-being. School curricula were enriched with cultural material designed to educate young Navajos as well as non-Indian students with respect to Indian traditions. Many young people graduated from high school and went on to attend the College of Eastern Utah. In fact, some 60 to 70 percent of the students at the Blanding campus were Indians. Nevertheless, San Juan County Commissioner Mark Maryboy, who was also education director for the Utah Navajo Development Council, complained in 1989 that even with their education young Navajos in the county were not able to find meaningful employment at the same rate as the white majority.[44]

The Navajo reservation was located mostly in Arizona and New Mexico, but Utah's Navajos were directly affected by the decisions, both federal and tribal, that affected the entire reservation. Originally one of their chief means of livelihood was raising sheep, but as both the human and sheep population increased the grasslands were practically destroyed. In 1935 the federal government decided to do something about the erosion by calling for massive stock reduction. For many Navajo families this was a disaster—their sheep were their total means of livelihood. The 1947 drought only added to the problems.

Navajo leaders, meanwhile, recognizing that the old pastoral economy could never survive, were determined to develop other resources. They asked for help from Secretary of the Interior J. A. Krug, who launched a major investigation. The report, issued in March 1948, revealed some startling conditions. Within the twenty-five thousand square miles that constituted the entire reservation, fewer than eight hundred residents had jobs while 7,841 were on welfare. In addition, there were only ninety-five miles of paved roads, three restaurants, 763 telephones, 466 hospital beds, and school facilities were minimal.[45] Within two months after the Krug report, a million-dollar emergency relief appropriation from Congress allowed the Navajos and the Hopis to begin work on road construction, soil conservation, irrigation, schools, and hospitals. The result was immediate financial relief for more than thirteen thousand Navajos who received at least temporary employment that year. In 1950 Congress passed a long-range Navajo and Hopi economic development program that authorized ninety million dollars more than a ten-year period for agricultural improvement as well as natural resource and industrial development. The resulting development of oil and gas, mineral, and lumber resources helped increase the wealth of the tribe as a corporate body. In 1970 the tribe was further enriched when the Indian Claims Commission ruled that it was entitled to compensation for over twelve million acres of land that had been taken from the original reservation outlined in the 1868 treaty. The funds were administered by the tribal council for whatever economic and social enterprises would benefit the Navajos as a whole.

In 1971 a private, nonprofit corporation, the Utah Navajo Development Council, was formed to direct available resources into such things as housing services, education, health, and natural resource development in the Utah part of the Navajo reservation (1.3 million acres). Funding came, in part, from various contracts with state, county, tribal, and federal agencies, and from the Utah Division of Indian Affairs, which administered more than a third of the royalties from the portion of the Aneth Oil fields that were on the reservation.

Educational opportunities for Navajos also improved. In the 1970s and 1980s two new high schools were erected, one in Montezuma Creek and the other in Monument Valley. This helped reduce dependence on boarding schools and, for those who stayed at home, eliminated the need for daily bussing to the northern end of San Juan County, a round trip that, in extreme cases, took eight hours a day.

It is a myth, however, that the Navajos became rich and comfortable. The money did not go directly to any family, and it took tremendous amounts even to bring about a modicum of improvement in general living standards and in education. In addition, the mineral wealth so carefully fostered by the tribal government was not renewable. By 1974 the per capita income among the Navajo was still only $1,000 annually, or about one-third the national average, and a third of the tribe was still unable to use English in a functional way.[46] In Utah in 1990, 75 percent of the Navajos on the reservation still did not have drinking water or electricity in their homes, 95 percent could not read, and unemployment rates were nearly triple those of the rest of the state.[47] They also suffered, comparatively, with poor nutrition and poor health. In addition, many whites did not yet understand the importance of allowing the Navajos, or any Native Americans, to retain their culture, and boarding schools and foster homes often still seemed to operate with the intent of eradicating that culture. The Navajos were still caught between two worlds.

The Uintah Reservation was created in 1861, but it took many years to persuade the Utes to settle there. In the early 1880s it was combined with the adjoining Ouray Reservation, but in 1905 the combined reservation was drastically reduced in size. The Uintah-Ouray Reservation, located in Duchesne, Uintah, and Grand counties, became the headquarters of the Northern Ute Tribe which, by the 1990s numbered about three thousand members. The Utes survived economically through working or leasing their land, working as laborers for whites, or through distributions from tribal funds. By the 1970s the tribe benefitted greatly from increased oil and gas development, which provided jobs as well as severance taxes, and from money received by allowing water to be diverted to the Central Utah Project.[48]

One of the internal problems confronting the Utes was the resentment many full-blooded tribesmen felt at sharing tribal money with mixed bloods (those with 50 percent or less Ute blood). The latter seemed to have more entré into white society, became better educated, and often broke completely with Ute family members. Those mixed bloods who remained active in tribal politics tended to dominate, contributing to a growing tension between the two groups. The rift came to a head in 1954, during the debates over termination policy, when BIA officials encouraged the expulsion of mixed bloods from the tribe. They considered this a first step in the termination of all the Utes. Mixed bloods accepted both termination and expulsion and formed an organization known as the Affiliated Ute Citizens. They took with them a claim to 27 percent of everything lager awarded to the Utes.

Another internal struggle came shortly after termination ended when a group calling itself the "True Utes" urged the disbanding of the tribe's Business Committee and the distribution of BIA-administered tribal funds to individual members rather than to projects that the committee determined were in the interest of the tribe as a whole. The True Utes were also concerned with revitalizing traditional teachings and ethics and wanted ultimately to disband not only the Business Committee but also tribal government itself. When True Utes actually assaulted the tribal offices at Fort Duchesne in June 1960, tribal police were forced to use tear gas and guns to disband and arrest them.[49]

Even though the federal government abandoned its ill-conceived termination policy in 1958, many people, including a small minority of Native Americans, continued to oppose government programs, particularly the Bureau of Indian Affairs. The BIA, they believed, was such a heavily layered bureaucracy that the cost of running it far exceeded the good it did. The issue came up again in 1981 when Utah's Representative James V. Hansen and other members of a Republican research committee examined the finances of thirteen Indian tribes, including the Utes. Hansen, claiming to be a friend of the Indians, believed they would be better off if the BIA were eliminated and the money distributed directly to individuals. An ill-worded letter to the Secretary of the Interior, however, seemed to represent all the insensitivity that Native Americans had been subject to for generations. Using the Utes as examples, Hansen described broken-down houses, beat-up pickup trucks, and yards stacked with junk. Living in squalor, he said, the Indians "have no incentive for betterment, and their personal habits have declined at a rapid rate." The Utes were the worst example of the effects of the welfare state, he complained, "more interested in shooting two deer a year than they are in their grazing, water and mineral rights."[50]

Hansen was really attacking the American welfare system rather than the Indians, but the letter left so many misleading impressions and was so fraught with possible consequences that it brought down the ire not only of Utes but also of Native Americans throughout the country. Some pointed out that instead of being better off after they accepted the termination policy of the 1950s, just the opposite had happened as families broke apart and a variety of social and economic problems ensued. Others responded by observing that Hansen had probably never visited the reservation. In contrast to the inaccurate picture he painted, they said, a trip into the Uintah-Ouray reservation would reveal a progressive community with new homes and cars and more buildings under construction. Further inside the reservation there was a mixture of the old and the new, including dilapidated buildings, but such scenes could be found also in many non-Indian communities. In addition, even though the BIA offered technical assistance, the tribe managed its own business activities, including cattle enterprises, a water system, agricultural activities, and energy and mineral resources. The Utes also had their own geologist, managed their own wildlife, and produced high-quality forest rangers. The tribe also contributed more than $10 million a year to the city of Roosevelt through its trade and business activities, and it employed many non-Indians. Admittedly, 45 percent of the members of the tribe were unemployed (partly because many whites still refused to employ Native Americans), but none were on welfare because dividends from natural resources made them ineligible.

One of the most sensitive issues was cultural. In response to the tribal view that the Utes constituted a "state within a state," Hansen argued that they must realize that they were part of the broader culture, too. "They don't go to medicine men," he said.

"They go to *our* doctors—and they have their own doctors." An understandably perturbed Ute medicine man correctly observed that Hansen, like so many other people, simply did not grasp the importance contemporary Indians attached to maintaining ties with tradition.

Such debates reflected the continuing challenge that complicated the relationship of most ethnic minorities to the larger economic and cultural setting—the problem of how to maintain pride in one's ethnic heritage, including the perpetuation of its traditions and beliefs, and still operate in the context of a different kind of society. However, many reservation Utes seemed successful in their efforts to combine the old and the new in their ways of life. A 1983 feature article in the *Deseret News* Magazine described what was happening in this land of contrasts.[51] Larry Cesspooch, for example, was the audio-visual director of the tribe's media studio and editor of its monthly newspaper, *The Ute Bulletin*. He lived comfortably in a modern home on the reservation, but he also wore braided hair in the tradition of the Plains Indians, had a sweat lodge in his backyard, and regularly participated in the strenuous annual Sun Dance, a high point in the religious tradition of many tribes. In addition, while many Utes lived in small towns or in the reservation hinterlands, maintaining their own culture, they also catered to tourism and operated a lakeside resort at Bottle Hollow.

The two worlds of the Utes were elegantly described in 1990 by Luke Duncan, chairman of the Northern Ute Tribe:

> I don't have time to just sit here and daydream. Always something going, always something moving. One day we're over in Salt Lake City negotiating for water and the next day I'm over here talking to the children. . . . I don't see anything more important than the other. They are all important, they're big business. . . .
>
> . . . . [With reference to disappearing culture,] The drum is the heartbeat of the tribe and as long as we have the drumbeat on the reservations and young boys singing, which we're seeing on our reservation now. Once you let the drum die on your reservation, the tribe is going to die.

.... Our young men at the pow-wows are singing and dancing and that's a step forward and that's just within the last fifteen and twenty years. You go to our pow-wow here, there's many dancers. I was proud to see so many of our kids dancing in competition and to hear their last names and to see they are part of us. Hey, that makes a guy feel good.[52]

A handful of other, very small, tribes also made their homes in Utah. At the beginning of the century, for example, there was a small Southern Paiute reservation at Shivwits, near St. George. Twenty-four families consisting of nearly one hundred people still lived there in 1950. Even smaller reservations, inhabited by fewer than fifty people, were established at Indian Peaks (1915), Koosharem (1928), and Kanosh (1929), while the Paiutes near Cedar City lived on land owned by the LDS Church.

In the 1940s, the group at Shivwits attempted to eke out a living by farming, but after going heavily into debt they finally leased their land to white cattlemen and began working for wages. In the 1950s the Paiutes fell victim to the federal termination policy, which took away all health services and other benefits and devastated them economically. Twenty years later, however, they received distributions of money awarded by the Indian Claims Commission. The Utah Paiute Tribal Council was formed in 1972, and soon, with the cooperation of the Department of Housing and Urban Development, 113 housing units were built at Richfield, Joseph, Shivwits, and Cedar City. In 1980 President Jimmy Carter signed a bill restoring federal status to the Paiutes, and in 1984 they were granted a reservation of 4,470 acres on poor land in southern Utah as well as a fund of $2.5 million for economic development. They soon built new homes and two sewing factories and enjoyed improved health care and economic opportunities.[53]

In San Juan County, near Blanding, a band of Southern Utes who refused to join the reservation system survived and kept their identity alive in a White Mesa–Allen Canyon area they called Avikan. Numbering approximately 250 people in 1949, they struggled through the rest of the century to maintain their cultural identity in the face of rapid incursions by whites and Navajos.

Although their life style changed several times, the Avikan Utes at least succeeded in keeping their distinctive native language alive and in maintaining some of their arts and crafts, such as basketry. They also retained the historic Bear Dance as well as the traditional courting flute, a uniquely styled flute used by young men to court their girlfriends. In 1990 eighty-five-year-old Billy Mike was one of the few remaining men who knew how to make these flutes, and that year the Utah Arts Council awarded him an apprenticeship grant to teach the craft to a grand-nephew. Others also began to learn to play the courting game.[54]

The Goshute[55] Indians were a small division of the Shoshonean family. They had two small reservations. One was on the Utah–Nevada border, at the base of the Deep Creek Mountains, with headquarters at Ibapah, Utah, in Juab County. The other was in Skull Valley, in Tooele County. By mid-century, both groups together totaled only about three hundred people.[56]

Most of the Goshute population was concentrated at or near Deep Creek.[57] Early in the century living conditions were still somewhat primitive but by the 1970s the community was characterized by modern lumber homes with indoor plumbing, a community center for tribal gatherings, and an industrial shop. However, by that time only eleven families remained on the reservation, while others were scattered around eastern Nevada and western Utah. A Goshute day school was combined with the Ibapah Elementary School at the end of the 1960s. High school students often boarded away from home, attending Wasatch Academy in Mount Pleasant or high schools in Tooele, Grantsville, Lehi, Salt Lake City, Delta, or Ely, Nevada. After 1977, however, they were bussed each day to Wendover. Some Deep Creek Goshutes gained their livelihood from agriculture while others found work in white communities and several remained on welfare. In 1969 a cooperative industry known as Goshute Enterprises was established, with federal assistance, in an effort to provide job training for tribal members and help them find work. The plant fabricated steel goods, such as trailers, cattle guards, handrails, and playground equipment.

How isolated the Deep Creek Goshutes were is illustrated by the fact that the first telephone in the area, a pay phone at Calloway Service and Grocery, was not installed until 1968. Before that anyone wanting to use a phone had to travel to a store thirty miles southeast or thirty-five miles northwest, to the Ferguson Springs road maintenance station. The first paved road came in about 1977. For the Goshutes, however, the solitude and stillness seemed preferable to the noise and pollution of the modern world that was all too quickly pressing in. The incursion of modernism seemed too close to reality in 1983 when the US Air Force sought permission to extend the practice area for its jets. Planes would make practice runs over the Deep Creek area, precipitating a thousand sonic booms a month. The Goshutes, along with other inhabitants, protested loudly.

There was little cooperation between the Goshutes at Deep Creek and those at Skull Valley. In the years before World War II, the BIA made several attempts to remove the tiny band of Skull Valley Goshutes to the reservation at Deep Creek.[58] Deeply devoted to its traditional homeland and adamantly committed to maintaining strong bloodlines, the Skull Valley group successfully fought off all such efforts. A final attempt to remove them came in 1954, at the time of the ill-fated termination policy, when the BIA recommended that the entire reservation be sold and the money distributed to tribal members to help them relocate. Goshute leaders were unyielding, refusing termination and reaffirming their unwavering attachment to traditional lands.

Economically, however, the Skull Valley band was in difficulty. In its isolated setting on land that had few natural resources, it had much less opportunity for economic development than other tribes. Some Goshutes tried their hand at farming, others tried sheepherding, but they continually looked for other economic opportunities. Land owned by the tribe, for example, was once leased to Hercules Aerospace for testing rockets, and some tribal members found employment with that company. Others moved elsewhere seeking work, and by the early 1980s there remained only four families, including about eighteen people, on the reservation.[59] In 1993 the Skull Valley tribe numbered about 112 people, with all but twenty-nine living off the reservation. But they remained fiercely independent, maintaining a separate tribal government and refusing to identify with the Confederated Tribes of the Goshute headquartered at Ipabah.[60]

Hispanics[61]

John Florez grew up in a boxcar on Salt Lake City's west side. His father was a section-gang worker on the railroad. Nine of John's eleven brothers and sisters died in their youth. When he started school in kindergarten, John immediately encountered a myriad of culture challenges. He could speak only Spanish in a school that taught only in English. Lessons on table manners and nutrition seemed strange when at home the family ate mainly beans with a tortilla for a utensil, as they had done in Mexico. In school he pretended that at home they ate like the others, but it seemed demeaning to his own customs to be taught that eating with fingers was somehow disgraceful. However, his parents encouraged him to get a good education and to excel, and John followed their advice. As a teenager in the 1950s, he played football at South High School and then attended Snow College on a football scholarship. He made up his mind to get a good education, become a social worker, and do everything in his power to ensure civil rights and adequate social services for all citizens. After graduating from college with a degree in sociology, he worked in prison probation, criminal justice, civil rights, youth employment, and juvenile justice. He received six national appointments, including an appointment to the Carter Task Force on Law and Criminal Justice. Between 1975 and 1981, he also served on twenty-seven local community service boards. In addition, he was a professor of social work at the University of Utah.[62]

Florez's experience was but one of the many notable examples in Utah's Hispanic community of the determination and ambition that helped young people raise themselves from deprivation to success in positions where they could be of inestimable service not only to their own people but to American society in general.

Hispanics constituted the largest ethnic group in Utah in 1990, totalling nearly 84,600 and comprising about 5 percent of the state's population. Most were concentrated in Salt Lake, Weber, Davis, and Utah counties. Theirs was not a monolithic cul-

Image A.3: The Guadalupe Center, founded by the Catholic Guadalupe Mission in 1966. Used by permission, Utah State Historical Society, all rights reserved.

ture, but, rather, one made up of diverse groups. Mexican-Americans, frequently referred to at that time as Chicanos, constituted the largest portion, while others were either born in or descended from immigrants from Peru, Chile, Guatemala, Argentina, Cuba, and other Central and South American countries. Many Chicanos were migrant workers, most of whom were not well off and whose children frequently lacked the educational opportunities needed to move them into higher socioeconomic patterns.[63] Other Hispanics were found in diverse professions, including all positions common to the rest of Utah's citizens. The main thing they had in common was the Spanish language, but despite their diverse Hispanic backgrounds they felt a cultural bond and frequently worked together for common ends. Notwithstanding their efforts at acculturation, especially in the first few decades after World War II, people in the larger society frequently did not take the time to distinguish middle-class Chicanos from migrant workers, making it difficult even for the middle class to be readily accepted into society.[64]

Utah's Hispanics were served by various organizations prior to World War II, but as their numbers increased after the war, several new associations appeared. These included the Centro Civico Mexicano in Salt Lake City, Sociedad Mexicana Cuahotemoc in

Carbon County, and Sociedad Fraternal Benito Juarez in Ogden. Chapters of the American G.I. Forum were established in Ogden and Salt Lake City in 1954 and 1955. This organization, founded by Hispanic World War II veterans in Texas, was formed to take both civil and political action against job discrimination and to provide scholarships to encourage young Hispanics to gain a better education. SOCIO (Spanish-speaking Organization for Community Integrity and Opportunity), founded in 1958 and made up of members from throughout the state, worked hard to promote equality, opportunity, and respect for its constituents.

Several churches also developed programs for, and in cooperation with, the Spanish-speaking people of Utah. The Guadalupe Center was founded by the Catholic Guadalupe Mission in 1966. There Mexican-American families, teenagers, and adults met and other people became involved in projects to meet Mexican-American needs. It provided youth sports activities as well as direction in educational pursuits. The La Morena Café, operated by the center, provided employment for Mexican-American youth and became a popular eating place for people of all cultures.[65] The café closed in 1986 although another with the same named opened elsewhere in 1995.

A 1972 study of Utah's social services suggested some of the problems that seemed to stand in the way of more rapid acceptance of Chicanos. Rightly or wrongly, Chicanos generally believed that employees and state welfare agencies were not really concerned with helping people get out of poverty, that there was too much emphasis in these agencies on abandoning Chicano culture, and that Chicano students did not do as well in school as their Anglo counterparts.[66] Other studies also emphasized the fact that Chicanos found it more difficult than their Anglo counterparts to achieve success in education. Reasons given for the inequality included a lower percentage of regular Hispanic attenders, although among regular attenders, grade point averages were similar to those of other students, a higher dropout rate, and a lack of intercultural understanding and communication.[67]

One problem was bilingualism—particularly the degree to which second- and third-generation Hispanics could or could not retain their ancestral language and, at the same time, be part of the American culture. Along the US–Mexican border, Mexican-Americans could get along without learning the English language at all. Businesses and government employees were proficient in both languages and all the media were readily available in both. This was not true in Utah, where many Hispanics used English as the language of communication outside the home and Spanish in the home and within their own cultural groups. But as the generations continued this practice became diluted, with parents speaking in Spanish and their children answering in English. Finally, many reached the point dubbed by one author as mere "vestigial bilingualism," where the youth retained only a few words or expressions as "ethnic markers" but no real understanding of the language.[68] Under these conditions Hispanic parents could hardly imbue their youth with some of the richest aspects of their heritage. The situation was not helped by the traditional insistence of schools and some churches that all minorities must learn the English language, and their seeming insistence that the mother tongue be left behind.

Meanwhile, a widespread movement, known popularly as the English-only movement, sought to make English the official language of the United States and of each of the states. On three different occasions the Utah legislature considered, but turned down, an English-only law. In November 2000, however, voters took matters into their own hands and approved an initiative that made Utah the twenty-sixth state to declare English as its official language. Utah's new law required that state and local governments conduct their official business almost exclusively in English, although exceptions were made with respect to health and public safety, some court proceedings, economic development, tourism, and education. The law also encouraged schools to adopt English as a Second Language programs.

By the 1980s, there seemed to be a Hispanic renaissance in the making. During the Rampton administration in the 1970s, there was a move toward both bilingual and bicultural education, beginning with day-care centers for migrant preschoolers. An increasing number of schools, from elementary through high school, taught more classes in Spanish and promoted bicultural understanding. Hispanics also found themselves more well represented in law enforcement as well as in state health and medical services. They also served on a variety of important councils and boards, including the School Textbook Commission, the State Manpower Council, the Family Services Board, the Comprehensive Health Planning Advisory Board, and the Weber State College Institutional Council.[69] Every governor beginning with Rampton paid special attention to the Hispanic community's needs, as well as those of other minorities. Equally important, Hispanic folklore, folk music, and folk dance became more popular, which helped foster knowledge of and pride in their heritage among Hispanic youth.

Between 1980 and 1990 there was a 40 percent jump in Utah's Hispanic population. One result of this remarkable growth was a marked upswing in the attention of retailers and other businesses. This, in turn, resulted in greater public awareness of and sensitivity to Hispanic culture and the founding, about 1988, of a Spanish-language newspaper, *America Unida*. It was founded and subsidized by Sonia Alcaron Parker. By 1992 this twelve-page weekly tabloid had a circulation of about three thousand. In addition to providing a linguistic tie among Hispanics, it helped them stay current with local, national, and international news of special interest to their community. It also helped with some of their financial needs. Banks ran advertisements in the paper, for example, directing Spanish-speaking people to particular branches and people who could most easily help them. The paper also helped Hispanics find real estate agents who could better communicate with them.[70]

Despite their progress, in the mid-1990s Utah's Spanish-speaking people still had concerns related to lingering racism and the lack of opportunity. As expressed in 1994 by William H. Gonzalez and Orlando Rivera,

> Hispanics currently have concerns about the public schools system's failure to educate their children, the exclusion of Hispanics from the higher education process, an unemployment rate three times that of the general population, sociological problems manifested by disproportionate numbers in the corrections system and on pub-

lic assistance, law enforcement profiling Hispanics, gang activity and adverse media reporting on youth accused of gang activity, English-only legislation, and immigration problems, among other basic human rights concerns.[71]

One particularly difficult problem was that of illegal immigrants, who came into the United States seeking work at a rate of more than a million a year in the 1970s. In 1979, it was reported that approximately two thousand people were apprehended each year in Utah and "voluntarily deported." Although critics argued that they took jobs from American citizens, in actuality these immigrants usually took jobs that no one else wanted. Utah farmers and fruit growers often insisted that they could not survive without them. While some people argued that illegals were a drain on the economy and must be deported, others produced statistics to demonstrate that they actually benefitted the economy.[72]

Most migrant workers in Utah were not illegal, however, and usually they were American citizens. They contributed significantly to the state's economy, even though it was frequently charged that they were shamelessly underpaid, often lived in unsanitary squalor, and that some employers showed little concern for their welfare. The Utah-Idaho Sugar Company was singled out in 1968 as one that refused to do anything about the fact that its migrant employees in northern Utah suffered totally inadequate housing.[73]

Whatever the truth was with respect to the sugar company, adequate housing was one of the chief problems facing the eighteen thousand seasonal migrant workers, mostly Hispanic, who usually lived in Utah for several months at a time. In 1993, for example, only one housing unit in Utah County, at Spring Lake, offered clean, heated apartments with modern plumbing. Subsidized partly by the federal Farmers' Home Administration, it offered affordable rates of $180 per month. However, there simply were not enough apartments to accommodate most of the 7,500 farm workers in the county, leaving the majority to live either in small, unsanitary, and unheated apartments at higher cost or in their own trucks or other vehicles.[74]

Hispanics often felt that law enforcement polices were biased against them, but by the mid-1990s the state and some local communities were taking steps to eliminate such problems. In Utah County, for example, law enforcement officials in both Provo and Orem cooperated with a Hispanic advocacy organization, Utah Latinos, to prevent officers from asking inappropriate questions, after adequate identification had been presented, in an effort to induce someone to produce a "green card." Utah Latinos also offered a five-month course of weekly Spanish classes to help officers communicate better with non-English-speaking Hispanics, focusing primarily on a vocabulary that would be useful in emergencies. Hispanic leaders also urged law enforcement to undergo more sensitivity training, in order to help protect the rights of dark-complexioned US citizens who may not be fluent in English.

Among the many strengths of the Hispanic community was its particularly strong family ties. In a society where their full acceptance was sometimes elusive, the family provided a sense of belonging that helped overcome many difficulties. One example was young John Florez, whose parents cherished their Mexican heritage so much that they returned to Mexico when John was nine years old. After only a year, however, his father realized that the children could never have the education he wanted for them. The final straw came when John needed medical attention. His father quickly put the family on the train and took them back to Utah, even though he knew that there he would always remain poor and never be allowed to advance in his work. But this did not destroy Florez's pride in his family and heritage. As Florez explained:

> It was my family that *instilled* my pride. In spite of poverty, I always had enough to eat; I was always clean. I was encouraged to get work as young as possible, and always had a job after that. My parents encouraged independence in us, and determination. They never hurt my pride—they were the reason for it.[75]

Asians and Pacific Islanders

Asians and Pacific Islanders comprised nearly 2 percent of the state's population in 1990, providing yet more diversity to Utah's vibrant cultural fabric. Located primarily in Salt Lake, Utah, Davis, Weber, and Cache counties, they included several nationalities: Japanese, Chinese, Korean, Southeast Asians, Hawaiians, Tongas, Samoans, New Zealanders, Tahitians, and those from other islands.

During World War II, as a result of the national government's relocation program, numerous Japanese-Americans were incarcerated at Topaz.[76] After the war, many who had originally lived on the West Coast remained in Utah, swelling the ranks of the small Japanese community that already existed in the state. Most lived in Salt Lake City and Ogden.

In an effort to gain redress for some of their losses, one Utah Japanese, Mike Masaoka, spearheaded the postwar effort of the Japanese-American Citizens' League that eventually resulted in the 1948 Evacuation Indemnity Act. Although less than 10 percent of the actual losses were repaid under that act, later national legislation approved more. As a result, $20,000 was appropriated for each survivor in 1989.

At the end of the twentieth century, the Japanese community in Utah included a handful of *issei* (first-generation Japanese immigrants) and many more *nisei* (second-generation), *sansei* (third-generation), and *yonsei* (fourth-generation). About half the *sansei* had married non-Japanese but continued to participate in Japanese activities. For the most part, Utah's Japanese were known for their high level of achievement despite the fact that they were often the victims of racial prejudice. Some achieved notable public recognition or made other significant contributions to the state. In 1947, for example, George Sibata of Garland became the first *nisei* to be appointed to the United States Military Academy at West Point, New York. Japanese were the leaders in planning an International Peace Garden in Salt Lake City's Jordan Park, and in 1947 their portion of the garden was the first to be dedicated. The park also drew international attention, resulting in the contribution of some lanterns, a statue of a peace goddess, and a tea house from Japan. In the 1960s three Utah Japanese received special awards from the Japanese government for their contributions toward improving Japanese-American relations: Henry Y. Kasai, for fostering understanding between Caucasians and Japanese-Americans (and who also was posthumously given Phi Delta Kappa's "Man of the Year" award for distinguishing himself in international education); Mrs. Kuniko Terasawa, publisher of *Utah Nippo*, for the many ways she used the press to help Utah's Japanese; and Mrs. Take Uchida, an educator who taught English to the *issei* and Japanese to the *nisei*. In addition, in 1968 Japan's Premier Eisaku Sato presented Mike Masaoka with the highest honor that Japan can bestow on a foreigner, the Order of the Rising Sun Third Class.[77] Some *nisei* and *sansei* found their way into mainstream politics and others into such prestigious professions as law, higher education, medicine, and many other fields.

The Japanese maintained a rich cultural tradition in Utah. This included two special festivals, New Year's Day and Obon, a midsummer festival on the occasion of a Buddhist memorial day. The Japanese community also fostered other activities, such as an annual picnic, where they participated in traditional games and activities. However, by the end of the century the Japanese were becoming more fully assimilated into the larger society than perhaps any other ethnic minority. And as the *issei* died off, many traditions went with them.[78]

Utah was also home to many Chinese people, located mainly around Salt Lake City. After World War II, changes in American immigration law opened the way for a sizable new wave of Chinese immigrants. The Chinese Exclusion Act was repealed during the war and the McCarran-Walter Act of 1952 approved Asian immigration. The Immigration Act of 1965 abolished quotas. Immigrants, many of them students, came from Hong Kong and Taiwan and, later in the century, from the Chinese mainland. In addition, many of the Vietnamese refugees who streamed to Utah after 1975 were of Chinese extraction. While there were only 1,281 Chinese-Americans in Utah in 1970, the total jumped to 5,322 by 1990.[79]

Chinese immigrants were ambitious, family-oriented, and hard-working, but some had problems accommodating to their new society. In some cases their inability to speak English kept them from finding jobs that paid livable wages. For that reason, many ended up as cooks or busboys in Chinese restaurants, usually working for relatives or friends.[80] Within Chinese families, communication was sometimes limited because, as one writer put it, "the parents learn only enough English to get by, while the children learn only enough Chinese to converse in household conversation."[81] The children were caught between the parents' desire to have them associate with and marry only Chinese and their own tendency to become more rapidly Americanized. But by the end of the century most of the Chinese population had accommodated well to the larger society.

There were also a small number of Koreans in Utah, centered mostly around Salt Lake City, Ogden, and Provo. Most arrived after the Korean War, some seeking employment opportunities and others seeking higher education. Brigham Young University, especially, attracted many Korean students as well as a few Korean professors. The main organization working for the betterment of the Korean community was the Utah Korean Association.

Koreans generally were known for their family cohesiveness, strong work ethic, and pride in accomplishment. They were also particularly well-educated. More than half of those who responded to a 1992 survey had received a four-year college education or more before they left Korea.[82] But more than half the respondents had difficulty understanding English, as spoken by Americans, even though all were convinced of the importance of learning English. As far as racial bias was concerned, only half had seldom, if ever, experienced it in Utah.[83]

Prior to the 1970s, Utah's Southeast Asian community was very small and came mostly from the Philippines and Thailand. But between 1975 and 1990, some twelve thousand refugees from Vietnam, Laos, and Cambodia came into the state in waves. The first were mostly Vietnamese from the cities. They were well educated and had been among the technical, managerial, and military elite of their country. They were followed by more Vietnamese plus a large number of farmers, fishermen, and mountain tribespeople from Laos and Cambodia. The next wave included ethnic Chinese and Hmong tribespeople who had been slated for extermination because they had collaborated with the American military.

Finally, in the early 1990s came people who had been detained in Communist reeducation camps, as well as many Amerasian children who had been fathered by American troops, along with their family members. However, more than half the refugees did not remain in Utah as weather, family ties elsewhere, and seemingly better economic opportunities lured them to southern California. In 1990 there were between eight and nine thousand Southeast Asians in the state.

In 1990, Utah's Filipino community numbered about 1,900. Most lived in urban areas, with the majority in Salt Lake City. Generally well-educated and productively employed in many professions, they also reflected the linguistic and cultural diversity of the Philippines. They maintained cultural ties through such organizations as the Philippine-American Association of Utah and the Philippine-American Bayanihan Association of Utah, which both sponsored a variety of fiestas, sports activities, and folk dancing.

The small Thai community in Utah consisted of about 150 families in 1990. Thais came seeking higher education, as military spouses, or as professional people who had educational or family ties in the state. Most were concentrated in the Layton area, near Hill Air Force Base. Most were Buddhists, and Layton was the location of Utah's only Thai Buddhist temple. Monks, periodically sent from Thailand to serve the Buddhist community, taught religion and conducted summer programs for children in the language and customs of Thailand.

When the Southeast Asian refugees began streaming into the state, they were relocated at first in the urban areas of northern Utah. The refugee resettlement program consisted of a network of public and private coordinating councils, voluntary agencies, churches, and numerous individuals who were committed to helping with this momentous challenge. For a time, beginning in 1979, the federal government provided approximately one million dollars annually to the Utah State Department of Social Services to help refugees in adjusting socially and culturally. Services provided by these funds included job counseling, vocational training, English language training, leadership development, and other programs.[84]

The major challenges faced by refugees included learning a new language and finding employment. They came with diverse educational and work experience, but most of those who remained in Utah eventually found work, some in agriculture but about half as skilled workers on production lines with companies such as Deseret Pharmaceutical, National Semiconductor, Kimball Draperies, and Marriott Flight Services. Some refugees opened successful family-operated restaurants specializing in Vietnamese and Chinese cuisine, while others opened specialized markets, thus contributing to increased cultural awareness among Utahns. In general, refugee employees received high evaluations from their employers.[85]

Helping refugees meet their needs and adapt to their new home were many public and private entities, including state social service agencies, Catholic Community Services, the LDS Church, the state's Office of Asian Affairs, created in 1983, and a number of volunteer groups such as the Utah Friends of the Refugees League. The Asian Association of Utah, a non-profit organization founded in 1977, played an especially important part in the process of helping all Asians find equal opportunity in immigration, employment, housing, education, and legal and social services.[86] Refugees sometimes made significant, if not highly public, contributions to Utah culture. For example, women among the Hmong, from Laos, brought with them a highly developed skill in needlework, an ancient art form that had special religious connotations. Accepting nothing less than perfection in their work, they painstakingly stitched their intricate and colorful designs into clothing worn at weddings, funerals, and religious festivals. Their work was also for sale.[87]

Churches played a vital role in the lives of most Asians. The Japanese were mostly Buddhist, and enjoyed the support of several Buddhist centers in Utah. There were also two Japanese congregations of the Church of Christ in the state, jointly sponsored by the Presbyterian church (see Appendix C). Utah's Koreans, on the other hand, were mostly Christianized. In 1992, well over half of them belonged to the LDS Church, while about 26 percent belonged to Protestant churches and 12 percent reported belonging to no church. Korean members of the LDS Church tended to integrate into regular wards, while other Koreans often formed their own congregations. Of the eight Korean Protestant congregations in 1992, one was in Ogden, one in Provo, one near Hill Air Force Base, and five in the Salt Lake area. Korean churches helped meet not just religious but also social, psychological, and personal needs of immigrants. This may help account for the fact that church attendance was higher among Korean immigrants in the United States than it was in Korea.[88]

Religion was also important to refugees from Southeast Asia. Most of them were Buddhists, who enjoyed fellowship and spiritual guidance at three temples in Utah: one in Sandy, another in the Guadalupe neighborhood in Salt Lake City, and a Cambodian temple at Salt Lake City's New Hope Multicultural Center. A significant minority, however, joined western Christian churches, partly because eastern religious groups and facilities were scarce and some ethnic Christian congregations provided valuable support networks. In addition, religion itself was important in the lives of refugees, who attended church services frequently and as family groups. By the early 1990s, approximately six hundred refugees were affiliated with the Mormon Church, and another two hundred, mostly Vietnamese and a few Hmong, were members of Catholic congregations.[89]

Utah was also home to a vibrant community of South Sea Islanders, most of whom originally came because of family and religious ties and to seek education and better employment opportunities. The 1990 census reported 3,904 people from Tonga, 1,570 from Samoa, and 1,396 from Hawaii. There were also an estimated six to seven hundred Maoris from New Zealand, close to two hundred Tahitians, nearly 150 from Guam, and a handful from some of the other South Pacific islands. Polynesians contested these figures, estimating much larger populations. The Tongans, for example, claimed to have between ten and twelve thousand people in Utah.[90] One estimate in 1994 indicated that there were between thirty-five and forty thousand Polynesians in the state. Such discrepancies may reflect not just mistakes on all sides but also the fact that many individuals arrived in the state on student visas and were not counted in the census but then remained.

Like the Asians and the Native Americans, the Polynesians hardly reflected a unified culture, for while there were obvious similarities there were also distinctions between the different customs and traditions of the islands. Nevertheless, for the sake of convenient summary, at least one author has pointed out that the Hawaiians, Maoris, and Tahitians represented a "more westernized" culture, while the other groups were "less westernized," leading to different experiences in Utah regarding assimilation, acculturation, and maintaining cultural traditions.[91]

Living in Utah's urban areas, mostly around the Salt Lake Valley, Hawaiians, Maoris, and Tahitians found work in every sector of the state's economy. Most were members of the LDS Church, and it was comparatively easy for them to integrate into their respective communities. At the same time, their interaction with other Polynesians through various ethnic organizations helped them maintain and transmit their cultural heritage. Theirs seemed to be one of the best examples of cultural pluralism—the ability to fit well into the larger society and at the same time retain many, if not most, of their distinctive cultural traits.

The other group, comprised mostly of Tongans and Samoans, were concentrated on the west side of Salt Lake Valley. They found employment mostly in the service sector of the economy, many of them as unskilled laborers. They maintained close ties with religion, affiliating with Mormon, Catholic, Seventh-Day Adventist, and other Christian groups, and had little to do with ethnic organizations. Originally the LDS Church attempted to integrate everyone into regular congregations, but a policy reversal in the 1970s led to the organization of ethnic wards authorized to conduct services in their native languages. A number of Methodist congregations also held services in native languages. This activity contributed greatly to the immigrants' ability to maintain their cultural traditions.

Among the organizations that helped perpetuate some aspects of Polynesian history and culture in Utah was the Iosepa Historical Society, founded in the mid-1980s. Iosepa (named for Joseph F. Smith, an early LDS missionary to Hawaii who became president of the church in 1901) was an ill-fated Hawaiian colony planted in a desolate area of Utah's Skull Valley in 1889. After its abandonment in 1915 the settlement disappeared except for a tiny cemetery that over the years was neglected and went to ruin. To the uninformed, it was a strange anomaly to see a tiny graveyard in the desert in which all the names were Hawaiian! The new historical society aimed to keep alive the memory of Iosepa and the struggles of its inhabitants. The society restored the cemetery and began an annual Memorial Day trek to clean up the area and decorate the graves. The site was placed on the National Register of Historical Places in 1971.

Also contributing to making the state more aware of some aspects of Polynesian culture was the Utah Polynesian Choir. Organized in 1989, the choir toured the state singing Mormon hymns in English, Hawaiian, Samoan, and Tongan. A governor's advisory council was also formed in the late 1980s consisting of representatives from various island groups. The council fostered the continuation of the annual Polynesian Day Celebration, where crowds enjoyed Polynesian music, dance, crafts, and food. Polynesians constituted a highly visible and well-liked subculture in Utah's diversified ethnic scene.

The Polynesian community was not without its problems, however, among which were difficulties in pursuing higher education. In the 1980s more than half of the Polynesian high school students wanted to continue on to higher education, but only 11.1 percent actually did so and less than 2 percent graduated from college. Teachers reported that many more students were capable of college work, but they seemed to be discouraged by academic difficulties in high school. One important factor was the lack of well-qualified Polynesian counselors. Other problems included the low economic status of many Polynesian families, with 34.6 percent considered to be at poverty level in the 1980s.[92]

The only state office set up to deal with these Polynesian concerns was the Office of Asian Affairs. But the Polynesian population was the fastest growing ethnic group in the state, and after the 1990 census Polynesian leaders began to press for their own office and budget. Finally, in an effort to distribute more state resources to aid in solving the challenges of the Polynesian community, Governor Mike Leavitt, in 1994, established a Governor's Advisory Council on Polynesian Affairs. He also appointed Fineasi

M. Nau, a native Tongan living in Provo, as the first director of the newly created Office of Polynesian Affairs. Nau was a skilled graphic designer and the first Tongan to graduate from Brigham Young University. "I am proud to be a member of Utah's Polynesian community and to have this chance to serve it," he said. "This office can help build unity among all members of our community and all Utahns as well." His top priority, he said, was to bridge the generation gap between Utah Polynesians born in the Pacific Islands and their children who were born in the state. "Many parents don't understand much about US culture or language," he observed. "So in some ways the children lead their parents. But we must remind ourselves and our children who we are and make them proud of their cultural identities."[93]

African Americans

African Americans constituted the smallest of the major ethnic minorities in Utah. In 1990, they made up a smaller percentage of the Utah population than of most other states, 0.6 percent compared with a national average of 12.1 percent. Only 40 percent of Utah's cities had any black population at all.[94] But in the years following World War II this group was the most discriminated against, both in Utah and in the nation at large. One unfortunate consequence of that discrimination was more than just a feeling of isolation and rejection but sometimes a seeming acceptance of the prevailing myth of black inferiority. To fight such stereotypes, blacks throughout the nation often responded enthusiastically to a variety of movements designed to build black pride and with it black self-confidence. Their efforts ranged from the peaceful civil disobedience fostered by Martin Luther King, Jr., to the militancy of the Black Panthers and the separatism of Black Muslim Malcolm X. It also included efforts in every camp to convince the younger generation that "Black Is Beautiful."

In 1972, a group of African American elementary school students in the central city area of Salt Lake City were asked to write what they felt about their blackness. Their replies were powerful reflections of what it meant to grow up as part of a minority who felt despised but, at the same time, had been imbued with deep racial pride. Wrote one ten-year-old boy:

> Black is beautiful, it is a being
> I mean what else would it be?
> You get called all kinds of names,
> but you know you're beautiful
> because your skin is black.
> I love you and I'll rap to you
> because we both know that
> Black is Beautiful.

In a slightly different vein, a girl of the same age wrote:

> People say Black is Beautiful
> But God didn't choose,
> Any kind of special color.
> So why is there hatred and trouble?[95]

Some Utahns tended to forget that blacks had been part of the Utah experience for as long as whites. James P. Beckwourth, a trapper, guide, and Indian fighter, was trapping and hunting with other early trappers in the Ogden-Salt Lake area as early as the mid-1820s. The first Mormon pioneer company, which arrived in 1847, included three black men, one of whom drove the wagon that carried Brigham Young into the Salt Lake Valley. By 1850 at least fifty black people, about half of them slaves, were residents of Utah Territory. In later years more arrived, though in small numbers, as railroad workers, cowboys, soldiers, and in other capacities, and in the late 1890s blacks began publishing their own newspaper in the state.

By 1940, there were more than 1,200 African Americans in Utah. The figure grew by more than 120 percent between 1940 and 1950, largely because of in-migration during World War II for employment opportunities in the defense industry.[96] Most lived in urban areas, particularly in and around Ogden and Salt Lake City, and that pattern continued through the rest of the century. The Salt Lake City chapter of the National Association of Colored

Image A.4: NAACP leaders James Dooley of Salt Lake City and Roy Wilkins of the national office, who visited Utah in 1971. Used by permission, Utah State Historical Society, all rights reserved.

People (NAACP) was organized in 1919 and the Ogden chapter in 1943.

At the end of the war discrimination against African Americans in Utah was considerably more pronounced than discrimination against other ethnic groups. As historian Ronald G. Coleman has noted, one of the ironies in black-white relationships was that even though whites flocked to hear black entertainers they would not allow them to stay in their hotels or eat in their restaurants.[97] Even Marian Anderson, one of the nation's most heralded concert singers in the 1950s, was permitted to stay overnight in the Hotel Utah only on condition that she use the freight elevator. Utah blacks did not always take such humiliation docilely, and some of them participated in protest demonstrations. In 1959, for example, Danny W. Burnett and Albert Fritz led a protest against three national chain stores in Salt Lake City that did not serve blacks at their lunch counters.[98]

Between 1950 and 1960 Utah's population grew by 29 percent but its black population increased by 52 percent. This increase was probably due to the continuing opportunity for employment, although the nature of that employment was gradually changing. In 1950 some 41 percent of blacks were employed in the service sector, usually as janitors, porters, waiters, etc., but this had dropped to 33 percent by 1950, while the number in the professions gradually rose. Income rates, however, remained highly uneven. In the 1950s the median African American income was $2,289 annually, compared with a state median of $3,007.[99] A quarter-century later, in 1975, relative income was still low, amounting to about $602 per month in Salt Lake County compared with an overall average of $1,081. Unemployment that year among blacks in Salt Lake City stood at 15.6 percent compared with 8.3 percent for the community as a whole. Although only four out of ten African Americans felt they were discriminated against in employment or when visiting public accommodations, most still felt that the black community had little or no opportunity for political participation.[100] A decade later it seemed apparent that black education and economic status had improved, but the Director of the Utah State Office of Black Affairs, Shauna M. Graves, feared that some of the data might be misleading. She observed that some students with high grade-point averages did not do well on national achievement tests, that African Americans were under-represented on college faculties, and that there was no significant growth in the number of black-owned businesses.[101]

In the last three decades of the twentieth century, there were encouraging signs of black progress in social, economic, and civic affairs, and of greater public acceptance of black people. After 1968, when federal fair housing legislation went into effect, several Utah blacks filed successful housing discrimination suits. The Rampton administration established a Black Policy Council within the state's Department of Community Affairs. In 1972, Donald L. Cope of Ogden was appointed as the first black ombudsman in the state. A year later, in August 1973, Governor Rampton issued an executive order creating the Governor's Advisory Council on Black Affairs.[102] By 1980 it appeared to Governor Scott M. Matheson that this twenty-four member council was too large to be productive. He dissolved it and appointed in its place a smaller Black Advisory Council. Six years later his successor, Norman H. Bangerter, set up separate Asian, black, and Hispanic advisory councils within the Department of Community and Economic Development. The directors were assigned to research major issues and to cooperate in prioritizing community needs.[103]

The first black legislator in Utah, the Reverend Robert Harris, was elected to Utah's House of Representatives in 1976.[104] In 1980 Terry Lee Williams was elected to the House, and then, in 1982, he became the first black to be elected to the Utah State Senate. Four years later Williams was instrumental in securing passage of a bill that made Martin Luther King, Jr.'s birthday a legal holiday in Utah. In 1984, Governor Scott Matheson named former Salt Lake County Attorney Tyrone E. Medley a judge in Utah's Fifth Circuit Court. In 1993 Medley was elevated to the Third District Court.

A number of other blacks achieved distinction in their fields and in public service. A few examples include elementary school principals Joyce M. Gray and Phyllis Fludd White; Afesa Marie Adams, associate vice-president for academic affairs at the University of Utah; Ronald G. Coleman, a University of Utah history professor whose Ph.D. dissertation was a particularly important study of blacks in Utah's heritage, and who became director of the university's Afro-American Studies Program, coordinator of the Ethnic Studies Program, and, in the mid-1990s, Associate Vice-President for Academic Affairs; Gail B. Dellapiana, a professor of architecture, who made notable contributions to the arts; nationally known and respected professional basketball players, such as Adrian Dantley and Karl Malone; and Utah's black ministers and civil rights leaders, such as James E. Dooley, who headed the Salt Lake Branch of the NAACP from 1968 to1980, and did yeoman service for the black community as well as the state in general.[105] In the world of business, Ike Spencer and Andrew Henderson founded Black Business Entrepreneurs (BBE) in 1992 to promote black business activities. The group worked to provide scholarships and summer work for college students and helped black professionals and business owners improve their economic understanding and opportunities. In 1994, there were more than fifty businesses in Utah owned by African Americans.[106]

When the University of Utah named her doctor of humane letters in 1971, Alberta Henry, a prominent social worker in the Salt Lake Valley, became the first black to receive an honorary degree from any Utah university. Nine years later she earned a bachelor's degree and in 1981 she became head of the state's NAACP. In addition, Henry was employed by the Salt Lake City School District for more than fourteen years, was the first black administrator in the district, and the first black to be inducted into the Salt Lake Council of Women's Hall of Fame. Henry's life story is not atypical of that of many blacks. She arrived in Utah a few years after World War II, but even though she had professional experience in other things, she found that the only jobs she could obtain were in janitorial or other kinds of services. Her first job was cooking, cleaning, and caring for children in a white family. It was a far cry from that position to the honors she later earned because of her great love for youth and her devotion to working with housing and other kinds of social welfare projects.[107]

E. Faye Wine arrived in Utah in 1966, and not long after that went to work for Utah Power. She soon discovered numerous black women who needed support groups. "When you are in a state that's predominantly white," she noted, "that can be a very lonely type of feeling." In 1990 Wine, a member of the Governor's Black Advisory Council, founded the Utah Coalition of African-American Women in order to provide help, resources, and support whenever they were needed. "In this society," she commented in 1994, "black women aren't revered as much as I feel they should be. I see black women who really need to be told they are somebody, that they're beautiful." Black women were also concerned with such important issues as education, better employment opportunities, programs for youth, black awareness of their own culture, and all the community problems that concerned every race. Wine's coalition of black women attempted to address these issues.[108]

A mainstay for many Utah blacks was their affiliation with a church (see Appendix C for comments on the African Methodist Episcopal Church and the Calvary Baptist Church in Salt Lake City).[109] Pastor David Wright of the Trinity African Methodist Church was apprehensive when he was initially assigned to Utah. He soon felt at home, however, and involved himself not just in pastoring but also in community social concerns such as employment and housing. The Reverend France Davis, pastor of Salt Lake's Calvary Baptist Church beginning in 1974, placed considerable emphasis on youth activity and developed an extensive youth recreation program. He noted in 1987 that 60 percent of his congregation was under thirty years of age.[110]

Within the LDS Church, many blacks had highly positive experiences despite the priesthood ban. Some, however, also found reason for discomfort, as illustrated by a widely publicized anti-discrimination suit in 1974. The Salt Lake chapter of the NAACP filed suit on behalf of two young blacks who were denied leadership positions in LDS Church-sponsored Boy Scout troops. The suit contended that the church's policy of denying priesthood to blacks kept the boys from becoming senior patrol leaders because that position was given to a boy holding a priesthood office. The suit did not actually come to trial, however, because the church quickly agreed to open all scouting positions to all boys, regardless of race.

Among the African-Americans who were deeply devoted to the LDS Church was Ruffin Bridgeforth, who was converted in 1953 and was, at the time, the only black member in his stake. A devout believer, he was highly concerned for the well-being of other black Mormons, who felt isolated. Ruffin and two other African Americans took their concerns to church leaders, who were responsive to their suggestion that a group be formed to serve the needs of the growing black Mormon community. On October 19, 1971, Elder Gordon B. Hinckley of the Quorum of the Twelve Apostles officially "set apart" Bridgeforth as president of the Genesis Branch. While this unique organization did not completely satisfy all of its members' concerns, it nevertheless played an important role in their lives. Ruffin was one of the first to receive the Mormon priesthood after the ban was lifted in 1978.[111]

Other Minorities

There were many other ethnic minorities in Utah but not in as large numbers as the groups already discussed above. The exception was the Jewish community (see discussion in Appendix B), which was estimated in the 1990s to number about five thousand people. Generally well-educated, Jews could be found in all the professions, including medicine, law, science, and both public and higher education.[112]

The Greek population that once existed in the state diminished greatly before World War II; after the war, however, there was a new influx of Greek immigrants. Ambitious and hardworking, they included skilled laborers, intellectuals, and entrepreneurs. They accommodated to American life more quickly and easily than their earlier counterparts, and at the same time they maintained the vitality of Greek culture in the state. People of Greek ancestry lived mainly in and around Salt Lake City, Price, and Ogden, where they added a great deal to the cultural and social well-being of the state.[113]

Utah also enjoyed the presence of immigrants from the Middle East, including Syrians, Assyrians, Lebanese, Armenians, Egyptians, Iranians, Palestinians, Iraqis, Jordanians, Turks, and Libyans. Those who came after World War II were mostly students or professional people and administrators seeking employment in the state. Among them were Palestinians who were displaced as a result of the creation of the state of Israel. Perhaps the largest Middle-Eastern workforce in the state was concentrated at the University of Utah. The Middle East Center at the university, which offered many courses from a prestigious faculty and produced a stream of impressive research, was one of the leading centers of its type in the nation.[114]

Concluding Observations

The dual quest of Utah's minorities to maintain distinctive ethnic identities and, at the same time, gain full acceptance into the dominant society was much closer to being fulfilled in the 1990s than it was in the 1950s. The "salad bowl" metaphor, although not necessarily a popular expression, characterized the way many minority citizens viewed their place in the economic, social, and political life of the state. On October 10, 1994, Judge José A. Cabranes of the US Court of Appeals for the Second Circuit was the keynote speaker at the Second Annual Cesar Chavez Peace and Justice

Awards Luncheon in Salt Lake City. Addressing the group first in Spanish and then in English, he declared that people of every ethnic background must value their own culture even while becoming part of the American mainstream. "Perhaps this tradition of looking backward and looking forward is what it means truly to be an American," he said as he told the Hispanics in attendance that they must maintain traditional values as well as take their places at the heart of the nation's economic and political life.

At the 1994 luncheon awards were given to four people who seemed to have accomplished both of Judge Cabranes' objectives. Preddy Osegura had lost the use of her native tongue when, as a child, she was not allowed to speak it in the schools of New Mexico. In 1970 she graduated from the University of Utah with a teaching degree and made up her mind to re-learn Spanish so she could teach it to her Hispanic pupils in an effort to help them value their own cultural heritage. In 1974 she was recruited by the Salt Lake School District to develop a bilingual education program. The other three awards went to Mike Martinez, an attorney, for his many services to Utah's Hispanic community; Maria Garciaz, executive director of Neighborhood Housing Services, Inc.; and Joe Pacheco, a state tax commissioner and adjunct University of Utah professor who consciously put himself in a position where he could be seen as a role model for other Hispanics. "I think it's important to know that all of us had a part in the history of the United States," he said.[115]

In that spirit, in the 1990s Utah's ethnic minorities were found in every profession, every socioeconomic group, every religion, every level of government, and practically everything else that occurred in the state. Their future looked bright, especially when their status was compared with that of their counterparts a generation earlier. In higher education, the number of minority students in Utah's colleges and universities increased by 60 percent, from 4,413 to 7,022, between 1983 and 1993, while the number of faculty jumped from 139 to 190. Minority representation on college faculties was about the same as that in the nation, except that Utah had a lower average of blacks.[116] In summary, no matter where one looked conditions seemed to be improving. Prejudice continued, the incidence of poverty among minorities remained significantly higher than among the general population,[117] and discrimination against minorities was still felt in many ways, but most believed that Utah was a better place to live for minorities in the mid-1990s than it had been three decades earlier. This was true not just from the perspective of civil rights but also in terms of broader association and improved communication between people of all races.

Notes

1. See, for example, the feelings of Yukus Inouye, a prominent second-generation Japanese-American, as expressed in an oral history interview by Geoffrey Crisp, October 17, 1979 (L. Tom Perry Special Collections, Harold B. Lee Library, Brigham oung University), 11.
2. "1990 Census Brief: Minorities of Utah," prepared by Demographic and Economic Analysis, Office of Planning and Budget (Salt Lake City: April 1991), iv. For a more detailed demographic profile of Utah's ethnic groups, see Cardall Jacobson, "Ethnic Groups in Utah," in *Utah in Demographic Perspective*, ed. Thomas K. Martin, Tim B. Heaton, and Stephen J. Bahr (Salt Lake City: Signature Books, 1987), 165–79.
3. For a somewhat embittered view of LDS policy in the 1960s, see David H. Oliver, *A Negro on Mormonism* (Salt Lake City: published by the author, 1963). For a different view see "Black, Female, and Mormon," *Intermountain Observer* 21 (February 6, 1971): 12, which tells the story of Wynetta Clark, a female African-American, who became a member of the Mormon Tabernacle Choir about 1970.
4. Elmer R. Smith, *The Status of the Negro in Utah* (Salt Lake City: prepared for the Salt Lake City Branch of the National Association for the Advancement of Colored People, 1956), 7.
5. Wallace R. Bennett, "The Negro in Utah," *Utah Law Review* 3 (Spring 1953): 340–41; J. Herschel Barnhill, "Civil Rights in Utah: The Mormon Way," *Journal of the West* 25 (October 1986): 22. The Barnhill article should be used with caution, not just because it displays a heavy anti-Utah bias but, more importantly, because it is factually wrong on some crucial issues.
6. Smith, *The Status of the Negro in Utah*, 7, 9–13. Other relevant commentaries on the status of blacks in Utah are found in "Symposium on the Negro in Utah," typescript, a series of papers presented at the fall meetings of the Utah Academy of Sciences, Arts, and Letters, Weber College, Ogden, November 20, 1954. Papers included "The Legal Status of the Negro in Utah," by Wallace R. Bennett, "*The Status of the Negro in Utah*," by Harmon O. Cole, "Moral and Religious Aspects of *the Status of the Negro in Utah*," by Gaylon L. Caldwell, and "The Social Status of the Negro in Utah," by Elmer R. Smith. Available Harold B. Lee Library, Brigham Young University.
7. Ronald G. Coleman, "Blacks in Utah History: An Unknown Legacy," in *The Peoples of Utah*, ed. Helen Z. Papanikolas (Salt Lake City: Utah State Historical Society, 1976), 136–37. See also *Utah's Black Legacy: A History of the Black Experience in Utah*," a viewer's guide to the television documentary "Utah's Black Legacy," pre-

miered by KUED, channel 7, February 18, 1987 (Salt Lake City: KUED 7, 1987). Coleman's article, slightly modified, is reproduced as part of this publication.
8. See John Spencer Kirkham, "A Study of Negro Housing in Salt Lake County" (honors thesis, University of Utah, 1968).
9. Helen Z. Papanikolas and Alice Kasi, "Japanese Life in Utah," in *The Peoples of Utah*, ed. Helen Z. Papanikolas, 359-60.
10. *Resource Catalog of Black Citizens in Utah* (Salt Lake City: State Economic Opportunity Office, 1975), 1.
11. For a general history of the Klan in Utah, see Larry R. Gerlach, *Blazing Crosses in Zion* (Logan, UT: Utah State University Press, 1981).
12. Lisa Riley Roach, "Utah Faiths Denounce Racist Fliers," *Deseret News*, April 6, 1991, B1.
13. See, for example, a letter of the First Presidency, "To General Authorities, Regional Representatives of the Twelve, Stake Presidents, Mission Presidents, and Bishops," *Ensign* 73 (February 1970): 70-71.
14. Utah State Board of Education, Division of Administration, *Services to Minorities and Concerns of Minorities* (Salt Lake City, published by the board, 1978), 1, 15-16.
15. "Minorities Fare Well in Utah Schools," *Daily Herald* (Provo, UT), July 26, 1993, C3.
16. Although problems continued to exist in Utah, they were no worse than in most other states, and perhaps not as prevalent as in some parts of the nation. Anglos seemed much less biased than they had been a half-century earlier, and also more interested in their ethnic neighbors. Utah was treated regularly to a variety of ethnic festivals and programs that provided numerous opportunities for heightening intercultural awareness and understanding. In 1987, for example, the Ogden Union Station hosted an eight-week activity in which each of eight ethnic groups had a week to display its heritage and to present special programs. In May 1994 the annual Living Traditions Festival, co-sponsored by the Salt Lake City Arts Council and the Folk Arts Program, highlighted the music, dance, foods, and crafts of numerous ethnic groups who made their homes in the Salt Lake Valley. During the three-day festival, which was free to the public, fifty music and dance groups performed, thirty artisans displayed their skills, and ethnic cuisine was prepared and sold by two dozen community groups. *Utah Folklife Bulletin* (Winter-Spring 1994).
17. For an excellent summary of the full history of Native Americans in Utah, see Forrest S. Cuch, ed., *A History of Utah's American Indians* (Salt Lake City: Utah State Division of Indian Affairs and Utah State Historical Society, 2003). This work includes chapters, by different authors, on each tribe. The final chapter, "Conclusion: The Contemporary Status of Utah Indians," by Robert S. McPherson, deals with the challenges faced by Native Americans in the last part of the twentieth century.
18. For brief summaries of these policies, and their effect on Utah Indians, as well as a general overview of the Native American experience in the state, see David Rich Lewis, "Native Americans in Utah," in *Utah History Encyclopedia*, ed. Allen Kent Powell (Salt Lake City: University of Utah Press, 1994), 389-91; Richard O. Ulibarri, "Utah's Ethnic Minorities: A Survey," *Utah Historical Quarterly* 40 (Summer 1972): 210-32; Richard O. Ulibarri, "Utah's Unassimilated Minorities," in *Utah's History*, ed. Richard D. Poll, Thomas G. Alexander, Eugene E. Campbell, David E. Miller (Logan, UT: Utah State University Press, 1989), 629-49; "The First Peoples of Utah," chap. in *The Peoples of Utah*, ed. Helen Z. Papanikolas (Salt Lake City: Utah State Historical Society, 1976), 11-59, which includes sections by Fred Con-

etah ("My Native Land"), Clyde J. Benally ("The Navajos"), and Floyd A. O'Neal ("The Utes, Southern Paiutes, and Gosiutes"); *Utah Historical Quarterly* 2 (Spring 1971), a special issue on Utah's Indians.

19. See Carolyn Grattan-Aiello, "Senator Arthur V. Watkins and the Termination of Utah's Southern Paiute Indians," *Utah Historical Quarterly* 63 (Summer 1995): 268–83. For an extended discussion of the impact of termination on one group, see R. Warren Metcalf, *Termination's Legacy: The Discarded Indians of Utah* (Lincoln: University of Nebraska Press, 2002).

20. Ulibarri, "Utah's Unassimilated Minorities," 646.

21. Much of the wording of the law is interesting. In justifying its action, Congress declared that "for many Indian people, the traditional ceremonial use of the peyote cactus as a religious sacrament has for centuries been integral to a way of life, and significant in perpetuating Indian tribes and cultures," and that the lack of uniformity among the states on the matter "has created hardship for Indian people who participate in such religious ceremonies." A full copy of the law is available online at http://www.fs.fed.us/spf/tribalrelations/documents/policy/statutes/American_Indian_Religous_Freedom_Act.pdf. Accessed December 12, 2014.

22. Manuel P. Guerrero, "Indian Child Welfare Act of 1978: A Response to the Threat to Indian Culture Caused by Foster and Adoptive Placements of Indian Children," *American Indian Law Review* 7 (1979): 52.

23. As one attorney has observed: "The wholesale separation of Indian children from their families ranks among the most tragic and destructive aspects of contemporary Indian life. State intrusion in parent-child relationships within the Indian culture impedes the ability of the tribe to perpetuate itself and is ultimately an unjustified coerced assimilation into the larger society." Guerrero, "Indian Child Welfare Act of 1978," 53, and note. Chapter 1 of Clarence R. Bishop, "A History of the Indian Placement Program" (master's thesis, University of Utah, 1967) includes a good summary of off-reservation educational programs for Indians, as of the 1960s.

24. The nature of the problem in boarding schools was illustrated by the experience of the Navajo girl who eventually became the catalyst for the foundation of a unique foster home program, the LDS Indian Student Placement Service (ISPS). In 1936, at about age six, Helen John found herself in a boarding school in Tuba City, Arizona. When two boys were caught committing the unpardonable sin of speaking Navajo, the principal washed their mouths out with soap, saying, "You know that what I am doing is to show you what we think of your talking Navajo. I'll just wash those words right out." One of Helen's teachers wondered silently "How can we teach these children to love the words we teach them when we show disdain for the only meaningful words they know?" But most had the attitude of the principal—the Navajo language, along with the culture it represented, had to go. This experience is recorded in Neil J. Birch, "Helen," unpublished manuscript, copy in possession of David J. Whittaker, 16–18.

25. Coleen Keane, "'Where Have All the Children Gone?' Controversy Over Native Child Placement by Mormon Church," *Wassaja* 9 (September–October 1982): 13.

26. As originally proposed, the act would have made it nearly impossible for the LDS Indian Student Placement program to continue, but a major lobbying effort on the part of the church resulted in an amendment that protected it. Lobbyists included the Washington law firm of Wilkinson, Cragun, and Barker, as well as Utah's Congressman Gunn McKay, the Director of the Washington D.C. LDS Social Services Agency (David Albrecht), and a Navajo—George P. Lee, a General Authority of the LDS Church and the church's show-piece so far as the placement program was con-

cerned. David M. Albrecht, interview by James B. Allen, September 3, 1992, notes in James B. Allen papers, L Tom Parry Special Collections, Harold B. Lee Library, Brigham Young University; Robert Gottlieb and Peter Wiley, *America's Saints: The Rise of Mormon Power* (New York: G. P. Putnam's Sons, 1984), 166.

27. For a brief history of this program see James B. Allen, "The Rise and Decline of the LDS Indian Student Placement Program, 1947–1996," in *Mormon Scripture and the Ancient World: Studies in Honor of John L. Sorenson*, ed. Davis Bitton (Provo: Foundation for Ancient Research and Mormon Studies, 1998), 85–119.See also Bishop, "A History of the Indian Placement Program"; Lynette A. Riggs, "The Church of Jesus Christ of Latter-day Saints' Indian Student Placement Service: A History" (Ph.D. dissertation, Utah State University, 2008); Matthew R. Garrett, "Mormons, Indians, and Lamanites: The Student Indian Placement Program, 1947–2000" (Ph.D. dissertation, Arizona State University, 2010); J. Neil Birch, "Helen John: The Beginnings of Indian Placement.," *Dialogue: A Journal of Mormon Thought* 18 (Winter 1985): 119-29.

28. Letter from Stephen L. Richards and J. Reuben Clark, Jr., August 10, 1954, as cited in Bishop, "A History of the Indian Placement Program," 43–44. It was sometimes a financial burden on the foster families, but in 1960 they received a little relief. Work by members of Utah's Congressional delegation resulted in an Internal Revenue Service policy that allowed an income tax exemption of up to $50 for each month a placement student was maintained in a home. Ibid., 75.

29. For a listing, see Bishop, "A History of the Indian Student Placement Program," 97.

30. This policy grew out of a lawsuit brought against the Washington County School District in 1990 by Raindancer Youth Services, Inc., an organization that brought Indian students from New Mexico and Arizona to St. George, where they received free public education. When the schools became overcrowded, however, school officials said that they would no longer provide education unless each student paid the required out-of-state tuition. Raindancer then brought suit, showing that 450 students in the LDS program throughout Utah and another one hundred students in a boarding school program in Sevier County also received free education. Raindancer demanded equal treatment. In a settlement worked out in 1992, the church agreed not to bring in any more out-of-state students. Marianne Funk, "Settlement May Spell End of Two Programs," *Deseret News* (September 30, 1992), B1–B2..

31. See Clarence R. Bishop, "An Evaluation of the Scholastic Achievement of Selected Indian Students Attending Elementary Public Schools of Utah" (master's thesis, Brigham Young University, 1960); Bruce A. Chadwick, Stan L. Albrecht, and Howard M. Bahr, "Evaluation of an Indian Student Placement Program," *Social Casework* 67 (November 1986): 515–24; Bert P. Cundick, Douglas K. Gottfredson and Linda Willson, "Changes in Scholastic Achievement and Intelligence of Indian Children Enrolled in a Foster Placement Program," *Developmental Psychology* 10 (1974): 815–20; Genevieve De Hoyos and Arturo De Hoyos, "The Indian Placement Program of The Church of Jesus Christ of Latter-day Saints: A Statistical and Analytical Study (First Draft)," (unpublished manuscript, May 1973, available L. Tom Perry Special Collections, Harold B. Lee Library, Brigham Young University.); Howard Rainer, "An Analysis of Attitudes Navajo Community Leaders Have Toward a Religion Sponsored Program Based Upon Membership of that Faith and Amount of Information Attained" (master's thesis, Brigham Young University, 1976); Dorothy Jensen Schimmelpfennig, "A Study of Cross-Cultural Problems in the L.D.S. Indian Student Placement Program in Davis County, Utah" (Ph.D. dissertation, University of Utah, 1971); Grant Hardy Taylor, "A Comparative Study of

Former LDS Placement and Non-Placement Navajo Students at Brigham Young University" (Ph.D. dissertation, Brigham Young University, 1981); Linda Ouida Willson, "Changes in Scholastic Achievement and Intelligence of Indian Children Enrolled in a Foster Placement Program" (master's thesis, Brigham Young University, 1973); Riggs, "The Church of Jesus Christ of Latter-day Saints' Indian Student Placement Service."

32. Chadwick, Albrecht, and Bahr, "Evaluation of an Indian Student Placement Program," 517. Forty percent of the students dropped out at their own request, most often because of the illness of a parent who needed help. Fifteen percent dropped out directly at their parents' request, while 8 percent were sent home by foster families. Especially significant, however, is the fact that even after dropping out of the program placement students went on to finish high school in significantly larger numbers than nonplacement Native Americans. Eighty-two percent of the participants finished high school, as compared with 45 percent in the control group studied. Bruce A. Chadwick and Stan L. Albrecht, "Mormons and Indians: Beliefs, Policies, Programs, and Practices" (unpublished manuscript, 1992, used by permission of the authors), 13.

33. See "Seeking Economic Independence," chapter 4 in Judith Harlan, *American Indians Today: Issues and Conflicts* (New York: Franklin Watts, 1987), 52–65.

34. See *Survey of Services to American Indians through Institutes of Higher Learning in Seven Northwestern States* (Salt Lake City: published by the Bureau of Indian Services, Division of Continuing Education, University of Utah, May 1970), 37–50.

35. For a brief discussion of these and other issues, see Jerry Spangler, "Tribal Rights Foster a Host of Problems," *Deseret News*, Extra, July 8, 1993, A13, A14.

36. Hagen v. Utah, 114 S. Ct. 958.

37. See discussions in John H. Allen, "Denial of Voting Rights to Reservation Indians," *Utah Law Review* 5 (Fall 1956): 247; Rothfels v. Southworth 356 P.2d 612.

38. Clyde J. Benally, "The Navajos," in *The Peoples of Utah*, ed. Helen Z. Papanikolas, 25.

39. Each was supported by four main posts, one on each corner, representing the gods in that particular direction (east, west, north, or south). The hogan always faced east, and the organization inside gathered around a central fireplace.

40. Benally, "The Navajos," 15. Benally's article includes a short but incisive description of Navajo religious customs.

41. Mary Shepardson and Blodwen Hammond, *The Navajo Mountain Community: Social Organization and Kinship Terminology* (Berkeley: University of California Press, 1970), 243.

42. For general treatments of the Navajo, see Raymond Friday Lock, *The Book of the Navajo* (Los Angeles: Mankind Publishing Company, 1989); Peter Iverson, *The Navajo Nation* (Westport, CN: Greenwood Press, 1981). For short general treatments of the Navajo in Utah, see Benally, "The Navajos"; Robert S. McPherson, "Navajo Indians," in *Utah History Encyclopedia*, ed. Powell, 391–93; Gregory C. Thompson, "Utah's Indian Country: The American Indian Experience in San Juan County, 1700–1980," in *San Juan County, Utah: People, Resources, and History*, ed. Allan Kent Powell (Salt Lake City: Utah State Historical Society, 1983): 51–67. Robert S. McPherson, *Sacred Land, Sacred View: Navajo Perceptions of the Four Corners Region* (Provo, UT: Charles Redd Center for Western Studies, Brigham Young University, 1992) is an impressive discussion of Navajo cultural traditions.

43. League of Women Voters of Salt Lake, "A Brief History and Description of Utah Indian Peoples" (1973), 2–3. See also Jeff Bork and Larry M. Blair, "San Juan County Navajos—Social and Economic Statistics," *Utah Economic and Business Review* 33 (August 1973):1-5.
44. Jerry Spangler, "Education Opening Doors for Indians?" *Deseret News*, November 13, 1989, B1.
45. Lock, *The Book of the Navajo*, 453.
46. Ibid., 458.
47. *High Country News*, July 30, 1990. For an extensive survey of Navajo economic conditions in the 1970s, see Jeffrey Holt Bork, "Income and Employment Status of the Navajo Indian in San Juan County, Utah" (master's thesis, University of Utah, 1973).
48. A fine history of the Ute people is Fred A. Conetah, *A History of the Northern Ute People* (Salt Lake City: Uintah–Ouray Ute Tribe, 1982). For a short summary of the Northern Utes, see David Rich Lewis, "Ute Indians—Northern," in *Utah History Encyclopedia*, ed. Powell, 608–9. A very insightful article on how public school policy affected Ute education is Kim M. Gruenwald, "American Indians and the Public School System: A Case Study of the Northern Utes," *Utah Historical Quarterly* 61 (Summer 1996), 246-63.
49. Conetah, *A History of the Northern Ute People*, 152–53.
50. See "The Front Page" section in *Utah Holiday* 10 (July 1982), 10–13, for a detailed discussion of Hansen's letter and the response to it.
51. Linda Sillitoe, "The Old and the New Come Together on the Reservation," *Deseret News* Magazine (September 25, 1983).
52. As quoted in Jan Pettit, *Utes: The Mountain People*, rev. ed. (Boulder, CO: Johnson Books, 1990), 158–59.
53. Ronald L. Holt, *Beneath These Red Cliffs: An Ethnohistory of the Utah Paiutes* (Albuquerque: University of New Mexico Press, 1992); Ronald L. Holt, "Paiute Indians of Utah," in *Utah History Encyclopedia*, ed. Powell, 408–10; Warren L. d'Asevedo, *Great Basin*, Vol. 11 of *Handbook of North American Indians*, ed. William C. Sturtevant (Washington, D. C. Smithsonian Institution, 1986), 576–77. See also Martha C. Knack, Life Is with People: Household Organization of the Contemporary Southern Paiute Indians (Socorro, NM: Ballena Press, 1980); Martha C. Knack, "Contemporary Southern Paiute Household Structure and Bilateral Kinship Structures (master's thesis, University of Michigan, 1975).
54. Mark Ashurst-McGee, "The Avikan Band of Utes and Their Cultural Survival in the Midst of Drastic Change," an anthropology term paper, Brigham Young University, 1994, copy in James B. Allen papers, L. Tom Perry Special Collections, Harold B. Lee Library, Brigham Young University. See also Robert McPherson, "Ute Indians—Southern," in *Utah History Encyclopedia*, ed. Powell, 609–11; "Some Historical Background on the San Juan County Utes," *Blue Mountain Shadows* 11 (Winter 1992): 4–5; Mary Jane Yazzie, "Life and Traditions of the Utes of Avikan," *Blue Mountain Shadows* 7 (Winter 1990): 25–33; Robert W. Delaney, *The Ute Mountain Utes* (Albuquerque: University of New Mexico Press, 1989). *The Ute Mountain Utes* are located mainly in Colorado, but the White Mesa (Avikan) Utes are associated with them historically.
55. The most common alternative spelling is Gosiute. For general nineteenth-century background, see James B. Allen and Ted J. Warner, "The Gosiute Indians in Pioneer Utah," *Utah Historical Quarterly* 39 (Spring 1971): 162–77.

56. Carling Malouf, "The Gosiute Indians," in *American Indian Ethnohistory: California and Basin-Plateau Indians*, ed. David Agee Horr (New York: Garland Publishing Co., 1974), 35.
57. For an extensive, sympathetic discussion of Goshute history and culture at Deep Creek, see Ronald R. Bateman, *Deep Creek Reflections: 125 Years at Ibapah, Utah, 1959-1984* (Salt Lake City: R. R. Bateman, 1984).
58. For an excellent treatment of the history of the Skull Valley group, see Steven J. Crum, "The Skull Valley Band of the Goshute Tribe—Deeply Attached to Their Native Homeland," *Utah Historical Quarterly* 55 (Summer 1978): 250-67.
59. Ibid., 267.
60. Leon Bear, Secretary-Treasurer of the Skull Valley Tribe, telephone interview by Mark Ashurst-McGee, July 31, 1993, notes in James B. Allen papers, L. Tom Perry Special Collections, Harold B. Lee Library, Brigham Young University. The Confederated Tribes of the Goshutes included Goshute, Paiute and Bannock peoples.
61. General treatments of the Hispanics in Utah include Jorge Iber, *Hispanics in the Mormon Zion 1912-1999* (College Station: Texas A&M University Press, 2000); Vincente V. Mayer, Jr., *Utah: A Hispanic History* (Salt Lake City: American West Center, University of Utah, 1975); Vincente V. Mayer, "After Escalante: The Spanish-Speaking People of Utah," chapter. in *The Peoples of Utah*, ed. Helen Z. Papanikolas, 437-68; Edward H. Mayer, "The Evolution of Culture and Tradition in Utah's Mexican-American Community," *Utah Historical Quarterly* 49 (Spring 1981): 133-44; Ann Nelson, "Spanish-Speaking Laborer in Utah 1950-1965," in "Working papers Toward a History of the Spanish-Speaking People of Utah," (manuscript, Salt Lake City: American West Center, Mexican-American Documentation Project, University of Utah, 1973), 63-111, copy in James B. Allen papers, L. Tom Perry Special Collections, Harold B. Lee Library, Brigham Young University; For a general treatment of Chicanos in the United States see Carey McWilliams, *North from Mexico: The Spanish-Speaking People of the United States* (New York: Greenwood Press, 1990).
62. See Patricia Maryon, "A Face in the Crowd," *Utah Holiday* 10 (April 1981): 18-22.
63. For a comprehensive treatment of migrant workers in Utah during a particular time period and some of their social and economic problems, see Nelson, "Spanish-Speaking Migrant Laborer in Utah 1950-1965."
64. Helen Mickelsen Crampton, "Acculturation of the Mexican-American in Salt Lake County, Utah" (Ph.D. dissertation, University of Utah, 1967), 90-92.
65. See Jerald A. Merrill, "Fifty Years with a Future: Salt Lake's Guadalupe Mission and Parish," *Utah Historical Quarterly* 40 (Summer 1972): 242-64.
66. D. Byrne, L. Maldando, and O. Rivera, *Chicanos in Utah* (Salt Lake City: The Utah State Board of Education, 1976), passim.
67. David Thomas Judd, "An Achievement Comparison between Anglos and Chicanos at Bingham and Hillcrest High Schools" (master's thesis, University of Utah, 1975); Douglas Bowen Luke, "Academic and Social Differences Study between Mexican and Non-Mexican Students at Layton High School" (master's thesis, University of Utah, 1971); James Francis Cushing, "A Comparison of Mexican American and Anglo American Tenth Grade Students in the West Complex of the Granite School District" (Ph.D. dissertation, University of Utah, 1975); Russell Harold Bishop, "A Status Study of Spanish-Speaking Students at Midvale Junior High School" (master's thesis, University of Utah, 1964).

68. Edward H. Mayer, "The Evolution of Culture and Tradition in Utah's Mexican-American Community," *Utah Historical Quarterly* 49 (Spring 1981): 137–38.
69. For a discussion of some of the efforts taking place during the Rampton administration, see Governor Calvin Rampton, "Utah's Efforts with Chicano Problems," in *The Spanish Speaking American Challenge: A Report of the Chicano Conference Held at BYU in 1974*, ed. L. Sid Shreeve and Merwin G. Fairbanks (Provo, UT: Latin American Studies, Brigham Young University, 1974), 23–58.
70. Marjorie Cortez, "Utah Business Reacts to Rapid Hispanic Growth, *Deseret News*, April 7, 1991; Milton Hollstein, "Media Brings News and Entertainment to Utah's Hispanics," *Deseret News*, February 10, 1992, C2.
71. William H. Gonzalez and Orlando Rivera, "Hispanics in Utah," in *Utah History Encyclopedia*, ed. Powell, 255–57.
72. Cynthia Gonzales, "'The Wetbacks are Coming!' 'The Wetbacks are Coming!'" *MountainWest Magazine* 5 (February 1979): 46–47.
73. See Sylvia Kronstadt, "Poverty, Ignorance Enslave Migrant," *The Daily Utah Chronicle*, October 30, 1968, 2, 4–5. See also Nelson, "Spanish-Speaking Migrant Laborer in Utah 1950-1965."
74. Jeff Vice, "Apartment Unit Fulfills a Dream for Migrants," *Deseret News*, November 19, 1993, B2; Sheila Sanchez, "County Examines Housing Needs for Farm Workers," *Daily Herald*, November 19, 1993, A1.
75. As quoted on Maryon, "A Face in the Crowd," 22.
76. For a history of the center at Topaz, see Leonard J. Arrington, *Price of Prejudice: The Japanese-American Relocation Center in Utah During World War II* (Logan, UT: The Faculty Association, Utah State University, 1962).
77. Helen Z. Papanikolas and Alice Kasai, "Japanese Life in Utah," in *The Peoples of Utah*, ed. Helen Z. Papanikolas, 361–62.
78. For a history of the Japanese in Utah see Ted Hagata, ed., *Japanese Americans in Utah* (Salt Lake City: JA Centennial Committee, 1966). See also Nancy J. Taniguchi, "Japanese Immigrants in Utah," in *Utah History Encyclopedia*, ed. Powell, 280–83; section on "Utah's Japanese" in Richard O. Ulibarri, "Utah's Unassimilated Minorities," in *Utah's History*, ed. Poll et al., 640–42; Helen Z. Papanikolas and Alice Kasai, "Japanese Life in Utah," chap. in The People's of Utah, ed. Helen Z. Papanikolas, 333–62; Elmer R. Smith, "The 'Japanese' in Utah (Part I)," and "The 'Japanese' in Utah (Part II)," *Utah Humanities Review* 2 (April, July 1948): 129–44, 208–30. More detailed sources for the Japanese in Utah may be found in two collections in Special Collections at the J. Willard Marriott, University of Utah: "Alice Kasai Papers, 1925–1988," and "Japanese in Utah Collection, 1971–1977." See also Mamoru Iga, "Acculturation of Japanese Population in Davis County, Utah" (Ph.D. dissertation, University of Utah, 1955); Hisa Aoki, "Functional Analysis of Mono-Racial In-Groups: *Nisei* Congeniality Primary Groups on the University of Utah Campus (master's thesis, University of Utah, 1950);
79. Don C. Conley, "The Chinese in Utah," in *Utah History Encyclopedia*, ed. Powell, 85–86. See also, Don C. Conley, "The Pioneer Chinese of Utah," chap. in *The Peoples of Utah*, ed. Helen Z. Papanikolas, 251–77.
80. Angela Chan Conley, "The Social Problems of the Chinese in Salt Lake County" (master's thesis, University of Utah, 1973), 30.
81. Conley, "The Social Problems of the Chinese in Salt Lake City," 24.

82. Sungup Moon, "The Linguistic Patterns of the Utah-Korean Community" (master's thesis, Brigham Young University, 1992), 41.
83. Ibid., 47–48, 51.
84. Mark W. Fraser, Peter J. Pecora, and Chirapat Popuang, "Self-Sufficiency among Indochinese Refugees: A Survey of Refugee Sponsors" (unpublished manuscript produced in the Social Research Institute, Graduate School of Social Work, University of Utah, January 1984), Introduction.
85. Brock Yancy, "Indochinese Refugees as Employees: Perceptions of Employers in Utah" (master's thesis, University of Utah, 1983), 50–51. The foregoing discussion of Utah's Southeast Asians is based almost wholly on Carol Edison, "Southeast Asians in Utah," in *Utah History Encyclopedia*, ed. Powell, 519–21. For a discussion of some success as well as problems and internal friction facing the Vietnam community in 1994, see Steve Fidel, "Utah's Refugees: A Culture Seeking Unity," *Deseret News*, Extra, June 16, 1994.
86. "The AAU: The Organization and It's Services," *AAU News* 1 (September 1985): 1. See also "The Voice of the Asian Community," *AAU News* 1 (September 1985): 2
87. Ann Kilbourn, "Hmong Residents Keep Traditions Alive Here," *Salt Lake Tribune*, May 6, 1984, W4.
88. Moon, "Linguistic Patterns," 58.
89. Edison, "Southeast Asians in Utah," 519–21; Robert E. Lewis, Mark W. Fraser, Peter J. Pecora, "Religiosity among Indochinese Refugees in Utah," *Journal for the Scientific Study of Religion* 27 (June 1988): 271–82. See summary statement on p. 281.
90. Carol Edison, "South Sea Islanders in Utah," in *Utah History Encyclopedia*, ed. Powell, 516–18.
91. Ibid. This discussion of South Sea Islanders is drawn primarily from this article.
92. Sione V. Hingano, "Social Cultural Problems of Polynesian High School Graduates Not Pursuing College Level Study" (Ed.D. dissertation, Brigham Young University, 1984), 81–82.
93. Michael Phillips, "Leavitt Names Director of Polynesian Affairs," *Salt Lake Tribune*, June 18, 1994, B5.
94. "1990 Census Brief: Minorities of Utah."
95. "Young Blacks on Blackness: Central City Youth on Being Black," typewritten booklet prepared by Clifford L. Williams, 1972. Available J. Willard Marriot Library, University of Utah.
96. James Boyd Christensen, "A Social Survey of the Negro Population of Salt Lake City, Utah" (master's thesis, University of Utah, 1948), 98; George Ramjoue, "The Negro in Utah: A Geographical Study in Population" (master's thesis, University of Utah, 1968), 26.
97. Coleman, "Blacks in Utah History," 136.
98. "Utah's Black Legacy," 5.
99. Ramjoue, "The Negro in Utah," 38.
100. For a report on these and other perceptions within the black community in the mid-1970s, see Dennis Geertsen, Harold Adams, David Gabriel, Theresa Breaux, and Paris Brown, "Needs Assessment of the Salt Lake City Black Community," Salt Lake Community Mental Health Center Program Evaluation and Research Department Report No. 2, April 1977
101. "Utah's Black Legacy," 6.

102. Ibid., 5.
103. Ibid., 6.
104. Klaus D. Gurgel, "Ethnic Minorities," in *Atlas of Utah*, ed. Wayne L. Wahlquist (Provo, UT: Brigham Young University Press, 1981), 122.
105. "Utah's Black Legacy," 7.
106. "Group Targets Education, Perceptions," *Deseret News* Extra, February 3, 1994, A16.
107. "After 45 Years, Alberta Henry Says She Still Has Work To Do," ibid., A15.
108. "Women Find Strength in Organization," ibid., A16.
109. See Geertsen et al., "Needs Assessment of the Salt Lake City Black Community."
110. "Utah's Black Legacy," 7.
111. See Peggy Olson, "Ruffin Bridgeforth: Leader and Father to Mormon Blacks," *This People* 1 (Winter 1980): 11-17.
112. See Ralph M. Tannenbaum, "The Jewish Community in Utah," in *Utah History Encyclopedia*, ed. Powell, 285-86.
113. See the discussion of the Greek Orthodox Church in Appendix B. See also Helen Z. Papanikolas, "The Exiled Greeks," chapter in *The Peoples of Utah*, ed. Helen Z. Papanikolas, 409-35; Helen Zeese Papanikolas, "The Greeks in Utah," in *Utah History Encyclopedia*, ed. Powell, 234-36.
114. See Robert F. Zeidner, "Middle Eastern Immigrants to Utah," in *Utah History Encyclopedia*, ed. Powell, 363-64; Robert F. Zeidner, "From Babylon to Babylon: Immigration from the Middle East," chapter in *The Peoples of Utah*, ed. Helen Z. Papanikolas, 385-408.
115. Amy Donaldson, "Minorities Urged to Value Cultures," *Deseret News*, October 11, 1994, B1.
116. Joe Costanzo, "Minorities Are Increasing on Utah College Campuses," *Deseret News*, January 26, 1995, B1.
117. See, for example, comments in *Poverty in Utah* (Salt Lake City: State Department of Community and Economic Development, Utah Issues Information Program, 1983), 96-97.

APPENDIX B

Utah and the Arts, 1945–1994[1]

The arts not only feed the soul, they spark the imagination. The measure of a civilization is the creativity of its people. Through the arts, Utah can inspire its men, women, and children to reach for the very best.

So said Utah Governor Norman L. Bangerter in the mid-1980s.[2] But Bangerter was not the only governor to recognize the arts as among the most vital elements of Utah culture. Beginning with the Rampton administration, all of Utah's governors paid special attention to the arts and also officially backed the process of public funding—something that had never been done before in Utah history. Spurred by this support as well as support from educational institutions, corporations, and private foundations, and invigorated by increasing artistic excellence, the arts literally flourished, especially after the mid-1970s. Public appreciation for art seemed to rise steadily as more painters and sculptors were able to earn a living through the sale of their works. By the 1990s, schoolchildren and small communities around the state were treated regularly to appearances by Utah's best performing groups and other artists; art museums dotted the state, enjoying a new sense of public appreciation; music, art, and film festivals attracted thousands, as did the nationally renowned annual Shakespearean Festival in

Cedar City; and Utahns regularly attended legitimate theater, ballet, and opera. Utah's literary artists, too, enjoyed a wider audience than ever before and were more diverse in their writing.

Whatever success the arts enjoyed did not come without some tension and controversy. The period following World War II was a time of new, often controversial, directions for the arts, and what happened in Utah was, in many ways, a microcosm of the larger American scene. There was sharp disagreement over modern artistic forms, for example. In addition, not everyone felt the same enthusiasm for all the arts or for public funding, resulting at times in objections to the use of tax money to support them. But despite the problems, by the 1990s the people of Utah seemed more interested in the arts than ever before in their history.

Fostering the Arts: Government, Private Institutions, and the Public

The first major effort by the federal government to support the arts came in the 1930s, during the Great Depression. Under the auspices of the Works Project Administration (WPA) the government officially sponsored a variety of historical and artistic programs through the Federal Arts Project and the Federal Writer's Project. These programs provided work for jobless writers, musicians, painters, and other artists. Before the program closed in 1941, the artists and writers involved produced thousands of works, some good and some bad. Murals were painted for public buildings in cities and towns that otherwise could never afford such art. Musicians enhanced the lives of people in communities throughout the nation. In Utah a symphony orchestra, forerunner of the Utah Symphony, was organized. The Historical Records Survey inventoried all county archives and published guides that became invaluable tools for historians. One of these was Dale Morgan's *Utah: A Guide to the State*, an important and well-written guide to *Utah's history* and to tours through all parts of the state.[3] In addition, historians helped preserve Utah's heritage by collecting and copying pioneer diaries for deposit in libraries and archives.

Except for the depression-born New Deal, there was never a major federal program dedicated specifically to promoting the arts. That absence of support ended in 1965 when, strongly encouraged by the Kennedy administration, Congress established the National Endowment for the Arts and the National Endowment for the Humanities. "It is necessary and appropriate," lawmakers said, "for the Federal Government to help create and sustain, not only the climate encouraging freedom of thought, imagination, and inquiry, but also the material conditions facilitating the release of this creative talent. It is necessary and appropriate for the Federal Government to complement, assist, and add to programs for the advancement of the humanities and the arts by local, State, regional, and private agencies and their organizations."[4] After that the nation and the state often acted as important partners with private institutions in fostering the arts.

The significance of public funding was partly illustrated through the numerous activities of the Utah Arts Council (previously known as the Utah State Institute of Fine Arts, then the Division of Fine Arts within the Department of Development Services, and then by its present name). In the years immediately after World War II this organization worked particularly hard to promote two of the state's most valuable artistic treasures, the Utah Symphony and Ballet West. Its ability to support these and other activities was strengthened in 1965 when national funding became available through the National Endowment for the Arts. As a result, the Arts Council helped not only these two groups but also the Repertory Dance Theater, the summer Shakespearean Festival in Cedar City, the Utah Opera Company, the Ririe-Woodbury Dance Company, and many other important arts programs. It also helped build the Pioneer Memorial Museum.[5] Ruth Draper, head of the Arts Council in the 1970s and early 1980s, was a particularly dynamic leader who directed the development of community outreach programs.

Among the Utah Arts Council's numerous activities was an outreach program, inaugurated in the 1970s, through which schools and communities were treated to fine performing artists and to exhibits of the visual arts. This replaced a similar program conducted earlier by the Utah Museum of Fine Arts. The council also supported such projects as the Utah Media Center, the US Film and Video Festival, the Salt Lake City Arts Council, and the annual Utah Arts Festival. Partly funded by the legislature, the latter was recognized as the only official state-sponsored arts festival in the nation.[6] Beginning in 1971, the Utah Arts Council sponsored an Artists in Education program designed to support artist residencies in schools and communities as well as specific, locally initiated art education programs. This was another effective way of introducing schoolchildren statewide to all the visual, performing, and literary arts.[7]

Beginning in 1975, the Utah Arts Council also promoted the *Utah Performing Arts Tour*, which took concerts, classes, workshops, and lecture-demonstrations to communities, both large and small, throughout the state. Being required to raise only one-third to one-half the normal cost, these communities enjoyed a wide variety of outstanding programs that included classical music, ballet, folk dance, modern dance, jazz and traditional music, bluegrass music, and theater. By 1993 the tour had cosponsored more than 1,350 performances in eighty communities and before more than half a million people. During the 1993–94 season twelve different performing groups were offered, including programs from the Children's Dance Theatre, Repertory Dance Theatre, Ririe-Woodbury Dance Company, and the Zivio Ethnic Arts Ensemble, which performed folk music and dance of Eastern Europe and the United States. The tour's theater offering included national stage, television, and film star Adilah Barnes, the University of Utah Classic Greek Theatre Festival, Sara Ransom (giving performances as well as workshops in the art of storytelling), the Sundance Children's Theatre, TheatreWorks West (which presented workshops as well as ten-minute plays written by Utah playwrights), and the Utah Opera.[8]

The Arts Council also encouraged Utah's flourishing interest in folk art. Many communities and ethnic groups held demonstrations, often annually, that portrayed indigenous crafts, cooking, music, dance, and storytelling. In 1984 the restored Chase Home in Liberty Park became the home of the Arts Council's Folk Arts Program, which included a museum. A concert series at the museum, "Mondays in the Park," demonstrated the rich variety of musical traditions in Utah, including Latin American, Japanese, and old-time American music. The council also sponsored numerous ethnic festivals, including the food, crafts, and culture of the Greek, Scottish, Irish, Asian, Chicano, Native American and other communities. Beginning in 1981, an annual Governor's Folk Art Award recognized individuals who made significant contributions to Utah's cultural heritage through their traditional art forms.[9]

Although most of the Arts Council's funding came from within the state, in the mid-1990s about 13 percent of its budget came from federal grants. Another source of funding for the arts began to open up between 1970 and 1975 when the National Endowment for the Humanities established volunteer humanities councils, with hired staffs, in every state, the District of Columbia, and three US protectorates. As a result, the Utah Endowment for the Humanities was created in the summer of 1975. Providing financial support for public programs, the Endowment focused at first on public policy issues, but it soon began to fund traditional humanities programs, including the arts.[10]

Meanwhile, many Utah schools did an outstanding job of introducing their students to the arts. In 1984, for example, Montezuma Creek Elementary School was one of eight schools in the nation to receive a $10,000 award from the Rockefeller Brothers Fund for Excellence in Art Education. The school offered an exceptional program in storytelling, creative writing, dance, and the visual arts, and the creative poetry produced by the students was particularly remarkable. As David Rockefeller said when he presented the award, "It is rare to find an elementary school which places so much importance on the arts, including the art of living, the most important art of all."[11]

Appreciation for the arts was also fostered by a growing number of art museums and centers in the state.[12] Utah's first art museum, still one of the premier galleries in the state, was the Springville Museum of Art.[13] Its history is an outstanding example of what can happen when a community becomes excited about and involved in such a project. Founded in 1903 by John Hafen and Cyrus E. Dallin, it was known originally as the Springville High School Art Gallery. Administered by the school faculty, it

Image B.1: The Springville Museum of Art. Courtesy of the Springville Museum of Art.

provided students and community volunteers with opportunities to assist in its operation. It was also the recipient of a number of significant art collections, as gifts. In 1967 the first full-time director was employed, and, after the Nebo School District relinquished its administrative role, the museum became the shared responsibility of the Springville High School Art Association (which consisted of dues-paying members and a board made up of citizens) and the City of Springville. Dr. Vern G. Swanson was hired as director of the museum in 1980,[14] and under his direction the art collection doubled, the budget tripled, the number of employees quadrupled, and a second annual show (the Autumn Exhibit) was inaugurated. Whereas the Spring Salon was a general exhibition, the Autumn Exhibit was more thematic. One indication of the growing prestige of the Springville museum was the fact that the 1995 Spring Salon received a record number of submissions—861—from which 241 were selected for display. This record may well have been related to the fact that two highly distinguished artists, Marcus C. G. Halliwell of London and Utah's H. Lee Deffebach, were the jurors.[15]

The museum housed a wide variety of art, representing virtually every form and style. It was remodeled in the 1980s in order to increase the space for exhibitions and support activities. In 1982 the board decided that it should also become a center for the history of Utah art. The result was the development of an extensive historical research library that by the 1990s made the museum an indispensable source of Utah art history. Among its many interesting exhibits was a collection of the works of Utah's women artists, displayed in 1984 and described in a museum booklet, *Women Artists in Utah*. In addition, director Vern Swanson co-authored a richly illustrated, detailed history of the visual arts in Utah, entitled *Utah Art*, funded by the George S. And Dolores Doré Eccles Foundation and published in 1991 by the Springville Museum of Art and Peregrine Smith Books.

The Springville Museum of Art was proudly supported by a public-spirited citizenry, and by a city government that, as of 1991, annually contributed $15.28 per capita to the fine and performing arts. This was the largest per capita contribution to the arts of any city in the United States. With its spacious halls, its important and varied collection that included Utah, American, and Soviet realism, and the numerous traveling exhibits presented there, the museum provided visitors an outstanding opportunity to view the works of nationally and internationally known painters and sculptors, as well as those of important local artists. It was also an elegant setting for balls, receptions, and other social activities.

In 1991, the state legislature and the state Board of Education funded the Statewide Art Partnership, centered at the Springville Museum of Art. Among its activities was a quarterly "Evening for Educators" held at the museum or other sites around the state. Open to all public school teachers, the program was designed to prepare educators to use Utah's visual arts throughout the curriculum. Art teachers from several school districts joined in providing instruction. Other institutions, such as the Utah Museum of Fine Arts, Brigham Young University, and the Braithwaite Gallery joined the Art Partnership in producing teacher packets, writing lesson plans, and hosting the evening for educators. In cooperation with the Springville Museum of Art, the partnership also began cataloging the extensive art collections held by most of Utah's schools. In addition, it provided more than $5,000 annually for the restoration and preparation of artwork in the schools. By 1996 more than two hundred paintings had been saved through this important program.[16]

The Springville Museum of Art was not the only noteworthy museum of its kind in Utah. The Salt Lake Art Center, a nonprofit organization founded in 1933, collected paintings, sculpture, prints, and drawings by contemporary Intermountain West artists. It also sponsored an annual arts festival. In Ogden, the Eccles Community Art Center, founded in 1959, promoted exhibitions of artists from around the state and conducted art classes, tours, and recitals. The Brigham City Museum-Gallery, located in the basement of the new city hall, came into existence in 1970. Its exhibits emphasized both the fine arts and historical artifacts. In Bountiful, the Bountiful/Davis Art Center, begun in cooperation with the art department and the Division of Continuing Education at the University of Utah, was opened in 1974. That year the center also inaugurated an annual LeConte Stewart Festival. The center became independent from the university in the 1983–84 school year.

Utah's colleges and universities were highly important centers for fostering, teaching, exhibiting, and performing works of art. The Utah Museum of Fine Arts at the University of Utah was founded in 1951 after Mrs. Richard Hudnut donated her collection of "old masters" to the university. Other donations followed and by the 1980s the museum boasted fine collections of Utah art, fifteenth to nineteenth-century European paintings, eighteenth-nineteenth-century American art, Native American art, primitive art from Africa and Oceania, Asian (especially southeast Asian) art, and ancient art objects. Because of its broad coverage of world art history, the museum became Utah's premier resource for studying the fine arts.[17] Its first professional director, Frank Sanguinetti, was named in 1967. The museum's collection was moved into a new building in 1970. In addition to displays from that collection, which grew at an unprecedented rate under Sanguinetti's hand, the museum brought in a dazzling array of temporary exhibits from around the world. These included, in the 1980s alone, works of Leonardo da Vinci, Henry Moore, and Thomas Hart Benton. The museum also brought many local and national performing artists to its galleries and its 420-seat auditorium. In addition, it provided traveling exhibitions from its collection, free of charge, to nonprofit Utah institutions such as schools, galleries, churches, and libraries.

In 1964, with the dedication of the Harris Fine Arts Center, the art department at Brigham Young University found a spacious new home and a choice place for artistic displays. In 1975 the department received curator responsibilities for the important collection housed in storage and in the various galleries of the Harris Fine Arts Center. The collection, rich in Asian, European, American, and Utah art, was moved to the university's impressive new Museum of Art in 1993. Long the dream of many art faculty members and others, the new museum was made a reality through the prodigious efforts of James Mason, dean of the College of Fine Arts, who became its first director. The building, financed entirely by private donations, covered one hundred thousand square feet and included several galleries and a cafeteria. The museum's inaugural six-month exhibit, "The Etruscans: Legacy of a Lost Civilization," was a 178-piece traveling exhibit that attracted nearly two hundred thousand visitors, including public school classes, from throughout the state. Other rotating exhibits came from the university's extensive collection as well as from many other places, and included all the visual arts. Beginning in December 1995, the museum sponsored another major exhibit, "Imperial Tombs of China," which attracted more than three hundred thousand visitors in four months.

In Cedar City, the Braithwaite Fine Arts Gallery at Southern Utah State College opened in 1976. The gallery exhibited works by faculty and students as well as traveling shows and its own permanent collection of nineteenth and twentieth-century European, American, and Utah art. At Utah State University, a major art museum was built with funds contributed by Nora Eccles Harrison. Opening in 1982, its emphasis was on twentieth-century American art and Native American ceramics.

In Salt Lake City, the LDS Church Museum of History and Art, directed by Glen M. Leonard, opened in 1983. Its permanent exhibit emphasized the lives of each of the presidents of the LDS Church, and its rotating exhibits featured the works of many Utah notables, including C. C. A. Christensen, LeConte Stewart, Minerva Teichert, and John Hafen. With a well-trained professional staff of art historians and curators and a cadre of docents to conduct visitors through the exhibitions, it soon became one of the most important and well attended art museums in the state. In 1987 and again in 1991, the church fostered international arts competitions, with the winning entries being shown at the Museum of History and Art. LDS artists from around the world displayed painting, sculpture, quilts, pottery, photography, and, beginning in 1991, multimedia presentations. The rich diversity of style, talent, and religious subject matter made these shows among the most interesting in the state.

There were numerous other galleries, not directly associated with universities or museums, where fine art was displayed and sold. In the mid-1990s the Salt Lake Gallery Association included twenty-four galleries that featured a wide variety of arts and crafts, including some produced by artists known nationally and internationally.[18] The Art Barn, founded in 1931 and later known as the Salt Lake Art Center, was a combination school and gallery that focused on contemporary art. It moved to the Salt Palace complex in 1979, and in 1965 its director, James L. Haseltine, published *100 Years of Utah Painting*, a seminal catalogue for those interested in Utah art history and collecting.

The Pioneer Craft House was founded in 1946 by Glen Beeley to continue the fostering of folk arts and crafts. The Atrium Gallery, founded in 1965 in the new Salt Lake City Public Library, became an important center for displaying contemporary Utah art. The Phillips Gallery, which specialized in modernist and avant-garde art, opened in 1965. In January 1994 the Hippodrome Gallery, located just off the main corridor of the FHP Hospital in Salt Lake City, displayed its inaugural exhibit. Entitled "This Is the Place," the exhibit celebrated the history of Salt Lake City and included both paintings and photographs.

Park City provided one of the most active art markets in the state. Several galleries, including the Meyer, Park City, and Saguaro galleries, displayed and sold the works of Utah and other artists. The Kimball Art Center focused on Utah and western regional art. It offered art classes and sponsored the Northwest Rendezvous annual exhibition. The Park City Annual Art Festival, begun in 1970, attracted tens of thousands of art lovers from around the state and elsewhere.

As the arts continued to flourish, the problem of adequate financial support became increasingly crucial. Purchases and ticket sales were important sources of revenue, but artists, museums, galleries, and performing companies all required other kinds of backing, including public funding. Government money did not support every artistic enterprise, however, and for those that it did help it provided only 10 to 30 percent of their expenses. Sometimes this was only seed money to help new programs get started, and it dried up after a few years. In most cases the money came as matching grants, which meant that patrons of the arts as well as the organizations themselves were required to raise matching funds.[19]

Because of the critical need for additional funding, the boards of Utah's major performing groups conducted professional, on-going fund-raising programs. The Utah Symphony, for example, was well served by the indefatigable efforts of board presidents such as Glenn Walker Wallace, J. Allen Crockett, T. Bowring "By" Woodbury, and Wendell Ashton. Wallace, who was elected president in 1948, even used her own funds to shore up the symphony in its early financial difficulties. A number of board members, including Morris Rosenblatt, Calvin Rawlings, James L. White, and Obert C. Tanner, were also effective in raising funds as well as very generous in their personal contributions.

A survey conducted among Utahns in mid-1985 indicated that 94 percent of them felt that art facilities such as museums and theaters were important to the state, and nearly 70 percent were willing to see more tax dollars spent on the arts.[20] Earlier that year, the legislature passed the Utah Percent-for-Art-Act that allocated public funding to incorporate works of art into new or newly renovated public buildings. Administered by the Utah Arts Council, by 1994 the fund had granted contracts to sixty-five different artists who had provided art work for forty-six buildings. In 1989 the old Union Pacific Depot was gifted to the state for the purpose of housing its fine art collection. The depot soon became the home of the Utah Museum Foundation and various Arts Council programs.

At the local level, Salt Lake City and Salt Lake County each had programs similar to that of the state.[21] In addition, in 1990 the legislature created a $2.3 million Utah Arts Endowment Fund, the first of its kind in the nation, which was enlarged by another $3 million in 1991.[22] But in 1993, when both the Utah Symphony and Ballet West were facing particularly severe financial problems, voters in Salt Lake County rejected a proposal that would have paved the way for the county to levy a one-tenth of one percent sales tax to help support those two organizations and more than one hundred others. Some opponents argued that the proposal would only tax the poor to support the interests of the rich. In reality, without more public support prices would go up and the poor would be even less able to afford tickets. In addition, performances in communities and schools around the state could be cut back because of lack of funds to pay the artists for extra work. It appeared, said the executive director of the Utah Symphony, that "the community wants the arts but doesn't want to pay for them."[23] The symphony and the ballet were rescued, at least temporarily, by a few generous philanthropists and by some financial concessions on the part of performers, but in the mid-1990s the organizations' continued economic viability remained precarious.

Despite financial problems, however, Utah's support of the arts was impressive enough to earn the state national praise, in 1986, as "an oasis for the arts in the West." Partners for Livable Places, based in Washington, D.C., named Salt Lake City as one of the sixteen most livable cities in the nation. It emphasized the city's diverse artistic culture, the money spent to send major performing groups throughout the state, the excellence of the three major dance companies, and the fact that the Utah Symphony, under the direction of Maestro Maurice Abravanel, had recently been named by both the *New York Times* and *Fortune Magazine* as one of the twelve best symphony orchestras in the nation.[24]

The Visual Arts: National Trends

The development of Utah's visual arts in the postwar world was multi-faceted, including traditional forms but also incorporating innovative, avant-garde ideas drawn from the larger world of art. The twentieth century was, in the words of one art historian, an "age of isms and schisms."[25] It was a time of war, revolution, automation, fast-paced social transformation, changing values, and a plethora of new social and philosophical dogmas. Artists in this new age often adopted new forms to express their responses to what they saw and felt around them. Some artistic movements were deliberate attempts to provoke discussion, even if it meant provoking the public. New works of art sometimes reflected only passing trends but there were also some memorable breakthroughs, seen, for example, in the works of abstract expressionists in painting, Frank Lloyd Wright in architecture, and Igor Stravinsky in music.

Partly because of the problems of World War II, some artists became alienated from their society, reflecting that alienation in new concepts and new art forms. Many European artists migrated to the United States, resulting in a combination of European and American talent and ideas that eventually thrust America into the forefront of world art. The New York School (a term that encompassed all the styles whose development centered on New York after 1945) soon replaced the School of Paris as the pacesetter of the international art world. The artists of the New York School were by no means unified in their styles and ideas but, rather, showed wide diversity.

One important development from the New York School was abstract impressionism. These artists drew from a variety of earlier forms that departed from any effort to represent the "real" world in traditional, realistic images, but their work also took on a new aura of action and spontaneity. For them, art was psychological, allowing the mind to expand in new directions and, through the imagination, to create paintings, sculpture, or music that evoked strong aesthetic or psychic feelings and moods. Each artist also insisted upon complete individuality, expressing his or her intense feelings through a variety of materials and approaches. The value of a painting was, for them, in the creation, not necessarily in the final result. Abstract impressionism was almost existential in nature for, as critic Harold Rosenberg once noted, each artist was "fatally aware that only what he constructs for himself will ever be real to him."[26]

Abstract impressionism was as diverse as the artists themselves. Jackson Pollock's "poured paintings" had no subject matter at all. Rather, the splatterings and lines of color reflected the movements of his arm and body as he applied paint to huge canvases lying on the floor, making his action itself part of the painting. The result was a highly complex composition of interwoven lines and colors that portrayed vigor and action but with no particular focal point. The observer became entranced with the action of the work rather than with any idea or representation.

Some artists, like Mark Rothko, Barnett Newman, and Franz Kline, relied on huge blocks of color juxtaposed in a variety of ways. Others, such as Adolph Gottlieb, used symbols, while Lee Krasner used abstract images drawn from ancient Irish and Persian manuscripts. Willem de Kooning, on the other hand, was one of a few abstract impressionists who continued to focus on a particular subject, such as the female form, though the form itself was highly abstract and not clearly discernible from the background. Abstract impressionism reached its international zenith in about 1958 when New York's Museum of Modern Art circulated its exhibition, "Abstract Painting in America," throughout Europe. The movement also evoked deep controversy, both inside the art world and among the general public. Its momentum was in decline by the early 1960s as it gradually gave way to other forms and new ideas.

One reaction to abstract impressionism was pop art, which, instead of rejecting mass culture, focused on its symbols: soda cans, Coke bottles, comic strips, hamburgers, billboards, and so forth. The public was enthralled with pop art because it was "fun" and because it reflected so much that was commonplace and easily recognizable. At the same time, some critics noted, it also revealed the cheapness and vulgarity inherent in much of popular culture. Prominent pop artists included painters Andy Warhol and Robert Rauschenberg and sculptor John Chamberlain. Chamberlain's *Silverheels*, which used discarded parts from an automobile chassis, represented a form of pop art sometimes called junk sculpture, which made statements about the throwaway aspects of modern urban society.

Pop art spawned its own reactionary movement, minimalism, or hard-edge art, which emphasized extreme simplicity of form. In sculpture, this meant reducing a work to an "irreducible minimum"—nothing more than a shape or outline that blended with rather than stood apart from its environment. Bernard Rosenthal's *Alamo*, for example, was simply a huge cube, constructed of painted steel, which became part of the total architectural environment when poised outdoors in New York's Astor Place.

In the late 1960s, there was also room in the modern art world for a return to realism. The new realism was a reaction, in part, to both abstractionism and photography. The new generation believed, the real world was worth studying and worth recording on canvas, not just through the eye of the camera. But the new realists did not entirely reject modernism. Their works did more than depict the world they portrayed—they analyzed it. Richard Estes's photo-like *Downtown*, for example, defined a cityscape so sharply that viewers, even those who lived in the area that was represented, saw things in the urban environment they had never seen before but which Estes wanted them to see. Any subject—still life, portraiture, ordinary people doing ordinary things, landscape, and more—fell under the scrutiny of the new realists.

By the 1990s, American art was characterized by wide diversity—a diversity that aptly symbolized modern society. Utah art was characterized by the same variety of forms and styles, as well as by the same disputes over modernistic trends.

The Visual Arts in Utah: The Battle of Styles and the Centers of Learning

As art historian Vern Swanson has written, in the year 1950 Utah, like the rest of the nation, seemed "poised on the edge of artistic maturity."[27] The traditional emphasis on representation and upon art that was "good" and "useful" remained, but some prominent artists, already known as modernists, were moving along some of the lines which developed in succeeding years. Young artists not only learned from them but also traveled to and were influenced by prestigious art schools in the East.

Much of the Utah public did not respond well to the most radical tendencies in twentieth-century modernism. For example, at the Salt Lake Fairgrounds Centennial exhibition in 1947 a number of nationally known artists, representing contemporary trends, were among the exhibitors. One was Max Weber, a New York expressionist, who gave Utahns what Swanson calls "a much-needed exposure to fresh new work." But Mayor Earl J. Glade, representing the prevailing popular response to avant-garde art, called it "a product of insanity." Young artists, especially, were outraged by the remark, and V. Douglas Snow, then nineteen, wrote a sharp letter to the mayor criticizing him for rejecting something he did not understand. Glade quickly apologized, but this incident was a dramatic illustration of the way public resistance could slow the acceptance of modern trends.[28] Most Utahns, it appeared, wanted their artists to remind them either of their pioneer heritage or of the natural wonders of the state.[29]

However, in 1953 the Utah State Institute of Fine Arts held an exhibit at the state capitol building in which modern art was given specific exhibition space as well as separate award categories. This was an important step forward for modernists and over the next decade traditionalists slowly began to lose out to contemporary art in Utah's annual shows.

The battle of styles was waged largely in Utah's colleges and universities which, at least until the 1980s, were the centers for most artistic development in the state. Art education (training art teachers for the public schools) was a major emphasis in all programs, but studio art (an emphasis on training professional artists) was also fostered. Several schools also developed art history programs.

Early in this period, a number of traditionalist teachers remained prominent. One was landscape artist LeConte Stewart, who, after helping to establish realism as the dominant form in Utah universities, retired from the University of Utah in 1956. Avard Fairbanks, a renowned sculptor on the faculty of the University of Michigan, was lured to the University of Utah in 1947. He served for the next eight years as dean of the newly-created School of Fine Arts. Fairbanks, a realist, was the outspoken leader in the fight against modernism, bashing it vociferously to students and public alike. As a teacher, meanwhile, he inspired numerous students who became important Utah sculptors. By the time Fairbanks resigned in 1967 the University of Utah was at the forefront of Utah modernism.

Alvin Gittins, who came from England, was also conservative in his personal approach to art but intellectually he was highly cosmopolitan and felt as much at home with young modernists as he did with Fairbanks and Stewart. Thus, in his classroom he broadened the perspectives of numerous young artists. In addition, in his capacity as department chair from 1956 to 1962, Gittins brought to the university a talented and avowed modernist sculptor, Angelo Caravaglia. Contemporary trends were reflected later in the work of some of Caravaglia's most prominent students, such as Franz M. Johansen at Brigham Young University and Larry Elsner at Utah State University. Another important modernist, V. Douglas Snow (whose letter had resulted in Mayor Glade's apology seven years earlier), joined the faculty in 1954. He worked closely with Gittins in an attempt to move the Utah audience out of its tradition-bound mold toward an acceptance of pluralism in art. For a time, however, it was a lonely battle.

In the 1960s, placing greater emphasis on studio art than on art education, the University of Utah added several faculty members. One of these was Earl Jones, who remained only from 1964 to 1970. Beginning as a modernist, Jones eventually returned to a more traditional approach—inspired by his early mentor LeConte Stewart—wherein his famous landscapes married tradition and contemporary art. In later years the *Deseret News* called him "a shining star in the pantheon of Utah artists."[30] Another faculty member was abstract impressionist Frank Anthony Smith. In 1981 Alvin Gittins suddenly died, leaving a serious void in the ranks of the realists. New faces in the department in the 1980s included abstractionist Sam Wilson and action-painter of still-lifes E. David Dornan.[31]

The battle over styles was less intense at Brigham Young University, where a climate conducive to experimentation and new ideas, if not to modernistic extremes, was established in the 1950s. The decade began with a small art faculty of five members, led by B. F. Larsen, which doubled in size by 1960. Originally a traditional landscape artist, by the 1950s Larsen had begun to experiment in modernist styles. J. Roman Andrus, a painter, lithographer, and art educator who joined the faculty in 1942, blended modernist and traditional elements. He became known particularly for his sweeping, abstract mountain scenes. Sculptor and painter Franz M. Johansen joined the faculty in the 1950s and is credited, along with Caravaglia, with producing the first nonobjective sculpture in the state. Johansen also helped foster appreciation for the sanctity of the human form, and he produced notable religious works. The teaching of art was enhanced during the 1950s with the addition of Conan E. Matthews and Frank M. Tippetts, who joined Andrus and Richard Gunn in the field of art education. Another outstanding teacher was Alex B. Darius, an abstract figurative painter. Francis R. Magleby and Floyd Breinholt maintained the strong realist landscape core of the art department. Wesley Burnside taught art history and education classes. BYU thus became an important center for the training of elementary and secondary teachers, in addition to its growing importance as a center of studio art.

By the end of the 1960s, the BYU art department boasted fourteen full-time faculty. During the following decade both the school and the department grew rapidly, adding a number of artists who became well known throughout the region and, in some cases, around the nation. These included Robert L. Marshall, who painted large oil paintings of close-ups of the western landscape; Trevor Southey, who remained only from 1969 to 1977; academic realist William F. Whittaker; fantasy artist James C. Christensen, and three artists who, with divergent styles and methods, helped carry on the Mormon art movement (see below): Wulf Erich Barsch, Bruce Hixon Smith, and Hagen Haltern. The latter developed an interesting style that sought to merge abstraction and realism. During the 1980s, under the chairmanship of Robert L. Marshall, the balance in BYU's art department changed in favor of professional studio art, though art education and graphic design also remained important. By the end of the decade the department rivaled the University of Utah in both size and quality.

At Utah State University, Everett Thorpe, who began his career as a traditionalist, continually updated his personal style and by the 1950s added abstraction to his repertoire. Thorpe left the university in the mid-1950s and was replaced by Harrison Thomas Groutage, a talented painter, watercolorist, and printmaker known particularly for his powerful Cache Valley landscapes. New faculty members in the 1950s began to add important diversity to the department. These included Jon I. Anderson in commercial art, Ralph T. Clark in photography, and Larry E. Elsner in sculpture and ceramics.

Replacing Twain Tippetts as department head in 1965, Harrison Groutage played an important role in upgrading the graduate program. The department also added other artists who worked in a variety of media and styles. Immediately after he joined the faculty in 1972, Ray W. Hellberg, a watercolorist, succeeded Groutage as department head. During his tenure the art wing of the Chase Fine Arts Center was constructed. He also added diversity to the department with the new people he brought in. These included Moishe Smith, whose sensitive appreciation for the mountains surrounding Cache Valley was admirably revealed in a series of etchings commissioned by the university in 1980. In the 1980s, USU continued to build its reputation in commercial art, as well as to hire new faculty from all over the United States who added more diversity.

The art department of Weber State University (then known as Weber College) began the 1950s with a very small art faculty and was known, at least for the next two decades, mostly for illustration and for art education. Among the early faculty members were David M. Strong, a modernist who retired in 1952, and Farrell R. Collett, who remained until 1976 and became Utah's premier wildlife painter. Richard Van Wagoner, who joined the faculty in 1959, taught a variety of subjects but, for his own work, paid increasing attention to painting the urban landscape. By the end of the 1960s the department was greatly enlarged and was characterized by a variety of artistic styles and teaching methods. Its teaching and production was spurred on by the completion of the Collett Art Building in 1964.

The Variety of Styles: Some Representative Artists

It is difficult, in the short space available here, to adequately portray the work of the many artists who contributed so much to Utah's cultural landscape in the last half of the twentieth century. Perhaps some commentary on a few representative artists will provide helpful insight into the rich diversity that characterized the period.

The gap between early and later generations of Utah modernists was bridged by Everett Thorpe and Donald Olsen. Olsen was more extreme in his protest against tradition than Thorpe. His abstract expressionism was dominated by unusual presentations of raw, unmixed color and revealed the excitement of self-discovery and self-revelation. "A painting reveals the internal expression of the artist," he stated in true expressionist fashion, "and has nothing to do with observation of visual fact."[32] In 1966 Olsen made a sudden change in style toward minimalism.

H. Lee Deffebach, originally from Texas, became one of Utah's premier abstractionists. She studied at the University of Utah and then in Florence, Italy, and New York. During the 1960s she was the major female abstractionist in Utah. She also became the first Utah artist to produce pop art, which says a great deal about her intellectual flexibility. In the 1970s she began to focus on mural-sized canvases of poured "spilled-paint" color and, with the help of a grant from the Western States Art Foundation, she produced several "vividly colored, translucent, acrylic-washed canvases. Like a veil of color, the exploratory, unmanipulated interaction of viscous paint spread translucently and transparently down a white canvas had an exhilarating effect."[33]

V. Douglas Snow, noted for his profound synthesis of traditional and expressionist styles, became one of the most popularly accepted modernists in the Utah art world. He acquired fame for his paintings of the Utah landscape, rendered with a surreal power and beauty that was appreciated by all camps. Utah's deserts, rugged mountains, and fantastic rock formations all provided subject matter for his elegant interpretation of nature.

Image B.2: LeConte Stewart (1891–1990), one of Utah's premier landscape artists. Used by permission, Utah State Historical Society, all rights reserved.

Modernism in Utah reached its zenith in the 1970s, after which the number of abstractionists in the state declined, giving way to a greater variety of styles. Even the remaining modernists represented a multiplicity of forms and techniques.[34] At the same time, Utah also saw the advent of a handful of "op" artists, such as Bonnie G. Phillips, whose application of scientific principles produced startling optical effects.

The reemphasis on realism in the 1950s and 1960s was led by Avard Fairbanks. When it came to receiving commissions, Fairbanks was the dominant Utah sculptor for two decades. He was best known within the state for his superb works depicting LDS Church history,[35] but his colossal *Head of Abraham Lincoln* was one of many pieces to gain wide national recognition. In addition, Fairbanks is credited for making the nude figure acceptable to the Utah public. Much of the public was still unable to accept the fact that the human figure was an important and ennobling object of art, and many galleries refused to exhibit nudes. Fairbanks, however, dealt with nudity in a delicate, unthreatening way. By the time the Springville Museum of Art acquired his tender 1928 work, *Mother and Child* (depicting a nursing mother), in 1951, the public mood had softened and the work was successfully displayed.

Alvin Gittins, meanwhile, used both oil paints and charcoal drawings to create realistic portraits, figures, and still life. He was admired as a master of observation and detail. He also helped elevate drawing from a mere artist's tool to an art form. Another realist of the 1960s and 1970s was Dale Fletcher, who painted amazingly lifelike pictures of tree houses and other familiar objects in nature. His changeable, moody, and puzzling personality, however, eventually led him away from studio art and finally, at the end of the 1970s, away from BYU and into a religious cult in Oregon.

Landscape painting also continued as a popular genre in Utah, dominated until the 1980s by the venerable LeConte Stewart, who left a remarkable legacy through his art and his teaching. A realist, Stewart was loved particularly for his portrayal of farmhouses, barns, country roads, and mountainsides, especially in winter, most of which he found in Davis County. He died in 1990.

Some artists were endowed with a healthy eclecticism and could achieve well in either modernist or realist styles. One was Denis Phillips, who was an abstract impressionist in the 1960s but in the 1970s turned to realism as well as abstraction in his landscapes. Another was Earl Jones (see above), who, after leaving the University Utah in 1970, became one of Utah's premier landscape artists, working and teaching in his own studio and, in a sense, carrying on the legacy of LeConte Stewart.

Two of the most important landscape artists in the 1980s were V. Douglas Snow (see above) and A. Valoy Eaton, both of whom combined traditional and modern styles. Another was Ken B. Baxter, a realist who rose to prominence in the 1970s with delightful historical portrayals of downtown Salt Lake City. Baxter was also founder of the Plein Air Painters of Utah, a group of artists who emphasized painting out-of-doors on location. Baxter and Earl Jones were said to be "the most influential teacher-painters on the Utah scene" during the 1980s.[36] But several other landscape artists dealt in various ways with Utah's inviting scenery. These included Thomas A. Leek, Marilee Campbell, Connie Borrup, Carol Petit Harding, James E. Jones, J. Thomas Mulder, Anton J. Rasmussen, Osral Allred, Carl L. Purcell, Bonnie Posselli, Kathryn Stats, Robert L. Marshall, Richard A. Murray, Steve Adams, George W. Handrahan, Phyllis Horne, D. Lynn Cozzens, and Frank Huff, Jr.[37]

In the early twentieth century, Utah did not have a strong tradition of western and cowboy art. Numerous painters beautifully portrayed Utah's landscape, but few artists or sculptors depicted the human characters and themes (including, surprisingly, Mormon religious themes) that were part of their society's mythos and tradition, as did other western artists such as Charles M. Russell of Montana. Among the outstanding exceptions were Cyrus E. Dallin, Paul Salisbury, Maynard Dixon, Mahonri M. Young, Arnold Friberg, Minerva Teichert, and Hughes Curtis. Dallin, noted nationally for his portrayal in sculpture of the noble Indian, and Young did most of their work in the East. Young and Teichert continued their work well into the postwar years, and during that time western and cowboy art grew into an important Utah genre.

Mahonri Young's most well-known (at least to Utahns) postwar works included the *This Is the Place Monument* (1947) and the *Brigham Young* statue in the Capitol Rotunda in Washington, D.C. (1949).[38] Minerva Teichert, who did much of her work while raising a large family on a ranch in Wyoming, developed a personal style of subdued detail but powerful feeling through the use of color and tone. She painted many of the grand themes of the Mormon religious experience, including fifty large-scale oils on the Book of Mormon, completed in 1950. National recognition of her outstanding artistry came slowly. Her Book of Mormon oils, for example, achieved national acclaim only after 1969, when they were donated to BYU. By the 1980s, however, she was well known far outside Utah and the West.[39]

Among Utah's foremost "cowboy and Indian" artists in the decades immediately following the war were Paul Salisbury and Arnold Friberg. Salisbury was also one of the few full-time professional artists not affiliated with a university. His paintings, such as *Riders of the Range*, were conservative in style and therefore highly popular among Utah's general public.

Arnold Friberg, who was raised in Arizona, taught at the University of Utah from 1949 to 1956 and was proudly adopted by Utahns as their own. His realistic style in his portrayals of cowboys, the American Indian, cavalry soldiers, saloons, locomotives, and other western themes endeared him to the public both in Utah and elsewhere. As Swanson aptly noted, he "portrayed the old West more authentically than ever it was in real life."[40] He also became well known nationwide for his heroic action pictures on national themes, such as his powerful *George Washington at Valley Forge*. In addition, Friberg received much of the credit for popularizing religious art in Utah. Although his early representations of Christ drew criticism from some LDS leaders, by the 1990s he was the "most beloved religious painter among the Mormons."[41] His most famous religious works include a series on the Book of Mormon for the LDS Church and the powerful paintings he did in connection with Cecil B. De Mille's film *The Ten Commandments*. While some critics disparagingly referred to him as an "illustrator," his work is now appreciated as fine art.[42]

Several Utah sculptors became prominent for their work in the western genre. Hughes Curtis became one of Utah's first notable cowboy sculptors and was co-founder of the first fine-art bronze foundry in the state. It was there that nationally known sculptors Grant Speed and Neil Hadlock obtained their early experience. Edward J. Fraughton, a student of Avard Fairbanks, was a realist who won wide acclaim, and numerous commissions, for his meticulously detailed, often heroic-size, bronzes. His bust of John F. Kennedy graces the Kennedy Memorial Library in Boston and a heroic-size bronze of a bucking horse and rider stands in front of the Wyoming state capitol in Laramie. By 1990 Fraughton had won four gold medals from the National Academy of Western Art.

Grant Speed, a former rodeo professional who moved to Lindon, Utah from Texas, became nationally known for his fine, action-packed sculptures depicting cowboy life. He served several different terms as president of the Cowboy Artists of America, one of the most prestigious groups of western artists in the nation. In his native Texas he was known particularly for his life-size bronco and rider at Texas Tech University and a sculpture of singer Buddy Holly located in Lubbock.

Stanley Wanlass, of Lehi, created more than western art, becoming known in both the US and Europe for his sculptures of cars. One of his most well-known works in the western genre was the monument at Fort Clatsop National Memorial commemorating the arrival of Lewis and Clark at the Pacific Ocean. Another Utahn, Clark Bronson, became known for his wildlife sculptures as well as his paintings, which were produced in his studio on the banks of the Provo River.

Wildlife painter Farrell Collett, at Weber State, was a realist who helped wildlife art become more acceptable in the state and led several young artists into this genre. Among them was Clark Bronson, who began as a painter but later moved to sculpting. Bronson was not only a realist but also a naturalist, giving his work no interpretation other than that implied by depicting his animals in their natural habitat. His sales, numerous awards, and membership in prestigious national and international organizations attest to his wide acceptance. Another wildlife artist to come into prominence in the 1970s, but who later left the state for Montana, was Nancy Glazier-Koehler, known particularly for her portrayal of buffalo, cougars, and other big game. Still another premier wildlife artist was Jan Henderson.

Perhaps the most widely popular, and financially successful, Utah painter of western scenes during and after the 1970s was former BYU student Michael Coleman. His compelling portrayal of western scenes, Indian life, and other topics were characterized by delicate colors and sensitive feeling somewhat reminiscent of the nineteenth-century Hudson River School.

The popularity of western art continued, perhaps even grew, in the 1980s and 1990s. Among the younger artists active in the genre by that time was John B. Jarvis who, like Michael Coleman, delighted in integrating figures, such as Indian encampments, into the western landscape. Others included Pete Plastow, E. Kimball Warren, James C. Norton, and Bruce Cheever. Another, Al Rounds, became particularly prominent for his authentic paintings of Utah's pioneer architecture. Utah western sculptors included Peter M. Fillerup, who produced a heroic scale *Kit Carson–Frontiersman* for the famous Whitney museum in Cody, Wyoming, Jeannine Young Newman, David W. Jackson, Clark Bronson, and Gary Lee Price. The latter attempted to balance realism, impressionism, and abstraction in his work.

A number of artists in the 1970s and 1980s moved from traditional western art into a figurative neorealism. Instead of simply seeing an illusion of reality, in neorealism one "senses, or feels, reality. Its essence is the heartfelt sentiment, not in mere nostalgia, and in expressive form, light and color rather than in mere didactic detail."[43] Gary E. Smith, originally from Oregon, remained in Utah after attending BYU in the 1970s and became one of America's most important neoregionalists. Early in his career he painted scenes of wheat harvesting, mining, and LDS Church history, but he soon developed a more metaphysical, metaphorical style as he painted farmers, laborers, and other ordinary westerners who had none of the glamour of the cowboy depicted by other artists but who became feeling-laden symbols of all the simple, beloved aspects of American life. Other Utah regionalists included Valoy Eaton (also a landscape artist), Arch D. Shaw, and Robert K. Duncan.[44]

Surrealism in various forms and styles also gained popularity in Utah during the last half of the twentieth century. This style is not easily categorized, although Swanson uses the phrase "metaphysical and metaphorical art" or sometimes the term "Art Extra-Ordinaire," to include a variety of styles: allegorical, mystical, fantasy, spiritualistic, symbolic, surrealistic, visionary, and many others that are "aesthetically beyond conventional or objective human experience."[45] Among the artists who produced paintings in such mystical, allegorical, or fantastical style in the 1950s and 1960s were Ruth Harwood, William J. Parkinson, and Ruth Wolf Smith. The latter's comical *Allegory of the 1960 Presidential Election* was a delightful piece of political satire depicting Richard Nixon and Henry Cabot Lodge (Republican presidential and vice-presidential candidates) riding an elephant, while Democratic Presidential candidate John F. Kennedy rode a donkey led by vice-presidential candidate Lyndon Johnson along a golden road to the White House. They were followed by a bandwagon, sheep, goats, and all the state delegates.

James C. Christensen, who joined BYU's art faculty in 1976, became one of the world's foremost fantasy painters. Prints of his whimsical representations of any and every kind of subject, from Santa Claus to Shakespeare and from storytellers to spoofs on technology, sold at handsome prices. One of his best-known works, *Fantasies of the Sea*, depicts a sea queen astride a huge fish, contentedly examining her realm while surrounded by mermaids as well as comical counselors, soldiers, and scouts riding various kinds of fish. Lurking in a dark recess, however, is a sinister-looking moray.

Other prominent metaphysical or metaphorical artists in the 1970s and 1980s included Francis Zimbeaux, Frank Anthony Smith, and Edith Tyler Roberson. Roberson, who originally came from Delaware, painted a wide variety of subjects and in a wide variety of styles. Whether they be of rusty tricycles, toys, antique clothing, or kitchen corkboards, it has been said that her works always catch "poignant melancholia" and "fool the eye and boggle the brain."[46]

More well known in the 1980s were Bruce H. Smith and Dennis V. Smith (not related). Deeply concerned with the spiritual dimension in life, Bruce Smith painted various objects and figures in brilliant color or in a kind of abstraction intended as representations of the process of life. "If I could set objective reality in a spiritual context," he said, "I would be very happy."[47] His life-size canvas *Jacob and Leah*, for example, reinterpreted this biblical story in a strictly modern context. Much of Dennis Smith's work was autobiographical in nature; it drew from his own past to create spiritual metaphors. His imagery was often expressed in mystical paintings, such as *Keeper of the Gate*, a colorful, symbolic landscape in which each part seems to represent some memory of the artist's past. But Smith became especially well known as a sculptor. His delightful, fanciful assemblage pieces often reminded viewers of nostalgic scenes from their own childhood. Perhaps his most-loved works, at least among the Mormon audience, were his tender, lifelike sculptures of people that exuded family and other religious values. Best known of these were his eleven of the thirteen sculptures of women in the garden of the LDS Visitors' Center in Nauvoo, Illinois.[48] The other two were sculpted by Florence Hansen.

Many other metaphorical, surrealistic artists made themselves known in Utah by the 1980s. Wulf Erich Barsch drew on ancient images and symbols as spiritual metaphors. H. Douglas Himes did something similar. Other such artists included Lee Udall Bennion, Steven James Fawson, Bonnie Sucec, Maureen O'Hare Ure, and Silvia Lis Davis.[49] Perhaps the most controversial, or at least enigmatic, modernistic sculpture in Utah, called *The Metaphor*, was erected in the mid-1980s by Karl Momen, a Swedish sculptor. Completed in two years at a cost of $1 million (mostly from Momen's own pocket), it stood seventy feet high and resembled a tree. It was located off Highway I-80 about ninety-five miles west of Salt Lake City.[50]

The 1960s saw the foundation of one of Utah's distinctive art movements, known as the Mormon Art and Belief Movement.[51] It began during the 1965–66 academic year, at a time when disillusionment with the Vietnam War and other perceived problems in society resulted in widespread student unrest and cynicism around the nation. The growing use of hallucinogenic drugs, "dropping out" of society into hippie communes, and wild expression of protest and dismay through psychedelic art were also symptomatic of this national unrest. At BYU, a number of art students clustered around Dale Fletcher, who joined the faculty in the fall of 1965. Trained as an abstractionist, Fletcher had undergone a spiritual transformation and had become a devout naturalist and realist. As a result of continuing informal discussions on art and religious values, Fletcher and his cadre of graduate students progressed to in-depth discussions on the question of whether there could be such a thing as Mormon art and, if so, what was it? Future "greats" such as Trevor Southey, Dennis Smith, Gary E. Smith, and Michael Clane Graves were among the excited young artists who became the nucleus of the movement, and Fletcher led them into the exciting realm of Egyptian art and the relationship between religion and art among the ancients.

A reaction to what seemed to be the decadence and ever-declining values of artists and others in the non-religious world, "Art and Belief" attempted to rally faithful artists to incorporating religious values, and particularly Mormon values, into their work. Devotees did not necessarily see eye-to-eye on all things. Some expected distinctive Mormon artistic forms to emerge, while others recognized the need for complete individuality of style. They were unified, however, in their quest for incorporating religious values into their work, and they were not averse to any artistic style that would enhance their efforts to do so. The movement contributed to the origin of the First Annual Festival of Mormon Art that opened on BYU campus in February 1969.[52] The festival, as well as the Art and Belief movement, grew to include all the arts. Although the movement itself became less formal after 1971, it continued to influence Utah's visual arts, even to the present time.

Trevor Southey was hired by BYU in 1969 to teach drawing and printmaking. However, he soon made a name for himself as he moved beyond his initial interest in Mormon art and developed a profound interest in art as metaphor. His nude paintings were profoundly allegorical in nature, but they also evoked heated controversy among the conservative Utah public. After a strained relationship with BYU's administration, he left the university in 1977 to work full-time in his studio at Alpine. He later moved to

California. One of his murals, depicting a nude male and a nude female flying in the air, was an elegant allegory suggesting the feeling and power of flight and, appropriately, hung in the Salt Lake City International Airport. Public outcry, however, finally contributed to its removal.

As the "battle of the styles" in the visual arts played itself out in Utah during the postwar decade, much of the public seemingly did not understand or appreciate the need for wide artistic diversity and the importance of freedom and self-expression in order for great art to develop and for artists to have an impact on society. The importance of this idea was summed up well by Vern Swanson, who ended his essay on the contemporary scene with what seemed like a little sermon to the public and the artist alike:

> Contemporary Utah has perhaps never really understood that artists make better journalists than historians. Our artists must increase their efforts in self-reflection, investigation, and articulation. Recognition of the artist as a leading agent of change, capable of transforming the way we feel, view, and understand our present world, is the raison d'être for future Utah art. Only the insightful eye can see clearly through the bewildering maze of the here and now, and only the insightful hand can arouse, inspire, and provoke new dimensions of reflection and experience.[53]

Nevertheless, he emphasized, Utah art had never been better.

The Performing Arts: Utah's Orchestras and Choirs

The performing arts, too, enjoyed a steadily improving vitality in the decades following World War II. The two most well-known performing groups were the Utah Symphony and the Mormon Tabernacle Choir, both of which became world-renowned.[54] More important than their fame, however, was the fact that Utahns supported them, attended their performances, and because of them learned to appreciate more fully the value of incorporating music into their lives.

Figure B.3: The Utah Symphony Orchestra, under the direction of Marice Abravanel, performed in Greece at the Athens Festival in 1966 and 1977. This photo was taken at one of those performances. Photo courtesy of Special Collections, J. Willard Marriott Library, University of Utah. Used with permission.

In the late nineteenth and early twentieth centuries, several sporadic attempts were made to organize a permanent symphony orchestra in Utah. Not until the WPA's Federal Music Project funds were made available during the Great Depression, however, was the Utah State Sinfonietta, the direct ancestor of the present Utah Symphony Orchestra, founded. Federal funding stopped in 1940, but the orchestra doggedly continued its performances anyway. Its name was changed to the Utah Symphony in 1946. The following year, even though it was plagued with serious financial problems, the orchestra board optimistically sought out a conductor who would be committed to Utah and to building a top-notch, permanent professional organization. That person was Maurice Abravanel. Born in Greece and reared in Switzerland, Abravanel studied music in Berlin and directed orchestras in Germany, Paris, and Australia. In 1933 he emigrated to New York City, where he became conductor of the Metropolitan Opera Orchestra, and later conductor of Broadway musicals. Propitiously, Abravanel was seeking an opportunity to build an orchestra of his own when the

Utah position came open, and he readily accepted it. He remained with the symphony for thirty-two years and was beloved throughout the state for his brilliance as a maestro and his dedication to Utah.

In order to build a first-class orchestra, Abravanel and the board realized that better funding was absolutely necessary. Help came in one form in 1948, when board president Glenn Walker Wallace used some of her own funds to support the struggling institution. Other philanthropists also donated funds. In addition, Abravanel realized that recordings would both bring in funds and establish a national reputation for the orchestra. Between 1957 and 1985, the orchestra recorded more than 120 albums, selling more than two million copies throughout the world. The Utah Symphony Orchestra was recognized, in particular, for its skill in performing the works of Gustav Mahler, recording all ten of his symphonies in one year. The orchestra was also one of the first western US symphonies to conduct international tours. The first one, a twenty-five day, eighteen thousand–mile European concert tour, took place in 1966. Appropriately, the first concert on foreign soil was conducted near the Acropolis in Athens, Greece, the homeland of Maurice Abravanel. "The Orchestra was worth waiting for," raved a critic in the *London Times*. It "achieved a high standard of playing as remarkable for its polished ensemble and rhythmic precision as for the general quality of its tone."[55] Other international tours followed.

Abravanel was also eager to help spread an appreciation for music to Utah's school children. Beginning with four school concerts in 1949, which grew to forty within twenty years, the orchestra's busy schedule regularly included schools and small communities throughout the state. Significantly, the Utah Symphony was the first professional symphony organization in the United States to present school concerts by a full orchestra.[56]

At first, the Utah Symphony conducted its regular concerts from the Mormon Tabernacle in Salt Lake City. By 1979, however, it had a new home, the $10 million Symphony Hall. Completed in time for the opening of the 1979–80 performing season, the hall was part of Utah's $18 million Bicentennial Arts Complex, built in commemoration of the nation's 1976 Bicentennial. Financed by county bond issues, state and federal grants, and numerous private contributors, the complex was built on land donated by the LDS Church, which had provided the Tabernacle rent-free for the previous thirty-two years.

Maurice Abravanel was not able to conduct the orchestra in the elegant new hall, however; he retired in 1979 for health reasons. By that time it was estimated that in his thirty-two years with the Utah Symphony he had conducted more than 3,100 concerts and traveled some 250,000 miles. In January 1993 the hall was appropriately renamed Abravanel Hall in honor of the beloved maestro, who died in September of that year at the age of ninety. Two years earlier Abravanel had received the prestigious National Medal of Arts at the White House from President George H. W. Bush. "Some conductors are able to interpret great music, others build orchestras," wrote the Utah Arts Council. "Maurice Abravanel did both, and he inspired and educated a multi-state audience in the bargain. That's a legacy richly deserving of the nation's thanks."[57]

Abravanel was succeeded in 1980 by Varujan Kohjian, who left after fulfilling his three-year contract. In 1983 the symphony board hired Joseph Silverstein on a trial basis, but before the year was out the board was so pleased with Silverstein's talents that it offered him a permanent position as music director and conductor. An accomplished violinist and conductor, Silverstein came to Utah after a distinguished career as concertmaster of the Boston Symphony, beginning in 1962, assistant conductor since 1971, interim director or director of other symphonies, and guest conductor with some twenty American orchestras. He brought not only professionalism but also a commitment to the community, and quickly won the hearts of the board, the orchestra, and Utah patrons. The orchestra had been divided and dispirited after three years under Kohjian, but Silverstein quickly turned that around during his trial year. As the *Salt Lake Tribune* observed, "He has impressed the Utah Symphony musicians with the depth of his knowledge, the breadth of his experience and his commitment to professionalism. He has proved worthy of their respect, and he has gotten it."[58] Under Silverstein's direction the orchestra expanded its activities to include chamber music and pop concerts. It continued presenting concerts throughout the state and elsewhere in what was recognized as the busiest schedule of any orchestra in the country–even traveling to Europe twice during the 1980s. The orchestra also continued to make noteworthy sound recordings. On February 1, 1986, the Utah Symphony reached a milestone—the performance of its five thousandth concert.

Despite the respect in which it was held, the Utah Symphony, like many other symphonies across the nation, had continuing financial difficulties. In 1993 both the Alabama and the Florida symphonies succumbed, but they were only the latest of more than half a dozen to disappear within a few years. In August, prior to the beginning of its 1993–94 concert year, the Utah Symphony found itself with an annual $1.2 million shortfall, a cumulative deficit of more than $3 million, and the prospect of abandoning the season if the budget could not be balanced. The musicians were already working harder than those in most of the nation but were at the bottom of the pay scale, which made it difficult to ask them to take a reduction in pay. The immediate problem was alleviated, however, by a compromise in which the board withdrew some restricted endowment money and the musicians took a 6 percent pay cut.

The season was saved, but the board stepped up its efforts to increase ticket sales and to find other ways of funding what was still a world-class orchestra. The refusal of Salt Lake County, earlier in the year, to approve a small sales tax hike for the benefit of the arts did not help, nor did the fact that attendance at the classical concerts dropped off slightly. The symphony endured, however, as innovative marketing and increased donations helped the budget. As similar crises occurred in subsequent seasons, various other approaches, including the possibility of shortening the season and canceling summer performances, were suggested. The 1995 summer season was saved only after two donors, Jon Huntsman and Spencer Eccles, contributed $100,000 each on behalf of their respective foundations, and a matching $200,000 was raised from other sources. A *Deseret News* editorial, however, scolded the Utah public for being so complacent as to allow such crises to occur year after year. Hopefully, the editorial said, there was time to make better plans for the following season, but more donations must be found, as well as some kind of governmental support. "Utahns need to support the symphony," the editor wrote. "It is an international jewel in the state's rich and varied artistic crown and can play an even brighter role in the future."[59] Unfortunately, a continuing lack of funds forced the orchestra to abbreviate its 1996 summer season.

The Mormon Tabernacle Choir was well-known long before World War II, partly because of its weekly Sunday broadcast, "Music and the Spoken Word," which began on NBC radio in 1929 and moved to CBS in 1932. The program made its television debut in 1962 and the choir aired its three-thousandth broadcast on the morning of February 17, 1987.

The Tabernacle Choir's public image extended far beyond its radio and television performances, however. Under the baton of J. Spencer Cornwall, who began conducting it in 1935, the choir became world renowned in the years following the war. Beginning with a tour of Europe in 1955, it frequently visited parts of the United States and the world, receiving enthusiastic plaudits wherever it went. After its 1955 performance in Munich, Germany, one listener told a reporter: "They are wonderful on the radio, to hear them in person is an incredible experience. It does not matter whether it is religious; only someone totally deaf could fail to be moved by their singing."[60]

Richard P. Condie replaced Cornwall in 1957, and it was under his direction that, in 1959, the choir received the coveted "Grammy" award from the recording industry for its most famous recording of "The Battle Hymn of the Republic." Between 1962 and 1974, the choir toured Canada three time, Mexico twice, and Europe once. It also appeared at five world fairs and joined with Eugene Ormandy and the Philadelphia Orchestra in creating some award-winning albums. In addition, the choir sang at the inaugurals of four American presidents (Lyndon Johnson in 1965, Richard Nixon in 1969, Ronald Reagan in 1981, and George H. W. Bush in 1989).

Jay Welch, a highly popular Utah conductor, replaced Condie in 1974, but a number of administrative problems led him to resign the same year. He was replaced by Jerold Ottley, who was soon credited with raising the choir to a new standard of excellence and adopting a more versatile style and a more varied repertoire. For church-related performances (such as the semiannual General Conferences), the choir placed more emphasis on the singing hymns. At the same time, LDS Church leaders deliberately expanded the choir's role as a cultural and spiritual ambassador for the church, which automatically augmented its role as a public relations group for the state of Utah. The choir's expanded repertoire included more classical masterworks as well as a wide variety of ethnic and folk music. In addition, it took on a greatly extended program of national and international tours.

Choir broadcasts from Salt Lake City also brought greater attention to the famed Tabernacle organ on Temple Square, although the organ itself was always an important attraction. Beginning in 1901, visitors were treated to organ recitals, at first twice a week and then daily at noon, except Sundays, during the summer months. In later years the recitals were performed during the entire year, with an added performance at 2:00 p.m. on Sundays.[61]

Utah also boasted other symphonic and choral groups. A few of them had concert seasons, but others usually performed only on special occasions, or by invitation, and were well appreciated in their communities. Members of these groups were not usually paid for their performances, or at least not paid substantively, but there were still expenses for hall rentals, advertising, printing of programs, and a variety of other necessities. Some were supported partly by grants from public funds (usually less than 10 percent of their total budget) and partly from corporate donations, but they also depended upon admissions for meeting their expenses.

The most long-standing independent choral organization in Utah was Salt Lake City's Oratorio Society of Utah, founded in 1914. By the 1990s it was the oldest continuously active choral society in the western United States and the only musical organization from Utah except the Utah Symphony and the Tabernacle Choir to be included in the *Encyclopedia Britannica*. The society performed in a number of places outside Utah, even touring the Holy Land in 1983.[62]

Among the other well-known, long-established groups were Pro Musica, the Utah Symphony Chorus (which annually at Christmastime performed with the Utah Symphony Orchestra in a sing-along of Handel's Messiah), the Mormon Youth Chorus, and the Jay Welch Chorale. Others, established later, included the Salt Lake Vocal Ensemble, the Utah Valley Choral Society, the Utah Chamber Artists, the West Valley Symphonic Orchestra, the Salt Lake Mens Chorus, the Eleanor Kennard Chorale, the Crossroads Choral Ensemble, the Oxford Chamber Choir, and the Southwest Symphony in St. George. One of the finest of the newer groups was the Utah Chamber Artists, led by Barlow Bradford, which by the early 1990s conducted a regular fall-winter season in Salt Lake City. Music was also important fare in the public schools. In the mid-1960s, for example, twenty-six out of Utah's eighty-four high schools conducted an orchestral music program.[63]

Although classical music did not always draw huge audiences, popular music usually did. When big-name stars came to perform, youth, especially, jammed the Salt Palace, the University of Utah Special Events Center, the Delta Center, and other auditoriums throughout the state. Among the many nationally and internationally popular artists to appear frequently was Utah's own Osmond family who, beginning in the 1960s, performed both as a group and as individuals on national radio and television and in films and popular recordings. In the 1980s, Park West became a favorite center for its outdoor concert stage, attracting such nationally popular entertainers as Muddy Waters, B. B. King, Bob Dylan, and the Grateful Dead.

By the 1990s, Utah could also boast of a number of its own young musicians and composers whose works were recognized nationally. Compositions by Tully Cathey of Salt Lake City and Phillip Kent Bimstein, mayor-elect of Springdale, appeared in 1993 on a classical rock CD by Windham Hill. In a more classical vein, Utah composers William Wallace and Henry Wolking also recorded CDs. A Utah expatriate, J. A. C. Redford, went to Hollywood in 1976, where he wrote music for several popular films and TV shows.[64] Other young composers whose works appealed to national as well as Utah audiences included guitarist Michael Dowdle, Sam Cardon, a pianist-composer whose contemporary jazz CD called *Serious Leisure* reached the number two spot on national radio, and Kurt Bestor, whose New Age recordings received popular acclaim nationwide.[65]

The Performing Arts: Opera, Theater, and Film[66]

Although Utahns were frequently treated to operatic productions, efforts to organize civic or community opera companies met with virtually no success until after World War II. In 1947, however, regular summer opera began in Stadium Bowl at the University of Utah. The first production, a light opera entitled *Promised Valley*, was staged in honor of the Pioneer Centennial. The music was written, appropriately, by a descendant of Brigham Young, Crawford Gates, who went on to become one of Utah's most acclaimed composers. Arnold Sundgaard provided the lyrics, and a New Yorker, Jay Blackton, conducted the orchestra. More light operas and musicals followed, attracting to the Utah stage such national stars as Beverly Sills, Robert Rounseville, and Kitty Carlisle.

At first the main support for opera came through Utah's universities, but in 1970s the dedication and hard work of many opera lovers and musicians, especially Glade Peterson, led to the formation of the Utah Opera Company. Peterson, a native of Utah who returned to the state after gaining operatic fame in the eastern states and in Europe, served as general director of the company and starred as lead vocalist in productions at the Pioneer Memorial Theatre and, later, in the renovated Capitol Theatre. Robert Peterson, another Utah singer who returned to the state after a successful career on Broadway, starred in numerous operas and light musicals and was a leader in the successful effort to broaden public acceptance of musical theater in Utah. The Utah Opera Company brought in several outstanding singers from outside the state, including Aprile Millo, who sang her first *Aida* with the Utah Opera in 1980 and soon became one of the fastest rising stars in New York's Metropolitan Opera. None was more impressive, however, than JoAnn Ottley, an outstanding local vocalist who performed not just with the opera but also as a soloist with the Tabernacle Choir and in Utah Symphony oratorio productions.[67] To the credit of Glade Peterson, when he died in 1989 the Utah Opera had been in the black for seven years in a row and had no major debt, even though most Utah performing groups and many opera companies around the nation were facing serious

Image B.4: The Pioneer Memorial Theater, completed on the University of Utah campus in 1962, is a replica of the historic Salt Lake Theater. Used by permission, Utah State Historical Society, all rights reserved.

financial difficulties. The three operas presented by the company each year were completely sold out. In 1990 Peterson was replaced as general director by Anne Ewers who, even though she was only thirty-eight years old, had a remarkable background in orchestra direction, administration, and fundraising.[68]

In Logan, in the 1980s, meanwhile, singers and other musicians at Utah State University, along with enthusiastic boosters from the community, began to work toward establishing an opera company there. Nationally prominent vocalist Michael Ballam, in particular, led out in founding the Utah Festival Opera, with the goal of raising a $7.5 million endowment fund. By the end of 1993 they were more than halfway toward that goal. That year, meanwhile, the beautifully restored Capitol Theater was reopened as the Ellen Eccles Theatre, home of the company's successful annual summer opera season.

Utahns also flocked in growing numbers to lighter musicals and to the legitimate theater, many of which were fostered through the state's colleges and universities.[69] In 1962 the Pioneer Memorial Theatre, a replica of the historic Salt Lake Theatre, was completed on the campus of the University of Utah. It housed two stages: the Babcock Theatre and the Lees Main Stage. Under the direction of Keith Engar, the theater soon became well known for its musicals and its excellent visiting and professional casts. During some years, in fact, more tickets were sold for theater presentations than for university sports events. Charles Morey, who replaced Engar as artistic director in 1984, helped form the Pioneer Theatre Company, Utah's first permanent professional acting company. In a subtle redefinition of the role of the theater, this group made a gradual shift away from musical comedy and toward more straight drama, producing plays in conjunction with outstanding visiting performers that rivaled those on Broadway.

After 1964 the Harris Fine Arts Center at Brigham Young University in Provo provided a wonderfully enhanced environment for its already prospering theater program. The DeJong Concert Hall boasted excellent facilities not just for concerts but also for operas and musicals, including many traveling shows. The Pardoe Drama Theatre became the setting for a full schedule of stage plays, the 250-seat Nelke Experimental Theatre presented experimental and other unique productions, and the Margetts Arena Theatre was a theater-in-the-round. Other successful college and university programs included Salt Lake Community College's Grand Theatre, the Westminster Playhouse and TheatreWorks West at Westminster College (where the $2.5 million Jewett Center for the Performing Arts opened in 1991), and active programs of theater production at Utah State University, Weber State University, Southern Utah University, and Dixie College.[70]

One of the jewels of Utah theater was the annual Utah Shakespearean Festival on the campus of Southern Utah University in Cedar City. Founded by Fred C. Adams in 1962, the goal of the festival was to present quality productions for visitors and to educate students in the value of the works of Shakespeare and other important dramatists. From a meager beginning of one week on a makeshift outdoor stage in 1962, attracting about one thousand people, the festival evolved to a world-renowned summer program that attracted an attendance of nearly 117,000 in 1993.

The Adams Shakespearean Theatre, dedicated in 1977, held eight hundred people and replicated as nearly as possible the Tudor design of Shakespeare's time. The Randall L. Jones Center Memorial Theatre opened in 1989 with the performances of plays by Moliere, Tennessee Williams, and Doug Christensen. As the program evolved, festival-goers were treated not only to plays by the English bard and other important playwrights but also to pre-performance music and dancing, backstage tours, workshops, a medieval banquet, and a high-school Shakespeare competition. The company of approximately fifty actors, chosen from hundreds of applicants, was supported by more than 250 additional people who were enthusiastic about their work in authentic costuming, staging, lighting, production, and public relations. One of the premier Shakespearean festivals in the world, the program brought a unique kind of public image to Southern Utah.[71]

Although the people in Utah's college and university communities showed great support for these theatrical activities, Utahns also supported independent theater groups in various locations around the state. In Logan, for example, the Old Lyric Repertory Company, formed in the 1960s, performed each summer in the Old Lyric Theatre. Other summer theaters included a varied program in the outdoor theater at Sundance Resort in Provo Canyon, melodrama in Kanab and Park City, and musicals at the Lagoon Opera House. In Salt Lake City, Theatre 138 was formed in he 1960s and for twenty years presented programs of popular comedy. About the time of Theatre 138's disappearance in the 1980s, another independent group, the Salt Lake Acting Company, was formed. It was described by one writer as "the most innovative and challenging theatrical enterprise in town."[72] At the same time, the restored Capitol Theatre presented an impressive schedule of professional road shows. These included, in the early 1990s, sold-out productions of the overwhelmingly popular musicals Les Miserables and Cats, brought to Salt Lake City by the newly formed Theater League of Utah. Other independent theater groups included the Pages Lane Theater in Centerville and the Desert Star Playhouse in Murray.[73]

Many theater and stage productions were aimed primarily at families. The Hale Center Theaters in Salt Lake City and Orem, for example, emphasized family entertainment and local talent. They produced some of the best Broadway plays as well as plays written by founders Ruth and Nathan Hale. Promised Valley Playhouse, a restored vaudeville-movie theater operated by the LDS Church, offered a variety of musical productions aimed at family entertainment and for years staged the traditional *Promised Valley* each summer. Also devoted to family entertainment was the SCERA Shell, in Orem. SCERA (Sharon Community Educational and Recreational Association) was founded as a nonprofit community enterprise during the Great Depression, providing wholesome family entertainment and recreation of all sorts. The Shell, an outdoor amphitheater where the audience was seated on the grass, opened in 1984 and conducted a full summer season of locally produced plays and musicals, as well as concerts by professional entertainers from around the country. Prominent local and national entertainers appearing in the 1980s and 1990s included the Utah Symphony, Robert Peterson, Mel Tormé, the Everly Brothers, Shirley Jones, the Kingston Trio, and the Osmond Brothers. "Our goal," said SCERA president Norm Nielsen in 1995, "is to have kids high on arts instead of high on drugs, and painting scenery, not graffiti."[74] In St. George, after fourteen years of planning, the year 1995 saw the opening of the $20 million Tuacahn Center for the Arts, with its magnificent outdoor stage set against the breathtaking background of southern Utah's red-rock mountains. The initial production, which the center planned to stage every summer for the benefit of tourists as well as the people of the state, was Utah!, an epic musical drama depicting the state's pioneer heritage.

The art of moviemaking, meanwhile, also found a welcome environment in Utah. In 1938, the state was discovered by filmmaker John Ford, who produced *Stagecoach* in the colorful Monument Valley and then returned there in the 1940s to film many other westerns. The incredibly scenic area around Moab also became popular for moviemakers in the years after World War II, and the region around Kanab continued to be known as Utah's "Little Hollywood." Among the popular movies that were at least partially filmed in Utah in the last third of the twentieth century were Redford's *Jeremiah Johnson* and *Butch Cassidy and the Sun-*

dance Kid, as well as *Indiana Jones and the Last Crusade, Geronimo: An American Legend, City Slickers II, Maverick,* and *Forrest Gump.*

In 1981, Robert Redford founded the Sundance Institute, which soon took over Park City's struggling US Film Festival. Renamed the Sundance Film Festival, it attracted filmmakers, both independent and major studios, from all over the world. By the mid-1990s it was the second most popular place in the world, behind only Cannes, France, for premiering new movies, the annual event pumping more than $6 million into the economy of Park City. For the state as a whole, movie making was an $89 million industry in 1993, although that figure dropped to $40 million the following year.[75]

The Performing Arts: Dance[76]

In 1949, Willam F. Christensen, cofounder of the San Francisco Ballet Company, returned to his native Utah to choreograph the University of Utah's summer festival productions. Two years later the university offered Christensen a full-time position as professor of ballet, charging him with founding a ballet school. As a result, the University Theatre Ballet, the first ballet school ever established at an American university, was inaugurated in 1952. Three years later the ballet teamed with the Utah Symphony to present *The Nutcracker*, which soon became a popular annual Christmas tradition.

Christensen had a more ambitious dream for the ballet, however. In 1963 he and Glenn Walker Wallace obtained a Ford Foundation grant of $175,000 for the purpose of establishing the Utah Civic Ballet, successor to the university's ballet. The first fully professional ballet company in the Intermountain West, the new organization's name was changed to Ballet West in 1968, after it was selected as the official ballet of the Federation of Rocky Mountain States.

It was not long before Ballet West, one of the most active companies of its kind in the nation, was recognized both nationally and internationally for its quality performances. Its summer residency program, established at Aspen, Colorado, in 1970, provided both instruction and professional performances. Its first of several successful European tours was conducted in 1971. Bruce Marks, an internationally acclaimed dancer and choreographer, joined the company five years later as co-artistic director, becoming full director when Christensen retired in 1978. Under Marks's guidance the ballet broadened its repertoire and achieved even greater national recognition in both classical and contemporary works. Some of its most noteworthy performances included *Sleeping Beauty*, *Abdallah* (performed at the Kennedy Center for the Performing Arts in Washington, D.C.), *Swan Lake*, *Études*, and *Billy the Kid*. Marks, who left the ballet for Boston in 1985, was replaced by John Hart, a distinguished dancer and ballet master from England, under whose guidance the ballet continued to excel.[77]

The Utah Ballet reached out to Utah's communities early in its career. In 1965, while still known as the Utah Civic Ballet, the company performed for two thousand students in two Southern Utah communities. The next year it began a lecture-demonstration program, under the auspices of a federal grant, in the Duchesne County Schools and also sent thirty dancers to perform in various gymnasiums in Uintah County for students ranging from kindergarten through high school. The response was so enthusiastic that the Salt Lake County schools asked for a similar program, obtaining a grant to help cover the costs. In 1968 the ballet performed for more than sixty-five thousand students in three states. The enthusiasm with which the program was received everywhere was typified by a second grade student in Richfield who, after watching a performance, declared, "Happiness is dancing!"[78] Dancers from the Utah Ballet continued to perform in schools around the state.

Utah also became known for its achievements in modern dance and in children's dance, initially under the inspiration of Virginia Tanner. A pioneer in modern dance, in 1935 Tanner began teaching children in her home. In 1949 she invited Doris Humphrey, her former teacher and one of the founders of modern dance, to come to Salt Lake City for the first formal performance of her Children's Dance Theatre. Humphrey was amazed at the artistry and charm of the children who, she said, "gave me a lift in spirit which I shall always remember."[79]

The Children's Dance Theatre soon received national exposure, and Ms. Tanner took her young performers to festivals in Connecticut, Massachusetts, and New York City in 1953 and 1960. "They looked like children and not like miniature adults," said one dance critic as he praised their performance. "The children danced as if they had faith in themselves, had love for those who were seeing them, actively believed in their God, and rejoiced in all these."[80] The program moved to the University of Utah in 1960, helping to attract the Rockefeller Foundation funds that led to the establishment of a modern dance program and a new professional adult company, the Repertory Dance Theatre. In 1979, Virginia Tanner died and was succeeded by Mary Ann Lee, a professional dancer who was also one of Tanner's former students. By 1995 the children's dance program had grown to eight hundred students and the Children's Dance Theatre was a company of two hundred performers who were seen by forty-one thousand Utahns annually as they toured the state. The company continued to travel both nationally and internationally as well.

Utah also boasted two professional modern dance companies. The Ririe-Woodbury Dance Company was created in the mid-1960s by Joan Jones Woodbury, a teacher of dance in the physical education department at the University of Utah, and Shirley Russon Ririe, also a member of the university dance staff. Each of the original team of eight members taught at the university but they practiced and performed during all the extra time they could muster. In 1966, thanks to the Rockefeller Foundation grant mentioned above, the university established a department of modern dance, with Woodbury as artistic director. Administrative duties forced Woodbury to withdraw from the company temporarily, but three years later she rejoined it. It was not long before the Ririe-Woodbury company was on the way to international fame, eventually performing in all fifty states, western and eastern Europe, the British Isles, Puerto Rico, South Africa, Hong Kong, and other parts of Asia. Its varied programs included not only concerts but also lectures, demonstrations, children's shows, and parent-child workshops. In 1989, this highly skilled, innovative dance company was the first American company in fifteen years to perform at the annual Berliner Festival in East Germany.

Anxious to help Utah's schoolchildren become acquainted with their art, the Ririe-Woodbury dancers spent a considerable amount of effort teaching and performing in Utah schools and small towns. In a typical program, the company sent two performers, usually a man and a woman, to each school. There they not only performed but also taught the elements of dance, choreography, and dance appreciation. These school performances were financed in part by grants from the National Endowment for the Arts (NEA), the Utah Arts Council, the state Board of Education, corporations, and private individuals, but they also required extra dedication on the part of the performers. The programs continued in the 1980s with no increase in fees, even though NEA grants were no longer forthcoming.[81]

The Repertory Dance Theatre (RDT) was founded in 1966 as a result of a cooperative effort involving Salt Lake City, the University of Utah, and the Rockefeller Foundation. Inspired by Virginia Tanner, its initial purpose was to preserve the unique achievements of American modern dance, which meant performing the works of the greatest American dance masters. The oldest and most successful company of its kind, RDT became a "living museum representing one hundred years of dance history, preserving the largest and most significant collection of American dance in the world."[82] The company was also dedicated to "artistic democracy," choosing its leadership from among its own ranks. In 1983 Linda C. Smith, a founding member of the company and a former student of Virginia Tanner, became artistic director.

In their effort to preserve dance history, and also partly in response to questions raised as they toured Utah's schools, in the 1980s RDT members scoured libraries, watched films, interviewed pupils of the great masters, and did what they could to make historic dance "photographs" come to life. Their performing collection, called *Then the Early Years*, began with the works of Isadora Duncan, founder of modern dance, and continued through the works of the 1950s.[83] The company achieved national acclaim, including the distinction of being featured in an article in the *Smithsonian Magazine*. It was also dedicated to preserving and performing important contemporary works, and frequently commissioned new works for its repertoire. Among these was *Centennial Suite*, created for the celebration of Utah's Centennial of Statehood.[84]

RDT was also one of Utah's premier musical ambassadors. By the 1990s it had performed in more than three hundred cities throughout the United States, Canada, and Europe. It was also committed to arts-in-education, providing workshops, lectures, and performances for more than thirty thousand students in Utah schools each year. One of its outstanding programs was a dance/drama, *Separate Journeys*, that celebrated the accomplishments of several Utah ethnic populations: Native American, Hispanic, Jewish, Japanese, and Greek. In the early 1990s the company moved into a new home, the Rose Wagner Performing Arts Center in downtown Salt Lake City, where it enjoyed facilities that enabled its potential to be expanded even further. With its commitment to preserving American cultural heritage as well as to innovation, and with its outstanding record of excellent performance, a *New York Post* columnist once called the Repertory Dance Theatre "A company all America should see."[85]

Dance found its way into Utah's communities not only through visits from professional dance companies but also through private dance schools that sprang up almost everywhere. Teachers of ballet, modern dance, clogging, and other forms of dance all found eager students waiting to learn. In Manti, for example, Vivian Kosan Bagnall began conducting the Central Utah Ballet School after she and her husband, Lewis, moved into town in 1987 and obtained funds to refurbish the old Manti city hall. When Bagnall directed the third annual Christmastime performance of *the Nutcracker* in 1991, the two hundred people participating in the production came from all over the county as well as some of the surrounding areas. In Logan, the Cache Valley Civic Ballet was formed in 1983, and by 1992 the company had four studios, six teachers and 260 students. Directed by Sandra Emile, it initially performed in the Chase Fine Arts Center at Utah State University, then at the Ellen Eccles Theatre after its completion. In 1984, the Ballet Repertory Ensemble, Inc., was created by Carolyn Gwyther, a teacher of dance at the College of Eastern Utah in Price. By 1992 there were seventy-five college students enrolled in dance classes, as well as more than one hundred students in a junior program. These were only a few indications of the fact that dance was enthusiastically supported by many people not only in Utah's large metropolitan communities but in smaller towns as well.[86]

Dance was also an important part of the curriculum and public programs of the University of Utah, Utah State University, and Brigham Young University,[87] each of which offered majors in dance. The Utah Ballet, based in the University of Utah's ballet department, conducted both winter and spring seasons of eight shows each. At BYU, several student entertainment groups frequently performed all over the nation and the world. Dance groups included the American Folk Dance Ensemble, the Dancers Company, and the Young Ambassadors.

Utahns also enjoyed other kinds of theatrical productions, including outdoor pageants and extravaganzas. Each summer thousands attended the *Mormon Miracle* pageant in Manti as well as pageants in Castle Dale and Clarkston also depicting LDS themes. In Logan, a grand pageant depicting western themes was presented at the annual Festival of the American West at Utah State University.

Historic Architecture and the Challenges of Preservation

As much as any other art form, architecture reflects the culture of its times and communicates thoughts and ideas. The creation of form and space for a particular purpose, whether as a dwelling, a place of worship, a public building, or an entire urban landscape, not only reflects the needs of a particular people in a particular time but also expresses the viewpoints of the architects about the society in which they work. The variety of buildings and styles produced throughout Utah's history thus constitute a rich and important cultural heritage. Nineteenth-century vernacular architecture included dwellings, barns, and other outbuildings that continue to inform us about pioneer life. Later, more highly stylistic structures reflected efforts to adapt the best contemporary architectural forms for use in Utah homes, churches, and public buildings of all sorts. Some of these became artistic treasures in their own right.[88]

Utah's architectural heritage included a few unique features attributable to Mormon town planning and religious architectural needs. For the most part, however, the state's architectural patterns reflected those of the rest of the nation. A good deal of Utah's nineteenth-century vernacular architecture still stands, including numerous adobe buildings, log buildings, Mormon forts, stone masonry buildings, and brick buildings. Many fine examples of important stylistic trends also remain. These include homes erected in the Federal style, featuring a symmetrical arrangement, a shallow pitched roof, and boxed cornice with a decorative frieze of some sort. The Greek Revival style was expressed in a number of elegant public and church buildings, including the Old City Hall in Salt Lake City and the Bountiful Tabernacle. At the same time, the popular Gothic Revival style appeared regularly between the 1860s and 1880s. Religious buildings exhibiting elements of that style included St. Mark's Episcopal Cathedral in Salt Lake City as well as all four Mormon temples built in Utah in the nineteenth century. Other examples included Brigham Young's Lion House and many other homes, both large and small, throughout the state.

Several other popular styles were reflected in Utah's homes, as well as its religious, public, and commercial buildings, but one of the most elegant was the Richardson Romanesque style, made popular by American architect Henry Hobson Richardson. It was characterized by large rounded arches, rock-faced masonry, weightiness, and massiveness. Peter Goss, one of Utah's premier architectural historians, identified the Salt Lake City and County Building, completed in 1894, as "the finest example of this style in the state."[89] Other important nineteenth-century styles reflected in buildings that still stand include: the Thomas Kearns Mansion (now the Governor's Mansion, in the Chateauesque style), the Salt Lake Public Library (now the O.C. Tanner Company Headquarters, in the Paris-inspired Beaux-Arts Classical style), the Utah State Capitol Building (Renaissance Revival style), the Utah County Courthouse in Provo (Neoclassical), St. Joseph's Catholic Church in Ogden (Gothic Revival), several Commercial Style buildings, many homes built in the style of the Prairie School inspired by Frank Lloyd Wright, a number of LDS Church buildings in the same style, and numerous homes that represent the so-called bungalow style.

Frank Lloyd Wright and his mentor, Louis Sullivan, were arguably the two most widely known American architects. Sullivan, called the "father of the skyscraper," designed public buildings characterized by "intricate and lavish arabesque decoration" on both the interior and exterior surfaces, flat roofs, extended cornices, and main entrances "usually emphasized by a large, round-arched opening on the ground floor, often accented with ornamentation." [90] A few buildings patterned after the Sullivan style were erected in Utah, but the Dooley Building in downtown Salt Lake City, designed by Sullivan himself in 1891, was one of only three actual Sullivan buildings in the West. It was demolished in 1961.

From the 1920s through the 1940s architectural design languished somewhat in Utah and did not follow the trends of other parts of the country. Two notable exceptions were the Ogden High School (1936) and the Ogden–Weber Municipal Building (1983), both in the Art Deco style. After 1945, however, Utah architects created a number of buildings in the new styles flourishing elsewhere. The Miesian style, following patterns established by Mies van der Rohe, emphasized the use of steel and glass and was represented by the Regis Medical Clinic in Holladay (1966). Buildings created in another style, New Formalism, are sometimes described as "free standing blocks containing symmetrical elevations and flat projecting roofs. Decoration, where present, consists of patterned screens of various materials. Columns used in supporting buildings of this style are often thicker or more exaggerated than those of other modern styles."[91] The LDS Church Office Building, completed in 1973, is a prominent example of New Formalism. In a style known as New Brutalism, unfinished building materials, such as rough-textured concrete, are often left exposed. Outstanding examples are the Behavioral Science Building and the Art and Architecture Center on the campus of the University of Utah.

In the latter part of the twentieth century, Utah architects, working with city planners, designers, artists, and business, civic, and cultural leaders, increasingly paid attention to the problem of creating well-planned, integrated urban landscapes that addressed a variety of cultural and ecological needs.[92] Among the many significant results were the development of a number of impressive downtown retail malls; the Delta Center in Salt Lake City; restoration and renovation of such important buildings as the Cathedral of the Madeleine, the Peery Hotel, and the Inn at Temple Square; a new baseball stadium in Salt Lake City; the Union Station Civic Center and the restoration of the Egyptian Theatre in Ogden; and the Dixie Center in St. George. Part of the object of these efforts was to incorporate local historical tradition as well as the natural environment into the planning. Robert Kimball Herman, prominent architect and civic leader in Ogden, wrote in 1993 that "perhaps for the first time in decades, Utah designers—like their progenitors—are effecting truly place-defining work that can celebrate their peculiar relationship with the land."[93]

In some instances unique waterworks were used to symbolize the importance of water in Utah's desert climate. The Seven Canyons Fountains in Salt Lake City's Liberty Park was an outstanding example. "Disposed like an amphitheater that mirrors the Salt Lake Valley topography," wrote Herman, "this absurdly wonderful piece creates a composite image of playground and didactic artifact that describes the cultivation of water as it emerges from the seven surrounding canyons and is then transformed by the grids and gutters of public works before being expelled into Great Salt Lake."[94] Other examples of the cooperative, environmentally conscious approach were the resort at Snowbird and the lodges at Deer Valley.

Meanwhile, as Utah's cities and towns became more congested, and as the needs and technology of modern society made older homes, churches, and public buildings appear outmoded, many of the state's historic architectural treasures seemed doomed to destruction. Beginning in the 1960s, however, Utahns mounted an increased effort to preserve their architectural heritage, recognizing that it was, in reality, an essential part of their historic and cultural legacy. This was partially a reflection of an important national trend, stimulated by the National Historic Preservation Act of 1966 which, among other things, provided for expanding the

Image B.5: The Logan Tabernacle, one of Utah's nineteenth-century architectural gems, went through several interior modifications but was saved from destruction when the LDS Church decided to restore it. The restoration was completed in 1989.

National Register of Historic Places. The issue became a matter of especially intense public interest and discussion after a number of architecturally important buildings in Salt Lake City were demolished, usually, it was said, because they were no longer functional and must be replaced by more modern facilities. Attitudes were changing, however, as seen in the fact that owners of many exceptional historic buildings increasingly chose to restore and utilize them rather than demolish and replace them. As one writer noted, this change in attitude "came barely in time to retain a part of the man-made charm of the state and nation."[95]

In 1965, long-time preservationists as well as numerous other civic-minded people throughout the state were shocked when they learned of the threatened destruction of one of Utah's architectural gems, the LDS Tabernacle in Heber City. An emotional public outcry, however, led to intense discussions during the winter of 1965–66 on how to restore the tabernacle and other buildings on the town square. The results were two-fold. The church turned the tabernacle over to the city and the Wasatch County chapter of the Utah State Historical Society, to be preserved as a public facility for such things as lectures and theatrical productions. This was precisely the kind of thing preservationists and architectural historians recommended for such buildings. In addition, the discussions led to the founding of a permanent organization, the Utah Heritage Foundation, established in 1966 as a voice for preservation. Depending heavily on the work of volunteers and on private contributions to support its small paid staff, the foundation also received a modest annual appropriation from the legislature that amounted to $10,000 in 1993.[96]

The Utah Heritage Foundation was unsuccessful, however, in its effort to save the Coalville Tabernacle which, for both aesthetic and cultural reasons, was considered by some to be one of the most important buildings in the state. In its original design, the tabernacle was one of those delightful examples of Gothic Revival architecture that, in and of themselves, seem to provide a religious experience. Such buildings, preservationists and architects often observed, were not only artistic jewels but were truly conducive to worship rather than simply utilitarian shelters for church programs. The tabernacle was characterized by graceful spires, Gothic windows, stained glass carrying Mormon motifs and symbols, a small rose window, simple but elegant interior columns, classical details around the windows, intricate wainscoting, and six brass lamps hanging from an elaborately decorated ceiling. The ceiling featured ornamental designs and scrollwork, as well as portraits of five Mormon leaders: Joseph Smith, Hyrum Smith, Brigham Young, John Taylor, and Wilford Woodruff.[97]

The tabernacle's unique architectural integrity was compromised as early as 1944, however, when the building was saved from destruction by being remodeled. The remodeling project divided the inspiring assembly hall horizontally by creating an upper floor, to be used as a recreation area, thus destroying the original aesthetic and spiritual effect of the interior. In addition, a stage on the new upper floor cut off the view of the portrait of Joseph Smith. Nevertheless, architectural historians still considered the tabernacle one of Utah's most important treasures, and the Utah Heritage Foundation called it "one of the four or five outstanding LDS buildings still standing." In 1970 it was officially listed on the Utah State Register of Historic Places. LDS Church leaders, however, determined that the building no longer met the needs of the church and that there was no alternative to razing it in order to make room for a more modern facility. Numerous people and organizations throughout the state attempted to stop the destruction, and one group even took the matter to court, but finally, in the pre-dawn hours of March 5, 1971, the demolition began.[98] The debate over the Coalville Tabernacle brought national attention, and the disappointed outcry went on for years.

It cannot be maintained that the Coalville controversy was the major factor in bringing about a change in LDS policy, but it is noteworthy that tensions eased in later years as the church established a policy of more careful consideration of each individual case. In southern Utah, the church preserved the Pine Valley Chapel (Greek Revival style), near St. George, to be used as both a place of worship and a visitor's center for tourists. The lovely Bountiful Tabernacle, also built in the elegant simplicity of the Greek Revival style and originally dedicated in 1863, was designated by the church for preservation in 1975. Structurally reinforced, restored, and refurbished, it continued to serve useful religious purposes. Tabernacles in Logan, Provo, and other parts of the state were likewise saved from destruction, and the beautiful Gothic Revival tabernacle in Brigham City seemed never to have been threatened. The historic Assembly Hall on Temple Square, a Gothic Revival structure that resembled the Coalville Tabernacle and provided an impressive setting for a regular concert series and other activities, was restored in the 1980s. In 1994 the church announced a unique and innovative plan for the eighty-five-year-old Uintah Stake Tabernacle in Vernal: it would be remodeled and become a temple, serving church members in east central Utah and parts of Wyoming and Colorado.

The Utah Heritage Foundation, meanwhile, created an inventory of state historic sites, conducted school programs aimed at helping students and teachers appreciate their architectural heritage, conducted tours of historic buildings, purchased selected buildings and resold them to people interested in restoring them for useful purposes, and sponsored lectures and other events.

The foundation also published a few books, including *Historic Buildings Along South Temple Street*. In 1976 the South Temple Historic District was established for the purpose of preserving and protecting important buildings along South Temple, the street that was once the city's premier residential boulevard. The area 's architecture represented an impressive variety of styles. Once known as Brigham Street, South Temple also included such important and architecturally elegant buildings as Brigham Young's Lion House, the Beehive House, the Alta Club, the Cathedral of the Madeleine, and the First Presbyterian Church. Other historic buildings in the area with significant architectural value included the Council Hall (the old Salt Lake City Hall, constructed in 1864 through 1868, dismantled in 1962 and restored on Capitol Hill), Hotel Utah (closed in 1987 but reopened in 1993 as the Joseph Smith Memorial Building), the Orpheum (Capitol) Theatre, the old Salt Lake Public Library (a 1905 building that, in 1965, became the Hansen Planetarium), the Denver and Rio Grande Railroad station (renovated in 1980 to become the home of the Utah State Historical Society), and the ZCMI building (which was demolished in the 1980s, but its unique cast-iron facade was preserved to grace the face of the new building).[99] In addition, after months of controversy over whether to replace it with a modern structure, the graceful Salt Lake City and County Building was restored and rededicated in 1989.

The growing sense of history also resulted in the preservation and restoration of numerous smaller homes and buildings that represented the special flavor of Utah's early life and architecture. The St. George Opera House, completed in 1880, was a delightful structure that served as both a theater and a social hall. Later, it was used for other purposes and finally languished for years as an unused eyesore. In the 1990s, citizens of St. George raised $1.5 million to create a Pioneer Cultural Center, with the beautifully restored Opera House as its centerpiece. Other examples included the Rockville telegraph office, built in the 1870s, the old LDS tithing house in Vernal, and the chapel in Spring City. Many other historic sites were restored and remodeled in such a way that they served useful, often economically profitable, purposes. Among them was Trolley Square in Salt Lake City, in which old trolley-car barns were turned into a unique shopping mall. In American Fork, the LDS Second Ward building, an example of Wright-inspired Prairie Style architecture, was once slated for demolition but then was restored and used by M. L. Bigelow & Co. as a place for building organs.

In Provo, however, citizens interested in preserving and restoring the graceful Victorian style buildings on Academy Square, site of the former Brigham Young Academy, met with continued frustration in their efforts to raise the necessary funds. After being sold by Brigham Young University in 1975, the square went through several owners, ending up in the hands of Provo City in 1994. But there was still no decision on what to do with the buildings. If no developer with plans and financial backing suitable to Provo City could be found, the city fathers said, the buildings would be demolished. However, a $16 million bond in 1997 paved the way for preserving and renovating the Education Building, which eventually became the city library. The other buildings were razed but the library began full operation in 2001.

The Literary Arts[100]

In the years following World War II, Utahns produced a rich flow of notable fiction, poetry, essays, dramas, and historical writings that also reflected the cross-currents and differing perspectives of Utah life. The most abundant, although not always the most critically acclaimed, might be called "insider" writings, produced by and for Mormons and published in LDS Church periodicals or by publishing houses that catered primarily to the LDS audience. Such writings, openly religious and frequently highly didactic in nature, provided welcome inspiration and support for faithful Mormons. Outlets included all the LDS periodicals, the church-owned publishing house Deseret Book Company, other publishers, such as Bookcraft, Aspen Books, Grandin Book Company, Horizon Publishers, Hawkes Publishing Company, Covenant Communications, and Olympic Publishers, that catered primarily to the LDS audience, and a variety of additional small publishers and vanity presses.

Another genre reflected efforts on the part of some Latter-day Saints to delve more deeply into their religious heritage, even if it raised controversial questions. Historical, philosophical, ethical, and theological issues were all explored in great detail not only by LDS writers but by non-Mormons as well. Their works often appeared in such journals as *Brigham Young University Studies* (founded in 1959), *Dialogue: A Journal of Mormon Thought* (founded in 1966), *Sunstone* (founded in 1974), the *Journal of Mormon History* (founded in 1974), and *Exponent II* (also founded in 1974). Many of these writings, often scholarly in their approach, also found their way into the hearts and minds of faithful Mormons, because they did not overtly raise fundamental questions about the validity of the faith. Others, however, became highly controversial.

At the same time, a wide range of literature reflected Utah, Western, and Mormon life but also explored much broader human themes and concerns and often became widely known outside the state. Utah publishers that catered to such works included the journals cited above as well as the *Western Humanities Review*, the *Rocky Mountain Review*, Brigham Young University Press (until its demise in the late 1970s), University of Utah Press, Utah

State University Press, the Utah State Historical Society, Peregrine Smith Publishers, Gibbs Smith Publisher, Signature Books, and a few of the other presses cited above. Popular periodicals such as *Mountain West* and *Utah Holiday* also published a variety of creative work by and/or about Utahns. In addition, the University of Illinois Press included Mormon studies as one of its specialities and published numerous books by Utah authors.

Eugene England, in a remarkably astute essay published in 1995, made a cogent observation on some differences of viewpoint within the Mormon literary community on what Mormon literature ought to be. One group, represented by Richard H. Cracroft, objected to recent trends in which, he believed, Mormon writers were too imitative of the flawed critical and moral trends of contemporary writers and thus untrue to traditional Mormon values. Mormon values, Cracroft felt, were unique, and Mormon literature should express that uniqueness. Others, represented by Bruce W. Jorgenson, felt that the new Mormon literature should be distinguished not by its doctrinal or didactic purposes but by the way it portrayed love for the world and by its rich diversity in style and content.[101] There were, of course, a variety of perspectives in between, but such discussions represented the continuing challenges facing Mormon writers attempting to remain true to their faith and, at the same time, respond to the ever-widening appeal for new ideas and fresh approaches.

England depicted four main periods in the history of Mormon literature, characterizing the fourth period, since 1960, as one of "slow growth and then flowering," in which good work in all genres "combines the best qualities and avoids the limitations of most past work, so that it is both faithful and critical, appreciated by a growing Mormon audience and also increasingly published and honored nationally."[102] This was, he said, a period of "faithful realism" in which Mormon writers produced works that were highly artistic, realistic, and sometimes even critical about the Mormon experience but still faithful to the visions and concerns of the Mormon founders.

At the same time, Utah literature in general was marked, as Thomas J. Lyon observed in 1995, "by the incursion of the relentless outer world into the Lombardy-poplar village, and the incor-

Image B.6: Wallace Stegner (1909–1993), a Utah expatriate who became famous for both his fiction and his historical writings. Used by permission, Utah State Historical Society, all rights reserved.

poration of Utah into the modern, industrial way of life and the global economy."[103] As noted throughout this history, the people of Utah were deeply affected by national economic, technological, political, and social crosscurrents, many of which changed the nature of both American and Utah society after World War II. Beginning with the dark and awesome possibilities seen in fallout from postwar nuclear testing, continuing through the technological miracles that brought Utah and the nation into the cyberworld of the 1990s, and responding to the ever-shrinking nature of the world because of rapid transportation and near-instant communication, the people of Utah experienced an unprecedented half-century of historical change and, in some ways, became less distinctive than ever before. But they also, as Lyon pointed out, faced a "splendid proliferation of possibilities" that helped enrich their literature. "There were simply more things to write about," he noted, "and more kinds of voices to write in," for they had "a kind of knowledge of the past, and of themselves, that wasn't possible until the state became more cosmopolitan."[104]

For whatever reason, the writing of poetry, essays, plays, and novels burgeoned in the last half of the twentieth century. Extensive listings of some of the most notable writers may be found in the bibliography of *Great and Peculiar Beauty: A Utah Reader*, an important anthology published in 1995 by Thomas Lyon and Terry Tempest Williams, and in several other sources. There is space here, unfortunately, to discuss only a representative few.[105]

In the years following World War II, several Utah expatriates achieved national reputations for their literary works. Among the most notable was Bernard DeVoto (1897-1955), well known for his columns in *Harper's Magazine*, for his editing of the *Saturday Review of Literature*, and for several works of both fiction and nonfiction. His important historical trilogy, *The Year of Decision: 1846* (1943), *Across the Wide Missouri* (1947), and *The Course of Empire* (1952) was especially well received. The second volume won the Pulitzer Prize in history. Wallace Stegner (1909-1993), reared in Salt Lake City, taught English at Stanford University. Like DeVoto, Stegner also became famous for both his fiction and his historical writings. His Utah-Western heritage was evident in many works, including his important historical books *Mormon Country* (1942), *The Gathering of Zion: The Story of the Mormon Trail* (1964), and *Beyond the Hundredth Meridian: John Wesley Powell and the Second Opening of the West* (1954). The same is true of his novels such as *Big Rock Candy Mountain* (1943) and *Recapitulation* (1979). The latter provided some powerful reflection on what it was like to grow up in Salt Lake City. Another novel, *Angle of Repose* (1971), won the Pulitzer Prize, and *The Spectator Bird* (1976) won the National Book Award.

Perhaps Utah's best-known poet in this era was May Swenson, who grew up in Logan but spent most of her adult years in New York. Among the books that brought her recognition as a major American poet were *To Mix with Time* (1963) and *In Other Words* (1987). Winner of the MacArthur Fellowship in 1987, which carried a stipend of $375,000, as well as several other highly prestigious prizes, Swenson published numerous volumes of poetry before her death in 1989. Much of her work reflected memories of her youth in the West. In "The Centaur," for example, she described the exciting ride of a ten-year-old astride her stick horse, while in the tender verses of "The Poplar's Shadow," published in her book *Nature* (1994), the scenes of the city reminded her of the poplar tree at home.[106]

Books by another expatriate, Rodello Hunter, became highly popular in Utah in the 1960s and 1970s. Based on her personal and family history, works such as *A House of Many Rooms* (1965), *Wyoming Wife* (1969), and *Daughter of Zion* (1970) appealed to readers because of their nostalgia as well as their wit. Still another expatriate, Samuel W. Taylor, became a novelist, screen writer, and historian.[107]

Among the younger generation of Utahns who lived outside the state and whose works appealed to a large Utah audience was Orson Scott Card, certainly the most prolific and widely-read Utah writer of his time. Becoming most well known for his science fiction and fantasy, he climbed to the top of his field when he won both the Hugo and Nebula Awards two years in a row, 1986 and 1987, first for the best-selling *Ender's Game* and then for its sequel, *Speaker for the Dead*. Returning to his roots, he also published a Mormon novel, *Woman of Destiny* (1984, republished as *Saints* in 1988), which traced the life of a British immigrant who ultimately became a plural wife of Joseph Smith and, later, Brigham Young. It dealt both frankly and sympathetically with all the feelings and emotions such nineteenth-century Mormon stalwarts experienced. While not overtly Mormon, *Seventh Son*, the first in a fantasy series called *The Tales of Alvin Maker*, clearly carried Mormon themes and values, as did its sequels.[108]

Among the literary figures who remained in Utah, BYU's Clinton F. Larson stood preeminent among poets in the 1960s and continued writing and publishing for more than three decades. He was credited by some as opening the modern era of Utah poetry or being the "spiritual father" of modern Utah literature. [109]*The Lord of Experience* (1967) and *Counterpoint* (1983) were among his several published collections. He also co-edited with William Stafford, in 1975, a collection of twentieth century poetry by various authors entitled *Modern Poetry of Western America*. Larson's ability to evoke almost any mood or feeling was demonstrated in a poem included in *The Lord of Experience*. "To a Dying Girl," characterized by Eugene England as "a perfectly cut jewel," tenderly but poignantly portrayed the experience of death.[110] In a different mode, his "Nuclear Winter" (1985) caught all the fears of a people who bitterly remembered the fallout from atomic testing in the 1950s and worried about the consequences if the Cold War should heat up.[111] In 1985, an unpublished collection of Larson's complete works comprised thirteen volumes. They included deeply religious poems and plays, such as "The Mantle of the Prophet" (a poetic play), directed especially to the Mormon audience, as well as poems on numerous other varied and sensitive themes.

One of Utah's most versatile writers was Brewster Ghiselin of the University of Utah, who founded the university's writers conference in 1947 and directed it for twenty years. He was also poetry editor for the *Rocky Mountain Review*. A writer of both fiction and poetry, he was the recipient of numerous prizes and awards, including a Ford Foundation Fellowship and the National Institute of Arts and Letters William Carlos Williams Award for *Windrose, Poems, 1929-1979*, published in 1980. His book *The Creative Process*, published in 1952, still remains in print.

Also at the University of Utah, François Camoin authored nationally recognized collections of short stories with such provocative titles as *The End of the World Is Los Angeles* (1982) and *Why Men Are Afraid of Women* (1984). The latter won the prestigious Flannery O'Connor Award for short fiction. Camoin, a native of France, endeared himself to the Utah literary community not only because of his artful writing but also because of his superb teaching and the outstanding contribution he made to the training of young writers.

Levi S. Peterson, professor of English at Weber State University, represented a new breed of "up-and-coming" Mormon writers who, through their short stories, explored the numerous conflicts, including theological conflicts, confronted by Mormon males in rural Utah. Witty, provocative, and sometimes controversial in the Utah context, Peterson often probed the depths of both joy and despair in both historic and contemporary times. His themes, however, were far from parochial. In works such as *The Backslider* (1986) he successfully did just what he said he wanted to accomplish with his characters: "reveal universal preoccupations and themes through them."[112] With the publication of *The Canyons of Grace*, winner of the short fiction prize of the University of Illinois Press in 1982, Peterson was the first of his generation of native Utah writers to publish a collection of stories through a national press. According to Eugene England, by the time he published *Night Soil: New Stories* in 1990, he was Utah's "most prolific author of high-quality contemporary Mormon fiction."[113]

Poet-essayist Emma Lou Thayne, who taught English for a time at the University of Utah, was the recipient of numerous honors and awards for her sensitive reflections on the people and culture of Utah. Honors included the David O. McKay Humanities Award from Brigham Young University and the Distinguished Alumna Award from the University of Utah. Among her most highly regarded books were *With Love, Mother* (1975), *How Much For the Earth?* (1983), and *Things Happen* (1991). The title poem in *Things Happen* was a penetrating reflection on an automobile accident that occurred while Thayne was driving and her son was reading the new automobile owner's "manual of how." In 1995, Thayne joined with Pulitzer-Prize winning historian Laurel Thatcher Ulrich[114] in publishing *All God's Critters Got a Place in the Choir*, a delightful book of provocative and entertaining personal essays and poems that often went to the very heart of the many crosscurrents in Utah/Mormon life.

Terry Tempest Williams, naturalist-in-residence at the Utah Museum of Natural History, was one of Utah's preeminent nature writers, as well as a writer on women's issues, in the 1980s and 1990s. Her first book, *Pieces of Shell: A Journey to Navajoland* (1984) won the Southwest Book Award. Her masterful *Refuge: An*

Unnatural History of Time and Place, published nationally in 1991, was a powerful yet tender autobiographical exploration of personal family relations, values, and nature. Set against the background of the Great Salt Lake and its wildlife, the book brought her immediate national attention. In 1991, this book, along with Thomas G. Alexander's *Things in Heaven and Earth: The Life and Times of Wilford Woodruff*, won the prestigious David W. and Beatrice C. Evans Biography Award. Williams's book also won the Association for Mormon Letters' best essay prize. In one provocative passage she reflected on the strength that can be drawn from being alone in the desert:

> .... You stand in the throbbing silence of the Great Basin, exposed and alone. On these occasions, I keep tight reins on my imagination. The pearl-handled pistol I carry in my car lends me no protection. Only the land's mercy and a calm mind can save my soul. And it is here I find grace.
>
> It's strange how deserts turn us into believers. I believe in walking in a landscape of mirages, because you learn humility. I believe in living in a land of little water because life is drawn together. And I believe in the gathering of bones as a testament to spirits that have moved on.
>
> If the desert is holy, it is because it is a forgotten place that allows us to remember the sacred. Perhaps that is why every pilgrimage to the desert is a pilgrimage to the self. There is no place to hide, and so we are found.
>
> In the severity of a salt desert, I am brought down to my knees by its beauty. My imagination is fired. My heart opens and my skin burns in the passion of these moments. I will have no other gods before me.
>
> Wilderness courts our souls. When I sat in church throughout my growing years, I listened to teachings about Christ in the wilderness for forty days and forty nights, reclaiming strength, where he was able to say to Satan, "Get thee hence." When I imagined Joseph Smith kneeling in a grove of trees as he received his vision to create a new religion, I believed their sojourns into nature were sacred. Are ours any less?[115]

Leslie Norris, a native of Wales and a Fellow of the Royal Society of Literature of Great Britain, was poet-in-residence at Brigham Young University and was named that school's Distinguished Faculty Lecturer in 1991. His book of short stories, *Sliding* (1971), won both the Chalmondeley Prize and the David Higham Award. Among his many other books were *Sequences*, a book of poetry published in 1988, and a collection of short stories, *Cardigan*, published the same year. Although most of his work did not deal with Utah themes, Norris eventually began incorporating them into some of his writing. His "Christmas in Utah," for example, beautifully caught the feeling of a winter day, perhaps a hundred years earlier, in Salt Lake City.[116]

Poet Edward L. Lueders, a faculty member at the University of Utah from 1966 to 1990, received the Utah Governor's Award in Humanities in 1992. His books included *The Clam Lake Papers: A Winter in the North Woods*, a metaphorical work (1982), and *The Wake of the General Bliss* (1989). Also on the faculty of the University of Utah was Mark Strand, a recipient of the prestigious MacArthur Foundation Fellowship. In 1990 he was appointed Poet Laureate Consultant in Poetry to the Library of Congress. *The Night Book* (1985) and *The Continuous Life* (1990) were among his many books. Another poet, Kenneth W. Brewer, who taught at Utah State University beginning in 1968 and headed that school's creative writing program, was also well-known nationally. His works included *The Collected Poems of Mongrel* (1981) and *To Remember What Is lost* (1982). He also regularly held poetry workshops throughout the state, where he endeared himself to the rising generation of writers. Katharine Coles taught at both the University of Utah and Westminster College, where she directed the Westminster Poetry Series. Her collection of poetry, *The One Right Touch* (1992), contains the powerful though somber "Love Poem for the Nuclear Age, Utah, 1950-[ ]," another reminder of the tensions of modern times. Linda Sillitoe, a fine freelance writer, received the Association of Mormon Letters Award for her 1987 novel *Sideways to the Sun*. Her other publications include a collection of short stories, *Windows on the Sea* (1989), a book of poetry, *Crazy for Living* (1991), and a novel, *Secrets Kept* (1995). Phyllis Barber, who spent much of her adult life in Utah but later moved to Colorado, won the Associated Writing Program Prize for Creative Nonfiction in 1991 for her autobiography, *How I Got Cultured: A Nevada Memoir* (published 1992). She also wrote successful fiction, such as her delightful book for children, *Legs, the Story of a Giraffe* (1991); a book of stories, *The School of Love* (1992); and *And the Desert Shall Blossom* (1993), a historical novel about the Hoover Dam project. Margaret Blair Young, a writing instructor at Brigham Young University, received two first prizes, one in the short story section and the other in the book section, in the 1989 Utah Arts Council contest. Her two novels, *House without Walls* (1991) and *Salvador* (1992), became highly popular among Utah readers.

Brigham Young University's Eugene England was known as a superb and provocative essayist as well as an important critic and historian of Utah and Mormon literature. Publishing frequently in various Utah journals and periodicals, he both inspired and provoked his Mormon audience with heartfelt reflections on the beauty of his faith as well as some of the intellectual and spiritual conflicts that grew out of his Mormon heritage. Two significant collections of his essays were *Dialogues with Myself* (1984) and *Making Peace* (1995), both published by Signature Books. Another, *The Quality of Mercy*, was published by Bookcraft in 1992. He also produced two important anthologies on Mormon literature: *Harvest: Contemporary Mormon Poems*, coedited with Dennis Clark (1989), and *Bright Angels and Familiars: Contemporary Mormon Stories* (1992). In 1996 he coedited, with Lavina Fielding Anderson, *Tending the Garden: Essays on Mormon Literature*.

Utah was also home to a number of fine dramatists and playwrights. One was Thomas Rogers of Brigham Young University. In his play *Huebener*, first produced in 1976, he reached perhaps his pinnacle of excellence as he explored the emotions and tragedy of conflicting views within the Mormon community in Nazi Germany during World War II. David Krane, meanwhile, was a gifted playwright at the University of Utah, as well as a writer of both fiction and nonfiction. In addition, he was artistic director of the Playwrights Conference at the Sundance Institute. James Arrington became particularly well known for his humorous depictions of Mormon history and life in his one-person plays. *Here's*

Brother Brigham entertained audiences of all ages throughout Utah as well as in other states, while *Farley Family Reunion* became a true classic for its comic insight into Mormon family life. It was considered by some, in fact, as among the best of authentic Mormon drama.[117]

History is not usually classified among the "arts," but it must be observed that the best historians are frequently also excellent writers, possessing an analytical and literary skill that often produces work of genuine literary merit. Even as they explore historical issues in detail and present significant new insights into past events, they sometimes capture the deepest concerns and emotions of the people they write about and portray the meaning of great events in as stimulating a fashion as writers of great poetry, plays, or novels. One of Utah's most nationally famous historians, LeRoy R. Hafen, described the ideal historian as a "person of literary ability" who would take time to do the necessary research, "and then produce history that is sound in appraisal, keen with insight, and also is crowned with artistic, literary presentation."[118] Among the historians who wrote about Utah history and whose works sometimes excelled in literary quality as well as academic excellence were Juanita Brooks, S. George Ellsworth, Davis Bitton, and Charles S. Peterson. Leonard J. Arrington, another fine literary stylist, became, along with Hafen, one of Utah's two most nationally well-known historians. In the spirit of Hafen's challenge to historians, Arrington's pathbreaking *Great Basin Kingdom: An Economic History of the Latter-day Saints, 1830–1900* (1958) was a highly readable exploration of the economic activities of the Mormons in the Great Basin, including both successes and failures. In 1972 Arrington became the Lemuel H. Redd, Jr., Professor of Western American History at BYU and, at the same time, was appointed LDS Church Historian. His later works included sensitive, well-written biographies of many prominent Utahns, including his *Brigham Young: American Moses* (1985).

Among the myriad kinds of historical writing, biography presents perhaps the greatest potential for literary achievement. As biographers sympathetically reconstruct individual lives, they often attempt to recreate in the hearts and minds of their readers all the feelings, moods, and emotions that made a difference to the historical characters they are portraying. Biography thus adds a richness and depth to history that could be captured in no other way. In 1983, in an effort to promote even better, more well-written biography, the David W. Evans family instituted a prestigious award, The David W. and Beatrice C. Evans Biography Award, given annually for the best biography about a person from "Mormon Country" (which, broadly interpreted, meant anywhere in the Intermountain West). By 1996 nine Utahns, or former Utahns, had received the award.[119]

Another important literary genre was folklore, and several Utah folklorists helped document the many tales, customs, and musical works that made up the perceptions and traditions of Utahns. Austin E. Fife's *Saints of Sage and Saddle* (1956), for example, was a masterful collection of early Mormon songs and folklore. Fife also published on cowboy folklore and songs, folklore relating to material culture such as gravestones and hay derricks, stories about the famous "Three Nephites" in Mormon tradition, and several other folk themes. Jan Brunvand, a very prolific modern folklorist, published *The Vanishing Hitchhiker: American Urban Legends and Their Meaning* (1981), *Curses, Broiled Again!: The Hottest Urban Legends Going* (1989), and *The Baby Train and Other Lusty Urban Legends* (1993), each of which was a delightful collection, with analysis, of American urban folklore. William A. Wilson, meanwhile, developed a unique and extensive collection of Mormon missionary folklore and became a popular writer and speaker throughout the state. His work also included folklore from various American ethnic groups as well as Finnish folklore. Another eminent folklorist was Barre Toelken, whose important historical critique of folksongs and poetry, *Morning Dew and Roses: Nuance, Metaphor, and Meaning in Folksongs*, was published by the University of Illinois Press in 1995. Toelken also wrote on Japanese folklore, life, and social customs in his book *Ghosts and the Japanese: Cultural Experience in Japanese Death Legends* (1994) and produced a nationally recognized text on methodology, *The Dynamics of Folklore* (1979). Hal Cannon was not only a folklorist but also a musician and poet. A leader in the revival of western music and cowboy poetry, his books include the best selling *Cowboy Poetry: A Gathering*. His honors include the Botkin Prize of the American Folklore Society, the Will Rogers Lifetime Achievement Award, and three Wrangler Awards from the National Cowboy Hall of Fame.

Concluding Observations

The last half of the twentieth century was good for the arts in Utah. With impressive public and private support, the visual arts, theater, dance, movie making, and the literary arts all flourished as never before. Much of what happened in Utah reflected national trends, including controversy over new artistic forms and genres. "Few things intimidate, confuse, and anger people as much as contemporary art they do not understand," wrote Carol Biddle in 1993. "And of all contemporary art, the so-called *new genres* are often the most difficult to figure out."[120] Among the new genres of the late twentieth century were a variety of unusual works displayed in outdoor settings as environmental art (often intended to make political and social statements), art that combines various genres in unusual and challenging presentations, and computer-generated art. Such work was on the cutting edge and was often misunderstood or rejected by much of the public, but for the artists it was a way of presenting new ideas about the challenges of the modern world. In addition, the changing nature of Utah-produced literature reflected changing political, social, and economic realities in America and the fact that Utah was increasingly affected by those historical circumstances. By the end of the century Utah artists in every field were known both nationally and internationally. The challenge was to continue to develop and maintain excellence in all fields, taking advantage of the cosmopolitan opportunities that were increasingly available, but at the same time retaining a distinctiveness that reflected both Utah's unique heritage and the desire of its people to face new challenges and concepts head-on. The best art, after all, reflect not just skill but also ideas and values.

Notes

1. The author expresses deep appreciation to Vern G. Swanson for critiquing the sections on fostering the arts and on the visual arts. Swanson offered many helpful

suggestions, and graciously helped reword some paragraphs. The author also expresses deep appreciation to the late Eugene England, who provided similar help respecting the literary arts, and to Shirley Britsch, who read the draft most recently and offered valuable suggestions. For a fine summary of the state of all the arts in Utah as of 1993, with listings of many prominent artists and groups not discussed in this appendix, see *Utah State of the Arts* (Ogden, UT: Meridian International, Inc., 1993). This handsome book contains fifteen short but authoritative essays and is richly illustrated. See also Vern G. Swanson, Robert S Olpin, and William C. Seifrit, *Utah Painting and Sculpture*, rev. ed. (Salt Lake City: Gibbs Smith, 1997); Vern G. Swanson, Robert S. Olpin, and Donna L. Poulton, *Utah Art, Utah Artists: 150 Year Survey* (Layton, UT: Gibbs Smith, 2001); Robert S. Olpin, William C. Seifrit, and Vern G. Swanson, *Artists of Utah* (Salt Lake City: Gibbs Smith, 1999).

2. Governor Norman L. Bangerter, as quoted on the title page of Utah Arts Council, *Annual Report, 1986-87*.

3. See the updated edition of that guide, Ward J. Roylance, *Utah: A Guide to the State*, rev. and enlarged (Salt Lake City: *Utah: A Guide to the State* Foundation, 1982), 203-4. For a more detailed evaluation of the Federal Art Project in Utah, see Will South, "The Federal Art Project in Utah: Out of Oblivion or More of the Same?" *Utah Historical Quarterly* 58 (Summer 1990): 277-95.

4. From the National Foundation on the Arts and the Humanities Act of 1965.

5. For a brief overview of the activities of the Utah Arts Council, see "90 Years in the Arts: A Renaissance with No Dark Ages," *Repertoire*, published by the Utah Arts Council (First quarter 1989).

6. The festival included paid theater performances, free street performances, a children's art yard, and numerous displays of the work of Utah artists. As Frank Sanguinetti, chairman of the festival board, explained in 1980, the primary function of the festival was "to engage as many people throughout the state as possible in a presentation of Utah's visual and performing arts, and to convince tourists that their destination must be Utah." *Repertoire* (Second quarter, 1980), 2.

7. In 1980, for example, dancer Arthur Hall, an American of African descent, spent two weeks at the Midvale Middle School, where he led students in an in-depth exploration of African culture. *Repertoire* (First quarter 1980), 7; Utah Arts Council, *Arts in Education Program: Guidelines and Artists Bank* (1992). In 1990, at the Central Elementary School in Vernal, Oregon writer and poet Ingrid Wendt introduced students to a variety of poets and poetic forms and then helped them, through their own imaginative powers, to create and share their own poetry. *Repertoire* (third quarter, 1990).

8. *Repertoire* (first quarter 1990); Utah Arts Council, *Utah Performing Arts Tour* (1993-94 brochure).

9. For an excellent, more extended discussion of the state of folk and ethnic arts and crafts in the 1990s, see Carol Edison, "Indian Baskets, Pioneer Quilts and Hispanic Music," in *Utah State of the Arts*, 129-50. For a discussion of crafts in general, see Carol Biddle, "Crafts: A Legacy of Tradition and a Search for New Forms," ibid., 83-96.

10. See Delmont R. Oswald, "Utah Humanities Council," in *Utah History Encyclopedia*, ed. Allen Kent Powell (Salt Lake City: University of Utah Press, 1994), 589-90.

11. *Repertoire* (third quarter 1984).

12. For a brief overview of some museums, including historical and archeological museums, not noted in this chapter, see Donald V. Hague, "Museums in Utah," in *Utah History Encyclopedia*, ed. Powell, 386–88.
13. For an overview of the history of the Springville Art Museum, see Yvonne Baker Johnson and Dianne Clyde Carr, "History of the Art Movement in Springville, Utah," in Vern G. Swanson, Robert S. Olpin, and William C. Seifrit, *Utah Painting and Sculpture* (Salt Lake City: Gibbs Smith Publisher, 1997), 281-83.
14. Swanson retired in 2012 and was replaced by Dr. Rita Wright.
15. For comments on the 1995 Salon, see Dave Gagon, "Spring Salon," *Deseret News*, April 30, 1995, E1–E2. Halliwell was from London, England. Deffebach is discussed in another part of this chapter.
16. Information provided to the author in the 1990s by Vern G. Swanson.
17. Donald V. Hague, "Museums on Utah," in *Utah History Encyclopedia*, ed. Powell, 388. For an important and beautifully illustrated history of Utah art since 1950, see Vern G. Swanson, "The Contemporary Scene: 1950-1992," in Swanson, Olpin, and Seifrit, *Utah Painting and Sculpture*, 181-266.. For an important earlier history of Utah painting, see James L. Haseltine, *One Hundred Years of Utah Painting* (Salt Lake City: Salt Lake City Art Center, 1965).
18. Members of the association included Art Access, Artspace Artists Association, Atrium Gallery, Dolores Chase Fine Art, D'Elegance International, Distinctive African American Art Works, Allen Dodworth Fine Arts Appraisal, Finch Lane Gallery, Gallery 56, Glendenning Gallery, Hippodrome Gallery of FHP Health Care, Leftbank at Pierpont, Loge Gallery, Marble House Gallery & Appraisal, Phillips Gallery, Repartee Gallery, Salt Lake Art Center, Sego Gallery, Southam Gallery, Tivoli Gallery, Utah Designer Crafts, Utah Museum of Fine Arts, F. Weixler Gallery, and Williams Fine Art.
19. A study published in 1981 compared public funding for the arts in Salt Lake City with several other metropolitan areas in the United States. Local government provided 6.3 percent of the funding for the institutions studied in Salt Lake City, state government provided 14.0 percent, and 11.5 percent came from the national government, for a total of 31.8 percent. When compared with the rest of the nation, Utah was about average. The study was limited in scope, but the Salt Lake City institutions included were Ballet West, the Pioneer Memorial Theatre, Repertory Dance Theatre, Salt Lake Art Center, Theatre 138, Tiffany's Attic, Utah Museum of Fine Arts, Utah Symphony, Utah Opera Company, and the Ririe-Woodbury Dance Company. *Economic Impact of Arts and Cultural Institutions: Case Studies in Columbus, Minneapolis, St. Paul, St. Louis, Salt Lake City, San Antonio, Springfield* (Washington, D.C., National Endowment for the Arts, 1981). Outside Salt Lake City, state and federal dollars represented a lower portion of total funding.
20. *Repertoire* (fourth quarter, 1985).
21. See Richard P. Christensen, "Art Commissions," *Deseret News*, February 13, 1994, E1–E2
22. *Community View*, published by the Utah Arts Council, 5 (Summer 1991), 1.
23. Bob Kuesterman, "Salt Lake County Voters Reject Arts Subsidy Tax," *Daily Herald* (Provo, UT), June 9, 1993, B3.
24. *Repertoire* (fourth quarter, 1986).
25. See William Fleming, *Arts and Ideas*, 6th ed. (New York: Holt, Rinehart and Winston, 1980), 405–09. Most of the following material on national art trends is based directly on Fleming.

26. As quoted in Fleming, *Arts and Ideas*, 446.
27. The material on visual arts in this chapter is based almost entirely on Vern G. Swanson, "The Contemporary Scene," in Swanson, Olpin, and Seifrit, *Utah Painting and Sculpture*, 181–266. The quotation above is on page 181. Numerous artists not mentioned here are discussed in some detail by Swanson. This large, handsome publication is a monumental work on the history of Utah art, and should be consulted for the numerous important details and interpretations that can only be suggested in the short space available here. The book contains numerous photographs, including 167 color plates. The periods before 1950 are covered by William Seifrit, "Pioneer Painters to Impressionism: 1847–1900," pp. 13–84, and Robert S. Olpin, "Tradition and the Lure of the Modern: 1900–1950," pp. 85–180. For more on contemporary Utah artists and sculptors, see Mary Francey, "Utah Art, toward a New Century," in *Utah State of the Arts*, 17–38; Steven W. Rosen, "Utah in Three Dimensions," ibid., 165–76. For a discussion of the state of photography not considered in this chapter, see John Telford, "Utah Photography: State of the Art," ibid., 201–18.
28. Swanson, "The Contemporary Scene," 182.
29. Marian Gresseth, "The Tyranny of Heritage: The Problems of the Utah Artist," *Pen* (Spring 1958): 23–24.
30. Dave Gagon, "The Art of Earl Jones," *Deseret News*, June 27, 2004.
31. For a brief discussion of Wilson and Dornan, see Swanson, 'The Contemporary Scene," 222.
32. Ibid., 196.
33. Ibid., 207.
34. For a discussion of several more modernists in this period who worked in a variety of styles and media, see ibid., 207–8, 210–13.
35. See Eugene F. Fairbanks, *A Sculptor's Testimony in Bronze and Stone: The Sacred Sculpture of Avard T. Fairbanks* (Salt Lake City: Publishers Press, 1972).
36. Swanson, "The Contemporary Scene," 203.
37. Most of these people and their works are discussed in ibid., 214–15.
38. For biographical studies of Young, see Wayne K. Hinton, "A Biographical History of Mahonri M. Young, A Western American Artist" (Ph.D. dissertation, Brigham Young University, 1974); Thomas Ernest Toone, *Mahonri Young: His Life and Art* (Salt Lake City: Signature Books, 1997).
39. See Museum of Church History and Art, *Rich in Story, Great in Faith: The Art of Minerva Kohlhepp Teichert* (Salt Lake City: The Church of Jesus Christ of Latter-day Saints, 1988). This was a book prepared to accompany the exhibition at the Museum of Church History and Art in 1988. It included essays by Laurie Teichert Eastwood, "My Mother—Minerva Kohlhepp Teichert," and Robert O. Davis, "I Must Paint." See also Marian Eastwood Wardle, "Minerva Teichert's Murals: The Motivation of Her Large-Scale Production" (master's thesis, Brigham Young University, 1988); Marian Ashby Johnson, "Minerva's Calling," *Dialogue: A Journal of Mormon Thought* 21 (Spring 1988): 127–43; Marian Ashby Johnson, "Minerva Teichert: Scriptorian and Artist," *BYU Studies* 30 (Summer 1990): 66–69.
40. Swanson, "The Contemporary Scene," 185.
41. Ibid.
42. Ibid., 190. See also Ted Schwarz, *Arnold Friberg: The Passion of a Modern Master* (Flagstaff, AZ: Northland Press, 1985).
43. Swanson, "The Contemporary Scene," 218.

44. Ibid., 218–19.
45. Ibid., 185.
46. Ibid., 206.
47. As quoted in ibid., 219.
48. For additional insight into Smith's recent work, see Jerry Johnston, "Dennis Smith and His Bronze Children," *This People* 16 (Holiday 1995): 46–52.
49. See Swanson, "The Contemporary Scene," 220–21.
50. "Pro or Con? Utah's Big New Sculpture?" *Sunset* 176 (April 1986): 46.
51. This movement is discussed in Swanson, "The Contemporary Scene," 194–95, but see also Vern G. Swanson, "Mormon Art and Belief Movement," *Southwest Art* 21 (December 1991): 66–70.
52. For some insight into the status of Mormon arts at the end of the 1960s, see Lorin F. Wheelwright and Lael J. Woodbury, eds., *Mormon Arts, Vol 1* (Provo, UT: Brigham Young University Press, 1972).
53. Swanson, "The Contemporary Scene," 228.
54. For histories of the Utah Symphony, see Conrad B. Harrison, *Five Thousand Concerts: A Commemorative History of the Utah Symphony* (Salt Lake City: Utah Symphony Society, 1986); Lowell M. Durham, *Abravanel!* (Salt Lake City: University of Utah Press, 1989). For the Mormon Tabernacle Choir, see Ray L. Bergman, *The Children Sing: The Life and Music of Evan Stephens and the Mormon Tabernacle Choir* (Salt Lake City: Northwest Publishing Inc., 1992); Charles Jeffrey Calman, *The Mormon Tabernacle Choir* (New York: Harper & Row, 1979); J. Spencer Cornwall, *A Century of Singing: The Salt Lake Mormon Tabernacle Choir* (Salt Lake City: Deseret Book, 1958); Michael Hicks, *Mormonism and Music: A History* (Urbana: University of Illinois Press, 19890); Gerald A. Peterson, *More Than Music: The Mormon Tabernacle Choir* (Provo, UT: Brigham Young University Press, 1979); Roger L. Miller, "Mormon Tabernacle Choir," in *Utah History Encyclopedia*, ed. Powell, 378–80. For a brief discussion of contemporary symphony and chamber music, see Paul Wetzel, "Great Basin Rhapsody," in *Utah State of the Arts*, 39–46.
55. As quoted in "Chance for Utah to Pay Debt to Symphony," *Salt Lake Tribune*, editorial, October 4, 1966, 14.
56. Shirl H. Swenson, "The Symphony Goes to the Schools," *Utah Educational Review* 61 (January–February 1968): 8–11.
57. *Repertoire* (fourth quarter 1991).
58. "Utah Symphony to Ring in New Year," *Salt Lake Tribune*, December 30, 1983, M2.
59. "Give Support to Utah Symphony," *Deseret News*, editorial, April 20, 1995, A20.
60. As quoted in Peterson, *More Than Music*, 35. David O. McKay, President of the LDS Church, saw what such a tour meant not only for the church but also for the state. "The money spent," he said, "is the best investment we have ever made in spreading goodwill for Utah, the US, and the Church." As quoted in Hicks, *Mormonism and Music*, 163.
61. Prominent organists included Alexander Shreiner, Frank Asper, Roy Darley, Robert Cundick, John Longhurst, Clay Christiansen, and Richard Elliott. In 1988 the magnificent Aeolian-Skinner pipe organ was renovated and enlarged to include 11,623 pipes in 206 ranks. For a history of the organ, see Barbara Owen, *The Mormon Tabernacle Organ: An American Classic* (Salt Lake City: The Church of Jesus Christ of Latter-day Saints, 1990).

62. For the story of the Oratorio Society of Utah, see Marcus Sidney Smith, *With Them Were 10,000 and More: The Authorized History of the Oratorio Society of Utah* (Salt Lake City: Actaeon Books, 1989). For a fine discussion and listing of various choral groups in Utah, many not listed in this discussion, see Edgar J. Thompson, "Choral Music: Break Forth Into Song," in *Utah State of the Arts*, 177–86.

63. See Wyatt J. Kondris, "A Survey of Orchestral Music Programs in the Senior High Schools of Utah" (master's thesis, Brigham Young University, 1968).

64. William S. Goodfellow, "Music Makes the Utah Connection," *Deseret News*, December 5, 1993, E1, E4; William S. Goodfellow, "Premiere to Focus on Composer's Choral Side," ibid., E4.

65. See Herschel Bullen, "Jazz, New Age, and Beyond in the Insular West," in *Utah State of the Arts*, 73-82, for a short but informative discussion of new directions in music

66. In addition to the secondary sources cited below, there are three fine essays on contemporary opera, theater, and moviemaking in *Utah State of the Arts*: Dorothy Stowe, "Opera Scales the Heights in Utah," 219-24; Nancy Melich, "A Theater Grows in Utah," 187-200; and Sharon Lee Swenson, "Oh Shoot! Filmmaking in Utah," 151–64

67. Roylance, *Utah: A Guide to the State*, 246; Paul Wetzel, "The '80s," feature article in *Salt Lake Tribune*, December 31, 1989, E1, E3.

68. "Utah Opera Company Picks Replacement for Peterson," *Deseret News*, December 28, 1990, A12.

69. See Morris Martin Clinger, "A History of the Theater in Mormon Colleges and Universities" (Ph.D. dissertation, University of Minnesota, 1963); Randall Lee Bernhard, "Contemporary Musical Theatre: History and Development in the Major Colleges and Universities of Utah" (Ph.D. dissertation, Brigham Young University, 1979).

70. For a full discussion of these and other programs, to 1979, see Randall Lee Bernhard, "Contemporary Musical Theatre: History and Development in the Major Colleges and Universities of Utah" (Ph.D. dissertation, Brigham Young University, 1979).

71. See Terrall Sam Lewis, "The Utah Shakespearean Festival: Twenty-five Years in Retrospect" (Ph.D. dissertation, Texas Tech University, 1991); Ann Engar, "Utah Shakespearean Festival," in *Utah History Encyclopedia*, ed. Powell, 495.

72. Wetzel, "The '80s," E3.

73. For a general overview of theater in Utah see Ann W. Engar, "Theater in Utah," in *Utah History Encyclopedia*, ed. Powell, 551-54.

74. "Show Time at the Scera," *Daily Herald*, April 30, 1995. E1.

75. Kimberly Murphy, "Local Firms Are Strong When Films Are Shooting," *Deseret News*, September 19, 1994, C4; Kimberly Murphy, "Utah Movie Equipment Companies Are Ready For Action" *Daily Herald*, September 19, 1994, B5.

76. In addition to the sources cited below, a short but informative essay on the state of dance in Utah in the 1990s is Dorothy Stowe, "State of the Dance in a Dancing State," in *Utah State of the Arts*, 57-72.

77. Cherie N. Willis, "Ballet West," in Utah History Encycwlopedia, ed. Powell, 25–26.

78. Alan Behunin, "Ballet Brings Joy to Students," *Utah Educational Review* 61 (May–June 1968), 10.

79. As quoted in "The Virginia Tanner Creative Dance Program and Children's Dance Theatre," brief historical material provided to James B. Allen by Mary Ann Lee, November 1995.
80. Ibid.
81. Information on the Ririe-Woodbury company is based on Anna Champena, "A Study of Utah's Professional Dance Companies Since 1950," a BYU History Department senior seminar paper written under the direction of James B. Allen, fall semester, 1991. The author of the paper received much of her information in a personal interview with Joan Woodbury.
82. Quoted from "Utah's Repertory Dance Theatre," a short unpublished history of the company provided to the author by Linda C. Smith, November, 1995, copy in James B. Allen papers, L. Tom Perry Special Collections, Harold B. Lee Library, Brigham Young University.
83. *Utah Chronicle*, February 12, 1986, as cited in Champena, "A Study of Utah's Professional Dance Companies Since 1950," 22.
84. The suite consisted of four dances honoring Utah's unique landscape. The first, "Erosion," was inspired by the red-rock country of southern Utah. The second, "Liquid Interior," honored other aspects of the stark Great Basin landscape and premiered in 1994. It was planned that all four dances would come together for the first time during the 1996 Centennial year. *Centennial Spirit* (Official publication of the Utah Statehood Centennial Commission) 2 (Winter 1995): 2.
85. Information on RDT is based primarily on the material provided by Linda C. Smith.
86. Dorothy Stowe, "Dance Blossoms around Utah: Companies Spring Up around Good Teachers," *Deseret News*, March 22, 1992, E1, E5.
87. For a discussion of dance at the University of Utah, see Margaret Tennant Waterfall, "A History of Dance at the University of Utah (1906–1968)" (master's thesis, University of Utah, 1968). For BYU, see Roxanne Smith, "The History of Ballet at Brigham Young University" (master's thesis, Brigham Young University, 1986); Denise P. Olsen, "An Historical Overview of Modern Dance at Brigham Young University from 1875 to 1986" (master's thesis, Brigham Young University, 1987).
88. See Peter L. Goss, "The Architectural History of Utah," *Utah Historical Quarterly* 43 (Summer 1975): 208-39. Much of what follows constitutes a very brief summary of that article. See also the entire Summer 1975 issue of the *Utah Historical Quarterly*, edited by Peter L. Goss under the title *Toward an Architectural Tradition;* Thomas Carter and Peter L. Goss, *Utah Historical Architecture, 1847-1940* (Salt Lake City: University of Utah Press, 1988); C. Mark Hamilton, *Nineteenth-Century Mormon Architecture and City Planning* (New York: Oxford University Press, 1995). For a discussion of Utah architects, see Peter L. Goss, "The Architectural Profession in Utah," in *Utah History Encyclopedia*, ed. Powell, 20–23. In addition, Mark Hamilton, "Utah Domestic Architecture," in *Utah History Encyclopedia*, ed. Powell, 18–20.
89. Goss, "The Architectural History of Utah," 223.
90. Ibid., 231.
91. Ibid., 238.
92. For an excellent discussion of this modern trend and important insight into the state of modern Utah architecture in the 1990s, see Robert Kimball Herman, "The State of the Place," in *Utah State of the Arts*, 97-120.

93. Ibid., 112.
94. Ibid.
95. Roylance, *Utah: A Guide to the State*, 268. For a general overview of historic preservation efforts to 1980, see John W. Haggerty, "Historic Preservation in Utah: 1960-1980" (master's thesis, Brigham Young University, 1980).
96. John S. McCormick, "Utah Heritage Foundation," in *Utah History Encyclopedia*, ed. Powell, 585-86.
97. For a sensitive discussion, with photographs, of the nature of the Coalville Tabernacle, see Thomas Wood and Douglas Hill, "The Coalville Tabernacle," *Dialogue: A Journal of Mormon Thought* 2 (Summer 1967): 61-74.
98. The portraits and stained glass were preserved, however, and some of the stained glass was used in the modern, utilitarian building that replaced the tabernacle. For discussions of the destruction of the tabernacle, see "The Coalville Tabernacle," a "Roundtable" with articles by Edward Geary, Paul G. Salisbury, and an anonymous writer, *Dialogue: A Journal of Mormon Thought* 5 (Winter 1970): 41-65
99. See Mark Hafey et al., *Historic Preservation: The South Temple Historic District* (Salt Lake City: published by the authors, 1975); Peter dePont Emerson, "The South Temple Historic District: Past, Present, Future" (master's thesis, University of Utah, 1979); Margaret D. Lester, *Brigham Street* (Salt Lake City: Utah State Historical Society, 1979); John S. McCormick, *Historic Buildings of Downtown Salt Lake City* (Salt Lake City: Utah State Historical Society, 1982).
100. In addition to the sources cited below, see Edward Leuders, "Wordscapes: The Literary Scene," in *Utah State of the Arts*, 121-28, for an insightful discussion of the state of the literary arts in the 1990s.
101. Eugene England, "Mormon Literature: Progress and Prospects," in David J. Whittaker, ed., *Mormon Americana: A Guide to Sources and Collections in the United States* (Provo, UT: BYU Studies, 1995), 455-505. The discussion above is found on pp. 456-58. This essay contains an extensive bibliography of Mormon literature.
102. Ibid., 462.
103. Thomas J. Lyon, "In the Valleys of the Mountains," in Thomas J. Lyon and Terry Tempest Williams, eds., *Great and Peculiar Beauty: A Utah Reader* (Salt Lake City: Gibbs Smith Publisher, 1995), 12.
104. Ibid.
105. See Joyce Kinkead, ed., *Literary Utah: A Bibliographic Guide* (Salt Lake City: Utah Council of Teachers of English, 1990); England, "Mormon Literature: Progress and Prospects"; Lavina Fielding Anderson, "Utah Literature," in *Utah History Encyclopedia*, ed. Powell, 328-33; "Literature, Mormon Writers of," in *Encyclopedia of Mormonism*, ed. Daniel H. Ludlow (New York: MacMillan, 1992), 2:837-44; Richard H. Cracroft and Neal E. Lambert, eds., *A Believing People: Literature of the Latter-day Saints* (Provo, UT: Brigham Young University Press, 1974); Lavina Fielding Anderson, "The Assimilation of Mormon History: Modern Mormon Historical Novels," *Mormon Letters Annual* (1983): 1-9; Richard H. Cracroft, "Seeking 'the Good, the Pure, the Elevating': A Short History of Mormon Fiction," *Ensign* 11 (June, July 1981): 56-62, 56-61; Eugene England, "The Dawning of a Brighter Day: Mormon Literature After 150 Years," in *After 150 Years: The Latter-day Saints in Sesquicentennial Perspective*, ed. Thomas G. Alexander and Jessie Embry (Provo, UT: Charles Redd Center for Western Studies, 1983): 97-146; Kenneth B. Hunsaker, "Mid-Century Mormon Novels," *Dialogue: A Journal of Mormon Thought* 4 (Autumn 1969): 123-28; Bruce W. Jorgensen, "Digging the Foundation: Making and Reading Mor-

mon Literature," *Dialogue: A Journal of Mormon Thought* 9 (Winter 1974): 50-61; Bruce W. Jorgensen, "A 'Smaller Canvass' of Mormon Short Story Since 1950," *Mormon Letters Annual* (1983): 10-31; Lavina Fielding Anderson, "Making the 'Good' Good for Something: A Direction for Mormon Literature," *Mormon Letters Annual* (1985): 150-64; Kenneth B. Hunsaker, "Mormon Novels," in *A Literary History of the American West*, ed. Thomas J. Lyon and others (Ft. Worth: Texas Christian University Press, 1987), 849-61; Richard H. Cracroft, "Attuning the Authentic Mormon Voice: Stemming the Sophic Tide in LDS Literature," *Sunstone* 16 (July 1993): 51-57; William A. Mulder, "'Essential Gestures': Craft and Calling in Contemporary Mormon Letters," *Weber Studies* 10 (Fall 1993): 7-25. Finally, see especially Lyon and Williams, eds., *Great and Peculiar Beauty*, the most comprehensive collection of Utah literature to date.

The author expresses appreciation to the late Eugene England for taking time to discuss Utah literature with him and to help him determine what writers to make note of here. The list of excellent, distinguished writers, however, is so long that no sampling can even begin to capture the depth and breadth of what has really happened in Utah literature. The reader is strongly urged to read the various bibliographic essays and anthologies listed above. See also Eugene England's two important anthologies on Mormon literature: *Harvest: Contemporary Mormon Poems*, co-edited with Dennis Clark (Salt Lake City: Signature Books, 1989), and *Bright Angels and Familiars: Contemporary Mormon Stories* (Salt Lake City: Signature Books, 1992). Both books contain carefully chosen selections from the works of several important writers not mentioned in this chapter.

106. These two poems are reproduced in Lyon and Williams, *Great and Peculiar Beauty*, 567-70.

107. A very interesting article on Taylor is Jean R. Paulson, "Samuel W. Taylor: Talented Native Son," *Utah Historical Quarterly* 67 (Summer 1997), 265-84.

108. Many of Card's other works, all of which sold well nationally as well as in Utah, were unabashedly Mormon-oriented. These included *The Folk of the Fringe* (1989), a series of Mormon science fiction stories, and his *Homecoming* series, clearly based on the narrative of the Book of Mormon.

109. Lyon and Williams, eds., *Great and Peculiar Beauty*, 1000; England, "Mormon Literature: Progress and Prospects," 471.

110. Discussed and reproduced in Eugene England, "The Dawning of a Brighter Day: Mormon Literature after 150 Years," *BYU Studies* 22 (Spring 1982): 151.

>How quickly must she go?
>She calls dark swans from mirrors everywhere:
>From halls and porticos, from pools of air.
>How quickly must she know?
>They wander through the fathoms of her eye,
>Waning southern until their cry
>>Is gone where she must go.
>>How quickly does the cloudfire streak the sky,
>Tremble on the peaks, then cool and die?
>She moves like evening into night,
>Forgetful as the swans forget their flight
>>Or spring the fragile snow,

>So quickly she must go.

111. Clinton F. Larson, "Nuclear Winter," *BYU Studies* 25 (Winter 1985), 99.
112. As quoted in Lyon and Williams, eds., *Great and Peculiar Beauty*, 1007.
113. England, ed., *Bright Angels and Familiars*, xv.
114. Although she grew up in Idaho and spent most of her adult life in New England, Ulrich was often claimed by Utahns because of her activity in the Mormon Church and because much of what she wrote, particularly about women, appealed to a Utah audience. She was a member of the history faculty of the University of New Hampshire and, later, the first woman to receive tenure in the history department at Harvard. Her first book, *Good Wives: Image and Reality in the Lives of Women in Northern New England 1650-1750* (New York: Knopf, 1982), was a pathbreaking social study in women's history. Another book, *A Midwife's Tale: The Life of Martha Ballard, Based on Her Diary, 1785-1812* (New York: Knopf, 1992), won the Pulitzer Prize in history. Here Ulrich's extraordinary research and compelling writing style provided fascinating and sympathetic detail not only on the life of a midwife in Maine but also on the lives and customs of the people of an entire community. Because of her continuing promise as a scholar and writer, Ulrich also received a MacArthur Fellowship, one of the most prestigious unrestricted research awards in America. In addition, Ulrich was a prominent Mormon essayist, whose writings in *Exponent II* and other places were widely read in Utah.
115. Terry Tempest Williams, *Refuge: An Unnatural History of Time and Place*, first Vintage Book edition (New York: Vintage Books, 1992), 148–49.
116. In barns turned from the wind
    the three-quarter horses
    twitch their laundered blankets.
    Three Steller's Jays,
    crests sharp as ice,
    bejewel the pine tree.
    Rough cold out of Idaho
    bundles irrational tumbleweed
    the length of Main Street.
    Higher than snowpeaks,
    shriller than the frost,
    a brazen angel blows his silent trumpet.

    As reproduced in Lyon and Williams, eds., *Great and Peculiar Beauty*, 243. For important analyses of Norris's work, see Eugene England and Peter Makuck, eds., *An Open World: Essays on Leslie Norris* (Columbia, SC: Camden House, 1994); James A. Davies, *Leslie Norris* (Cardiff: University of Wales Press, 1991).
117. England, "Mormon Literature: Progress and Prospects," 480.
118. LeRoy R. Hafen, "Joys of Discovery--Historical Research and Writing," *BYU Studies* 7 (Spring-Summer 1966): 182.
119. Those recipients from Utah during the years covered by this book, and when the awards were received, were Leonard J. Arrington, for *Brigham Young: American Moses* (1983); Richard L. Bushman, for *Joseph Smith and the Beginnings of Mormonism* (1984); Linda King Newell and Valeen Tippetts Avery, for *Mormon Enigma: Emma Hale Smith* (1984); James B. Allen, for *Trials of Discipleship: The Story of William Clayton, A Mormon* (1987); Levi S. Peterson, for *Juanita Brooks: Mormon*

Woman Historian (1988); Thomas G. Alexander, for *Things in Heaven and Earth: The Life and Times of Wilford Woodruff* (1991); Terry Tempest Williams, for *Refuge: An Unnatural History of Family and Place* (1991); Robert Alan Goldberg, for *Barry Goldwater* (1995); Mary Lythgoe Bradford, for *Lowell L. Bennion: Teacher, Counselor, Humanitarian* (1995).

120. For an interesting discussion of contemporary new genres, see Carl Biddle, "New Genres: The Orphans of Discipline," in *Utah State of the Arts*, 47–56. The quotation above is on page 47.

APPENDIX C

Notes on Utah's Religions, 1945–1995

Religion has always played a central role in the life of Utahns, even though the subject was dealt with only incidentally in the major chapters of this book. For that reason we have prepared this appendix. The following brief sketches focus on the post-World War II activities of several of Utah's religious bodies. and their status as of 1995.

The Church of Jesus Christ of Latter-day Saints remained predominant, but other denominations were an increasingly significant presence.[1] The Catholic Church, a few Protestant denominations, and a Jewish community were well established in the state before World War II. With the outbreak of the war, prospects for these and other non-Mormon churches improved as the growth of defense industries attracted numerous people from outside the state.[2] The growth of other industries in later years aided even more in-migration. Between 1971 and 1990 the number of religious denominations in the state jumped from twenty-six to thirty-four. In 1986 an unpublished directory of Protestant and Roman Catholic churches in Utah listed 377 congregations scattered throughout the state. It also listed forty-nine service institutions that were related to religious groups. These included the American Bible Society, rescue missions and various other ministries and groups designed to offer charitable assistance and training to those in need, Bible study fellowships, the Boy Scout and Girl Scout organizations, four book stores (in addition to those associated with certain special ministries), and campus ministries at the University of Utah, Utah State University, and Brigham Young University. There were also thirty-one Christian schools, three chapels on military bases, and thirty-four other places where non-Mormon denominations sponsored some kind of Christian ministry.[3]

The Church of Jesus Christ of Latter-day Saints[4]

The history of The Church of Jesus Christ of Latter-day Saints after World War II was characterized by rapid growth in numbers, accelerated expansion worldwide, and numerous administrative and program changes. Between 1950 and 1993, total membership grew from about 1,111,000 to 8,689,000 while the number of Mormons in Utah increased from about five hundred thousand to an estimated 1,425,000. In fact, the proportion of Utah's population made up of Latter-day Saints increased from 66.45 percent in 1940 to about 75.7 percent in 1990.[5] In the early 1990s Utah had the highest concentration in the nation of a single religious body and in only five other states was there a group that made up more than 50 per cent of the total population.[5]

More significant for the church, however, was the fact that the proportion of its total membership living outside Utah rose from 55 percent in 1950 to 83 percent in 1990. The remarkable worldwide expansion really constituted the major story of the church during these years. However, the focus here is on the church in Utah.

Mormon Church leaders played significant roles in Utah public life, not only because of their prominence as leaders of the dominant church but also because of their personal interest and leadership in supporting public policies designed to improve the well-being of all Utah citizens. For example, President David O. McKay, who led the church from 1951 to 1970, had a particularly positive working relationship with Gus P. Backman, executive secretary of Salt Lake City's Chamber of Commerce, and John F. Fitzpatrick, editor of the *Salt Lake Tribune*. In their frequent meetings they shared views on the important issues affecting the city and the state.[7]

Much of the church's extraordinary growth was the result of a burgeoning missionary program, especially after the mid-1950s.[8] This program had a direct effect on Utah in many ways. One was simply the fact that each year thousands of Utahns left to serve as missionaries in various parts of the world. Young men were gone for two years, young women for eighteen months, and retired couples for various periods ranging from one to two years. A second effect occurred after the missionaries who went to non-English speaking missions came home. Their language skills, along with those of hundreds of returned missionaries who were not from Utah but were attending school in the state, made Utah the most linguistically proficient state in the nation. As a result, Utah became an important recruiting spot for businesses and government agencies involved in international activities.

A third way in which the missionary program affected Utah was through the activities of the Missionary Training Center in Provo. The center began in 1966 as the Language Training Mission at Brigham Young University, but in 1974 a new $15 million facility was erected away from the campus. In 1978, the name was changed to the Missionary Training Center after the instructional activity was expanded to serve all missionaries. There, newly called missionaries received up to two months of intensive missionary instruction and language training before going to their assigned fields of labor. In the mid-1990s, approximately two thousand missionaries were in residence at the center at any given time. Beyond the religious aspects of such a program, the economic consequences were significant not only for local business but also for the airlines that flew hundreds of missionaries in and out of Salt Lake City's International Airport every week.

Finally, the missionary program had another kind of effect on Utah when, in 1975, the Utah Salt Lake City mission was organized, the first time a mission had been created within the state. The results were remarkable. This mission was soon among the top in the world as far as the number of convert baptisms was concerned. The mission was divided in 1980 and again in 1989.

Church growth was accompanied by several significant changes in organization. These changes included the organization of the First and Second Quorums of the Seventy, in 1975 and 1989, respectively. Members of these quorums became General Authorities, acting under the direction of the Quorum of the Twelve Apostles. Meanwhile, the church divided the world into "areas," each presided over by members of the Quorums of the Seventy. In 1994 there were twenty-two such areas worldwide, two of them in Utah.

During this same period, beginning in the 1970s, the church's huge administrative structure was refined, making it more professional and, ideally, more effective in carrying out its many programs that were intended to enhance the lives of members worldwide. These programs, headquartered in Salt Lake City, included education, social services, family history (genealogy) services, a building department, publishing, missionary administration, financial services, computer services, library and archival services, and numerous others.

One of Mormonism's most rapidly expanding programs was education, and particularly religious education. An early morning seminary program expanded to include hundreds of thousands of students worldwide. In Utah, released time seminary enrollment reached nearly sixty-four thousand by 1986.[9] Classes were conducted in seminary buildings adjacent to high schools. The state discontinued its practice of allowing high school credit for Bible classes, but school administrators often expressed gratitude for the released time arrangement, which helped avert a crisis in the number of available classrooms.

Meanwhile, Brigham Young University, with its authorized enrollment of twenty-seven thousand full-time students, remained the largest university in Utah and the largest privately-owned institution of higher learning in the United States. The church also operated the LDS Business College in Salt Lake City.

As a result of the heavy emphasis Mormons placed on genealogical research, after World War II the church dramatically broadened its program of microfilming genealogical records, eventually extending this work to many parts of the globe. The church's massive archive of vital records soon became the most extensive and well-known collection in the world. To house the master copies of the microfilms, as well as other important documents, a massive storage vault was constructed, carved into a granite cliff in Little Cottonwood Canyon. The vault was dedicated in 1966. The unique location and facilities of the Granite Mountain Vault provided the humidity and temperature control needed to maintain the priceless records on a permanent basis. One result of making the huge collection available to researchers of all sorts, was that genealogists, historians, people interested in medical research, and scholars from a variety of other disciplines found their way to the Family History Library in Salt Lake City.[10]

Meanwhile, the building of Mormon temples, the most important physical symbol of the presence of the church, increased in Utah and beyond. By the end of 1998, there were fifty-three temples in operation worldwide. Of the eleven temples located in Utah, seven had been dedicated since World War II: Ogden (1972); Provo (1972); Jordan River (1981); Bountiful (1995); Mount Timpanogos, in American Fork (1996); Vernal (1997), and Monticello (1998).

The church also became more diverse in its ethnic and cultural makeup. This change contributed to a continuing reexamination by leaders of various policies and programs, as well as reevaluation by many church members of their personal attitudes toward other races and cultures. A major step toward greater intercultural understanding and more equality of opportunity within the church came in June 1978, when President Spencer W. Kimball announced that he had received a revelation extending the priesthood to all worthy male members of the church, regardless of race. African-American Mormons in Utah and elsewhere were elated. Now they could fully enjoy everything the church had to offer, including the temples.

Mormon influence in Utah could be seen in many other ways. The twenty-eight-story Church Office Building, completed in 1972, dominated Salt Lake City's skyline, while LDS meetinghouses were prominent features in the landscape of nearly every Utah community. A variety of church-sponsored dances, plays, and other social activities were important elements in the life of the state. Beginning in 1964, the religious needs of LDS students

Figure C.1: The LDS Church's Temple Square remains one of Utah's top tourist attractions. Used by permission, Utah State Historical Society, all rights reserved.

in Utah's colleges and universities were more fully served by the organization of student wards and stakes. In 1965 the church re-emphasized its family home evening program, urging its members to set aside one evening a week for family activity and suggesting that Monday evening was an appropriate time. As a result, many movie houses, recreational facilities, and eating establishments offered special family rates on Monday evenings. During the first week of every April and October, the semiannual general conferences of the church attracted visitors from around the world and, at the same time, stimulated business in Salt Lake City.

Economically, LDS building programs, educational institutions, and other activities were important to the state. Church-owned business institutions, such as Deseret Book Company, the *Deseret News*, Bonneville International Corporation (an international broadcasting facility), and several other businesses in which the church held major shares, provided employment as well as an important tax base. In fact, with all of its Utah-based activities, the church itself became the largest employer in the state.

The LDS welfare program had a particularly important economic and social impact in Utah. The program provided emergency care for many Utahns who otherwise might be on state welfare rolls. Bishop's storehouses, from which welfare supplies were distributed to the needy, as recommended by their bishops, dotted the state. So, too, did welfare farms and orchards, where Mormons regularly donated their time to plant, trim, cultivate, irrigate, and harvest various crops. A prominent symbol of the program was Welfare Square in Salt Lake City, where these crops were processed into canned goods and other products.

The church's social outreach went far beyond physical goods. Its Social Services Department established programs throughout the state and elsewhere to counsel and assist those with a variety of social needs: help for unwed mothers, career counseling, medical assistance, health education, employment, and other kinds of assistance. In addition, the church's Deseret Industries collected used goods of every kind and cleaning and repairing these goods for sale to the public provided employment for many people, including some with disabilities or special needs. The church also became increasingly involved with other churches and civic groups in efforts to promote the social and cultural well-being of the community at large.

The LDS Church brought national and international attention to Utah. Temple square remained one of the top tourist attractions in the state, drawing approximately 5 million visitors a year in the 1990s. Brigham Young University's Young Ambassadors and other entertainment groups regularly toured many parts of the world, bringing acclaim to themselves and recognition to Utah. The most well-known LDS performing group was the Mormon Tabernacle Choir. (For a discussion of the choir, see Appendix B, "Utah and the Arts.")

Mormon Splinter Groups and Anti-Mormon Evangelism

The LDS Church spawned numerous splinter groups. Some of these offshoots arose for reasons related to the Mormon abandonment of plural marriage while others sprang up for a variety of other reasons. One ironic result was that even though the church abandoned polygamy a century earlier, and throughout the twentieth century excommunicated anyone found practicing it, in the 1990s Utah continued to be home to many families who, for religious reasons, continued the practice.[11]

Most of the Mormon splinter groups were very small, but a brief listing of some of them is instructive. The Aaronic Order, the only significant nonpolygamous offshoot since the 1890 "Manifesto," was founded by Maurice Glendenning in 1942. At the end of the century the group was based in Murray. The Church of Jesus Christ was founded in the 1980s by Art Bulla, who claimed to be the "One Mighty and Strong" spoken of in LDS scriptures. The School of the Prophets was founded by R. C. Crossfield in 1982 and established its headquarters in Salem. Another group known as the School of the Prophets was founded in 1986 by Archie Dean Wood and was headquartered in Idaho.

The Fundamentalist Church of Jesus Christ of Latter-day Saints descended from a movement organized in 1929 by Lorin C. Woolley. It became the largest group to practice polygamy, with perhaps as many as ten thousand members in the 1990s. A communal living program sponsored by that church was known as the United Effort Plan. The church was headquartered in Colorado City, Arizona but a large number of members lived in Hilldale, Utah. A split in this group in the 1950s resulted in the eventual founding of The Apostolic United Brethren. Popularly referred to as the "Allred Group," the United Brethren was incorporated in 1975 by Rulon Allred. In 1995 it had a mailing address in Bluffdale, but there were seven thousand members in five American centers and in England and Mexico. Another group, Christ's Church, was founded in 1978 in Provo by Gerald W. Peterson, Sr. The Church of the First Born of the Fullness of Times was a break-off from the Allred group in Mexico and was led by members of the LeBaron family. The Church of the Lamb of God was a splinter group from the Church of the First Born of the Fullness of Times. The Confederate Nations of Israel, an offshoot of the Apostolic United Brethren, was founded by Alex Joseph in the 1970s and by the 1990s had about 250 members. These polygamists were located chiefly in Big Water, Utah. A group known as the True and Living Church of Jesus Christ of Saints of the Last Days, was founded in Manti in the early 1990s. These were only a few of the numerous splinter groups that seemed to pop up regularly and add a peculiar zest to the story of religion in Utah.[12]

Members from the Mormon community were sometimes drawn to the offshoots because they claimed to be the true successors to Joseph Smith or, at least, taught principles and practices they felt were more consistent with those of nineteenth-century Mormonism. Other Christians sincerely believed that the Book of Mormon and LDS claims to modern revelation were fraudulent and that Mormon theology ran counter to true Christianity. However, they were somewhat discouraged in their postwar evangelistic efforts among the Mormons. A 1951 survey showed that Baptists converted some forty to sixty Mormons each year, but, as the executive secretary of the American Baptist Home Missionary Society wrote on October 30, 1951, "The results are not spectacular and I am sure that we are not going to wipe out the Mormon empire within the foreseeable future." Other churches reported similar results with respect to missionary efforts, but Dr. A. Walton Roth, a field representative of the Presbyterian Church, noted that even though the numbers were small his church received four times as many members from among the Mormons as it lost to them.[13]

By the end of the twentieth century specific efforts by major denominations to proselytize the Mormons were largely a thing of the past. There were a handful of independent missions, though, that carried out intensive, and sometimes effective, proselytizing. One was the Utah Christian Mission, Inc., of Phoenix, Arizona, founded about mid-century. This mission distributed evangelistic Christian literature, and its representatives often appeared in Salt Lake City in April and October, passing out tracts to Mormons attending LDS semiannual conferences. But the most prominent and prolific anti-Mormon press in Utah was the Utah Lighthouse Ministry. Founded in 1982 by former LDS Church members Gerald and Sandra Tanner, this nonprofit ministry was built on their earlier operation, Modern Microfilm, producing books, pamphlets, and a newsletter, all aimed at undermining the credibility of the LDS Church and persuading Mormons toward more traditional Christianity.

The Roman Catholics[14]

The Roman Catholic Church was the largest non-Mormon denomination in Utah. By 1995 there were more than seventy-five thousand Catholics in forty-three parishes, an increase of more than fifty-five thousand since World War II, constituting about 5 percent of the state's population. Catholics and their various social programs were served by ninety priests and ninety-five women in religious orders.[15] They came under the direction of the Diocese of Salt Lake City, the borders of which were contiguous with those of the state.

Bishop of the diocese at the beginning of the post-World War II era was the Most Reverend Duane G. Hunt. Among his many public activities was a series of addresses over KSL Radio, that were continued on a regular basis until 1952. One project that concerned him greatly was expanding the diocese through missionary efforts. He founded fifteen new parishes in the state, from which priests often traveled long distances to offer mass to scattered Catholics. In addition, during his tenure several orders of nuns arrived in Utah to conduct missionary work and teach in Catholic schools. These orders included the Missionary Sisters, with convents in Salt Lake City, Ogden, and Bingham; the Sisters of St. Francis of Perpetual Adoration, with a convent in Provo; the Sisters of the Atonement, with convents in Bingham, Dragerton (now East Carbon City), and Roosevelt; the Carmelite Sisters in Salt Lake County; and the Sisters of the Holy Family, who conducted their work in Tooele and Helper.

Before becoming parishes, many areas underwent a mission stage. Since the limited membership could not support a priest, priests from established parishes commuted to say mass, take confessions, and perform other essential services. During the 1940s, for example, Father Blase Shumaker, a pilot, flew from mission to mission in the Uintah Basin and northwestern Colorado. In 1941 St. Thomas Aquinas Parish was established in Logan, but its first pastor, Father Joseph H. Valine, and his assistant, Reverend Colin V. McEachen, also served Catholics elsewhere in Cache County as well as in Box Elder and Rich counties. Until there were enough members in a particular community to establish a parish and erect a building, visiting priests offered mass wherever they could, including private homes, the facilities of other denominations, American Legion or other organizational halls, and city halls.

Bishop Hunt played a significant role in founding a Trappist monastery, the Abbey of Our Lady of the Holy Trinity, near Huntsville in 1947. Initially, thirty-four monks took up residency in Quonset huts. Within ten years the monastery accommodated sixteen priests and forty-four lay brothers who were preparing for the priesthood or to become members of the Trappist brotherhood. Having dedicated their lives to God, the Trappists devoted themselves to prayer, silence, and labor.

Bishop Hunt was succeeded in 1960 by Bishop Joseph Federal, auxiliary bishop of Salt Lake since 1951. Federal gradually shifted the emphasis from missionary work to internal growth and organizational solidarity. In addition, he participated in the pivotal second Vatican Council (1962-75) and became responsible for interpreting and implementing in Utah that council's final decrees. These included significant revisions in the liturgy that, among other things, allowed the language to be changed from Latin to the vernacular.

Bishop Federal established various programs and policies to cope with the rapidly changing patterns and challenges of American life. One was a broadening of lay participation in church affairs, symbolized by the establishment of a permanent diaconate. Catholics taught that deacons held a special place in the early church, along with bishops and priests, but their role gradually diminished until the diaconate became little more than a step toward ordination as a priest. In 1964, the Second Vatican Council authorized the restoration of the permanent diaconate, open to both single and married men. Ten years later, on September 28,

1974, Bishop Federal established the diaconate in the Diocese of Salt Lake City. The deacons, most of whom were family men with permanent secular occupations, were carefully trained in liturgy and pastoral work and ordained as ministers. They were thus empowered to administer baptisms, perform marriages, preach, distribute communion, and teach the Catholic faith.

Bishop Federal also led out in instituting a Hispanic ministry in the Diocese of Salt Lake City. With more than half the Catholic population of the state composed of Hispanics, in 1972 Bishop Federal established the Diocesan Office of the Spanish-speaking. Its first director, Ruben Jiminez, participated in the founding of such groups as SOCIO (Spanish-speaking Organization for Community, Integrity and Opportunity), Citizens Congress, and the Utah Immigration Project. The office also focused on the spiritual life of Utah's scattered Hispanic Catholics, sponsoring a liturgical team that traveled the state providing Spanish mass and other religious needs. The name of the office was eventually changed to the Office of Hispanic Affairs, and in 1981 a full-time director was appointed. In 1985 Spanish masses were held weekly in fourteen areas, monthly in four areas, and occasionally in six others. In addition, there were eighteen Hispanic choirs in the diocese. In 1986, the Office of Hispanic Affairs began working closely with the Utah Immigration Project in training volunteers to help process immigrants and assist in the legalization process.

In 1994, during a celebration honoring Bishop Federal's sixtieth year as a priest, Monsignor J. Terrance Fitzgerald emphasized the effectiveness of Bishop Federal's leadership: "His ability to keep us together in difficult times, to gradually implement the decisions of the Second Vatican Council without the great dishevel seen elsewhere and his patience with our human limitations were his hallmarks and virtues that endeared him to us as an effective leader."[16]

Bishop Federal retired in 1980 and was replaced by Bishop William K. Weigand. Bishop Weigand was noted especially for his concern for the poor, the underprivileged, and minorities. He personally offered mass annually to each ethnic minority in the diocese. He also appointed chaplains for the Vietnamese, Laotians, and Tongans, and established special ministries among Native Americans.

Prior to his appointment to the Salt Lake diocese, Bishop Weigand had spent ten years in Cali, Columbia, working among the poor. This experience made him especially sensitive to the needs of the poor and somewhat outspoken on issues relating to the needy. He was well prepared, therefore, for the appointment that came to him in November 1980 to serve on a committee chosen to draft a pastoral letter on justice and the United States economy. The work of the committee finally resulted in a historic document, "Economic Justice for All: Catholic Social Teaching and the U. S. Economy," promulgated by the United States Conference of Catholic Bishops in 1986. Bishop Weigand's continuing efforts to improve the lot of those struggling for equality and economic opportunity was recognized in 1987 when he was awarded the Silver Citizenship Medal of the Utah Society of the Sons of the American Revolution.

Among Bishop Weigand's other contributions to strengthening the church in Utah was the founding of three new parishes, the establishment of about a dozen chapels in outlying areas, initiating construction of two new elementary schools, and establishing the Marillac House for Homeless Women. He also initiated the massive fund-raising project for the renovation of the Cathedral of the Madeleine. In January 1994 he assumed a new post as bishop of the Diocese of Sacramento. He was succeeded by Bishop George H. Niederauer, who was ordained on January 25, 1995.

An ongoing concern for the Catholic Church was its schools. In 1967 the church operated eleven parochial grade schools and five high schools in the state but rising costs and changing educational patterns forced some of them to close. Nevertheless, in 1993 the church still served approximately 3,800 students in nine elementary and two high schools. Some three to four hundred more were on a waiting list each year.[17] The largest Catholic school in the state was Judge Memorial High School in Salt Lake City. About 30 percent of the students at Judge Memorial were non-Catholic, with LDS students constituting the largest such group.[18]

The Catholic Church operated two colleges in Utah early in the twentieth century, but the last one, St.-Mary-of-the-Wasatch, discontinued its collegiate work in 1959. It continued as a high school until 1970. The church showed its concern for the well-being of its college students through organizations, known as Newman Centers, on the campuses of Utah's college and universities. They provided a social setting as well as religious services, instruction, and counseling.

The church also established two Catholic Indian centers for the benefit of Native American high school students: one in Brigham City and the other on the Ute Reservation at Fort Duchesne. In 1950, the Our Lady of Victory Missionary Sisters began to work with the Catholic students at the newly opened Intermountain Indian School in Brigham City. In 1978, regular religion classes, begun in 1954 by priests of the Society of Jesus, were moved to the new Catholic Indian Center across from the entrance to the school. It remained open until the Intermountain School closed in 1984. Meanwhile, in 1982, the Kateri Tekakwitha Indian Center was established on the Ute Reservation, providing both instruction and social opportunities for Catholic and other youth on the reservation.

The Catholic Church also sponsored numerous charitable and social welfare programs. One was Catholic Community Services, founded in 1945 to provide basic services to the needy. It began in a small office in Salt Lake City and eventually expanded to four sites along the Wasatch Front and in northern Utah. Its work eventually included transient and emergency services, a soup kitchen, adoption services, a refugee program, outreach to the elderly, immigration services, and other important charitable work.[19]

The Guadalupe Center, opened in 1966, focused on the concerns of Hispanics, whether Catholic or not, and provided a gathering place as well as various social programs. (For more detail, see Appendix A.)

St. Joseph's Villa, a home for the aged in Salt Lake City, was founded in 1947 by the Sisters of Charity of the Incarnate Word. In 1993 St. Joseph's had 170 beds, was one of two nonprofit organizations of its type in Utah, and was the largest nursing home in the state. A large addition, completed in 1995, greatly increased the number of beds and provided several additional services and facilities. These included a senior health clinic, rehabilitation equipment, apartments for seniors who could care for themselves but needed health care facilities nearby, transitional care, and a special unit for those with Alzheimer's and related illnesses. and expanded long-term care.[20]

In 1967, the Daughters of Charity of St. Vincent de Paul opened St. Vincent de Paul Thrift Store to supply affordable clothing to the indigent of Salt Lake City. However, the staff and volunteers soon felt the need to provide sandwiches for the homeless who frequented the store. The store eventually grew into one of the largest soup kitchens in the metropolitan area, serving several hundred meals daily as well as providing a wide range of services to the elderly. It was supported by a number of different denominations. When it was destroyed by fire in 1986, a fund-raising drive to build a new facility brought support from all over the community, including sizeable donations from other denominations.

Another type of charity originated with the work of James Hale, sometimes called "Big Jim." Hale, who had once experienced severe poverty, wanted to provide a way to help needy men obtain food and housing and, more important, to develop spiritually and dedicate themselves to helping others. With the cooperation of the pastor and parishioners in Our Lady of Guadalupe Parish, he opened St. Thomas House in a donated home. A board of advisors was formed in 1966 and the following year the name was changed to St. Mary's Home for Men. Incorporated as a nonprofit organization in 1974 and housed in a renovated home on Second South in Salt Lake City, St. Mary's continued to provide a haven for homeless men, regardless of race or creed, who were indigent or dying, as well as self-help programs for those trying to get back on their feet.

These were only a few of the many social welfare programs, too numerous to detail here, that were sponsored by various Catholic organizations.[21]

Another important Catholic contribution to the well-being of Utah was the continued operation of two hospitals, Holy Cross in Salt Lake City and St. Benedict's in Ogden. Holy Cross, founded in 1875, became a 380-bed facility by the time an expansion proj-

Image C.2: The Cathedral of the Madeleine, completed in 1909, is one of the elegant landmarks of Salt Lake City. Used by permission, Utah State Historical Society, all rights reserved.

ect was completed in 1968. It housed both research and care facilities and, until 1973, conducted an accredited school of nursing. St. Benedict's Hospital, dedicated in 1946 by Bishop Hunt, was a 150-bed facility operated by the Sisters of St. Benedict. In 1947 the hospital established a school of nursing that endured for some twenty years. In 1977, with the construction of a new facility, St. Benedict's moved to Weber County's Washington Terrace.

The most visible and well-known physical symbol of the Catholic presence in Utah was the Cathedral of the Madeleine, one of Salt Lake City's principal landmarks. Noted for its elegant Gothic architecture, fine statuary, beautiful stained glass, and art masterpieces, the cathedral served as a center for both Catholic and community activities. In the mid-1980s, the church initiated a massive renovation project. However, unable to raise the necessary $9 million, the Catholics appealed to the community. The effort quickly took on the aura of a community project, with half of those on the fund-raising committee not of the Catholic faith. Many Utah citizens as well as a number of religious and business institutions, contributed generously.

Renovation finally began in 1991. The building was thoroughly cleaned inside and out, frescoes and paintings were restored, and a new altar, baptismal font, and organ were installed. On February 20, 1993, the cathedral was re-dedicated by Bishop Weigand. Symbolic of the friendly relations existing between the Catholic Church and other religious and civic groups was the fact that several other religious and community leaders participated in the dedication services. The Most Reverend Archbishop Agostino Cacciavillan, representing Pope John Paul II, noted in his address that many outside the Catholic community, including the LDS Church and the Episcopal Church, were among the donors. Another speaker was President Thomas S. Monson of the First Presidency of the LDS Church. The restored Cathedral of the Madeleine provided an elegant religious home for a people who continued to add much to Utah's religious environment and appealing way of life.

Baptists in Utah[22]

The first Baptist church in Utah was founded in Ogden in 1880, and a century later, with more than twenty thousand members, the Baptists constituted the largest Protestant denomination in Utah. However, the Baptist label covered several different bodies, including the Southern, American, Independent, and Conservative Baptist conventions, as well as a few smaller groups. Furthermore, their independent form of government resulted in significant differences between congregations in both practice and belief.

During the mid-1950s, the First Baptist Church of Salt Lake City had as many as 1,800 people attending services, forcing it to use a public address system to bring the services to people outside the building. However, attendance dropped in later years. The church also served as the mother church for the First Baptist Church of Bountiful, which was incorporated in 1958.[23]

In the 1990s, the largest and fastest growing group in the state was the Southern Baptist Convention, which began in Roosevelt, Utah in the early 1940s. The number of Southern Baptists grew from 140 members in 1950 to 14,227 by 1990. The Black Baptist and the American Baptist churches made up the next largest bodies, with 3,134 and 2,775 members, respectively, in 1990. There were three Independent Baptist congregations in the state in 1986, and in 1994 eight Conservative Baptist congregations.[24]

In terms of theological issues and church practice, the Independent and Southern Baptists were generally more conservative, while the American and, ironically, the Conservative Baptists were somewhat more liberal. For example, the American Baptists were less doctrinally fundamental than the Southern Baptists, more ecumenical in nature, more willing to become involved in social causes, more ready to work with other churches, and more willing to ordain women. In 1994 the First Baptist Church in Salt Lake City, part of the American Baptist Convention, was copastored by Reverend Stanley Smith and his wife, Reverend Nancy Darnell.

Baptist congregations in Utah often sponsored notable religious activities beyond regular worship services. Some supported missionaries in the United States as well as in foreign countries. From time to time, several Baptist congregations also sponsored revivals, which were intended not only to spread their message but also to fortify their members. Baptists also conducted services at the state prison, for both male and female prisoners.[25] In addition, the Southern Baptist Convention sponsored a number of local radio and television broadcasts intended to strengthen Christians in general.[26]

In 1991, the Southern Baptist Convention announced that it had selected Salt Lake City as the site for its annual meeting in

1998. Some twenty-five thousand Southern Baptists were expected to attend, bringing to the state not only the spiritual rejuvenation that attends such gatherings but also millions of dollars in business activity.[27]

Utah's Baptists were highly active in important community programs. Many helped staff local soup kitchens, shelters, and counseling centers. They also participated in other social programs intended to promote the general welfare of Utahns. One was an adult literacy program, the Literary Action Center, begun in the mid-1980s by the First Baptist Church of Salt Lake City. The Center became independent in the 1990s, continuing to serve some two hundred clients.[28] The American Baptists worked with Shared Ministry in Utah in an effort to propagate Christian ideals and positions on various issues. Baptists participated actively in the March of the Cross during Eastertime to commemorate Christ's passion. In addition, they supported campus ministries at the University of Utah and at Brigham Young University. Student ministers, some of whom planned to become full-time clergy, were recent college graduates who worked with local congregations. The fifty-acre camp UTABA (Utah American Baptist Assembly), located near Liberty, east of Ogden, provided a place for youth meetings and retreats.[29]

Salt Lake City was the home of Calvary Baptist Church, one of the oldest African American Baptist congregations in the intermountain area.[30] With roots dating back to 1892, the church was plagued by financial troubles for years but eventually became secure, obtained a building of its own, purchased a church van, and in 1989 dedicated Calvary Towers, a low-income housing facility for the elderly. Calvary Baptist also managed a college scholarship fund for its members and a mentor program whereby church youth worked with adult members of the congregation in various careers. France Davis, Calvary's pastor beginning in 1974, continued in the 1990s to work actively with about a dozen other African American congregations in Utah, Idaho, and Wyoming. He was also active in the Salt Lake Ministerial Association and the National Council of Christians and Jews, on the board of directors of the Salt Lake Convention and Visitors Bureau, chairman of the board of the Salt Lake City Housing Authority, and vice-chairman of the board of the Salt Lake County Career Service Council.[31] In the 1990s the Calvary Baptist Church had a thriving congregation with a positive outlook for continued growth.

Lutherans[32]

Lutherans arrived in Utah during the nineteenth century, but they were divided by the fact that their various synods catered mostly to specific language and ethnic groups. Eventually eleven synods were established but in some areas hard feelings arose between them. The barriers eventually broke down in the early twentieth century, and soon the various small groups began to consolidate into a few larger ones. By the 1990s, the Evangelical Lutheran Church in America, the Lutheran Church—Missouri Synod, and the Wisconsin Evangelical Lutheran Synod encompassed nearly ten thousand members in twenty-nine Utah congregations. This made the Lutheran Church as a conglomerate the fourth largest religious group in the state.

In the initial stages of their ministry in Utah, Lutherans sponsored a number of schools in an effort to proselytize Mormon children, but most of these schools shut down around the turn of the century. However, in the 1990s Lutherans still maintained four elementary schools: one each in Murray, Sandy, Salt Lake City, and St. George. Students of all faiths could attend, and only about a third or less came from the Lutheran tradition. These schools fed into the Salt Lake Lutheran High School, where some 55 percent of the students came from a Lutheran background.[33]

Utah's Lutherans were involved in various charitable organizations, including the Crossroads Urban Center. A number of Lutheran churches frequently pooled their resources to buy several tons of turkey for the local homeless shelters and soup kitchens. Students at the Salt Lake Lutheran High School were required to give a certain number of service hours annually, and many of them worked through charitable organizations in their communities. Several Lutheran churches cooperated to distribute gift baskets with food and toys each Christmas. A voucher system, providing a number of necessary services, was available through the Lutherans to travelers who experienced problem while passing through the state. Lutheran congregations also sponsored refugees from countries, such as Vietnam and Korea, where war had disrupted their lives.[34]

In addition to their social outreach programs, Lutherans participated in joint activities such as the Key 73 campaign in 1973, an interdenominational effort to share Christ with every person in North America. In addition, they sometimes held joint Lenten services with other Protestant and Catholic groups.[35] As they overcame their internal differences, Utah's Lutherans effectively focused their energies into becoming a positive force in the community at large.

Greek Orthodox[36]

The first Greeks to migrate to Utah came around the turn of the twentieth century. As the Greek population grew, two churches were established: the Holy Trinity Greek Orthodox Church in Salt Lake City (1905, with a new edifice dedicated in 1925) and the Annunciation Church in Price (1915). The Greek population experienced a surge after World War II, necessitating more Greek Orthodox worship facilities. In 1962, the Greek community of Ogden built and consecrated the Transfiguration Greek Orthodox Church. Meanwhile, the community in Salt Lake City outgrew its facilities.. With some seven hundred children attending Sunday school in the early 1960s, the building simply could not accommodate them. Not wanting to divide the parish, the community received permission from the archdiocese to erect a second church building, to be governed by the same parish council. The Prophet Elias Greek Orthodox Church opened its doors in December 1969.

In the late 1980s, a third Salt Lake City congregation, Saints Peter and Paul Antiochian Orthodox Church, was established. This branch of the church had its roots in an Arabic tradition, although in 1994 only one Arabic family attended services in Salt Lake City. About 60 percent of those regularly attending were Russian immigrants.[37] The congregation included many converts and families with mixed marriages, and the liturgy was performed entirely in English. Holy Trinity and Prophet Elias, on the other hand, performed as much as half of its liturgical service in Greek. In addition, the Orthodox Church of America supported a mission church in Utah, with bimonthly services for immigrants from Eastern Europe.

Utah's Greek Orthodox community, the largest such group between San Francisco and Chicago, continued in the 1990s to add much to Utah's cultural and social well-being. The Hellenic Memorial Cultural Center, housed at the Holy Trinity Church, was an ethnic Greek museum dedicated to those Greeks who lost their lives during both world wars. It was said to be one of the finest museums of its type in the United States. An active Greek Orthodox youth program, organized in Utah in 1947, eventually resulted in the formation of the Greek Orthodox Youth of America, which held large conventions for young members of Greek communities across the nation. The annual Greek Festival in Salt Lake City, put on by the Philoptochos Society, attracted some thirty to forty thousand visitors each year. Proceeds from the festival helped fund programs such as Sunday schools within the Orthodox community, as well as a few outside charities such as the Red Cross. Beginning in the early 1980s, the Greek community of Salt Lake City put on an annual sit-down dinner for the indigent in the area, serving up to 1,500 people.

Even though the Greeks, like other minorities, experienced some discrimination in the early years of the century, by the end of the century things had improved markedly. A number of Greeks served in Utah's legislature. Greek Orthodox leaders also participated in the National Council of Christians and Jews, designed to develop better understanding between the various religious and ethnic groups. The Greek Orthodox community of the 1990s, which numbered a possible seven thousand people, constituted still another vital element in the life of the state.[38]

Presbyterians

The first Presbyterian congregation in Utah took root in 1870 in the non-Mormon town of Corinne. By the 1990s there were nearly 6,700 Presbyterians in the state in twenty-three congregations. Two of these congregations catered to Utah's Japanese community and operated jointly with the United Church of Christ. The Kanab congregation functioned under the auspices of the Presbyterians, the United Methodists, the Disciples of Christ, and the United Church of Christ. One of the Salt Lake congregations principally served Koreans.[39]

In their early efforts to establish themselves in Utah, Presbyterians devoted a considerable amount of energy to setting up an educational system. They established several grammar schools, four academies, and a college. By the 1990s, however, only two of these schools remained, both of which became independent in 1974: Wasatch Academy, a high school in Mount Pleasant, and Westminster College in Salt Lake City.

Utah's Presbyterians were highly involved in ecumenical activities, participating in a number of partnerships, joint ministries, and associations. One of these partnerships began in 1960 when the Presbyterians and the United Methodist Church formed the United Ministries Council. Later they were joined by the United Church of Christ, the American Baptist churches, and the Christian Church (Disciple of Christ). In 1977 the group changed its name to Shared Ministry of Utah. They were joined by the African Methodist Episcopal Church in 1990. Shared Ministry allowed the churches to coordinate mission outreach efforts and the allocation of resources. Such a ministerial partnership was unique in the United States.[40] Shared Ministry was dissolved in 1996 as the six participating denominations decided to restructure their ecumenical efforts.[41]

Utah's Presbyterian clergy also worked with local ministerial associations, including the Central Salt Lake City Council of Churches. This council organized the March of the Cross, an Easter procession through Salt Lake City, as well as Christmas Eve worship services and participation in National Bible Week. It also informed the public about the position of Salt Lake City's churches on issues that concerned them and that they could agree upon.[42]

Like members of other denominations, Presbyterians took part in various community and social improvement projects. They were involved in the YWCA, in the Women in Jeopardy program, in providing worship services at the state prison, with the Crossroads Urban Center, in Boy Scouts and Girl Scouts, with the

Salvation Army's meal program, in providing gasoline for stranded motorists, and with the Ulster project to help Irish teens.[43]

Presbyterians also established a large ministry to Native Americans at the Intermountain Indian School in Brigham City, eventually building a facility there to provide religious instruction as well as a place for socializing. They also supported interdenominational campus ministries at the University of Utah and Utah State University.[44] These and other such efforts helped make the Presbyterians another continuing force for good in Utah.

Pentecostal and Holiness Churches

The Pentecostal movement began in the United States in the late nineteenth and early twentieth centuries after many Christians became convinced of the need to have the same charismatic experiences as those of the early Christians. As recorded in the Bible, after the dramatic outpouring of the Holy Spirit at the feast of Pentecost, many were endowed with spiritual gifts and powers such as speaking in tongues and healing. There was no single Pentecostal denomination but rather a variety of groups who believed in the need for the Pentecostal experience but differed in other matters of doctrine, organization, and forms of worship. These groups included the Assemblies of God, the Church of God, the Church of God in Christ, the International Church of the Foursquare Gospel, the Pentecostal Church of God in America, the Pentecostal Holiness Church, and the United Pentecostal Church. The larger groups were loosely associated in the Pentecostal World Conference. In the 1990s, at least three different Pentecostal groups were found in Utah, the largest being the Assemblies of God.

Holiness churches held doctrines somewhat similar to those of the Pentecostals, and were sometimes confused with them. But the holiness tradition stemmed more directly from John Wesley, founder of Methodism, who taught that human perfection, or holiness, could be achieved within an individual's lifetime but as a gift from God, not as a human achievement. There were various holiness groups, a few of which found their way into Utah.

Assemblies of God

Assemblies of God were first established in Utah in the 1940s. Membership grew slowly until the 1970s and then began a rapid upward climb. In 1991, the Assemblies of God counted twenty-three congregations, with the number increasing to thirty-three by 1994.[45] Some congregations, such as the Salt Lake Christian Center, were quite large, with several hundred members. Total Utah membership as of 1990 was 6,450.

Members of the Assemblies of God were concerned not only with their own salvation but also with the moral and ethical well-being of their society. As a result, they regularly participated in a number of community action programs. These included the Right to Life movement, crisis pregnancy counseling and assistance, volunteer work at homeless shelters, and anti-gang activity. The Assemblies also conducted strong social programs within the church, sponsoring various ministries for children, youths, and adults. Among these ministries were a summer camp, Bible schools, camp meetings, the "Royal Rangers" (equivalent to Boy Scouts), and "Missionettes" (equivalent to Girl Scouts).

The Assemblies sponsored two schools in Utah in the 1990s: the Valley Christian School in West Valley City and the Layton Christian Academy in Layton. Students at both schools came from all different denominations. The Valley school included day care for some 160 children and facilities for 140 students in grades kindergarten through twelve. In 1994, construction for a new wing was in progress. With this addition, school officials planned to enroll some two hundred day care students and four to five hundred regular students.[46] In 1994, the Layton Academy expanded from preschool and kindergarten, serving approximately 35 students, to facilities that would also accommodate approximately 150 students in grades one through six.[47]

Members of the Assemblies of God were not reluctant to become involves in political and civic activities. James Ferguson, a member of Provo's Rock Canyon Assembly of God, served as mayor of Provo between 1978 and 1985. He won his second election by more than a two to one margin.[48]

International Church of the Foursquare Gospel

The International Church of the Foursquare Gospel began in the early twentieth century in Los Angeles, California, through the efforts of Aimee Semple McPherson.[49] The church came to Utah in 1983 when a previously non-aligned independent church in Salt Lake City chose to join with the Foursquare movement. In 1990 total membership in the state was listed at 739. In 1995 there were ten Foursquare congregations in Utah: five in the Salt Lake area, two in Ogden, one in Roy, one in Logan, and one in Provo.[50]

Pentecostal Church of God

The Pentecostal Church of God was founded in the mid-1950s through the efforts of Willie James Peterson. Predominantly African American, the church emphasized turning away from the things of the world, including the "false" teachings (such as trinitarianism) of some Protestant and Catholic churches and participation in several holiday celebrations. Members accepted Peterson as a divinely appointed apostle of God, were baptized by immersion in the name of Jesus, and did not participate in man-made governments.[51]

The first Pentecostal Church of God to take root in Utah was organized in Dragerton in the early 1940s, but it later disbanded. In 1994 there were three Pentecostal congregations in the state: one in Roosevelt, one in East Carbon, and one in Ogden. The Ogden congregation was founded in 1951.[52] Total Utah membership in 1990 was 384.

Church of God (Cleveland, Tennessee) and the Church of God of Prophecy

The Church of God (Cleveland, Tennessee) and the Church of God of Prophecy both grew out of a Pentecostal movement that had its roots in Georgia and Tennessee. Ambrose J. Tomlinson, of Cleveland, Tennessee is credited with founding the Church of God, hence the name for one branch of the movement. In 1952, the suffix "of Prophecy" was added by another group in order to distinguish itself from the many organizations that were, by that time, using the phrase "Church of God" in their names. Fundamentalist and evangelistic in nature, the Churches of God emphasized personal commitment to God and the importance of spiritual gifts, such as speaking in tongues and healing. They also practiced foot washing, did not use cosmetics, and the women did not wear slacks or shorts. Members also abstained from intoxicating beverages and tobacco.[53]

As of 1990, there were three congregations of the Church of God (Cleveland, Tennessee) in Weber County, while the Church of God of Prophecy maintained one congregation in Weber County, three in Salt Lake County, one in Grand County and one in Carbon County.[54] There were 265 members of the Tennessee group and 181 in the Church of God of Prophecy.

Church of the Nazarene

The Church of the Nazarene, one of the largest holiness denominations, originated with a split in Methodism over the holiness issue and a merger of two holiness groups in 1907. Nazarenes believed in healing and spiritual gifts, but their major emphasis was on personal holiness. Church government was representative in nature.[55] The first Nazarene church in Utah was founded in 1911 in Salt Lake City. In 1994 there were four congregations: two in the Salt Lake area, one in Provo, and one in Layton.[56]

Christian and Missionary Alliance

Another holiness group, the Christian and Missionary Alliance (C&MA), began as an evangelical movement in New York in the 1880s. At first the movement spawned two groups, the Christian Alliance and the Missionary Alliance, but the two joined together in 1897. The C&MA became a recognized denomination in 1974, although its various congregations maintained their independence.[57]

The first Christian and Missionary Alliance congregation in Utah was founded in United States Fuel's company-owned mining town of Hiawatha in 1940. At the request of the people of Hiawatha, Reverend Thomas Constance and his wife, Nelly, who lived in Price, came to give Bible classes and to conduct Sunday School. Also in 1940 the Constances began to offer instruction in the town of Columbia. When the mine in Hiawatha closed,

Reverend Constance established a church in Price, constructing a building in 1952.

In 1990, there were 441 members of the C&MA in Utah. In 1994 there were four congregations in the state: one in Salt Lake City, one in East Carbon City, one in Price, and one in St. George.[58]

Methodists[59]

The first Methodist congregation in Utah took root about 1870. By 1994 there were nearly twenty Methodist congregations throughout the state, and approximately seven thousand members. Several congregations served minority communities. The African Methodist Episcopal churches in Ogden and in Salt Lake City, for instance, catered to Utah's black Methodists. Trinity African Methodist Episcopal Church, established in the 1880s, was the oldest black congregation in the state and served as a gathering place for many people in the black community. Tongan Methodists met at the Tongan United Methodist Church in Salt Lake City, and a ministry for Koreans began in Ogden in 1991.[60]

Among the many social action programs sponsored by American Methodists were living centers for single working women who wished to live in a Christian environment. Founded by the Women's Home Missionary Society, these were called Esther Halls. In 1970 Ogden's Esther Hall, founded in 1914, provided bedrooms for some twenty-three women, as well as an additional full apartment. From 1965 until 1978 a portion of the building was also used as a counseling facility, where women could receive help on such issues as marriage counseling, parent-child relationships, premarital counseling, geriatric concerns, and single-parent problems. In 1968 a similar counseling facility was set up in Davis County. Ogden's Esther Hall was discontinued in the mid-1970s. Another Esther Hall was established in Salt Lake City in 1937 and closed in 1965.

In 1966, with the aim of helping Salt Lake City's homeless and poor, the United Methodist Church opened the Crossroads Urban Center. The center focused on preteen and predelinquent outreach and social welfare. Its facilities included a thrift store, a clothing distribution program, and an emergency food pantry. In

1994 it was one of the largest facilities of its type in Utah. It drew support from a wide array of donors, and many local churches participated in its programs.

In 1968, Methodists initiated the formation of the Cooperative Christian Ministry in Southern Utah. Recognizing that each of them had a limited number of members from which to form a congregation, as well as a limited pool of available funds, seven Protestant denominations worked out an agreement to rotate a few clergymen through five specific worship groups. This allowed members to have the services of clergy without the accompanying burden of maintaining a full-time minister. In addition to this cooperative ministry, Methodists also participated in local ministerial associations and Shared Ministry.

Episcopalians

The Protestant Episcopal Church was first established in Utah in 1867. It grew slowly but steadily and between 1940 and 1990, its membership increased from 2,200 to 5,400, an increase of 69 percent in fifty years. In 1994 there were twenty-one parishes and missions in the state, about half of them along the Wasatch Front.[61]

Episcopalians made significant contributions to the state in education as well as other areas. While many denominational schools died out after the passage of the public school law in 1890, Rowland Hall–St. Mark's School (now known as Rowland Hall), considered one of the finest schools in Utah, survived in Salt Lake City. It is the oldest coeducational college-preparatory school in the state. In the 1980s it served some five hundred students in prekindergarten through grade twelve[62] and grew to an enrollment of over a thousand.

Another particularly noteworthy contribution was the founding and continued operation of St. Mark's Hospital in Salt Lake City. Originally organized as a facility for miners and railroad workers, the hospital grew rapidly and its location was moved several times. From 1894 until 1970 the hospital operated a school of nursing, training a large number of people for service both in Utah and outside the state. The nursing school was succeeded by the St. Mark's Hospital School of Baccalaureate Nursing

Image C.3: St. Mark's Episcopal Cathedral, Salt Lake City, built in 1871, is the third oldest Episcopal Cathedral in the United State. Used by permission, Utah State Historical Society, all rights reserved.

of Westminster College, a cooperative venture between the hospital and the college.[63] In 1987 the diocese chose to sell St. Mark's, with more than three hundred beds, to the Hospital Corporation of America.

The sale of St. Marks gave the Episcopal diocese a huge windfall of millions of dollars, which it decided to use for charitable grants in Utah. In March 1988, Bishop George E. Bates pledged a donation of $600,000 to the Salt Lake Area Shelter Homeless Committee. Intended to help raise $4 million to build and operate homeless shelters in the city, this was the largest donation offered by any group. Also that year another $400,000 was given to other social service agencies. In 1989, $622,000 in grants went to fifty-five groups and organizations, with 32 percent of the money going to agencies that helped the homeless and poverty-stricken. The church also provided funds to the Indian Urban Center, various youth programs, the Indigent Health Care Fund, and the nursing program at Westminster College, and aided the remodeling of church facilities throughout the state.[64]

In June 1977, the Church of the Good Shepherd, an Episcopalian congregation in Ogden, signed a covenant agreement with St. Joseph's Roman Catholic Church. In a healthy ecumenical spirit, the congregations agreed to work together as a single community in outreach programs, conduct joint services, and publish an ecumenical newsletter. The agreement, intended to last only two years, was later renewed for an indefinite period of time.[65]

In 1978, in cooperation with the US Department of Housing and Urban Development, Utah's Episcopal diocese began construction of a one hundred–unit high-rise home for the elderly. After that home was completed, three other facilities for the elderly were opened, one in Kaysville, one in Brigham City, and another in South Salt Lake City.[66]

In 1990, Reverend Quentin Kolb founded the Outreach Center in Salt Lake City. Established for the benefit of displaced Native Americans of any denomination, the center gave them a place to gather and served as an information clearinghouse with respect to jobs, housing and transportation. It was fully funded by the Episcopal Church.[67]

Jehovah's Witnesses[68]

Jehovah's Witnesses taught that the invisible Kingdom of God was established in the heavens in 1914, that the final "battle of Armageddon" heralding the end of the world was near, and that the Earth will be reconstituted as a paradise for believers. Because of their emphasis on the Kingdom of God, Witnesses consciously dissociated themselves from political activities, refusing to vote, run for public offices, serve in the armed forces, or take part in patriotic exercises. A number of cases involving Jehovah's Witnesses went to the United States Supreme Court, resulting in some significant decisions relating to the First Amendment that, among other things, upheld their refusal to recite the Pledge of Allegiance in school.

Because they would not enter the armed forces, Jehovah's Witnesses became unpopular and, unfortunately, the victims of verbal abuse in parts of Utah during World War II. Discrimination continued after the war, especially in the schools, partly because of misunderstanding about why Witnesses refused to participate in flag ceremonies. But by the 1980s there was a general feeling among the Witnesses that discrimination had subsided and that there was much more understanding and toleration.

Meanwhile, Utah "publishers" (members who spent ten to twelve hours a month spreading the Jehovah's Witnesses message) went about their work. They made some converts among the Mormons, but most new members came from among people who moved into the state because of employment opportunities. At first the members met in homes or rented facilities, but as their numbers grew they were able to erect their own buildings, called Kingdom Halls, and to divide their congregations. The first hall was erected in Salt Lake City in 1947. By 1994 there were six Kingdom Halls in the Salt Lake Valley accommodating eleven congregations. Ogden's first Kingdom Hall was built in the 1950s. By 1994 there were four congregations in Ogden sharing two halls, plus other congregations and halls in nearby communities. That year there were more than thirty congregations throughout the state and approximately four thousand members.

Jehovah's Witnesses did not participate in ecumenical activities, preferring to spend their time trying to share their own un-

Image C.4: The B'Nai Israel Jewish Temple, Salt Lake City, was built in 1891. Used by permission, Utah State Historical Society, all rights reserved.

derstanding of truth. Their numbers were small, but most people in the state were well aware of them. They frequently appeared in Utah neighborhoods, usually in pairs, politely witnessing of the Kingdom of God and the coming Armageddon.

Judasim[69]

The first Jewish congregation in Utah, B'nai Israel, was incorporated in 1881. Congregation Montefiore, founded in 1899, provided an orthodox counterpart to the more liberal B'nai congregation.

These two groups remained completely separate until 1959, when they jointly opened a Jewish Community Center in Salt Lake City. Later, in 1969, they also combined their educational facilities to improve the quality of their children's instruction. Finally, in 1972, the two congregations merged to form the Kol Ami ("All My People") Congregation, housed in a new synagogue. There was also a Jewish synagogue in Ogden, Congregation B'rith Sholem. It was estimated that nearly five thousand Jews resided in the state at the end of 1994.

Utah's Jews were involved in a number of important public service activities. They became particularly active in helping Jewish refugees, both those coming into the United States and those in Europe. They also sent assistance to Jews in the newly created nation of Israel.

Utah Jews were highly active in the National Council of Christians and Jews, which established an office in Salt Lake City in 1954. This organization helped many of Utah's religious groups to better understand each other and opened up lines of communication and cooperation on a variety of issues.

The Jewish experience in Utah differed in some respects from that of Jews in other areas of the United States. Because of the Mormons' unusually strong theological emphasis on Old Testament traditions, and also because of the similarity between Jews' and Mormons' historical experiences, Mormons felt a close kinship to the Jews and often drew parallels between themselves and the Jewish people. In fact, Mormons have been described as "Judeophiles."[70] Even though this comparison was not readily accepted by Jews, it created a positive atmosphere in which Jews could flourish in Utah. Some anti-Semitism existed, but it was not fostered by the Latter-day Saints, and the level of it in Utah seemed to be somewhat lower than in other areas.[71]

Perhaps one of the greatest challenges for the Jewish community was to maintain its identity as a group. Jewish life revolved around a community, with many of the key rituals and activities requiring the participation of several people. As one Jewish scholar in Utah explained, Jewish identity was hard to separate from Jewish community. "Thus, the effects on Jewish children of *not* being in a Jewish community are easy to predict: without formal and informal Jewish education, they are likely to be assimilated even without attempts at conversion. A certain amount can be taught at home, but without group experiences and without other Jewish adult role models around, it is hard to 'become' Jewish as one grows up."[72] Nevertheless, in the 1990s Utah's Jewish community continued to flourish.

United Church of Christ

The United Church of Christ (UCC) traces its roots back to the work of John Calvin and Ulrich Zwingli in the sixteenth century. Most such denominations use the term Reformed, Presbyterian, or Congregational in their names. The United Church of Christ came into being in 1957 with a merger of the Evangelical and Reformed Church and the Congregational Christian Churches. Individual congregations could choose either to enter the new fellowship or to remain independent. In the mid-1990s, there were eight United Church of Christ congregations in Utah, including a Japanese church in Ogden and another in Salt Lake City, both jointly sponsored by the Presbyterian Church.[73] Membership exceeded 2,200. The Congregational Church of Provo, which had been in existence since the mid-1880s, became associated with the UCC in the 1957 merger, as did the congregation in Holladay and more in several other communities. Some, such as the First Congregational Church of Salt Lake, did not officially join the UCC, even though they maintained ties to that organization.[74]

Members of the United Church of Christ participated actively in public affairs,. During the Vietnam War, for example, several UCC members spoke out for peace. One member of the Holladay congregation, retired Marine Corps Major General William Fairbourne, became increasingly uneasy about the war and joined with Ed Firmage of the University of Utah in traveling throughout the country and speaking out against war generally.[75]

Members of the United Church of Christ helped finance and voluntarily staff numerous social programs in the state, many of which focused on helping the indigent. These included Utahns Against Hunger, the Crossroads Urban Center, the Family Support

Center of Salt Lake, and Utah Issues.[76] Ecumenical organizations such as Shared Ministry in Utah also attracted UCC participation.

In general, the United Church of Christ tended toward theological liberalism. Not adhering to rigid dogma, it encouraged its members to question their assumptions, examine their beliefs, and form personal opinions. The more conservative element among them may not have felt comfortable with such a liberal approach, but many UCC members saw this flexibility as a great strength and something that would continue to make the church appealing to those in the community who craved open religious discussion.

Seventh-day Adventists

The Seventh-day Adventist Church took its name from an emphasis on the second advent, or coming, of Christ and on the seventh day of the week (Saturday), which they viewed as the proper Sabbath. Organized in 1863, the church's first missionaries appeared in Utah in the late 1880s. As of 1990, there were fourteen congregations in Utah, with more than 1,800 members.[77]

In some ways the Adventists had much in common with the Mormon population. Emphasizing the sanctity of the human body, they followed dietary rules even more strict than those of the Mormons. In addition to shunning narcotics and stimulants such as tea and coffee, they ate no meat. They also tithed (gave one-tenth of their incomes) to support the worldwide social programs of the church. In addition, not unlike the Mormons, they were the objects of ridicule and discrimination because of their beliefs and practices.

The Central Seventh-day Adventist Church in Salt Lake City began in 1925, after several black members of the Salt Lake congregation petitioned to have their own congregation. They reasoned that their acquaintances, who felt uncomfortable attending the mostly white Salt Lake church, would more readily attend a predominantly black church. The mission headquarters agreed. The congregation continued to consist mostly of African Americans and Hispanics, but some Caucasians attended this congregations because of the convenient location.[78]

Seventh-day Adventists usually established small schools in connection with each congregation. Although they catered specifically to Adventist children, these schools also accepted students of other faiths, providing they agreed to abide by school standards. In 1994 there were Adventist schools in Provo, Ogden, Monument Valley, and Castle Valley. All four schools supported grades one through eight, with the exception of the Castle Valley school, which supported grades one through twelve. A junior academy, with grades one through twelve, served some eighty-seven students in Salt Lake City.[79]

Adventists also worked with the Christian Braille Association, a group dedicated to the production of the Bible and other Christian literature in braille. They also managed an annual summer camp for the blind. The camp, located in Hobble Creek Canyon near Springville, cost the participants nothing and focused on teaching practical living skills, as well as such things as CPR.[80]

Adventists actively supported a large number of hospitals around the world, and Utah benefitted from this service. In 1950, Harry Goulding, a trading post operator in southern Utah, contacted the Adventists and offered to donate ten acres of land if the church would set up a mission with a medical clinic to serve the Navajos in that area. By 1952 a small clinic had been constructed. By 1958 fund-raising efforts succeeded in raising some $150,000, half of which came from the Indian Affairs Commission.[81] This money permitted an expansion of the clinic's services, turning it into a small hospital with a maternity ward, nursery, X-ray equipment, and a generator to supply power. Two full-time residential doctors and several nurses staffed the facility, assisted by student volunteers during the summer months. The staff members also performed several thousand outpatient calls every year.[82]

Adventists also engaged in a number of other community activities, including giving support to several local shelters and soup kitchens, operating a prison outreach program, collecting funds for disaster relief, conducting stop-smoking classes, and giving aid to unwed teenage mothers. The Salt Lake Ministerial Association also attracted Adventist participation and was, at one time, headed by an Adventist pastor.[83]

Buddhists[84]

As Japanese Buddhists came to Utah in the late nineteenth and early twentieth centuries, two independent Buddhist congregations took root, one in Ogden and another in Salt Lake City. A temple was built in Salt Lake City in the mid-1920s. The Ogden congregation bought its first facility in 1937, then built a temple to its own specifications in 1964. For a while, during World War II, the headquarters of the Buddhist Mission of North America was located at the Japanese relocation center in Topaz.

Early in 1962, in response to the need for expansion that had long been felt by temple patrons, a new Buddhist temple was dedicated in Salt Lake City. In addition to its religious function, for many years the temple continued to provide an environment where Japanese-Americans could preserve their culture as well as their personal ties. It also served as a kind of bastion against influences that the *issei*, or first generation Japanese, feared would adversely influence their children. However, as later generations become assimilated into American culture the temple became more of a spiritual than a cultural center.[85]

In the mid-1990s, the Salt Lake Buddhist congregation included approximately two hundred families. The temple sponsored organizations for children, youth, and women. The Buddhists did not involve themselves in the community at large as actively as some other groups did, although they participated in the Japanese-Americans' Citizens League and the Senior Citizens' League.[86] The Buddhists also sponsored an annual Obon festival, or "Festival of Souls," which commemorated deceased ancestors. The festival became somewhat of a tourist attraction, offering Japanese foods and dancing displays.

Although the temple in Salt Lake City was the largest in terms of participation, there were other Buddhist centers in Utah. The very active Ogden temple supported a branch in Corinne, where a building was erected in 1944. The Ogden temple also once supported a branch in Honeyville, but that congregation became independent in 1971. Other Buddhist centers included a Thai Buddhist temple in Logan, founded in the mid-1970s and boasting about five hundred members by the mid-1990s, another Thai temple in Layton, and a Zen meditation center in Salt Lake

City. At the end of 1994, there were an estimated one thousand Buddhists statewide.[87]

Evangelical Free Church[88]

The Evangelical Free Church in America resulted from the 1950 merger of the Swedish Evangelical Free Church of America and the Norwegian-Danish Evangelical Free Church. Both denominations had splintered from the Lutheran Church. Evangelical Free congregations governed themselves quite independently and subscribed to a range of theological positions, although they held to a core statement of faith that listed twelve elements considered necessary for inclusion in the Body of Christ.[89] In the early 1960s the Salt Lake congregation constructed a new facility with seating for some 160 people.

In late 1965, the Provo Bible Church, a nondenominational body, built a new facility in Orem and then aligned with the Evangelical Free Church.[90] In the early 1980s, a seed church began in Ogden and then later moved to Roy. Also in the 1980s and early 1990s, several independent churches became aligned with the Evangelical Free Church. These included the Cache Valley Community Church, the San Juan Community Church in Monticello, the Cornerstone Community Church in Salt Lake City, and a group from Park City. In 1988, a church plant (a small congregation sponsored by a larger group), later known as the South Valley Evangelical Free Church, was started in West Jordan.

In 1979, the Salt Lake congregation took the first steps toward establishing a school. Under Pastor Reginald McLindon, the congregation began with a preschool, but the facility was eventually expanded to serve children from kindergarten through grade twelve and became known as the Intermountain Christian School. A new facility in southeast Salt Lake City opened in 1991. That school soon served some 370 students from fourteen different denominations in its two preschool grades and grades kindergarten through twelve.[91]

Evangelical Free Church participation in social programs and ministries usually came from the independent action of church members. They worked with the Salt Lake Rescue Mission, took part in the Days of '47 Youth Parade, and were involved in various other community projects. Although ecumenical work was not common among Evangelical Free churches, the Orem church worked with several other denominations in its area to more effectively communicate a common message to the surrounding community

Because of its emphasis on congregational autonomy and its willingness to accept differences in theological persuasion, the Evangelical Free Church experienced a fair amount of growth in Utah. In the 1990s there were two congregations in Salt Lake City and others in Logan, Roy, Monticello, Orem, Park City, and West Jordan. Combined Utah membership was estimated at some 1,200 people.[92]

Unitarian-Universalist Churches[93]

In 1961, the American Unitarian Association and the Universalist Church of America joined together to form the American Unitarian Universalist Association. There was, at the time, one Unitarian congregation in Salt Lake City, the First Unitarian Society. The following year the congregation changed its name to the First Unitarian Church of Salt Lake City. In April 1983, a second congregation, the South Valley Unitarian Society, was formed in the area. During the next decade churches were established also in Park City and Ogden.[94] As of 1990, there were 718 Unitarians in the state.

Unitarianism took a very liberal approach to religion and theology, allowing each member to use his or her own intellect to develop personal faith. This perspective appealed to many intellectuals, among others, who did not hold to the orthodoxy of mainstream churches. Unitarianism thus drew much of its membership from the University of Utah community. A number of Unitarian ministers held degrees in theology and philosophy, and some lectured in philosophy at the university.

Unitarians were involved in a number of social issues in Utah, including the movement against the Vietnam War. At one time, they passed a resolution to provide symbolic sanctuary for those who wished to avoid the draft, but this sanctuary was never actually provided. Unitarians also worked with abortion counseling and Planned Parenthood, made their facilities available to Utah's minorities. They also provided support for local rescue missions, the Crossroads Urban Center, and other facilities for the homeless and the indigent. In addition, they led out in efforts to address many other social issues, including women's rights, minority rights, gay rights, the peace movement, and environmental issues.

Christian Church (Disciples of Christ) and Churches of Christ

The Christian Church (Disciples of Christ) came into existence in 1832 after Alexander Campbell joined with Barton Stone to found a movement that emphasized the need to restore the simple truths of New Testament Christianity. However, because of certain doctrinal differences three modern religious groups actually stemmed from the original movement: the Christian Church (Disciples of Christ), the Churches of Christ, and a fellowship known as the Christian Churches and Churches of Christ. The Christian Church (Disciples of Christ) advocated a greater degree of organization than the others. Local congregations were independent, but there was a corporate unity through national and international conventions to which separate congregations sent representatives. The Churches of Christ, on the other hand, were strictly congregational, with no national organization at all, while the Christian Churches (Disciples of Christ) and Churches of Christ developed a loosely related national fellowship.

The first Utah congregation of the Christian Church (Disciples of Christ) was formed in Salt Lake City in mid-1890. The Ogden congregation took root in October of that same year.[95] In 1995 there were four Christian Church (Disciples of Christ) congregations in Utah: two in the Salt Lake area, one in Weber County, and one in Kanab, which operated jointly with the United Church of Christ, the United Methodists, the Presbyterians, and the American Baptists. There were 769 members in Utah in 1993.[96] Members of the Churches of Christ numbered 912 in 1990, in seventeen congregations around the state.

Church of Christ

In 1990, with a total of 949 members, there were seventeen congregations of the Church of Christ in Utah: three in Salt Lake County, two in Davis County, two in San Juan County, and one each in Box Elder, Cache, Carbon, Grand, Iron, Millard, Tooele, Utah, Uintah, and Weber counties.[97]

The Church of Christ was often confused with the Churches of Christ, but it was a distinctive group not descended from the Campbell-Stone movement. It consisted of independent congregations who held no specific written creed except the New Testament. Members believed that their non-credal position was necessary for the promotion of unity among Christians. Congregations cooperated in certain social ministries but could refrain from joint actions if they so chose. Their religion was strictly Bible-centered and members modeled their lives and worship services on what they found in the scriptures.[98]

Christian Reformed Church

The Christian Reformed Church, growing from the same reform tradition as Presbyterianism, Congregationalism, and the United Church of Christ, leaned toward Calvinist teachings. They emphasized education and operated a number of colleges throughout the United States. Clergy were required to have college degrees. They worked with several ecumenical organizations around the world.[99]

The first Christian Reformed Church in Utah began with meetings in homes during the late 1940s. For a time, the members were allowed the use of a Seventh-day Adventist sanctuary, but in 1953 they purchased a Methodist building for their own use. Later, a new Salt Lake sanctuary was built on the same piece of property. The church became a legally incorporated body in 1957. In 1994 there were five Christian Reformed congregations in Utah: three in the Salt Lake area, one of which was a Native American congregation and one Cambodian, one in Ogden, and one in Brigham City.[100] Total membership in 1990 was listed at 602.

The Reorganized Church of Jesus Christ of Latter Day Saints

The Reorganized Church of Jesus Christ of Latter Day Saints (RLDS) was founded on the belief that Joseph Smith III was his father's true successor to church leadership. In 1994 there were three RLDS congregations in the state, one each in Salt Lake City, Ogden, and Orem, with membership estimated at 570.[101]

At first, the Salt Lake City congregation worshiped in a facility purchased from the Methodists in 1920, but in 1966 it moved into a new chapel. The Orem congregation built a chapel in 1969. From 1969 to 1973, this group sponsored an annual summer camp for children with cystic fibrosis, as well as a weeklong camp for church members. In 1984, the RLDS Church leased some land near Huntsville. There it opened a camp, known as Camp Radcliffe, which was used throughout the summer by members of the church as well as by health organizations who conducted camps for cancer patients, cystic fibrosis patients, diabetics, and patients with other serious illnesses.[102]

Among other things, the RLDS Church provided a place for estranged Mormons, and much of its membership came from that source. Over the years, however, the church moved away from the distinctive teachings of Joseph Smith and more toward mainstream Protestant theology and practice. It also placed less emphasis on the historical authenticity of the Book of Mormon, and in the 1980s it adopted the practice of ordaining women to the priesthood. These changes did not sit well with the more conservatives members, who sometimes banded together and formed restoration or independent branches. They remained on RLDS rolls but had little contact with RLDS leadership. In the 1990s there were restoration branches of the RLDS Church in the Provo and Orem area and in Salt Lake City.[103] In the year 2000 members at the RLDS world conference voted to change the church's name to Community of Christ, effective January 1, 2001.

Christian Science

Christian Science got its start in 1879 through the work of Mary Baker Eddy, whose basic teachings may be found in her book *Science and Health with Key to the Scriptures*. The first Christian Science church in Utah was formed in the 1890s.[104]

Christian Scientists emphasize the life and teachings of Jesus. The term Christian Science refers to their belief in spiritual, prayer-based healing. In 1994 there were an estimated 150 members in seven Christian Science congregations in Utah: three in the Salt Lake area, one in Park City, one in St. George, one in Weber County, and one in Utah County.

Society of Friends (Quakers)[105]

The Society of Friends, more commonly known as the Quakers, first formalized an independent Utah Meeting (congregation) in Logan in 1974. The Logan Meeting then took a small group of Quakers in Salt Lake City under its wing until that group became independent in 1979. Later the Salt Lake Meeting began to oversee another fledgling group in Moab. As of 1990, some 120 Friends resided in Utah.

In general, Quakers were very active in community affairs, though they did not specifically draw attention to themselves. The Salt Lake Meeting's Peace and Social Concerns Committee sponsored a number of non-violence training seminars at prisons in Utah, aimed at teaching inmates and prison workers effective ways of diffusing confrontation without recourse to violence. The state's Department of Corrections publicly recognized the Friends for this work.

Individual Friends worked at various homeless shelters and soup kitchens, and the group involved itself in giving aid to refugees in Utah. In the 1990s, the Salt Lake Meeting shared its building with a Jewish group, and sometimes the two participated in joint gatherings.

The Salvation Army

The Salvation Army was founded in 1878 in England and came to the United States in 1880. Actually a holiness church in terms of its religious doctrine, the Army was known in particular for its social welfare programs. These included, but were not limited to, family welfare, aid to transients and to the indigent, work with alcoholics, homeless shelters, low-cost residences for working women, and emergency service in the wake of disasters. Its support came not just from members of the Army but also from voluntary contributions by other members of the community as well as from various community chests and united funds.[106]

The first congregation of the Salvation Army in Utah was established in Salt Lake City just after the turn of the century. In 1995 there were three congregations: one in Ogden and two in Salt Lake City, one of which served the Hispanic community. The combined membership of the two Salt Lake congregations was around eighty.[107] However, the public was more aware of the Army than its numbers would imply because of its well-known charitable service and its public appeals for funds at Christmastime.

Christ Catholic Church

Christ Catholic Church got its start in the late 1960s through the efforts of Reverend Karl Pruter, a Congregationalist minister. The church emphasized personal contemplation and meditation, mysticism, and experiential faith. Its liturgy came from the Old Catholic tradition, though both clergy and lay persons could decide on their personal beliefs.[108] As of 1990, Utah had a single Christ Catholic congregation, located in Salt Lake City, with twenty-eight members.[109]

Apostolic Christian Church

The Apostolic Christian Church grew out of a protest movement within the Reformed Church in Switzerland in 1830. The first congregation in the United States was founded in the 1840s. Borrowing from the traditions of the Mennonites and the Reformed

Church, Apostolic Christians taught that a change of heart through regeneration, and a godly life through the Holy Spirit were needed for the soul to be saved. They also practiced pacifism, though they were loyal citizens of the United States.[110] As of 1990, a single Apostolic Christian congregation, with six members, could be found in Salt Lake City.[111]

Hare Krishna

Krishna, one of the most widely revered gods in Hinduism, was the focus of numerous devotional groups. One of them, the International Society for Krishna Consciousness, was founded in the United States in 1966 by the swami Prabhupada (A. C. Bhaktivedanta). It became popularly known as Hare Krishna because of its chants. Devotees sought to attain ultimate peace and happiness by returning to an original relationship with their god, called Krishna Consciousness. Achieving this state came through practicing a type of yoga, called bhakti yoga, and doing Krishna's work with no thought of personal reward. Members lived in communes, or temples, where unmarried men and women practiced strict celibacy and where gambling, alcohol, and eating meat were forbidden. Each commune was self-supporting, usually by selling the society's publications. The movement appealed particularly to young people, who soon made themselves known to the public by singing, dancing, or chanting on street corners and by soliciting funds in railroad stations and airports. By the early 1990s there were over three hundred Hare Krishna centers worldwide.

Krishna devotees appeared in Utah in the mid-1970s. Some were natives of India who had come to America for various reasons, while others were American converts. Often they were seen in the Salt Lake City International Airport selling flowers as well as copies of the *Bhagavad Gita*, one of their principle books of scripture.

In the late 1970s, two attempts were made to establish a Krishna temple in the Salt Lake area, but neither succeeded.[112] In 1981, however, Caru Das and his wife, Vaibhavi Dasi, arrived in Spanish Fork with the goal of establishing a temple there. They purchased a local AM station (KHQN 1480) to support their effort and to raise "God consciousness" in Utah. The couple supported the station, the only one of its type in the United States, partly from the proceeds of their vegetarian food catering business in Los Angeles.[113] They also operated a llama farm near Spanish Fork.

A temporary temple, located next to the radio station, was completed in 1977. Weekly worship services held there attracted worshipers from both Utah and Salt Lake Counties, and were open to the public. By the mid-1990s, Caru estimated, there were approximately one thousand devotees in the state.

From 1981 to 1993, a traveling Krishna festival was headquartered near the temple in Spanish Fork. The festival, with its busses and tents, traveled around the country during the summer months teaching devotion to Krishna and about the society's core beliefs. It remained in Spanish Fork during the winter months, repairing equipment and preparing for the next season of travel.

Beginning in 1987, the society hosted an annual festival at the temple. There the Ramayana, an Indian religious story, was reenacted, dances were performed, and vegetarian cuisine was served. Even though the traveling festival moved its headquarters elsewhere after 1993, it returned to Utah each year. The festival grew in popularity and, by the mid-1990s, attracted thousands of people annually.

At the same time, Caru and the Krishna community began gathering funds for a new temple. As they envisioned it, the edifice would be built in traditional Indian architectural style, with seventy-five columns and fifteen domes. In 1995 funds were being raised from Govinda's Buffet (a vegetarian restaurant in Provo), the rental and sale of llamas, the radio station, and bake sales. In addition, Caru himself, age forty-eight, helped raise funds by running marathons. By 1995 he had finished twenty-six marathons, with a personal-best time of 3:01.11. The only one of its kind between Pennsylvania and California, the elegant new building would serve not just as a center for worship but also as a cultural and performing arts center. It would also include a gift shop, a marriage hall, and a vegetarian restaurant, and would undoubtedly bring tourists to Spanish Fork.[114] The beautiful Lotus Temple was completed in 2002.

Interfaith Efforts in Utah

Partly because of the predominance of the LDS faith, the general relationship between all the churches in Utah was somewhat different than that in other states. Historically, interfaith efforts among non-LDS churches was an outgrowth of their efforts, as minorities, to more effectively help their members find spiritual strength. In 1915, for example, the Home Missions Council was established by Utah's Protestant churches to coordinate efforts between them where limited resources and members existed. Shared Ministry of Utah was established in 1977 to provide the same kind of service. In the 1990s, some sixty-eight congregations from six mainline Protestant denominations participated in Shared Ministry, which coordinated mission efforts, helped establish new churches, provided ecclesiastical training, and drafted public position statements. It held three meetings a year.[115] In addition, churches in various communities supported local ministerial associations in an effort to bring about better interfaith understanding and cooperation. All of the clergy and laypersons interviewed in the course of doing research for this study characterized the atmosphere for inter-church cooperation in Utah as favorable.[116] Some even said that churches cooperated more closely in Utah than in other areas where they had lived.

In the late nineteenth and early twentieth centuries, the LDS Church participated only perfunctorily in such interfaith activities, but that gradually changed. An impressive sign of this was seen in 1970 when the youth of 566 LDS wards in the Salt Lake area joined with the youth of Deliverance Temple, Church of God in Christ, a black church, to raise over $33,000 to erect a new Deliverance Temple. At a banquet celebrating the event, President Harold B. Lee of the First Presidency of the LDS Church made some heartfelt comments. "Let this be the beginning of a kind of brotherhood that will be evident to all," he said. "We will stand by your side and encourage you and bless you with love and fellowship—and may the Lord be with you always."[117]

By the 1990s various Mormon leaders and laypersons took part in local ministerial associations and in discussion groups with their counterparts from other denominations. For example, representatives of several faiths, including the LDS Church, participated in the Utah Valley Ministerial Association. The association provided an opportunity for better understanding each other's faiths, and also conducted a Food and Shelter Coalition.[118]

Some denominations with close theological ties sponsored joint Bible classes for adults, Bible schools for children, combined training meetings, and joint evangelistic efforts. Some even conducted joint worship services. In November, 1993, during a national campaign known as "Win Our City to Jesus," volunteers from over thirty Utah churches spent one day visiting over nine hundred homes in Salt Lake Valley, asking residents to share any life-changing experiences had with Jesus. It was reported that 225 people were "won" to Jesus through that effort.[119]

However, some religious groups shunned participation in joint services or teaching activities, feeling that such cooperation could lead to unwanted modification of theologies. Such separatism, said one Utah minister in 1994, was necessary to keep people from being confused about what to believe.[120]

At the same time, various social ministries garnered great support from a wide number of denominations. Many shelters, soup kitchens, and clothing distribution centers were recipients of much denominational aid both in terms of volunteer time and financial donations. Representatives from various churches met to discuss how to confront, within the community, such pressing social issues as child abuse, abortion, and capital punishment.[121] Volunteers from several denominations participated in Prison Fellowship, a national program for helping prison inmates rehabilitate themselves.[122] In Salt Lake City, an association of local churches known as Salt Lake Urban Social Ministries involved itself in a number of social outreach services. In 1990, for example, this ministry received a major grant from the Episcopal Diocese of Utah aimed toward establishing a Dignity in Work Program designed to help the needy obtain financial help through working. Other groups participating in this program included the Salvation Army (who helped provide jobs), Catholics, Methodists, Presbyterians, Lutherans, and the African Methodist Episcopal Church.[123] The AIDS crisis also led to cooperative activity among Utah churches. An AIDS coalition in Provo, for example, was supported by St. Mary's Episcopal Church, the Provo Community

Church, and others interested in educating the public. In 1992 the coalition held a public AIDS sensitivity training session and also encouraged AIDS education at colleges and university.[124] During AIDS Awareness Month that year an interfaith religious service was held at the First Presbyterian Church in Salt Lake City. This and separate services in twenty other congregations were designed to help church members and others better understand AIDS and how to help those afflicted with it.[125]

Natural disasters also provided a rallying point for interfaith cooperation. During the 1983 floods in the Salt Lake Valley, Mormons, Catholics, Jews, and several Protestant denominations all joined in relief efforts. The Greek Orthodox community, for example, sandbagged for several days and organized a kitchen to feed those who were doing the sandbagging. The First Baptist Church of Salt Lake City provided food for sandbaggers in the canyons, while the Bountiful Community Church organized neighborhood sandbagging groups and sent three busloads of youth to help out with the Farmington mudslides.[126]

Utah churches cooperated in various other ways. In the 1970s, low church attendance in Brigham City led the Presbyterians, Lutherans, and Methodists to form the Christian Ministry Council. Weekly religion classes sponsored by the council used materials drawn from the catechisms and Bible study courses of all three groups.[127] In 1985, Presbyterian, Episcopalian, United Methodist, Catholic, Assembly of God, Greek Orthodox, Lutheran, and Black Baptist congregations in central Salt Lake City formed the Central Salt Lake Council of Churches. Its purpose was to provide interdenominational social opportunities for parishioners of all faiths, to support and educate the clergy involved, and to create a Christian community with a common voice.[128]

A number of special events in the 1980s and 1990s symbolized the unfeigned effort on the part of Utah's religious leaders to demonstrate good will toward each other. In 1980, for example, Catholic Bishop Joseph Federal attended the installation of Rabbi Eric Silver at the Synagogue of Kol Ami. In November 1982, Bishop Federal and Episcopal Bishop Otis E. Chandler preached from each other's pulpits in Salt Lake City. In 1983 several religious leaders joined together to proclaim December 4–10 of that year as Peace Week. In February 1993, various denominational leaders attended the rededication of the Cathedral of the Madeleine. In May of that same year, in an address at Utah's annual Episcopal convention, Episcopal Bishop George E. Bates discussed the need to accept community and religious differences and to be Christian to one another.[129]

Good feelings and cooperation between most churches became one of the positive features of the Utah religious scene. It contributed much in terms of alleviating human suffering and in other ways making the state a better place to live. Despite their differences, Utah's religions shared that common goal.

Notes

1. There is no adequate, full-length study on religions in Utah. Principal sources for several of the sketches here are the congregational, diocesan, and presbytery histories that the various groups have written about themselves. Some are very incomplete. In addition, there are full-length books relating to the Mormons, Catholics, and Unitarians in the state, and a few articles, some of them very sketchy on this period, in a handful of books and journals. Many of Utah's denominations, however, particularly those organized in the last twenty or thirty years of the twentieth century, do not have any published information about their history or activities. A number of interviews were conducted by the author's research assistant, Jesse S. Bushman, to gather material about some of these groups, as well as to supplement the sparse written information available on others. A few newspaper articles added to the picture. General background information on the origin and teachings of various groups was obtained from William B. Williamson, ed., *An Encyclopedia of Religions in the United States: One Hundred Religious Groups Speak for Themselves* (New York: The Crossroads Publishing Company, 1992); J. Gordon Melton, *Encyclopedia of American Religions*, 4th ed. (Detroit: Gale Research Inc., 1993); *Compton's Encyclopedia*, Online Edition, downloaded from America Online. The author expresses special appreciation to Jesse S. Bushman, who not only spent considerable time gathering information on non-LDS churches but also prepared the original draft for the section of this chapter dealing with non-Mormons. With Mr. Bushman's permission, portions of that draft are used almost verbatim herein. After the first draft of this book was written, Mr. Bushman completed his master's thesis. See Jesse Smith Bushman, "A Qualitative Analysis of the Non-LDS Experience in Utah" (master's thesis, Brigham Young University, 1995).
2. See Milford Randall Rathjen, "The Distribution of Major Non-Mormon Denominations in Utah" (master's thesis, University of Utah, 1966).
3. The churches were categorized and listed as follows: Assembly of God, 31; Baptist, 13; American Baptist, 11; Conservative Baptist, 10; Fundamental Baptist, 1; Independent Baptist, 3; Southern Baptist, 43; Bible, 32; Christian and Missionary Alliance, 2; Calvary Chapel, 3; Roman Catholic, 43; Charismatic, 2; Christian, 4; Christian (Disciples of Christ), 3; Christian, Independent, 3; Christian Reformed, 5; Church of Christ, 10; Church of God, 4; Church of God in Christ, 3; Church of

God of Prophecy, 2; Congregational, 1; Episcopal, 17; Evangelical Free, 3; Foursquare, 5; Lutheran, A.L.C., 4; Lutheran, L.C.A., 8; Lutheran, Missouri Synod, 18; Lutheran, Wisconsin Synod, 1; Methodist, A.M.E., 2; United Methodist, 15; Nazarene, 5; Non-Denominational, 22; Eastern Orthodox, 4; Pentecostal, 8; Presbyterian, 21; Salvation Army, 2; Seventh-day Adventist, 7; United Church of Christ, 6. Intermountain Book Store, Inc., "1986 Utah Directory of Church and Related Institutions: Protestant and Roman Catholic," unpublished directory, copy located in James B. Allen papers, L. Tom Perry Special Collections, Harold B. Lee Library, Brigham Young University.

4. For a general history of The Church of Jesus Christ of Latter-day Saints, see James B. Allen and Glen M. Leonard, *The Story of the Latter-Day Saints*, 2nd ed., rev. and enl. (Salt Lake City: Deseret Book Company, 1992). For continuing updates on statistical and other kinds of important information, see the bi-annual editions of the *Deseret News Church Almanac* (Salt Lake City: *Deseret News*).

5. 1993 statistics based on figures reported in *Deseret News 1995 Church Almanac*, 172. This is higher than other published estimates, but the difficulty of arriving at a correct figure for 1990 illustrates a persistent problem in obtaining accurate statistics. The 1990 Utah population, according to the US Census, was 1,722,850. The church's Statistical Department provided the author with a 1990 *year-end* figure of 1,329,375 members in the state. Comparing these two numbers resulted in an estimate of 80.10 percent LDS. This seemed excessively high, but the fact that the US Census reflected the population near the *beginning* of the year probably caused a discrepancy. Recognizing this, the author consulted the *1991-1992 Deseret News Church Almanac*, which estimated Utah's 1989 *year-end* population at 1.69 million (p. 109) and listed the LDS 1989 *year-end* population at 1,305,000 (p. 332). This resulted in a figure of 77.22 percent LDS at the end of 1989. This figure still seemed high so a reasonable compromise estimate was arrived at by dividing the 1989 *year-end* figure provided by the church (1,305,000) by the 1990 US Census figure for Utah (1,722,850). This resulted in the 75.7 percent reported in the text.

6. As reported in Barry A. Kosmin and Seymour P. Lachman, *One Nation Under God: Religion in Contemporary American Society* (New York: Harmony Books, 1993), 88-98. While the result of their statistics was different from those reported elsewhere, their reported result of 69.2 percent LDS in Utah was at least close to the author's estimate of 75.7 percent. Rhode Island, with a 61.7 percent Roman Catholic population, most closely approximated the situation in Utah. Furthermore, of all the adherents to Mormonism in the United States, 34.5 percent lived in Utah. The only other groups that reflected this type of membership concentration were the Buddhists, with 38 per cent of their American membership in California, and the Hindus, with 34.7 percent of their American membership in New York. The Buddhists and Hindus, however, made up only a small proportion of the total population of these two states, at 0.7 per cent and 0.6 percent respectively.

7. Thomas G. Alexander and James B. Allen, *Mormons and Gentiles: A History of Salt Lake City* (Denver: Pruett Publishing Company, 1984), 263-65.

8. Between 1950 and 1993, the number of full-time LDS missionaries worldwide grew from five thousand to 48,700. See Allen and Leonard, *Story of the Latter-day Saints*, 560-61, 565; *Deseret News 1995-96 Church Almanac*, 412-20.

9. William E. Berrett, *A Miracle in Weekday Religious Education: A History of the Church Educational System* (Salt Lake City: privately published, 1988), 245; *Deseret News 1995-96 Church Almanac*, 6.

10. For a general history of the genealogical activities of the church, including its vast microfilming program, see James B. Allen, Jessie L. Embry, and Kahlile B. Mehr, *Hearts Turned to the Fathers: A History of the Genealogical Society of Utah, 1894–1994* (Provo, UT: BYU Studies, 1995).
11. For insight into the nature of contemporary polygamous relationships, see Irwin Altman and Joseph Giant, *Polygamous Families in Contemporary Society* (New York: Cambridge University Press, 1996).
12. The summary above is largely based on the excellent overview of numerous Mormon schismatic groups found in Melton, *Encyclopedia of American Religions*, 617–41. The author also thanks one of his students, Don Bradley, who has studied many of these schismatic groups in depth.
13. Louis M. Ader, "Evangelical Missions among the Mormons," *Review & Expositor* 49 (July 1952), 320-21.
14. Unless otherwise noted, most of the following information on the Roman Catholic Church in Utah is based on Bernice Maher Mooney, *Salt of the Earth: The History of the Catholic Church in Utah, 1776–1987* (Salt Lake City: Catholic Diocese of Salt Lake City, 1992). Some is also based on James B. Allen, "Religion in Twentieth-century Utah," in *Utah's History*, ed. Richard D. Poll, Thomas G. Alexander, Eugene E. Campbell, David E. Miller (Logan, UT: Utah State University Press, 1989), 614-17. See also Bernice Maher Mooney, *The Story of the Cathedral of the Madeleine* (Salt Lake City: Litho Graphics, 1981); Bernice M. Mooney, "Duane Garrison Hunt," in *Utah History Encyclopedia*, ed. Allen Kent Powell (Salt Lake City: University of Utah Press, 1994), 264.
15. Linda Martinez (Salt Lake City), telephone interview by Jesse S. Bushman, January 3, 1995; Deacon Silvio Mayo (Salt Lake City), telephone interview by Jesse S. Bushman, January 3, 1995; notes in James B. Allen papers, L. Tom Perry Special Collections, Harold B. Lee Library, Brigham Young University; Bernice M. Mooney, "The Catholic Church in Utah," in *Utah History Encyclopedia*, ed. Powell, 78–79.
16. Brooke Adams, "The Bishop," *Deseret News* Extra, January 19, 1995, A21.
17. Jerry Spangler, "Catholic Schools Restore Opposition to Elitism," *Deseret News*, November 1, 1992, B13. The elementary schools were Cosgriff Memorial School, Our Lady of Lourdes School, St. Ann's School, and St. Vincent's School, all in Salt Lake City; Notre Dame School in Price, St. Francis Xavier School in Kearns; St. Joseph's Elementary School in Ogden, St. Olaf's School in Bountiful; and Blessed Sacrament School in Sandy. The high schools were Judge Memorial Catholic School in Salt Lake City and St. Joseph High School in Ogden. These and other religious schools in the state are listed in Intermountain Book Store, Inc., "1986 Utah Directory of Churches and Related Institutions."
18. Tim Fitzpatrick, "Non-Catholics Flock to Judge Memorial," *Salt Lake Tribune*, April 14, 1991, A1, A3.
19. See this organization's website at www.ccsutah.org. Accessed January 9, 2015.
20. Douglas Palmer, "Construction Set to Start for New St. Joseph Center," *Deseret News*, May 29, 1993, A12; Douglas D. Palmer, "Sisters' Values Still at Heart of Expanded St. Joseph Villa," *Deseret News*, April 15, 1995, E1; Lori Peterson (Salt Lake City), telephone interview by Jesse S. Bushman, January 10, 1995, notes in James B. Allen papers, L. Tom Perry Special Collections, Harold B. Lee Library, Brigham Young University.
21. Many more are described in the pages of Mooney, *Salt of the Earth*.

22. There are no published histories of the Baptists dealing extensively with the post-World War II era. Information for this section comes from interviews, unpublished congregational histories, and a few telephone conversations. For a general overview, see David L. Schirer, "Baptists in Utah," in *Utah History Encyclopedia*, ed. Powell, 31-33.
23. "First Baptist Marks Its First 100 Years," *Salt Lake Tribune* May 14, 1983, 2; Mrs. A. F. Martin, *Ten Years of Devotion and Sacrifice of the First Baptist Church of Bountiful, Utah* (Bountiful, UT: First Baptist Church of Bountiful, 1967), 3.
24. Rathjen, "Distribution of Major Non-Mormon Denominations," 62; Martin B. Bradley, Norman M. Green, Jr., Dale E. Jones, Mac Lynn, and Lou McNeil, eds. and comps., *Churches and Church Membership in the United States, 1990: An Enumeration by Region, State, and County, Based on Data Reported for 133 Church Groupings* (Atlanta: Glenmary Research Center, 1992), 392-94; Intermountain Book Store, Inc., "1986 Utah Directory of Churches and Related Institutions." The directory lists ten Conservative Baptist congregations, but two have since been disbanded.
25. Lynn Arave, "Layton Hills Baptist Church Plans August Revivals," *Deseret News*, August 17, 1991, A8.
26. David M. Walden, "First Baptist Church," in *Protestant and Catholic Churches of Provo*, ed. David M. Walden (Provo, UT: Center for Family and Community History, Brigham Young University, 1986), 178.
27. Peggy Fletcher Stack, "S. L. Strikes Gold After Losing Olympics: 25,000 Baptists Say 'This Is the Place,'" *Salt Lake Tribune*, June 18, 1991, A1. The convention actually attracted more than twenty thousand Baptists, who were cordially welcomed by the Mormons even though the period of the convention became a time of heavy proselytizing among the Mormons. On the weekend before the convention, thousands of missionary-minded Baptists went from door to door in Utah. However, contrary to some reports and what some people expected, there was no open conflict, and the week of the convention ended in very amicable Mormon-Baptist relations.
28. Reverend Stanley Smith (Salt Lake City), interview by Jesse S. Bushman, October 26, 1994, tape in James B. Allen papers, L. Tom Perry Special Collections, Harold B. Lee Library, Brigham Young University.
29. Joan E. Stewart, Bountiful, Utah, to Jesse S. Bushman, December 6, 1994, letter in James B. Allen papers, L. Tom Perry Special Collections, Harold B. Lee Library, Brigham Young University.
30. Calvary is one of the few congregations that has documented its history. The congregation's story can be found in *Calvary Missionary Baptist Church, 1899–1976* (Salt Lake City: privately published by Calvary Baptist Church, 1976), available in Special Collections, J. Willard Marriott Library, University of Utah. For a very brief history of the church, see "Celebrating 119 Years of Faith, Glory, and Honor to God," program for the Calvary Baptist Church Revival and Anniversary, November 6–13, 2011, at www.calvaryslc.com/documents/pdf/119anniversary.pdf. Accessed January 13, 2015.
31. Reverend France Davis (Salt Lake City), interview by Jesse S. Bushman, October 28, 1994, tape in James B. Allen papers, L. Tom Perry Special Collections, Harold B. Lee Library, Brigham Young University. See also France Davis, *France Davis: An American Story Told* (Salt Lake City, University of Utah Press, 2006).
32. For a general overview of the Lutherans, to 1975, see Ronnie L. Stellhorn, "A History of the Lutheran Church in Utah" (master's thesis, Utah State University, 1975).

33. "Redeemer School Offers Alternative," *Salt Lake Tribune*, February 9, 1980, B2; Jan Bowker (Provo, Ut, telephone interview by Jesse S. Bushman, December 21, 1994, notes in James B. Allen papers, L. Tom Perry Special Collections, Harold B. Lee Library, Brigham Young University.
34. Reverend Mark G. Bellow (Salt Lake City), interview by Jesse S. Bushman, October 12, 1994, tape and transcription in James B. Allen papers, L. Tom Perry Special Collections, Harold B. Lee Library, Brigham Young University; See also Paul A. Mogren, *Zion Lutheran Church, Salt Lake City, Utah: A Centennial History, 1882-1982* (Salt Lake City: Zion Lutheran Church, 1982).
35. Ibid.
36. The most definitive study of the Greek community in Utah is Helen Papanikolas, *Toil and Rage in a New Land: The Greek Immigrants in Utah*, 2nd ed. rev. (Salt Lake City: Utah State Historical Society, 1974). Most of the information for this section has been taken from Constantine Skedros, "History of the Greek Orthodox Community of Greater Salt Lake City," a short, unpublished history written for the members of Holy Trinity Greek Orthodox Cathedral, available from Holy Trinity Greek Orthodox Cathedral, copy in James B. Allen papers, L. Tom Perry Special Collections, Harold B. Lee Library, Brigham Young University. Mr. Skedros is the congregational historian of Holy Trinity Greek Orthodox Cathedral. These two sources were supplemented and updated by Constantine Skedros (Salt Lake City), interview by Jesse S. Bushman, October 21, 1994, tape in James B. Allen papers, L. Tom Perry Special Collections, Harold B. Lee Library, Brigham Young University.
37. Father Basil Hartung of Saints Peter and Paul Antiochian Diocese (Salt Lake City), telephone interview with Jesse S. Bushman, January 20, 1995, notes in James B. Allen papers, L. Tom Perry Special Collections, Harold B. Lee Library, Brigham Young University.
38. There are no accurate population figures available. The above is based on Father Dean Panagos (Holy Trinity Greek Orthodox Church, Salt Lake City), telephone interview by Jesse S. Bushman, January 13, 1995; Sandy Senson (member of the board and treasurer of Assumption of the Blessed Virgin Mary Greek Orthodox Church, Price, Ut, telephone interview by Jesse S. Bushman, January 20, 1995; Father Basil Hartung interview; notes in James B. Allen papers, L. Tom Perry Special Collections, Harold B. Lee Library, Brigham Young University. Father Panagos estimated that there were between five and seven thousand members in the Salt Lake Valley. The other interviewees estimated very small numbers for their groups. It appears, therefore, that seven thousand might be a reasonable estimate for the state as a whole.
39. *Presbytery of Utah Directory, September 1994* (Salt Lake City: Presbytery of Utah, 1994).
40. H. Jeffrey Silliman, "The Presbyterian Church in Utah," in *Utah History Encyclopedia*, ed. Powell, 442-43.
41. Joe Costanzo, "Shared Ministry of Utah Closes after 25 Years," *Deseret News*, November 18, 1996, B4.
42. Reverend Donald Baird (Salt Lake City), interview by Jesse S. Bushman, November 7, 1994, tape in James B. Allen papers, L. Tom Perry Special Collections, Harold B. Lee Library, Brigham Young University.
43. Ibid.; Rev. Howard Jeffrey Silliman (Salt Lake City), interview by Jesse S. Bushman, November 2, 1994, tape in James B. Allen papers, L. Tom Perry Special Collections, Harold B. Lee Library, Brigham Young University.

44. Walton A. Roth, *A Century of Service in Utah, 1869-1969* (Salt Lake City: Presbytery of Utah, 1969), 19.
45. Pastor Noel Ravan (Salt Lake City), interview by Jesse S. Bushman, October, 19, 1994, tape in James B. Allen papers, L. Tom Perry Special Collections, Harold B. Lee Library, Brigham Young University.
46. Pastor Robert J. Smith (Provo, Ut, telephone interview by Jesse S. Bushman, December 15, 1994, notes in James B. Allen papers, L. Tom Perry Special Collections, Harold B. Lee Library, Brigham Young University.
47. Karen Miller (Provo, Ut, telephone interview by Jesse S. Bushman, December 16, 1994, notes in James B. Allen papers, L. Tom Perry Special Collections, Harold B. Lee Library, Brigham Young University.
48. Charles Hidenshield, "Rock Canyon Assembly of God," in *Protestant and Catholic Churches of Provo*, ed. Walden, 147.
49. Williamson, ed., *Encyclopedia of Religions in the United States*, 160–62.
50. Pastor Steve Mullen (Salt Lake City), telephone interview by Jesse S. Bushman, January 3, 1995, notes in James B. Allen papers, L. Tom Perry Special Collections, Harold B. Lee Library, Brigham Young University.
51. Melton, *Encyclopedia of American Religions*, 439–40.
52. Pastor Lee Todd (Ogden, Ut, telephone interview by Jesse S. Bushman, January 6, 1995, notes in James B. Allen papers, L. Tom Perry Special Collections, Harold B. Lee Library, Brigham Young University.
53. Melton, *Encyclopedia of American Religions*, 403–4, 406–7.
54. Bradley et al., eds., *Churches and Church Membership*, 392–94.
55. Melton, *Encyclopedia of American Religions*, 378–79.
56. Pastor Brian Deacon (Salt Lake City), telephone interview by Jesse S. Bushman, December 30, 1994, notes in James B. Allen papers, L. Tom Perry Special Collections, Harold B. Lee Library, Brigham Young University.
57. Melton, *Encyclopedia of American Religions*, 374–75.
58. Reverend Thomas Constance (Salt Lake City), by Jesse S. Bushman, January 3, 1995; Pastor Steve Meltzer (Salt Lake City), telephone interview by Jesse S. Bushman, January 3, 1995; notes in James B. Allen papers, L. Tom Perry Special Collections, Harold B. Lee Library, Brigham Young University.
59. The following information was gleaned from *The First Century of the Methodist Church in Utah* (Salt Lake City: Utah Methodism Centennial Committee, 1970); Bradley et al., eds, *Churches and Church Membership*, 392–94; Connie Fife, "Methodists," in *Utah History Encyclopedia*, ed. Powell, 361–63; "A History From the Past Will Come the Future," on the website of the First United Methodist Church of Ogden, at www.fumcogdenut.org/history.htm (accessed January 9, 2015).
60. Beverly Devoy, "S. Korean to Develop Ministry in Weber,"*Deseret News*, September 14, 1991, B4.
61. *The Episcopal Church Annual, 1994* (Ridgefield, Connecticut: Morehouse Publishing, 1994), 302. For a brief commentary on the administration of the various Episcopal bishops in Utah, see A. J. Simmonds, "The Eight Bishops of Utah," a series of historical vignettes presented to the 81st Convention of the church in the Diocese of Utah, June 20–22, 1986, available in Special Collections, Merrill-Cazier Library, Utah State University. See also James W. Beless, Jr., "The Episcopal Church in Utah: Seven Bishops and One Hundred Years," *Utah Historical Quarterly* 36 (Winter 1968): 76–96.

62. *A Rational and Thoughtful Alternative: The Episcopal Church in Utah* (Salt Lake City: The Episcopal Diocese of Utah, 1984).
63. A brief overview of the history of St. Mark's is in a pamphlet prepared by the Board of St. Mark's Hospital, 1973; available in the archives of the Episcopal Diocese of Utah, Salt Lake City, Utah.
64. "Church Diocese to Donate $600,000 to Homeless Shelter," *Salt Lake Tribune*, March 26, 1988, B1; "Agencies to Aid Homeless and Poverty-Stricken Get 32% of Episcopal Grants," *Deseret News*, October 28, 1989, E2; Katherine L. Miller (archives of the Episcopal Diocese of Salt Lake City), telephone interview by Jesse S. Bushman, November 2, 1994, notes in James B. Allen papers, L. Tom Perry Special Collections, Harold B. Lee Library, Brigham Young University.
65. Thelma Ellis, *Church of the Good Shepherd, Ogden, Utah* (Ogden, UT: The Church of the Good Shepherd, 1993), 46-47.
66. *Through the Eyes of Many Faiths*, 2nd ed. (Salt Lake City: The Utah Heritage Foundation, 1990), 33.
67. Karl Coates, "Ministry Lends a Hand to Dispossessed Indians," *Deseret News*, February 6, 1993, A8.
68. For general information on Jehovah's Witnesses, see William B. Williamson, *Encyclopedia of Religions in the United States*, 174-76; David M. Walden, "Jehovah's Witnesses," in *Protestant and Catholic Churches in Provo*, ed. Walden, 117-31. Other information on Jehovah's Witnessers in Utah was obtained from Francis Swingle (Sandy, UT), telephone interview by Jesse S. Bushman, January 28, 1995, notes in James B. Allen papers, L. Tom Perry Special Collections, Harold B. Lee Library, Brigham Young University; Takeshi Mori (Salt Lake City), telephone interview by Jesse S. Bushman, January 28, 1995, notes in James B. Allen papers, L. Tom Perry Special Collections, Harold B. Lee Library, Brigham Young University; Al Williams (Ogden, UT), telephone interview by Jesse S. Bushman, January 28, 1995, notes in James B. Allen papers, L. Tom Perry Special Collections, Harold B. Lee Library, Brigham Young University; Noel F. Capson (a local elder and overseer of Jehovah's Witnesses in Salt Lake City), telephone interview by James B. Allen, January 27, 1995, notes in James B. Allen papers, L. Tom Perry Special Collections, Harold B. Lee Library, Brigham Young University. Mr. Capson listed congregations in the following communities: Kanab, Moab, Cedar City, Hurricane, Beaver, Richfield, Delta, Roosevelt, Vernal, Sandy, Midvale, Holladay, West Jordan, Kearns, West Valley, Magna, Tooele, Sugar House, Mill Creek, downtown Salt Lake City (two congregations, one of which was Spanish-speaking), Spanish Fork (two congregations, one of which was Spanish-speaking), Provo, American Fork, Ogden (four congregations, including one Spanish-speaking), Brigham City, Logan.
69. See Robert A. Goldberg, "The Jewish Community in Utah," (unpublished paper written for a local newsletter, 1994), 9, copy in James B. Allen papers, L. Tom Perry Special Collections, Harold B. Lee Library, Brigham Young University. Mr. Goldberg is a professor of history at the University of Utah. Rudolf Glanz, *Jew and Mormon: Historic Group Relations and Religious Outlook* (New York: Walden Press, 1963), deals extensively with the relation between the two groups, showing how it arose, and what effect it has had on Mormon-Jewish interaction and Jewish life in Utah.
70. Dyan Zaslowsky, "Letter from Salt Lake City: Who, or What, Is a Gentile?" *Hadassah Magazine* (November 1982): 12.

71. A Jewish professor at Utah State University made a telling comment about the cultural but unconscious anti-Semitism that some Utahns have. "I was told before I moved to Utah that I would encounter something called 'philo-Semitism' (as opposed to anti-Semitism). Given a choice, there is no doubt which I would prefer! Nonetheless, there is always the danger of exoticizing and stereotyping members of others groups....

    "Moreover, anti-Semitism does exist in Utah, and it is especially painful for children. I am grateful that anti-Semitism is not LDS policy. In fact, just the opposite is true. But anti-Semitism remains at an unconscious level, carried forward by language, probably the unfortunate inheritance of European and Euro-American converts and their descendants. Quite recently a student of mine told me that someone could have 'jewed him out' of something. We all know what that means, but we rarely examine its insidiousness. The student and I were alone in my office, and so it was easy for me to make him aware of what he had said. He was embarrassed and hadn't ever realized the stereotyped prejudice that lay behind that expression." Steve Siporin, "A Jew Among Mormons," *Dialogue: A Journal of Mormon Thought* 24 (Winter 1991): 115.

72. Ibid., 121.
73. Bradley, et al., eds., *Churches and Church Membership*, 392–94.
74. *History of the First Congregational Church, Salt Lake City, Utah* (n.p.: n.d.), 31. Available in L. Tome Perry Special Collections, Harold B. Lee Library, Brigham Young University.
75. Horace McMullen to Jesse S. Bushman, June 2, 1995. Copy in James B. Allen papers, L. Tom Perry Special Collections, Harold B. Lee Library, Brigham Young University.
76. Reverend Michael G. Jackson (Salt Lake City), interview by Jesse S. Bushman, October 14, 1994, tape in James B. Allen papers, L. Tom Perry Special Collections, Harold B. Lee Library, Brigham Young University.
77. Bradley et al., eds., *Churches and Church Membership*, 392–94.
78. William A. MacCarty, "Statistical History of the Wasatch Hills Church to 1976," copy in James B. Allen papers, L. Tom Perry Special Collections, Harold B. Lee Library, Brigham Young University. This unpublished paper is an extract of a graduate research paper entitled "Installing Lay Ministry: A Retrospective Analysis," by the same author, who served as pastor for both the Provo and Wasatch Adventist congregations. See also "History of the SLC Central DSA Church," on the website of the Salt Lake City Central Seventh Day Adventist Church at www.centralsda.com. Accessed January 9, 2015.
79. Francis Barron (principal Adventist school, Provo, UT), telephone interview by Jesse S. Bushman, December 20, 1994; John Rowe (principal of Adventist school in Monument Valley, UT), telephone interview by Jesse S. Bushman, December 20, 1994; Dean Ruddle (principal of Adventist school in Ogden, UT), telephone interview by Jesse S. Bushman, December, 20, 1994; notes in James B. Allen papers, L. Tom Perry Special Collections, Harold B. Lee Library, Brigham Young University. Dean Ruddle served as principal for the Salt Lake Junior Academy before transferring to Ogden in 1994.
80. Clark Caras, "Hobble Creek Camp Helps Blind Learn, Have Fun," *Daily Herald* (Provo, UT), July 13, 1983, 4.
81. "Adventists to Hear of Navajo Mission Project," *Daily Herald*, July 25, 1967, 2.

82. Floyd D. Glissmeyer, "A Historical Study of the Religious Education Program of the Seventh-day Adventist Church in Utah" (master's thesis, Brigham Young University, 1970), 31–32.
83. Dean Ruddle, telephone interview.
84. Information on the Buddhists comes mainly from Masami Hayashi, George Tohinaka, and Mrs. Ritsuko Hayashi, "Salt Lake Buddhist Church, Salt Lake City, Utah," in *Buddhist Churches of America Vol I: 75 Year History 1899-1974* (Chicago: Nobart, Inc., 1974), 242-49.
85. Reverend Jerry K. Hirano, "Birth and Death, Changes Are Going to Come, *Buddhist Thoughts* (newsletter of the Salt Lake City Buddhist temple), April–May, 1994.
86. Reverend Jerry K. Hirano, interview by Jesse S. Bushman, Salt Lake City, October 19, 1994, tape in James B. Allen papers, L. Tom Perry Special Collections, Harold B. Lee Library, Brigham Young University.
87. Phramaha Somjit (priest of Thai Buddhist Temple in Logan, UT), telephone interview by Jesse S. Bushman, January 20, 1995, notes in James B. Allen papers, L. Tom Perry Special Collections, Harold B. Lee Library, Brigham Young University.; Rev. Jerry K. Hirano, interview. Somjit estimated about five hundred members in Logan, while Hirano estimated 220 active members with some two hundred families in Salt Lake City. Estimates for other areas were not available; the above is the author's best approximation.
88. Unless otherwise noted, information for this section comes from Arnold Brown (Provo, UT), interview by Jesse S. Bushman, January, 7, 1995, tape in James B. Allen papers, L. Tom Perry Special Collections, Harold B. Lee Library, Brigham Young University.
89. Williamson, ed., *Encyclopedia of Religions in the United States*, 141–43. See also David M. Walden, "The Evangelical Free Church," in *Protestant and Catholic Churches of Provo*, ed. Walden, 150–59. For the current statement of faith (adopted 2008) see "EFCA Statement of Faith" at http://go.efca.org/resources/document/efca-statement-faith. Accessed January 9, 2015.
90. Walden, "The Evangelical Free Church," 157.
91. Patty Horton (Salt Lake City), telephone interview by Jesse S. Bushman, January 10, 1995, notes in James B. Allen papers, L. Tom Perry Special Collections, Harold B. Lee Library, Brigham Young University.
92. Ann Carpenter (Salt Lake City), telephone interview by Jesse S. Bushman, December 29, 1994, notes in James B. Allen papers, L. Tom Perry Special Collections, Harold B. Lee Library, Brigham Young University; Arnold Brown (Salt Lake City), telephone interview by Jesse S. Bushman, January 10, 1995, notes in James B. Allen papers, L. Tom Perry Special Collections, Harold B. Lee Library, Brigham Young University. It is recognized that this estimate seems high when compared with the 1990 figure of six hundred reported by the Glenmary Research Center and used in Table 1. This is simply another illustration of the difficulty of acquiring accurate figures. The general impression is that Glenmary tends to be conservative while denominational representatives tend to be optimistic in their estimates.
93. See Stan Larson and Lorille Horne Miller, *Unitarianism in Utah: A Gentile Religion in Salt Lake City, 1891–1991* (Salt Lake City: Freethinker Press, 1991).
94. Lucille Miller, "The Unitarian Association of Churches in Utah," in *Utah History Encyclopedia*, ed. Powell, 574–75.
95. Pastor Steve Sandlin (Salt Lake City), telephone interview by Jesse S. Bushman, January 6, 1995; Pastor Steve Dobbins (Ogden, UT), telephone interview by Jesse

S. Bushman, January 3, 1995; notes in James B. Allen papers, L. Tom Perry Special Collections, Harold B. Lee Library, Brigham Young University.

96. Reverend Dave Barnes (Granger, UT, telephone interview by Jesse S. Bushman, January 3, 1995, notes in James B. Allen papers, L. Tom Perry Special Collections, Harold B. Lee Library, Brigham Young University.
97. Bradley et al., eds. *Churches and Church Membership*, 392–94.
98. Williamson, *Encyclopedia of Religions in the United States*, 76–79.
99. Williamson, *Encyclopedia of Religions in the United States*, 274–80.
100. Pastor David Crump (Ogden, UT, telephone interview by Jesse S. Bushman, January 10, 1995; Pastor Gary Ofland (Salt Lake City), telephone interview by Jesse S. Bushman, January 10, 1995; notes in James B. Allen papers, L. Tom Perry Special Collections, Harold B. Lee Library, Brigham Young University.
101. See Roger D. Launius, "The Reorganized Church of Jesus Christ of Latter Day Saints," in *Utah History Encyclopedia*, ed. Powell, 459–61; David M. Walden, "The Reorganized Church of Jesus Christ of Latter Day Saints," in *Protestant and Catholic Churches of Provo*, ed. Walden, 1–17. Membership estimate from RLDS stake president Sidney Troyer, telephone interview by Jesse S. Bushman, January 23, 1995, notes in James B. Allen papers, L. Tom Perry Special Collections, Harold B. Lee Library, Brigham Young University.
102. Sidney Troyer, interview.
103. *Utah County Journal* (Provo, UT), September 15, 1991.
104. *Through the Eyes of Many Faiths*, 71.
105. There is no printed history of Quakers in Utah. Information for this short sketch was taken almost entirely from Kate MacLeod (Salt Lake City), interview by Jesse S. Bushman, November 2, 1994, tape in James B. Allen papers, L. Tom Perry Special Collections, Harold B. Lee Library, Brigham Young University.
106. Melton, *Encyclopedia of American Religions*, 385–86.
107. Major Dell Brockleman (Salt Lake City), telephone interview by Jesse S. Bushman, January 6, 1995, notes in James B. Allen papers, L. Tom Perry Special Collections, Harold B. Lee Library, Brigham Young University.
108. Melton, *Encyclopedia of American Religions*, 231–32.
109. Bradley et al., eds., *Churches and Church Membership*, 392–94.
110. Melton, *Encyclopedia of American Religions*, 500.
111. Bradley et. al., eds., *Churches and Church Membership*, 392–94.
112. Caru Das and Vaibhavi Dasi (Spanish Fork, UT, interview by Jesse S. Bushman, May 4, 1995, notes in James B. Allen papers, L. Tom Perry Special Collections, Harold B. Lee Library, Brigham Young University.
113. John VeDevilbiss, "Hare Krishna," *Ogden Standard Examiner*, September 17, 1988.
114. Ed Carter, "Local Hare Krishna Concert Attracts Hundreds," *Daily Herald* (Provo, UT), May 13, 1995 A7; Michael Rosen, "Krishnas in Zion," videocassette, produced by KUTV Channel 2 News, 1995.
115. Genelle Larsen, "68 Shared Ministry Congregations Will Meet," *Deseret News*, May 19, 1990. B8.
116. These interviews, by Jesse S. Bushman, include all those cited in this chapter as well as a few not cited.
117. Paul Swenson, "Operation Good Samaritan," *Deseret News*, June 11, 1970, B1.
118. Jeff Vice, "Group Unifies Religious Leaders," *Deseret News*, May 8, 1993, A12.

119. Gina Howard, "Methods Differ in Evangelizing," *Deseret News*, November 21, 1992, B5.
120. Reverend Mark G. Bellow, interview.
121. David Briggs, "Various Religious Leaders Call on US to Stop the Slaughter," *Deseret News*, May 15, 1993, A2; "Clerics Back Abortion Law," ibid., April 4, 1992, B1; Scott Iwasaki, "Members of Varied Religions Call for a Consistent Life Ethic," ibid., July 17, 1993, B8.
122. Douglas D. Palmer, "Volunteers Use Christian Fellowship to Change Inmate Lives," *Deseret News*, November 11, 1989, D5.
123. Douglas D. Palmer, "Dignity in Work Program Offers Temporary Jobs for Individuals in Crisis," *Deseret News*, May 12, 1990, D5.
124. Ganelle Pugmire, "Combined Utah Churches Form Aids Coalition," *Deseret News*, August 1, 1992, A8
125. "Services Target AIDS," *Deseret News*, October 17, 1992, A10.
126. Mary Finch, "Members of Area Churches Leap into Flood Breach," *Deseret News* June 11, 1983, A12.
127. Patricia McCoy, "3 Congregations Join in Church Program," *Salt Lake Tribune*, November 14, 1970, 8.
128. "Central Salt Lake Council of Churches Conducts First Public Meeting," *Salt Lake Tribune*, October 19, 1985. B3.
129. Lezlee Whiting, "Uintah Basin Hosts Annual Convention of Episcopal Diocese," *Deseret News*, May 29, 1993, A12.

BIBLIOGRAPHY

The number of books devoted specifically to aspects of Utah history in the last half of the twentieth century are minimal but there are numerous articles that focus on events of this period. I have also used contemporary newspaper accounts as well as reports by various government and private agencies. The newspaper and magazine articles cited in the text ar not listed separately below, but these publications include *The Salt Lake Tribune, Deseret News, Daily Herald* (Provo, UT), *New York Times, Washington Star, Time, Business Week, US News and World Report, Saturday Evening Post, Portsmouth Time* (Portsmouth, OH), *The Daily Times* (New Philadelphia, OH), *Daily Universe* (Brigham Young University), *High Country News, AAU News; Episcopal Church Annual,* and *Utah Folklife Bulletin*. In addition, numerous helpful reports and articles, not listed separately here but cited in the notes, are found in the *Utah Economic and Business Review*, the *Research Briefs* and other bulletins and reports of the Utah Foundation, in *Utah's Health: An Annual Review* (published by University of Utah's FHP Center for Health Care Studies); in *Repertoire* and *Community View* (published by the Utah Arts Council); *Annual Report* of the Utah Arts Council; annual reports (variously titled) of the State Superintendent of Public Instruction; *Centennial Spirit* (official publication of the Utah Statehood Centennial Commission); *Deseret News Church Almanac*; and *Utah County Journal*.

A few edited works are devoted exclusively to Utah history and include chapters or articles on the period covered here. Specific chapters or articles in these works are cited in the chapter notes but not listed separately here. These books include Richard D. Poll, et. al, *Utah's History*; Helen Z. Papanikolas, ed. *The Peoples of Utah*; *Utah History Encyclopedia*, ed. Allen Kent Powell; and *Utah State of the Arts*.

Other sources used include a few miscellaneous letters and unpublished notes, as indicated in the chapter endnotes. In addition, the internet is of great value, and several items not otherwise readily available, including a handful of items from non-Utah newspapers, are cited in the chapters of the book but not listed below. In addition, some items are listed in the notes as further references to a topic but since they were not actually used in preparing this publication they are not listed here.

Books and Monographs Cited

1969 Statistical Abstract of Utah. Salt Lake City: Bureau of Business and Economic Research, University of Utah, 1969.

A Rational and Thoughtful Alternative: The Episcopal Church in Utah. Salt Lake City: The Episcopal Diocese of Utah, 1984.

Abrams, Douglas M. *Conflict, Competition, or Cooperation? Dilemmas of State Education Policymaking*. New York: State University of New York Press, 1993.

Alexander, Thomas G., and James B. Allen. *Mormons and Gentiles: A History of Salt Lake City*. Denver: Pruett Publishing Company, 1984.

Alexander, Thomas G. : *The Official Centennial History*. Salt Lake City: Gibbs Smith Publisher, 1995.

Allen, James B., and Glen M. Leonard. *The Story of the Latter-Day Saints*. 2nd ed., rev. and enl., Salt Lake City: Deseret Book Company, 1992.

Allen, James B., Jessie L. Embry, and Kahlile B. Mehr. *Hearts Turned to the Fathers: A History of the Genealogical Society of Utah, 1894–1994*. Provo, UT: BYU Studies, 1995.

Altman, Irwin, and Joseph Giant. *Polygamous Families in Contemporary Society*. New York: Cambridge University Press, 1996.

Anderson, Loren R. *The Utah Landslides, Debris Flows, and Floods of May and June 1983*. Springfield, VA: National Technical Information Service, 1984.

Anderson, Scott. *The 4 O'Clock Murders: A True Story of a Mormon Family's Vengeance*. New York: Doubleday, 1993.

Arrington, Leonard J. Arrington. *The Hotel: Salt Lake's Classy Lady, the Hotel Utah, 1911–1986*. Salt Lake City: Westin Hotel Utah, 1986.

Arrington, Leonard J., and George Jensen. *The Defense Industry of Utah*. Logan, UT: Department of Economics, Utah State University, 1965.

Arrington, Leonard J. *: A History of the Governors' Mansion*. Salt Lake City: Governor's Mansion Foundation, 1987.

Arrington, Leonard J. *Beet Sugar in the West: A History of the Utah-Idaho Sugar Company, 1891–1966*. Seattle: University of Washington Press, 1966.

Arrington, Leonard J. *Price of Prejudice: The Japanese-American Relocation Center in Utah During World War II*. Logan, UT: The Faculty Association, Utah State University, 1962.

Bateman, Ronald R. *Deep Creek Reflections: 125 Years at Ibapah, Utah, 1959–1984*. Salt Lake City: R. R. Bateman, 1984.

Benson, Ezra Taft. *Cross Fire: The Eight Years with Eisenhower*. Garden City, NY: Doubleday, 1962.

Bergman, Ray L. *The Children Sing: The Life and Music of Evan Stephens and the Mormon Tabernacle Choir*. Salt Lake City: Northwest Publishing Inc..1992.

Berrett, William E. *A Miracle in Weekday Religious Education: A History of the Church Educational System*. Salt Lake City: privately published, 1988.

Berry, Mary Francis. *Why ERA Failed: Politics, Women's Rights, and the Amending Process of the Constitution*. Bloomington: Indiana University Press, 1986.

Bradley, Martin B., Norman M. Green, Jr., Dale E. Jones, Mac Lynn, and Lou McNeil, eds. and comps. *Churches and Church Membership in the United States, 1990: An Enumeration by Region, State, and County, Based on Data Reported for 133 Church Groupings*. Atlanta: Glenmary Research Center, 1992.

Bradley, Ben, Jr., and Dale Van Atta. *Prophet of Blood: The Untold Story of Ervil LeBaron and the Lambs of God*. New York, G. P. Putnam's Sons, 1981.

Building a Better Utah: The Bangerter Administration 1985–1992. Salt Lake City: Office of the Governor?, 1992?

Bushnell, Eleanor, ed. *Impact of Reapportionment on the Thirteen Western States*. Salt Lake City: University of Utah Press, 1970.

Calman, Charles Jeffrey. *The Mormon Tabernacle Choir*. New York: Harper & Row.1979.

Calvary Missionary Baptist Church, 1899–1976. Salt Lake City: privately published by Calvary Baptist Church, 1976.

Carter, Thomas, and Peter L. Goss. *Utah Historical Architecture.1847-1940*. Salt Lake City: University of Utah Press.1988.

Cawley, R. McGreggor. *Federal Land, Western Anger: The Sagebrush Rebellion and Environmental Politics*. Lawrence: University Press of Kansas, 1993.

Christensen, Edward L. *Snow College Historical Highlights: The First 100 Years*. Ephraim, UT: Snow College, 1988.

Clopton, Beverly B. *Her Honor, the Judge: The Story of Reva Beck Bosone.* Ames, IA: The Iowa State University Press, 1980.

Conetah, Fred A. *A History of the Northern Ute People.* Salt Lake City: Uintah-Ouray Ute Tribe, 1982.

Cornwall, J. Spencer. *A Century of Singing: The Salt Lake Mormon Tabernacle Choir.* Salt Lake City: Deseret Book.1958.

Cracroft, Richard H., and Neal E. Lambert, eds..*A Believing People: Literature of the Latter-day Saints.* Provo. UT: Brigham Young University Press.1974.

Much, Forrest S. ed. *A History of Utah's American Indians.* Salt Lake City: Utah State Division of Indian Affairs and Utah State Historical Society, 2003.

d'Asevedo, Warren L. *Great Basin.* Vol. 11, *Handbook of North American Indians*, ed. William C. Sturtevant. Washington, D.C.: Smithsonian Institution, 1986.

Davies, James A. *Leslie Norris.* Cardiff: University of Wales Press, 1991.

Davis, France Davis. *France Davis: An American Story Told.* Salt Lake City, University of Utah Press, 2006.

Delaney, Robert W. *The Ute Mountain Utes.* Albuquerque: University of New Mexico Press, 1989.

Durham, Lowell M. *Abravanel!* Salt Lake City: University of Utah Press.1989.

Economic Impact of Arts and Cultural Institutions: Case Studies in Columbus, Minneapolis, St. Paul, St. Louis, Salt Lake City, San Antonio, Springfield. Washington. D.C.:National Endowment for the Arts.1981.

Ellis, Thelma. *Church of the Good Shepherd, Ogden, Utah.* Ogden, UT: The Church of the Good Shepherd, 1993. 46-47.

England, Eugene, and Peter Makuck, eds. *An Open World: Essays on Leslie Norris.* Columbia, SC: Camden House.1994.

Eubank, Mark. *Mark Eubank's Utah Weather.* Bountiful, UT: Horizon Publishers, 1979.

Fairbanks, Eugene F..*A Sculptor's Testimony in Bronze and Stone: The Sacred Sculpture of Avard T. Fairbanks.* Salt Lake City: Publishers Press.1972.

Farmer, Jared. *Glen Canyon Damned: Inventing Lake Powell and the Canyon Country.* Tucson: University of Arizona Press, 1999.

Fleisher, David. *Death of An American: The Killing of John Singer.* New York: Continuum, 1983.

Fleming, William. *Arts and Ideas.* 6th ed.. New York: Holt. Rinehart and Winston.1980.

Fox, Renée C. *Spare Parts: Organ Replacement in American Society.* New York: Oxford University Press, 1992.

Fradkin, Philip L. *Fallout: An American Nuclear Tragedy.* Tucson: University of Arizona Press, 1989.

Fuller, John G. *The Day We Bombed Utah: America's Most Lethal Secret.* New York: New American Library, 1984.

Gallagher, Carole. *American Ground Zero: The Secret Nuclear War.* Cambridge, MA: MIT Press, 1993.

Gerlach, Larry R. *Blazing Crosses in Zion.* Logan, UT: Utah State University Press, 1981.

Glanz, Rudolf. *Jew and Mormon: Historic Group Relations and Religious Outlook.* New York: Walden Press, 1963.

Glass, Matthew. *Citizens Against the MX: Public Languages in the Nuclear Age.* Urbana: University of Illinois Press, 1993.

Gordon, Melton, J. *Encyclopedia of American Religions.* 4th ed. Detroit: Gale Research Inc., 1993.

Gottlieb, Robert, and Peter Wiley. *America's Saints: The Rise of Mormon Power.* New York: G. P. Putnam's Sons, 1984.

Greer, Deon C. et al. *Atlas of Utah.* Ogden, UT, and Provo, UT: Weber State College and BYU Press, 1981.

Hafey, Mark et al. *Historic Preservation: The South Temple Historic District.* Salt Lake City: published by the authors.1975.

Hagata, Ted, ed. *Japanese Americans in Utah.* Salt Lake City: JA Centennial Committee, 1966.

Hamilton, C. Mark *Nineteenth-Century Mormon Architecture and City Planning.* New York: Oxford University Press.1995.

Harlan, Judith. *American Indians Today: Issues and Conflicts.* New York: Franklin Watts, 1987.

Harrison, Conrad B. *Five Thousand Concerts: A Commemorative History of the Utah Symphony.* Salt Lake City: Utah Symphony Society, 1986.

Harvey, Mark W. T. *A Symbol of Wilderness: Echo Park and the American Conservation Movement.* Albuquerque: University of New Mexico Press, 1994.

Haseltine, James L. *One Hundred Years of Utah Painting.* Salt Lake City: Salt Lake City Art Center, 1965.

Hicks, Michael. *Mormonism and Music: A History.* Urbana: University of Illinois Press.1989).

History of the First Congregational Church. Salt Lake City, Utah. n.p.: n.d. Copy in L. Tom Perry Special Collections, Harold B. Lee Library, Brigham Young University.

Hodson, Paul W. *Crisis on Campus: The Exciting Years of Campus Development at the University of Utah.* Salt Lake City: Keeban Corporation, 1987.

Holt, Ronald L. *Beneath These Red Cliffs: An Ethnohistory of the Utah Paiutes.* Albuquerque: University of New Mexico Press, 1992.

Hughes, Trevor C. *Utah's 1977 Drought.* Logan, UT: Water Research Laboratory, College of Engineering, Utah State University, 1978.

Hughes, Raymond, and William Lancelot, *Education: America's Magic.* Ames, IA: Iowa State College Press, 1946.

Hunsaker, Kenneth B. "Mormon Novels." In *A Literary History of the American West.* ed. Thomas J. Lyon et. al. Ft. Worth: Texas Christian University Press.1987).849-61.

Iber, Jorge. *Hispanics in the Mormon Zion 1912–1999.* College Station: Texas A&M University Press, 2000.

Iverson, Peter. *The Navajo Nation*. Westport, CN: Greenwood Press, 1981.
Jensen, George, and Leonard J. Arrington. *Impact of Defense Spending on the Economy of Utah*. Logan, UT: Department of Economics, Utah State University 1967.
Jepperson, Ronald. *The Kaiparowits Coal Project and the Environment: A Case Study*. Ann Arbor: Ann Arbor Science Publishers, 1981.
Jonas, Frank H. *The Story of a Political Hoax*. Salt Lake City: Research Monograph No. 8, Institute of Government, University of Utah, 1966.
Jonas, Frank H., ed. *Politics in the American West*. Salt Lake City: University of Utah Press, 1969.
Jonas, Frank H. ed. *Political Dynamiting*. Salt Lake City: University of Utah Press, 1970.
Kinkead, Joyce, ed. *Literary Utah: A Bibliographic Guide*. Salt Lake City: Utah Council of Teachers of English, 1990.
Knack, Martha C. *Life Is with People: Household Organization of the Contemporary Southern Paiute Indians*. Socorro, NM: Ballena Press, 1980.
Knowlton, Ezra Clark. *History of Highway Development in Utah*. Salt Lake City: Utah State Department of Highways, 1967.
Kosmin, Barry A., and Seymour P. Lachman. *One Nation Under God: Religion in Contemporary American Society*. New York: Harmony Books, 1993.
Larson, Stan, and Lorille Horne Miller. *Unitarianism in Utah: A Gentile Religion in Salt Lake City, 1891–1991*. Salt Lake City: Freethinker Press, 1991.
League of Women Voters in Utah. *Reapportionment in Utah: Political Game or Fair Representation?* Salt Lake City: League of Women Voters of Utah, 1980.
Lee, Rex E. *A Lawyer Looks at the Equal Rights Amendment*. Provo, UT: Brigham Young University Press, 1980.
Leonard, Glen M. *A History of Davis County*. Salt Lake City: Utah State Historical Society, 1999.
Lester, Margaret D. *Brigham Street*. Salt Lake City: Utah State Historical Society.1979.
Lock, Raymond Friday. *The Book of the Navajo*. Los Angeles: Mankind Publishing Company, 1989,
Luger, Michael I., and Harvey A. Goldstein. *Technology in the Garden: Research Parks and Regional Economic Development*. Chapel Hill: University of North Carolina Press, 1991.
Lythgoe, Dennis L. *Let 'Em Holler: A Political Biography of J. Bracken Lee*. Salt Lake City: Utah State Historical Society, 1982.
Martin, Mrs. A. F. *Ten Years of Devotion and Sacrifice of the First Baptist Church of Bountiful, Utah*. Bountiful, UT: First Baptist Church of Bountiful, 1967.
Matheson, Scott M., with James Edwin Kee, *Out of Balance* (Salt Lake City: Gibbs M. Smith, Inc., Peregrine Smith Books, 1986.

Mayer, Vincente V., *Utah: A Hispanic History.* Salt Lake City: American West Center, University of Utah, 1975.

McCormick, John S. *Historic Buildings of Downtown Salt Lake City.* Salt Lake City: Utah State Historical Society.1982.

McPherson, Robert S. *Sacred Land, Sacred View: Navajo Perceptions of the Four Corners Region.* Provo, UT: Charles Redd Center for Western Studies, Brigham Young University, 1992.

McWilliams, Carey. *North from Mexico: The Spanish-Speaking People of the United States.* New York: Greenwood Press, 1990.

Merrill, Milton R. "The 1954 Elections in the Eleven Western States." *Western Political Quarterly* 7 (December 1954): 588–635.

Mooney, Bernice Maher. *Salt of the Earth: The History of the Catholic Church in Utah, 1776–1987.* Salt Lake City: Catholic Diocese of Salt Lake City, 1992.

Mooney, Bernice Maher. *The Story of the Cathedral of the Madeleine.* Salt Lake City: Litho Graphics, 1981.

Morgan, Paul A. *Zion Lutheran Church, Salt Lake City, Utah: A Centennial History, 1882–1982.* Salt Lake City: Zion Lutheran Church, 1982.

Museum of Church History and Art. *Rich in Story. Great in Faith: The Art of Minerva Kohlhepp Teichert.* Salt Lake City: The Church of Jesus Christ of Latter-day Saints.1988.

Nelson, Elroy. *Utah's Economic Patterns.* Salt Lake City: University of Utah Press, 1956.

Nelson, Jay L. *The First Thirty Years: A History of Utah Technical College.* Salt Lake City: Utah Technical College at Salt Lake, 1982.

Nelson, Elroy, and Osmond S. Harline. *Utah's Changing Economic Patterns 1964.* Salt Lake City: University of Utah Press, 1964.

Oliver, David H. *A Negro on Mormonism.* Salt Lake City: published by the author, 1963.

Olpin, Robert S., William C. Seifrit, and Vern G. Swanson. *Artists of Utah.* Salt Lake City: Gibbs Smith, 1999.

Owen, Barbara. *The Mormon Tabernacle Organ: An American Classic.* Salt Lake City: The Church of Jesus Christ of Latter-day Saints.1990.

Papanikolas, Helen Z., ed. *The Peoples of Utah.* Salt Lake City: Utah State Historical Society, 1976.

Papanikolas, Helen. *Toil and Rage in a New Land: The Greek Immigrants in Utah.* 2nd ed. rev., Salt Lake City: Utah State Historical Society, 1974.

Parks, Lecia. *At Your Service: A Look at Utah's Service Economy*, Salt Lake City: Utah Department of Employment Security, January 1987.

Peterson, Gerald A. *More Than Music: The Mormon Tabernacle Choir.* Provo. UT: Brigham Young University Press.1979.

Petit, Jan. *Utes: The Mountain People.* Rev ed. Boulder, CO: Johnson Books, 1990.

Poll, Richard D., Thomas G. Alexander, Eugene E. Campbell, and David E Miller. *Utah's History*. Logan, UT: Utah State University Press, 1989.
Presbytery of Utah Directory, September 1994. Salt Lake City: Presbytery of Utah, 1994.
Priest, Ivy Baker. *Green Grows Ivy*. New York: McGraw-Hill Book Company, 1958.
Prince, Gregory A., and Wm. Robert Wright. *David O. McKay and the Rise of Modern Mormonism*. Salt Lake City: University of Utah Press, 2005.
Protestant and Catholic Churches of Provo, ed. David M. Walden. Provo, Utah: Center for Family and Community History, Brigham Young University, 1986.
Rampton, Calvin L. *As I Recall*. Ed. Floyd A. O'Neil and Gregory C. Thompson. Salt Lake City: University of Utah Press, 1989.
Rawlen, Edwin U. *A Decade in Review and a Look Ahead*. Salt Lake City: Utah State Department of Natural Resources, Division of Wildlife Resources, 1975.
Rhodes, Bernie. *D.B. Cooper: The Real McCoy*. Salt Lake City: University of Utah Press, 1991.
Ringholz, Raye C. *Uranium Frenzy: Saga of the Nuclear West*. Logan: Utah State University Press, 2002.
Roth, Walton A. *A Century of Service in Utah, 1869-1969*. Salt Lake City: Presbytery of Utah, 1969.
Roy, Denny, Grant Paul Skabelund, and Ray C Hillam. *A Time To Kill: Reflections on War*. Salt Lake City: Signature Books, 1992.
Roylance, Ward J. *Utah: A Guide to the State*. Rev. and enlarged. Salt Lake City: *Utah: A Guide to the State* Foundation.1982.
Russell, George B. *J. Bracken Lee: The Taxpayer's Champion*. New York: Robert Speller & Sons, 1961.
Sadler, Richard W., ed. *Weber State College: A Centennial History*. Ogden, UT: Weber State College, 1988.
Schapsmeir, Edward L. and Frederick H. Schapsmeier. *Ezra Taft Benson and the Politics of Agriculture: The Eisenhower Years, 1953-1961*. Danville, IL: Interstate Printers & Publishers, 1975.
Schwarz, Ted. *Arnold Friberg: The Passion of a Modern Master*. Flagstaff, AZ: Northland Press.1985.
Shaw, Margery W., ed. *After Barney Clark: Reflections on the Utah Artificial Heart Program* (Austin: University of Texas Press, 1984).
Shepard son, Mary, and Blodwen Hammond, *The Navajo Mountain Community: Social Organization and Kinship Terminology*. Berkeley: University of California Press, 1970.
Sillitoe, Linda, and Allen Roberts. *Salamander: The Story of the Mormon Forger Murders*. Salt Lake City: Signature Books, 1988.

Smith, Elmer R. *The Status of the Negro in Utah*. Salt Lake City: prepared for the Salt Lake City Branch of the National Association for the Advancement of Colored People, 1956.

Smith, Marcus Sidney. *With Them Were 10,000 and More: The Authorized History of the Oratorio Society of Utah*. Salt Lake City: Actaeon Books,1989.

Sorenson, Wilson W. *A Miracle in Utah Valley: The Story of Utah Technical College 1941-1982*. Provo, UT: Utah Technical College at Provo, 1985.

Statistical Abstract of Utah 1993. Salt Lake City: Bureau of Economic and Business Research, David Eccles School of Business, University of Utah, 1993.

Swanson, Vern G., Robert S Olpin, and William C. Seifrit. *Utah Painting and Sculpture*. Rev. ed. Salt Lake City: Gibbs Smith.1997.

Swanson,Vern G., Robert S. Olpin, and Donna L. Poulton. *Utah Art. Utah Artists: 150 Year Survey*. Layton. UT: Gibbs Smith.2001.

The First Century of the Methodist Church in Utah. Salt Lake City: Utah Methodism Centennial Committee, 1970.

Through the Eyes of Many Faiths. 2nd ed.. Salt Lake City: The Utah Heritage Foundation, 1990. 33.

Titus, A. Costandina. *Bombs in the Backyard: Atomic Testing and American Politics*. Reno and Las Vegas: University of Nevada Press, 1986.

Toone, Thomas Ernest. *Mahonri Young: His Life and Art*. Salt Lake City: Signature Books.1997.

Turley, Richard E. Turley, Jr. *Victims: The LDS Church and the Mark Hofmann Case*. Urbana: University of Illinois Press, 1992.

Udall, Stewart L. *The Quiet Crisis*. New York: Avon Books, 1963.

Utah History Encyclopedia, ed. Allen Kent Powell. Salt Lake City: University of Utah Press, 1994.

Utah State of the Arts (Ogden, UT: Meridian International, Inc., 1993.

Watkins, Arthur V. *Enough Rope*. Englewood Cliffs, NJ: Prentice-Hall, Inc., 1969.

Wheelwright, Lorin F., and Lael J. Woodbury, eds..*Mormon Arts*. Vol 1. Provo. UT: Brigham Young University Press.1972.

White, Jean Bickmore. *The Utah State Constitution: A Reference Guide*. Greenwood Press: Westport, Connecticut, 1998.

Wiley, Peter, and Robert Gottlieb. *Empires in the Sun: The Rise of the New American West*. New York: G. P. Putnam's Sons, 1982.

Wiley, Peter, and Robert Gottlieb. *Empires in the Sun: The Rise of the New American West*. New York: G. T. Putnam's Sons, 1982.

Williams, Terry Tempest. *Refuge: An Unnatural History of Time and Place*. First Vintage Book edition. New York: Vintage Books.1992.

Williamson, William B., ed. *An Encyclopedia of Religions in the United States: One Hundred Religious Groups Speak for Themselves*. New York: The Crossroads Publishing Company, 1992.

Articles and Book Chapters

Adams, Susan. "Rescue Mission." *The American Lawyer* (December 1987): 83-86.

Ader, Louis M. "Evangelical Missions among the Mormons." *Review & Expositor* 49 (July 1952): 313-26.

Alexander, Thomas G. "An Investment in Progress: Utah's First Federal Reclamation Project, The Strawberry Valley Project." *Utah Historical Quarterly* 39 (Summer 1971): 286-304.

Alexander, Thomas G. "The Emergence of a Republican Majority in Utah, 1970-1992." In *Politics in the Postwar American West*, ed. Richard Lowitt. Norman: University of Oklahoma Press, 1995: 260-76.

Allen, James B. "The Rise and Decline of the LDS Indian Student Placement Program, 1947-1996." In *Mormon Scripture and the Ancient World: Studies in Honor of John L. Sorenson*, ed. Davis Bitton, 85-119. Provo, UT: Foundation for Ancient Research and Mormon Studies, 1998.

Allen, James B. "Crisis on the Home Front: The Federal Government and Utah's Defense Housing in World War II." *Pacific Historical Review* 38 (November1969): 407-28.

Allen, James B., and Ted J. Warner. "The Gosiute Indians in Pioneer Utah." *Utah Historical Quarterly* 39 (Spring 1971): 162-77.

Allen, James B. "The Evolution of County Boundaries in Utah." *Utah Historical Quarterly* 23 (July 1955): 261-78.

Anderson, Lavina Fielding. "The Assimilation of Mormon History: Modern Mormon Historical Novels." *Mormon Letters Annual* (1983): 1-9.

Anderson, Lavina Fielding. "Making the 'Good' Good for Something: A Direction for Mormon Literature." *Mormon Letters Annual* (1985): 150-64.

Arrington, Leonard J. and Jon G. Perry. "Utah's Spectacular Missiles Industry: Its History and Impact." *Utah Historical Quarterly* 30 (Winter 1962): 3-39.

Bahr, Howard M. "The Declining Distinctiveness of Utah's Working Women." *BYU Studies* 10 (Summer 1979): 525-43.

Barnhill, J. Herschel. "Civil Rights in Utah: The Mormon Way." *Journal of the West* 25 (October 1986): 21-27.

Behunin, Alan. "Ballet Brings Joy to Students." *Utah Educational Review* 61 (May-June 1968): 10.

Belssa, James W., Jr. "The Episcopal Church in Utah: Seven Bishops and One Hundred Years." *Utah Historical Quarterly* 36 (Winter 1968): 76-96.

Bennett, Wallace R. "The Negro in Utah." *Utah Law Review* 3 (Spring 1953): 340-48.

Bennion, Lowell C., and Merrill K. Ridd. "Utah's Dynamic Dixie: Satellite of Salt Lake, Las Vegas, or Los Angeles?" *Utah Historical Quarterly* 47 (Summer 1979): 311-27.

Bergera, Gary James. "'A Sad and Expensive Experience': Ernest L. Wilkinson's 1964 Bid for the US Senate." *Utah Historical Quarterly* 61 (Fall 1993): 304-24.

Birch, J. Neil. "Helen John: The Beginnings of Indian Placement." *Dialogue: A Journal of Mormon Thought* 18 (Winter 1985): 119-29.

"Black, Female, and Mormon." *Intermountain Observer* 21 (February 6, 1971):1, 12.

Bradley, Martha Sonntag. "The Mormon Relief Society and the International Women's Year." *Journal of Mormon History* 21 (Spring 1995): 115–18.

Bradley, Martha Sonntag. "The Mormon Relief Society and the International Women's Year." *Journal of Mormon History* 21 (Spring 1995): 105–67.

"Cable Television: United States." In *Encyclopedia of Television*. 2ᵈ ed. Ed. Horace Newcomb. New York: Fitzroy Dearborn and the Museum of Broadcast Communications, 2004): 393.

Campbell, Beverly. "A Conversation with Beverly Campbell." *Dialogue: A Journal of Mormon Thought* 14 (Spring 1981): 45-57.

Carroll, Howard J. "Sanctions Work in Utah," *Michigan Educational Journal* (May 1965): 8–9, 74.

Chadwick, Bruce A., Stan L. Albrecht, and Howard M. Bahr. "Evaluation of an Indian Student Placement Program." *Social Casework* 67 (November 1986): 515–24.

Condie, Spencer J., and Thomas K. Martin. "Crime." chapter III in *Utah in Demographic Perspective: Regional and National Contrasts*, ed. Howard M. Bahr. Provo, UT: Family and Demographic Research Institute, Brigham Young University, 1981.

Cracroft, Richard H. "Attuning the Authentic Mormon Voice: Stemming the Sophic Tide in LDS Literature." *Sunstone* 16 (July 1993): 51-57.

Cracroft, Richard H. "Seeking 'the Good, the Pure, the Elevating': A Short History of Mormon Fiction." *Ensign* 11 (June, July 1981): 56-62, 56-61.

Crum, Steven J. "The Skull Valley Band of the Goshute Tribe—Deeply Attached to Their Native Homeland." *Utah Historical Quarterly* 55 (Summer 1978): 250–67.

Cundick, Bert P., Douglas K. Gottfredson, and Linda Willson. "Changes in Scholastic Achievement and Intelligence of Indian Children Enrolled in a Foster Placement Program." *Developmental Psychology* 10 (1974): 815–20.

Davies, J. Kenneth. "Mormonism and the Closed Shop." *Labor History* 3 (Spring 1962): 169–87.

Davies, J. Kenneth. "The Accommodation of Mormonism and Politico-Economic Reality." *Dialogue: A Journal of Mormon Thought* 3 (Spring 1968): 42–54.

Davis, Gode. "Biomedical Breakthroughs: Utah's Bionic Valley Needs A Venture-Capital Boost." *Utah Holiday* (January 1988): 30–37.

Dean, Suzanne. "Utah Fights the Drug War: Testing in the Workplace." *Utah Holiday* 19 (October 1989): 10- 11.

Dwore, Richard B. "A Case Study of the 1976 Referendum in Utah on Fluoridation." *Public Health Reports* 93 (January–February 1978), 73–78.

Elbert, Joan. "Mormons and the MX Missile." *Christian Century* 98 (July 15–22, 1981): 725–26.

England, Eugene. "Mormon Literature: Progress and Prospects." In David J. Whittaker, ed., *Mormon Americana: A Guide to Sources and Collections in the United States* (Provo, UT: BYU Studies, 1995): 455–505.

England, Eugene. "The Dawning of a Brighter Day: Mormon Literature After 150 Years." In *After 150 Years: The Latter-day Saints in Sesquicentennial Perspective*, ed. Thomas G. Alexander and Jessie Embry (Provo, UT: Charles Redd Center for Western Studies, 1983): 97–146.

England, Eugene. "The Dawning of a Brighter Day: Mormon Literature after 150 Years." *BYU Studies* 22 (Spring 1982): 151.

Geis, Gilbert. "Do Utah Schools Face the Race Problems?" *Utah Educational Review* 42 (January 1950): 20, 32.

"Geneva Resurrection." *Intermountain Contractor* 39 (September 5, 1988): 8–10.

Goss, Peter L. "The Architectural History of Utah." *Utah Historical Quarterly* 43 (Summer 1975): 208–39.

Gresseth, Marian. "The Tyranny of Heritage: The Problems of the *Utah Art*ist." *Pen* (Spring 1958): 23–24.

Grow, Stewart L. "The 1962 Election in Utah." *Western Political Quarterly* 16 (June 1963): 460–66.

Gruenwald, Kim M. "American Indians and the Public School System: A Case Study of the Northern Utes." *Utah Historical Quarterly* 61 (Summer 1996), 246–63.

Guerrero, Manuel P. "Indian Child Welfare Act of 1978: A Response to the Threat to Indian Culture Caused by Foster and Adoptive Placements of Indian Children." *American Indian Law Review* 7 (1979): 51–77.

Hafen, LeRoy R. "Joys of Discovery--Historical Research and Writing." *BYU Studies* 7 (Spring–Summer 1966): 171-87.

Harvey, Mark W. T. "Echo Park, Glen Canyon, and the Postwar Wilderness Movement." *Pacific Historical Review* 60 (February 1991): 43–67.

Harvey, Mark W. T. "Utah, the National Park Service, and Dinosaur National Monument." *Utah Historical Quarterly* 59 (Summer 1991): 242–63.

Hayashi, Masami, George Tohinaka, and Mrs. Ritsuko Hayashi. "Salt Lake Buddhist Church, Salt Lake City, Utah." In *Buddhist Churches of America Vol I: 75 Year History 1899-1974*. Chicago: Nobart, Inc., 1974: 242-49.

Head, Derin Lea. "At the Helm of an (Academic) Empire." *This People* (February 1984): 40–41.

Hector, Gary. "S&Ls: Where Did All Those Billions Go?" *Fortune* (September 10, 1990), 82–88.

Hickman, Diane. "Riding Out a Deseret Tide." *This People* 6 (September 1983): 27–29, 49, 51.

Hidenshield, Charles. "Rock Canyon Assembly of God." In *Protestant and Catholic Churches of Provo*, ed. David M. Walden, 147. Provo, UT; Center for Family and Community History, Brigham Young University, 1986.

Hildreth, Steven A. "The First Presidency Statement on MX in Perspective." *BYU Studies* 22 (Spring 1982): 215–25.

Hildreth, Steven A. "Mormon Concerns over MX: Parochialism or Enduring Mormon Theology." *Journal of Church and State* 26 (1984): 227–55.

Hirano, Reverend Jerry K. "Birth and Death, Changes Are Going to Come, *Buddhist Thoughts* (newsletter of the Salt Lake City Buddhist temple), April–May, 1994.

Hrebenar, Ronald J. "Utah: The Most Republican State in the Union." *The Social Science Journal* 18 (October 1981): 103–14.

Huefner, Dixie Snow. "Church and Politics at the Utah IWY Conference." *Dialogue: A Journal of Mormon Thought* 11 (Spring 1978): 58–75.

Hunsaker, Kenneth B. "Mid-Century Mormon Novels," *Dialogue: A Journal of Mormon Thought* 4 (Autumn 1969): 123–28.

Jacobson, Cardall. "Ethnic Groups in Utah." In *Utah in Demographic Perspective*, ed. Thomas K. Martin, Tim B. Heaton, and Stephen J. Bahr. Salt Lake City: Signature Books, 1987: 165–79.

Johnson, Yvonne Baker, and Dianne Clyde Carr, "History of the Art Movement in Springville, Utah." In Vern G. Swanson, Robert S. Olpin, and William C. Seifrit, *Utah Painting and Sculpture* (Salt Lake City: Gibbs Smith Publisher, 1997): 281-83

Johnson, Marian Ashby. "Minerva's Calling." *Dialogue: A Journal of Mormon Thought* 21 (Spring 1988): 127–43.

Johnson, Marian Ashby. "Minerva Teichert: Scriptorian and Artist." *BYU Studies* 30 (Summer 1990): 66–69.

Johnston, Jerry. "Dennis Smith and His Bronze Children." *This People* 16 (Holiday 1995): 46–52.

Jonas, Frank H. "The 1958 Election in Utah." *Western Political Quarterly* 12 (March1959): 345–54.

Jonas, Frank H. "President Lyndon Johnson, the Mormon Church and the 1964 Political Campaign." *Proceedings of the Utah Academy of Sciences, Arts and Letters* 44 (1967): 67–90.

Jonas, Frank H. "The Third Man in Utah Politics." *Proceedings of the Utah Academy of Sciences, Arts and Letters* 37 (1960): 103–25.

Jonas, Frank H. "The 1964 Election in Utah." *Western Political Quarterly* 18 (June 1965): 509–13.

Jonas, Frank H., and Dan E. Jones, "The 1970 Election in Utah." *Western Political Quarterly* 24 (June 1971): 339–49.

Jonas, Frank H. "The 1956 Election in Utah." *Western Historical Quarterly* 10 (March 1957): 151–60.

Jonas, Frank H. "The 1954 Elections in Utah." *Proceedings of the Utah Academy of Sciences, Arts, and Letters* 32 (1955): 155–69.

Jonas, Frank H. "The Mormon Church and *Political Dynamiting* in the 1950 Election in Utah." *Proceedings of the Utah Academy of Sciences, Arts, and Letters* 40 (1962-63): 94-108.

Jonas, Frank H. "The 1966 Election in Utah." *Utah Historical Quarterly* 20 (June 1967): 602-6.

Jonas, Frank H. "Reapportionment in Utah and the Mormon Church." *Proceedings of the Utah Academy of Sciences, Arts and Letters* 46 (1969): 11-26.

Jonas, Frank H. "The Mormon Church and J. Bracken Lee," *Proceedings of the Utah Academy of Sciences, Arts, and Letters* 36 (1959): 145-69.

Jonas, Frank H. "The 1950 Election in Utah." *Western Historical Quarterly* 4 (March 1951): 90-91.

Jonas, Frank H. "J. Bracken Lee and the Mormon Church." *Proceedings of the Utah Academy of Sciences, Arts, and Letters* 34 (1957): 109-25.

Jorgensen, Bruce W. "Digging the Foundation: Making and Reading Mormon Literature," *Dialogue: A Journal of Mormon Thought* 9 (Winter 1974): 50-61.

Jorgensen, Bruce W. "A 'Smaller Canvass' of Mormon Short Story Since 1950." *Mormon Letters Annual* (1983): 10-31.

Keane, Coleen. "'Where Have All the Children Gone?' Controversy Over Native Child Placement by Mormon Church." *Wassaja* 9 (September-October 1982): 12-13.

Knight, Amberly. "Hot Rocks Make Big Waves: The Impact of the Uranium Boom on Moab, Utah, 1948-57," *Utah Historical Quarterly* 69 (Winter 2001): 29-45.

Knowlton, David. "Missionaries and Terror: The Assassination of Two Elders in Bolivia," *Sunstone* 13 (August 1989): 10-15.

Kraut, Ogden. "The Singer/Swapp Siege: Revelation or Retaliation?" *Sunstone* 12 (November 1988): 10-17.

Kuida, Hirosho, "Cardiology." In *Medicine in the Beehive State, 1940-1990*, ed. Henry P. Plenk. Salt Lake City: Utah Medical Association, LDS Hospital-Deseret Foundation, University of Utah Health Sciences Center, 1992: 107-111.

Kunz, Phillip R. and Merlin B. Brinkerhoff. *Utah in Numbers: Comparisons, Trends, and Descriptions*. Provo: Brigham Young University Press, 1969.

Larson, Clinton F. "Nuclear Winter." *BYU Studies* 25 (Winter 1985), 99.

Lewis, Robert E., Mark W. Fraser, and Peter J. Pecora. "Religiosity among Indochinese Refugees in Utah." *Journal for the Scientific Study of Religion* 27 (June 1988): 271-82.

Lyon, Thomas J. "In the Valleys of the Mountains." In Thomas J. Lyon and Terry Tempest Williams, eds., *Great and Peculiar Beauty: A Utah Reader*, 5-13. Salt Lake City: Gibbs Smith Publisher, 1995.

Lythgoe, Dennis. "Political Feud in Salt Lake City: J. Bracken Lee and the Firing of W. Cleon Skousen." *Utah Historical Quarterly* 42 (Fall 1974): 316-43.

Lythgoe, Dennis L. "A Special Relationship: J. Bracken Lee and the Mormon Church." *Dialogue: A Journal of Mormon Thought* 11 (Winter 1978): 71-87.

Malouf, Carling. "The Gosiute Indians." In *American Indian Ethnohistory: California and Basin-Plateau Indians*, ed. David Agee Horr, 35. New York: Garland Publishing Co., 1974.

Mann, Dean E. "Mormon Attitudes toward the Political Roles of Church Leaders." *Dialogue: A Journal of Mormon Thought* 2 (Summer 1967):32-48.

Mayer, Edward H. "The Evolution of Culture and Tradition in Utah's Mexican-American Community." *Utah Historical Quarterly* 49 (Spring 1981): 133-44.

McCullough, C. W. "Utah Valley Teems with Action." *Utah Magazine* 8 (1946): 43-44.

Mulder, William A. "'Essential Gestures': Craft and Calling in Contemporary Mormon Letters." *Weber Studies* 10 (Fall 1993): 7-25.

Nixon, Robert W. "Anti-Sunday-Law Strategy Forecast in Utah Governor's Veto." *Liberty* 63 (January-February 1968): 20-22

O. Kendall White, Jr., "Overt and Covert Politics: The Mormon Church's Anti-ERA Campaign in Virginia." *Virginia Social Science Journal* 19 (Winter 1984): 11-16.

Olson, Peggy Olson. "Ruffin Bridgeforth: Leader and Father to Mormon Blacks." *This People* 1 (Winter 1980): 11-17.

Partridge, Elinore H. "A. Ray Olpin and the Postwar Emergency at the University of Utah." *Utah Historical Quarterly* 48 (Spring 1980): 193-206.

Paulson, Jean R. "Samuel W. Taylor: Talented Native Son." *Utah Historical Quarterly* 67 (Summer 1997): 265-84.

Peterson, F. Ross. "McCarthyism in the Mountains, 1950-1954." In *Essays in the American West, 1974-75*, ed. Thomas G. Alexander, Provo, UT: BYU Press, 1976: 47-77.

Peterson, F. Ross. "'Blindside': Utah on the Eve of *Brown v. Board of Education*." *Utah Historical Quarterly* 73 (Winter 2005), 4-20.

Plenk, Henry P. "Early History of the Four-Year Medical School of the University of Utah, 1942-1952," In *Medicine in the Beehive State, 1940-1990*, ed. Henry P. Plenk. Salt Lake City: Utah Medical Association, LDS Hospital-Deseret Foundation, University of Utah Health Sciences Center, 1992: 3-59.

Quinn, D. Michael. "The LDS Church's Campaign Against the Equal Rights Amendment." *Journal of Mormon History* 20 (Fall 1994): 85-155.

Reilly, P. T. "The Lost World of Glen Canyon." *Utah Historical Quarterly* 62 (Spring 1995): 122-34.

Ringholz, Raye G. "Armageddon at Marion, Utah." Parts I and II. *Utah Holiday* (January 1979): 39-48 and (February 1979): 36-41.

Ringholz, Raye C. "Utah's Uranium Boom." *Beehive History* 16 (1990): 25-27.

Rogers, Jedediah Smart. "'When the People Speak': Mormons and the 1954 Redistricting Campaign in Utah." *Utah Historical Quarterly* 71 (Summer 2003),:233–49.

Sandiford, Glenn. "Bernard DeVoto and His Forgotten Contribution to Echo Park." *Utah Historical Quarterly* 59 (Winter 1991): 72–86.

Schapsmeier, Edward L. and Frederick H. Schapsmeier. "Eisenhower and Ezra Taft Benson: Farm Policy in the 1950s." *Agricultural History* 44 (October 1970): 369–78.

Schapsmeier, Edward L. and Frederick H. Schapsmeier. "Religion and Reform: A Case Study of Henry A. Wallace and Ezra Taft Benson." *Journal of Church and State* 21 (1979): 525–35.

Sheldon, Ken. "First in Finance," *Utah Business* 6 (August 1991): 32–36.

Sherlock, Richard. "Supreme Court Challenge: Inside the Making of the Utah Abortion Law." *Policy Review* 56 (Spring 1991): 85–87.

Sillitoe, Linda. "Inside Utah's IWY Conference: Women Scorned." *Utah Holiday* 6 (August 1977): 26.

Sillitoe, Linda Sillitoe. "A Foot in Both Camps, an Interview with Jan Tyler." *Sunstone* 3 (January/February 1979): 11–14.

Sillitoe, Linda. "Fear and Anger in Virginia: The New Mormon Activists (Part II)." *Utah Holiday* 8 (April 1979): 9–10, 12.

Sillitoe. Linda. "The New Mormon Activists: Fighting the ERA in Virginia." *Utah Holiday* 8 (March 1979): 12, 14.

Siporin, Steve. "A Jew Among Mormons." *Dialogue: A Journal of Mormon Thought* 24 (Winter 1991): 113-22.

Smith, Elmer R. "The 'Japanese' in Utah (Part I)" and "The 'Japanese' in Utah (Part II)." *Utah Humanities Review* 2 (April, July 1948): 129–44, 208–30.

Smith, Thomas G. "The Canyonlands National Park Controversy, 1961-64" *Utah Historical Quarterly* 59 (Summer 1991): 216–42.

"Some Historical Background on the San Juan County Utes." *Blue Mountain Shadows* 11 (Winter 1992): 4–5.

South, Will. "The Federal Art Project in Utah: Out of Oblivion or More of the Same?" *Utah Historical Quarterly* 58 (Summer 1990): 277–95.

Sprout, David Kent. "Environmentalism and th Kaiparowits Power Project." *Utah Historical Quarterly* 70 (Fall 2002), 356–71.

Stern, Richard L., and Toddi Gutner. "A Helluva Place to Have a Business." *Forbes* 15 (December 21, 1992): 114–36.

Swanson, Vern G. "Mormon Art and Belief Movement." *Southwest Art* 21 (December 1991): 66–70.

Swanson, Vern G. "The Contemporary Scene." In Vern G. Swanson, Robert S. Olpin, and William C. Seifrit, *Utah Art* (Salt Lake City: Peregrine Smith Books, 1991): 186-266.

Sweden, Eric G. "Thiokol in Utah." *Utah Historical Quarterly* 75 (Winter 2007): 63-77.

Tanner, Jordan. "Smoking and Health: Showdown on Utah's Capitol Hill." *The Religious Educator* 9:3 (2008): 85-90.

"The Front Page." *Utah Holiday* 10 (July 1982): 10–13.

"The Coalville Tabernacle." a "Roundtable" with articles by Edward Geary, Paul G. Salisbury, and an anonymous writer. *Dialogue: A Journal of Mormon Thought* 5 (Winter 1970): 41–65.

Thompson, Gregory C. "Utah's Indian Country: The American Indian Experience in San Juan County, 1700–1980." In *San Juan County, Utah: People, Resources, and History*, ed. Allan Kent Powell, 51-67. Salt Lake City: Utah State Historical Society, 1983.

Trevithick, David R. "Utah's Centennial Celebration" *Utah Humanities Review* 1 (October 1947): 355–60.

"US Steel Abandons Utah." *The Progressive* (May 1986): 19.

Ulibarri, Richard O. "Utah's Ethnic Minorities: A Survey." *Utah Historical Quarterly* 40 (Summer 1972): 210–32.

Utah Arts Council. *Arts in Education Program: Guidelines and Artists Bank* (1992).

Utah Arts Council, *Utah Performing Arts Tour* (1993–94 brochure).

Wahlquist, John T. "Utah Schools Rank High." *Utah Educational Review* 41 (December 1947): 20–21, 30.

Wahlquist, John T. "Status of Education in Utah." *Proceedings of the Utah Academy of Sciences, Arts, and Letters* 24 (1947): 109–131.

Wahlquist, John T. "Education in Utah, 1947." *Utah Educational Review* 40 (September–October 1947): 11–13, 38.

Walden, David M. "The Reorganized Church of Jesus Christ of Latter Day Saints." in *Protestant and Catholic Churches of Provo*, ed. Walden, 1–17.

Walden, David M. "The Evangelical Free Church." In *Protestant and Catholic Churches of Provo*, ed. David M. Walden, 150-59. Provo, UT: Center for Family and Community History, Brigham Young University, 1986.

Walden, David M. "Jehovah's Witnesses." In *Protestant and Catholic Churches of Provo*, ed. David M. Walden, 117-31. Provo, UT: Center for Family and Community History, Brigham Young University, 1986.

White, O. Kendall, Jr. "Mormonism and the Equal Rights Amendment." *Journal of Church and State* 31 (Spring 1989): 249– 67.

White, O. Kendall, Jr. "A Feminist Challenge: 'Mormons for ERA' as an Internal Social Movement." *Journal of Ethnic Studies* 13 (Spring 1985): 29–50.

Wilkins, Richard G. Wilkins. "One Moment Please: Private Devotion in the Public Schools." *The BYU Journal of Public Law* 2 (1988): 1–13.

Winder, Lorie. "LDS Position on the ERA: An Historical View." *Exponent II* 6 (Winter 1980): 6–7.

Wood, Thomas, and Douglas Hill. "The Coalville Tabernacle." *Dialogue: A Journal of Mormon Thought* 2 (Summer 1967): 61-74.

Yazzie, Mary Jane. "Life and Traditions of the Utes of Avikan." *Blue Mountain Shadows* 7 (Winter 1990): 25–33.

Zaslowsky, Dyan. "Letter from Salt Lake City: Who, or What, Is a Gentile?" *Hadassah Magazine*. (November 1982): 12.

Theses and Dissertations

Aoki, Hisa. "Functional Analysis of Mono-Racial In-Groups: *Nisei* Congeniality Primary Groups on the University of Utah Campus." Master's thesis, University of Utah, 1950.

Beckham, Raymond E. "The Utah Newspaper War of 1968: Liquor-by-the-Drink." Master's thesis, Brigham Young University, 1969.

Bernhard, Randall Lee. "Contemporary Musical Theatre: History and Development in the Major Colleges and Universities of Utah. " Ph.D. dissertation, Brigham Young University, 1979.

Bishop, Clarence R. "An Evaluation of the Scholastic Achievement of Selected Indian Students Attending Elementary Public Schools of Utah." Master's thesis, Brigham Young University, 1960.

Bishop, Clarence R. "A History of the Indian Placement Program." Master's thesis, University of Utah, 1967.

Bushman, Jesse Smith. "A Qualitative Analysis of the Non-LDS Experience in Utah," Master's thesis, Brigham Young University, 1995.

Clinger, Morris Martin. "A History of the Theater in Mormon Colleges and Universities." Ph.D. dissertation, University of Minnesota, 1963.

Conley, Angela Chan. "The Social Problems of the Chinese in Salt Lake County." Master's thesis, University of Utah, 1973.

Garrett, Matthew R. "Mormons, Indians, and Lamanites: The Student Indian Placement Program, 1947–2000." Ph.D. dissertation, Arizona State University, 2010.

Glissmeyer, Floyd D. Glissmeyer. "A Historical Study of the Religious Education Program of the Seventh-day Adventist Church in Utah." Master's thesis, Brigham Young University 1970.

Haggerty, John W. "Historic Preservation in Utah: 1960-1980." Master's thesis, Brigham Young University, 1980.

Hainsworth, Brad. "Reapportionment in Utah, 1954–1965." Master's thesis, University of Utah, 1966).

Hair, Mary Jane Stewart. "History of the Efforts to Coordinate Higher Education in Utah." Ph.D. dissertation, University of Utah, 1974.

Harvey, Mark W. T. "The Echo Park Controversy and the American Conservation Movement." Ph.D. dissertation, University of Wyoming, 1986.

Hingano, Sione V. "Social Cultural Problems of Polynesian High School Graduates Not Pursuing College Level Study." Ed.D. dissertation, Brigham Young University, 1984.

Hinton, Wayne K. "A Biographical History of Mahonri M. Young, a Western American Artist." Ph.D. dissertation, Brigham Young University, 1974.

Hughes, Donald L. "Aspirations and Goals of 1976 Utah Women Educators for Public School Administration." Ed.D. dissertation, Brigham Young University, 1976.

Iga, Mamoru. "Acculturation of Japanese Population in Davis County, Utah." Ph.D. dissertation, University of Utah, 1955.

Kirkham, John Spencer. "A Study of Negro Housing in Salt Lake County." Honors thesis, University of Utah, 1968.

Knack, Martha C. "Contemporary Southern Paiute Household Structure and Bilateral Kinship Structures." Master's thesis, University of Michigan, 1975.

Lewis, Terrall Sam. "The Utah Shakespearean Festival: Twenty-five Years in Retrospect" Ph.D. dissertation, Texas Tech University, 1991.

Madsen, Roger Bryan. "Analysis of the 1958 Senatorial Campaign in Utah." Master's thesis, Brigham Young University, 1973.

Michael, William R. "High Technology Industries in Utah Valley: A Survey and Needs Analysis for Growth and Development." Master's thesis, Brigham Young University, 1986.

Moon, Sungup. "The Linguistic Patterns of the Utah-Korean Community." Master's thesis, Brigham Young University, 1992.

Neel, Susan Rhodes. "Irreconcilable Differences: Reclamation, Preservation, and the Origins of the Echo Dam Controversy." Ph.D. dissertation, University of California at Los Angeles, 1989.

Neel, Susan Mae. "Utah and the Echo Park Dam Controversy." Master's Thesis, University of Utah, 1980.

Olsen, Denise P. "An Historical Overview of Modern Dance at Brigham Young University from 1875 to 1986," Master's thesis, Brigham Young University, 1987.

Peter dePont Emerson, "The South Temple Historic District: Past, Present, Future. Master's thesis, University of Utah, 1979.

Piedras, Daniel. "An Analysis of Downtown Revitalization in Salt Lake City." Master's thesis, Brigham Young University, 1992.

Rainer, Howard. "An Analysis of Attitudes Navajo Community Leaders Have Toward a Religion Sponsored Program Based Upon Membership of that Faith and Amount of Information Attained." Master's thesis, Brigham Young University, 1976.

Rathjen, Milford Randall. "The Distribution of Major Non-Mormon Denominations in Utah." Master's thesis, University of Utah, 1966).

Reynolds, Edwin Lee. "J. Bracken Lee and Utah Public Education" Master's thesis, Brigham Young University, 1973.

Riggs, Lynette A. "The Church of Jesus Christ of Latter-day Saints' Indian Student Placement Service: A History." Ph.D. dissertation, Utah State University, 2008.

Schimmelpfennig, Dorothy Jensen. "A Study of Cross-Cultural Problems in the L.D.S. Indian Student Placement Program in Davis County, Utah." Ph.D. dissertation, University of Utah, 1971.

Smith, Roxanne. "The History of Ballet at Brigham Young University." Master's thesis, Brigham Young University, 1986.
Stellhorn, Ronnie L. "A History of the Lutheran Church in Utah. Master's thesis, Utah State University, 1975.
Swanson, Richard. "McCarthyism in Utah." Master's thesis, Brigham Young University, 1977.
Taylor, Grant Hardy. "A Comparative Study of Former LDS Placement and Non-Placement Navajo Students at Brigham Young University." Ph.D. dissertation, Brigham Young University, 1981.
Walden, David M. "Utah's Health Care Revolution: Pluralism and Professionalization Since World War II." Master's thesis, Brigham Young University, 1989.
Wardle, Marian Eastwood. "Minerva Teichert's Murals: The Motivation of Her Large-Scale Production." Master's thesis, Brigham Young University, 1988.
Waterfall, Margaret Tennant. "A History of Dance at the University of Utah (1906–1968." Master's thesis, University of Utah, 1968.
Wilcox, Floyd Samuel. "The Major Financial Policies of Governor J. Braken Lee of Utah, 1949–1957." Master's thesis, University of Utah, 1967.
Wilson, Linda Ouida. "Changes in Scholastic Achievement and Intelligence of Indian Children Enrolled in a Foster Placement Program." Master's thesis, Brigham Young University, 1973.
Wyatt J. Kondris. "A Survey of Orchestral Music Programs in the Senior High Schools of Utah." Master's thesis, Brigham Young University, 1968.
Yancey, Brock. "Indochinese Refugees as Employees: Perceptions of Employers in Utah." Master's thesis, University of Utah, 1983.

Miscellaneous Government Reports and Publications
"But What about Utah's Vital 80%?" *1970 Annual Report, Utah State Advisory Council for Vocational and Technical Education*. Salt Lake City: January 1971.
"CUP History." Central Utah Project, Bureau of Reclamation, 1973 (an eleven-page report).
1994 Economic Report to the Governor. Salt Lake City: Office of the Governor, 1994.
1995 Economic Report to the Governor. Salt Lake City: Office of the Governor, 1995.
A Review of the Federal and State Funded Utah Drug Abuse Education Project, 1970–1976. Salt Lake City: State Board of Education, 1976.
Dawson, William A. "Memoirs of William A. Dawson." Typescript, 1972. Available L. Tom Perry Special Collections, Harold B. Lee Library, Brigham Young University.
Developing Utah's Economy: Guidelines, Policies and Plans, Executive Summary. Salt Lake City: Department of Community and Economic Development, November 26, 1985.

Division of Family Services, State of Utah Department of Human Services, *Report on Child Abuse and Neglect* (1990).

Economic Diversification: Utah's Adjustment to Declining Defense Spending. Prepared for the Department of Community and Economic Development. Salt Lake City: Bureau of Economic and Business Research, University of Utah, December 1990.

Engle v. Vitale, 370 US 421 (1962).

Geersten, Dennis, Harold Adams, David Gabriel, Theresa Breaux, and Paris Brown. "Needs Assessment of the Salt Lake City Black Community." Salt Lake Community Mental Health Center Program Evaluation and Research Department Report No. 2, April 1977.

Governor's Commission for Women and the Family. *Utah Women and the Law: A Resource Handbook.* 2d ed., rev. Salt Lake City: University of Utah Press, 1991.

Governor's Securities Fraud Task Force. *Report.* Salt Lake City: The Task Force, 1984.

Governor's Task Force on Health Care Costs. "Report of the Governor's Task Force on Health Care Costs: Executive Summary." Salt Lake City: Governor's Task Force on Health Care Costs and Utah Department of Health, Bureau of Health Planning and Policy Analysis, 1988.

Higher Education in Utah: Facts for Master Planning for the Decade Ahead. Salt Lake City: Utah Coordinating Council of Higher Education, 1967.

Langston, Lecia Parks. *Hard at Work: Women in the Utah Labor Force.* Salt Lake City: Labor Market Information Services, Utah Department of Employment Security, 1989.

McNab, Scott. "Geneva and the Environment" Unpublished working paper prepared for Garth L. Mangum. Copy in James B. Allen papers, L. Tom Perry Special Collections, Harold B. Lee Library, Brigham Young University. Used by permission.

Migrant Education in Utah: Portraits of Success. Salt Lake City: Migrant Education Section, Curriculum and Instruction, Utah State Office of Education, 1985.

Nelson, David E. *Utah Educational Quality Indicators,* No. 3. In *How Good are Utah Public Schools?* series. Salt Lake City: Utah State Board of Education, 1974), 93–95, 100–101.

Office of the Governor. *A Utah Perspective on the National Education Goals.* Salt Lake City, Utah Office of the Governor and Utah State Office of Education, 1992.

Parks, Lecia. *Hard at Work: Women in the Utah Labor Force.* Salt Lake City: Labor Market Information Services, Utah Department of Employment Security, 1985.

Poverty in Utah. (Salt Lake City: State Department of Community and Economic Development, Utah Issues Information Program, 1983.

Resource Catalog of Black Citizens in Utah. Salt Lake City: State Economic Opportunity Office, 1975.

State Superintendent of Public Instruction. *Utah School Report, 1962-64.* Salt Lake City: Utah State Department of Public Instruction, 1964.
State Superintendent of Public Instruction. *Utah School Report, 1969-70.* Salt Lake City: Utah State Department of Public Instruction, 1970.
State Superintendent of Public Instruction. *School Report, 1978-79.* Salt Lake City: Utah State Department of Public Instruction, 1979.
State Superintendent of Public Instruction. *Utah School Report, 1958-1960.* Salt Lake City: Utah State Department of Public Instruction, 1960.
Survey of Services to American Indians through Institutes of Higher Learning in Seven Northwestern States. Salt Lake City: published by the Bureau of Indian Services, Division of Continuing Education, University of Utah, May 1970.
Survival Communication Instruction for Classroom Teachers of Students with Limited English Proficiency (LEP). Salt Lake City: Utah State Office of Education, Division of Program Administration, 1981.
Teenage Pregnancy in Utah 1975-1981. Salt Lake City: Utah Department of Health, Office of Management Planning and Division of Family Health Services, 1983.
Twelfth Annual Report of the Superintendent of Public Instruction of the State of Utah, for the Period Ending June 30, 1984.
Uniform Crime Reports of the United States, printed annually by the Federal Bureau of Investigation, US Department of Justice, Washington, D.C.
Utah State Board of Education. Division of Administration. *Services to Minorities and Concerns of Minorities.* Salt Lake City, published by the board, 1978.
Utah Coordinating Council of Higher Education. *News of Higher Education* 1 (June 1968).
Utah Centennial Commission. "General Report." Salt Lake City: 1947.
Utah Centennial Commission. "Utah Centennial Programs, Magazine Articles, and Newspaper Clippings, 1947."
Utah State Department of Publicity and Industrial Development. "After Victory: Plans for Utah and the Wasatch Front: Report of the Cooperative Planning Program, Compiled Under the Direction of Ora Bundy." Salt Lake City: Utah State Department of Publicity and Industrial Development, 1943.
Utah Legislature, Handicapped Children's Research Team. "Utah Schools Special Education Study: A Report to the Education Study Committee of the Utah State Legislature." Salt Lake City (1977?).
Utah Task Force on Gender and Justice: Report to the Judicial Council. March 1990.
Utah Coordinating Council of Higher Education. "Coordination of Utah Higher Education." Salt Lake City: n.p., 1963.
Utah State Board of Regents. *Annual Report to the Governor and the Legislature.* 1978-79.

Utah Department of Employment Security, *Women in the Labor Force, 1950–1980*. Salt Lake City: Utah Department of Employment Security, 1981.

Utah Department of Human Services, Division of Family Services, *Report on Child Abuse and Neglect*. Salt Lake City: The Division, 1984.

Women in Utah's Labor Force 1950–1980. Salt Lake City: Utah Department of Employment Security, Labor Market Information Services Section, 1981.

Women in Utah [1966]. Report of the Governor's Committee on the Status of Women in Utah, June 15, 1966.

Wyatt, Spencer. "Comparative Study of the 1962–1963 School District Expenditures for Eight Rocky Mountain States." Salt Lake City: Utah State Department of Public Instruction, 1964.

Interviews and Oral Histories

Albrecht, David M. Interview by James B. Allen, September 3, 1992. Notes in James B. Allen papers, L Tom Parry Special Collections, Harold B. Lee Library, Brigham Young University.

Baird, Rev. Donald, Salt Lake City. Interview by Jesse S. Bushman, November 7, 1994. Tape in James B. Allen papers, L. Tom Perry Special Collections, Harold B. Lee Library, Brigham Young University.

Barnes, Reverend Dave. Granger, UT. Telephone interview by Jesse S. Bushman, January 3, 1995. Notes in James B. Allen papers, L. Tom Perry Special Collections, Harold B. Lee Library, Brigham Young University.

Barron, Francis, principal, Adventist school, Provo, UT. Telephone interview by Jesse S. Bushman, December 20, 1994. Notes in James B. Allen papers, L. Tom Perry Special Collections, Harold B. Lee Library, Brigham Young University.

Bear, Leon, Secretary-Treasurer of the Skull Valley Tribe. Telephone interview by Mark Ashurst-McGee, July 31, 1993. Notes in James B. Allen papers, L. Tom Perry Special Collections, Harold B. Lee Library, Brigham Young University.

Bellow, Reverend Mark G. Bellow, Salt Lake City. Interview by Jesse S. Bushman, October 12, 1994. Tape and transcription in James B. Allen papers, L. Tom Perry Special Collections, Harold B. Lee Library, Brigham Young University.

Brockleman, Major Dell, Salt Lake City. Telephone interview by Jesse S. Bushman, January 6, 1995. Notes in James B. Allen papers, L. Tom Perry Special Collections, Harold B. Lee Library, Brigham Young University.

Brown, Arnold. Provo, UT. Interview by Jesse S. Bushman, January, 7, 1995. Tape in James B. Allen papers, L. Tom Perry Special Collections, Harold B. Lee Library, Brigham Young University.

Brown, Arnold, Salt Lake City. Telephone interview by Jesse S. Bushman, January 10, 1995. Notes in James B. Allen papers, L. Tom Perry Special Collections, Harold B. Lee Library, Brigham Young University.

Capson, Noel F. Capson. (A local elder and overseer of Jehovah's Witnesses in Salt Lake City.) Telephone interview by James B. Allen, January 27, 1995. Notes in James B. Allen papers, L. Tom Perry Special Collections, Harold B. Lee Library, Brigham Young University.

Carpenter, Ann, Salt Lake City. Telephone interview by Jesse S. Bushman, December 29, 1994. Notes in James B. Allen papers, L. Tom Perry Special Collections, Harold B. Lee Library, Brigham Young University.

Clyde, Ora P. Oral history interview by Keith Melville, November 23, 1979. Brigham Young University Archives.

Constance, Reverend Thomas, Salt Lake City. Telephone interview by Jesse S. Bushman, January 3, 1995. Notes in James B. Allen papers, L. Tom Perry Special Collections, Harold B. Lee Library, Brigham Young University.

Crump, Pastor David, Ogden, UT. Telephone interview by Jesse S. Bushman, January 10, 1995. Notes in James B. Allen papers, L. Tom Perry Special Collections, Harold B. Lee Library, Brigham Young University.

Das, Caru, and Vaibhavi Dasi, Spanish Fork, UT. Interview by Jesse S. Bushman, May 4, 1995. Notes in James B. Allen papers, L. Tom Perry Special Collections, Harold B. Lee Library, Brigham Young University.

Davis, Reverend France, Salt Lake City. Interview by Jesse S. Bushman, October 8, 1994. Tape in James B. Allen papers, L. Tom Perry Special Collections, Harold B. Lee Library, Brigham Young University.

Deacon, Pastor Brian Deacon, Salt Lake City. Telephone interview by Jesse S. Bushman, December 30, 1994. Notes in James B. Allen papers, L. Tom Perry Special Collections, Harold B. Lee Library, Brigham Young University.

Dobbins, Pastor Steve, Ogden, UT. Telephone interview by Jesse S. Bushman, January 3, 1995. notes in James B. Allen papers, L. Tom Perry Special Collections, Harold B. Lee Library, Brigham Young University.

Hartig, Father Basil, Saints Peter and Paul Antiochian Diocese, Salt Lake City. Telephone interview with Jesse S. Bushman, January 20, 1995. Notes in James B. Allen papers, L. Tom Perry Special Collections, Harold B. Lee Library, Brigham Young University.

Hirano, Reverend Jerry K., Salt Lake City. Interview by Jesse S. Bushman, October 19, 1994. Tape in James B. Allen papers, L. Tom Perry Special Collections, Harold B. Lee Library, Brigham Young University.

Horton, Patty, Salt Lake City. Telephone interview by Jesse S. Bushman, January 10, 1995. Notes in James B. Allen papers, L. Tom Perry Special Collections, Harold B. Lee Library, Brigham Young University.

Inouye, Auks. Oral history interview by Geoffrey Crisp, October 17, 1979. L. Tom Perry Special Collections, Harold B. Lee Library, Brigham Young University.

Jackson, Reverend Michael G. Salt Lake City. Interview by Jesse S. Bushman, October 14, 1994. Tape in James B. Allen papers, L. Tom Perry Special Collections, Harold B. Lee Library, Brigham Young University.

Julander, Rod. Telephone interview by James B. Allen, January 25, 1996. Notes in James B. Allen papers, L. Tom Perry Special Collections, Harold B. Lee Library, Brigham Young University.

Macleod, Kate, Salt Lake City. Interview by Jesse S. Bushman, November 2, 1994 Tape in James B. Allen papers, L. Tom Perry Special Collections, Harold B. Lee Library, Brigham Young University.

Martinez, Linda, Salt Lake City. Telephone interview by Jesse S. Bushman, January 3, 1995. Notes in James B. Allen papers, L. Tom Perry Special Collections, Harold B. Lee Library, Brigham Young University.

Mayo, Deacon Silvio, Salt Lake City. Telephone interview by Jesse S. Bushman, January 3, 1995. Notes in James B. Allen papers, L. Tom Perry Special Collections, Harold B. Lee Library, Brigham Young University.

Meltzer, Pastor Steve, Salt Lake City. Telephone interview by Jesse S. Bushman, January 3, 1995). Notes in James B. Allen papers, L. Tom Perry Special Collections, Harold B. Lee Library, Brigham Young University.

Miller, Karen, Provo, UT. Telephone interview by Jesse S. Bushman, December 16, 1994. Notes in James B. Allen papers, L. Tom Perry Special Collections, Harold B. Lee Library, Brigham Young University.

Miller, Katherine L. Archives of the Episcopal Diocese of Salt Lake City. Telephone interview by Jesse S. Bushman, November 2, 1994. Notes in James B. Allen papers, L. Tom Perry Special Collections, Harold B. Lee Library, Brigham Young University.

Mori, Takeshi Mori, Salt Lake City. Telephone interview by Jesse S. Bushman, January 28, 1995. Notes in James B. Allen papers, L. Tom Perry Special Collections, Harold B. Lee Library, Brigham Young University.

Mullen, Pastor Steve, Salt Lake City. Telephone interview by Jesse S. Bushman, January 3, 1995. Notes in James B. Allen papers, L. Tom Perry Special Collections, Harold B. Lee Library, Brigham Young University.

Ofland, Pastor Gary, Salt Lake City. Telephone interview by Jesse S. Bushman, January 10, 1995. Notes in James B. Allen papers, L. Tom Perry Special Collections, Harold B. Lee Library, Brigham Young University.

Panagos, Father Dean, Holy Trinity Greek Orthodox Church, Salt Lake City. Telephone interview by Jesse S. Bushman, January 13, 1995. Notes in James B. Allen papers, L. Tom Perry Special Collections, Harold B. Lee Library, Brigham Young University.

Peterson, Lori, Salt Lake City. Telephone interview by Jesse S. Bushman, January 10, 1995. Notes in James B. Allen papers, L. Tom Perry Special Collections, Harold B. Lee Library, Brigham Young University.

Ravan, Pastor Noel, Salt Lake City. Interview by Jesse S. Bushman, October, 19, 1994. Tape in James B. Allen papers, L. Tom Perry Special Collections, Harold B. Lee Library, Brigham Young University.

Rowe, John, principal, Adventist school, Monument Valley, UT. Telephone interview by Jesse S. Bushman, December 20, 1994. Notes in James B. Allen papers, L. Tom Perry Special Collections, Harold B. Lee Library, Brigham Young University.

Ruddle, Dean, principal, Adventist school, Ogden, UT. Telephone interview by Jesse S. Bushman, December, 20, 1994. Notes in James B. Allen papers, L. Tom Perry Special Collections, Harold B. Lee Library, Brigham Young University.

Sandlin, Pastor Steve, Salt Lake City. Telephone interview by Jesse S. Bushman, January 6, 1995. Notes in James B. Allen papers, L. Tom Perry Special Collections, Harold B. Lee Library, Brigham Young University.

Senson, Sandy. Member of the board and treasurer of Assumption of the Blessed Virgin Mary Greek Orthodox Church, Price, UT. Telephone interview by Jesse S. Bushman, January 20, 1995. Notes in James B. Allen papers, L. Tom Perry Special Collections, Harold B. Lee Library, Brigham Young University.

Silliman, Rev. Howard Jeffrey, Salt Lake City. Interview by Jesse S. Bushman, November 2, 1994. Tape in James B. Allen papers, L. Tom Perry Special Collections, Harold B. Lee Library, Brigham Young University.

Skedros, Constantine, Salt Lake City. Interview by Jesse S. Bushman, October 21, 1994. Tape in James B. Allen papers, L. Tom Perry Special Collections, Harold B. Lee Library, Brigham Young University.

Smith, Reverend Stanley, Salt Lake City. Interview by Jesse S. Bushman, October 26, 1994. Tape in James B. Allen papers, L. Tom Perry Special Collections, Harold B. Lee Library, Brigham Young University.

Smith, Pastor Robert J., Provo, UT. Telephone interview by Jesse S. Bushman, December 15, 1994. Notes in James B. Allen papers, L. Tom Perry Special Collections, Harold B. Lee Library, Brigham Young University.

Snow, Karl N. Interview by James B. Allen, February 5, 1996. Notes in James B. Allen papers, L. Tom Perry Special Collections, Harold B. Lee Library, Brigham Young University.

Somjit, Phramaha, priest of Thai Buddhist Temple in Logan, UT. Telephone interview by Jesse S. Bushman, January 20, 1995. Notes in James B. Allen papers, L. Tom Perry Special Collections, Harold B. Lee Library, Brigham Young University.

Swingle, Francis Swingle (Sandy, UT). Telephone interview by Jesse S. Bushman, January 28, 1995. Notes in James B. Allen papers, L. Tom Perry Special Collections, Harold B. Lee Library, Brigham Young University.

Todd, Pastor Lee. Ogden, UT. Telephone interview by Jesse S. Bushman, January 6, 1995. Notes in James B. Allen papers, L. Tom Perry Special Collections, Harold B. Lee Library, Brigham Young University.

Troyes, President Sidney. Telephone interview by Jesse S. Bushman, January 23, 1995. Notes in James B. Allen papers, L. Tom Perry Special Collections, Harold B. Lee Library, Brigham Young University.

Williams, Al, Ogden, UT. Telephone interview by Jesse S. Bushman, January 28, 1995. Notes in James B. Allen papers, L. Tom Perry Special Collections, Harold B. Lee Library, Brigham Young University.

Other Unpublished Material

Ashurst-McGee, Mark. "The Avikan Band of Utes and Their Cultural Survival in the Midst of Drastic Change." Anthropology term paper, Brigham Young University, 1994. Copy in James B. Allen papers, L. Tom Perry Special Collections, Harold B. Lee Library, Brigham Young University.

Birch, Neil J. "Helen." unpublished manuscript, copy in possession of David J. Whittaker, Orem, UT.

Chadwick, Bruce A., and Stan L. Albrecht. "Mormons and Indians: Beliefs, Policies, Programs, and Practices." Unpublished manuscript, 1992, used by permission of the authors.

Champena, Anna. "A Study of Utah's Professional Dance Companies Since 1950." BYU History Department senior seminar paper written under the direction of James B. Allen, fall semester, 1991. The author of the paper received much of her information in a personal interview with Joan Woodbury.

Clarke, Darral G., Gene W. Dalton, W. Gibb Dyer, and Alan L. Wilkins, "High Tech Business in Utah Valley: A Multidisciplinary Study for the Utah Technology Finance Corporation." Provo, UT: J. Willard and Alice S. Marriott School of Management, Brigham Young University, 1989. Manuscript available Harold B. Lee Library, Brigham Young University.

De Hoyos, Genevieve and Arturo De Hoyos. "The Indian Placement Program of The Church of Jesus Christ of Latter-day Saints: A Statistical and Analytical Study (First Draft)." Unpublished manuscript, May 1973. Available L. Tom Perry Special Collections, Harold B. Lee Library, Brigham Young University.

Fraser, Mark W., Peter J. Pecora, and Chirapat Popuang. "Self-Sufficiency among Indochinese Refugees: A Survey of Refugee Sponsors." Unpublished manuscript produced in the Social Research Institute, Graduate School of Social Work, University of Utah, January 1984.

Goldberg, Robert A. "The Jewish Community in Utah." Unpublished paper written for a local newsletter, 1994. Copy in James B. Allen papers, L. Tom Perry Special Collections, Harold B. Lee Library, Brigham Young University.

Intermountain Book Store, Inc. "1986 Utah Directory of Church and Related Institutions: Protestant and Roman Catholic." Copy located in James B. Allen papers, L. Tom Perry Special Collections, Harold B. Lee Library, Brigham Young University.

League of Women Voters of Salt Lake. "A Brief History and Description of Utah Indian Peoples" (1973). Copy in James B. Allen papers, L. Tom Perry Special Collections, Harold B. Lee Library, Brigham Young University.

MacCarty, William A. "Statistical History of the Wasatch Hills Church to 1976." Copy in James B. Allen papers, L. Tom Perry Special Collections, Harold B. Lee Library, Brigham Young University.

Nelson, Ann. " Spanish-Speaking Migrant Laborer in Utah 1950-1965," in "Working Papers Toward a History of the Spanish-Speaking People of Utah." Manuscript, Salt Lake City: American West Center, Mexican-American Documentation Project, University of Utah, 1973, 63-111. Copy in James B. Allen papers, L. Tom Perry Special Collections, Harold B. Lee Library, Brigham Young University.

Robson, R. Thayne and Boyd Fjeldsted. "Kennecott Corporation and the Utah Economy." Paper prepared under the auspices of the Bureau of Economic and Business Research, University of Utah, December 1991. Copy in James B. Allen papers, L. Tom Perry Special Collections, Harold B. Lee Library, Brigham Young University.

Skedros, Constantine. "History of the Greek Orthodox Community of Greater Salt Lake City." A short, unpublished history written for the members of Holy Trinity Greek Orthodox Cathedral. Available from Holy Trinity Greek Orthodox Cathedral. Copy in James B. Allen papers, L. Tom Perry Special Collections, Harold B. Lee Library, Brigham Young University.

"Symposium on the Negro in Utah." Typescript. A series of papers presented at the fall meetings of the Utah Academy of Sciences, Arts, and Letters, Weber College, Ogden UT, November 20, 1954. Copy available at Harold B. Lee Library, Brigham Young University.

"The Virginia Tanner Creative Dance Program and Children's Dance Theatre." brief historical material provided to James B. Allen by Mary Ann Lee, November 1995. Copy in James B. Allen papers, L. Tom Perry Special Collections, Harold B. Lee Library, Brigham Young University.

"Utah's Repertory Dance Theatre." a short unpublished history of the company provided to the author by Linda C. Smith, November, 1995. Copy in James B. Allen papers, L. Tom Perry Special Collections, Harold B. Lee Library, Brigham Young University.

Utah's Black Legacy: A History of the Black Experience in Utah, a viewer's guide to the television documentary "Utah's Black Legacy" premiered by KUED, channel 7, February 18, 1987. Salt Lake City: KUED 7, 1987.

"Young Blacks on Blackness: Central City Youth on Being Black." Typewritten booklet prepared by Clifford L. Williams, 1972. Available J. Willard Marriot Library, University of Utah.

INDEX

Abbey of Our Lady of the Holy Trinity (Trappist monastery), 569
abortion, 337-40, 396
Abravanel, Maurice, 491, 510-12
Academy Square (Provo), 535-36
Adams, Afesa Marie, 465
Affleck, C. Grant, 249
African Americans, 461-67, 577-78
agriculture, 26, 327
aids, 348
Alexander, Thomas G., Utah, The Right Place, 1, 413
Allred, Rulon, 245
Alpine School District, 367-69
Amber Alert system, 248
American Folk Dance Ensemble, 527
American G.I. Forum, 448
Anderson, Jon I, 498
Andrus, J. Roman, 497
Apostolic Christian Church, 603-604
architecture, 527-536

Arrington, James, 546
Arrington, Leonard J., 546
Art Barn. See Salt Lake Art Center
artificial heart, see Clark, Dr. Barney
arts, Appendix B. See also specific artists, schools, galleries, and art forms
Ashman, Debbie, 340
Ashton, Alan, 331, 419n
Ashton, Wendell, 490
Assembly Hall on Temple Square, 534
atomic testing. See nuclear testing program
Atrium Gallery, 489
Backman, Gus, 168. 560-61
Bagnall, Vivian Kosan, 526
Ballam, Michael, 518
Ballet Repertory Ensemble, Inc., 527
Ballet West, 482, 522-23

Index

Bangerter, Norman H., 301, 311-13, 319, 336, 338, 343, 357-58, 371, 372, 465, 481; and economic issues, 318; and state politics, 357-58. See chapter 6 for Utah history generally during the Bangerter administration.
banking industry, 17
Baptists, 575-78
Barber, Phyllis, 545
Barker, Bart, 359
Barlocker, William, 141
Barsch, Wulf Erich, 497, 507
Basic Manufacturing and Technologies of Utah, 320
Bastion, Bruce, 331
Bateman, E. Allen, 67-69
Battisone, Sam, 326
Baxter, Ken B., 502
Beeley, Glen, 489
Bell, Terrell H., 178, 392
Bennett, Robert F., 362, 364
Bennett, Wallace F., 92-93, 142, 194, 218
Bennion, Adam S., 71, 102n,
Bennion, Lee Udall, 507
Benson, Ezra Taft, 84-8 6, 219
Benson, Reed, 143
Bernhard, John T., 69-70
Bestor, Kurt, 517
Bimstein, Phillip Kent, 516
Bishop, Arthur Gary, 248
Bitton, Davis, 546
Black, Parnell, 92.
Black, Shirley, 246
Bonneville International Corporation, 212
Bosone, Reva Beck, 19-21, 94-95
Bountiful/Davis Art Center, 487
Bountiful Tabernacle, 528
Bowen, Albert R., 97
Bradford, Barlow, 516
Braithwaite Fine Arts Gallery, 488

Breinholt, Floyd, 497
Brewer, Kenneth W., 544
Bridgeforth, Ruffin, 467
Brigham City Museum-Gallery, 487
Brigham City Tabernacle, 534
Brigham Young University, 76, 187, 318, 326, 527; art department, 496-98, 508. 562
Bronson, Clark, 505
Brooks, Juanita, 546
Brown, Hugh B., 141, 146
Brunvand, Jan, 547
Bryce Canyon National Park, 390
Buchanan, Golden, 431
Buddhists, 596-97
Buehner, Carl W., 217-18
Bullen, Reed, 162
Bundy, Theodore, 211-12
Burnett, Danny W., 463
Burns, Scott, 365
Burton, Laurence J., 142-43, 216, 218
Cabranes, José A., 468-69
Cache Valley Civic Ballet, 526-27
Callister, A. Cyril, 75
Cambodians. See Southeast Asians
Camoin, François, 541-42
Cannon, Hal, 548
Cannon, Joseph A., 320-21, 364
Canyonlands, 133-36
Capitol Theater (Logan), 519
Capitol Theatre (Salt Lake City), 517, 520, 534
Carbon College, 76, 114
Card, Orson Scott, 540-41
Cardon, Sam, 516-17
Cathedral of the Madeleine, 574, 575
Cathey, Tully, 516
Cedar City, 90
Cedar Mesa, 391
Centennial Schools, 408-409
Central Utah Ballet School, 526

649

Central Utah Project, 27-28, 122-24, 271, 323-24
Chase, Daryl, 76
Cheever, Bruce, 505
chemical testing and sheep deaths, 203
Chicanos. See Hispanics
child abuse, 344-46
Children's Dance Theatre, 524
Chinese, 454-55
Christ Catholic Church, 603
Christensen, James C., 497, 506
Christensen, Steven C., 342
Christensen, William F., 522-23
Christian Reformed Church, 600
Christian Science, 602
Church of Christ, 600
Church of Jesus Christ of Latter-day Saints, 208, 212: and politics, 35-38, 142, 143-44, 145-48, 195-97, 208, 212; Welfare Department, 41; and blacks, 186-87, 292, 426, 467; and Equal Rights Amendment, 195-97; and MX missile controversy, 260-61; opposition to gambling, 369; Church-owned businesses, 564-65; welfare program, 565; Social Services Department, 565. See also Bonneville International Corporation; International Women's Year conference; LDS Relief Society; LDS Rural Health Project; LDS Special Affairs Committee; school prayer; other listings beginning with LDS
civil rights, 124-27, 185-87
Clark, Dr. Barney, 293
Clark, Robert T., 498
Clayton, James L., 200
Clyde, Aileen H., 192

Clyde, George D., 97-98, 107-124, 129, 141, 144; elected governor, 97-98; and education, 109-15; and law and order, 115-119; and economic development, 119-24; reelection, 141. See chapter 3 for Utah history generally during the Clyde administration.
Coalville Tabernacle, 532-33
Cold War, 37-40
Coleman, Michael, 505
Coleman, Ronald G., 465
Coles, Katharine, 544
Collard, Kathy, 195-96
College of Eastern Utah, 180, 181-82
College of Southern Utah, 180
Collett, Farrell, 498, 504
Colorado River storage project, 62, 88
Condie, Richard P., 514
Congressional representation, 152
constitutional revision, 164-68, 250-54
Cook, Merrill, 357, 358, 360, 361, 364-65
Cooper, D.B., 234
Cope, Donald L., 464
Cornwall, J. Spencer, 514
Corradini, Deedee, 341, 361
Council Hall, 534
Cracroft, Richard H., 537
Crockett, J. Allen, 490
Crossroads Choral Ensemble, 516
Cuban missile crisis, 130
Curtis, Hughes, 502, 504
Cyprus High School, 407
Dallin, Cyrus E., 485, 502
dance, 522-27
Dancers Company (BYU), 527
Dantley, Adrian, 465
Darius, Alex B., 47
Daughters of Utah Pioneers, 414

David W. and Beatrice C. Evans Biography Award, 547, 557-58n
Davis, France, 467, 577
Davis, Silvia Lis, 507
Dawson, William A., 94-95, 139-40
death penalty, 243-45
Deep Creek. See Goshutes
Deffebach, H. Lee, 485, 499
Dellapiana, Gail B., 465
Delta Center, 326-27, 530
demographics, 392. See also population; social and cultural life; social issues
Denver and Rio Grande Railroad station, 534-35
DePaulis, Palmer, 357
Deseret Management Corporation, 212
Desert Star Playhouse, 521
Detmer, Ty, 326
DeVoto, Bernard, 88, 539
DeVries, Dr. William, 293, 309n
Dewey, Thomas E, 42, 43, 45
Disciples of Christ and Churches of Christ, 599
divorce, 295, 397
Dixie Center, 530
Dixie College, 76, 114, 180
Dixon, Henry Aldous, 76, 95, 139
Dixon, Maynard, 502
Dooley, James E., 465
Dornan, E. David, 496
Dowdle, Michael, 516
Draper, Ruth, 482
drug abuse, 179, 296, 350
Dugway Proving Ground, 203
Duncan, Luke, 442-43
Duncan, Robert K., 506
Durham, Christine Meaders, 189-90
Eaton, A. Valoy, 502, 506
Eccles Community Art Center, 487
Eccles, Mariner S.,200

Echo Park, 88-89
economic growth, issues, and activities, 15-17, 21-29. 58-64, 119-24, 170-73. 278-80, 327-30, 388-92, 392-95. See also industry; roads and highways
education, 31-33, 67-77, 109-15, 144-45, 177-83, 286-92, 351-57, 406-409. See also religion in public schools; school prayer
Egyptian Theatre (Ogden), 530
Eisenhower, Dwight D., 32 – 33
Eleanor Kennard Choral, 516
electronics industry, 171
Elgren, Lorenzo E., 31
Ellen Eccles Theatre, 519, 527
Ellsworth, S. George, 546
Elsner, Larry E., 496, 498
Emery County, 413
employment, federal, 171-72
Engar, Keith, 519
England, Eugene, 537, 545
environmental issues, 86-91; 131-33, 201-207, 273-77, 333-37, 402
Environmental Protection Agency, 204-206
Episcopalians, 587-89
Equal Rights Amendment, 193-97
Evangelical Free Church, 597-98
Evans and Sutherland, 331
Evans, John, 178
Ewers, Anne, 518
Fairbanks, Avard, 501
Farley, Frances, 302
Faust, James E., 212, 250
Fawson, Steven James, 507
Federal, Bishop Joseph, 569-70
federal-state relations, 237-38, 254-62, 400-401, 409-12
Fife, Austin, 547
Filipinos. See Southeast Asians
Fillerup, Peter M., 505
Fillmore, 413

651

Fingerhut Companies, Inc., 388
Fitzpatrick, John F., 560-61
Flaming Gorge Dam, 123
Flaming Gorge National Recreation Area, 390
Fletcher, Dale, 501, 508
Fletcher, James C.
Florez, John, 446, 452
fluoridation, 137, 208 –209
Fort Douglas, 32-33
Fourth Street Clinic, 297, 310n
Foxley, Cecilia H., 409
Fraughton, Edward J., 504
freeport law, 162, 168-69, 171
Friberg, Arnold, 502, 503
Fritz, Albert, 463
Fugal, Lavina Christensen, 98
gambling, 117, 119, 146-47, 369-70, 404-405
Garciaz, Maria, 469
Gardner, David P., 292
Garn, E. J. (Jake), 185, 220-222, 261, 299, 314, 324, 357
Gates, Crawford, 517
Gateway Amendment, 166-68
Geneva Steel, 14, 22-24, 25, 122, 128, 205-206, 273-75, 280, 318, 320-23, 335, 384, 273-75, 335
George S. Eccles Foundation, 296-97
Ghiselin, Brewster, 541
Gilmore, Gary, 243-45
Gittins, Alvin, 496, 501
Glade, Earl J., 32, 95, 495
Glazier-Koehler, Nancy, 505
Glen Canyon Dam, 62, 89, 122-23
Glen Canyon National Recreation Area, 390
Golden Spike National Historic Site, 177
Goshutes, 428, 443-46
Governor's Mansion, 238-36, 240, 386-87, 528

Graham, Jan, 365-66, 399
Granger, Walter K. , 94, 95
Granite Mountain Vault, 562-63
Granite School District, 367-68
Graves, Michael Clane, 508
Graves, Shauna M., 464
Gray, Joyce M., 465
Great Salt Lake, 336-37
Greek Orthodox Church, 579-80
Greeks, 468
Greene, Enid, 363
Gregory, Thomas J., 198-99
Groutage, Harrison Thomas, 498
Guadalupe Center, 447, 448, 572
gun control, 398-400
Gunn, Richard, 497
Gwyther, Carolyn, 527
Hadlock, Neil, 504
Hafen, LeRoy R., 546
Haight, David B., 212
Hale Center Theaters, 521
Hale, James ("Big Jim"), 573
Hall, Gordon R., 192, 250
Haltern, Hagen, 497
Halversen, Gail, 39-40
Hansen, James V., 300, 301, 357, 364, 440-42
Hansen, Lisa and Elisa, 293
Hansen, Phil, 218
Hansen, Stewart, 364-65
Hare Krishna, 604-605
Harmer, John L., 266, 360
Harmsen, Stephen, 223
Harrington, Richard, 363
Harris Fine Arts Center, 488, 519
Harris, Robert, 225, 465
Harwood, Ruth, 506
Haseltine, James L., 489
Hatch, Orrin G, 221, 224. 264, 299, 301, 314, 358
Hawaiians. See South Sea Islanders
hazardous waste, 335-36

Index

health and medicine, 136-38, 207-209, 293, 346-49, 397-98
Heber City Tabernacle, 531
Hebner, William Logan and Angie, 315-16
Hecht, Dr. Hans H., 138
Hellberg, Ray W., 498
Henderson, Andrew, 465
Henderson, Jan, 505
Henry, Alberta, 466
Hercules Powder Company, 120, 316
Herman, Robert Kimball, 530
Hill Air Force Base, 170
Himes, H. Douglas, 507
Hinckley, Gordon B., 212
Hippodrome Gallery, 489
Hispanics, 446-53; organizations, 447-48
historic preservation, 527-36
Hoffmann, Mark, 342-43
Hogle Zoo, 390
homelessness, 347
Horiuchi, Randy, 359
Hotel Utah, 370-71, 534
House, Fred, 344
Howe, Allen T., 223-24
Howlett, G. Edward, 200
Hudnut, Mrs. Richard, 487
Humphrey, Hubert, 219
Hunt, Most Reverend Duane G., 568-69
Hunter, Rodello, 540
Huntsman, John, 358
Hutchins, Coleen, 98
immunization program, 348
Indian Child Welfare Act, 431
industrial development, see industry
Industrial Promotion Commission, 168
industry, 21-25, 168-70. See also economic issues and activities

interfaith activities, 606-609
Intermountain Health Care, Inc., 208
Intermountain Indian School, 430
Intermountain Power Project, 272-73
international trade, 329-30, 389
International Women's Year Conference, 280-85
Iosepa, 459-60
Jackson, David W., 505
Japanese-Americans, 453-54
Jarvis, John B., 505
Jay Welch Chorale, 516
Jehovah's Witnesses, 590-91
Jensen, Golden, 155n
Jewish Center for the Performing Arts, 519
Johansen, Franz M., 497
John, Helen, 431
Johnson, Lady Bird, 144
Johnson, Lyndon B., 143, 144
Jonas, Frank H., 36-37
Jones, Earl, 496, 502
Jordanelle Dam, 324
Joseph Smith Memorial Building, 370-71
Judaism in Utah, 591-93
Julander, Paula, 366
Kaiparowits power plant proposal, 206-207
Kane County, 413-14
KBYU-TV, 115
Kennecott Copper Corporation, 61, 122, 128, 206, 209, 279, 280, 318, 328, 384,
Kennedy, John F., 141-42.
Kerr, William Rolfe, 356
Kimball Art Center, 489
Kimball, Spencer W., 41, 292, 431
King, David S., 139-41, 143, 184, 216
King, Martin Luther, Jr., 125.

653

Kohjian, Varujan, 512
Korean war, 77-79, 89
Koreans, 455
Krane, David, 545-46
Kraut, Ogden, 343
Ku Klux Klan, 426
KUED, 115
labor relations, 34-37, 96, 128-29, 279
Lafferty, Brenda Wright, 248
Lafferty, Dan, 248-49
Lafferty, Ron, 248-49
Lagoon, 390, 425
Lagoon Opera House, 520
land-use planning, 215-16
landscape artists, 501-502
Laotians. See Southeast Asians
Larsen, B. F., 497
Larson, Clinton F., 541
law and order, 115-19, 209-212, 243-50.340-44, 398-400
Layden, Frank, 341
LDS Church Museum of History and Art, 488-89
LDS Church Office Building, 529
LDS Health Services Corporation, 207
LDS Indian Placement Program, 431-33
LDS Relief Society, 191, 432: and International Women's Year conference, 282-84
LDS Rural Health Project, 207
LDS Second Ward building (Salt Lake City), 535
LDS seminaries, 286
LDS Special Affairs Committee, 212
LDS Temple Square, 390, 565
Leavitt, Michael O., 364-65, 382-83. 386, 389, 392, 401, 407, 409-12, 415-17; 417n. See chapter 7 for Utah history generally during Leavitt's first term as governor.

LeBaron, Ervil, 245
Lee, J. Bracken, 44-46, 53-77, 83-84, 91-92, 95, 96-98, 104n, 107,139, 141, 142, 143, 144-45, 149, 184-85, 299; elected governor, 44-46; goals as governor, 54-56; and liquor control, 56-58; and the economy, 58-64; tax rebel, 64-65; and Utah highways, 65-67; and education, 67-77; and state politics, 91-92, 95, 95-98. See chapter 2 for Utah history generally during the Lee' first term as governor.
Lee, Mary Ann, 524
Leonard, Glen M., 488
Lind, Don, 314
Lion House, 528
liquor control, 45, 56-58, 214-15
Literary arts, 536-48
Little Hoover Commission, 164-65.
livestock industry, 26, 327-28
Lloyd, Sherman P., 142, 145, 194, 216, 218, 222
Logan tabernacle, 531
Long, Darrold, 178
Lueders, Edward L., 544
Lutherans, 578-79
Madsen, Louis L., 75-76
Magleby, Francis R., 497
Mahoney, J. R., economic forecasts, 16-17
Majerus, Rick, 341
Malone, Karl, 465
Maoris. See South Sea Islanders
Marks, Bruce, 523
Marriott, Dan, 298, 301, 302
Marshall, Robert L., 497
Martinez, Mike, 469
Maryboy, Mark, 437
Masaoka, Mike, 453, 454
Mason, James, 488
Master Plan for Higher Education, 182

Index

Matheson, Norma, 282
Matheson, Scott M., 224-25, 237-39, 244-47, 250, 254-71, 277-78, 301-302, 464; and quest for federal-state balance, 237-38, 254-62; and nuclear testing, 255-57; and MX controversy, 257-61; and Weteye bombs, 261-62; and Sagebrush Rebellion, 266-67; and wilderness, 268-70; and water policy 270- 71; and regional cooperation, 277-78; and state politics, 300, 301, 302. See chapter 5 for Utah history generally during the Matheson administration.
Matthews, Conan E., 497
Maw, Herbert B., 15-16, 43-44, 45-46. See chapter 1 for Utah history generally during Governor Maw's second administration.
Maxwell, Neal A.,166-68, 212
McCarthy, Joseph R., 79 – 81.
McCoy, Richard Floyd, 211, 234n
McGovern, George, 223
McKay, David O., 141-42, 144, 219, 560
McKay, Gunn, 194 220, 223, 224, 259, 298, 300
McMurrin, Sterling M., 113
Medley, Tyrone E., 465
Melich, Mitchell, 145
Merrill, Frances Hatch, 366
Merrill, Joseph F, 35-37
Methodists, 586-87
Micron Technology, 388-89
Miller, Clyde, 218
Miller, Hack, 199
mine disaster, 276-77
mining, 25-26, 326
minorities, 31, Appendix A. See also specific minority groups
missile industry, 120-21
modernism in Utah art, 499-501

Momen, Karl, 507
Monson, David S., 302
Montezuma Creek Elementary School, 484
Morey, Charles, 519
Morgan, Dale, 481
Mormon Art and Belief Movement, 507-508
Mormon splinter groups, 566-67
Mormon Tabernacle Choir, 98, 144, 509, 514-15,
Mormon Youth Course, 516
Moss, Frank, 134-36. 139-40, 143, 194, 220, 224
moviemaking, 521-22
MX missile controversy, 257-61
Native Americans, 40-42, 427-46
Nau, Fineasi M., 460-61
Navajos, 436-39
neorealism, 505-506
Newman, Jeannine Young, 505
Nielson, Howard, 301, 357
Nixon, Richard M., 142, 219-20, 222
Noorda, David, 332
Norris, Leslie, 544
Norton, James C., 505
Novell, Inc., 331-32
nuclear testing program, 89-91, 132-33, 255-57, 314-15
Oaks, Dallin H, 250
Ogden, 415
Ogden High School building, 529
Ogden-Weber Municipal Building, 529
Old City Hall (Salt Lake City), 528, 534
Old Lyric Repertory Company, 520
Olpin, A. Ray, 32-33, 115
Olsen, Donald, 499
Operation Desert Storm, See Persian Gulf War
Oratorio Society of Utah, 515

Orem High School, 368-69
Orton, William, 359-60, 361-63
Osegura, Preddy, 469
Ottley, Jerold, 515
Ottley, JoAnn, 517-18
Owens, Wayne, 222, 223, 301, 314, 357, 359, 363, 364
Oxford Chamber Choir 516
Pacheco, Joe, 469
Packard Bell, 388
pageants, 527
Pages Lane Theater, 521
Palmer, Brent, 414
pari-mutual betting. See gambling
Park City, 390
Park City art galleries, 489-90
Parkinson, William J., 506
Peery Hotel, 530
Pentecostal and Holiness churches, 582-86
performing arts, 509-27
periodicals (Utah-oriented), 536-37
Persian Gulf War, 317
Peterson, Charles S., 546
Peterson, Georgia B., 283
Peterson, Glade, 517, 518
Peterson, Levi S., 542
Peterson, N. Blaine, 141
peyote, 429-30
philanthropy, 398, 419n
Phillips, Bonnie G., 501
Phillips Gallery, 489
Pine Valley Chapel, 533-34
Pioneer Centennial, 29
Pioneer Craft House, 489
Pioneer Memorial Museum, 482
Pioneer Memorial Theatre, 519
Pioneer Theatre Company, 519
Plastow, Pete, 505
Plein Air Painters of Utah, 502
polio, 136-37

politics, national, 37-42, 77-86, 124-31, 183-202, 239-43, 312, 314-16, 396-97, 401, 412-13
politics, state and local, 18, 42-47, 91-98, 138-51, 212-25, 298-303, 357-66, 412. See also school prayer
pollution. See environmental issues
Polynesians. See South Sea Islanders
population, 9-10, 19, 387-88, 48n, 152, 258, 387-88
population, minorities, 31, 423
poverty, 394
Presbyterians, 580-82
Price, Gary Lee, 505
Priest, Ivy Baker, 84, 85
Project BOLD, 267
Promised Valley, 517, 521
Promised Valley Playhouse, 521
Provo-Orem area, 372
Quail Creek Dam, 323
racial equality, efforts to achieve, 423-27
racism, 81-83.
Rampton, Calvin L., 145, 157n, 159-70, 220, 299; governorship begins, 159-64; and industrial development, 168-70; and education, 177-78, 182; and state politics, 212-14, 217-18, 222, 224; faith in democratic government, 226. See chapter 4 for Utah history generally during the Rampton administration.
Rampton, Lucybeth, 163
Rampton's Raiders, 169
Rawlings, Calvin, 490
realism in Utah art, 501
reapportionment, 148-52, 300-301
Redford, J. A. C., 516
Redford, Robert, 522
refugees, 297, 455-58
Regis Medical Clinic building, 529

Relief Society. See LDS Relief Society
religion in public schools, 405-406. See also school prayer
religions in Utah. See chapter 7
Reorganized Church of Jesus Christ of Latter Day Saints, 601
Repertory Dance Theater, 482, 524, 524-26
Richards, Richard, 220
right-to-work-law, 147
Ririe, Shirley Russon, 524
Ririe-Woodbury Dance Company, 482, 524-25
Ritter, Willis W., 244-45
roads and highways, 21, 65-67, 122, 174-75, 402-403
Roberson, Edith Tyler, 506
Rocky Mountain Helicopters, 207
Roe v. Wade. See abortion
Rogers, Thomas, 545
Rollins, Jeffrey A., 317
Roman Catholic Church, 568-75; various orders of nuns, 568; St. Thomas Aquinas Parish (Logan), 569; Catholic schools, 571-72; Catholic Indian centers, 572; social welfare programs, 572-73; Catholic hospitals, 573-74
Rose Wagner Performing Arts Center, 526
Rosenblatt, Morris, 490
Rounds, Al, 505
Roy Municipal Elementary School, 407
Runyon, Rachel, 247
Sagebrush Rebellion, 263-67
Salisbury, Paul, 502, 503
Salt Lake Acting Company, 520
Salt Lake Art Center, 487, 489
Salt Lake Christian Association, 340
Salt Lake City and County Building, 535

Salt Lake City International Airport, 171, 390
Salt Lake City, 19, 391-92, 414, 491
Salt Lake Community College, 114, 181, 353
Salt Lake Fairground Centennial Exhibition (1947), 495
Salt Lake Gallery Association, 489
Salt Lake Men's Chorus, 516
Salt Lake Public Library (old), 528-29, 534
Salt Lake Trade Technical Institute, 114, 180-181
Salt Lake Vocal Ensemble, 516
Salt Palace, 176
Salvation Army, 603
same-sex marriage, 397
Samoans. See South Sea Islanders
Sanguinetti, Frank, 487
SCERA Shell, 521
school prayer, 366-69, 405
Schreuder, Frances, 248
Selvin, Sol J., 31
Seven Canyons Fountain (Liberty Park), 530
Seventh-day Adventists, 594-95
Shakespearean Festival, See Utah Shakespearean Festival
Shaw, Arch D., 506
Shedd, William E., 32-33
Sheets, Kathleen W., 342
Shepherd, Karen, 363, 365
Shimzu, Tom, 357
Sillitoe, Linda, 544-45
Silverstein, Joseph, 512-13
Singer, John, 245-47, 343
Singer, John Timothy, 344
Singer, Vickie, 245-47, 343, 344
Single Parent Employment Demonstration, 394-95
skiing, 176-77, 325, 390
Skousen, Cleon, 117-19
Skull Valley. See Goshutes

Smith, Barbara B., 195-96, 282, 284
Smith, Bruce H., 497. 507
Smith, Dennis V., 507, 508
Smith, Frank Anthony, 506
Smith, Gary E., 505, 508
Smith, Ruth Wolf, 506
Snow, Carl, 359-60
Snow College, 76, 114, 180
Snow, V. Douglas, 495, 496, 499-501, 502
social and cultural life, 31-33, 383-86. See also Appendix A. ("Utah's Ethnic Minorities and the Quest for a Pluralistic Society"); Appendix B ("Utah and the Arts, 1945-1994"); Appendix C ("Notes on Utah's Religions, 1945-1995")
social issues, 292-98, 346-49, 396-400. See also abortion; child abuse; education; health and medicine; women
Society of Friends (Quakers), 602
SOCIO, 448
South Sea Islanders, 458-61
South Temple Historic District, 534
Southeast Asians, 455-58
Southern Paiutes, 419, 443
Southern Utah State College. See Southern Utah State University
Southern Utah University, 356, 488, 519
Southern Utes, 443-44
Southey, Trevor, 497, 508-509
Southwest Symphony, 516
Spafford, Belle Smith,191, 282
Speed, Grant, 504
Spencer, Ike, 465
sports and recreation, 325-27
Springville Museum of Art, 484-87
St. George, 172
St. George Opera House, 535

St. Joseph's Catholic Church (Ogden), 529
St. Joseph's Villa, 572
St. Mark's Episcopal Cathedral, 528, 588
State Capitol Building, 529
state prison reforms, 116-17
state prison riot, 115-16
state symbols, 8-9
statehood centennial commemoration, 6-7, 371, 413-15
states-rights, 150-51, 259
Steen, Charles, 64
Stegner, Wallace, 539-40
Stephenson, Dion J., 317
Stewart, LeConte, 495-96. 500, 501-502
Strand, Mark, 544
Strike, Nicholas, 222
Stringfellow, Douglas R., 95
Strong, David M., 498
Sucec, Bonnie, 507
Sundance Institute, 522
Sundance Outdoor Theater, 520
Sunday closing, 147, 213-14
Sundgaard, Arnold, 517
surrealism, 506
Swanson, Vern G., 485, 486, 550n
Swapp, Addam, 343-44
Swapp, Jonathan, 344
Swenson, May, 540
Symphony Hall, 511
Tahitians. See South Sea Islanders
Tanner, Gerald and Sandra, 568
Tanner, N. Eldon, 217
Tanner, Obert C., 176, 490
Tanner, Virginia, 524
Taylor, Milton B., 91-92.
technology, 330-33, 352-53
teenage pregnancy, 295-96
Teichert, Minerva, 502
television, as a social problem, 294

Temple Square. See LDS Temple Square
Terasawa, Mrs. Kuniko, 454
termination policy, 427-28
Thailanders. See Southeast Asians
Thanksgiving Point, 419n
Thayne, Emma Lou, 542
Theatre 138, 520
Thiokol Corporation, 120
"This is the Place" Monument, 30-31
Thistle, 274, 275-76
Thomas, Elbert D., 92-93
Thorpe, Everett, 498, 499
Tippetts, Frank M., 497
Tippetts, Twain, 498
Toelken, Barre, 547
Tongans. See South Sea Islanders
Topaz, 453
tourism. See travel and tourism
transportation industry, 171
travel and tourism, 28-29, 175-77, 324-25, 390
TRAX, 404
Trolley Square, 535
Truman, Harry, 44-45
Tuacahn Center for the Arts, 521
Tyler, Jan, 282-85
Uchida, Mrs. Take, 454
Udall, Stewart L., 133-34.
Uintah Stake Tabernacle, 534
Uintah-Ouray Reservation, 439
Ulibarri, John, 225
Ulrich, Laurel Thatcher, 542, 557n
Union Station Civic Center, 530
Unitarian-Universal churches, 598-99
United Church of Christ, 593-94
United Methodist Church, 340
University of Utah medical school, 74-75, 138., 207
University of Utah, 318. 326, 527, 530

University of Utah Research Park, 331
urban renewal 184-85
urbanization and suburbanization, 173-74
Ure, Maureen O'Hare, 507
Urie, Rita, 194
Utah Air National Guard, 199, 317
Utah Anti–Discrimination Act, 188
Utah Arts Council, 482-84
Utah Centers of Excellence Program, 318
Utah Chamber Artists, 516
Utah Christian Mission, 567
Utah Civic Ballet. See Ballet West
Utah: converting to peace after World War II. See chapter 1
Utah County Courthouse, 529
Utah Festival Opera, 518-19
Utah Jazz, 326, 390
Utah Lighthouse Ministry, 568
Utah Museum of Fine Arts, 487-88
Utah, national image, 372-73
Utah Opera Company, 482, 517
Utah Polynesian Choir, 460
Utah Procurement Outreach, 318
Utah Shakespearean Festival, , 482, 519-20
Utah State Agricultural College, 68, 75-76
Utah State Institute of Fine Arts, 495
Utah State University, 113, 318; art department, 498, 518, 519, 527; See also Utah State Agricultural College
Utah Symphony, 176, 509, 510-14
Utah Symphony, 482
Utah Symphony, 490, 491
Utah Symphony Chorus, 516
Utah Technical College at Salt Lake, 114, 181

Utah Trade Technical Institute, 180-81
Utah Valley Choral Society, 516
Utah Valley Community College (now Utah Valley University), 181, 335
Utah Vietnam Veterans Memorial, 201
Utes, 428, 439-43
Van Dam, Paul, 339, 358
Van Wagoner, Richard, 498
Vernal Tabernacle. See Uintah Stake Tabernacle
Vietnam war, 130-31, 199-202
Vietnamese. See Southeast Asians
visual arts in Utah, 494-509
visual arts, national trends, 492-94
Walker, Olene, 366
Wallace, George C., 219
Wallace, Glenn Walker, 490, 511, 522
Wallace, William, 516
Wanlass, Stanley, 504
Warren, E. Kimball, 505
Washington County, 172, 387, 414
water policy, 270-71; see also Central Utah Project
Watergate scandal, 197-99
Watkins, Arthur V., 80, 81, 139-40, 427, 430
Watson, Dave, 357
"We the People," 299
weather. See environmental issues
Weber State College. See Weber State University
Weber State University, 76, 114, 318, 356 519; art department, 498
Weigand, Bishop William K., 570-71
Weilenman,, Milton L., 218, 228n
Welch, Jay, 514-15
Wells, Sharlene, 242-43

West, Allan M., 69-70
West Desert Project, 337
West High School, 406
West Valley City, 299
West Valley Symphonic Orchestra, 516
western and cowboy art, 502-505
Western Governor's Conference, 278
Western Governor's Policy Office, 278
Westminster College, 519
Westwood, Jean, 222
Weteye bombs, 261-62
White, James L., 490
White, Phyllis Fludd, 465
Whittaker, William E., 497
wholesale and retail trade, 171
wilderness, 268-70
Wilkinson, David L., 358
Wilkinson, Ernest L., 145
Williams, Terry Lee, 465
Williams, Terry Tempest, 542-43
Wilson, Sam, 496
Wilson, Ted, 297, 299, 357, 358
Wilson, William A., 547
Wine, E. Faye, 466
Winter Olympics, 325-26, 391-92, 418n
Wolfe, James M., 104n
Wolking, Henry, 516
women, 187- 97; in World War II, 15. See also Equal Rights Amendment; International Women's Year Conference
Wood, Mary Ann, 339
Woodbury, Joan Jones, 524
Woodbury, T. Bowring, 490
WordPerfect Corporation, 331-32.
Works Progress Administration, 481
World War II: end of, 12-13, impact on Utah, 14-15

Wright, David, 466
Wright, Robert, 300
Young Ambassadors, 527
Young, Mahonri M., 502, 503
Young, Margaret Blair, 545
ZCMI building, 535
Zimbeaux, Francis, 506
Zion National Park, 390
Zion's Securities Corporation, 212

www.ingramcontent.com/pod-product-compliance
Lightning Source LLC
Chambersburg PA
CBHW030428010526
44118CB00011B/548